15.50

WITHDRAWN

The Victoria History of the Counties of England

EDITED BY WILLIAM PAGE, F.S.A.

A HISTORY OF
MIDDLESEX

VOLUME II

THE
VICTORIA HISTORY
OF THE COUNTIES
OF ENGLAND

MIDDLESEX

PUBLISHED FOR
THE UNIVERSITY OF LONDON
INSTITUTE OF HISTORICAL RESEARCH
REPRINTED FROM THE ORIGINAL EDITION OF 1911
BY
DAWSONS OF PALL MALL
FOLKESTONE & LONDON
1970

Issued by
Archibald Constable and Company Limited
in 1911

Reprinted for the University of London
Institute of Historical Research
by
Dawsons of Pall Mall
Cannon House
Folkestone, Kent, England
1970

ISBN 0 7129 0448 4

Printed in Great Britain
by photolithography
Unwin Brothers Limited
Woking and London

INSCRIBED
TO THE MEMORY OF
HER LATE MAJESTY
QUEEN VICTORIA
WHO GRACIOUSLY GAVE
THE TITLE TO AND
ACCEPTED THE
DEDICATION OF
THIS HISTORY

Hampton Court Palace

From an Engraving by J. Rigaud 1736

THE
VICTORIA HISTORY
OF THE COUNTY OF
MIDDLESEX

EDITED BY

WILLIAM PAGE, F.S.A.

VOLUME TWO

PUBLISHED FOR

THE UNIVERSITY OF LONDON
INSTITUTE OF HISTORICAL RESEARCH

REPRINTED BY

DAWSONS OF PALL MALL
FOLKESTONE & LONDON

CONTENTS OF VOLUME TWO

CONTENTS OF VOLUME TWO

LIST OF ILLUSTRATIONS

LIST OF MAPS

EDITORIAL NOTE

THE Editor wishes to express his thanks to all those who have assisted in the compilation of this volume, but particularly to Mr. H. B. Walters, M.A., F.S.A., Mr. A. F. Hill, F.S.A., and Mr. William Dale, F.S.A., for information and assistance regarding the Industries of the county. He is also indebted to Mr. Ernest Law, B.A., F.S.A., for reading the proofs and offering suggestions regarding the history of Hampton Court Palace, and to Mr. W. Lempriere, senior assistant clerk at Christ's Hospital, for information supplied for the topographical section.

A HISTORY OF
MIDDLESEX

ANCIENT EARTHWORKS

ALTHOUGH earthworks are the most durable of all man's handiwork when exposed to Nature alone, they cannot withstand
the encroachments of the builder. With the continual spread
of habitations for the workers of commercial London, and the
surrounding cultivation of the land for the vegetable supply of so great a
host, there is little cause for wonder that the few works which are known
to have existed in the county of Middlesex have been all but obliterated.
When we consider the exceptionally small size of Middlesex as a county,
that it contains the two cities of London and Westminster, and the amazing
extension of their borders, the marvel is that any ancient works remain.

The natural features of the county lent themselves to no mighty
defensive works; it was no locality for habitations, seeing that it was
generally of a marshy nature and subject to great inundations, it was itself
a defence for more inland territories. Guest remarks, 'I have little doubt
that between Brockley Hill [1] and the Thames all was wilderness from the
Lea to the Brent.' Prehistoric and Roman camps were apparently few; the
Roman stations at Staines (*Pontes*) on the Thames, and Brockley Hill (*Sul-
lonicae*) near Elstree, have no earthworks to indicate their former sites; while
the fosse formerly surrounding the walls of London now no longer remains.

One great dyke in part remains to record the boundary line between
British tribes or Saxon provinces; but the only type of earthwork much in
evidence in the county is that of Homestead Moats, and those are fast
disappearing beneath the foundations of houses.

Moats are more thickly clustered on the north of London than elsewhere; they surround the sites of manor houses and farmsteads in close
proximity to the neighbourhood of Barnet. When it is remembered that
this was the scene of two engagements during the Wars of the Roses, that
two other battles were fought within a short distance at St. Albans, and
how marauding bands were the certain accompaniment of fighting forces in
those days, it will be seen how necessary a precaution it was for people of
substance to safeguard their property by the best means then known.

The surface of the county, however, has altogether changed since
Nichols described the moated mansion of Balmes within the parish of St. Leonard Shoreditch. Whilst passing over Willoughbys and other demolished
earthworks, we cannot ignore those that have disappeared in more recent
years, otherwise our task would be light; yet the few remaining works are apparently doomed in the near future unless the growth of London be arrested.

[1] *Origines Celticæ.*

From the general classification of earthworks it is needful to quote those classes only which are represented in this county.

Class C.—Rectangular or other simple inclosures, including forts and towns of the Romano-British period.

Class F.—Homestead Moats, such as abound in some lowland districts, consisting of simple inclosures formed into artificial islands by water moats.

Class G.—Inclosures, mostly rectangular, partaking of the form of F, but protected by stronger defensive works, ramparted and fossed, and in some instances provided with outworks.

Class X.—Defensive works which fall under none of these headings.

To which is added T for Tumuli.

Out of the four examples of Class C until recently existing one only in part remains, the other three have been obliterated, one of them as late as the year 1906.

The greatest number of earthworks remaining are of Class F, among them are some representative examples, whether surrounding the grounds as that at Fulham Palace, or washing the walls of the house, as Headstone.

In class G two examples are placed, one of them surrounding the formerly strong fortress of the Tower.

The most stupendous earthwork of Middlesex is found in Class X, and the Grimes Dyke will probably survive all other works of this nature.

One tumulus survives, possibly the most ancient earthen monument in the county.

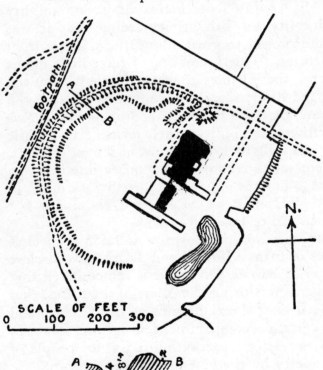

ENFIELD CAMP

SIMPLE DEFENSIVE INCLOSURES

[CLASS C]

ENFIELD (vii, 6 and 7).—In Old Park, nearly a mile south-west of Enfield Town Station, is the most extensive fragment of a camp in the whole county. Its existence is due to a situation in private grounds whilst its partial demolition is owing to the laying out of a garden to the house within the circuit of the camp over a century ago.

A little more than a semicircle—the north, west, and south-west—remains of a circular camp upon the top of a shallow hill. The extant portion consists of a vallum and fosse. The vallum rises from the ground

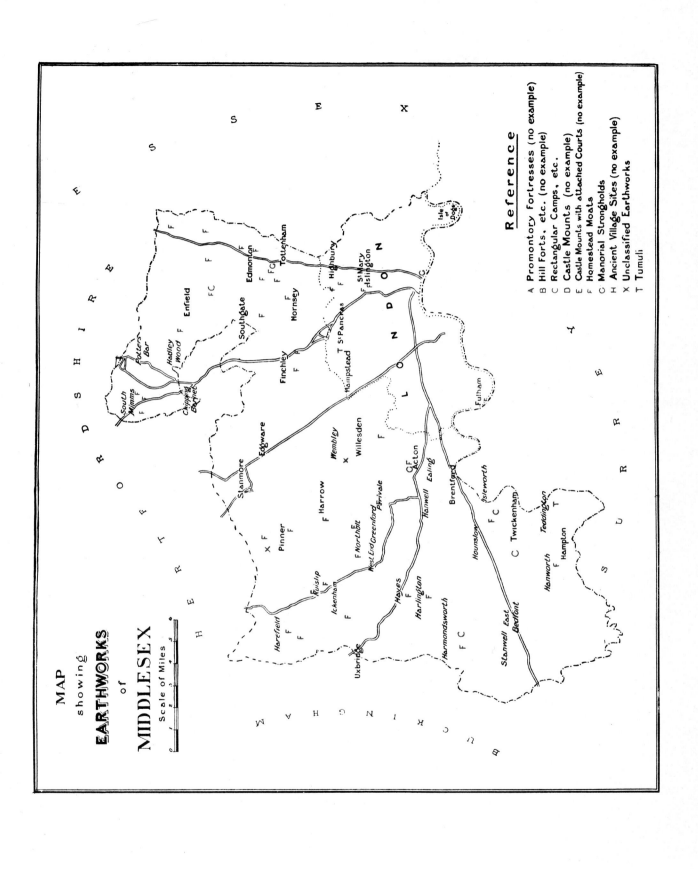

MAP
showing
EARTHWORKS
of
MIDDLESEX

Scale of Miles

Reference

A Promontory Fortresses (no example)
B Hill Forts, etc. (no example)
C Rectangular Camps, etc.
D Castle Mounts (no example)
E Castle Mounts with attached Courts (no example)
F Homestead Moats
G Manorial Strongholds
H Ancient Village Sites (no example)
X Unclassified Earthworks
T Tumuli

level on the south and quickly attains a height of 5 ft. ; in the middle of the western side it rises to 8 ft., declining somewhat towards the north it again rises towards its termination at the north-east. The vallum is broad and a path has been made on the top, probably at the expense of a greater original height, which is now about 2 ft. above the interior area except at the north where the vallum stands boldly above the ground which is the same internally and externally at this spot. A path pierces the vallum at the north-east, but a very small portion of the latter remains on the eastern side of the path. The plan of the works in the neighbourhood of the path is in perfect harmony with an original entrance between an inturned vallum, containing a guard-room within the curve and a platform obtained by the widening of the vallum ; at the same time this arrangement may possibly have been made when the house was built, whereby an even pathway might be obtained, and by the removal of soil from the interior area a garden bower formed—on the site of the possible guard-room—for which purpose this hollow is now used. Around the north-west is a portion of the fosse, from 3 ft. to 4 ft. deep, which has been raised above its original depth to form a gravelled path. On the south-east is a modern pond, fed by a spring in its northern part, at a spot which would have been immediately outside the original circuit of the vallum, and therefore in the fosse. Thus the constructors of the camp may have provided a water-girt stronghold in addition to a water supply. A bank on the north-east of the pond is modern.

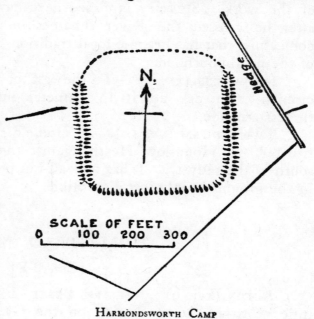

SCALE OF FEET
0   100   200   300

HARMONDSWORTH CAMP

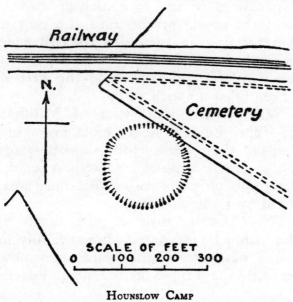

SCALE OF FEET
0   100   200   300

HOUNSLOW CAMP

HARMONDSWORTH (xix, 8).—Three quarters of a mile north-east from Heath Row, immediately south of the

3

Bath Road, a small square camp, about 380 ft. square, was extant until the autumn of 1906. It is now ploughed perfectly flat, leaving no trace of the work. Stukeley supposed it to have been one of Cæsar's stations after he crossed the River Thames in pursuit of Cassivellaunus; a conjecture that has become local tradition, firmly held by the inhabitants of the neighbourhood.

ISLEWORTH (xx, 3).—To the east of OSTERLEY PARK was a small circular earthwork 200 ft. in diameter inclusive, with the entrance on the eastern side.

TWICKENHAM (xx, 10).—A circular camp 200 ft. in diameter was situated on Hounslow Heath against the boundary of the cemetery, south of the railway. It has now all but perished, the slightest depression in the ground is only just discernible.

HOMESTEAD MOATS
[CLASS F]

ACTON (xvi, 9) : 'FRIARS' PLACE FARM.' Within a quarter of a mile north of Acton Station on the Great Western Railway are the remains of two moats, of which one will be classified under G. That which we now consider is a water moat, but only two sides remain, the southern, which is about 50 ft. wide, and the western, which is considerably narrower. Lysons, in the *Environs of London*, considers this to have formed part of the lands given by Adam de Hervynton to the prior and convent of St. Bartholomew in Smithfield.

EDMONTON (vii, 12) : MOAT HOUSE FARM, Marsh side, to the east of Lower Edmonton. The old Moat House was demolished in 1906 but the moat at present remains. This is a large oblong in plan, and although varying in breadth it averages about 20 ft., and is 8 ft. deep. The south-western side has been narrowed by the formation of a road. Near the north angle the water of the moat intrudes into the central area in a semicircular course, thus forming an islet. In the Ordnance Survey two small islands are erroneously inserted.

EDMONTON (vii, 16).—A small quadrangular moat to the west of Angel Road Station has recently been filled up with earth.

EDMONTON (vii, 15).—At WEIR HALL, south-west of Millfield Training School, in the district of Upper Edmonton, is a moat, averaging 30ft. wide. The banks—a foot above the water—gently slope upwards towards the centre of the interior site, where a modern house now stands. At the south-eastern angle the water cuts off a corner of the inner area, thereby forming an island. It is fed by Pymmes Brook.

ENFIELD (vii, 8).—'DURANT'S ARBOUR,' half a mile north of Ponders End, was the name of the manor house of the Durant family in the fourteenth century. The name has survived the house and is now applied to the large square moat with the bridge on the north-eastern side.

ENFIELD (vii, 7).—A large moat formerly situated on the south-east of Enfield Town Station has recently been filled in and is now built over.

ENFIELD (vii, 6).—West of OLD PARK FARM, upon the Golf Links, is a diamond-shaped moat surrounding a small elevated area. At the western end is a cutting through which the moat is fed by a small stream which flows into the River Lea.

ENFIELD (ii, 16).—North-east of Enfield Lock Station, on Plantation Farm, is a quadrangular moat crossed by two bridges on the southern and eastern sides respectively.

ENFIELD (ii, 13) : 'CAMLET MOAT.' In Moat Wood, north of Trent Park and south of Enfield Chase is a large moat, oblong in plan, with the entrance on the east. The house has long since been demolished. In the time of Sir Walter Scott it must have presented a similar appearance as now, for he mentions it as a place 'little more than a mound, partly surrounded by a ditch, from which it derived the name of Camlet Moat.'[2]

FINCHLEY (xi, 8).—One mile south of Finchley is the long rectangular moat of the ancient manor house. It incloses a large oblong area but is divided by a public road. To the south of it, traces of other artificial work are being obliterated and it is difficult to determine their original form or use ; but it is possibly the site of fish ponds.

FINCHLEY (xii, 10) : 'DUCKETTS' or 'DOVECOTS,' north-east of St. Mary's Church, Hornsey. The site of the manor house is surrounded by a narrow moat which is fed by water from the New River. A portion on the east has been filled in, and the bridge is on the western side.

FINCHLEY (xi, 8).—Norden, in his *Speculum Britannica*, 1593, states that

> a hill or fort in Hornesey Park, and so called Lodge Hill, for that thereon for some time stood a lodge, when the park was replenished with deare ; but it seemeth by the foundation it was rather a castle than a lodge, for the hill is at this time trenched with two deep ditches, now olde and overgrown with bushes.

This lodge, which was the property of the See of London from the twelfth to the fourteenth century, occupied a site to the south-west of the Manor Farm house on the north-east of Bishop's Wood, between Highgate and Finchley. Although it appears that the lodge was pulled down in the fourteenth century on account of its great age; traces of the moat are visible, from which it would seem that it was square in plan with sides 210 ft. in length. The moat was fed by a spring which still flows.

FULHAM (xxi, 7).—The grounds of the Bishop of London's palace at Fulham are entirely surrounded by a moat which is crossed by two bridges. The moat is nearly a mile in circuit and incloses an area of 37 acres. It has been suggested that the moat was originally the fosse made for the protection of the Danish camp in A.D. 879 ; a conjecture

[2] *Fortunes of Nigel*, chap. 36.

formed solely on the Anglo-Saxon Chronicle, wherein it is stated that this year a body of those pirates camped at Fulham.

HANWORTH (xxv, 2): HANWORTH CASTLE MOAT.—Why the moat should be known by this name is not apparent. It is situated in the grounds attached to the ruins of the Tudor building in which some of the youthful days of Queen Elizabeth were spent. A large square area, perfectly flat, and at a slightly lower level than the exterior banks, is surrounded by a moat averaging 45 ft. in width ; each angle being broadened by the rounding of the angles of the interior site. At the south-eastern corner is a culvert, at which point the moat is supplied by water through a cutting locally called the 'Queen's River,' from its associations with Elizabeth, and the 'Cardinal's River,' from the belief that it was made by the order of Wolsey.

HAREFIELD (ix, 12).—At BRACKENBURY FARM, 1 mile north-west from Ickenham, near the western bank of the River Pinn and fed by its waters, is a quadrangular moat inclosing a considerable area. The widest and deepest part is on the south, where it is 24 ft. broad, but it narrows to 9 ft. in width around the western side. The outer bank rises above the general level on the north side. The eastern side has been filled in within the last fifty years to enlarge the surface of the garden.

HAREFIELD (ix, 12).—A quarter of a mile south-west of the last mentioned a small but perfect moat lies within a bend of the River Pinn, by which it is supplied. By being thus situated the eastern side and its two angles of the interior area are protected by two widths of water. The moat, which is walled on the inner side to a height of 6 ft., is 18 ft. wide, broadening to 28 ft. at the south-eastern corner. Access to the interior is gained on the western side.

HARMONDSWORTH (xix, 3).—On the site of an Alien Priory—a cell to Rouen—and west of the ancient Tithe Barn, the course of a large rectangular moat may yet be traced, although all but a small portion at the north-east has been filled in. The remaining fragment is nearly 24 ft. wide. Although situated close to the River Colne the moat was supplied with water from the 'Duke's River,' on the west, and a spring rising on the southern side flows into the former, by which the interior site was doubly protected on the south-west.

HARROW ON THE HILL (x, 11).—On the west side of the hill, on the lower ground of the slope and west of the Northolt Road, a small moat remains in a perfect state in the grounds of The Grange. It is square with slightly rounded angles, 20 ft. wide between the sloping banks, which gently rise to 4 ft. 6 in. above the water.

HAYES (xv, 13).—One mile south-east of Hayes Station, and on the eastern side of the River Crane, a small moat surrounds the remains of the old house which was formerly the property of the archbishop of Canterbury. Rectangular at its two southern angles—where the entrance is situated—the moat narrows on the northern side, where it assumes an almost semicircular course.

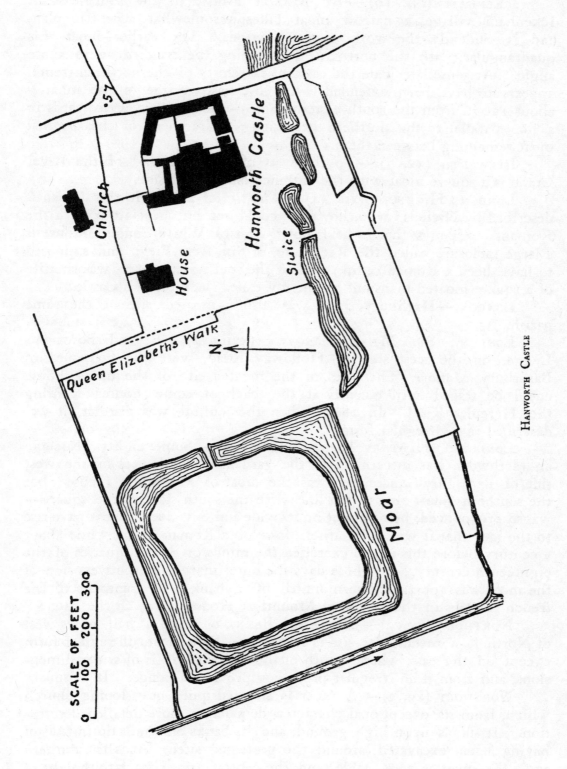

SCALE OF FEET
0   100   200   300

N.

Queen Elizabeth's Walk

Church

House

Hanworth Castle

Sluice

Moat

·57·

HANWORTH CASTLE

7

ICKENHAM (ix, 16).—At MANOR FARM, to the south-east of Ickenham village, a narrow moat takes a somewhat eccentric plan, and is evidently the work of two periods. The earlier moat was quadrangular, with the northern side joining the western at an acute angle. At some later date the eastern extremity of the northern trench appears to have been extended, while the eastern side of the moat— about 120 ft. from the south-eastern angle—was also turned eastwards in a line parallel to the northern extension ; a fragment of the original moat remaining between them.

ISLEWORTH (xx, 7).—To the west of Isleworth and of the River Crane is a square moat with the entrance on the east side.

LONDON : HIGHBURY (xii, 14).—The site of a moat in this parish is described by Nichols,[3] who, however, could not but associate it with the Romans. He says that in fields north-west of White Conduit House is a large inclosure called the Reedmote, or Six Acre Field, and supposed to have been a Roman camp ; and at the south-east corner was the site of a square moated mansion, commonly called Jack Straw's Castle.

LONDON.—Highbury Barn was also a moated site in the same parish.

LONDON : ST. MARY ISLINGTON (xvii, 2).—Beyond Bowman's Lodge, on the west side of Holloway Road, were the demesnes of Barnsbury Manor. The lines of the moated site of the manor-house could be traced until recently at the back of some houses fronting the Hercules Road. In 1835, when the outline was distinct, it was described as of irregular form.

LONDON : ST. MARY ISLINGTON (xvii, 2).—Some eighty years ago an earthwork was discernible in the gardens of the houses on the west side of Barnsbury Square. It was the moat of Mountfort House ; but the southern side—almost in a line with the south side or the square— was so pronounced, being about 20 ft. wide and 8 ft. deep, that it gave rise to the idea that it was the southern fosse of a Roman camp, while about a century before this it had exercised the minds of the antiquaries of the eighteenth century. In those days the outer margin of the west side of the moat was apparently surmounted by a bank.[4] A fragment of the trench remains in the garden of Mountfort House.

NORTHOLT (xv, 2).—At DOWN BARNS, one and a half miles west of Northolt, a rectangular site is surrounded by a moat, of regular form except on the east, where, south of the entrance, it is of wider dimensions, and from it an irregular projection provides a pond.

NORTHOLT (xv, 3).—A moat is situated quite near to the church which, from its exceptional character, demands a more detailed description. It stands upon high ground, and its banks are built up instead of having been excavated around the protected site. At the southern angle the moat is 12 ft. wide, and the central area rises to a height of 5 ft., overlooking the outer bank which is 4 ft. 6 in. high. The south-

[3] *Bibliotheca Topographica Britannica*, A.D. 1782.
[4] Nichols, *Literary Illustrations of Hist.* v, 283.

eastern side varies in width from 9 ft. to 12 ft. The western angle is 36 ft. wide, narrowing towards the northern corner, where it is from 28 ft. to 30 ft. broad. On this north-western side the interior ground continues its former height; but the external bank is only 4 ft. in height. At the north the moat is again about 36 ft. wide, but the inner area attains a height of 7 ft. 6 in., while the outer bank is but 3 ft. At this point the water of the moat is drained into a pond 60 ft. distant, and although water is retained in the north-eastern side it is reduced in bulk. On the north-east, between the angle and the entrance, the moat is from 9 ft. to 10 ft. wide, the interior site is 8 ft. high, but this is the highest point in the outer bank, which is 6 ft. to 7 ft. 6 in. in height. The entrance is by a causeway 21 ft. broad. The site of the ancient house commands an extensive view of the surrounding country.

PERIVALE (xv, 4).—In a field west of the church and north-east of HORSENDON FARM, may be seen the depressions in the land which mark the site of the old manor-house of Greenford Parva. The house has long since been demolished, but the moat still remains on three sides. The northern portion was filled up some fifty years ago.

PINNER (x, 3).—'HEADSTONE' MANOR, about a mile west of Holy Trinity Church, Wealdstone, was part of the archiepiscopal manor of Harrow. A notice of the house in 1344 opens the probability of the moat dating from about that time.

PINNER (v, 15).—A fragment of a circular moat is crossed by a road from Pinner to Harrow Weald. The southerly portion is 20 ft. wide, the northerly is serpentine in form, and the north-eastern has been filled up and farm buildings cover the site.

RUISLIP (x, 9).—At MANOR FARM, on the site of an Alien Priory that was a cell of the abbey of Bec, is an oval moat, surrounding an area of 350 ft. by 200 ft. The two entrances are on opposite sides of the long axis.

RUISLIP (x, 9).—At SOUTHCOTE FARM, half a mile south-west of Ruislip Reservoir is a quadrangular moat inclosing a site about 200 ft. long by 100 ft. broad; with the bridge on the south-western side.

SOUTHGATE (vii, 14).—In the grounds of BOWES MANOR, north-east of St. Michael's Church, is a small irregular square moat around an islet measuring about 100 ft. across.

SOUTH MIMMS (vi, 3).—OLD FOLD MANOR FARM, north-west of Hadley Green, occupies ground formerly protected by a well-defined moat. The eastern side has been filled in and cow-houses occupy the site; but otherwise it retains its ancient appearance. On the southern side the moat is 18 ft. broad, increasing to 28 ft. on the west and the north. The depth to the water is from 4 ft. on the north, to 5 ft. on the south, the banks prettily clothed with wood and undergrowth.

SOUTH MIMMS (vi, 3).—At OLD FOLD FARM, about one and a half miles from the last mentioned, in a westerly direction and close to the county border, is another moat of smaller size but more complete in its extant four sides. It is of oblong plan with a rounded broadening at the north-west corner. The entrance is on the east towards the south-eastern angle.

SOUTH MIMMS (i, 10).—At BLANCHE FARM, to the south of St. Monica's Priory, are the remains of that which was undoubtedly a moat, although the north-west and south-east are the only two extant sides.

TOTTENHAM (xii, 3).—BRUCE CASTLE and BRUCE PARK formed one-third of the ancient manor of Tottenham. The spread of London's population is responsible for the recent levelling of the moat.

TOTTENHAM (xii, 3).—'MOCKINGS' was a sub-manor formed from that of Bruce, lying north of the high road. The moated manor-house stood on the south side of Marsh Lane.

WILLESDEN (xvi, 6).—A moat similar to that in the moated meadow at Acton was situated near Willesden Junction until finally obliterated about the year 1890.

[CLASS G]

ACTON (xvi, 9).—A quarter of a mile north of Acton Station on the Great Western Railway, in a field called 'Moated Meadow,' two fields westward of 'Friars' Place Farm,' are the remains of an earthwork which the Ordnance Surveyors have marked as a moat. From the slight indications extant it might possibly have formed a camp; but not enough remains to decide its original use.

The work occupies a slight eminence and consists of a shallow fosse, or dry moat, surrounding a quadrangular area. The two short sides—the western and eastern—are nearly parallel, the west is 89 ft. long, the east 136 ft. Of the two long sides the southern, 235 ft., is at right angles to the east and west ; but the northern, 240 ft., takes a course to the north-east-by-east. The fosse varies from 41 ft. broad at the south-east, to 60 ft. at the north-west. On the north side, where the higher ground on the exterior makes it more assailable, is found the deepest part, which is 6 ft. A bank has surmounted the outer edge of the fosse, this is still discernible on all sides but the south, and averages 15 ft. wide. The latter feature may have led Lysons to speak of it as 'a deep trench enclosing a parallelogram (sic) . . . supposed to have been a Roman camp.'

LONDON : THE TOWER MOAT.—The precincts of the Tower of London are partly within London, but the greater eastern portion is in Middlesex. The first castle on this spot was built by the conquering Norman.

No account of earthen ramparts has been bequeathed to us, and the earliest mention of a fosse is of the twelfth century.

In 1190 William Longchamp, bishop of Ely and justiciary of England, while acting as regent during the absence of Richard in Palestine, caused a deep trench to be dug round the Tower of London, hoping to bring the waters of the Thames into the City, but after

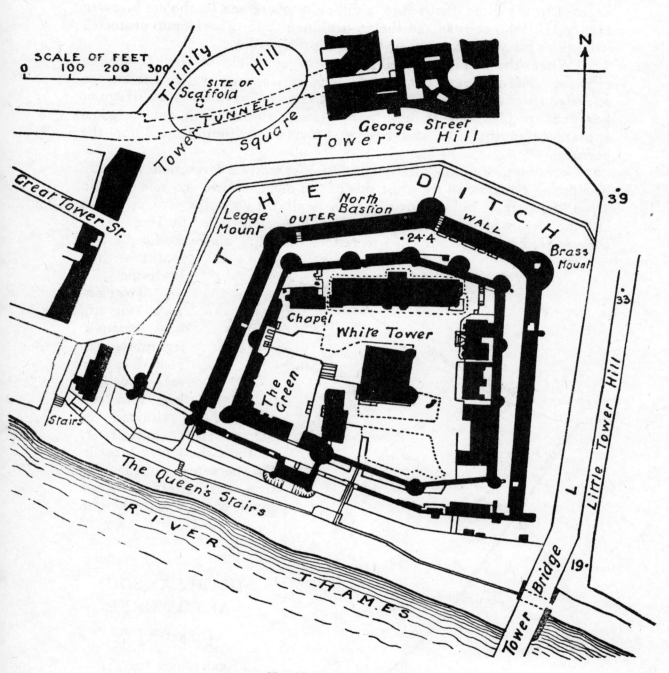

The Tower of London

11

expending much from the treasury his labours proved fruitless.[5] It would be interesting to know the cause of this failure ; possibly Longchamp could not complete the circuit on the river side, where it was exposed to the force of the tide, a difficulty overcome by the engineers of Henry III, who constructed the embankment and wharf, and protected it by piles ; a work completed by his son Edward I.

When the Duke of Wellington was constable of the Tower he cleansed and deepened the moat ; but its stagnant waters became so offensive that it was finally drained in 1843. The fosse is an irregular hexagon in plan, but it has been greatly altered from its original appearance in the sides and base to provide a drilling-ground for the garrison.

A vallum, of unknown dimensions, apparently a revetment, formerly occupied a position on the west side of the moat, for we are told that in 1316 the citizens pulled down a mud wall between the Tower Ditch and the city, which was supposed to have been constructed by Henry III ; they were, however, compelled to restore the same, and were fined 1,000 marks for their lawlessness.

TOTTENHAM (xii, 7).—A rectangular moat, surrounding an area now broken into two portions, is situated on 'Down Hills,' immediately south of the River Moselle. On the exterior of the western and eastern sides are broad banks 2 ft. in height.

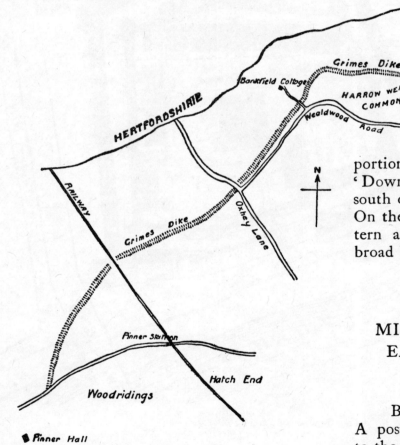

PLAN OF GRIMES DYKE THROUGH HARROW WEALD AND PINNER

MISCELLANEOUS EARTHWORKS

[CLASS X]

BRENTFORD (xxi, i).—A possible line of defence to the Brent Ford is traced by Mr. Montague Sharpe, of which no definite signs exist ; even the 'Old

[5] Roger of Wendover, A.D. 1190.

Ditch,' two sides of a rectangular fosse on the slope of Cuckoo Hill at the western extremity of Hanwell Ridge, and in a curve of the River Brent, is no more.

HARROW WEALD AND PINNER (v and x) : GRIMES DYKE.—Fragments of a boundary earthwork are in evidence over a distance of three miles within, and close to, the border of the counties of Middlesex and Hertfordshire, extending from Pinner Green to Bentley Priory. It consists of a vallum and fosse, the latter on the south-eastern side suggests that it was part of the south-eastern defence of the territories of the British tribe of the Catuvellauni.

The dyke appears to have been supported at the south-west extremity by the woodland of the Colne valley, and the other end was possibly connected with the ancient works on Brockley Hill. Thus the position of the dyke looked out upon the marshland which extended generally to the River Thames, and from the Brent to the Lea.

The work is most clearly to be seen to the south of Wealdstone Common, where the vallum rises 5 ft. from the interior, on the Hertfordshire side, is 63 ft. wide at the base, and has an escarpment of 12 ft. into the fosse ; the latter has been too greatly disturbed to form an adequate idea of its former strength, but it is 5 ft. at its deepest part, and averages 15 ft. broad.

Passing the common, where the rights of carrying gravel have injured the configuration of the land, the most perfect section is found in private grounds ; here the base of the vallum retains the same width, but is 15 ft. in height—now broken by a path on its escarpment, and the fosse widens to 21 ft ; at one part this has been doubly dammed to form an artificial lake.

PINNER.—*See* HARROW WEALD.

WEMBLEY (xv, 4).—HORSA-DUN HILL, south-east of Harrow, shows slight traces of defensive works in two terraces on the southern side.

TUMULI

LONDON : ST. PANCRAS (xvii).—On Hampstead Heath, between Hampstead Ponds on the west and Highgate Ponds on the east, on a ridge of hill running north and south is a bowl-shaped tumulus, known as 'Boadicea's Grave.' It is a gradually sloping mound 10 ft. in height, with diameters—including the surrounding ditch—north to south 145 ft. and east to west 135 ft. The original ditch was within the cincture of the present one, which is modern. It was opened in 1894 by Mr. C. H. Read, who thinks it is a monument of pre-Roman burial by inhumation.

TEDDINGTON (xxv, 8).—Formerly situated in a field known as 'Barrow Field,' between Hampton Wick and Bushey, was a bowl-shaped barrow, 96 ft. in diameter and 12 ft. 3 in. high. The tumulus, composed of burnt sand, was explored in 1854, when three interments were found, two after cremation and one by inhumation. The first on the ground level was accompanied by flint flakes and the bronze blade of a weapon; with the second, 4 ft. below the apex, were fragments of a very large half-baked urn and a flint hatchet-head; whilst in the third case the bones of an adult were buried superficially.

INDEX

OF THE

PARISHES IN WHICH EARTHWORKS ARE SITUATED, WITH THE LETTER OF THE CLASS
TO WHICH THEY BELONG

POLITICAL HISTORY

MIDDLESEX is bounded on the south, east, and west sides by the rivers Thames, Lea, and Colne respectively. The district thus formed seems to have been an uninhabited borderland in British times,[1] a desolate tract round Roman London,[2] and presents itself later as the portion left over when the neighbouring counties had been colonized by the Anglo-Saxons. The three rivers formed the natural boundaries to a physically unattractive country, over which stretched a mass of forest in the north, a marsh in the southeast, and a barren heath in the south-west. The northern boundary points to a later period, to the time when manorial estates were formed. The irregular outline seems to make a special effort to exclude Totteridge, High and East Barnet, and Monken Hadley from Middlesex, and includes South Mimms, while leaving North Mimms to Hertfordshire. This irregularity is explained when we find that the entire north-eastern portion of Middlesex consisted of the manors of Enfield and Edmonton, including South Mimms. These large and thinly populated manors stretched into the forest which was known later as Enfield Chase, until they met the confines of Totteridge, an outlying portion of the bishop of Ely's manor of Hatfield ;[3] of High and East Barnet, which belonged to the abbey of St. Albans ; of Hadley and North Mimms, which were given by Geoffrey de Mandeville to Walden Abbey. Friern Barnet is thus cut off from the other Barnets, and lies in Middlesex, because it formed part of the manor of Whetstone and belonged to the priory of St. John of Jerusalem at Clerkenwell.[4]

It is uncertain when Middlesex was divided into hundreds. Six appear in the Domesday Survey and six remain to-day, although 'Houeslaw' (Hounslow) Hundred is now called Isleworth, and a large portion of Ossulstone Hundred has been included in the county of London since 1888.

London has naturally been the all-dominating factor in the political history of Middlesex, although the City is not in Middlesex. We see her influence in the lack of independent county history ; in the smallness of the population in early times, as well as in the ever-increasing multitudes of to-day ; in the absence of county nobility and gentry, as well as in the unimportance of her towns.

Little is known of the early history of Middlesex. The marshy valley of the Lea, and the forest stretching northwards from the heights

---

[1] Guest, *Origines Celticae,* ii, 390, 403.
[2] Scarth, *Roman Britain,* 38 ; *Journ. Arch. Inst.* xxiii, 180.
[3] *Domesday Bk.* (Rec. Com.), i, 135.   [4] Lysons, *Environs of London* (1795), ii, 21.

of Hampstead and Highgate, saved it for a time from the incursions of the East Saxons, and the wide channel of the Thames and the fortifications of London, from the settlers in Kent and Sussex.[5] It was only after South Britain had been conquered, and the advance of the East Saxons up the Essex river valleys had led to the fall of Verulamium, that the tide of invasion trickled into Middlesex from the north-west, down the great Roman road, Watling Street. London fell before 552, and whether inhabited or not during the next fifty years,[6] it is certain that it was in the hands of the East Saxons in 604,[7] so that the colonization of Middlesex must have taken place during the latter half of the sixth century. The settlers in the district west of London are known afterwards as the Middle Saxons, but it is clear that they were only an offshoot of the East Saxons from the fact that, with London, they always belonged to the kingdom of Essex, and that Middlesex formed part of the East Saxon bishopric of London.[8] Thus Middlesex was never a separate kingdom. The first contemporary mention shows it to be already under double subjection, for in 704 the king of the East Saxons, himself a tributary of Mercia, granted a piece of land in Twickenham, 'in provincia quae nuncapatur Middelseaxon.'[9] It was indeed but sparsely inhabited, the settlers dwelling far apart along the banks of the Thames, and still farther apart in the valleys of the Brent and the Colne, and the tributaries of the Lea.

Middlesex suffered terribly and consecutively from the Danish invasions, chiefly because the Thames offered so excellent a winter harbour for the invaders, and London was the goal of many an expedition.

In 879 a body of Vikings, coming from Chippenham and Cirencester where the main army was assembled, 'sat down at Fulham on the Thames.'[11] These were there joined by another army which had been driven out of Flanders by Charles II, and after both forces had spent the winter at Fulham, they departed in the spring to make a renewed attack on Ghent.[12] According to the Treaty of Wedmore in 879, the boundary between Danes and English was fixed at the River Lea,[13] but the district between the Lea and the Brent seems to have remained in Danish hands until 886,[14] when Alfred gained possession of London (and therefore of Middlesex), and was in a position to restore or 're-settle it.'[15]

In 1009, after harassing the south-eastern counties, the Danes took up their winter quarters on the Thames.[16] After mid-winter they went through the Chilterns to plunder the country round Oxford. As they

---

[5] Green, *Making of Engl.* i, 124–5, 155 ; Robinson, *Hist. Hackney.*
[6] Guest, *Origines Celticae,* ii, 311.　　　　[7] Bede, *Hist. Eccl.* (ed. Plummer), i, 85.
[8] Freeman, *Norman Conq.* i, 23–7 ; Green, *Making of Engl.* i, 227.
[9] Kemble, *Codex Dipl.* i, 59.
[11] *Angl.-Sax. Chron.* (Rolls Ser.), ii, 65 ; Hen. of Hunt. *Hist. Angl.* (Rolls Ser.), 147–8.
[12] *Angl.-Sax. Chron.* (Rolls Ser.), ii, 65 ; Hen. of Hunt. *Hist. Angl.* (Rolls Ser.), 147–8.
[13] Stubbs, *Select Charters,* 63. 'Concerning our land boundaries ; up on the Thames, and then up on the Lea, and along the Lea unto the source. . . .'
[14] Freeman, *Norman Conq.* i, 56.
[15] Hen. of Hunt. *Hist. Angl.* (Rolls Ser.), 148 ; *Angl.-Sax. Chron.* (Rolls Ser.), ii, 67 ; Flor. Worc. *Chron.* (Engl. Hist. Soc.), i, 101.
[16] Hen. of Hunt. *Hist. Angl.* (Rolls Ser.), 179.

were returning in two divisions, as though to attack London, they were met by the news that a force was gathered against them in London. The northern division therefore crossed the Thames at Staines, and both went back through Surrey to their ships to spend Lent in repairing them, but Middlesex was again ravaged during the year.[17] In Edmund Ironside's campaign against Cnut in 1016 the last of his four great battles was fought at Brentford. Edmund had set out to recover Wessex from the Danes after he had been chosen king by the citizens of London. He had gained two victories at Penselwood and at Sherston, but while he was collecting fresh forces Cnut had laid siege to London. Edmund with his reinforcements marched along the north bank of the Thames[18] and won a third battle, which compelled the Danes to raise the siege and flee to their ships. Two days later he defeated them for a fourth time, and drove them in flight across the Thames.[19] Apparently a great number of the English pressed the pursuit in advance of their main body, and in their eagerness to spoil the enemy were by their own carelessness drowned in the river. This battle did not finally disperse the enemy, however, for as soon as Edmund had departed into Wessex, London was again besieged, 'but Almighty God saved it.'[20]

Middlesex is not mentioned in the list of shires whose troops mustered at Hastings, but the sheriff of the Middle Saxons, the Staller Esegar, played a prominent part as leader of the London contingent.[21] He was wounded in the battle, and was carried back to London to conduct its defence against the Conqueror. William marched westward from Southwark to Wallingford, and then northward to Berkhampstead, in order that his triumphant progress might isolate London, and bring it to submission rather by intimidation than by direct attack. When his army entered Middlesex from the north-west London had already come to terms, so that though the northern districts round Enfield, Edmonton, and Tottenham suffered from the passage of his army, yet his march was on the whole peaceful.[22]

The Norman Conquest brought perhaps less change to Middlesex than to any county. It is said that William gave to Geoffrey de Mandeville all the lands which had been held by the Staller Esegar,[23] and apparently Geoffrey occupied much the same position with regard to London and Middlesex as was filled by the Staller before the Conquest. His son and heir, William de Mandeville, was made Constable of the Tower.[24] The greater part of the land in Middlesex had been, and continued to be, in ecclesiastical hands. The king held no manor in the

[17] *Angl.-Sax. Chron.* (Rolls Ser.), ii, 115 ; Freeman, op. cit. i, 377.
[18] Flor. Worc. op. cit. 176. ' Exercitus vice tertiâ congregato.'
[19] Hen. of Hunt. *Hist. Angl.* (Rolls Ser.), 183 ; Freeman, op. cit. i, 426.
[20] *Angl.-Sax. Chron.* (Rolls Ser.), ii, 116.
[21] Sharpe, *London and the Kingdom,* i, 32 ; Freeman, op. cit. iii, 486.
[22] Wm. of Malmesbury, *Gesta Regum* (Rolls Ser.), ii, 307 ; cf. Flor. Worc. *Chron.* (Engl. Hist. Soc.), i, 228. See an interesting article on the subject by F. Baring, ' The Conqueror's Footprints in Domesday,' *Engl. Hist. Rev.* 1898.
[23] *Waltham Chron. de Indentione* (ed. Stubbs), cap. **xiv.**
[24] Ordericus Vitalis, *Hist. Eccl.* (Soc. de l'Histoire de France), iv, 108.

county, and had only a few houses and some acres of 'No man's land.'[25] There were only twenty-four tenants-in-chief. The lay holders, either English or Norman, held a very small proportion of the land compared with the large holdings of the bishop of London and the abbot of Westminster,[26] and many of the lay tenants, such as Geoffrey de Mandeville and Earl Roger, possessed vastly greater estates in other counties than those which they held in Middlesex.

Owing to the unimportance of the lay tenures, it was saved from the evils which attended the building of feudal castles, not one being raised within its boundaries.

In William II's reign the only incident of importance connected with Middlesex occurred in 1095. The quarrel between the king and Archbishop Anselm was then at its height, and the Council of Rockingham had been held in the spring of that year to discuss the question of the recognition of Urban II as pope. Anselm kept Whitsuntide at Mortlake, but immediately after the festival he was summoned to the neighbourhood of Windsor where the king then held his court, and therefore came to his manor of Hayes. He was visited there the day after his arrival by nearly all the bishops, who tried to prevail on him to make his peace by a payment of money to the king.[27] He refused to buy the king's friendship, and refused also to accept the *pallium* which had been sent privately to William from Rome. The bishops retired discomfited, and William, realizing that Anselm was inflexible, and being already concerned with Mowbray's threatened rebellion in the north, sent messages of reconciliation to Hayes.[28] A few days later the king and archbishop met publicly as friends at Windsor.

The most important aspect of the history of Middlesex under the Normans and Angevins is to be found in the definition of the county's relation to London. Henry I granted Middlesex to the city of London to farm for £300 per annum, and granted to the citizens the right to appoint from among themselves whom they would to be sheriff.[29] It cannot be said that the grant of the sheriffwick made the county a dependency of the City, but rather that London and Middlesex were from that time to be regarded as one from an administrative point of view.[30] The citizens were to be responsible for the City and shire as a unity, not for the City and its dependency.[31] Both the 'firma' and the shrievalty are spoken of sometimes as of 'London,'[32] sometimes as of 'Middlesex,' and sometimes as of 'London and Middlesex,'[33] but 'for fiscal purposes, London and Middlesex under any name are indivisible.'[34] The relation between the City and shire remained on this basis until the Local

---

[25] *Domesday Bk.* (Rec. Com.), i, 127.
[26] Ibid. ii, 57–63 ; ibid. i, 23–5, 34, 44.
[27] Eadmer, *Hist. Novorum* (ed. M. Rule), 70.
[28] Ibid. 71.
[29] *Liber Albus* (Rolls Ser.), i, 128–9 ; Rymer, *Foed.* (Rec. Com.), i, 11.
[30] Cf. *Hund. R. of Edw. I* (Rec. Com.), ii, 403 sqq.
[31] Round, *Geoffrey de Mandeville*, 347 seq. ; cf. Sharpe, *London and the Kingdom*, i, 42 ; Stubbs, *Const. Hist.* i, 439.
[32] *Pipe R.* (Rec. Com.), 31 Hen. I, 143.
[33] Pipe R. 8 Ric. I.
[34] Round, *Geoffrey de Mandeville,* 347.

Government Act of 1888, although the grant was a frequent cause of dispute between London and the crown, and was on occasion temporarily withdrawn. As early as 1130 the citizens had been deprived of their right to elect the sheriff, for in that year they paid 100 marks that they might have a sheriff of their own choice.[35]

The Civil War of Stephen's reign fell as heavily on Middlesex as on the rest of England. In the summer of 1141 the empress came towards London after the election at Winchester. She received a deputation of Londoners at St. Albans, and then leaving the abbey proceeded by the old Roman road through Edgeware towards Westminster.[36] She was met by the citizens and rulers of London when nearing the City.[37] Geoffrey de Mandeville, grandson of the Geoffrey of the time of William I, was then at the height of his power. He was practically master of London as hereditary constable of the Tower, and one of the empress's first acts was to confirm the charter of the earldom and shrievalty of Essex granted to him by Stephen.[38] Meanwhile the queen was marching on London from Kent. She crossed the Thames and, ravaging Middlesex, spread a belt of desolation round the City.[39] The Londoners, who were already incensed against the empress, rose in arms for the queen. Matilda was forced to leave the City with all haste, and having galloped clear of the suburbs, her followers fleeing in all directions, she took the road towards Oxford.[40]

London admitted the queen, and Geoffrey de Mandeville made his peace with her likewise. To signalize his defection from the empress, he sallied out of the Tower and seized Sigillo, whom Matilda had lately installed as bishop of London,[41] and who was then at the episcopal manor of Fulham.[42] It is said that he held Sigillo to ransom for an enormous sum, but the bishop was present at Matilda's court a month later.[43] After Geoffrey had assisted at the liberation of Stephen,[44] and after the latter had been crowned for the second time at Canterbury, the king granted him the shrievalty of London and Middlesex, and of Herts. as well as that of Essex, which he already held.[45] Even these privileges could not hold him to Stephen's side. He deserted to the empress in six months' time, but after she left England he was captured and deprived of his lands by Stephen. From that time until his tragic death in September, 1143, his power was broken. Of his estates in Middlesex he gave the churches of Enfield, Edmonton, South Mimms, Northolt, with the hermitage of Hadley, to endow Walden Abbey,[46] which he had founded in 1136.

The effect of the military operations in Middlesex and of the continual anarchy of Stephen's reign is shown in the Pipe Rolls under Henry II. Of the £85 0s. 6d. danegeld due from the county in Henry's

---

[35] *Pipe R.* (Rec. Com.), 31 Hen. I, 143, 145.   [36] *Cont. Flor. Worc.* (Engl. Hist. Soc.), 131.
[37] Ibid.   [38] Round, *Geoffrey de Mandeville*, 88–95.   [39] *Gesta Stephani* (Rolls Ser.), 78.
[40] Ibid. 79.   [41] *Cont. Flor. Worc.* (Engl. Hist. Soc.), 131.
[42] Trivet, *Annals* (Engl. Hist. Soc.), 13.   [43] *Cont. Flor. Worc.* (Engl. Hist. Soc.), 131.
[44] Will. of Malmesbury, *Hist. Nov.* ii, 580.   [45] Round, *Geoffrey de Mandeville*, 138–44.
[46] Walden Abbey Chronicle, Harl. MS. 3697, fol. 1, cart. 1.

second year, £10 or nearly one-eighth of the whole, comes under the heading *in wasto*.[47]

We hear nothing of Middlesex during the reign of Henry II except in connexion with the demands made by the king upon London. The yearly farm for the City and shire was raised above the original sum of £300, and was not reduced until John's reign. The right to appoint the sheriffs was not exercised by the Londoners under Henry and his successor, and in the charter granted by Henry to the citizens no mention is made of Middlesex being let to farm.[48] The king strengthened his hold on the City and shire just as he increased his control over the barons. In 1174 Brichter de Haverhalle and Peter Fitz Walter held office, not as sheriffs, but as 'custodes,' showing that they were acting as the direct agents of the crown. Two years later the farm was raised to £490. John was frequently at Fulham during the early part of his reign,[49] but nothing of importance occurred in the county until the crisis of 1215 drew near. In May, 1215, safe-conduct was granted to the archbishop to come to Staines to treat of peace with the barons.[50] On 8 June safe-conduct was granted to all who would come to treat with the king at Staines,[51] but the signing of the Great Charter took place just beyond our boundaries. During the nominal peace which followed London remained in the hands of the barons until 15 August.[52] Fitz Walter, the baronial leader, was so fearful of treachery on the king's part that he thought it wiser to postpone the tournament fixed at Stamford for the Monday of the Feast of Sts. Peter and Paul, and ordered that it should be held instead on Hounslow Heath,[53] so that the barons should be in a better position to protect London if need arose. To this tournament came Walter de Albini by special invitation, for he represented the barons who were less hostile to the king.[54]

When Louis of France was called upon to act as arbitrator between the two parties, a conference was held at Hounslow during the first months of the reign of Henry III. Safe-conduct was granted to four peers and twenty knights on the Dauphin's side, to meet an equal number of peers and knights representing the king.[55] The conference known as the Treaty of Lambeth was possibly held at Staines, when Henry under the guidance of William Earl Marshal concluded peace with Louis and the baronial party.[56]

There was a continual struggle between the king and the Londoners during the early part of Henry's reign. In 1227 the citizens secured a reduction of the farm for London and Middlesex to £300,[57] but the disputes with regard to the shrievalty soon broke out again, and Henry took the City into his own hand on the least excuse. About 1250 a quarrel arose between the citizens and the abbot of Westminster over a concession made by the king to the abbot which in some way infringed

[47] *Pipe R.* (Pipe R. Soc.), 2 Hen. II, 5.

[48] Charter preserved in the Guildhall.

[49] *Rot. Lit. Pat.* (Rec. Com.), i, pt. 1. Itinerary.

[50] Ibid. i, 142.

[51] Rymer, *Foed.* (Rec. Com.), i, 129.

[52] Ibid. 133.   [53] Ibid. 134.

[54] Ibid.

[55] Pat. 1 Hen. III, m. 6.

[56] Rymer, *Foed.* i, 148.

[57] Chart. R. 11 Hen. III, m. 16.

the rights of the citizens in the county of Middlesex.[58] The king had recourse to his usual expedient, and took the City into his hand, and the dispute lasted for fifteen years, at the end of which the Exchequer Court decided in favour of the Londoners.[59]

The later struggle between Henry and the barons came to a crisis in the summer of 1263, when the king refused to confirm the Provisions of Oxford, and Simon de Montfort raised the banner of revolt. The king's brother Richard, earl of Cornwall and king of the Romans, took upon himself the post of arbitrator. Henry had granted him the large manor of Isleworth,[60] and during the negotiations held from 29 June to 15 July, Simon de Montfort lay at Isleworth, probably Richard's palace, while his adherents pitched their tents in Isleworth or 'Thistleworthe' Park.[61] A temporary peace was concluded on 15 July,[62] by which the barons gained their demands, Hugh le Despenser being confirmed in the office of justiciar, and the Tower of London being given into his custody, while Henry returned to Westminster. Simon de Montfort was practically ruler of the kingdom, and throughout July and August[63] he remained at Isleworth conducting negotiations with the Welsh. The following February the king of the Romans was at Windsor, organizing resistance to the barons with Prince Edward.[64] London declared energetically for de Montfort, and was greatly incensed with Richard for his espousal of the king's cause, for which he was denounced by the patriotic song writers of the day.[65] On 31 March 1264 the Londoners, led by Hugh Despenser, Thomas Piwelsdon, and Stephen Bukerelle, set out for Isleworth,[66] and there laid waste the whole manor, set fire to the manor-place and destroyed the 'water-mills and other commodities' belonging to the king of the Romans.[67] After this act of violence Richard threw himself vigorously into the campaign on the king's side,[68] and was present shortly afterwards with Henry at the taking of Northampton.[69] The citizens were punished for the outrage when Henry had regained the upper hand, and were forced to pay 1,000 marks for Richard's losses at Isleworth.[70] Richard was indeed loaded with debt before the war ended, for he supplied Henry with money and provisions for the campaign against the 'Disinherited' in the Isle of Ely.[71]

While this campaign was still in progress the earl of Gloucester, who had retired to his estates to mark his dissatisfaction with the terms of the Dictum of Kenilworth,[72] marched suddenly upon London, and

---

[58] Matt. Paris, *Chron. Maj.* (Rolls Ser.), iii, 62, 80–1.
[59] Fitz Thedmar, *Chron. of the Mayors and Sheriffs* (Camd. Soc.), 16, 17, 61.
[60] Lysons, *Environs of London* (1795), iii, 94.
[61] T. Wykes, *Chron.* (Rolls Ser.), 135; Prothero, *Simon de Montfort*, 250; Stow, *Annals*, 193.
[62] Rymer, *Foed.* (Rec. Com.) i, 427.   [63] T. Wykes, *Chron.* (Rolls Ser.), 135.
[64] *Royal Letters*, ii, 247–9.   [65] Rishanger, *De Bellis* (Rolls Ser.), 140.
[66] *Chron. of the Mayors and Sheriffs of London*, 65.
[67] T. Wykes, *Chron.* (Rolls Ser.), 140; *Ann. Dunst.* (Rolls Ser.), 221; Holinshed, *Chron.* iii, 460.
[68] Holinshed, *Chron.* iii, 460. 'Some think that this was the cause of the war which followed, because till this time the king of Almaine, through alliance with the earl of Gloucester, had been continually treating for peace; but after this time he was a bitter enemy of the barons.'
[69] T. Wykes, *Chron.* (Rolls Ser.), 145; Prothero, *Simon de Montfort*, 268.
[70] *Liber de Ant. Leg.* 94–5.   [71] Rymer, *Foed.* (Rec. Com.), i, 466.   [72] 31 Oct. 1266.

demanded the removal of aliens and the restitution of their lands to the 'Disinherited.'[73] London admitted him on 8 April.[74] Four days later he was joined by D'Eyville and other disinherited lords from the north, but he forced them to remain outside the City until after Easter (17 April).[75] Hearing of Gloucester's action, the king marched south, raising as many men as he could by borrowing on the shrines, jewels, and relics of Westminster.[76] He met Prince Edward at Cambridge, and together they went to Windsor, where the royal army daily increased.[77] Gloucester and his friends were somewhat dismayed and sent overtures of peace which, however, were not well received. Whereupon they 'appointed' to give the king battle upon Hounslow Heath on 5 May. Their hearts failed them, however, for 'the king coming thither in the morning found no man to resist him,' and after he had stayed there awhile, he marched towards London and passing into Essex, took up his abode at Stratford Abbey, while his army encamped about (East) Ham.[78] The king of the Romans again acted as mediator, and after several weeks of negotiation peace was concluded,[79] the earl of Gloucester receiving liberal terms for himself and the 'Disinherited,' and a pardon for the citizens of London who had taken his part.[80]

We hear nothing of Middlesex during the early years of Edward I. During the latter half of his reign the effects of the king's pecuniary difficulties fell on the county as on the rest of England. Repeated orders were sent to the sheriff for the enforcement of knighthood. In one instance, in February, 1292, all freeholders of land of the annual value of £40 were ordered to receive knighthood, and in January, 1293, the estates of defaulters were seized by the king's orders.[81] In 1294 war was declared against France, and Middlesex sent a quota of men to follow the king into Gascony.[82] The following year 4,000 cross-bow men and archers were supplied by Middlesex, with Essex, Herts. and London, to meet at Winchelsea in readiness to cross the seas.[83]

Edward was forced, by the need of money for the Scottish war, to promise the re-confirmation of the charters on his return from the Scottish campaign of 1298. A great council, therefore, was held at Stepney on 8 March, 1299, in the house of Henry Walleis, mayor of London.[84] The earls pressed Edward to fulfil his promise, but the king refused to give his answer till the following day. In the night he left the City and took up his quarters in the suburbs,[85] declaring to the lords who followed him, the next day, that he removed for the sake of the purer air. He agreed to the confirmation of the charters, however, and it was not until the people were assembled at St. Paul's Churchyard that

---

[73] Rishanger, *Chron.* (Camd. Soc.), 59.
[74] Stow, *Annals*, 196 ; Matt. Westm. *Flor. Hist.* (Rolls Ser.), iii, 15.
[75] *Dict. Nat. Biog.* x, 340.   [76] Holinshed, *Chron.* ii, 471.
[77] Matt. Westm. *Flor. Hist.* (Rolls Ser.), iii, 15.
[78] T. Wykes, *Chron.* 202 ; Stow, *Annals*, 196.
[79] 16 June, 1266.   [80] Stow, *Annals*, 196 ; Holinshed, *Chron.* ii, 472.
[81] Writ to the Sheriff of Middlesex, Letter-Book K, fol. 25.
[82] Palgrave, *Parl. Writs* (Rec. Com.), i, 259.   [83] Ibid. i, 270.
[84] Stow, *Annals*, 207.   [85] W. Hemingburgh, *Chron.* (Engl. Hist. Soc.), ii, 183.

they discovered his addition to the Charter of Forests—'saving the rights of the crown.'[86]

There is nothing of interest to record in the history of Middlesex during the early part of the fourteenth century. The burden of the Scottish and Welsh wars fell on the county, although it was beyond the region of actual warfare. Orders for the distraint of knighthood and summonses for the county's quota to appear on either border form the chief records during this period. Those specially summoned to serve against the Scots in 1301 were Richard de Windsor, who had already represented Middlesex in the Parliaments of 1297–9, Henry de Enfield, who had attended the Parliament at Salisbury amongst other justices of the peace in 1277, John de Bello Campo, and Adam Badyk.[87]

The Mandeville estates were at this time held by the Bohuns, earls of Hereford, a Humphrey de Bohun having married Maud, the Mandeville heiress. The Humphrey de Bohun of the reign of Edward III, who had succeeded to the title and lands of the earls of Essex and of Hereford in 1335,[88] served the king in France in the expedition for the relief of Aiguillon. On his return to England he obtained a licence to fortify and embattle his manor-house at Enfield.[89]

Middlesex was the scene of the climax of the Peasant Revolt in 1381. The Commons of Essex entered the county on the Festival of Corpus Christi (13 June).[90] On that morning they went to Highbury, led by Jack Straw, and there set fire to the hospital of St. John of Clerkenwell, causing much damage and loss to the Hospitallers.[91] Some of the Commons then returned to London, but the greater number remained on the scene of the outrage, surrounding the ruined house which had lately been built for the hospital by Sir Robert Hales,[92] and the remains of which came to be known as 'Jack Straw's Castle.'[93] On the following morning (Friday), the peasants of St. Albans and Barnet, marching into London, found the Essex insurgents still gathered round the burning ruins.[94] Jack Straw, as leader, received the new comers, and immediately exacted from them an oath of fealty to King Richard and the Commons of England.[95] Meanwhile the peasants of Kent and Surrey had entered London, and after committing many outrages in the City and in Westminster, they finally passed through Holborn and burnt the hospital of St. John at Clerkenwell.[96] That night, the insurgents were in three bodies: those who were still burning and wrecking in Highbury and Clerkenwell; and those who were encamped at Mile End, and on Tower Hill respectively.

The Mile End insurgents demanded that the king should come to them in person, immediately and unarmed.[97] Accordingly he rode out at

[86] W. Hemingburgh, *Chron.* (Engl. Hist. Soc.), ii, 183.

[87] Palgrave, *Parl. Writs* (Rec. Com.), i, 270.   [88] Inq. p.m. 10 Edw. III, No. 62.

[89] Pat. 21 Edw. III, pt. 3, m. 4. Camlet moat in Trent Park is supposed to mark the site of the Bohun manor-house.

[90] 'Anominalle Cronicle,' printed in *Engl. Hist. Rev.* July, 1898.

[91] Stow, *Annals*, 285.   [92] Lingard, *Hist. of Engl.* iii, 290.

[93] Lewis, *Hist. of Islington*, 4.   [94] Walsingham, *Hist. Angl.* (Rolls Ser.), i, 458.

[95] Ibid. i, 468.   [96] 'Anominalle Cronicle,' *ut supra.*   [97] Stow, *Annals*, 286.

seven o'clock in the morning, accompanied by his mother in a 'whir-lecote,' the mayor of London, and many earls, knights, and esquires.[98] He was surrounded by 60,000 petitioners, who demanded the abolition of slavery, the reduction of rents, and free liberty to buy and sell at fairs and markets.[99] By granting their demands and by giving a charter of liberties to each parish, Richard persuaded the Commons to return to their homes, not, however, before they had dragged the archbishop of Canterbury and the prior of St. John of Clerkenwell from the Tower, and summarily beheaded them.[100]

On the following day the king proclaimed that he would meet the remainder of the insurgents two miles beyond the North-West gate.[101] He rode to the appointed place in the morning and took up his position, surrounded by the nobles, near the priory of St. Bartholomew, the Commons being drawn up to the west and further from the City.[102] The story is well known of how Wat Tyler rode up to the king and saluting him familiarly, rehearsed the demands of the peasants, and then having threatened the valet de Kent, who stood among the king's retinue, was struck to the ground by William Walworth, mayor of London.[103] The king's marvellous presence of mind saved the situation, and while he led the Commons to the field of St. John of Clerkenwell,[104] the mayor rode with all haste to London for armed help. Tyler was carried into St. Bartholomew's priory, but on Walworth's return he was brought out and executed, and his head and that of Jack Straw replaced those of the archbishop and the prior of St. John's on London Bridge.[105] The mass of the Commons were meanwhile surrounded in Clerkenwell Fields, and would have been slaughtered if the king had not intervened to spare them.[106] After quiet was restored, he knighted the mayor, Nicholas Brembre, John Philpot, and Ralph Laundre, beneath the standard.[107]

At the end of the same reign, during the struggle between Richard II and the barons, the latter marched into Middlesex under Thomas of Woodstock, duke of Gloucester. The king had spent the year in a royal progress with the object of consolidating his friends, and in the late summer had gained the favourable decision of the five judges at Nottingham, which declared the Commission of Regency to be illegal.[108] In November he marched into London intending to prevent by force the renewal of the Commission, and to punish as traitors those who had originated it. News of his intention reached the duke of Gloucester, and on 12 November the king was surprised to learn that he and Warwick were marching on London with an armed force, and were already only a few miles north of the City.[109] The earl of Arundel joined

[98] 'Anominalle Cronicle,' *ut supra.* [99] Lingard, *Hist. of Engl.* iii, 291.
[100] Riley, *Mems. of Lond.* 449. [101] 'Anominalle Cronicle,' *ut supra.* [102] Stow, *Annals.*
[103] 'Anominalle Cronicle,' *ut supra* ; Walsingham, *Hist. Angl.* i, 43, 389 ; Knighton, *Chron.* (Twysden), 2637. [104] Riley, *Mems. of Lond.* 450.
[105] 'Anominalle Cronicle,' *ut supra.* [106] Riley, *Mems. of Lond.* 450.
[107] 'Anominalle Cronicle' ; cf. *Three Fifteenth Century Chronicles* (Camd. Soc.), 48.
[108] Stubbs, *Const. Hist.* ii, 266 ; Lingard, *Hist. of Engl.* iii, 328.
[109] *Mon. Evesh.* (ed. Hearne), 90 ; Walsingham, *Hist. Angl.* (Rolls Ser.), ii, 163.

them at their camp in Hornsey Park near Highgate.[110] The king thought of resistance, but London refused to fight, and Richard's adherents sympathized too keenly with Gloucester's demand for the removal of the aliens 'to get their heads broken for de Veer's sake,' as the earl of Northumberland said.[111] Richard could only issue a proclamation forbidding the citizens to assist or sell provisions to the enemy. This was met on the part of the barons by an advance to Hackney with 4,000 men. They dispatched a letter to the mayor and aldermen assuring the City that their only object was to deliver the king from traitors. On 13 November they were joined by the earls of Derby and Nottingham,[112] and on the following day at Waltham Abbey, just beyond the north-east boundary of Middlesex, they 'appealed' five of the king's favourites of treason, which charge they repeated three days later at Westminster.[113]

The accession of Henry of Lancaster to the throne led to the increase of royal influence in Middlesex. Before he came to the throne Henry had married Mary, one of the de Bohun heiresses,[114] and thus the manor of Enfield came into the hands of the crown. The whole estate, that is from Barnet to Enfield, and from Potters Bar to Winchmore Hill and Southgate, was strictly preserved, and became a favourite royal hunting-ground.

The rebellions and wars of the reign of Henry IV scarcely affected Middlesex, and we hear very little of it during the early fifteenth century. In 1414 a great meeting was secretly arranged by the Lollards to be held in St. Giles's Fields.[115] Their intention was said to be to seize and even to put to death the king and his brothers, to destroy Westminster Abbey and St. Paul's, and to proclaim Sir John Oldcastle as Regent.[116] It was expected that thousands of apprentices from London would muster in the fields, and that Oldcastle would place himself at the head of the insurgents. The date and place of the meeting were, however, made known to the king. He came quietly to Westminster from Eltham where he had been keeping Christmas, and on the evening fixed, the Sunday after Twelfth Day, he set out for St. Giles' Fields with a small body of companions.[117] Panic seized the rebels on the news of his approach, and they scattered in all haste, though many were killed and others taken prisoners.[118]

Jack Cade's rebellion, in the following reign, had little to do with the county. Apparently no Middlesex men joined the rebels.[119] Cade and the men of Kent and Sussex entered London from Southwark, and Mile End seems to have been the only place north of the river that was affected by the insurrection.[120] On the same day on which Lord Say was

[110] Walsingham, op. cit. (Rolls Ser.), ii, 164.
[111] Knighton, *Chron.* (Twysden), 2698.
[112] Knighton, *Chron.* (Twysden), 2700.
[113] Lingard, op. cit. iii, 328.
[114] Inq. p.m. 47 Edw. III, m. 10.
[115] *Gesta Henrici V.* (Engl. Hist. Soc.), 4.
[116] *Rot. Parl.* (Rec. Com.), iv, 108.
[117] Elmham, *Vita Hen. V.* (ed. Hearne), 31.
[118] Walsingham, *Hist. Angl.* (Rolls Ser.), ii, 298.
[119] Owridge, *Illus. of Jack Cade's Rebellion*, 73.
[120] A great number of the Commons of Essex encamped there on the same day that Jack Cade entered Southwark. Fabyan, *Chron.* (1811), 623.

executed in Cheapside, his son-in-law Cromer, the former sheriff of Kent, who had been committed to the Fleet prison for extortion,[121] was led out by the rebels to Mile End, and there, without any judgement, his head was smitten off in Cade's presence.[122] Cade and his followers seem then to have returned to the City bearing the heads of Cromer and Lord Say on poles to London Bridge.

Middlesex suffered but little during the Wars of the Roses, having no great baronial houses to lose, and being overshadowed by London's predilection for the White Rose. Except for the passage of armies to and from London, and in 1461, when the county was in danger of devastation after the second battle of St. Albans, the tide of war did not come very near our boundaries during the early part of the war. On the latter occasion, the known hostility of the Londoners deterred the queen from nearer approach to the city.[124] On 25 February, 1461, Edward of York entered London, and the men of all the neighbouring counties flocked to his standard. On 2 March an enthusiastic crowd offered him the crown at Clerkenwell, and he was crowned on the following day at Westminster.[125] Four years later Henry VI was brought a prisoner to London after his capture in Lancashire. He was met on 24 July by the earl of Warwick at Islington,[126] where his gilt spurs were struck from his feet, and he was taken in bonds and under strong escort to the Tower.[127] The short period of his restoration in 1471 brought about the most important battle to which Middlesex can lay claim.

Edward of York landed in March of that year after his brief exile. He was proclaimed king at Nottingham, and marched towards London, closely followed by the earl of Warwick. London admitted the Yorkist army on Maundy Thursday (11 April).[128] Warwick hoped that Edward would keep Easter in London, and that he might then take him by surprise. In this, however, he was disappointed. Edward allowed his forces to rest on Good Friday, but on the Saturday set out to meet the enemy.[129] Knowing that his throne hung upon the forthcoming battle, he spared no pains to render his army efficient. 'Harness, weapons, horses, all engines, instruments meet for the war, he neither forgot nor slackly furnished. What shall I say more? He determined clearly to spend all his riches, yea all that he could imagine upon the chance of this battle; firmly believing that this conflict should knit up all his labour and bring him to quietness.'[130] Henry VI, again dethroned and a prisoner, went in his train, both as a precaution against treachery in his rear, and as a protection in case the battle should go against him.[131]

[121] Engl. Chron. Three Fifteenth Cent. Chron. (Camd. Soc.), 67. [122] Ibid.

[124] Chron. of Ric. II, &c. (ed. Davies), 107 ; Whethamstede, Reg. (ed. Hearne), i, 391.

[125] Pink, Hist. of Clerkenwell, 612–13.

[126] Three Fifteenth Cent. Chron. (Camd. Soc.), 80.

[127] Holinshed, Chron. iii ; Hall's Chron. 285 ; Ramsay, York and Lanc. ii, 317.

[128] Chron. of the White Rose (Camd. Soc.), 58 ; Ann. of Edw. IV, 18.

[129] Warkworth, Chron. (Camd. Soc.), 15 ; Three Fifteenth Cent. Chron. (Camd. Soc.), 184 ; Chron. of the White Rose, 61. [130] Hall, Chron. 295.

[131] Ibid ; Warkworth, Chron. 15 ; Chron. of the White Rose, 61.

Warwick had marched meanwhile from St. Albans, and had taken up a position on Gladesmore Heath, on the northern outskirts of Barnet.[132] He encamped there on the night of Easter Eve, hoping from that position to take the enemy's troops in detail as they came out of the narrow village of Barnet. Edward was too wary a soldier to be caught in this trap. Marching north towards Barnet he sent his advance-guard to drive Warwick's outposts from the town, but would allow none of his main body to enter it.[133] He drew his forces under cover of darkness very quietly to the right and took up a position on the then uninclosed slopes which fell eastward from the Hatfield-Barnet road on which Warwick's left was stationed.[134] But the manœuvre was not effected so quietly that Warwick did not detect it. He accordingly opened fire on the unseen foe, but not until Edward's forces were mostly under cover of the hill, so that the Lancastrian guns overshot their mark,[135] and Warwick had to be content to draw up his troops along the high road, where they passed the night under the hedge-side.[136] Edward would allow no guns to be fired in reply, so that his exact position should not be betrayed. He ordered the advance before sunrise on Easter morning,[137] and without any blowing of trumpets, and taking advantage of the thick mist,[138] the Yorkists fell upon the enemy. Warwick's right wing under the earl of Oxford and Lord Montagu swept across the heath and overpowered Hastings on the Yorkist left, driving him from the field.[139] His troops fled through Barnet, and spread the news even as far as London that Edward was already defeated.[140] Similar misfortune befell the Lancastrian left under the duke of Exeter, for they were driven back and overpowered by Gloucester on the Yorkist right. Consequently the positions of the forces were now so altered that the Yorkists faced south and the Lancastrians faced north.[141] Meanwhile the fight in the centre raged fiercely, Edward himself displaying great prowess.[142] The mist had lain so thick on the ground that the centre was unconscious of the triumph of the Lancastrian left, and Oxford's men returning from the pursuit of Edward's right wing were themselves mistaken for Yorkists, and before the mistake could be discovered, Warwick's men had fallen upon them. Oxford raised the cry of treason and fled from the field.[143] Edward, quick to take advantage of the confusion, pressed the attack hard, and after heavy fighting won the day. The Kingmaker was among the slain, but accounts vary as to the manner in which he met his

---

[132] Ramsay, *York and Lanc.* ii, 370 ; Hall, *Chron.* 295 ; cf. *Paston Letters* (ed. Gairdner), ii, 4.

[133] *Chron. of the White Rose*, 62 ; Warkworth, op. cit. 15, says that Edward reached Barnet first and that, therefore, Warwick stayed without the town.

[134] Ramsay, loc. cit. Edward's left was on the cross road to Monken Hadley (Herts.) and his right stretched northwards over the Middlesex border along the slopes towards Wrotham Park.

[135] *Chron. of the White Rose*, 62.

[136] *Arrivall of Edw. IV* (Camd. Soc.), 18.

[137] Waurin, *Anchiennes Cronicques d'Engleterre* (ed. Dupont), iii, 125.

[138] Fabyan, *Chron.* 661. The mist was ascribed to the incantation of Friar Bungay.

[139] Hall, *Chron.* 296.   [140] *Chron. of the White Rose*, 63.

[141] Waurin, op. cit. iii, 213.   [142] *Arrivall of Edw. IV* (Camd. Soc.), 20.

[143] Warkworth, *Chron.* (Camd. Soc.) 15. Oxford's livery was a star with streams, the Radiant Star of the de Veers. Edward's was a sun with streams.

death.[144] That commonly accepted is that he was fighting on toot, but when he saw that the day was lost, he hurried to his horse which was tethered near a wood, intending to escape, but encumbered by his heavy armour, he could not ride away before he was surrounded by the enemy and slain.[145] Whatever the manner of his death, his body and that of his brother Montagu were taken to London by the victorious Yorkists, and there exposed for several days. Of the Lancastrian leaders, Oxford alone escaped unhurt.[146] The duke of Exeter was badly wounded ; Sir William Tyrell, Sir Lewis Johns and many knights were killed. Edward also lost many adherents, among them Lord Cromwell, Lord Berners, Lord Say, and many others.[147]

The battle over, Edward refreshed himself at Barnet and proceeded to London.[148] A dozen years later his son passed along the same road to his coronation. He was in the charge of Richard of Gloucester, who had led the Yorkist right at Barnet, and who had just gained possession of his nephew's person by taking him from the guardianship of the Woodvilles. The royal party was met at Hornsey Park by the mayor and 500 citizens of London,[149] who escorted the boy-king to the capital, whence his mother had fled to sanctuary at Westminster on hearing that Gloucester, and not her brother, was approaching in charge of her son.

Under the Tudors, Middlesex began to assume its modern aspect. The Dissolution of the Monasteries was the first step towards transforming the county into a residential neighbourhood for London. The Church continued to be a great landowner in the county, but many small estates came into the hands of the king, who would grant them for short periods to favourites, statesmen or merchants of London. There was hardly a man of distinction who did not at some time in his career build a house or own a small property in Middlesex. These small estates, however, were so continually changing hands, so frequently falling to the crown and being re-granted, so often sold, divided, and forfeited, as practically to prevent the growth of a county gentry,[150] and thus to keep Middlesex from taking an independent part in the history of the time. The growing importance of London brought greater natural prosperity and increasing civilization to the county, but little corporate unity.

On the other hand, Middlesex saw much of the personages if not of the events of the time. Naturally the sovereign was continually passing through the county on his way to and from the capital. Thus in August, 1487, Henry VII was welcomed at Islington on his return from suppressing Lambert Simnel's rebellion.[151] In November of the same year, when he was journeying to London for the coronation of

---

[144] According to Hall (*Chron.* 296), Warwick rushed into the thick of the battle to encourage his troops and died covered with wounds. For other accounts see *Chron. of the White Rose*, 64 note.

[145] Warkworth, *Chron.* 16 ; *Chron. of the White Rose*, 65 ; *Arrivall of Edw. IV* (Camd. Soc.), 20.

[146] *Paston Letters*, ii, 5.   [147] Warkworth, *Chron.* (Camd. Soc.), 16.

[148] *Arrivall of Edw. IV* (Camd. Soc.), 21.

[149] Fabyan, *Chron.* 668 ; Kennet, *Hist. of Engl.* i, 482 ; *Cont. Hist. of Engl.* 565.

[150] Compare the list of the gentry in Fuller's *Worthies*, Midd. with that made three hundred years later in Norden, *Spec. Brit.* and with the names of noblemen and knights in the *Antiquarian Repertory*, iii, 107.   [151] Stow, *Annals*, 472.

the queen, they were both met at Hornsey Park by sheriffs, with the mayor and principal commoners of London.[152] Under Henry VIII Middlesex became very popular with the royal family, both as a nursery for the younger members and as a place of recreation for those whom affairs of state kept within a day's journey from Westminster. In 1514 Wolsey obtained a ninety-nine years' lease of Hampton Manor from the priory of St. John of Jerusalem,[153] and began to build his magnificent palace, so magnificent that he found it prudent to offer it as a present to the king a year after it was completed. Wolsey was still allowed to use the palace himself on occasions, and in 1527, by the king's desire, he entertained Montmorenci, the French ambassador, in gorgeous state.[154] Three years later the cardinal passed through the county on his way to York, in deep disgrace and in comparative poverty. Nevertheless his train numbered a hundred and threescore persons, and he had twelve carts to carry 'his stuffe of his owne' and three score other carts for his 'daily carriage of necessities.' Coming from Richmond at the beginning of Passion Week he stayed for a night at the abbot of Westminster's house at Hendon,[155] and passed on the next day to a 'place where my lady Parry lay, called the Rye,' never to journey so far south again. Very different was the exit from our stage of Wolsey's successor to the chancellorship. Sir Thomas More passed the period after his retirement from public life at Chelsea on the estate which he had bought about 1520.[156] Very soon after the passing of the Act of Supremacy, he was summoned to take the oath at Lambeth.[157] Before setting out he went to Chelsea parish church 'to be confessed, to heare masse, and to be housed,' and then with foreboding in his heart, bade farewell to his wife and family. Accompanied by his son-in-law, Roper, and his four servants, he took boat for Lambeth 'wherein sitting still sadly awhile, at the last he suddenly sounded me in the ear and said " Son Roper, I thank my God the field is won." ' [158] Henry VIII spent much of his time at Hampton Court after Wolsey's death. Here Edward was born,[159] and here twelve days later Jane Seymour died. Here Catherine Howard was disgraced, and here Henry married his sixth wife. The unfortunate Catherine Howard was confined at Syon House[160] from 14 November until three days before her execution, where she was 'kept very strict, but served as a queen.'[161] In 1547, Henry's corpse rested at Syon as the magnificent funeral procession was on its way to Windsor.[162] The heir to the throne was at Hertford when Henry died, whence he was brought

---

[152] Stow, *Annals*, 473.   [153] Lysons, *Environs of Lond.* (1800), v, 52.
[154] Cavendish, *Life of Wolsey* (ed. Holmes), 110–15 ; Harl. MSS. No. 428.
[155] Cavendish, *Life of Wolsey* (ed. Holmes), 209.
[156] Faulkner, *Chelsea*, 92 ; Roper, *Life of Sir Thomas More*, 61–70.
[157] Gairdner, *L. and P. Hen. VIII*, vii, 112.
[158] Roper, *Life of Sir Thomas More*, 80–7.   [159] 12 Oct. 1537.
[160] The monastery of Syon is erroneously said by Burnet to have been suppressed in 1532 for harbouring the king's enemies, and of being in league with the Maid of Kent. (*Hist. of the Reformation*, ii, 340.) It was dissolved in 1539 and remained in the hands of the crown until the end of the reign.
[161] Holinshed, *Chron.* iii, 1582.
[162] Lysons, *Environs of Lond.* (1795), iii, 87.

privately to Enfield by the earl of Hertford and Sir Anthony Browne.[163] There he and his sister Elizabeth heard with many tears the news of their father's death, and on the following day (31 January), Edward made his state entry into London.[164]

Edward VI spent the summers of his reign at Hampton Court. He was there also in the October of 1549 when Somerset's ecclesiastical and economic policy brought his Protectorate to a close. The council was assembled in London 'thinking to meet with the Lord Protector to make him amend his disorders.'[165] Somerset wrote from Hampton Court in Edward's name asking why they gathered together their 'powers' and requesting that they should come peaceably to consult with him. But the following day, having heard how closely the council consulted together,[166] and guessing the hostility of their intentions towards him, he made ready to defend himself at Hampton Court. He had the palace gates repaired and brought down about five hundred 'harnesses' from the armoury for his own and the king's men.[167] He raised the country side, summoning all the king's loving subjects to repair to Hampton Court, 'in most defensible array, with harness and weapons to defend his most royal person and his most entirely beloved uncle, the Lord Protector,' against whom a conspiracy was suspected.[168] He requested the aid of the earl of Oxford's servants, asked Sir Henry Seymour to levy horse and foot, and wrote under the king's signet to the mayor, aldermen and citizens of London to send one thousand men 'well harnessed and with good and convenient weapons' to Hampton Court.[169] Then not content with these precautions, he decided to remove the king to Windsor.[170] Accordingly they set out between nine and ten o'clock of the same evening (6 October). He was subsequently charged with having alarmed the king by telling him that his life was in danger, and with having injured his health by the hasty removal to Windsor.[171] Somerset treated with the council by letter,[172] but on 14 October the lords came in person to the castle and carried him a prisoner through Holborn to the Tower.[173] The king returned the same day to Hampton Court, seemingly little affected by his uncle's fate, and the council met on 15 October to reorganize the government in the favour of Warwick. One of those who gained by this *coup d'état* was Sir Thomas Wroth of Durrants near Enfield, who was then made one of the four principal gentlemen of the king's privy chamber. It was the duty of two of these gentlemen to be always with the king, and in consideration of 'the singular care and travail that they should have about the king's person,' and also to secure

---

[163] *Literary Remains of Edw. VI* (ed. J. G. Nichols), 210.
[164] Strickland, *Lives of the Queens of Engl.* vi, 20–1.
[165] Edw. VI's Journal in *Literary Remains of Edw. VI*, 233.
[166] Tytler, *Engl. under Edw. VI and Mary*, i, 249. Somerset's suspicions were aroused by hearing that the councillors dined every day at one another's houses.
[167] *Literary Remains of Edw. VI*, 235. [168] Ibid. ; Tytler, op. cit. i, 205.
[169] Strype, *Eccl. Mem.* ii, App. 44 ; Ellis, *Letters,* i (2), 166.
[170] *Literary Remains of Edw. VI*, 235.
[171] *Acts of the P.C.* 1547–50, pp. 341–2.   [172] Ibid. 333, 337–40.
[173] *Literary Remains of Edw. VI*, 255.

POLITICAL HISTORY

their fidelity to Warwick, their salaries of £50 were increased by yet another £50.[175] Wroth was already a favourite of the king, having been appointed a gentleman of the chamber to Edward before his accession, a post which he owed to Cranmer's influence.[176] During the campaign of Pinkie, Wroth had been sent to Scotland in order that Edward might have a full and trustworthy account of the war.[177] After Somerset's fall he was made keeper of Syon House, which then reverted to the king until 1553, when it was granted to the duke of Northumberland.[178] Wroth was an ardent Protestant, and as such was privy to Northumberland's schemes to continue the Protestant succession after Edward's death.

Lady Jane Grey spent the greater part of her life in Middlesex.[179] She entered the household of Queen Catherine Parr when barely nine years old, and continued to live with Catherine and her second husband, Lord Thomas Seymour, both at Chelsea and at Hanworth.[180] After Seymour's impeachment and the fall of his brother Somerset, Jane's father allied himself closely with the Dudleys, and in 1553 brought his family to East Sheen, on the Surrey side of the river, in order to be near Northumberland's house at Syon. A marriage was arranged for Jane with Northumberland's fourth son, Guildford Dudley, as part of the plot to win the succession from the Tudors to the Dudleys. The marriage took place on Whit-Sunday (21 May, 1553) at Northumberland's London house in the Strand,[181] after which Jane went to live with her husband's parents in order that she might be at hand when Edward should die. She detested the duke and duchess, and after some trouble, obtained permission to retire 'for recreation' to Chelsea Place, which then belonged to Northumberland.[182] She was taken so ill there as to imagine herself to be poisoned.[183]

Edward VI died on 6 July.[184] Northumberland took great precautions that the news of the king's death might be kept secret, in order to secure the persons of his sisters, so no public announcement was made until 8 July.[185] Jane was still at Chelsea. Thither came Lady Sidney[186] on the ninth, with the news that Jane must repair the same night to Syon House,[187] where she must appear before the assembled council. They went up the river in a barge, the tide running so strongly that it was two hours before they reached Syon House. Lady Jane has herself described the scene which followed ; the deference of Northampton, Arundel, and Pembroke ; her astonishment when her own mother and mother-in-law paid their homage.[188] Finally, the duke of Northumberland, as president of the council, declared the death of the king, and that Edward had left

[175] *Acts of the P.C.* 1547–50, p. 345.
[176] *Dict. Nat. Biog.* lxiii, 164.
[177] *Literary Remains of Edw. VI*, 50.
[178] Lysons, *Environs of Lond.* (1795), iii, 87.
[179] Strickland, *Tudor Princesses*, 97.
[180] Howard, *Life of Lady Jane Grey*, 156 ; Strickland, *Lives of the Queens of Engl.* iii, 246.
[181] Durham House.
[182] Strickland, *Tudor Princesses*, 141.
[183] Pollino, *L'Historia Ecclesiastica della Revoluzion d'Inghilterra*, 335–8.
[184] *Literary Remains of Edw. VI*, cxix.
[185] Lingard, *Hist. of Engl.* v, 370.
[186] The sister of Robert Dudley, earl of Leicester, and mother of Sir Philip Sidney.
[187] Strickland, *Tudor Princesses*, 143 ; cf. *Gent. Mag.* May, 1847, p. 491.
[188] Pollino, op. cit. 335–8.

the crown by his will to Lady Jane. The lords of the council then performed their homage, swearing to support her to the death, 'whilst I having heard all this, remained as stunned, and out of myself.' Bewildered and full of foreboding, surrounded by those she hated and feared, yet unable, a girl of sixteen, to withstand their will, Lady Jane fell to the ground, wept, lamented the death of the king, swooned—and submitted.[189] The next day she was conducted to Westminster and then to the Tower, as much a prisoner then, as the gorgeous procession swept down the river, as when, the nine days' reign at an end, she was at the mercy of Queen Mary.[190]

All the lords and ladies near London flocked in to see the coronation, but the popular feeling in Middlesex ran very strongly against Northumberland. As he rode out through Shoreditch a few days later on his mission to fetch Mary from Newmarket he remarked to one who rode near him 'The people press to see us, but not one sayeth God spede us.'[191] When, as Mary's prisoner, he again passed through the place, 'all the people reviled him and called him traitor and heretic.'[192] Mary's triumphant entry took place on 30 July. The last miles of her progress through Middlesex were thronged with crowds, whose enthusiasm left no doubt as to the popularity of her cause. The Princess Elizabeth rode out from Somerset House to meet her sister, and at Whitechapel the mayor and aldermen delivered up the sword of the City to the new queen.[193]

It was fortunate for Sir Thomas Wroth that he was not one of those who suffered for the attempt to oust Mary from the throne. He must have been acquainted with the whole scheme, as he was in attendance on Edward VI till the last,[194] and signed the letters patent limiting the crown to Lady Jane Grey, but fortunately for himself he took no active part in the rebellion. He was sent to the Tower on 27 July, but was very soon released. In January, 1553–4, when Suffolk was meditating the second rising, Wroth was urged to join, but he prudently refrained. Bishop Gardiner proposed his arrest,[195] but Wroth escaped, probably through the influence of his son-in-law, Lord Rich, and he spent the remainder of Mary's reign abroad, mostly at Frankfort and Strasburg.[196]

In February, 1553–4, the queen's intended marriage with Philip of Spain brought about the rebellion of Wyatt and the men of Kent.[197] On the night of Shrove Tuesday (6 February) the insurgents crossed the Thames at Kingston, intending to pass quickly through southern Middlesex and to gain an entrance to the City in the early morning.[198]

[189] Strickland, *Tudor Princesses*, 144 ; Tytler, *Engl. under Edw. VI and Mary*, ii, 188.
[190] Strickland, *Tudor Princesses*, 144 ; Howard, *Life of Lady Jane Grey*, 235.
[191] *Chron. of the Grey Friars* (Camd. Soc.), 58 ; *Chron. of Queen Jane* (Camd. Soc.), 8.
[192] *Chron. of the Grey Friars* (Camd. Soc.), 81.   [193] Ibid.
[194] Edward died in his arms ; *Literary Remains of Edw. VI*, cxcix.
[195] Wroth was one of the witnesses against Gardiner for the latter's sermon at St. Paul's in July, 1548.
[196] *Dict. Nat. Biog.*   [197] *Machyn's Diary* (Camd. Soc.), 54.
[198] Grafton, *Chron.* (1809), 538.

But before they reached Brentford their advance was discovered;[199] and the news being carried to London, the queen's forces had ample time in which to take up a strong position across the road by which Wyatt must advance.[200] As Wyatt had been delayed by the dismounting of a piece of artillery, when he heard that London was already warned of his approach, he encamped for the night to refresh his men, who were very weary and faint from want of food.[201] By ten o'clock the following morning Wyatt was advancing through Kensington, and on reaching the corner of Hyde Park he found the queen's troops, under the earl of Pembroke, drawn up across his path. After a sharp skirmish Wyatt's little force was cut in two. Those in the rear found it impossible to rejoin their leader and as many as were able fled back, along the way they had come, to Brentford.[202] Wyatt still went forward, but the story of his subsequent battle at Charing Cross[203] and of his disappointment at Ludgate belong to the history of Westminster and London.[204]

Wyatt's rebellion nearly cost Princess Elizabeth her life. The queen sent for her sister to come from Ashridge, Hertfordshire, to answer the charge of implication in the plot, and sent the royal physician to see that Elizabeth did not evade the command by pleading illness.[205] Starting on the day of Lady Jane Grey's execution,[206] and travelling very slowly, Elizabeth came on the third night of her journey to ' Mr. Dodd's at Mimms,' and on the fourth to Mr. Cholmeley's at Highgate, where she stayed for more than a week, too ill to proceed.[207] It is little wonder that Elizabeth journeyed slowly, nor that she could truly plead ill-health, for the future looked black enough. There were gibbets at each of the City gates, and the public buildings were crowded with the heads of the noblest in the land.[208] Whatever her fears, Elizabeth showed a brave front. On the day on which she entered London, the same morning that Suffolk was executed, the road from Highgate was thronged with gazing and weeping crowds.[209] She bade her attendants uncover the litter in which she was carried so that the people might see her as she sat clothed in white ; and though her countenance was pale, her bearing was ' proud, lofty, and disdainful, by which she endeavoured to conceal her trouble.'[210] Elizabeth's popularity, as well as her own prudence and wit, saved her life; but the following Christmas she was again journeying through Middlesex uncertain of her fate, this time to appear before Mary

---

[199] *Chron. of Queen Jane and Queen Mary* (Camd. Soc.), 47. Before coming to Brentford they were seen by one of the queen's scouts, ' who then by chance meeting Brett and his company, the said Brett said to the scout, " Back, villain : if thou go further to discover any company here, thou shalt die out of hand." The scout returned in great haste.'

[200] Grafton, *Chron.* 539.

[201] *Chron. of Queen Jane and Queen Mary* (Camd. Soc.), 48.

[202] Grafton, *Chron.* 541.   [203] *Chron. of the Grey Friars* (Camd. Soc.), 87.

[204] *Chron. of Queen Jane and Queen Mary* (Camd. Soc.), 48–9 ; and Appendix, 131.

[205] Nichols, *Progresses of Queen Eliz.* i, 6.

[206] Lodge, *Illus. of Brit. Hist.* i, 190. Robert Swift to the earl of Shrewsbury.

[207] Holinshed, *Chron.* iii, 1151 ; cf. Tytler, *Engl. under Edw. VI and Mary*, ii, 426.

[208] Noailles, *Ambassades en Angleterre*, iii, 83.

[209] Nichols, *Progresses of Queen Eliz.* i, 6 (note).

[210] Simon Renard to Chas. V, cited by Strickland, *Queens of Engl.* vi, 66.

at Hampton Court. She was brought under strong escort from Woodstock, and on her way stayed for a night at the George Inn at Colnbrook, on the borders of Middlesex and Buckinghamshire.[211] There she was met by sixty gentlemen and yeomen from her own retinue at Somerset House, 'much to all their comforts,' for they had not seen her for several months.[212] They were not to receive much comfort from their meeting, for Sir Henry Benefield, who had the custody of Elizabeth, would not allow them to approach near enough to speak to her, but commanded them in the queen's name immediately to leave the town, 'to both their own and her grace's no little heaviness.'[213] Hardly reassured by this incident, Elizabeth reached Hampton Court the next night, and found herself installed in 'the prince's lodgings,' with the doors locked and guarded. She was left for several days to wonder what fate was in store for her, occasionally visited by Bishop Gardiner, who vainly tried to extort from her some confession of conspiracy against the queen.[214] Her suspense was ended one night when at ten o'clock she received a summons to the queen's presence. Imagining herself to be in great danger, and requesting the prayers of her attendant—'for she could not tell if she should ever see her again'—she followed Sir Henry Benefield through the garden and up the stairs which led to the queen's lodgings.[215] But her fears proved groundless. The expectation of an heir to the throne made the queen look upon her sister as a far less dangerous rival than hitherto, and Philip of Spain was anxious to please the English people, and that the popular princess should join the royal festivities at Christmastide. A reconciliation took place between the sisters,[216] and throughout the brilliant scenes of the following days Elizabeth was recognized as the second royal personage in the realm.[217]

Elizabeth was always a familiar and popular figure in Middlesex. She had spent the greater part of her youth at Chelsea[218] and at Enfield,[219] and during Mary's reign she was allowed to hunt in Enfield Chase.[220] On her accession in November, 1558, huge multitudes crowded to welcome her at Highgate, and to witness the procession of bishops kneel by the wayside to offer their allegiance; which was graciously accepted except in the case of Bishop Bonner, to whom Elizabeth refused her hand.[221]

During the early part of her reign Elizabeth often returned to Elsing Hall at Enfield,[222] and in 1578 she honoured Sir Thomas Gresham, at Osterley, with a visit, when he entertained her with great magnificence.[223] Hampton Court was one of her favourite residences, and she kept Christmas there in 1572 and 1593.

---

[211] Holinshed, *Chron.* iii, 1158.
[213] Holinshed, *Chron.* iii, 1158.
[215] Ibid. 1158–9.
[216] It was at this interview that Philip is supposed to have been hidden behind the tapestry ; Strickland, *Lives of the Queens of Engl.* vi, 117.
[218] With Catherine Howard.
[220] Nichols, *Progresses of Queen Eliz.* i, 17, 102.
[222] Strype, *Annals,* i, 270 ; *Burghley Papers,* ii, 763.
[223] Nichols, *Progresses of Queen Eliz.* ii, 279.

[212] Nichols, *Progresses of Queen Eliz.* i, 12.
[214] Ibid.
[217] Ibid. 118.
[219] Strype, *Annals,* i, 236.
[221] Holinshed, *Chron.* iii, 1784.

POLITICAL HISTORY

Great indignation was aroused in 1586 by Babington's conspiracy against the queen's life. Babington had been detained at Walsingham's house in London, apparently as his guest, until one night he discovered that the all-powerful minister was fully informed of his intention to assassinate the queen.[224] Babington immediately took to flight, and having warned his fellow-conspirators they all fled to St. John's Wood,[225] which then afforded good covert to robbers and outlaws. To disguise Babington his friends cut off his hair and 'besmeared and soiled the natural beauty of his face with green walnut shells.'[226] 'Being constrained by famine' they went to Okington at Harrow-on-the-Hill, a house belonging to a Roman Catholic family of the name of Bellamy. There they were hidden in a barn, fed, and clothed 'in rusticall habit.' Warrants had been issued for their arrest, and such was the popular indignation aroused by Walsingham's exaggerated reports of the plot[227] that the fugitives did not dare try to make their escape. When they had been in hiding for ten days, however, they were discovered, and were taken to London for their trial. Suspicion fell heavily on all recusants living within a few miles to the north of London.[228] Many houses were searched,[229] and many persons examined. The Bellamies suffered severely for having aided the fugitives; Mrs. Bellamy was committed to the Fleet Prison, and her son Jerome was executed on the charge of having 'aided and relieved Babington, Barnewell, and Dune in the woods and in his mother's hay-barn after that he understood that search was made for them as traitors for conspiring the death of the queen's majesty.'[230]

Two years later the whole county was in a bustle of preparation to resist the Spanish invasion. The conduct of military affairs in Middlesex lay mostly in the hands of Sir Gilbert Gerard, Sir Robert Wroth, and Sir Owen Hopton.[231] Under their direction, the quota of men for the county was drilled for many months before the invader sailed.[232] In April 1,500 men were raised, in June 1,000 more, and in July, thirty-five lances, and eighty-eight light horse.[233] Middlesex with Warwickshire and Leicestershire supplied the guard for the queen's person, and in July, 1,000 of the county's trained bands were specially detailed for this purpose.[234] When the army was finally mustered, it was quartered

---

[224] Camden, *Annals*, 305.   [225] Ibid. 306; Mackintosh, *Hist. of Engl.* iii, 309.
[226] Camden, *Annals*, 306.
[227] Nevertheless Burghley found reason to complain of the way in which the search was prosecuted. On his way from London to Theobald's he noticed groups of men standing about in the villages. At last, in Enfield, he asked some of these what they did, and was told that they were searching for three young men. He asked how they would identify them, and was answered, 'Marry, my lord, by their favour.' 'What mean you by that?' he asked. 'Marry,' said they, 'one of the party hath a hooked nose.' 'And have you no other mark?' enquired Burghley. 'No,' said they.—Burghley to Walsingham, 10 Aug. 1536; Cooper, *Notices of Anthony Babington of Dethick*, 178.
[228] *Cal. S.P. Dom.* 1581–90, pp. 345–7.
[229] Cooper, *Notices of Anthony Babington of Dethick*, 183.
[230] *Cal. S.P. Dom.* 1581–90, p. 347.
[231] *Acts of the P.C.* 1588, p. 219.   [232] *Cal. S.P. Dom.* 1581–90, pp. 271, 442.
[233] *Acts of the P.C.* 1588, pp. 25, 144, 169. There was some difficulty in raising these, for though the people were willing to serve, they were not well able to bear the expense, the citizens of London who held lands in Middlesex were also taxed in the City, and the inhabitants of the Tower Hamlets already served in the Tower.   [234] Ibid. 202.

largely in East Ham and Hackney, to protect the queen, and to defend Kent and Essex as need arose.[235]   The tense expectation ended at last, the enemy hove in sight, the long-prepared beacons were lighted, and ' high on bleak Hampstead's swarthy moor, they started for the North.'

We hear little of Middlesex during the rest of Elizabeth's reign, and as little during the reign of her successor.   James was given a hearty welcome on his accession, when he journeyed from Scotland to London. At Theobalds (Hertfordshire) he created many new knights, among whom was Sir Vincent Skinner of Middlesex.   On his way thence to London (7 May) he was met on the boundaries of the county by the sheriffs of London and Middlesex, and at Stamford Hill by the chief gentlemen of the hundreds.   Of these, Sir Thomas Fowler, Sir Hugh Losse, and Sir Arthur Attie were knighted at the Charterhouse on 11 May.[236]   James took such a fancy to Theobalds, when he stayed there on his way to London, that he took possession of it, giving the Cecils, to whom it belonged, their present estate at Hatfield.   In 1608 he caused his house at Enfield to be pulled down, and the materials removed to Theobalds,[237] so that Enfield did not see so much of court life as hitherto.

Some scenes of the conspiracy of 1605 took place in the county, though none of the plotters were Middlesex men.   Garnet had lodgings at Enfield, where the conspirators occasionally met.[238]   During the ten days before Parliament assembled, Catesby and Fawkes came to White Webbes, a house in Enfield Chase, where they were visited by Thomas Winter.[239]   The famous letter by which Tresham conveyed his mysterious warning to Lord Monteagle was received by the latter at his house in Hoxton, where he dined on the evening of 26 October.[240] The following morning, Winter went to White Webbes to tell Catesby his suspicions of Tresham, and to entreat him to give up the enterprise, and flee the country.   Catesby, however, was cool and firm and decided to wait until the 30 October, when Fawkes would rejoin him, and could be sent to examine the cellar at Westminster.   A week later, the conspirators were riding for their lives along the road from London to Ashby St. Legers—Catesby and John Wright first, then Christopher Wright and Percy; in the afternoon Rokewood overtook Keyes at Highgate, and lastly came Winter.   Percy had promised to give all he could get from the earl of Northumberland's rents to the cause, and expected to raise about £4,000.[241]   For this reason he went to Syon House on 4 November, on the night of which Fawkes was seized in the cellar.   Syon House and Isleworth manor had only been granted to Northumberland the preceding year, and he was now ' treated with uncommon rigour by the Star Chamber, for what at most amounted to a presumption of being privy to the Gunpowder Plot.'[242]   Feeling ran so

[235] *S.P. Misc.* (ed. Hardwicke), i, 575.
[237] *Cal. S.P. Dom.* 1603–10, p. 419.
[239] Thomas Winter's Confession.
[241] Bishop Williams of Chichester, *The Gunpowder Treason,* 56.
[242] Lysons, *Environs of London* (1795), iii, 95.
[236] Nichols, *Progresses of James I,* i, 112–13.
[238] Ibid. 247.
[240] *State Trials,* ii, 195.

high at the time, that even a ' presumption ' was sufficient on which to fine the earl £30,000, and to confine him in the Tower for fifteen years. Northumberland offered his Isleworth estates to the king in payment of the fine, but they were not accepted, and he was forced to remain a prisoner until 1621.[243]

During the reign of Charles I, there was a great deal of opposition in Middlesex to the king's methods of raising money. The committee raised to collect the forced loan of September, 1626, reported in October that John Brookes, Edward Bastwick, and William Webb had contemptuously refused to contribute.[244] To which the king replied that those who would not serve him with their purses should serve with their persons, and ordered that they should be enrolled forthwith among the soldiers.[245] Thirteen more persons ' all of reasonable ability ' refused to contribute on the following day, and warrants were issued against them.[246] The burden of ship-money [247] was felt all the more severely in Middlesex because the county suffered severely at this time from repeated visits of the plague. The districts round London naturally suffered most both from depopulation and from the interruption to trade.[248] The county had originally been assessed at £5,500, but the sum was reduced to £5,000.[249] The whole abatement of £500 was taken off the hundred of Ossulstone, upon which there arose great outcry from the hundreds of Elthorne, Spelthorne, and Isleworth, urging that those hundreds had to bear the charges of watch and ward at Hampton Court, as well as the extraordinary carriage for His Majesty's provisions to the Court,[250] and that therefore they were as much entitled to share the abatement as was the hundred of Ossulstone. Complaints did not only come from the poverty stricken. In 1636, the inhabitants of Chelsea, a suburb which was then increasing in favour with the well-to-do, discovered that they were taxed at a higher rate than the larger district of Acton.[251] The sheriffs replied to their complaints that Chelsea was rated so highly because of the persons of honour and quality who had summer houses there, and who owned land and property elsewhere.[252] In 1639, there was actual resistance to the collectors of ship-money in the hundred of Gore, and no less than forty distresses were taken at Harrow-on-the-Hill alone.[253]

In 1640, the levies for the Scottish War and the demand for coat-and-conduct money were greatly resented,[254] and such was the state of discontent in Middlesex, that in May the trained bands were ordered to be exercised on all holidays, in order to prevent riots.[255]

In January, 1642, some of the Middlesex trained bands were stationed in the new guard-house built by the king at Whitehall,[256] which

---

[243] *Hist. MSS. Com. Rep.* vi, 229–31.
[244] *Cal. S.P. Dom.* 1625–6, p. 458.
[245] Ibid. 459.
[246] Ibid. 460.
[247] William Noy, who discovered ' the precedent for ship-money among the records in the Tower,' lived at Brentford ; *Strafford's Letters*, i, 262. He was one of the Commissioners to raise the forced loan of 1626 in Middlesex ; *Cal. S.P. Dom.* 1625–6, p. 435.
[248] Ibid. 1636–7, pp. 155, 286.
[249] Ibid. 152.
[250] Ibid. 290.
[251] Ibid. 1635–6, p. 344.
[252] Ibid.
[253] Ibid. 1639, p. 434.
[254] Ibid. 1640, pp. 68, 155, 164, 228.
[255] Ibid. 167, 201.
[256] Ibid. 1641–3, p. 241.

it was said so frightened the Commons that they decided to hold their Committee meetings at the Guildhall. On the occasion of the attempted arrest of the five members, the Commons 'who had been very high before the King came,' sent for troops to the City. But failing to obtain them, they sent to the trained bands in the corps-de-garde at Whitehall, 'but they (the trained bands), stayed still.'[257] Two days later, the Committee of the Commons, sitting at the Guildhall, stated that it was necessary for the safety of both Houses of Parliament that the sheriffs of Middlesex and London should attend with the 'posse comitatus.'[258]

As far as Middlesex was concerned, the crisis of the Civil War came very early in the struggle. In September, 1642, Essex passed through on his way to face the king, taking with him his coffin, scutcheon and winding-sheet as a sign that he would be faithful to the death.[259] Then came Edgehill, and then the king's march southward. London was in a panic, and when the king reached Reading on 2 November, the news was received 'with the greatest horror.' The peace-party, led by the earl of Northumberland, hourly increased in power. Negotiations were opened with Charles, but he received them coldly. He had information each night of what passed in Parliament during the day, and to quicken the desire for peace, he advanced to Colnbrook,[260] 'this indeed exalted their appetite to peace.'[261] On 11 November, an embassy was sent to Colnbrook, consisting of the earls of Northumberland and Pembroke, Lord Wenman, William Pierpoint, and Sir John Hippesley, carrying a petition from Parliament 'for the removal of these bloody distempers.'[262] On receiving the petition, Charles tried to gain some immediate advantage by proposing that Windsor should be yielded to him as a convenient place from which negotiations might be held. To the surprise of Parliament, Charles said nothing about a cessation of arms pending the negotiations. Therefore the Houses thought it prudent to order Essex (who had just brought back the remnant of his army from Edgehill), to take the field; but they ordered that he should abstain from any open act of hostility while they sent again to the king to point out these omissions.[263] Clarendon admits that Charles had returned such an answer to Parliament as would lead them to suppose that he would approach no nearer to London while negotiations were pending. But he says that Prince Rupert had already advanced towards Brentford, that the king was bound to follow him in order to support the cavalry.[264] Charles himself wrote on the following day that on the night of 11 November, 'after the departure of the Committee of both Houses with our gracious answer to their petition, we received certain information that the earl of Essex had drawn his forces out of London towards us, which has necessitated our sudden resolution to march with our forces to Brainceford.'[265] He still protested his

[257] *Cal. S.P. Dom.* 1641–3, pp. 241–2.
[258] Ibid. 247.
[259] Gardiner, *Hist. of Gt. Civil War*, i, 21.
[260] Clarendon, *Hist. of the Rebellion*, ii, 392.
[261] *Cal. S.P. Dom.* 1641–3, p. 405. Petition that extreme measures might be taken to secure the safety of the City.
[262] *Lords' Journ.* v, 442.
[263] Ibid.
[264] Clarendon, op. cit. ii, 389–90.
[265] *Cal. S.P. Dom.* 1641–3, p. 406.

readiness to negotiate, and stated that he would receive terms at Brentford. Parliament then sent to the king to explain that their forces were instructed not to open hostilities, but the messenger found an engagement already in progress, and returned without fulfilling his mission.[266]

Whatever the explanation, the facts were that on the morning of 12 November, Rupert appeared suddenly through the mist[267] which lay heavily on the ground near the river, and fell on Hollis's regiment,[268] which had taken up a position just west of Brentford. Hollis was forced back into the town, where Brook's regiment was quartered. Here the two regiments maintained an unequal fight, having barricaded the narrow entrance to the town, and 'cast up some little breastwork at the most convenient places.'[269] The whole of Charles's army seems to have come up before the place was taken.[270] A Welsh regiment which had been 'faulty' at Edgehill, now recovered its honour and forced the barricades. 'After a very warm service, the King's troops entered the town.'[271] The chief officers and many soldiers on the Parliamentary side were killed, besides many who were drowned in the river in their attempts to escape; eleven colours and fifteen pieces of cannon, besides large quantities of ammunition were captured by the Royalists.[272] The town was plundered unmercifully, and before nightfall was thoroughly sacked.[273] That night most of the king's army 'lay in the cold fields.'[274]

During the day of this attack on Brentford the Parliamentary army in and about London drew together with all haste. The life guards were already mustered in Chelsea Fields when they heard the sound of the volleys in the west.[275] 'With unspeakable expedition' Essex gathered the trained bands together 'with their brightest equipage.'[276] All through the evening of 12 November, his forces streamed out along the Bath road, until by eight o'clock on the morning of the thirteenth, a large body of troops was drawn up on Turnham Green.[277] This army was nearly twice the size of the king's, but was of very mixed composition. There were a few veterans who had fought at Edgehill, but the greater part consisted of trained bands, and untrained volunteers, who were incapable of the complicated evolutions necessary for a successful attack on the enemy. On the defensive, the stubborn spirit of the troops made them a formidable array, nerved as they were by the popular report that if the king once entered London, he would allow Rupert to pillage the City unrestrained.

The king was in a difficult position. It would be madness to attack Essex's superior force, for 'he had no convenient place for his

---

[266] Clarendon, op. cit. ii, 395.   [267] Ludlow, *Memoirs*, i, 53.
[268] 'Those honest, religious soldiers.' Pamphlet describing the battle of Brentford, cited by Gardiner, op. cit. i, 47.
[269] Clarendon, op. cit. ii, 395.   [270] Ashmole MS. No. 830, fol. 85, cited by Lysons.
[271] Clarendon, op. cit. ii, 395.   [272] Ludlow, *Memoirs*, i, 53–4.
[273] 'A True and Perfect Relation of the barbarous and cruell Passages of the King's Army at Old Brainceford, near London.'   [274] Ashmole MS. No. 830.
[275] Ludlow, *Memoirs*, i, 54.   [276] Clarendon, op. cit. ii, 395.   [277] Ludlow, *Memoirs*, i, 54.

horse (which is the greatest pillar of the army to fight).' [278] Yet it was useless to stay where he was, while the enemy increased the strength of their position, and while a force of 3,000 men was stationed under Sir John Ramsay in his rear, holding the bridge at Kingston for the Parliament. [279] Essex was strongly urged to order Ramsay to attack the king's rear, but the professional soldiers in the army were much opposed to the scheme, and finally Ramsay was ordered to fall back along the south side of the Thames to defend London Bridge. [280] Later in the day Essex sent Hampden to sweep round the flank of the king's army, and it was probably this force which took part in the skirmish on a hill near Acton ; but the professionals prevailed upon Essex to recall Hampden before the manœuvre was complete. [281] The armies remained facing one another all that day, a few cannon shots only being exchanged, and many were the complaints of inactivity among the Parliamentarians. [282] A great number of spectators had ridden out of London to see the fight, and these were bold enough when all was quiet, but hastily galloped away whenever the king's army showed signs of movement—to the demoralization of the recruits, a few of whom took the opportunity to decamp at each stampede. [283]

Towards evening, as the king found that Essex did not mean to attack him, he drew off his troops towards Kingston, leaving only a small force between Old and New Brentford to cover his retreat. [284] These followed the main body as soon as they were fired upon, and Essex took possession of Brentford without striking a blow. [285] He was at once surrounded by a hungry crowd of the plundered townspeople, who declared that the town had been stripped and clamoured for food. Fortunately the wives and sisters of the citizens in the trained bands had provided a goodly supply of loaves for their husbands and brothers, and these were devoted to the stricken inhabitants of Brentford. [286]

The Royalists in Kingston welcomed Charles and gave him the command of the bridge (the first above the City in those days). Essex feared that the king meant to make his way into Kent where he had many partisans among the gentry. The earl therefore threw a bridge of boats across the Thames from Fulham to Putney, so that he could speedily transfer his army to Surrey if necessary. [287] But Charles made no attempt to go into Kent. The army took up its quarters in Kingston, while he stayed the night at Hampton Court [288] before removing to Oatlands. His troops shortly withdrew to Reading, and on 29 November Oxford became the royal head quarters.

The engagement at Brentford and the action of the following day formed a turning-point in the struggle between the king and the Parliament. It was now certain that the war must be prolonged. Charles's march towards London had seemed like a triumphal progress, but it had been

[278] Ashmole MS. No. 830.
[279] Gardiner, op. cit. 59.
[280] Ludlow, *Memoirs*, i, 54.
[281] Ibid. [282] Whitelocke, *Mem.* 65.
[283] Gardiner, op. cit. i, 59.
[284] Clarendon, op. cit. ii, 397.
[285] Ludlow, *Memoirs*, i, 55.
[286] 'A True and Perfect Relation.'
[287] Ludlow, *Memoirs*, i, 55.
[288] Clarendon, op. cit. ii, 397.

checked by a hastily gathered army, and his troops never again approached so near to the capital. His conduct in ordering or allowing the attack on Brentford while negotiations were pending, though no doubt defensible on military grounds, was most strongly resented both in London and Middlesex, and did much to turn the scale of favour against him.[289] The petition of the plundered inhabitants of Brentford, and the generous response to the order for a collection to be made in their aid, show with what feelings Middlesex regarded the royal army.[290]

Although after November, 1642, the royal cause had little chance of success in Middlesex, yet many of the gentry of the county belonged to the king's party and followed him to Oxford. Sir Arthur Aston of Fulham distinguished himself at Edgehill by driving the right wing of the Parliamentary army from the field.[291] He was made commander of Reading when the king went to Oxford, and was probably at the taking of Bristol. Later he was made governor of Oxford, where he was much hated for his cruelty and imperious temper.[292] Among those who followed the king to Oxford were John Cary of Marylebone Park, Sir Francis Rowse of Hedgstone Manor, Harrow, and Sir Henry Wroth of Durrants. Sir Henry Spiller of Laleham took up arms for the king, as did also Sir Robert Fenn and his son, and Sir John Kaye.[293] One of the most conspicuous figures in Middlesex at this time was Henry Rich, earl of Holland, who owned Holland House in Kensington. He was a man of ability, and had been prominent at court during the early part of the reign, but his lack of principle and instability of character prevented him when the crisis came from serving either side with success or fidelity. Before the war he had attached himself to the queen's party, and was made general of the horse when war broke out with Scotland.[294] When the army was disbanded he retired to Holland House, having received some imaginary cause for offence.[295] At the opening of the Civil War, Holland sided with the Parliament, and was present with Essex at the battle of Turnham Green; indeed the Parliamentary historians lay it to his account that Essex made no decisive action against the king that day.[296] In August, 1643, when the peers who had remained at Westminster began to leave their seats, Holland set out with Bedford to join the king at Oxford.[297] They were stopped at Wallingford while the king deliberated whether they should be received or not. All considerations of prudence counselled a warm welcome, but the Royalist hopes were high at that time, and under the queen's influence the majority of the council urged that the fugitives should be

---

[289] 'If your majesty had prevailed it is easy to imagine what a miserable peace we should have had.' Letter from the Houses of Parliament, 16 Nov. 1642.

[290] *Cal. S.P. Dom.* 1641–3, p. 417.

[291] Clarendon, op. cit. ii, 358, 361.

[292] In November, 1646, he was sent to Ireland with the marquis of Ormonde, and was left to defend Drogheda with 3,000 men. When the town fell in September, 1647, Aston was butchered with the rest of the garrison. (*Dict. Nat. Biog.*)

[293] *Cal. Com. for Comp.* ii, 1145, 1312, 1402, 1482, 1567.

[294] *Strafford Letters,* ii, 276.   [295] Clarendon, op. cit. i, 295.

[296] Ludlow, *Memoirs,* i, 54.   [297] Gardiner, op. cit. i, 199.

treated with scorn.[298]   Charles took a middle course.   The earls were to be allowed to come to Oxford, but every one was to treat them as he thought best.   Holland received nothing but cold looks, and though he followed the king to Colchester and was present at Newbury, he was disappointed in the hope that he would be restored to his office as groom of the stole.   He still refused to acknowledge that he had committed any offence in siding with the rebels, and leaving the king's party on 6 November he threw himself at the feet of Parliament, 'which after a short imprisonment gave him leave to live in his own house without further considering him as a man able to do little good or harm.'[299] He employed his time in publishing a declaration of the causes of his going to and returning from Oxford, which lost him the regard of the few friends he still retained.

After Brentford, Middlesex was completely at the disposal of Parliament.   The proceedings of the Committee for the Advance of Money fell very heavily on the county in 1643.   The object of the committee was to furnish the sinews of war, and at first its exactions fell mainly on those within a twenty-mile radius of London.   No distinction of party was made in the first instances, but gradually delinquents came to be more frequently and heavily taxed.   In April, 1643, Sir Nicholas Crispe, whose house in Lime Street was sold 'by the candle,' also had his estate at Hammersmith despoiled, and his goods carried to London for the use of the Parliament.[300]   Sir Thomas Allen, who lived at Finchley, was assessed at £1,000, and his household goods were distrained for arrears.[301]   There is a long list of those who were called upon to pay sums varying from £200 to £2,000.[302]   Sir John Wolfenstone of Stanmore was said to have lost £100,000 during the war by fines, and by the seizure of his estates.[303]

The country round London, and especially the south-western portion of Middlesex, was used as a camping and recruiting ground for the Parliamentary armies.   In August, 1643, when Essex was about to raise the siege of Gloucester, the rendezvous for the army was appointed for Hounslow Heath.   Some of the Commons who rode out to inspect the troops reported them to be 'a very shattered and broken body,' and found their general in a very dispirited condition.[304]   They used every effort to recruit the army[305] and such was their energy that in three weeks three regiments of auxiliary forces had been raised, and these with three regiments of London trained bands gave Essex an additional 5,000 men.[306]   On Saturday, 26 August, he broke camp from his last stations at Colnbrook and Uxbridge with an army 'so full of patience as that with one fortnight's pay (being much in arrears) they were content to march against all these difficulties.'[307]

[298] Clarendon, op. cit. ii, 146–51.
[300] *Cal. Com. for Advance of Money*, 21 April, 1643.
[302] *Cal. S.P. Dom.* 1641–3, p. 474.
[304] Ludlow, *Memoirs*, i, 65.
[306] *Com. Journ.* 3, 15, 16 August.

[299] Ibid. 156, 191–9.
[301] Ibid. 21 June.
[303] Lysons, op. cit. iii, 400.
[305] Washbourn, *Bibl. Glouc.* lxv.
[307] Washbourn, *Bibl. Glouc.* 253.

When Essex returned in triumph at the end of September, he held a review of all the London trained bands in Finsbury Fields.

In May, 1643, great alarm was felt lest the king should march against London, and trenches were hastily made on all the approaches to the City, such as at Islington, in the fields near St. Pancras, and at Mile End, at which men, and even women and children, worked day and night.[308] There was another alarm in the campaign of 1644, when Essex and Waller had separated and the king entered Buckinghamshire with Waller hopelessly in the rear. A force was hastily collected, with which Major-general Browne was ordered to defend the country between London and the king. On 25 June Sir Gilbert Gerrard reported four thousand men to be ready in Middlesex.[309] Two days earlier his own regiment, which he had raised in the county, was ordered to march to Hertford under Browne.[310] The rest of the force was composed of men from the eastern counties of a non-military character, but luckily for Browne's little force the king could not shake off Waller and on 29 June fought at Cropredy Bridge.

Middlesex supplied many men during that year for the Parliamentary armies. In March sixty horse were sent into the field.[311] After the second battle of Newbury all the forces of the county were drawn to Staines to defend the western approaches to London.[312] During the winter of 1644–5 Middlesex men were in garrison at Windsor Castle.[313] In March, 1645, 2,500 men were raised in Middlesex with London, Westminster and Southwark, and in June an additional 800 to recruit Fairfax's army.[314] A troop of forty horse were with Major-general Browne at Abingdon in January, 1644–5, when he complained of frequent desertions because of the straitness of their quarters, the scantiness of victuals, and the lack of money;[315] 200 more were sent to him in June.[316] Four hundred foot joined Cromwell before Oxford,[317] and in June the county forces marched under Colonel Massey to relieve Taunton, and 'went forth with much cheerfulness.' When Fairfax's army was at Reading during the summer of 1645 recruiting went on apace in Middlesex.

The county suffered not only from the continual drain of men and money, but also from the billeting of troops. In January, 1643–4, a petition was presented to Parliament from the inhabitants of Middlesex and other of the south and eastern counties,[318] against 'the intolerable oppression and undoing grievance of Free Quarter' which 'has rendered us no better than mere conquered slaves' of the soldiers, who 'like so many Egyptian locusts feed so long upon us at free costs.'[319] In November, 1644, the gentlemen of Middlesex again petitioned, and

---

[308] *Lords' Journ.* v, 419 ; *Perfect Diurnall*, May, June, 1643.
[309] *Cal. S.P. Dom.* 1644, p. 274.
[310] Ibid. 265.
[311] Ibid. 77.
[312] Ibid. 1644–5, p. 136.
[313] Ibid. 124, 134, 327.
[314] Ibid. 359, 625.
[315] Ibid. 247.
[316] Ibid. 555.
[317] Ibid. 550.
[318] *Hist. MSS. Com. Rep.* vi, 3.
[319] 'Petition of the inhabitants of Middlesex,' &c., B.M.

Essex was desired to punish the 'particular insolencies' which were complained of.[320] In the following April Fairfax was commanded to remove his forces which lay in Middlesex, and the county was empowered to refuse lodging to such officers and soldiers as had not proper warrant from their superior officers.[321]

In 1644–5 was held that abortive conference known as the Treaty of Uxbridge. The Commissioners met on 29 January. Those representing the king were quartered on the south side of the town, those representing the Parliament were on the north side,[322] each party having a 'best inn' reserved for their use.[323] On the evening of their arrival the two parties exchanged visits.[324] Sir John Bennet's house at the Buckinghamshire end of the town was appointed as a 'treaty house,' and it was arranged that the king's party should come in by the 'foreway' and the Parliament's by the 'backway,' a room in the middle of the house having been arranged for the meetings.[325] Uxbridge was in the Parliamentary country, and the Royalists were treated as guests, but Clarendon declares that the townspeople observed that the Parliament's men did not look as much at home as did the cavaliers, and adds that the former had not that 'alacrity and serenity of mind as men use to have who do not believe themselves to be at fault.'[326] The conference was to last twenty days, not counting the days of coming and returning, nor the days spent in devotion, 'there falling out three Sundays and one fast day in those first twenty days.' On the first morning of the conference Christopher Love, a celebrated Puritan divine, preached the usual market-day sermon. He told the large congregation that the king's commissioners were come with 'hearts of blood,' and that there was as great a distance between the Treaty and peace as between heaven and hell. The Cavaliers complained, but the Parliamentarians disowned him, and he was afterwards reprimanded by Parliament.[327]

The discussions and wranglings over ecclesiastical, military and Irish questions do not belong to the history of Middlesex. The negotiations from the first were hopeless, and early served to show how unlikely was the chance of any settlement between Charles and the Parliament. The main proceedings had opened on 31 January, and they came to an end on Saturday, 22 February. On the Sunday both sides rested in the town, and spent the afternoon in exchanging farewells, 'parting with such dryness towards each other as if they scarce hoped to meet again.' The Parliament had allowed two days for the Royalists to return to Oxford as the time of year was bad for travelling, but the king's commissioners were so unwilling to run the risk of being caught on the road after the armistice ended, that they were in their coaches early enough on the Monday morning to kiss the king's hand at Oxford that night.[328]

---

[320] *Cal. S.P. Dom.* 1644–5, p. 144.
[322] Lysons, *Environs of Lond.* (1800), v, 179.
[323] Whitelocke, *Mem.* 127.
[324] Clarendon, op. cit. ii, 472.
[326] Clarendon, op. cit. iii, 472.

[321] Ibid. 441, 443 (39).
[325] Whitelocke, *Mem.* 127.
[327] Ibid. 474.
[328] Ibid. 501.

In 1647 came the struggle between the Presbyterians in Parliament and the Independents in the army, the bone of contention which brought matters to a crisis being the control of the City Militia. There were stormy scenes in Parliament on 26 July,[329] and when the Houses met again after a four days' adjournment it was found that the Independent members with the two speakers, Lenthall and Manchester, had fled to the army.[330]

The army under Fairfax had left Bedford on 29 July *en route* for London, and disregarding the order of Parliament that the army should remain fifty miles from the City, Fairfax had reached Uxbridge after a hard march on 30 July.[331] A meeting was held privately at Syon House between Fairfax with his officers on the one side and the earl of Northumberland, Lord Saye and Sele, Lord Wharton, with the speakers and other members, on the other.[332] Meanwhile the Independent party in London had grown bolder, and the City had become tired of anarchy and riots, and a deputation, therefore, waited on Fairfax at his quarters on 3 August.[333] The general stated in a long declaration that the army was about to march on London, and that the eleven members of Parliament who had been previously impeached by the army must be given up immediately.[334] Then followed a dramatic scene which is supposed to have been pre-arranged. The whole army, 20,000 strong, was drawn up on Hounslow Heath[335] in battalions which stretched near a mile and a half in length.[336] Fairfax rode on to the Heath accompanied by the earls of Northumberland, Salisbury and Kent, Lord Grey of Wark, Lord Howard of Escrick, Lords Wharton, Saye and Sele, and Mulgrove, besides the two speakers and about a hundred members of the House of Commons.[337] The General accompanied by the said lords and gentlemen then rode along the entire length of the army from regiment to regiment. They were received with tumultuous enthusiasm, and with cries of 'Lords and Commons and a free Parliament.'[338] After this demonstration, the fugitive members took their leave of the army, some going to Syon House with the earl of Northumberland, and some to Stanwell with Lord Saye and Sele. Later in the day the Elector Palatine came on to the heath, and reviewed the army in company with Fairfax and many other gentlemen, and was also warmly greeted.[339]

Fairfax was now assured of success. Southwark had sent a message imploring his aid, and he had dispatched Colonel Raynesborough with a brigade of horse, foot and cannon from Hampton Court to take possession.[340] On the afternoon of 3 August the City surrendered, and a letter was written to Fairfax announcing this decision. He received

---

[329] *Lords' Journ.* ix, 143 ; *Com. Journ.* v, 256–9. [330] Ludlow, *Memoirs*, i, 207.
[331] Whitelocke, *Mem.* 262. Fairfax's quarters were at Colnbrook, 'at one Mr. Wilson's neere the bridge whither he came Sunday night' (1 Aug.). *Perfect Diurnall*, 2 Aug.
[332] Ludlow, *Memoirs*, i, 208–9.
[333] *Com. Journ.* v, 266. *Perfect Diurnall*, 3 Aug. [334] Whitelocke, *Mem.* 263.
[335] The army was then quartered at Brentford and Twickenham. Clarendon, op. cit. iv, 246.
[336] *Perfect Diurnall*, 2–9 Aug. [337] Ibid. [338] Whitelocke, *Mem.* 263.
[339] Rushworth, *Coll.* vii, 743–51. [340] Clarendon, op. cit. iv, 247.

it on the morning of the 4th at Isleworth, whither he had removed on the previous day.[341]   On the 5th the whole army moved nearer to London, the General taking up his quarters at Hammersmith in the house of Sir Nicholas Crispe, who had fled to France.[342]   He met the commissioners from the City at the end of the town that morning, and they announced the surrender of the forts along the river.   On 6 August the fugitive members met Fairfax at the earl of Holland's house at Kensington, where they subscribed to a declaration expressing their agreement with the army in its late proceedings.[343]   The whole army then marched in triumphal procession into London ; Fairfax, with the Lords and Commons, was surrounded by a guard three deep, and every soldier in the force was crowned with laurels.[344]

Meanwhile the king had been taken to Stoke Abbey when the army entered Middlesex, but as soon as Fairfax had come to an agreement with the City, Charles was removed to Hampton Court.[345]   Except that he must remain at the Palace, Charles was allowed absolute freedom. His friends and servants had free access to his person, and the citizens of London rode out frequently to Hampton as they had been used to do at the end of a progress.[346]   Lord Capel came with news of the Royalists in Jersey,[347] and the marquis of Ormond with news from Ireland.[348]   Charles was allowed also to see his children whom Parliament had placed under the care of the earl of Northumberland.   They had been removed from Whitehall to Northumberland's house at Syon on account of the plague, and were within easy riding distance of Hampton Court.[349]

The months which followed were passed in negotiations with the army and with the Scots.   At first Cromwell came often from his quarters at Putney to see the king, but after the latter's refusal of the Heads of Proposals, the feeling of the army rose hotly against Charles, and the Scots grew proportionately more pressing in their demands that he should throw himself into their hands.   On 22 October Loudoun, Lauderdale and Lanark presented themselves at Hampton Court with a written assurance that the Scots were prepared to assist Charles in the recovery of his throne.[350]   They came again on the following day, accompanied by fifty horse, and urged the king to escape under their escort.[351]   Charles, however, would not take so decided a step, and when at length he decided on escape, only Ashburnham, Berkeley and Legge were in the secret.[352]   His first preparations aroused the suspicions of Colonel Whalley, who was in command of the guard at the palace.   At the end of October, therefore, he posted guards within as well as without, and on 1 November Ashburnham

[341] *Perfect Diurnall*, 2–9 Aug.
[342] Ibid.
[343] Whitelocke, *Mem.* 263–4.
[344] *Perfect Diurnall*, 2–9 Aug.
[345] Clarendon, op. cit. iv, 244.
[346] Ibid. 247–50.
[347] Ashburnham, *Narrative*, i, 104.
[348] Warwick, *Memoirs*, 302–3.
[349] Whitelocke, *Mem.* 260.
[350] *Clarendon State Papers*, ii, 380.
[351] Burnet, *Hist. of his own Time*, v, 123.
[352] Ashburnham, *Narrative*, ii, 100 ; Berkeley, *Memoirs*, 47.

and most of the king's attendants were removed from Hampton Court.[353] On 9 November Charles received a mysterious letter informing him that the Levellers, his enemies in the army, had resolved on his death.[354] He could still communicate with Ashburnham, and that night Berkeley was brought secretly to the palace and final preparations were made for the escape.[355] On the Thursday, 11 November, the king retired early to his room;[356] horses were brought to the back door of the garden, to which there was a passage from the king's room,[357] and accompanied by Ashburnham, Berkeley and Legge he made his escape unnoticed.[358]

The alarm was given within half an hour of his departure, but the king and the fugitives were already across the river. The officers who broke into the king's apartments found only some letters on the table in the king's handwriting, and a cloak cast aside on the way to the water.[359] Colonel Whalley immediately sent word to Cromwell at Putney, who apparently hastened over to Hampton Court, and having assured himself of the king's escape dispatched the news to Speaker Lenthall.[360]

Middlesex seems to have shared the general Royalist reaction which preceded the second Civil War. The county joined with Kent, Essex, and Surrey in a declaration to the army under Fairfax in which were rehearsed the 'many miseries' of the time, and the attempts to restore prosperity to the nation by the proposed 're-establishment of his Majesty unto his royal rights, the Settlement of Religion and Liberty according unto the known received Laws, and (upon payment of their arrears) the disbanding of the army.'[361] Having affirmed the failure of the Parliament to attain 'the ends for which we first engaged them,' and that the Parliament had 'for divers years continued free-born people of England in a greater servitude than at any time since the Norman Conquest,' the gentlemen of the county announced their intention to arm, and 'by our power (God assisting) to command what we could not entreat.' To this end they 'heartily and seriously' invited the soldiers of the army either to 'repair unto us with your horses and arms,' or to go to their own homes, in which case their whole arrears should be paid.[362] Little result seems to have come of the Declaration. The second Civil War was soon over as far as Middlesex was concerned.

A general rising was planned by the queen and Jermyn, which was to follow the appearance of the Scots in England. The earl of Holland, who through the influence of the lord of Carlisle had made his peace

---

[353] Ashburnham, *Narrative*, ii, 100.   [354] Ibid. 105.   [355] Berkeley, *Memoirs*, 161.
[356] Clarendon, op. cit. iv, 263, says that Charles pretended indisposition, but Berkeley (*Memoirs*, 50) that it was his custom to retire early on Thursday to write letters for the foreign post.
[357] Clarendon, op. cit. iv, 263.   [358] Warwick, *Memoirs*, 305.
[359] Bulstrode, *Memoirs*, 162.
[360] *Com. Journ.* v, 350; Rushworth, *Coll.* vii, 871; Carlyle, *Cromwell's Letters*, i, 264. Dated 'Hampton Court, Twelve at night, 11 Nov. 1647.'
[361] 'The joint declaration of the several Counties of Kent, Essex, Middlesex, and Surrey, unto the soldiers of the army, now under the command of the Lord Fairfax' (B.M.).
[362] 'The joint Declaration.'

with the Royalists, was appointed commander-in-chief.[363] The general scheme was rendered hopeless, however, by the premature rising in Kent (21 May, 1648). After his defeat at Maidstone, Norwich, to whom Holland had given the command in Kent, heard that thousands had risen for the king in Essex, and that there were 2,000 men in arms at Bow.[364] The City refused to let him pass through, so he decided to cross the Thames below London.[365] He intended to go only to Bow and Stratford, but finding that his news had been false and that there was no force gathered to receive him, he went on to Chelmsford. About 500 men had followed him, crossing the river in boats, with their horses swimming.[366] They meant to land in Essex, but on the morning of the 4 June they found themselves in Middlesex under the Hamlets of the Tower. Here they were confronted by the regiment of the Hamletteers. Their leader, Sir William Compton, prevailed upon the regiment to let them pass on a promise to disband, but when they reached Bow Bridge they forced the turn-pike to let them through into Essex, and met Norwich, on his return from Chelmsford, at Stratford.[367] Fairfax had meanwhile sent Colonel Whalley in pursuit of the Royalists.[368] He pressed after them, but was beaten back and pursued to Mile End, where the pursuers themselves fell into an ambuscade, and were forced to retreat. The Hamletteers then returned to the attack, but were surrounded in Bow church, where they had taken refuge, and were finally released on condition that they returned to their homes. The Royalists retired behind the Lea, setting guards at the fords over the river ; and when a Parliamentary force of dragoons was collected on Mile End Green, they withdrew to Stratford.[369] There were a few skirmishes at ' Bow Townes End ' until 7 June, when the rising passed into Essex.[370] The earl of Holland took the field on 4 July, being forced to act prematurely because the committee at Derby House had knowledge of his intended rising. He appeared in arms at Kingston, but after four days' skirmishing in Surrey he gave up all hope of success, for he found that the Royalists did not join him, and that the number of his followers dwindled daily.[371] On 7 July the deputy-lieutenant of Middlesex was ordered to guard the bridges and ferries over the Thames, and to secure the boats on his side of the river.[372] Guards were posted in the county to prevent any person from joining the rising in Surrey.[373] Holland entered Middlesex with a small following, but without attempting an action ; he pushed through the narrow lanes about Harrow on his way to St. Albans.[374] The insurrection was finally ended by his capture on 9 July at St. Neots.[375]

---

[363] Gardiner, op. cit. iv, 138.   [364] Carter, *A Most True and Exact Narrative*, 102.   [365] Ibid.
[366] Gardiner, op. cit. iv, 138 ; cf. Carter, *Narrative*, 32 ; Clarendon, op. cit. iv, 358.
[367] Carter, *Narrative*, 107–11.   [368] Ludlow, *Memoirs*, i, 250.
[369] Carter, *Narrative*, 111–14.
[370] On 5 June Parliament passed an Act of Indemnity for all, except Norwich, who would lay down arms ; *Com. Journ.* v, 586. On 7 June Sir William Hicks and others submitted ; Whitelocke, *Mem.* 310.
[371] Ludlow, *Memoirs*, i, 255.   [372] *Cal. S.P. Dom.* 1648–9, p. 169.
[373] Ibid. 93.   [374] Whitelocke, *Mem.* 318.
[375] Ludlow, *Memoirs*, i, 255.

POLITICAL HISTORY

He was condemned to death by the High Court of Justice,[376] and his firmness on the scaffold, as well as his last attempt in the king's cause, went some way towards making the Royalists forget his earlier vacillation.[377]

After the king's death Middlesex settled down quietly under the Commonwealth. Several prominent republicans lived in the county. Lambert was quartered at Holland House in 1649,[378] where, owing to his deafness, Cromwell insisted that their conference should be held in the meadow. After his difference with Cromwell, Fairfax inhabited Holland House until it was restored to the countess of Holland. Sir William Waller lived at Osterley [379] until his death in 1668. Of the regicides, Owen Rowe and Colonel John Okey lived at Hackney.[380] Many of the Royalists made their peace with the government and returned to their estates. Of these, Lord Campden, who had been a zealous Royalist, compounded for £9,000, and lived at Campden House during the Protectorate.[381] Sir John Thorowgood of Kensington, a gentleman-pensioner of Charles I, joined the republicans during the interregnum. Several Parliamentarians bought land in Middlesex during the sale of church lands, and of these Sir William Roberts, who held the manor of Neasden,[382] represented Middlesex in the Parliament which gave Cromwell the title of Protector. Some little agitation was caused in 1650 when Parliament proceeded to break up Enfield Chase into small lots, and to sell these to soldiers who had fought on the revolutionary side in the war. The inhabitants of Enfield claimed the right of common, and the rioters broke down the inclosures in the Chase.[383] Four files of soldiers were sent against them, and two petitions were sent to Parliament: one from the officers who had bought lands, the other from the inhabitants of Enfield and Edmonton.[384]

Great alarm was felt in August, 1651, when the Scots advanced into England. Barnet was appointed as the rendezvous for the forces in the south, and Middlesex was represented there by 1,000 men from the militia.[385] The news soon came of Cromwell's victory at Worcester, and the 500 Middlesex men who had marched out to Uxbridge were ordered to return home, though for over a week troops kept guard on all the main roads in the county.[386]

When Monk marched south in February, 1660, he broke up his last camp at Barnet on the third, and marched that day into London.[387] Before coming to Highgate the general drew up his forces which consisted of four regiments of foot and three of horse, 5,800 men in all, with whom he entered the City by Gray's Inn Lane and Holborn Bars.[388]

[376] Clarendon, op. cit. iii, 174, 271.
[377] Andrews, *Bygone Middlesex*, 119.
[378] *Perfect Diurnall*, 9 July, 1649.
[379] Lysons, *Environs of Lond.* (1795), iii, 27.
[380] Ibid. Hackney.
[381] Ibid. iii, 179.
[382] Ibid. 613.
[383] Ibid. ii, 286–7.
[384] *Cal. S.P. Dom.* 1658–9, pp. 363, 368 (30).
[385] Ibid. 1651, pp. 325, 346.
[386] Ibid. 411–12.
[387] Ludlow, *Memoirs*, 818.
[388] Price, *Mystery and Method of His Majesty's Restoration*, 757.

49

After the Restoration Court life returned to Middlesex. Charles II was frequently at Hampton Court,[389] which had fortunately escaped the fate of other crown lands, for Cromwell took a fancy to it and reserved it for his own use during the Protectorate.

By 1686 James II had succeeded in estranging every class in England by his over-zeal for the re-establishment of Roman Catholicism. Riots took place all over the country on account of the favour shown to Roman Catholics. London especially was in great excitement when the chapel in Lime Street was opened for the Elector Palatine, and the City-trained bands could not be relied upon to quell the frequent riots. In the early summer of that year the king formed the idea of establishing a large military camp on Hounslow Heath, chiefly with the object of overawing London. The army was always dear to the king's heart, and he showed the greatest interest in the formation of the camp. As early as 16 April he rode out to Hounslow himself to choose a suitable position on the Heath.[390] Here between 13,000 and 16,000 men were collected in the circumference of about 2½ miles; fourteen battalions of foot, thirty-two squadrons of horse, twenty-six pieces of artillery, besides the quantities of guns and ammunition which were dragged hither from the Tower.[391] The camp was established during May and June, and the first great review was held on 30 June. It was made an occasion of great state, and a gallery was raised for the queen, the queen dowager, and her ladies. James himself led the troops until he had passed the queens, when he dismounted, and the commander-in-chief, Lord Feversham, marched before them.[392] On another occasion, in July, the king, 'as a piece of gallantry,' made all his 4,000 horse march at two o'clock in the morning into Staines meadow to attend the queen from thence to the Heath, where she honoured Lord Arran by dining with him.[393]

The general suspicion with which the king's love for his troops was regarded made James think their presence all the more necessary. He spared no pains to render the force efficient, and gave his attention even to details of clothing, arms, and discipline. The army was soon a 'very compleat body of men.' It had the reputation of being the best paid, best equipped, and 'most sightly body of troops of any in Europe,' and raised the king's and the kingdom's credit to no little extent abroad.[394] So proud was James of his army that he could not refrain from 'descanting in his letters to the Prince of Orange on the beauty of his troops, not without a secret pleasure for the reflection that the exultation could give no great pleasure to the Prince.'[395] London had at first regarded the camp with awe, but the king's frequent visits to Hounslow and their

[389] *Hist. MSS. Com. Rep.* v, 153. He went there as early as 9 June, 1660, 'and had by the way a great fall of his horse, but God be thanked no hurt.'

[390] Reresby's *Memoirs*, 360. 'I waited upon His Majesty to Hounslow Heath. . . . He was afterwards entertained at dinner by Mr. Shales, the provider, in a little house built there for the convenience of this business, where his Majesty was more pleasant and entertaining to all the company than he used to be.'

[391] *Ellis Corres.* i, 125, 271.   [392] Sir John Bramston, *Autobiography*, 234.   [393] *Ellis Corres.* i, 125.
[394] J. S. Clarke, *Life of Jas. II*, ii, 71.   [395] Dalrymple, *Memoirs*, pt. 1, bk. iv, p. 103.

attendant gaieties soon brought the citizens to look upon Hounslow Heath as a pleasure resort.

> Mingled with the musketeers and dragoons, a multitude of fine ladies and gentlemen from Soho Square, sharpers from Whitefriars, invalids in sedans, monks in hoods and gowns, lacqueys in rich liveries, pedlars, orange girls, mischievous apprentices, and gaping clowns, were constantly passing and re-passing through the long lanes of tents . . . In truth the place was merely a gay suburb of the capital.[396]

Familiarity had the proverbial result, and London no longer feared the army, which indeed, soon ceased to be a menace to its safety. The troops on which the king had so greatly depended, and whose welfare he had rightly cherished as his own, became imbued with the temper of the City and of the nation.[397] A strong Protestant bias made itself felt among the soldiers and ' it appeared on many occasions that the army had a great animadvertence to the King's religion.'[398]

The Roman Catholic officers, whose admission to the army the king had gained by the suspension of the Test Act, were very few in number. James had a chapel in the camp, but few officers or men heard mass there, and those few were treated with great scorn by their fellows.[399] Protestant tracts were freely circulated, in which the troops were exhorted to use their arms in defence of the Bible, the Great Charter, and the Petition of Right.[400] As the crisis of 1688 drew near it became evident that the army could not be trusted if trouble arose. James still went frequently to the camp, driving there as a rule twice a week, sometimes with Major-General Worden,[401] and sometimes with the future duke of Marlborough, then Lord Churchill.[402] He went to Hounslow on the morning of the last day of the trial of the Seven Bishops.[403] Sunderland sent a courier with news of the acquittal, who was brought before the king while he was in Lord Feversham's tent. On hearing the news James exclaimed fiercely, ' So much the worse for them.' He set out shortly afterwards for London, and scarcely had he left the camp when a great shout broke out from the soldiers. The king asked what noise was that, and was answered that it was ' Nothing, that the soldiers were glad that the Bishops were acquitted.' Then James broke out, ' Do you call that nothing ?' and again said gloomily, ' So much the worse for them.'[404] The news was received with even more acclamation at the camp than elsewhere,[405] and the soldiers were soon more dreaded by the Court than ever they had been by the City. James went several times to Hounslow during July,[406] but he saw fit to break up the camp early in August.[407] The troops were scattered over the country on the excuse that they would be needed to keep order at the approaching elections, but in reality because they had become more a danger than a protection to the king.[408]

[396] Macaulay, *Hist. of Engl.* ii, 102.
[397] Bramston, *Autobiog.* 234.
[398] Burnet, *Hist. of His Own Time*, iii, 154.
[399] Clarke, *Life of Jas. II*, ii, 70.
[400] Macaulay, op. cit. ii, 103.
[401] *Ellis Corres.* ii, 24.
[402] Ibid. ii, 1.
[403] Ibid. ii, 2. The jury for the trial was drawn from Middlesex.
[404] Macaulay, op. cit. ii, 388.
[405] Clarke, *Life of Jas. II*, ii, 163.
[406] Reresby's *Memoirs*, 397, 399.
[407] *Ellis Corres.* ii, 116.
[408] Ibid. ii, 139.

After the Revolution Middlesex was connected even more intimately than before with the life of the Court. William III very soon discovered a predilection for Hampton Court, and after he had altered and added to the palace he was seldom in London. The king's Dutch friends formed quite a colony in southern Middlesex, and after the duke of Schomberg received an English peerage he took his title from Brentford. The Princess Anne also lived at Hampton Court during the early part of the reign, and until her relations with the queen made it desirable that she should find a house of her own. While the question of her income was before Parliament she withdrew to Lord Craven's house at Kensington Gravel Pits, which he had lent as a nursery for her son, the duke of Gloucester.

Another royal palace was built by William III at Kensington. It was near enough to London for all business of state and yet it was free from the smoke which so much affected the king's asthma. Early in 1690 he bought the lease of Lord Nottingham's house at Kensington, and the palace was hastily finished on his return from the Irish campaign.[409] The political intrigues of the reign centred round Kensington and Hampton Court Palaces. The feud between the queen and Princess Anne still continued, and after the duke of Marlborough's disgrace and the duchess's subsequent exclusion from the queen's presence at Kensington, Anne fled from Hampton Court and took refuge at Syon House,[410] the property of the duke of Somerset since his marriage with the heiress of the Percies. During the winter of 1693-4 the queen was at Kensington Palace, while Anne was at Berkeley House and her son at Campden House, but as her quarrel with Queen Mary still continued, the entrée to Kensington was barred to her although open to her son. On 28 December, 1694 (O.S.), the Queen died at Kensington. Immediately after her death Somers negotiated a reconciliation between the king and his sister-in-law.[411] Anne came to Campden House, whence she was carried in a sedan chair, for she could not walk, into the presence of the king at Kensington. Her political interests as heir-apparent being now the same as the king's, they agreed to sink the memory of many mutual injuries.[412]

On 31 December the House of Peers went in a body to Kensington to present an address to the king deploring the death of Queen Mary. The same afternoon the Commons came with a still longer address and a still more urgent appeal that the king would direct his attention to his own preservation.[413] William lived indeed in great danger of assassination by the Jacobites, and one of the many plots against his life was connected with Middlesex. In 1696 Sir George Barclay came to England from the court of St. Germains, bearing a commission from James II requiring all his loving subjects to rise in arms on his behalf.[414] Barclay interpreted his commission to mean that he should get rid of the usurper as best he could. He gathered about him a band of forty conspirators,

[409] Dalrymple, *Memoirs*, App. ii, 150.
[410] *Lond. Gaz.* No. 2758.
[411] *Conduct of the Duchess of Marlborough*, 108.
[412] *Evelyn's Diary* (ed. Bray), 505.
[413] White Kennet, *Hist. of Engl.* iii, 674.
[414] Wilson, *Memoirs of the Duke of Berwick*, i, 134.

composed of English and Irish Roman Catholics, Non-jurors, and Jacobites.[415] The place chosen for the attempt was Turnham Green, the day 15 February. The king intended to drive from Kensington Palace to hunt in Richmond Park. It was agreed that the conspirators should go in parties of two and three, some to inns at Brentford, some to inns at Turnham Green. As the king returned to the ferry at Brentford those who were posted there should ride back towards Turnham Green, and the whole band would fall upon the royal party in the lane between the two places, where the road was too narrow and the ditches too deep for the coach to turn round.[416] On the appointed day, when all was ready as arranged, news reached Barclay that the king had already returned in haste to Kensington. Information of the plot had been given by two of the conspirators, Prendergast and La Rue, and though Barclay escaped to France many of his subordinates were captured.[417] The attempt roused the greatest agitation in London, and led to the formation of the association for the protection of the king's person.[418]

The accident which caused William's death took place at Hampton Court as he was riding in the park.[419] He died at Kensington Palace, and Anne aroused great indignation among his Dutch friends by causing his body to be removed at once to Westminster, so that she might take immediate possession of Kensington Palace.

Perhaps the most conspicuous figure in Middlesex during the reign of William III was Charles Mordaunt, earl of Peterborough, admiral, general and diplomatist, who had inherited the Carey house at Fulham from his mother. In his younger days he had been an opponent of James II,[420] and at the Revolution he had been in close attendance on the Prince of Orange.[421] He held many court appointments under William, and in all his dealings—and he had much to do with the distribution of patronage—he was known as a man at once liberal and scrupulously honest. During the wars under Queen Anne Peterborough was granted a commission as admiral and commander-in-chief of the fleet with Sir Cloudesley Shovell. His greatest achievement was the siege of Barcelona, where he displayed great generalship as well as the highest personal valour.[422]

With the advent of the Hanoverian dynasty Middlesex seems to lose more and more of its individual history, and to become altogether merged in London and in the kingdom generally. The first two Georges went frequently to Hampton Court and Kensington Palace, but these ceased to be royal residences under George III. The many statesmen and men of distinction whom we find in Middlesex during the eighteenth century lived there for short periods only, and looked upon it merely as a place of residence, so they did not contribute much to the history of the county. In early Georgian times Holland House was famous for its political gatherings. Even before

[415] *Evelyn's Diary*, 509.
[417] Ibid. 553.
[419] Burnet, *Hist. of His Own Time*, iv, 558.
[421] *Hist. MSS. Com. Rep.* v, 136.
[416] Clarke, *Life of Jas. II*, ii, 550.
[418] *Evelyn's Diary*, 509.
[420] Macaulay, op. cit. ii, 287.
[422] Burnet, *Hist. of His Own Time*, v, 214.

Addison's marriage with the dowager countess of Holland, he had had a retirement near Chelsea, within an easy walk over the fields from Holland House.[423] His marriage in 1716, though it did not conduce to his happiness, probably facilitated his official advancement. In 1717 he was Secretary of State in Sunderland's ministry, but he retired the following year and died at Holland House in 1719.

Walpole was much at Chelsea during the reign of George II.[424] News of the sudden death of George I reached him there on 14 June, 1727. Walpole's fortunes were then passing through a crisis, and his position had been greatly damaged by the invectives of the Opposition in the *Craftsman*. Thoroughly aware of the importance of first audience with the new king, he is said to have killed two horses in carrying the tidings of the death of George I to his successor at Richmond.[425] Meanwhile Walpole's great opponent, Bolingbroke, was settled on the other side of the county, at Dawley near Uxbridge. Here he acted the part of a country gentleman with great spirit, and had his hall painted with rakes and spades 'to countenance his calling it a farm.'[426] All the time he was taking an important though obscure part in politics, leading the attacks on Walpole in the *Craftsman*.[427] In the new reign, while still at Dawley, he wrote the articles signed 'John Trot' which contained such virulent attacks on Walpole's foreign policy. In 1730 he was working to bring about the combination between the opposition Whigs and the Tories, led by Sir William Wyndham, and in 1733 it was from Dawley that he inspired Wyndham's speeches on the Excise Bill. He did not leave Dawley until he retired altogether from politics to live in France.

The rebellion of 1715 had not disturbed Middlesex, and that in 1745 affected it but little. When the news reached London that the enemy was advancing south, a small army, poorly and hastily equipped, was mustered on Finchley Common,[428] whence the duke of Cumberland travelled to Culloden. The rebellion had this result: that the ensuing elections proved a great victory for the Whigs in Middlesex, owing to the publication of the lists of subscriptions which had been raised for the defence of the kingdom, whereby Jacobite proclivities were rendered only too conspicuous. Sir Roger Newdigate of Harefield had represented Middlesex since 1741. So high a Tory was he that Horace Walpole speaks of him as a half-converted Jacobite. In 1747 he made way for Sir William Beauchamp Proctor.

In 1780, when the Gordon Riots reduced London to a state of panic, 11,000 troops were gathered round the City.[429] The Queen's Regiment and the South Hants Militia were quartered on Finchley Common.[430]

At the beginning of the nineteenth century the duke of Orleans settled at Twickenham with the duke of Montpensier and the comte de

[423] Swift, *Journ. to Stella*, 18 Sept. 1710.
[425] Pinkerton, *Walpoliana*, i, 86.
[427] Coxe, *Memoir of Sir R. Walpole*, ii, 344, 571.
[429] Walpole, *Journ.* ii, 409 ; *Ann. Reg.* (1780), 3 June.

[424] *Gent. Mag.* 1737, p. 514.
[426] Pope to Swift, 28 June, 1728.
[428] H. Walpole, *Journ.* ii.
[430] Lysons, *Environs of Lond.* ii, 335.

Beaujolais. Orleans returned after Napoleon's escape from Elba, and stayed until he was called to take the throne of France as Louis Philippe.[431] His house was sold to the earl of Kilmorey, who sold it again to the exiled king in 1852 for the use of the latter's son, the duc d'Aumale. From that time until 1871 Orleans House was the centre of the French loyalists. The comte de Paris lived at York House near by, the prince of Joinville at Mount Lebanon ; the duc de Nemours lived at Bushey Park.

The introduction of railways has converted so large a portion of Middlesex into metropolitan suburb that the history of the latter half of the nineteenth century is somewhat barren except from a social and economic point of view. The Local Government Act of 1888 marked a new era in the county's history.[432] The Act made two great changes.[433] In the first place, a new county of London was formed, which includes a large district formerly belonging to Middlesex. London now stretches to the River Lea on the east, and northwards to include Stoke Newington, Upper Holloway, and Hampstead, and westward beyond Hammersmith. Any future alteration in the boundaries will naturally be at the expense of Middlesex.[434]

The second change made by the Local Government Act was in the appointment of the sheriff. The right to appoint the sheriff still remained in the hands of the citizens of London, but by the Act the right was transferred to the hands of the crown, as in the case of other counties. The sheriffs of London ceased to have any jurisdiction in Middlesex on the day when the first sheriff of Middlesex entered into office.[435]

The parliamentary history of Middlesex dates from 1282, when the counties south of the Trent were summoned to send representatives to Northampton.[436] Middlesex also sent representatives to the assemblies of 1283 and 1290.[437] In 1295 William de Brook and Stephen de Gravesend were chosen for the county.[438] Richard le Rous sat for Middlesex in every Parliament during the remainder of the reign of Edward I, his fellow-representative being on most occasions Richard de Windsor. The names le Rous, de Windsor, de Enefield (or de Enefeud), and de Badyk occur frequently during the fourteenth century. In 1324 the representatives are described as two of the best and most discreet, but are not designated as knights.[438a] John de Wrotham sat for Middlesex in many of the Parliaments of Edward III. There were few occasions under the Tudors when one of the Wroths, his descendants, did not represent the county. Sir Robert Wroth sat in the Reformation Parliament. His son, Sir Thomas, was first returned in 1544, and with the exception of the Parliaments of the reign of Mary, he represented Middlesex practically without intermission till his death

[431] Michaud, *Public and Private Life of Louis Philippe*, 271.
[432] Pub. Gen. Stat. xxv, cap. 262.   [433] Clause 40 (2).
[434] The county of London and the county of Middlesex are considered as one county for the purpose of all legal proceedings, civil or criminal ; clause 89 (3).   [435] Clause 113 (2).
[436] Palgrave, *Parl. Writs* (Rec. Com.), i, 10.   [437] Ibid. 16, 21.   [438] Ibid. 39.   [438a] Ibid. ii, 321.

in 1573. His son, a second Sir Robert Wroth, was first returned in 1572, and again in 1585, 1588, 1601, and 1602. Sir Gilbert Gerrard represented Middlesex throughout the Long Parliament, and Sir Thomas Allen and Sir Launcelot Lake in the Restoration Parliament.

The most familiar name in connexion with Middlesex politics is that of 'Jack' Wilkes. When Wilkes offered himself as candidate for Middlesex in the general election of 1768, he had just been defeated as candidate for the City. He had already been prosecuted in 1763 for his criticism of the king's speech in No. 45 of the *North Briton*.[439] He had been attacked by the House of Lords for the 'Essay on Woman' (November, 1763),[440] and expelled by the Commons (he was member for Aylesbury), on account of No. 45, on 19 January, 1764.[441] On 21 February of that year he had been condemned by the Court of King's Bench as a libeller and as the author of an obscene poem, and he had later been outlawed for duelling and forced to flee to France.[442] His character was certainly not of the highest, and his personality was most unattractive. Yet when he returned from France in 1768, he found himself exalted to the position of popular idol. Technically he had suffered injustice, because the liberty of the subject had been outraged by his arrest under a general warrant for the publication of No. 45; and the privilege of Parliament had been denied him by his imprisonment in the Tower. But what appealed to the people was that an unpopular court, the adherents of an unpopular king, had pursued him with unexampled animosity. The country was just entering on that period of unrest and smouldering revolution in which it continued until the Reform Bill of 1832: the period which beheld the rise of democracy and the expansion of a formidable party of reform. Wilkes, the son of a rich distiller of Clerkenwell, an atheist, and a notorious evil-liver, yet appealed to the people as one who, himself a victim of tyranny, might lead them to fuller freedom.[443] He was supported because of his indomitable resistance to a king who was hated as much for the corruption by which he controlled Parliament as for the policy by which he had brought about the war with the American colonies.

In 1768, then, Wilkes was elected for Middlesex by a large majority in opposition to the established interest of men who already represented the county, and who, besides having considerable fortunes in connexion with Middlesex, were supported by the whole interest of the court. Wilkes's partisans were jubilant, forcing even the inhabitants of London to celebrate his triumph, and marking every door with the popular number '45.'[444] Their champion had, however, to appear before the Court of King's Bench on his outlawry, and he was committed on a *capias utlagatum*. He was rescued by the mob, but again surrendered himself. His outlawry was reversed, but he was sentenced to two

---

[439] Erskine May, *Const. Hist.* i, cap. x.   [440] *Parl. Hist.* xv, 1346.
[441] *Com. Journ.* xxix, 689.   [442] *Grenville Papers*, ii, 155.
[443] *Hist. MSS. Com. Rep.* iii, 415. Lord Hardwicke to President Dundas, 16 Mar. 1762 : 'We are now got into a strange flame about an object, in himself of no great consequence, Mr. Wilkes, and it has spread far and wide.'   [444] Erskine May, op. cit. i, 391.

years' imprisonment for libel, and to a fine of £1,000. Riots took place in his favour, and an unhappy collision between the mob and the military occurred in St. George's Fields.

Owing to his imprisonment, Wilkes was unable to take his seat in the first session of Parliament. In the second session he was expelled by the Commons on four charges, for the first three of which he had already suffered, and for the fourth (that of libel on the Secretary of State) it was not within the province of the Commons to punish him. The reason for this unconstitutional action was that the court party, to whom the Commons were bound by a process of corruption and bribery, were determined that no amount of popularity should prevail against their own dignity. The weakness and irregularity of the Commons' action was proclaimed even in the House itself by a powerful party, led by Burke, Pitt, Dowdeswell, and George Greville.[445] Wilkes's constituents were by no means overawed by the attitude of the authorities. His supporters raised £20,000 to pay his debts, and he was immediately re-elected for Middlesex. Parliament declared his election to be void. With increasing popularity, Wilkes was again elected without opposition, and again his election was declared void.[446] To prevent a repetition of the farce, Colonel Luttrell vacated his seat and offered himself as candidate for Middlesex. He obtained only 296 votes to Wilkes's 1,143,[447] but the Commons rejected Wilkes and declared Colonel Luttrell to be returned. A petition of the freeholders of Middlesex was presented to Parliament on 24 May, 1769, by Mr. Serjeant Glynn and others,[448] in which they pleaded against having a candidate forced upon the county,[449] but Colonel Luttrell's election was confirmed. As evidence of Wilkes's continued popularity he was elected successively [450] alderman, sheriff, and Lord Mayor of London, and a subscription was again raised to pay his debts. In 1774 he was returned for Middlesex and took his seat unmolested.

An exciting contest took place in 1802 between Sir Francis Burdett and Mr. William Mainwaring. Burdett was already well known as the champion of liberty of speech ; he was foremost among the opposers of the government, had exposed the grievances of war taxation, and the abuse of power over those who were offensive to the ministry.[451] He had just rendered great service to the public by obtaining an inquiry into the mismanagement of Coldbath Fields Prison, where suspected persons were detained under the Habeas Corpus Suspension Acts ; when it was shown that no distinction had been made between the treatment of these persons and that accorded to convicted felons. His opponent, Mainwaring, was the magistrate who had most strenuously objected to the investigation of the prison abuses, and true to their liberal principles,

[445] Cavendish, *Debates*, i, 151.   [446] Ibid. 345 ; Feb. 17, 1769.
[447] Erskine May, op. cit. i, 397.   [448] Political Tracts, 8, Signed by 1,565 freeholders.
[449] 'The case of the late Election for the County of Middlesex condemned on the Principles of the Constitution and the Authorities of the Law' (1769).
[450] 'The Sentiments of an English Freeholder on the Late Decision of the Middlesex Election.'
[451] *Dict. Nat. Biog.* vii, 297.

the freeholders of Middlesex returned Burdett by a considerable majority.[452] He sat for nearly two years, during which legal proceedings were taken for nullifying his election. In 1804 his election was declared void. There was a new contest between Burdett and Mainwaring's son,[453] which the latter won by five votes. This decision was amended in Burdett's favour the following year, but in 1806 Burdett was finally excluded, Mr. William Mellish (Mr. G. B. Mainwaring having withdrawn) and Mr. George Byng being returned after a sixteen days' poll.[454] Mr. William Mellish, who was now elected, represented Middlesex for several years. During the election of 1818 he was spoken of by *The Times* as ' a thick and thin man for the government and a jolly, comely, hereditary Protestant.'[455]

Mr. George Byng of Wrotham Park, a descendant of Admiral Byng, was first returned for Middlesex in the Whig interest in 1790.[456] He represented the county without intermission for fifty-six years, and was the father of the House of Commons when he died in 1847.[457] The Reform Bill of 1832 created three metropolitan boroughs, Finsbury and Marylebone, to each of which two members were assigned, and the Tower Hamlets, which returned one representative.[458] The population did not begin to increase rapidly until after the establishment of railways. The market-towns of Uxbridge, Staines, and Brentford, were still little better than villages, and only in the immediate neighbourhood of London was there any urgent need for further representation. During the next fifty years, however, the circumstances were immensely altered. Chelsea was given two members in 1867, and the Tower Hamlets was divided into two districts under the names of Hackney and the Tower Hamlets, each returning one member.[459] But further complete representation was badly needed. Twickenham, Hanwell, and Brentford now contained a large manufacturing population. The residential suburbs of London had increased tremendously. There were only two county members to represent a population of 70,000 voters.[460] By the Redistribution of Seats Act of 1884, fifteen new metropolitan boroughs were created, and the representatives of the Tower Hamlets were increased to seven. The county outside the metropolitan area was divided into seven electoral districts, Enfield, Tottenham, Hornsey, Harrow, Ealing, Brentford, and Uxbridge, each of which returns one member.

The trained bands of Middlesex ceased to exist on 25 March, 1663, when the County Militia was reorganized.[461] The trained bands of the Tower division of Middlesex, known as the Tower Hamlets, were on the other hand retained, and continued to be levied, the reason being that the Tower Hamlets were, and always had been, under the command of the constable of the Tower.[462] Future legislation continued to treat

[452] ' Full Account of the Proceedings at the Middlesex Election,' Political Tracts.
[453] *Dict. Nat. Biog.* vii, 297.
[454] ' Westminster and Middlesex Election.'
[455] *The Times*, Saturday, 27 June, 1818.
[456] *Parliamentary Touchstone and Political Guide*, 20.
[457] *Gent. Mag.* xxvii, 307.
[458] Stat. 2 & 3 Will. IV, cap. 45.
[459] Representation of the People Act, 1867.
[460] Hansard, *Reports* (3rd Ser.), ccxciii, 1195.
[461] Stat. 13 & 14 Car. II, cap. 3, sect. 20.
[462] Ibid. sect. 31.

the Hamlets apart from the rest of Middlesex. When the militia was reconstituted under George II, in 1757, the number of men appointed to be raised in Middlesex was 1,160 and in the Tower Hamlets 1,600.[463] At the beginning of the next reign the quota for the county was raised to 1,600.[464] By this Act separate provision is made for the necessary qualifications of officers in the Tower Hamlets,[465] the militia of which remained on the same basis as in the time of Charles II, and consisted of two regiments of eight companies each.[466] It was reorganized in 1797, when the number of men to be levied in each parish within the division was fixed.[467] Two regiments were raised as formerly, and it was provided that one or other of these should stay always in the Tower division, whilst the other might be put under the command of such general officers as the king should be pleased to appoint, and might be required to serve at a distance not exceeding twelve miles from London.[468] By 1802 the number of men in the Middlesex Militia had fallen to 338,[469] but six years later, when England was in the stress of the Napoleonic War, the number was raised to 2,024,[470] and in 1812 to 12,162,[471] with 4,480 for the Tower Hamlets and liberties of the Tower.[472]

During the revolutionary wars at the close of the eighteenth century, several 'Loyal Associations' were formed in Middlesex. These were volunteer infantry corps on a small scale, to serve in parishes, and mainly to assist the civil authorities. The earliest of these was the Tottenham Loyal Association,[473] which was formed in 1792, and drilled regularly for three or four years.[474] The 'Hadley and South Mimms Volunteers' were among the forces reviewed in Hyde Park by George III, on 21 June, 1799.[475] The Hampstead Loyal Association was also reviewed on that occasion. It numbered probably 150 men, under the command of Josiah Boydell, esq.[476]

Middlesex also furnished a corps of volunteer cavalry, numbering 830 men, 300 of whom were members of the London and Westminster Light Horse Volunteers. Other cavalry corps were raised at Uxbridge, Islington, and Twickenham.[477] The associations were disbanded in 1802 after the Peace of Amiens, but when Napoleon threatened invasion in 1803, the Defence Act was passed, by which the lords lieutenant were empowered to raise forces in each county. The Hampstead Loyal Volunteer Infantry was then formed,[478] and a force of 108 men was raised in Barnet and district, and three companies were raised by Mr. Nathaniel Haden at Highgate.[479] There also existed at this time a mounted force, raised in Edmonton, Kensington, Ealing, and Brentford.[480] These corps were in turn disbanded in 1813–14.

[463] Stat. 30 Geo. II, cap. 25.
[464] Stat. 2 Geo. III, cap. 20, sect. 13.
[465] Ibid. sect. 41.
[466] Stat. 26 Geo. III, cap. 107, sect. 111.
[467] Stat. 37 Geo. III, cap. 25.
[468] Ibid. sect. 6.
[469] Stat. 42 Geo. III, cap. 90.
[470] Stat. 48 Geo. III, cap. 90.
[471] Stat. 52 Geo. III, cap. 38, sect. 14, 16.
[472] Ibid. sect. 169.
[473] Robinson, *Hist. of Tottenham*, 72–3.
[474] G. T. Evans, *Records of the 3rd Middlesex Rifle Volunteers*, 136.
[475] Ibid. 64.
[476] Ibid. 36.
[477] Ibid. 5.
[478] Ibid. 38.
[479] Ibid. 65–7.
[480] Ibid. 46.

The volunteer movement of 1859–60 was taken up with the greatest warmth in Middlesex, rifle corps being formed in almost every village.[481]

When the line regiments of the British Army were territorialized the old 57th became the 1st Battalion, and the old 77th the 2nd Battalion of the Duke of Cambridge's Own Middlesex Regiment. Both regiments brought great traditions of the Peninsular, Crimean, and South African (1879) wars.[482] The Royal Elthorne Militia and the Royal East Middlesex Militia now form respectively the 5th and 6th Battalions. The line and militia, with the three volunteer battalions, served in the South African War, 1900–2.

[481] Evans, op. cit. 48, 70, 86, 112, 141 ; *The West Middlesex Herald*, 1860–1.
[482] H. M. Chichester and G. Burges-Short, *Records and Badges of the British Army*. At the Battle of Albuera (1811) the 57th gained the name of the ' Die-Hards.'

SOCIAL AND ECONOMIC HISTORY

UNTIL it was flooded by the suburban expansion of London Middlesex was an exclusively agricultural county, the near neighbourhood of the cities of London and Westminster preventing any great development of urban life or urban manufacture. There was no incorporate town in the county, and no trade but agriculture attained any degree of importance. But, containing as it did, some of the best arable land in the kingdom, within such easy reach of the London market; having also a sufficiency of good pasture and meadow land, and in the northern parts some valuable woodland, Middlesex, in the fourteenth century, was the second richest county in the kingdom.[1] When the wool tax of 1341 (15 Edward III) was levied, Middlesex [2] was assessed at 236 sacks, or one sack to 760 acres. The assessment of the richest county—Norfolk—was one to 610, and the counties which were the immediate neighbours of Middlesex were assessed at: Hertfordshire, one to 1,200 acres; Buckinghamshire, one to 1,260 acres; Essex, one to 1,580 acres; Surrey, one to 1,250 acres.

The Domesday Survey of Middlesex distinguishes three categories of servile tenants: villeins, bordars, and cottars. Of slaves proper there are only 104 in the whole county, and they make no further appearance in its history. Nor do we hear any more of the 'bordarii,' unless we may regard as their successors the holders of 'Bordlond' at Twickenham. Of the 2,132 tenants who are enumerated on the several manors in the six hundreds of the county, 1,936 are villeins (1,133), bordars (342), and cottars (461). The only free tenants mentioned in the survey are: 13 knights, 1 *francus*, 12 priests, 10 foreigners (*francigenae*), and 46 *burgenses* at Staines, nothing being said as to the status of 23 *homines* at St. Pancras who rendered 30s. a year. In the later records, on the contrary, from the time of Henry I onwards, free as well as servile tenants are mentioned on nearly all the manors of which we have any account. Already in the reign of Henry I there were at Harmondsworth free and custumary tenants and cottars.[3] At Kensington in 1263–4 the rents of the free tenants amounted to £4 15s., so that there must have been a certain number of them. The villein tenants held

---

[1] Prof. Thorold Rogers, *Hist. of Agric. and Prices*, i, 107; *Rot. Parl.* (Rec. Com.), ii, 131.
[2] Exclusive of London.   [3] P.R.O. Rentals and Surv. ptfo. 11, No. 20.

21 virgates, their money rents amounting to £2 19s. 4½d., and there were two cottars.[4]

According to a Westminster Abbey custumal, in the reign of Henry III there were at Teddington five free tenants holding among them 10 virgates, and 15 custumary tenants holding 16½ virgates, besides five cottars whose holdings varied from 1 to 6 acres. Of the three other manors in the custumal, free tenants are mentioned on one only, Greenford. At Hayes and Paddington there appear to have been only custumers.[5] The survey of the St. Paul's manors of Drayton and Sutton in 1222 does not specify the status of the tenants, distinguishing only at Drayton twenty-nine tenants of demesne land and twenty-four of *terra assiza*. The demesne tenants have mostly small holdings, some paying money rents only, while some are *posita ad operationem*. The holdings of assized land are larger; one is a whole hide, two are half hides. There is one of 2 virgates, twelve of 1 virgate, and eight half virgates. The tenants all pay rents, generally at the rate of 4s. for a virgate, and render various services, but no week work.[6] A Drayton court roll of the time of Richard II in the library of St. Paul's cathedral mentions free tenants on the manor. In 1276–7 there is mention of seven free tenants on the manor of Edgeware.[6a]

At Sutton there are three categories of tenants: seven demesne tenants who hold small tenements for rents and services; thirty-two tenants of assize land, one holding 3 virgates, four 1 virgate, ten half a virgate, and seventeen with smaller holdings. They hold at a variety of rents and services, some paying malt-silver (½d. to 5d.), and giving 8d. or 10d. *de dono* as well, and two paying 2d. ward-penny. Some of these holdings are in the hands of demesne tenants. Thirdly, there are eight *operarii* who hold 5 acres each, for weekly and boon works, paying no rent, but giving 5d. *de dono*, and 2½ malt-silver. Two of them, who hold assart lands as well as their 5 acres, pay rent only for them.[7]

The number of free tenants at Isleworth varies somewhat. In the time of Edward I there were four free and twenty custumary cottars,[8] while in 1315–16 nine free tenants superintended the mowing and reaping.[8a] A rental of the parsonage[9] in the reign of Edward III enumerates nineteen free tenants, and a minister's account of the same reign mentions thirty-seven free virgaters.[9a] According to a custumal quoted in the Historical Manuscripts' Commissioners' Report on the manuscripts at Syon House, there were also *burgenses* who held *per cartam*, and some of the free tenants were tallageable.[10] At Fulham by the reign of Richard II, at Stepney by the time of Edward III, and by the same reign at Kempton, where they are expressly stated to hold by socage tenure, the existence of free tenants is recorded.[11] Lastly, at

[4] P.R.O. Inq. p.m. Hen. III, No. 26.
[5] B.M. Add. Chart. 8139.
[6] *Domesday of St. Paul's* (Camd. Soc.).
[6a] P.R.O. Rentals and Surv. 5 Edw. I, rot. 395.
[7] *Domesday of St. Paul's*, 1222 Surv. of Sutton.
[8] P.R.O. Inq. 28 Edw. I, No. 44.
[8a] P.R.O. Mins. Accts. bdle. 916, No. 12 (8–9, Edw. II.)
[9] P.R.O. Rental, ptfo. 11, No. 26.
[9a] P.R.O. Mins. Accts. bdle. 916, No. 17.
[10] *Hist. MSS. Com. Rep.* vi, App. 232.
[11] P.R.O. Ct. R. bdle. 191, No. 60; bdle. 191, No. 41; bdle. 188, No. 65.

Enfield,[12] though no free tenants are mentioned in our earliest account of the manor in the time of Henry VI, in an Elizabethan syllabus of all the free tenants in Middlesex, twenty-three are enumerated there ; seven at Drayton ; four at Fulham ; eleven at Stepney and Hackney ; and four at Harmondsworth. Neither Isleworth, Teddington, nor Kensington is given in the list at all.[13]

On some manors there were special tenures as to which the information derived from compotus rolls and even from custumals is not always very definite. Generally they are differentiated from the other tenants by doing a given number of works at a particular season, sometimes by different customs as to heriot and inheritance. Thus at Harmondsworth there are seven tenants, undistinguished by any special name, who render two works weekly between Michaelmas and Martinmas.[14]

There are several of these tenures at Isleworth. Eight custumary tenants held Forapellond. They had to attend the waterbedrippe, and they paid money rents as well.[15]

'Bordlond' was held by twenty-one custumary tenants in Twickenham. Their united rents amounted to £5 15s. 6d., and the net value of their services was 5d. a head. They held at a certain rent and tallage, and paid heriots of 2s. or 1s. according to the size of their holdings. They paid pannage and had to plough and harrow half an acre each at the winter sowing, fetching the seed from the grange ; in return for which they each received 1d. ; besides sending two men to one bedrippe at the lord's expense.[16] 'Bordlond' occurs at Fulham, but is only mentioned in the court rolls without any details as to the nature of the tenure there.

The tenants of 'Werklond' did the same ploughing works as the holders of 'Bordlond,' and they rendered 420 works during the fourteen weeks between Midsummer and Michaelmas, at the rate of three half days a week, in return for an allowance of half their rent, amounting to 1s. 3d. for each virgate.[17] The nature of the works done varied considerably, probably at the discretion of the reeve. Should they be kept beyond noon, they received 1d. each. These holdings passed by inheritance to the youngest son.

There were also at Isleworth six villein holdings, held for rent and services, 'misfre' or 'unfre' lands. The tenants ploughed, harrowed, sowed and carried grain to the field, receiving 2d. each, and sent two men to two bedrippes, who had one meal of bread, fish and cheese. If they had no beast they paid money heriots of 2s. for a virgate and 1s. for half a virgate. The eldest sons inherited.[18] In the Isleworth accounts for the reign of Edward III custumers called 'gader-

---

[12] P.R.O. Mins. Accts. (Duchy of Lanc.), bdle. 42, No. 825.
[13] B.M. Harl. MS. 1711.   [14] P.R.O. Rentals and Surv. ptfo. 11, No. 25.
[15] P.R.O. Inq. 28 Edw. I, No. 44 ; *Hist. MSS. Com. Rep.* vi, App. 232.
[16] *Hist. MSS. Com. Rep.* vi, App. 232 ; P.R.O. Inq. 28 Edw. I, No. 44.
[17] P.R.O. Mins. Accts. bdle. 916, Nos. 11, 12, 17, 18, 19, 20.
[18] *Hist. MSS. Com. Rep.* vi, App. 232.

zerdus' put in an appearance, rendering with the cottars fifteen works at the ale-bedrippe and fifty-two at the water-bedrippe. They seem to have done no other works, and whether they paid rents or not, or what was the size of their holdings, does not appear.[19] An unexplained custom called a 'mismene' is mentioned in one compotus roll as yielding 6s. 8d.[20]

In the Teddington manor rolls tenants called 'hesebonds' or 'house-bonds' appear who are mentioned neither in the Westminster custumal, nor in a rental of the time of Richard II. Nothing is said as to their status, and it is not easy to account for the land they held. At one time there are nine of them, at another fifteen. They do boon works only, it being expressly provided that they do not reap, but only follow the reapers, rod in hand, to superintend the work.[21] Certain tenants here rendered two unexplained customs called 'cherne' and 'russic.'

At Stepney, in the time of Edward I,[21a] there were 10½ virgates of 'Shirlond,' 15 virgates of 'Cotlond,' and also 'Mollond' and 'Hydlond,' the virgate, for all four tenures, containing 20 acres.[22] One holding of a virgate containing 25 acres is noted as rendering the same services as the 'Mollond' virgates. The shirmen and cotmen owed weekly works for eleven weeks and three days in each year; six works a week being exacted from 8½ virgates, and three a week from the other 2 virgates of the Shirlond; while of the cotlond, 12 virgates owed five, and 3 virgates four days weekly. Instead of a corresponding number of these weekly works, the shirmen had to do 'redeherth' ploughing. The 'Hydmen' and 'Molmen,' on the other hand, rendered no weekly works, their services being confined to a certain tale of ploughing works and 'wodelods,' and to stacking corn, the amounts due differing for the two tenures.

In the accounts for 1392[22a] and later, the *redditus assisi* is entered in three sums, as accruing from free tenants (£17 14s. 11d.), custumary tenants (£1 6s. 5d.), and from 'Molelond' (£13 15s. 2d.). But 'Molelond' was held by freemen and custumers, 16½ acres being let on lease to custumers in 1362,[23] while in 1392 12 virgates were in the hands of free tenants. There were 'Molmen' at Enfield as well as at Stepney, but they are explicitly specified as custumers. Like the molmen at Stepney, the twenty-two 'molmen and cottars' at Enfield,[23a] who differed from one another only in the amount, not in the nature of their holdings, did no weekly works, but sent twenty-six men, among them, to weed the lord's corn for one day (one man apiece from eighteen holdings, and two among the remaining four, probably the cottars', holdings) and

---

[19] P.R.O. Mins. Accts. 17 Edw. III, bdle. 916, No. 17.

[20] Ibid. bdle. 1126, No. 5.

[21] Ibid. bdle. 918, Nos. 1–25; bdle. 919, Nos. 1–11.

[21a] Mins. Accts. of the manor of Stepney in the Library of St. Paul's Cathedral.

[22] In an account of 1362–3 five half-virgate holdings of 'Shirlond' are estimated at 12 acres to the half-virgate, but the amount of the rent is corrected to that corresponding to a half-virgate of 10 acres, as if this were an error. There are several allowances for overcharges in the account.

[22a] P.R.O. Mins. Accts. bdle. 1139, No. 20, 15–16 Ric. II.

[23] Ibid. bdle. 1139, No. 18, 36 Edw. III.

[23a] Ibid. 7 Hen. V, bdle. 915, No. 26; 17 Hen. VI (Duchy of Lanc.), bdle. 42, No. 825.

mowed 23½ acres of meadow,[23b] in the proportion of 2 acres per virgate for eighteen holdings and half an acre for the others. They also rendered, among them, twenty autumn boon-works, four tenants sending among them one man for two days at the lord's cost and the remaining eighteen each one man for one day. Thirteen of them also owed eleven carrying works (on foot). In view of the accepted definition of mol (or mal) men as custumary tenants, whose early release from servile works has reacted on their status in the direction of freedom,[24] it is curious to note that at Enfield the molmen, whose servile status is expressly asserted, were actually, in 1419, the only tenants on the manor who rendered works at all; while at Stepney, where the services generally were commuted very early, there is nothing to show that the mollond works were commuted earlier, or more completely, than those of the other tenures. In the *Victoria History* of county Durham [24a] it is pointed out that the Hatfield Survey equates *firmarius* to *malmannus* (*malmanni sive firmarii*), and it is suggested that the malmen were farmers of portions of the demesne land, their services being, by special arrangement, extensively commuted for money payments. But at Stepney, as we have seen, though some mollond was let on lease, the commutation of molmen works proceeded *pari passu* with, and at Enfield was actually later than, those of the other holdings. Neither is there anything to show that the mollond was essentially, though some of it might be occasionally, demesne land. In one Stepney account one acre of mollond is mentioned under the heading of *firme* of demesne lands. Certainly at Enfield the molmen were not *firmarii*, for they rendered the same services before and after the leasing of the demesne, with the sole difference that afterwards their services belonged to the demesne farmer instead of to the lord of the manor. Now the demesne lease explicitly conveyed to the farmer all the weeding, mowing, and reaping works *not let on lease* (*ad firmam non dimissis*) *nor commuted* (*necque arrentatis*),[25] and these, as the accounts show, were precisely the works actually rendered to the firmarius by the twenty-two molmen.

'Acre ware' occur at Isleworth, Blanchappelton (a Duchy of Lancaster manor), and Fulham, but, unfortunately, not in a way to throw any illumination on that much-discussed term. At Stepney land is measured by 'day-work acres,' and on several manors in 'pyghtellings.'

On the two St. Paul's manors of Drayton and Sutton a portion of the land is distinguished as 'solanda' or 'scholanda.' This was identified erroneously by Archdeacon Hales [26] with the Kentish 'sulung' or 'solinus,' but Mr. Round has shown that it has no connexion with sulung,

---

[23b] The account does not expressly state that these mowing works were rendered by the molmen, but it is clear that this was the case from the proportion in which the works are allotted to the holdings, and from the identity of the names of tenants for whose works allowances are made with those rendering specified mollond services.

[24] Vinogradoff, *Villeinage in England*, 183; *Engl. Hist. Rev.* i, 734.

[24a] *V.C.H. Dur.* i, 280–2.

[25] P.R.O. Mins. Accts. (Duchy of Lanc.), bdle. 53, No. 1010. [26] *Domesday of St. Paul's.*

and is not a measure of land at all, but means a prebend, implying that the estates in question were prebends of St. Paul's.[27]

There are indications that the virgate represented a variable number of actual acres on different manors, and even, as at Stepney, on different holdings of the same manor. It is noted in the survey of Drayton of 1222 that the virgate there contained 16 acres, and at Teddington in the reign of Edward III one or two virgate holdings are stated to contain 16½ acres, and half-virgate holdings 8½ acres. At Harmondsworth, where there was a great deal of sub-letting, a holding generally continued to be called a virgate however much its actual contents had been reduced by subdivision.

The earliest custumal we possess for any Middlesex manor is one of Harmondsworth of 11 Henry I (1110–11), which is transcribed in a valor of the reign of Richard II. It is the sworn verdict of twelve jurors on the customs and services owed by the tenants to the abbot of Saint Katherine's of Rouen,[28] the lord of the manor, and gives the services in great detail.

At the time of sowing, every villein tenant who owned a plough had to plough and harrow 2 acres, one for corn and one for oats. The lord supplied the seed, and his servant sowed it, but the tenant had to fetch the seed from the grange and cart it to the field. Of whatever kind the seed might be, the tenant's horse must not have a feed from it, but if any remained over after the sowing it was to be taken back to the grange by the servant. Those villeins who had no plough were to thrash in the grange till vespers instead of ploughing.

At the hay harvest all the villeins, except the cottars, must mow for one day at their own cost, it being understood that they are bound to complete the mowing of the meadow, and that the lord is bound to find two mowers to help them. Custumers who do not come the first day may do their mowing on the morrow or at the lord's pleasure without fine. At vespers, after the day's mowing, each tenant receives as much grass as he can lift on the heft of his scythe in the presence of the lord or his ministers. But if the scythe break he loses the hay, and is fined into the bargain. When all the mowing is finished the tenants receive from the lord a ram or 13d. in lieu thereof.

All villein tenants, including the cottars, must attend or send one man to lift, load, and stack the hay, bringing with them any tenants they may have. For this work they are at their own expense. Every tenant who possesses a cart or wagon must carry three loads of hay to the grange, where those tenants who have no carts stack it, each working for the time occupied on its three journeys by the cart with which he came. Should the rain prevent the completion of this task, the tenants must make good the hours that are lacking either on the morrow or at the lord's pleasure. Any carrying works which may not be needed at hay-time must be made up, load for load, at the corn-harvest cartings. There were three *precariae* at Harmondsworth: a

[27] Round, *Feud. Engl.* 103. [28] P.R.O. Rentals and Surv. ptfo. 11, No. 20, Ric. II.

water-bedrippe, the Great *Precaria*, and a third and very ill-named love-bedrippe, for it was a never-ending source of contention between the lord and his tenants. Every tenant had to attend the first boon day, when summoned by the crier, coming at the hour of prime with all his servants and tenants, and working till vespers. At noon every thirteen reapers received three loaves made from one bushel of corn. To the great bedrippe all the free and villein tenants and cottars were summoned to reap from prime until vespers at the lord's cost. After the day's work they had a supper in the hall, consisting of broth of peas or beans, bread, cheese and beer in sufficient quantity, and a dish of meat or fish to the value of $1\frac{1}{2}d$. for every two men. Those who were tired out (*gravati*) by their task and could not sup with the others might carry their portions home with them. The superintendents of the reapers had beer in the hall at noon as well. They were responsible for any damage accruing from bad work.

For the third or love-bedrippe every tenant had to provide one man to bind the corn from prime; one meal in the hall being provided for each man. All villein tenants who had carts or wagons must carry three loads to the grange, without food or drink, and their horses must not eat of the sheaves. If any tenant worked otherwhere than in the lord's fields on the days of the first two bedrippes he was in the lord's mercy. After the wheat was carried the animals of the vill commoned on the fields.

Except the free tenants and the cottars all must provide one man to weed and one to clean the ponds (*riperia*) every three years, receiving one meal each of bread, cheese and beer, and a dish of meat or fish for every two men.

Every hide of bond-land must fence one perch every three years right round the manor, each tenant fetching the pales from the manor and fencing in proportion to the amount of his holding. The only week work done on the manor is by seven tenants who render two days a week from Michaelmas to Martinmas, four of the holdings rendering twelve, and two six days; the seventh is quit of his works. A later compotus states that they must do any kind of work which the reeve may impose on them.

All the native tenants and the tenants of the freemen whose holdings border on the woods have a right to wood and pannage, and whether there be mast in the wood or no they must pay for pannage $1d$. on every pig over a year old and $\frac{1}{2}d$. on all younger. All the villeins must bring their pigs to the court at Martinmas and pay their pannage, and if the lord be in doubt as to the age of any pig its owner is to be quit on oath and for $1\frac{1}{2}d$. The lord is bound to provide a herd to watch the pigs while they are in the woods and to bring them home.

Every tenant in Harmondsworth and Ruislip, man or woman, bond or free, owes at his or her death a heriot of the best beast on the holding, and on changing hands the holding must be redeemed by a fine at the lord's discretion. No bondage tenant may marry son or daughter within or without the vill except by the lord's licence, for which he must fine at the lord's will, nor may any villein enter holy orders or leave the vill without his lord's permission. Nor may they let their lands out of the lord's dominion, nor place metes and bounds without leave and under the supervision of the lord's servants. Every bondage tenant is tallageable at the lord's will and pleasure either annually or when he comes over sea.

No tenant—bond or free—may shake down mast in the woods or thrash in Ruislip woods, on pain of having their teams confiscated by the forester till they have fined to the lord for their transgression. Neither may any tenant fish in the lord's water except for a dish of fish for the diet of himself and his wife, and then any fish more than a foot long goes to the lord.

The lord may seize the teams—oxen or horses—of any tenants, who, owing rent at Trinity, have not paid by the day after the feast, detaining the teams for a day and a night, after which time, unless the tenant have redeemed it by paying the rent, the lord may take the team to his own use.

Any villein tenant must serve as reeve or crier at the appointment of his lord, being quit of all other service and rent for his holding during his term of office.[29] The reeve and the crier either dined daily at the lord's table, or received a weekly allowance of a bushel of wheat apiece, 'and nothing more save by the lord's grace.' The crier had charge of the hay while it was in cocks, and was responsible for any damage to it. While watching the hay he had his lodging in the meadow.

The smith also held his tenement in return for the special services of his trade, being quit of all other obligations, except a yearly rent of 2s. He had to repair and replace the shares of the demesne ploughs, the lord providing the necessary iron and steel, to sharpen the tenants' scythes when they mowed for the lord, and to shoe the front feet of two beasts all the year round, keeping as his perquisite the old shoes, if they were still on the feet. In 1434 the smith's duties were not rendered because there was no one on the manor of that custom, and the tenement was ruinous.[30] So that evidently the smith's duties were accredited to a particular holding. The manor smiths were sometimes paid a regular stipend as at Isleworth and Paddington.[31] On the latter manor the smith's stipend is 18s. 'by custom,' and he makes as well as repairs the ploughs. At Isleworth he gets 6s. 8d. for repairing the ploughs, including the materials.

The Harmondsworth custumal does not mention how the forester of the manor was appointed. On some manors any villein had to serve in this capacity, too, if appointed by the lord. This was the case at Sutton,[32] where the forester, who was apparently one of the *operarii*,

[29] At Edgeware in 1279–80 (P.R.O. Ct. R. bdle. 188, No. 54) a tenant was fined for making himself reeve.

[30] P.R.O. Mins. Accts. 12–13 Hen. VI, bdle. 1126, No. 7.

[31] Ibid. bdle. 917, No. 25.   [32] *Domesday of St. Paul's,* Surv. 1222.

held his 5 acres free of all works in return for his services as woodward, and also at Paddington, where the woodward had 2 acres free of all services, pasture in the woods, and the loppings of the timber felled for the lord's ploughs.[33] Sometimes the office was, or tended to become hereditary. At Sutton it is particularly stated that the woodward had no hereditary right to the office and its emoluments. His father, it is recorded, had 28*d.* a year as stipend, he lost and never recovered the 5 acres, and was dismissed from the office. At Harmondsworth, on the contrary, it was hereditary. In 1383–4 the horn of office was successfully claimed by the cousin and heir of the late forester,[34] and later on it actually passed by inheritance to the second husband of the incumbent's widow. In the time of Henry VIII [35] one William Norton was forester, who held a 'principal tenement' of 160 acres by military tenure and also a small holding, whether bond or free is not stated, called a 'tile-place,' with a 'tile-house.' If the office of woodward was connected with any holding, it must have been with this latter one, as this one only passed at his death to his widow. The widow re-married within a year of her husband's death, and her second husband succeeded to the office of woodward *jure uxoris suae*.

At much less length, and with far less detail, than the Harmondsworth record, a custumal of Westminster Abbey states the rents and services due from the abbot's tenants in his Middlesex estates in the time of Henry III.[36] The Harmondsworth customs are fairly typical of the services rendered on the different manors, though there is some variation in the amount of ploughing and the number of boon-days exacted and in the amount and nature of the extra works and weekly works.[37] With few exceptions, such as the holders of half virgates at Teddington, and the *operarii* at Sutton, who pay no rent, the tenants render money rents as well as services; tallage is mentioned nearly everywhere and remained nominally constant over very long periods, though sometimes lowered 'by the lord's grace' in bad times. 'Gersilver' or 'gerspeni' or pannage is paid nearly everywhere, generally at the rate of 1*d.* or ½*d.* for each pig according to its age; but at Paddington the tenants pay a round sum, 19*s.*, among them, and at Greenford it is ½*d.* for every pig, and at Enfield it is 4*d.* and 3*d.* per pig.

Of dues in kind, at Greenford the tenants brought ten eggs at Easter and the Hanwell tenants paid the fourth part of a quarter of wheat once a year. A bushel of barley and five eggs at Easter were exacted from each tenant at Teddington, as well as a hen from every two at Christmas, and they paid a certain number of sheaves of wheat and barley as a composition for trespassing fines. The Kensington

---

[33] Abbey of Westminster Custumal, Hen. III, B.M. Add. Chart. 8139.
[34] P.R.O. Ct. R. bdle. 191, No. 14, Ric. II.
[35] Ibid. Hen. VIII, bdle. 191, No. 31.   [36] B.M. Add. Chart. 8139.
[37] For customs at Paddington, Greenford, Hayes and Teddington B.M. Add. Chart. 8139. For Teddington also P.R.O. Mins. Accts. bdle. 918, Nos. 20, 22; bdle. 919, Nos. 1, 3, 7, 8. For Drayton and Sutton, see *Domesday of St. Paul's* Survey of 1222. For Kensington P.R.O. Midd. Hund. R.; Rentals and Surv. 445; Inq. p.m. 48 Hen. III, file 31. For Isleworth P.R.O. Mins. Accts. bdle. 916, No. 12; bdle. 916, Nos. 17, 18.

tenants rendered sixteen and a half lambs, thirty-three hens, and 415 eggs among them.

As to the ploughing works, the tenants at Paddington ploughed, sowed and harrowed twice a year, while at Greenford the free tenants ploughed one acre, except one of them who ploughed two; one for wheat and one for oats; and even a third if exacted by the lord. This tenant and another defended the manor in the county and hundred courts. Four acres to plough and three to harrow was the allowance at Teddington; two acres for every half virgate at Sutton; at Drayton one acre for each holding. The tenants at Isleworth in the time of Edward III ploughed half an acre for each half virgate, fetching and carrying the seed, and received 2d. for every acre ploughed.

No weekly services are mentioned either at Paddington or at Drayton; at Isleworth they are confined to the holders of Werk and Akerlonds, and at Sutton to the *operarii*. The custumers at Teddington rendered three works in every fortnight—Monday and Friday one week, Wednesday the next—except from Midsummer to autumn, when they did only one weekly work, and during the six autumn weeks, when they rendered three days in each week. At Greenford they did five works in each month, except during the autumn weeks, when an extra day in the week was required. At Hayes and Kensington one day a week all the year round was exacted, with a second between 1 August and Michaelmas.

No weekly works are mentioned in an extent of the manor of Edgeware in the year 1276.[37a] There the majority of virgaters paid a money rent of 5s. 11½d., and rendered works valued at 1s. 6d.: namely, four men to reap in autumn, one at their own and three at the lord's expense; one day's carting at the lord's expense, and two half-days' binding sheaves; two half-days' weeding, one half-day's harrowing, and a half-day's fencing, and four carrying works (*averagia*). The rent of the half-virgate holdings was 2s. 11½d., and their works were worth 9½d., as they sent four men (three *ad cibum domini*) to reap instead of five, did only half-a-day's carting and no *averagia*. All the tenants had to mow the meadow (6½ acres 1 rod) among them.

The extra works were heaviest at Greenford, where they included besides two days each at harrowing, weeding and thrashing, the hay harvest of two meadows, a day's carting after the autumn *precariae* and half a day's fencing in Easter or Whit-week. At Drayton and Sutton the two 'firme' which each manor rendered in kind for the canons' table at St. Paul's had to be carried to London by the tenants, besides the usual weeding, thrashing, and carting wood and manures. Washing and shearing sheep was another extra service, sometimes performed by the cottars, sometimes by particular custumers. The harvest of one and sometimes two meadows had to be completed by the tenants on all the manors. At Teddington the hay-makers received from the lord a *dignarium*, at Paddington 17d. and a cheese worth 4d.; while at Drayton

---

[37a] P.R.O. Rentals and Surv. rot. 439 (5 Edw. I).

they had half a load of wheat, a sheep, and a 'scultellata' of salt, and at Edgeware 6d., a cheese worth 2d., and salt to the value of ½d.

The usual number of boon-days is either three, as at Paddington, Kensington, and Teddington, where the free tenants only attend two, while the custumers send six men to three; or two, as at Drayton, the one with food being attended by all the tenants' servants as well as by the tenants themselves. At Sutton the tenants send one man to the dry and two to the 'wet precaria'; and at Isleworth, where again the free tenants attend as overseers only one bedrippe and have three meals a day of bread, cheese, and beer, at the lord's cost, the custumers have to attend two, receiving only one similar meal in the day, but without beer at the second bedrippe. At Greenford the free tenants attend one 'precaria,' while there are six—four being dry—for the custumers; but these probably include ploughing days, which were sometimes called 'precariae,' and are not otherwhere mentioned for the Greenford custumers. At Hayes no boon-days are mentioned.

The food provided at the 'precariae' is carefully specified at Teddington, where at the first 'precaria' the servants had a meal of bread, water and two dishes, and the masters received 30 gallons of beer. Masters and servants had bread, water and two dishes at the second 'precaria.' At the great 'precaria' the masters had a *dignarium* of bread and cheese and beer, the servants had water and two dishes, and masters and servants supped together, provided with a sufficiency of beer. On the second day of the great 'precaria' all the 'consuetudinarii' dined together, and when the harvest was finished they received a measure (*sectariam*) of beer. The fare provided for the tenants on all the manors was ample in quantity and quality. Bread and cheese with either fish or meat was the usual dinner, and at supper there was often a pottage of beans or peas as well. At Harmondsworth in 1434 the provisions laid in, either from the stock of the manor or by purchase, for the autumn boon-days included bread, cheese, milk and butter and eggs, beer, beef, pork and other meat, ducks, salt-fish, and herrings. If the usual diet of the tenants at their own tables was in anything like the same proportion, there would seem to be some justification for Froissart's surprise at the 'grant aisse et craisse' in which the English peasant lived, and in which the chronicler, who was not remarkable for democratic sympathies, saw the source and origin of their turbulence at the 'hurling-time.'[38]

Although the works were apportioned to the separate holdings, there was a certain amount of joint responsibility for certain services. Thus it was generally understood that the mowing and carting of the hay from the whole meadow must be completed, and if tenements were in the lord's hands, he had to provide substitutes for a corresponding share of this work. Again at Kensington all the tenants were responsible for the ploughing of a given number of acres, and at Isleworth when the number of cottars fell from five to four, the four had to do the same

[38] Froissart, *Chroniques* (ed. Soc. de l'Hist. de France, Luce), x, 94.

amount of stacking hay that was formerly done by the five. This common liability is illustrated by an Isleworth inquisition [39] into the status of a certain Nicholas Est of Heston, who complained that being of free status he had been presented at the court not by his lord but by the villein tenants of the manor for failing to render villein services.

Though there are many cases in the records of tenants being not 'heriotable,' as a general rule heriots were paid by free and bondage tenants alike. Even on the same manor there would seem to be a certain variation in the heriots, and sometimes special classes of tenants paid special heriots, as we have seen was the case with some of the Isleworth tenures. At Harmondsworth it is stated to be the 'custom of the manor' that no heriot accrued when there was neither live stock nor chattels on the holding ; but nevertheless there are a great many instances of money heriots paid because there is no animal on the holding, and often heriots are paid in money without any reason being assigned. In a few cases the heriot consisted of clothing, as for instance a 'russet kirtle' and a tunic 'blodii coloris' lined with white lambskin. In one case a table and a scythe were given because there was no beast on the holding. There would seem to be no fixed amount here for the money heriots, but in one or two cases the amount of the heriot was specified when the holding was granted to the tenant. A heriot of 6d. is accepted from one tenant, 'quia pauper,' and in the time of Edward IV an apparently accepted heriot of a 'horscolt' is stated to be of no value because it is dead. According to the custom of the manor, when a holding was held jointly by husband and wife the heriot only accrued at the death of the survivor, because on the death of the first co-tenant the holding does not change hands. Nevertheless instances occur in the rolls of heriots paid at the first death, and there is at least one of heriots paid at both deaths. At Harmondsworth, where disputes were always plenty, there was a good deal of trouble in obtaining the heriots from the tenants in the fifteenth century, and orders to distrain for them are frequent, though more often made and repeated than executed.

It is more than once stated that according to the custom of the manor a widow's free bench consisted of a fourth part of her husband's holding, and in the fifteenth century a widower claimed the fourth part of his late wife's holding, ' per legem Anglie,' and 'according to the custom of the manor.' In many instances, however, the wife would seem to inherit the entire holding.

At Fulham the heriot for every holding on which there was no stock was 3s. 4d. Here a widow had a third of her husband's holding as free bench.

At Drayton and at Stepney the rule no animal, no heriot, applies, though there are two cases at Drayton, in a court roll at St. Paul's, where there being no animal a payment was made ' tam per finem quam per heriot.' We have already noted the special heriots paid by holders of Bordlond and 'unfre lond' at Isleworth of 2s. or 1s. accord-

[39] P.R.O. Inq. 1 Ric. II, No. 146a.

ing to the size of their holdings. The usual cottar's heriot here was 3*d.*

At Kempton a money payment was made in the absence of live stock, and the amount would seem to be proportioned to the rent ; in one case where the rent was 8*d.* the heriot was the same sum, and in two others, a virgate and a two-virgate holding paid 5*s.* 1*d.* and 10*s.* 1*d.* respectively, which would be roughly equal to the usual rent.

The history of the process by which the services on the Middlesex manors were commuted for money payments aptly illustrates the wisdom of Dr. Maitland's warning against facile generalizations from the history of particular manors to the history of 'the manor.' In Middlesex at any rate it is impossible to generalize at all as to commutation ; each manor went its own way, some commuted earlier, some later, some by the gradual sale of services, some by a formal agreement, some by the grant of leases at money rents. One would expect *a priori* the neighbourhood of London, by providing the tenants with a market and the landlords with a source of supply for free labour, to accelerate the process of commutation, and tempt the tenants to desert the manors. As a matter of fact commutation in Middlesex on the whole was later instead of earlier than in other counties, and there are very few cases in the manor rolls of either fugitive tenants or tenants fining to remain away.

The earliest commutation of which the writer has found a record occurred on the manor of Harmondsworth shortly before 1110–11.[40] One of the seven tenants who rendered weekly works between Michaelmas and Martinmas was released from his six days' work by the prior then in office, in return for a yearly rent of 12*d.* Another early, but only temporary, commutation on the same manor is mentioned in 1390,[41] in a dispute as to the rent and status of a tenant whom the abbot claimed as his villein and attached for withholding 12*d.* a year rent as well as for 'diverse rebellions.' Walter atte Nasshe, on the other hand, asserted that he was free as were his predecessors, and that he held a virgate of land as heir to a certain Roger de Fraxino, who came to the manor as a stranger and took from the lord a messuage and virgate for an annual rent of 6*s.* and all the custumary services. At what date the said Roger came to Harmondsworth is not stated, but it is clear that there was more than one tenant between him and Walter atte Nasshe. Subsequently Roger obtained the land 'per cartam' at a composition rent of 7*s.* in lieu of all services and customs. Roger's heirs, however, reverted after his death to the original tenure, paying 6*s.* rent and performing the services due from a virgate of land according to the custom of the manor. And by this tenure Walter atte Nasshe claims and apparently desires to hold the virgate, unless indeed the alternative sought to be imposed on him by the lord was the payment of the higher rent and the performance of the services as well. After this there were practically only a few temporary commutations at Harmondsworth until

[40] P.R.O. Rentals and Surv. ptfo. 11, No. 20 (11 Hen. I).
[41] P.R.O. Ct. R. 14 Ric. II, bdle. 191, No. 15.

after the time of Henry VI.   In the reign of Richard II [42] the services rendered on the manor coincided absolutely with those enumerated in the custumal of the twelfth century, and in 1433–4 (12–13 Henry VI) [43] the same number of holdings is rendering exactly the same works as their predecessors rendered three hundred years before, and receiving the same dues in return.   The mowers still get their heft load of hay each, and the 13d. for their 'mederam.'   It is quite clear from the terms of the account in 1434 that the works were actually performed, and that the statement is not a mere survival of a formula with no real meaning.   The expenses of the autumn 'precariae' are accounted for ; it is noted that the custumary works sufficed for the mowing, and an allowance is made for the works of three holdings which are in the lord's hands.   Only two tenants pay for their works, Roger Tenterden 3s. 4d. and Robert Hiton 12d.   The latter made this arrangement in 1421,[44] in which year he covenanted with the lord to give a capon in lieu of services, and in the future to pay for them 12d. a year.   This survival of services is the more remarkable that, although the formal number of holdings is unaltered, the actual distribution of them has been much modified by sub-letting, of which there was a great deal on this manor, subdividing, and consolidating the holdings.   During the reign of Henry VI two or three tenants took up a good many holdings ; Roger Hubard, the 'prepositus' of this very account, for one.   A good many leases had also been granted and continued to be granted by this time.   In this matter of commutation, Ruislip, which belonged to Harmondsworth, is a great contrast to it.   In 1434–6, when the tenants on the latter manor were rendering all their services, the Ruislip tenants were quit of all theirs, some being sold and some definitely commuted under a new rental.[45]   A curious arrangement made with a tenant in 1417 illustrates the reluctance with which the lord conceded commutations at Harmondsworth.   In that year a certain John Samon took over a toft and half virgate which had escheated to the lord at the death of the last tenant. The holding was granted to Samon for five years at a rent of 7s. instead of all services and customs, always provided that the lord did not, during that term, concede it to a tenant holding according to the custom of the manor for rent and services, in which case Samon's lease was to determine.[46]   Another rather curious case occurred in 1428.[47]   Three tenants of Stanwell were sentenced to a fine of 2s. for trespassing and cutting thorns on the Harmondsworth demesne.   Subsequently, at the special prayer of several of his own tenants, the lord remitted the fine on condition that each of the men should do one day's work at the following autumn bedrippe.   And yet at this time some of the services were actually not profitable.   In the reeve's account for 1433–4 [48] it is stated that the

[42] P.R.O. Rentals and Surv. Ric. II, ptfo. 11, No. 20.
[43] P.R.O. Mins. Accts. 12–13 Hen. VI, bdle. 1126, No. 7.
[44] P.R.O. Ct. R. Hen. V, bdle. 191, No. 20.
[45] P.R.O. Mins. Accts. 13–15 Hen. VI, bdle. 917, Nos. 26 and 27.
[46] P.R.O. Ct. R. Hen. V, bdle. 191, No. 20.   [47] Ibid. 6 Hen. VI, bdle. 191, No. 21.
[48] P.R.O. Mins. Accts. 12–13 Hen. VI, bdle. 1126, No. 7.

SOCIAL AND ECONOMIC HISTORY

expenses of the scouring works exceeded their value, therefore only so many tenants as were absolutely required for the work were summoned, the others being quit. The expenses of the great boon-day also were in excess of the value of the works, in spite of which the works continued to be exacted and rendered.

In 1446 [49] an arrangement was made in full court between the lord and his steward on the one hand, with the assent of the tenants on the other, that every tenant might pay for his autumn works at the rate of 2d. a day, the money to be paid to the bailiff or some other of the lord's ministers yearly at the feast of St. Peter in Chains (1 August), or on the Sunday next following, any tenants not paying at this time to be charged at a double rate. But later than this agreement, tenants still took up holdings on the express condition of rendering autumn services ; two years later, in February, 1448, Robert Iver, Edward Bokeland and Thomas Ravener were summoned to Westminster to have the amount of their autumn work determined, and in the following October they submitted themselves to the lord's mercy and petitioned for leave to perform their services and to be no longer disquieted for those previously withheld.[50] As late as 1455 and 1471 tenants were presented for not doing works, and in 1492 two tenants paid for their services.[51] No mention of such payments is made in the two court rolls of the reign of Henry VIII,[52] but no conclusion as to the absence of commutations can be deduced from the fact that the holdings in Henry VIII's rolls are still said to be granted for ' all services and customs due by law and custom,' or *inde prius debita*. The survival of this formula in the court rolls is very misleading, and continues long after it has any meaning in actual fact. It is used in court rolls of the Stuart reigns, and of the Commonwealth, and the tenants are still spoken of as *custumarii*. The same formula is used in the leases of manors granted by the Hospitallers in the reign of Henry VIII.[52a] And in Sutton rolls [53] the formula is still regularly recited after the Restoration, and at Stepney [53a] in the time of Henry VIII, although by the reign of Henry VI no more services were rendered on the manor.

At Sutton we find an early commutation in 1222,[54] a tenant holding ' per cartam ' for a rent of 5s. instead of services, and by this time no new services were imposed, for, as we have already noticed, the assart lands held by two *operarii* were paid for by a money rent only. In 1408–9 no account of works appears in the rolls ; [55] the demesne is let on lease, and there is an entry of £4 11s. 1d. from the sale of autumn works. A receipt of £7 8s. 10d. from the lord for the expenses of the autumn works is noted, and entries of expenses are made. So that evidently some are still rendered.

[49] P.R.O. Ct. R. Hen. VI, bdle. 191, No. 23.
[50] Ibid. bdle. 191, No. 23.
[51] Ibid. Hen. VII, bdle. 191, No. 28.
[52] Ibid. Hen. VIII, bdle. 191, Nos. 30 and 31.
[52a] B.M. Chart. of Hospitallers, Cott. MS. Claud. E. vi.
[53] Ct. R. at St. Paul's.
[53a] P.R.O. Ct. R. (1 Hen. VIII), bdle. 191, No. 63.
[54] *Domesday of St. Paul's.* Survey of Sutton.
[55] St. Paul's Library, Mins. Accts. 9 or 10 Hen. IV.

By 1283-4 six out of the ten and a half virgates of 'Shirlond' at Stepney were definitely *posita ad denarium*, and thirty-five more works were sold, accounting for 449 out of a total of 658½ works due. 450½ cotmen's works out of 854 were sold, as well as the great majority of Hydlond and Mollond works. In and after 1362 the rolls contain no *compotus operum*, but instead account for all the works due from the four classes of holdings under the heading *de operis arrentatis*. There was a dispute this year about the commutation of works due from twelve virgates of mollond held by free tenants, the homage declaring that the tenants had not been a party to the arrangement, and an allowance for an overcharge was made to them. In 1464 the accounts cease to distinguish the *redditus assisi* of the mollond, and only free and custumary tenants are mentioned.[56] Stepney suffered badly from the Black Death, and afterwards a good deal of land was let on lease, the rents of *terre dimisse* amounting to £43 14s. 6d. in 1352–3.[57]

As we have already seen, certain molmen's works only were rendered at Enfield in and after 1419. By 1439 the *situs manerii*, the demesne, was let on a six years' lease with the garden, pasture, all demesne and meadow land, all the custumers' weeding, mowing and reaping works and the profits of the first annual hunt in the chase. A house over the gateway, with some adjoining rooms and the stables were reserved for the king. A good deal of bondage land was also let on lease. The carrying works due to the firmarius from certain of the molmen were sold by him at 3¼d. each.[58]

Although many commutations were made with the granting of leases at Fulham between 1384 and 1396, services were still rendered on the manor at the latter date, for there is a note in an account of that year that tenants who had no horses paid 4d. instead of harrowing. The same account contains a list of custumary holdings, consisting of from five to twenty-six 'akerware' each, in Acton and Drayton,[59] and giving their payments for rents, works and customs to Fulham manor and to Ealing. The demesne was leased in 1401 for seven years with 40 cows and 251 sheep, and in 1439–40 the manor was leased for nine years with all demesne land, meadows, pasture, the profits of the court-leet and all services. The bishop reserved to himself the advowson of the church, the hall and all buildings and gardens within the lower gate, the great garden, one grange and all the stables, 6 acres of meadow, the fishponds and woods and all the judicial rights of the lord of the manor.[60]

A few payments for release from works occur in the Edgeware rolls from 1268, and the sums received do not vary greatly in the few years during which we have any account of the manor. A certain amount of land

[56] Compotus roll in St. Paul's Library, dated *anno 12 regis Edwardi;* P.R.O. Mins. Accts. bdle. 1139, Nos. 18–24; bdle. 1140, No. 24 (4–5 Edw. IV).

[57] P.R.O. Mins. Accts. bdle. 1139, No. 18.

[58] Ibid. bdle. 915, No. 26 (7 Hen. V); Mins. Accts. (Duchy of Lanc.), bdle. 42, No. 825; bdle. 53, Nos. 1010 and 1014.

[59] Not to be confused with the St. Paul's Manor of Drayton. This is a small place near Hanwell. P.R.O. Ct. R. 8–19 Ric. II, bdle. 188, Nos. 65–7; Mins. Accts. 19 Ric. II, bdle. 1138, No. 18.

[60] P.R.O. Mins. Accts. bdle. 1138, Nos. 22 and 23.

is let on lease 'at the lord's will,' for which the rents amount in 1268 to £1 4s. 6d., and in 1279 to £3 4s. 6d. There are also lands *dimissae ad seminand'*.[61]

The custumal and rental of the manor of Friern Barnet[62] was revised in 1506–7. In all but four cases the tenants paid a money rent and were charged with carrying and ploughing services and boon-works as well. Two holdings paid a money rent only, and two paid no rent and owed only carrying services. None of the services were sold except the carrying services, which were all sold at 4d. a load ; and it is clear from the terms of the custumal that the other works were actually rendered. By a lease of 1519 granted by the Hospitallers, the 'firmarius' was bound to collect for the prior all 'rents, carriage-moneys, work-silver and fines.'[63]

At Barnes in 1460–1 services were still rendered, except for the lands let on lease, but in the time of Henry VIII no works are mentioned.[64] In 1434–5 at Uxbridge it was apparently left to the tenants' discretion whether they rendered the boon services or paid for them at the rate of 5d. for one, and 10d. for two bedrippes.[65]

At Kensington the services were in process of commutation during the reign of Henry VI, and a valor of that reign gives the money value of all the works. In 1406 the person and goods of a tenant described as *nativus domini de sanguine* are ordered to be seized for living out of the manor without paying chevage.[66]

A large number of works appear as sold at Isleworth in 1314–15 and subsequent years, all the superintending works being regularly sold. In 1361–2 a very large proportion of the works was sold ; some of the aker- and werklond services and some ale-bedrippes being all that were rendered, besides the harvest works and sheep-shearing. Three years before, 145 acres were let on five-year leases in small holdings at rents of 6s. and 7s. per acre. Much the same proportion of works was sold in 1383–4, all the werk- and akerlond services being sold this year. Six tenants were presented for withholding works during the reign of Henry VI, and a compotus of 1462–3 shows the same proportion of works sold and rendered as in 1383–4. The demesne was let on lease, the house being reserved for the abbess of Syon. Indeed, to judge by the sum entered for *opera vendita* in a collector's account of 1484–6 the process of commutation does not seem to have made much progress.[67] In the inquiry already mentioned into the status of Nicholas Est,[68] he asserted that it was the custom of the manor for free tenants who, like himself, held bondage

---

[61] P.R.O. Mins. Accts. Hen. III and Edw. I, bdle. 915, Nos. 2, 3, 4, 12 ; Rentals and Surv. 5 Edw. I, rot. 439.

[62] St. Paul's Library, Custumal 22 Hen. VII.

[63] B.M. Chartul. of the Hospitallers, Cott. MS. Claud. E. vi.

[64] St. Paul's Library, Compotus Rolls, 39 Hen. VI and Hen. VIII.

[65] B.M. Rental 13 Hen. VI. Harl. Roll D 22.

[66] P.R.O. Ct. R. bdle. 191, Nos. 44, 45, Hen. VI ; Rental rot. 445.

[67] P.R.O. Mins. Accts. bdle. 916, Nos. 11 (8 Edw. II), 18 (35–6 Edw. III), 19 (7–8 Ric. II), 22 (2–3 Edw. IV), 25 (2 Ric. III–1 Hen. VII).

[68] P.R.O. Inq. 1 Ric. II, No. 146a.

land as well, to pay a certain yearly increment in order to be quit of all villeinage. The verdict passed over this assertion and decided his freedom on the usual ground that one of his predecessors was an ' adventitius.'

At Teddington the first sale of works (258) occurs in 1313–14, and after that the numbers sold vary a good deal in different years; in 1324–5 ninety-eight were sold, and the next year seventy; the year after the Black Death only one and a-half. In 1372–3 the demesne was let to the prepositus on a fifteen-year lease at a rent of 80 quarters of barley, equivalent at the current price (4s. 6d. a quarter) to £18. The works then accrued to him, and he rendered no further account of them. A rental of Richard II, however, shows them in process of commutation. Six of the free tenants have commuted their suit of court and boon-works for 12d. The eight holdings which are let on lease by 1373–4 are all let at a rent covering all services, from 10s. to 13s. 4d. for a virgate of 16½ acres; for half a virgate (8½ acres) 4s. 6d. In 1379-80 seven holdings are still held for services with or without a money rent. Two holdings have been forfeited for non-performance of services, and in both cases the new tenant has commuted. One of the half virgates still pays no rent, but does all services,[69] and three cotmen are still doing their works. Finally, a rental of 1434 [70] does not mention works at all—the land is all let for money rents: virgates at £1 to £1 6s. 8d., and half virgates from 12s. to 13s. 4d.

Owing to the scarcity of early court rolls we are left very much in ignorance of the effects of the Black Death in Middlesex.[71] The only court roll in the Record Office for the plague year belongs to the manor of Stepney,[72] and witnesses to an appalling mortality. At the court held on the feast of St. Fabian and St. Sebastian (20 January), 1349, nine tenements were reported in the lord's hands owing to the death of the tenants. In December, 1348, four members of one family— mother and daughter and two sons—have died, a third son dies in the following February, and later in the year three more members of the family are reported to be dead and the holdings passed to heirs of a different name. After Easter, 1349, the ale-tasters in Stratford, Aldgate Street and Halliwell Street are all reported to be dead. The plague was at its worst during the summer and early autumn of 1349: between February and Michaelmas in that year 105 tenements were vacated by the death of the tenants, 121 deaths being recorded in connexion with the vacancies, as in some cases joint tenants, and in others the heirs, have died as well. Nor must it be forgotten that only the deaths of tenants and heirs to holdings are recorded in the rolls, and even this list is not complete, for the rolls are torn off at Hokeday, St. Peter in Chains and Michaelmas 1349, and it is impossible to know how many entries are lost.

[69] P.R.O. Mins. Accts. Edw. II, Edw. III, bdle. 918, Nos. 12–25; bdle. 919, Nos. 1–11; Rental 3 Ric. II, No. 456.

[70] St. Paul's Library, Rental 12 Hen. VI.

[71] See Appendix I.   [72] P.R.O. Ct. R. 22 & 23 Edw. III, bdle. 191, No. 60.

Nothing comparable to these conditions is revealed in the Teddington manor accounts for the years after the plague.[73] There is no account for the years 1347–9, but as there is a gap in the series from 13 & 14 till 23 & 24 Edward III, it does not by any means follow that the account was not kept in those years. In the account for the year, Michaelmas 1349 to Michaelmas 1350, five custumers out of fifteen are reported as dead, and evidently left no heirs, for their holdings remain in the lord's hands and an allowance is made for their share of services. The number of hesebonders decreases in this year from fifteen to nine, but it is not stated that they are dead. There is also a decrease from five or six to only three and a half in the plough-teams owned by the tenants, as if they were not so well off. So far as we can see the manor was in its usual working order; tallage £1 13s. 2d. was paid in full, and all the works, with the exception of those of the five dead tenants, are rendered as due. Nevertheless, as may be seen from the following table, the profits of the manor show a decrease of over £11 compared with those realized in 1339–40 (from £13 18s. 5d. to £2 2s. 8¼d.), and of £9 compared with the average of all the preceding years on record. The profits of the manor of Paddington for the same year [74] are very small, £2 3s. 0½d.,

YEARLY PROFITS OF THE MANOR OF TEDDINGTON

Years	Receipts			Expenses			Profit		
	£	s.	d.	£	s.	d.	£	s.	d.
3–4 Edw. I	18	10	2½	9	4	2¾	9	5	11¾
28–29 Edw. I	17	17	3¼	8	12	11¼	9	4	4
29–30 Edw. I	20	17	7¼	10	8	2¾	10	9	4½
4–5 Edw. II	18	19	9	8	8	1¼	10	11	7¾
5–6 Edw. II	15	4	7	5	19	11½	9	4	7½
9–10 Edw. III	23	2	0	7	2	1¾	15	19	10¼
13–14 Edw. III	20	7	1	6	8	8	13	18	5
23–24 Edw. III	14	19	7½	12	16	11¼	2	2	8¼
24–25 Edw. III	17	4	3	11	11	5¼	5	12	9¾
							Demesne farmed at lease		
47–48 Edw. III	31	1	6¼	1	2	6½	29	18	11¾
48–49 Edw. III	24	3	2	1	2	7	23	0	7
49–50 Edw. III	21	11	10	1	2	7½	20	9	2½

but as we only possess this one compotus for the manor, there are no figures for comparison. There are three holdings in the lord's hand at Paddington, no reason being given, and it is remarked in accounting for the servants' expenses at Christmas and Easter that there were fewer

[73] P.R.O. Mins. Accts. 23–26 Edw. III, bdle. 918, Nos. 22–24.
[74] Ibid. 23 & 24 Edw. III, bdle. 917, No. 25.

servants than usual. Walsingham, in the *Gesta Abbatum*,[75] asserts that the tenants of the St. Albans manor of Barnet in Middlesex took advantage of the disorganization caused by the Black Death—'when hardly any reeves or cellarer survived, and certainly could not care for such transitory and mortal things'—to tamper with the manor rolls.

The accounts of Paddington and Teddington show a sudden rise of wages immediately after the Black Death. In 1335–6 at Teddington, the chief ploughman had 6s., the fugator 5s., carters and herds 4s. 6d., and the 'daye' 2s. a year each; the same wages having been paid as far back as 1275–7. The year after the Black Death, ploughmen, carters, and herds all have 11s. a year and the 'daye' 4s. The price of thrashing wheat has risen from 2½d. to 4d. a quarter, and barley from 1½d. to 3d. At Paddington the ploughmen get 11s., and a maid to look after the poultry and winnow the corn has 5s. In 1351–2, in obedience to the statute, the wages fall again, the ploughmen, carters and herds getting 7s., while the 'daye' remains at 4s.; but a substantial rise over the earlier rates is still maintained. Another effect of the Black Death was to give an impetus to the letting of land on lease. On most manors we find leases increasing during the latter years of the reign of Edward III. The five holdings left vacant by the Black Death at Teddington remained in the lord's hands (excepting a small portion of one, let in 1351–2) for years. The first of them was leased for a term of seven years in 1368–9 and the others gradually after that. By 1373–4 eight holdings are let on leases of varying lengths—for the life of the tenant, for seven, sixteen, twenty years.

So far as the paucity of information allows us to judge, in Middlesex, at any rate, the Black Death promoted the granting of leases far more effectually than the Peasants' Revolt. But before we follow the course of the revolt in Middlesex we must notice some earlier disputes between landlord and tenants. In all the rolls, more or less, there are the usual fines for trespassing in the woods and in the lord's fields, for overcharging commons and pastures, for withholding suit of court and other services, and orders to distrain for rents and heriots. The leniency with which these orders are repeated and apparently disregarded at court after court is very striking, so that there are instances in the rolls of tenants being ten, twenty and even thirty years in arrears with their rents. On no other manor in the county of which we have records was there anything like the constant disputes and insubordination which appear in the Harmondsworth Court Rolls.[76] Troubles between the abbot and his tenants began very early, and by the time of Henry III had been carried to the royal courts for settlement. The tenants asserted that the manor was ancient demesne and that the abbot was infringing their rights as ancient demesne tenants by exacting from them services and tallage to which they had not been subjected when the manor was in the king's hands. The plea was heard by William of Raseley, the chief justice, in 1233 and was given against the tenants, it being

[75] Oman, *The Peasants' Revolt*, 328.   [76] P.R.O. Rentals and Surv. rot. 444.

decided that the manor was not ancient demesne, that the abbot and his predecessors were seised of the tallage and merchet of the tenants ; he was therefore to recover seisin, and the men to be fined 5 marks.

In 1276 the tenants returned to the charge. Walter de Lestile, Walter le Disine, Roger le Paternoster, and other men of Harmondsworth attacked the abbot on the same grounds as before. This time the abbot refused to plead on the ground that the manor not being ancient demesne the men were his villeins and could not sue him at law. The court declared that a jury of the county could not decide whether the manor were or were not ancient demesne, because rights of the crown which went back beyond the memory of man could not be determined by a reference to that memory. A reference to Domesday was made by the lords of the Exchequer, who found that Harmondsworth was not amongst the manors of ancient demesne entered in Domesday. The court therefore confirmed William of Raseley's verdict that the men were tallageable at will and bound to redeem their flesh and blood.

In this decision the tenants were not by any means minded to acquiesce. With 'presumptuous and inveterate fatuity' they flatly refused the disputed customs, 'saying they would rather die than render them.' When the abbot distrained their teams, they took them back by force *vi et armis* ; openly threatened no less than to burn down his house, and committed 'various homicides and other enormities.' The abbot was powerless and appealed to the king, 'lest by their insolence and rebellion worse should befall his prior' at Harmondsworth. In May, 1277, Edward II dispatched Geoffrey de Pyncheford, the constable of Windsor, *in propria persona*, to the aid of the prior ; and a year later the sheriff of Middlesex was sent on the same errand. But the men of Harmondsworth persisted in their 'pristine malice and rebellion,' so that later in that year or in the next the king sent Robert Fulton and Roger de Bechesworth with orders to call the tenants before them, and, if they persisted in their disobedience, to assist the abbot in enforcing his rights and to punish the men with a severity calculated to deter them from a repetition of their wrong-doing.

Apparently these drastic measures produced the desired effect, for there seems to have been no further litigation until ten years later. In 1289 the abbot proceeded against twenty-five tenants for withholding services and customs which they and their predecessors had rendered until two years before. The services claimed are practically those of the custumal ; ploughing, sowing, weeding, mowing, carting hay and corn, attendance at bedrippes, and the obligation to tallage, merchet, and 'grasenese.' The defendants recognized all the works except sowing—which they claimed (and the custumal states) should be done by the abbot's servants—the third or love-bedrippe and the obligation to bring their cottars to help with the hay-carting. They also disputed their responsibility for the adequate performance of the ploughing, their obligation to pay merchet and tallage (*auxilium*) and to obtain licence to sell horse or ox. But once more the jury found for the abbot and placed the tenants in mercy.

After this there appears to have been no further litigation *coram rege*, but at the beginning of the reign of Richard II the first court roll[77] discovers a good deal of insubordination amongst the tenants. At the Martinmas Court in 1377, Roger Fayrher, Thomas Hyne, Walter Langleye, Robert Baker, William Hiton and Nicholas Houtchon were fined 1*d.* each for not coming to the haymaking ; John Austyn the same sum for not carting hay, and also, together with Walter Robyn and Roger Janyn, for reaping his own corn on the day of the great precaria. Roger Janyn and John Austyn, Walter Smith, Ralph Jurdan, Godfrey Atte Pyrie, John Pelling and Roger Cook were further fined for not coming to superintend the reapers as they were ' by law and custom bound.' John Essex, Richard Sheter and Nicholas Herbert were each fined 6*d.* for non-attendance at a bedrippe ; William Pompe and Robert Freke for not obeying the bailiff's summons ; and Roger Cook for a deficiency of one work, piling wheat in the grange. It is evident that there was something like organized opposition to the lord ; indeed, Robert Baker so far forgot himself as to upbraid the jury in full court, and in the presence of the seneschal, accusing them of finding a false verdict ; while Walter Breuer disturbed the court with his scornful words, and would not be prevailed on by the seneschal to behave himself reasonably as beseemed him (*rationabiliter modo prout decebit*). At the same time a good many tenants were letting their land without leave, there is a long list of trespassers in the woods, some one has been poaching in the abbot's private waters, and one tenant is a fugitive and undiscovered in spite of reiterated orders to search for him. The next year the servant of one of the tenants opened the lord's sluices so that the hay was flooded. Thomas Reynolds and Nicholas Herberd were fined 12*d.* each at Ascension-tide 1379 for abusing the lord's servants. On St. Luke's day in the same year four tenants were fined for not coming to load hay, by which default hay to the value of 1*s.* 8*d.* was lost, and William Boyland's land was ordered to be seized, because he withheld services and customs. It is not surprising under the circumstances to find that the reeve, elected at this court, fined 13*s.* 4*d.* to be absolved from the office. A year later at the St. Luke's court of 1380, Walter Frensch, Robert Freke, senior and junior, John Attenelme, Walter Breuer, Walter Holder, William Atte Hatche, William Boyland and Roger Taylor were fined for not coming to superintend the reapers ; seven tenants worked in their own fields on the day of the great bedrippe, two tenants did not attend the love-bedrippe, and four came late to their autumn works. Thomas Reynolds, it must be supposed for further ' contempts,' had forfeited his land and had to pledge himself to the amount of 100*s.* to get it back. Again the elected reeve prudently preferred to decline the office even at the cost of a fine of £1 6*s.* 8*d.*

[77] P.R.O. Ct. R. Ric. II, bdle. 191, No. 14.

In the following spring the Peasants' Revolt broke out, and it would seem as if the ferment of the rebellion had been already at work at Harmondsworth.[78]

It is unnecessary to repeat here the account of the burning of the Savoy, of the Temple, of the Hospital of St. John at Clerkenwell, of the manor house of the Hospitallers at Highbury, of the properties of the under-sheriff of Middlesex at Eybury, Tothill, and Knightsbridge, and of the climax of the rebellion at Mile End,[79] which have no special connexion with the county, belonging rather to the general history of the revolt.

Although there does not appear to have been anything like a general Middlesex rising, there is evidence of sporadic outbreaks on several manors, and the Middlesex men must have taken their full share in the rebellion, for the list of exclusions from the general pardon is longer for that small county than for any other, except for London itself.[80] Twenty-three Middlesex rebels were excluded from the amnesty, from fifteen different parishes,[81] but so far as the evidence goes only two of them were convicted and outlawed ; eleven were subsequently acquitted in 1386-7, and the remainder were, it must be supposed, never brought to justice, as there is no record of their conviction or acquittal. Of the two who were outlawed,[82] Peter Walshe held a cottage and 1⅓ acres in Chiswick, and was found to possess no goods or chattels ; of the other outlaw, Thomas Bedford of Holborn, the goods seized by the escheator were valued at 4s., being chiefly small household utensils—most of them ' debil.' Only one other rebel figures in this Middlesex escheator's account : John Stackpole, described as of Middlesex, was beheaded as one of the principal insurgents in the Corpus Christi rising, and is mentioned in an inquiry carried out by the sheriffs in November, 1382, as being with Walter Tyler, one of the leaders of the rebels at Blackheath. His goods and chattels are valued at 18s., amongst them being a red and green cloth gown worth 8s. and ' unius cithere et gyterne, precium 16d.'[83] William Peche, clerk of St. Clements, accused of being with the rebels at Knightsbridge, Eybury, and Tothill ; John Hore, of Knightsbridge, for burning the under-sheriffs' houses ; Robert Gardiner (or Rob. Poltayne gardener) of Holborn, accused of joining in the burning of St. John's Clerkenwell, of slaying seven Flemings there and stealing a cup, and Thomas Clerke of Algate Street, butcher—all pleaded the general pardon; and John Norman of Hammersmith, John Smart and John Neue of Lilleston, and John Brewer of Hoxton do not appear to have been caught at all.[84] Thus it will be seen that Middlesex was no exception to the

---

[78] See Appendix I.   [79] See ' Political History.'   [80] *Rot. Parl.* (Rec. Com.), iii, 111.

[81] This hardly seems sufficient justification for Prof. Oman's statement (*Peasants' Revolt*, 91) that ' inhabitants of *almost every* parish in Middlesex ' are to be found in the list of exclusions.

[82] P.R.O. Coram Rege R. East. 9 Ric. II, m. 2 (rex), m. 16 (rex) *r. d.;* Trin. 9–10 Ric. II, m. 8 (rex) ; Mich. 10 Ric. II, ms. 20 (rex), 23 (rex) *d.* and 25 (rex) ; Hil. 11 Ric. II, m. 7 (rex) ; Esch. Acct. 5–6 Ric. II (John de Newinton). *Bona et catalla proditorum.*

[83] Réville, *Soulèvement des Travailleurs*, pp. lxxvi note 2 and 192 ; Esch. Accts. as above.

[84] P.R.O. Coram Rege R. Hil. 5 Ric. II, m. 9 (rex); Trin. 5 Ric. II, m. 34 (rex); Mich. 8 Ric. II, m. 14 (rex) ; Trin. 6–7 Ric. II, m. 2 (rex) ; Mich. 6 Ric. II, m. 15 (rex) *d.*

general rule of leniency in the suppression of the revolt. As to the local outbreaks in the county we have little more than the scantiest information. The disturbances at Pinner were sufficiently serious to warrant a royal inquiry, the manor of Harrow being in the king's hands as part of the temporalities of the see of Canterbury during the vacancy caused by the murder of Simon of Sudbury.[85] An entry in a Fulham court roll of 1392 states that the court rolls were burnt *tempore rumoris*.[86] Amongst the exclusions from the pardon are men from Hendon, Hounslow, Ruislip, Greenford, Twickenham, Fulham, Chelsea, Charing and Heston; but it does not appear whether they were engaged in local disturbances or in the London rebellion. At Heston the tenants seized the opportunity to pay off their old score against Nicholas Est. William Weyland, John Walter and Richard Umfray attacked Est on 5 June, 1381, with swords and staves, abused and wounded him, and finally imprisoned him for a day and night, until Nicholas paid 40s. for his freedom. When the latter brought an action against them in 1383, the three men pleaded—and brought four credible witnesses in support of their plea—that they had not acted of their own free will, but by the orders of Jack Straw, Walter Tyler, and other insurgents. The acceptance of this plea entitled them to benefit by the general pardon and they were actually dismissed *sine die*.[87] That an outbreak occurred at Harmondsworth is clear, for Walter Come, Richard Gode and Robert Freke, junior, forfeited their lands for rebellion against the prior and the king's peace, and William Pompe's and John Pellyng's lands were also seized for the same reason. It seems probable that the manor rolls were burnt, for the early custumals are extant, not in the originals, but in transcripts of the reign of Richard II, and with the exception of one roll of the time of Edward I there are no earlier court rolls of the manor extant than the one actually in use at the time of the rebellion. The prior was evidently not disposed to be harsh—indeed, it was far from the interests of the landlords to prevent a quiet settlement to the *statu quo*—for William Pompe got his land back a few months later, and at the instance of his friends the prior reduced his fine from 40s. to 40d. John Pellyng's land was given back to him in 1383 at the prayer of two of the tenants. Robert Freke, junior, is again in possession in 1385 and again does not come to superintend the reapers, and in 1386 Richard Gode is once more in a position to come late to the autumn bedrippe.[88] Indeed, things went on at Harmondsworth after the rebellion just as they did before. There were quite as many defaults at bedrippes and superintending works, and the same names recur amongst the defaulters—John Austyn, Thomas Hyne, William Pompe, John Attehelme, Nicholas Herbard, Roger Fayrer and Robert Freke. The position of reeve was so unpopular that William Boyland fined 10 marks to escape it, although diligently required by the steward to accept the

---

[85] P.R.O. Pat. 5 Ric. II.   [86] P.R.O. Ct. R. 16 Ric. II, bdle. 188, No. 66.
[87] Cf. *ante*, p. 72, and Inq. 1 Ric. II, No. 146*a* ; Coram Rege R. Trin. 7 Ric. II, m. 23 (rex).
[88] P.R.O. Ct. R. 1–9 Ric. II, bdle. 191, No. 14.

office. In 1399 Roger Cook, when summoned to cart wheat, at first would not come, and when he did, flung his first load on the tithe heap and his second on the ground, so that all the sheaves were broken, and the carts had to pass over them to get into the grange; but the proceedings against him were stayed by the homage finding he 'had done all things well.' And so it goes on until in the fifteenth century the unquiet annals of the manor settle down, except for occasional defaults and troubles about the heriots. There are always long lists of defaulters from suit of court, and in 1462 they were called before the steward and allowed their obligation to render all dues, customs and services owing to the lord, promising faithfully to observe them in future and placing themselves in mercy for their past faults; which did not prevent most of them being in default again at the next court.[89]

As to the effects of the Peasants' Revolt on the economic conditions of Middlesex, it is difficult to see that they were great, though this conclusion may partly be due to the paucity of our information. The granting of leases was more advanced by the Black Death than by the revolt, and as for the extinction of base services, commutations had begun on some manors long before, and in others only commenced long after the rebellion.

The Middlesex markets and fairs are not of any great importance or special interest. Henry III and the three Edwards granted charters founding or confirming grants of seven markets and nine fairs, with all the liberties and free customs usually appertaining to them. Norden, in the *Speculum*, only mentions four market towns, Brentford, Staines, Uxbridge, and Harrow, but Middleton in 1798[90] gives ten fairs and nine weekly markets, namely, Barnet, Southall, Finchley, Uxbridge, Brentford, Hounslow, Edgeware, Staines and Enfield.

Henry III, in 1228, granted an annual fair at Staines to the abbot of Westminster to last for four days at Ascensiontide.[91] But in his reply to a *Quo Warranto* inquisition of 1293–4, the abbot claimed by grant of Henry III a four days' fair at the Feast of the Nativity of the Virgin (8 September), as well as a weekly market which he had had time out of mind and which was altered from Sunday to Friday by Henry III in 1218.[92] The grants were inspected and confirmed by Edward I.

Henry III also granted to the archbishop of Canterbury a Monday market at his manor of Harrow, and a three days' fair at the Nativity of the Virgin.[93] Edward II's only grant of a market in Middlesex was to the archbishop, of a Wednesday market and of a two days' fair at the Feast of the Nativity;[94] and finally the archbishop obtained from Edward III in 1336 a Wednesday market and two fairs at Pinner—for three days at the Nativity and for two at the Decollation of St. John Baptist (24 June and 29 August.)[95]

[89] P.R.O. Ct. R. Ric. II, bdle. 191, Nos. 14–17, 22.
[90] *Agric. in Midd.*   [91] Chart. R. 12 Hen. III, m. 7.
[92] *Plac. de quo Warr.* (Rec. Com.), 476 ; Close, 2 Hen. III ; P.R.O. Cal. 381.
[93] *Cal. of Chart.* R. ii, 38.   [94] P.R.O. Chart. R. 8 Edw. II, No. 10.
[95] Chart. R. 10 Edw. III, No. 31.

Henry de Lacy, earl of Lincoln, who held the manors of Colham and Edgeware by his wife's right, claimed that his predecessors had had a Thursday market at Uxbridge, which was a member of Colham, and a three days' fair there at the Feast of St. Margaret (12 July), time out of mind.[96]   In the same year Edward I granted him a Monday market and a two days' fair at Michaelmas.[97]   Edward I also granted a Tuesday market and an eight days' fair at Trinity to the brothers of Holy Trinity of Hounslow;[98] and to Humfry de Bohun, earl of Hereford and Essex, and his wife the countess of Holland, a Monday market and two three days' fairs on St. Andrew's day and the Assumption (29 November and 15 August), at Enfield;[99] and lastly a Tuesday market and a six days' fair at Brentford at the Feast of St. Lawrence (11 August), to the prioress and nuns of St. Helens.[100]   These ancient rights were surrendered to Charles I in 1635 by a certain Mr. Valentine Saunders, who then held the manor of Brentford, in return for a grant of a Tuesday market and two fairs to last six days each, beginning on 7 May and 1 September respectively, for which he was to pay 20s. a year.[101]   He also had leave to enlarge on his own ground the market-place, which was too small to contain the concourse of people frequenting the town and passing on the London road.   In a charter roll of 4 Edward III there is a grant of a yearly fair lasting seventeen days at Michaelmas at his manor of 'Scrine in com. Mid'. to 'francisco de feipo.'[102]   I have been quite unable to identify either the manor or its owner.   The entry is copied without comment by Palmer in his Index to Markets and Fairs, and from him by the commissioners on *Market Rights and Tolls*.

A probably not uncommon institution was a Sunday meat market, held in the churchyard before service at Enfield, for the retention of which ' old and ancient usage ' the queen's tenants and inhabitants of Her Majesty's decayed town of Enfield, in 1586, petitioned Burghley, who was high steward of the manor.[103]   The petitioners complained bitterly of the conduct of their minister, Leonard Thickpenny, 'set on we beleeve by the vicar,' who in ' a very outragious manner very evyll beseamynge a man of the churche, in a maddynge mode most ruffynlike ' seized the butcher's meat one Sunday and threw it on the ground, 'most pyttyfull to beholde.'   He then in the presence of a great many ' honest poore men ' abused the butcher, threatening to kill him ' if he hanged for it half an hour afterwards.'   Later in the forenoon the vicar improved the occasion by preaching on the subject of the ' marquet ' in a 'most mallancolly and angrye vayne.'   They have many such sermons, they concluded sadly, so that ' in church they wish themselves at home.'   Burghley, it would appear, was minded to allow the market on which the men of Enfield set such store.

Owen's *New Book of Fairs* gives a list of seventeen fairs as existing in Middlesex in 1772 : Bow, Beggar's Bush, Brentford (two), Chiswick,

[96] *Plac. de quo Warr.* 476, 22 Edw. I, 1293–4.
[97] Chart. R. 22 Edw. I, No. 23.
[98] Chart. R. 24 Edw. I, No. 21.
[99] Ibid. 31 Edw. I, No. 33.
[100] Ibid. 35 Edw. I, No. 49.
[101] P.R.O. Privy Seal Doc. 10 June, 11 Chas. I.
[102] Chart. R. 4 Edw. III, No. 46.
[103] B.M. Lansdowne MS. 47.

SOCIAL AND ECONOMIC HISTORY

Edgeware, Edmonton, Enfield, Hammersmith, Hounslow (two), Staines (two), and Uxbridge (four). Of these, only the two Brentford fairs, one at Staines, one at Enfield, and one at Hounslow, were still held in 1888.

Elizabethan Middlesex was still a corn-growing county and famous for the quality of the wheat it produced. Norden in his *Speculum Britanniae* highly praises the fertility of the soil. 'Although it is so small a shire, yet for the quantetie of it the qualetie may compare with anie other shire in this lande.' The soil is 'excellent fat and fertile' and in parts of the county about Perivale, Heston and Harrow, there is what he calls a 'vayne' of some of the best wheat grown in England. Heston may be accounted 'the garner or store howse of the most fayre wheate and pure in this land.' So much so indeed that the 'marchet and cheate' for the queen's own diet are said to be specially made from Heston wheat. Times have changed in Middlesex since Norden could admire from Harrow Hill in harvest time how 'the feyldes round about so sweetely addresse themselves to the sicle and scythe, with such comfortable aboundance of all kinde of grayne, that it maketh the inhabitantes to clappe theyr handes for joy.'

He also notes with approval the good pasture, but regrets that 'things are more confounded by ignorance and evel husbandrye in this shire then in anie other shire that I knowe.' This he attributes to the large number of country seats owned by citizens of London—'prebends, gentlemen, and merchants'—which afford, with their fair houses, gardens, and orchards, a fine ornament to the country side, but are less advantageous to its cultivation, the land being 'noethinge husbandlyke manured.'

Husbandry and the carrying of its produce to London by land and water were then the only trade and occupation of importance in the county. Nothing in the way of a manufacture is noted by Norden except a copper and brass mill at Isleworth, where he admires the ingenuity with which bellows, hammers and snippers are moved by water power by means of an 'artificiall engine.'

The northern parts of the shire which used to be well timbered were in his time 'but poorly' wooded. In spite of reiterated orders [104] for the better preservation of Enfield Chase made by Henry VIII and Elizabeth, the depredations of keepers and commoners alike have so reduced it that Norden says it will hardly continue to provide fuel for the inhabitants. 'Cutting green boughs for sale in London' had apparently become a trade in Enfield. As for the Hornsey woods, their decrease was largely due to Aylmer, bishop of London, into whose inroads on the episcopal timber Cecil caused an inquiry to be made.[104a]

Norden was no friend to inclosures; he praised the 'good store of lardge commons' in the shire, 'the best and most comfortable neighbours for poore men,' and noted with satisfaction that the 'many parks erected chiefly for deer now fall to decay and are converted to better uses.' Amongst these was the chase made by Henry VIII at Hampton Court,

[104] B.M. Harl. MS. 368, fol. 104; Lansdowne MS. 105, Nos. 1, 12.
[104a] S.P. Dom. Eliz. vol. 137, Nos. 9, 10, 12, 73.

which was disparked in the time of Edward VI, at the petition of the inhabitants, who surmise that a younger king will prefer to seek better sport further afield. The land was re-let to the former tenants at the old rents,[105] just as Henry III granted [106] to the county of Middlesex, in 1227, that the warren of Staines should be disafforested 'so that all men may cultivate their lands and assart their woods therein.'

Long before inclosures became a source of contention, pasture and common rights were a frequent subject of dispute. There are constant entries in the court rolls, especially in the fifteenth century, of tenants fined for overcharging the commons, and pasturing on them beasts not their own property for which they were paid. The right of the animals of the vill to pasture on the arable after the harvest was lifted, and the periodical opening as common for the manor of the 'Lammas' fields often led to trouble, and there was the further complication of common rights enjoyed on one manor by the tenants of another. Thus the men of Drayton and Herdington exercised pasture rights on the Harmondsworth stubble fields, and in 1414, at the instigation of some of the Harmondsworth tenants, 140 men of Drayton and Herdington came into the manor, 'armed with bows and arrows, swords, staves and bills,' and with their teams and swine trampled and depastured the corn and hay where they had no right to common till the corn was cut and carried; neither the bailiff nor the hayward nor any other of the lord's ministers daring to oppose them for fear of death.[107] On the other hand the Harmondsworth tenants had the right of mast pasture in the Drayton Woods, and it was reported to the court of the manor in 1521–2, as an infringement of these rights, that the bailiff of Drayton manor had felled some twenty oaks in the wood there.[108] At Isleworth in 1445–6 the court was informed that the abbess of Syon had inclosed and kept separate two pastures which were always open from the Feast of St. Peter in Chains to the Purification (2 February) or the Annunciation (28 March), and in which two other persons, the prior of St. Walery and Emma de Ayston, shared her rights.[109]

The quality of the Middlesex land was so much better adapted to arable than to pasture farming that comparatively little was inclosed for pasture. But the rapid expansion of London made land in the neighbourhood of the City valuable, and most of the inclosures near the walls were probably made rather with a view to building than for any agricultural purpose.

Parts of the depopulation returns made for Middlesex by the inclosure commission of Henry VIII in 1517 are preserved in the Record Office.[110] There are only two membranes, a considerable piece being torn away from the right-hand side of each. They are headed ' Inquisitio indentata et prima capta apud Hendon in com. Mid. die Lune, 28

[105] B.M. Harl. MS. 6195, fol. 3.
[106] P.R.O. Chart. R. 11 Hen. III, pt. 2.
[107] P.R.O. Ct. R. Hen. V, bdle. 191, No. 20.
[108] Ibid. Hen. VIII, bdle. 191, No. 30.
[109] Ibid. Hen. VI, bdle. 191, No. 36.
[110] Chan. Misc. 7, No. 2 (2). Compare also Leadam, *Domesday of Inclosures* (Roy. Hist. Soc.) and Gay, ' Depopulation Inquisition, 1507,' *Roy. Hist. Soc. Trans.* (New Ser.), xiv.

die Septembris anno 9 Hen: VIII.' The Middlesex commissioners were John, abbot of Westminster, Sir Thomas Lovell, Sir Thomas Nevell and John Heron.[110a] The opening meeting and the appointment of the jury were held at Hendon, after which the commissioners adjourned to Westminster to receive the sworn returns of the jurors. Subjoined are tabulated the inclosures given in the return, and the number of ploughs put down in consequence. The incompleteness of the returns prevents, of course, anything like an exact estimate of the amount inclosed, but they suffice to show that the quantity is not very considerable.

DEPOPULATION RETURN, 1517

Place	Object	Acreage	'Aratra' destroyed	Persons dispossessed
South Mimms	Not stated	80	2	6
Ruislip	Pasture	(Torn off)	4	12
Hedgeley	,,	140	3	6
Stanwell	,,	(Torn off)	½	2
East Bedfont	,,	16	½ (?)	—
Hendon	Deer park	20	—	—
Hanworth	,,	200	6	12
Twickenham	,,	80	2	4
Hampton	,,	300	6	12
,,	(Second imparking, jury do not know how much)			
Dawley	Pasture	60 ? (or 100 ?)	2	12
		Three messuages ruined		
Hackney	Not stated	100	—	—
,,	,,	10	—	—
,,	,,	3	—	—
,,	,,	9	—	—
,,	(Two more amounts illegible)			
Ickenham	Park	9	—	—
(Name gone)	Pasture	10	½	2
Edmonton	,,	10	½	2
,,	,,	A 'campus'	½	2
,,	,,	12	½	2
,,	,,	40 and 14	½	2
Harrow	,,	20	½	4
Willesden (Brownswood)	,,	160	½	12

Messuages allowed to be ruinous—
    Ruislip, four (worth 40s. per ann.). 'The people turned out and the praise of God decayed.'
    East Bedfont tenements ruinous. Three persons turned out.
    Harrow cot and messuage (worth 20s.). Three people turned out.

A Lansdowne manuscript in the British Museum[111] contains a fragment of a list of inclosures in the suburbs of London, bound up with no heading, between the returns for the Isle of Wight and Staffordshire. The inclosures are in Hackney and, with the exception of one of 100 acres made by the prior of St. Helen's Bishopsgate, which is entered among the commissioners' returns in the inquisition at the Record Office,

[110a] Pat. 9 Hen. VIII, pt. 2, m. 6 d.
[111] B.M. Lansdowne MS. i, fol. 177; see also Leadam and Gay as above.

are of small amounts. Altogether, leaving out these 100 acres, 174 acres of arable land were inclosed in twenty-five separate inclosures. The object of the inclosures is not stated, but it seems likely that they were for building.

The inclosure of the commons and waste lands, of which, as we have seen, there was a considerable amount in the county, provoked, as usual, much opposition and in consequence made little progress, though the great stretches of waste land so near the City harboured very many undesirable rogues and vagabonds ; indeed, the neighbourhood of London was far from safe, and the county sessions rolls contain a large number of indictments for highway robberies in Tudor and Stuart times. In February, 1591, a true bill was found against a band of seven highwaymen for robberies at Islington, and in November, 1594, a band of four was apprehended at Hayes. In 1693 highwaymen were indicted for robberies on the road between Bow and Mile End.[112] Small bands of robbers preyed upon the roads in the suburbs; there are robberies at Notting Hill, at Tottenham, and at Knightsbridge, and the fields between Gray's Inn and Paddington were infested with footpads. In 1690 complaints were made that the watches in the county were set too late and discharged too early, so a double watch was ordered to be kept from 9 p.m. till 5 a.m. and ward in the daytime from 5 a.m. to 9 p.m. There having been robberies in the Strand before the watch was set, it was ordered, in 1691, that four 'able and sufficient' men were to be placed at convenient stands in the High Street till the watch was set at 10 o'clock by the constables. The same year [113] the inhabitants of St. Giles in the Fields and St. Clement Danes obtained leave to set an extra watch, at their own expense, and the next year Chelsea made a similar appeal.[114] Norden in his *Speculum* warns his readers against 'walking too late' in the neighbourhood of the old church at Pancras, which stands all alone and utterly forsaken, the buildings which used to surround it 'all removed and fled,' and is the haunt of very undesirable company. Even in the further parts of the county robberies were not infrequent on the roads ; there are indictments for robberies at Enfield, Edmonton and Hayes, sometimes three or four in a day, and many of course at Hounslow.[115] Even in the early years of the nineteenth century, George IV and the duke of York are said to have been stopped in a hackney coach and robbed on Hay Hill, Berkeley Square. And it was the custom, on Sunday evenings at Kensington, to ring a bell to muster people returning to town.

Henry VIII, in an Act which 'in spirit anticipated the private inclosure Acts of the eighteenth century,'[116] made an attempt in 1545 to encourage the inclosure of Hounslow Heath,[117] which had come into his possession with the estates of Syon Abbey at the dissolution of the

[112] Jeaffreson, *Midd. Sess. Rolls* (Midd. Rec. Soc.) ; Hardy, *Midd. Sess. Rolls*, 96.
[113] Hardy, *Midd. Sess. Rolls* (Midd. Rec. Soc.), 12, 27, 30, 31.
[114] Ibid. 87.　　　　　　　　　　　　[115] Jeaffreson, *Sess. Rolls.*
[116] Scrutton, *Commons and Common Fields.*
[117] Act for the Partition of Hounslow Heath, 37 Hen. VIII, cap. 2, *Statutes of the Realm*, 986.

monasteries, and contained 4,293 acres of waste, extending into fourteen parishes and hamlets. The king considering that the

> barrenness and infertility thereof by want of industry and diligence of men . . . . breadithe as well scarsitye and lacke of all manner of grayne, grasse, woode, and other necessarie thinges amonges thinhabitauntes of the said Parishes ; . . . . even so the conversion thereof into tyllage and severall pasture by men's labor and paynes, besides that it shall be an exile of ydlenes in those parties, must of necessitye cause and bringe furthe to all his saide subjectes plentye and haboundance of all the thinges above remembred,

has had portions of the heath assigned to each parish, and it is enacted that the waste and heath can be inclosed by decision of four commissioners and shall immediately be and remain perpetually copyhold land, or it may be held on lease for twenty-one years, the tenants to improve at will.

In 1575 the tenants at Enfield petitioned [118] the queen against an inclosure of 53 acres, made by the lessee of the manor, of land which had beyond the memory of man lain open as common once a year. This 'evil example has given courage' to one of the keepers of the chase to inclose 12 acres of common land. They, the tenants, are charged with carrying duties to the royal household ; 'to remove your Majesty with 12 carts in summer and eight in winter, either lying at Endfield or within 20 miles of London,' besides 400 horse-loads of wheat and grain, and carrying of poultry, 'which service to doo and see performyd they shall not be hable if the said Taylor and Holt be sufferyd to inclose their commen.' In 1589, 90 acres of a piece of ground, which the tenants claim as common, having been inclosed by nine different owners in pieces varying from 50 to 2 acres, a feminine riot ensued, 'certain women of the town' to the number of twenty-four, the wives of labourers and tradesmen of Enfield, 'assembled themselves riotously and in warlike manner, being armed with swords, daggers, staves, knives, and other weapons,' [119] broke into one of the inclosures and plucked up the fencing. The women, some of whom were 'greate with child and expecting every hour to travaile,' were in danger of imprisonment for the offence, and the inhabitants and the queen's tenants of Enfield petition Burghley to interfere in their favour and to get the common back. [120] What the results were on these two occasions we do not know, but the persistent opposition of the Enfield tenants did succeed in impeding the progress of hedge and pale, as is shown by the report to the Board of Agriculture in 1795. There are many indictments in the sessions rolls for breaking into inclosures in different parts of the county, of 'gentlemen' as well as of 'yomen' and labourers.

The Londoners saw with equal disfavour the inclosure of waste lands near the City walls, which they had been accustomed to use for their recreation and their archery practice. So 'on a morning' in 1513 'they assembled themselves and went with spades and shovels,'

[118] B.M. Lansdowne MS. 105, No. 7. [119] Jeaffreson, *Midd. Sess. Rolls* (Midd. Rec. Soc.), i, 188.
[120] B.M. Lansdowne MS. 59, fols. 30–1.

to some inclosures which had been made in the common fields about Islington, Hoxton and Shoreditch,

> and there, like diligent workmen, so bestirred themselves, that within a short space all the hedges about those townes were cast downe and the ditches filled. The king's councell comming to the graie friars, to understand what was meant by this dooing were so answered by the maior of councell of the citie, that the matter was dissembled, and so when the workmen had done their worke, they came home in a quiet manner, and the fields were neuer after hedged.[121]

Indeed the necessity for maintaining open spaces round the City became very present to Elizabeth's careful government, to whom the expansion and overcrowding of London and the rural exodus to the City were a source of great disquiet. At the county sessions of the peace in May, 1561, John Draney, citizen and clothier of London, was fined for inclosing an open field in Stepney, through which the citizens were wont to pass freely to their archery practices.[122] And in the Act[122a] by which the government tried to stem the further growth and overcrowding of the City by limiting the building of new houses within and without the walls, the inclosure of commons and waste grounds within three miles of the City gates was prohibited, as interfering with the mustering of soldiers, the practice of archery, and the recreation, comfort, and health of the people inhabiting the cities of London and Westminster.

The problem of providing for the poor of the county was complicated for Middlesex by the neighbourhood of London. London was one of the first of English towns to provide for itself an organized local system of poor relief.[123] But this had the disadvantage of attracting a hungry immigration from less advanced districts, which defied the terrors of Tudor settlement laws, and flooded the adjoining counties with undesirable vagrants, to provide for and deal with whom quite overtaxed their resources. It is not surprising to find from the county sessions rolls that the Middlesex justices were at once active and uncompromising in the execution of the Vagrant Act. In 1572 they reported to the Privy Council[124] that they had caused privy searches to be made on 20 March and 20 April in all the hundreds of the county, by which a number of rogues and vagabonds of both sexes have been taken, and have been 'ordered and ponyshed,' according to the statute. That is to say that those who were not taken into service by some employer who would make himself responsible for them were whipped and branded, and if found again wandering, hanged. Three relapsed vagrants found wandering in the parish of St. Giles were sentenced to be hanged in June, 1575.[125]

The sessions rolls for 1572–3 contain twenty-eight, and those for 1574–5 thirty-five convictions for vagrancy, and in ten weeks of the year 1589–90 seventy-one persons were sentenced to be whipped and

---

[121] Holinshed, *Chron.* (1808), iii, 599.
[122a] 35 Eliz. cap. 6.
[124] S.P. Dom. Eliz. vol. 86, Nos. 21, 28.
[122] *Midd. County Sess. Rolls* (Midd. Rec. Soc.), i, 38.
[123] Leonard, *Early Hist. of Poor Relief.*
[125] Jeaffreson, *Midd. Sess. Rolls,* i, 81, 94, 101, 103.

branded for that offence.[126]   Four years later the Privy Council ordered
the City authorities to confer with the Middlesex justices as to the adoption of joint action for the repression of vagrancy,[127] and about 1600 the
Lord Chief Justice at the queen's request called a meeting of the justices
of Middlesex and Surrey and of representatives of the City [127a] to consider
what joint measures should be adopted.   The best method of dealing
with the vagrants was considered to be the institution of a house of
correction in each of the two counties at a capital expenditure of £4,000
and a yearly allowance of £150 each, and as it was 'very apparent' that
London really was the main source of this concourse of beggars, the
representatives of the City consented that they ought to make some
contribution to charges which exceeded the county resources.   Con-
fiding in this agreement the counties leased suitable premises and
entered into agreements with 'undertakers' to take charge of and
employ at suitable trades the vagrants committed to them.   Amongst
the Caesar papers in the British Museum [128] there is a scheme submitted
to the justices of Middlesex in 1602 by the undertakers of the poor for
employing pauper children from the age of seven at pin-making.   The
undertakers ask for a 'convenient stock of money' to take and
furnish a house and clothe and provide for the children, who at first,
of course, will be able to earn nothing, and they suggest a quarterly
levy for this purpose at the rate of 4d. for every one rated at £10,
and 1d. weekly contribution to the poor's rate.   Apparently adult
vagrants were to be taken in as well and employed as servants to the
children, and in spinning and weaving linen and wool, making clothes,
and knitting stockings for the house.   The house is to be 'ordered like
a college or hospital, whereby the whole nomber may learne exsample
of religion and civilitie.'   The children were to wear 'a clean shirt or
smock fyttinge their age,' they are to rise at 5 a.m. and work till 9 p.m.,
and if they misdemean themselves to have 'reasonable correction according
to discretion.'   When they have served their time each is to receive
'double apparrell, and each man a new broad cloth cloke and each
mayde a new gown,' and, it was hoped, be sent out into the world with
the excellent prospect of soon being 'liable themselves to three or four
servants.'

Meanwhile the promised contributions from the City were conspicuous by their absence, the undertakers were unpaid and petitioned
the king for the reimbursement of money expended by them, and in
1603 James I appointed a commission of four—the earl of Shrewsbury,
Sir John Fortescue, chancellor of the Duchy of Lancaster, Sir John
Popham, the chief justice, and Sir John Stanhope, the vice-chamberlain,
to inquire into the matter.   Their report emphasized the greatness of
the evil and the necessity for the co-operation of the City, which the
latter obstinately continued to refuse.   The king himself addressed a letter
to the City urging on them their obligations, and in June, 1605, the

---

[126] Jeaffreson, *Sess. R.* i, 190.   [127] Leonard, op. cit. 93 ; Everall, *Analytical Index to Remembrancia*, 358.
[127a] B.M. MS. 12503, fol. 278–84 (Caesar papers).   [128] B.M. MS. 12497, fol. 187.

City sent a petition to the king, in reply, in which many protestations of their humble duty barely veiled a sufficiently round refusal. No grant, they submit, can be made without the consent of the commons, and this is not an opportune moment to make such an application when they have just been put to great expense in fitting out galleys and soldiers for the Irish wars, towards which the two counties had persistently refused the contribution to which they were bound.[129]

In 1614 the justices levied by a 'rate and taxation' £200 for the building and furnishing of a house of correction,[130] and at the same time appointed a commission of five gentlemen: Sir George Coppyn, Sir William Smythe, Sir Baptist Hickes, Mr. Edmond Dobbleday and Mr. Francis Mitchell, to collect voluntary contributions from 'well-affected persons' with what—if any—success is not on record. The rate was less popular in the county than with the justices, but they made short and exemplary work with grumblers, and in 1615 the house was finished. The justices appointed as governor, at a salary of 40 marks, one John (or Jacob) Stoyte, whose petition for the post is preserved amongst the Caesar papers in the British Museum,[131] in which he asserts that he 'has been trained up most part of his life in the said service.' That sanguine ideal of self-supporting pauperism, which Tudor and Stuart Poor Law administration strove vainly to realize, dictated the order that the inmates must earn their food by their labour, and that, except in case of sickness, they were to have no more than they earned. Stoyte undertook to 'keepe and maintain the exercise of trades of weaving and spinning of cotton, wooles for drapery, and all other manufactures fit for their employment and labour,' and some attempt was evidently made to put them to work, for there are orders for the repair of spinning wheels and hemp mills, and a new mill was to be provided so that more might be employed. The inmates were to have fresh straw every month, and warm pottage thrice a week, and their 'lynnen (if any they have)' was to be washed. But the house seems to have been little more than a prison, and not well managed in spite of reiterated orders for its better government issued by the justices, and an attempt at some sort of classification of the inmates does not seem to have been realized in practice.

At Clerkenwell in 1666 a 'workhouse' was built at an expenditure of £2,002 levied on the parishes within the Bills of Mortality by the 'Governors of the Corporation of the Poor,' to accommodate 600 blind, impotent, and aged poor as well as able-bodied paupers,[132] in which some advance seems to have been made towards differentiating paupers and criminals at any rate. It proved, however, so very expensive to maintain that it was closed and the county exempted for the future from any workhouse rate by Act of Parliament in 1675. The workhouse itself was let for £30 a year to one Sir Thomas Rowe, who turned it into a charity school.

---

[129] B.M. MS. 12503, fol. 278–84.   [130] Jeaffreson, *Midd. Sess. R.* ii, 102, 103, 105, 120, 130; iii, 7.
[131] B.M. MS. 12496, No. 256 (it is here dated 1626).
[132] Hardy, *Sess. R.* 296; Jeaffreson, *Sess. R.* iii, 337.

SOCIAL AND ECONOMIC HISTORY

A certain number of aged and impotent poor were relieved by pensions of 2s. 6d. a month or 1s. or 1s. 6d. a week. In 1690 the parish of St. Andrew Holborn complained that owing to the great increase of the pensioned poor the available money is insufficient to maintain them. In 1701 Ealing attempted to replace these pensions by indoor-relief, and obtained leave to accommodate eight of their pensioned poor in a house, and to levy for this purpose a rate of 3d. in the pound, hoping to effect a saving of £12 a year.[132a] Invalided soldiers also were provided for under an Act of Queen Elizabeth's reign by pensions of about 40s. a year, raised by a special county rate managed by two county treasurers. As these pensions were given without any inquiry there was a great deal of abuse and fraud, and in 1623 the treasurers were ordered to give no pensions without strict investigation.[133]

To meet the expense of the poor, besides the special rates levied for the purpose, certain fines were apportioned to the justices, such as the fines for not taking the oath and the fines levied on alehouse-keepers for using false measures.[133a] In 1631 [134] the justices sent into the Council the accounts of the expenditure of £92 received from such fines in the parishes of St. Sepulchre, Clerkenwell, St. Giles Cripplegate, Islington, Hornsey, Finchley, and Friern Barnet, reporting that they have apprenticed twenty children of poor men, that they are 'maintaining a manufacture' in the house of correction, founded by a 'stock' of £100 given by Sir John Fenner, by which an artisan is to instruct in the said manufacture twenty poor orphans, 'such as before wandered in the streets,' and that they have dispatched many idle and loose persons to serve with His Majesty of Sweden, besides distributions of money to the poor 'at their discretion.'

In consequence of many complaints of the inequality and uncertainty of the rates and charges for the poor and the highways, an assessment was ordered to be made according to an equal pound rate on the yearly value of the houses.[134a] The increase of the poor, ' owing to the present war ' led the churchwardens in Ratcliff to apply for an extra assessment in 1694, and a similar request was made by the parish of St. Clement Danes.

Special endowments for the benefit of the poor were often bequeathed to their parishes by well-to-do parishioners. A list of such benefactions belonging to the parish of Enfield in 1709 is in the British Museum,[135] amounting to a capital sum of £184, besides yearly income to the amount of £119 7s. 6d. Of this some is to be spent in distributions of money or bread or clothes to the poor ; some is for the maintenance of poor

---

[132a] Hardy, *Midd. Sess. R.* 229. [133] Jeaffreson, *Midd. Sess. R.* ii, 142, 164, 176 ; iii, 2, 25.

[133a] Elizabeth's act forbidding inclosures near London (35 Eliz. cap. 6) allotted a moiety of the fines imposed, viz. £5 for every inclosure, and £5 for every month it was kept inclosed, to the churchwardens of the parish in which the inclosure was made, for the benefit of the poor.

[134] S.P. Dom. Chas. I, vol. 202, No. 20.

[134a] Hardy, *Midd. Sess. R.* 33, 107, 119.

[135] B.M. Egerton Library, No. 2267.

widows, impotent men and orphans, and for apprenticing and schooling of the latter; £1 7s. 6d. is left in consideration of an inclosure made by the testator, and £22 is to keep a competent master for the new free school just built by the parish, to teach the children 'The Cross Row and the arts of writing, grammar and arithmetic.'

The plague epidemics were another frequent charge on the poor's rates. Sporadic cases of plague were of constant occurrence, and the authorities seem always to have had the fear of an epidemic before their eyes. In 1607–9 the Sessions Acts contain orders against the plague, enforcing the strict seclusion of infected persons in their houses, and forbidding the importation of rags from London for paper-making; and on one occasion eleven persons were actually committed to Newgate for attending the funeral of a victim of the plague.[135a] In 1625 the Cockpit Theatre in Whitehall was closed for fear of infection.[136] In the same year there was an outbreak at Enfield, and in 1630 at Edgeware.[137] In 1636–7 there was a serious outbreak in and round London. Except for an isolated parish here and there the plague at this time and in the great outbreak of 1665 was chiefly severe in London and its immediate suburbs, the only rural parish for which the weekly assessment was made in 1637 being Isleworth.[138] This assessment was levied on the county for the relief of the affected parishes in sums varying from 10s. to £3. The plague was worst in Stepney, and the 'Green goose fair' held there in Whit week was prohibited for fear of spreading the infection.[139]

After the Great Plague in 1665 the overseers of the poor in St. Katharine's, Ratcliff, Whitechapel, and Limehouse were called upon to answer for refusing to make an assessment in their districts.[140]

During the latter half of the sixteenth century the persecutions of Protestants in France and the Netherlands led to a considerable immigration of refugees from both countries into the suburbs of London,[141] where a small alien population was already settled, protected by Tudor governments both as Protestants and as the importers of new and improved methods in the various trades they plied. The new comers settled chiefly in the parish of St. Katharine by the Tower, where in 1583, 285 foreigners were living; in East Smithfield, where there were 445; in Whitechapel 146, in Halliwell Street 152, in Blackfriars 275, and in the adjoining parishes,[142] making altogether a population of 1,604 foreigners. A small number were more or less substantial merchants, but the great majority were wage-earning servants and artisans of a great variety of trades.

The revocation of the Edict of Nantes in 1685 caused a fresh immigration, this time from France, the great majority of the immigrants belonging to the silk-weaving industry and trades connected

[135a] Jeaffreson, *Midd. Sess. R.* ii, 31, 41, 50; iii, 167.
[136] *Midd. Sess. R.* iii, 3, 4, 6.
[137] Ibid. iii, 33.
[138] Ibid. iii, 62, 63.
[139] Ibid. iii, 62.
[140] Ibid. iii, 387.
[141] Burn, *Hist. of Foreign Protestant Refugees in Engl.*; *Returns of Aliens in Lond.* (Huguenot Soc.).
[142] *Returns of Aliens in Lond.* (Huguenot Soc.), x (2), Cecil MSS. 208–14.

therewith. They settled chiefly in Spitalfields and its neighbourhood.[143] Strype writes :

> The north-west parts of this parish became a great harbour for poor protestant strangers, who have been forced to become exiles from their own country for the avoiding of cruel persecution. Here they found Quiet and Security and settled themselves in their several trades and occupations, weavers especially. Whereby God's Blessing surely is not only upon the Parish, but also a great advantage hath accrued to the whole Nation by the rich Manufactures of weaving silks and stuffs and camlets : which art they brought along with them. And this benefit to the neighbourhood, that these strangers may serve for patterns of Thrift, Honesty, Industry, and Sobriety as well.

And indeed it is a fact that foreign names are of the rarest occurrence in the indictments of the county sessions. But the introduction of the silk-weaving industry cannot have been so entirely their work as Strype states. Even camlets were introduced by earlier immigrants, if we may trust an entry in Evelyn's Diary on 30 May, 1652 : ' Inspected the manner of chambletting silks and grograms at one Mr. La Doree's in Moorefields.' And a decade before the Revocation, in 1675, the Shoreditch and Spitalfields silk weavers indulged in an anticipation on a small scale of the future frame-breaking riots.[144] For three days, the 9, 10, and 11 August, bands of from 30 to 200 persons went about Stepney, Shoreditch, Whitechapel, Hoxton, and Clerkenwell breaking into houses, carrying out the obnoxious ' wooden machines called engine weaving looms,' which they smashed and burnt in the streets. Now it is curious to note that none of the indicted rioters, and none of the owners whose machines they destroyed, bear foreign names. The riots were easily suppressed, and the ringleaders sentenced to heavy fines and stations in the pillories in different parts of London.

Middlesex, as described in the reports on the county drawn up for the Board of Agriculture at the end of the eighteenth century, differs a good deal from the corn-producing county described by Norden two centuries before. The subordination of the whole county to the rapidly expanding capital has increased. That city which already in Norden's day ' draweth unto it as an adamant all other partes of the land,' still ' attracts people so strongly from every part of the kingdom that no large towns can exist in its neighbourhood.'[145] ' The whole county may be very properly considered as a sort of demesne to the metropolis, being covered with its villas, intersected with innumerable roads leading to it, and laid out in gardens, pastures and inclosures of all sorts for its convenience and support.'

These reports commend the fertility of the soil as emphatically, though not so picturesquely, as Norden. The best wheat was still grown at Heston and towards the western boundaries of the shire, but most of the highly cultivated ground beyond Hounslow was given up to growing hay for the London market, and between this and London, from Kensington to Hounslow, ' is one great garden for the supply of London.' On the north-eastern side, about Islington and Hackney, a great deal of ground

---

[143] *Huguenot Soc. Publ.* vol. xi.   [144] Jeaffreson, *Midd. Sess. R.* iv, 60–65.
[145] *Rep. to the Bd. of Agric.* 1793–5 ; also Middleton, *Agric. in Midd.* published by the Bd. of Agric.

was occupied by cow-keepers, and to the east, by Bethnal Green and Stepney, there was nursery ground again, chiefly devoted to the raising of trees and plants. To the west, 'about a mile along the Kingsland Road there are some 1,000 acres of valuable brick fields.' The reports compute the number of acres in the county at 250,000, and of these 130,000 were meadow or pasture and 50,000 nursery gardens and pleasure grounds. The land had greatly increased in value, and 'as is natural in the neighbourhood of a large city' was held in small portions by a number of proprietors. Rents varied a good deal—near London under leases the land stood at about 50s. an acre, and inclosed garden ground was worth from £5 to £8 an acre, and near Chelsea and Kensington even to £10, and in the common fields near Fulham £3.

The woods and copses of the county were nearly annihilated ; there were still a few acres left on the northern slopes of Hampstead and Highgate, and about 100 acres on the east side of Finchley Common, 1,000 in Enfield Chase, and 2,000 on the west side of Ruislip. The hills about Copt Hall and Hornsey which were wood a few years before were then meadow.

Inclosure being, to the reporters of the Board of Agriculture, the one saving grace of rural economy, the uninclosed condition of much of the Middlesex arable appeared very unsatisfactory. 'It is hardly to be credited [146] so near the metropolis, yet certain it is that there are still many common fields in the county.' Middleton [147] calculated that out of a total arable acreage of 23,000,[148] 20,000 acres were still in common fields, and not producing sufficient wheat to supply one-fiftieth of the inhabitants with bread. At Enfield, Edmonton, Tottenham, and Chiswick, there were still meadows held by the old Lammas tenure.[149] In 1789 Stanwell inclosed 200 acres of its common fields, thereby increasing their value almost immediately from 14s. to 20s. the acre.[150]

Thirty acres were set apart and let at a rent of 20s. an acre and the rent divided among those cottagers of the parish who did not pay above £5 a year rent and were not in receipt of public alms.

The condition of the waste lands and commons was as unsatisfactory to the reporters as that of the cultivated land.

> To the reproach of the inhabitants and to the utter astonishment of every foreigner who visits us, the county contains many thousand acres, still in a state of nature, though within a few miles of the capital, as little improved by the labour of man, as if they belonged to the Cherokees.[151]

By which neglect a yearly income of some thirty to fifty thousand pounds is thrown away. Middleton [152] estimates the uncultivated soil at 17,000 acres, something like a tenth part of the entire acreage of the county distributed among the following commons :

Hounslow, Finchley (1,240 acres), the remains of Enfield Chase, Harrow Weald and part of Bushey Heath (1,500 acres), besides eight smaller commons in the parish of Harrow. Uxbridge Moor and

---

[146] Baird, *Rep. on Midd.* (1793). [147] *Agric. in Midd.* (1798), 138.
[148] In 1827 Porter estimates the cultivated land of the county at 155,000 ac.; *Progress of the Nation*, (1851), 158. [149] *Rep. to Bd. of Agric.* (1794). [150] Ibid. (1793). [151] Ibid. (1795). [152] Ibid.

SOCIAL AND ECONOMIC HISTORY

Common (350 acres), Hillingdon Heath (160 acres), Ruislip Common (1,500 acres), Sunbury (1,400 acres), Memsey Moor, Goulds Green, Peil Heath, Hanwell Common, Wormwood Shrubs in the parish of Fulham, and between 400 and 500 acres of waste in Hendon.

The good intentions of Henry VIII evidently bore but little fruit, for Hounslow Heath was far the largest waste, still containing in 1754 over 6,000 acres. According to the reports the common rights were profitable only to a few wealthy farmers, borderers on the heath, who overcharged the pasture with immense numbers of ' grey-hound-like sheep ' ; and to a few cottagers who cut turf and fuel for sale. In 1789 Stanwell inclosed its share of the heath, and 300 acres of practically valueless land was by 1793 worth from 15s. to 25s. the acre.

There still remained of Enfield Chase some 3,000 to 4,000 acres uninclosed of ' good soil and improvable,' thanks mainly to the tenacity with which the Enfield tenants, like their Elizabethan predecessors, clung to their common rights, which their unstinted exploitation had reduced to little more than scanty and very unhealthy pasture for a few half-starved cattle. They badly needed small inclosed fields, but the Enfield commoners may, not unwisely, have reflected that inclosure was by no means certain to bring the desired inclosed fields into their hands. A considerable portion of the chase was inclosed by Act of Parliament in 1777, as the reporter allows, not profitably ; a failure which he attributes to bad management. Better success attended an inclosure made by the parish of South Mimms (nearly 1,000 acres) which raised the annual yield of the land from 2s. to 15s. the acre.[153] Practically the whole chase, 3,540 acres, was inclosed in 1801 (see table).

Finchley Common, which in 1754 contained 1,243 uninclosed acres, was reported to be good soil for cultivation, though part of it was excellent road gravel. 900 acres were inclosed here in 1811 (see table). The annexed table of inclosures in Middlesex[154] has been put together from a list of Inclosure Acts 1702–1876 in Clifford's *Private Bill Legislation*,[155] and a list of Middlesex inclosures in the *Middlesex and Hertford Notes and Queries*, supplemented from the tables in Dr. Slater's *The English Peasantry and the Inclosure of Common Fields*.[156] The table shows that a great deal of land was inclosed in Middlesex during the latter years of George III's reign. As the increased inclosures so near London began to assume a less admirable complexion, the necessity of maintaining open spaces round the City—which had been so clear to Elizabeth's ministers—once more impressed a less far-seeing public opinion, and an Inclosure Act of 1854 prohibited the inclosure of common fields within ten miles of London. The general Inclosure Act of 1845 required the special consent of Parliament for inclosures of wastes within fifteen miles of the capital. And the later history of Middlesex inclosures is that of the struggle for open spaces led by the Commons Preservation Society.

[153] *Rep. to Bd. of Agric.* (1794).   [154] App. III.   [155] Op. cit. i, App. B. ii, 495 seq.
[156] Op. cit. i, 55. Between 1702 and 1796 five private inclosure Acts were passed for Middlesex, inclosing among them 7,875 acres. Dr. Slater states the area inclosed by these five Acts at 11,854 acres.

99

In the eighteenth and nineteenth centuries Middlesex was not exempt from the enormous increase of pauperism due to the demoralizing effects of the unreformed poor law.

In 1798, in his report on the county,[157] Middleton draws attention to the

> numerous efficient and comfortable funds raised for the support of the idle poor in this county, which operate against the general industry of the labouring poor. The thriftless pauper in the workhouse was better housed and fed than the industrious labourer and his family. In some parishes the paupers cost 15·15 guineas a head, while their earnings did not reach 8s., at a time when the ordinary labourer's family of five or more persons had to subsist on thirty. Charity added to the evil by raising voluntary contributions during every temporary inconvenience, and by the constant clothing of upwards of ten thousand of the children of the labouring poor in this county.[158]

The report on the Poor Laws of 1834[159] states the cost of the workhouse poor in the rural districts of the county at from 4s. to 5s. a head, whether farmed or not. Not very much seems to have been done towards the sixteenth-century ideal of ' setting the poor on work.' At some workhouses the inmates cultivated a garden ; at Harrow the paupers were employed in picking oakum and at a corn-mill ; at Isleworth any parishioner could have a pauper out of the house to work at 1s. a day: but in general the report states that no parish was in a situation to put able-bodied paupers to profitable work.

The standard of comfort in the workhouses was high. At Sunbury the paupers had beer every day, and at Isleworth the victuals and comfort were so excellent that people went in, especially for the winter, and it was very difficult to get them out again. Here in 1821, 28 out of the 130 persons in the house were children. At Staines the children went out to school, and here also a successful trial of allotments had been made to stop the increase of out-door pauperism.[160] The apprenticing of children to trades was hardly practised at all. The annexed table gives the poor law expenditure of the hundreds and of the county from 1776–1841.

POOR LAW EXPENDITURE, 1776–1803[161]

Hundred	Total, 1803	Total, 1776	Number relieved, 1803	Children in School of Industry
	£	£		
Edmonton	10,700	3,200	1,375	85
Elthorne	9,200	3,500	855	15
Gore	3,900	2,000	275	128
Isleworth	6,600	2,500	548	54
Spelthorne	7,400	2,400	721	49
Ossulstone (Finsbury Division) .	41,900	11,800	14,692	330
,, (Holborn ,,) .	84,200	22,500	8,069	629
,, (Kensington ,,) .	24,100	7,264	6,879	214
,, (Tower ,,) .	59,800	35,400	6,773	305

[157] Rep. to the Bd. of Agric. (1798).
[158] Agric. in Midd. 63.
[159] Poor Law Rep. 1834, App. to 1st Rep. pp. 530, 531.
[160] Rep. p. 576.
[161] From State of Population and Poor and Poor Rates in Middlesex, 1805.

SOCIAL AND ECONOMIC HISTORY

MIDDLESEX EXPENDITURE ON POOR [162]

	Expended on Poor	Average per Head of Population	
	£	s.	d.
1801	349,200	8	6
1811	502,900	10	6
1821	582,000	10	2
1831	681,500	10	0
1841	476,200	6	0

The general history of the county during the latter half of the nineteenth century is simply the record of the suburban expansion of London, effacing all local distinctions and characteristics under an undistinguished chaos of villas and streets. The 'huge and growing wen,' which so powerfully impressed the imagination of Cobbett, has almost absorbed the entire county, so that it appears at the present day, not as it did to Middleton, as 'the demesne of the Metropolis,' but almost as a part of that Metropolis itself.

[162] From Porter's *Progress of the Nation*, 1851, p. 96.

APPENDIX I

MATERIALS FOR THE ECONOMIC HISTORY OF MIDDLESEX

The materials available for the economic history of Middlesex are neither copious nor consecutive. Of the Hundred Rolls—usually such a valuable source of information—only two fragments are extant,[162a] and yield little or nothing to the purpose. The first membrane contains a list of persons holding land to the value of £20 who are not knights; and on the second, Kensington is the only manor described with any particularity. The majority of the Court Rolls at the Record Office are too late to be interesting, and it is only for the one manor of Harmondsworth that there is a consecutive series long enough and early enough to be valuable.

While the earliest roll of this manor belongs to the reign of Edward I and contains nothing of interest, there is a complete series of eighteen rolls, extending from 1 Richard II to 21 Henry VIII,[163] which, with a couple of custumals and some rentals and ministers' accounts, give with some detail an interesting history of an interesting manor. There is a very complete custumal of the time of Henry I, and rentals of the reign of Edward III, Richard II, Henry VI, and Henry VIII; and although the two earlier compotus rolls, of dates in the reigns of Edward II and Richard II respectively, yield little beyond prices and wages, a third, dating from the time of Henry VII, contains a full account of the tenants' services.[164]

Seeing the paucity of the available material, it is particularly regrettable that the fine custumal and almost complete series of Court Rolls of the manor of Isleworth, belonging to the duke of Northumberland at Syon House, are not accessible for research. Only a rather disjointed account of the manor can be derived from the brief summary of the Syon Manuscripts published by the Historical Manuscripts Commission,[165] and the materials at the Record Office, where there are Court Rolls for periods in the reigns of Edward III, Henry VI, Edward IV, Richard III, and Henry VIII, besides some useful ministers' accounts for the reigns of Edward III and Richard II. An inquisition of 28 Edward I would afford much valuable information as to the tenures, were it not unfortunately so badly torn and discoloured as to be practically useless. Another Isleworth inquisition throws light incidentally on one of the indictments of the Peasants' Revolt.[166]

Teddington is the only other manor of which we have any consecutive account; and that only for the reigns of the three Edwards, in a series of compotus rolls extending—with a good many breaks—from 3 Edward I to 50 Edward III.[167] These are usefully supplemented by a rental of 3 Richard II, and a custumal of the manor in a Westminster Abbey custumal of the time of Henry III, in the British Museum,[168] which also contains accounts of the tenants and services on the manors of Paddington and Knightsbridge, Greenford and Hayes. For no other manors are there more than isolated documents, and for many only rolls too late to be of any use. The *Domesday of St. Paul's*, published by Archdeacon Hales for the Camden Society, includes two Middlesex manors—Sutton and Drayton—and for both there are later Court Rolls, and for Sutton a minister's account, in the library at St. Paul's Cathedral, which by the kindness of the librarian I was permitted to examine. The numerous prebendal manors, held in Middlesex by canons of the cathedral, are not included in the *Domesday*.

For the period of the Black Death we are practically reduced to such information as may be derived from one Court Roll of the manor of Stepney, and from some compotus rolls of

[162a] In the Public Record Office. They have not been printed.

[163] P.R.O. Ct. R. bdle. 191, Nos. 13–31.

[164] P.R.O. Rentals and Surv. ptfo. 11, No. 20; rot. 443, 444, 446, 449; Mins. Accts. bdle. 1126, Nos. 5, 6, 7.

[165] *Hist. MSS. Com. Rep.* vi, Appendix 232 (Syon House MSS.).

[166] P.R.O. Ct. R. bdle. 191, Nos. 33–40; Inquisitions, 41 Edw. III, No. 49 and 1 Ric. II, 146a; Mins. Accts. bdle. 916, Nos. 17–20.

[167] P.R.O. Mins. Accts. bdle. 918, Nos. 1–25; bdle. 919, Nos. 1–11 : Rental No. 456.

[168] B.M. Add. Chart. 8139.

SOCIAL AND ECONOMIC HISTORY

Teddington for the years immediately following the plague year. The post mortem inquisitions do not help us at all; there are no more of them for 1348 and 1349 than for other years, and the owners of estates who died held lands in other counties as well, and it is not certain, and in some cases not even probable, that they died in Middlesex at all. Then the registers of institutions to benefices, which are generally so useful in estimating the plague mortality (Seebohm and Rogers, *Fortnightly Rev.* ii, iii, iv), are missing for the diocese of London for the years 1337–61. Materials for the history of the Peasants' Revolt, so far as it concerns Middlesex and Middlesex men, are found in Walsingham's *Historia Anglicana* and the *Gesta Abbatum*, in John of Malvern, in Froissart, and in the *Anominalle Cronicle*, first printed in the original French by Trevelyan (*Engl. Hist. Rev.* 1898), and in a translation by Professor Oman in his *Peasants' Revolt*. There is also an account of the burning of the houses at Highbury and Knightsbridge in Stow's *Annals*. The two latest modern authorities on the rebellion are, of course, the late André Réville and Professor Oman. The former writer (Réville, *Le Soulèvement des Travailleurs d'Angleterre en* 1381, App. ii, 199–215, 225, &c.) has collected and printed all the unpublished records concerning the revolt in the several districts. These consist chiefly in the indictments in the king's courts of the rebels, in escheators' accounts of their confiscated effects, and in Patent and Close Rolls containing orders for inquiries, appointments of commissions to try the rebels and of keepers of the peace. A list of the rebels excluded from the general pardon is printed in the *Rolls of Parliament*. The poll tax returns for the county are not extant. (Oman, *Peasants' Revolt*, 158.)

For the Markets and Fairs Palmer's *Index* (and the *Report of the Commission on Market Rights and Tolls*, vol. liii, 188) gives a list of all grants and references to the originals in Charter and Close Rolls, &c., and Middleton's *Agriculture in Middlesex* and Owen's *New Book of Fairs* record the later survivals of these early markets.

Norden in his *Speculum Britanniae* gives a good general description of the county, but no details as to inclosures. For these there are only two mutilated membranes, in the Record Office, of the depopulation returns made by Henry VIII's commission in 1517, as well as a list, also fragmentary, of suburban inclosures in a Lansdowne manuscript in the British Museum. Another Lansdowne paper contains some information about inclosure disputes and regulations for the preservation of the chase at Enfield. Middlesex owes to the Middlesex Record Society the publication of an abstract of the County Sessions Rolls, from the reign of Edward VI to 1709, made by Messrs. Jeaffreson (4 volumes) and Hardy (1 volume). These rolls are a mine of valuable information as to vagrant and poor laws, plague measures, the dangers of the neighbourhood of London owing to highway robbery, &c. Some Caesar papers in the British Museum contain valuable information about the poor law and so do the Domestic State Papers.

A good deal of information about the alien immigrations into the suburbs of London has been brought together by the Huguenot Society, in their Publications, chiefly derived from returns of Aliens and Lay Subsidy Rolls.

Finally, the reports on the county made to the Board of Agriculture in the later years of the eighteenth, and early years of the succeeding century are our chief sources of information for the agricultural conditions in the county, inclosures and wages at that period.

APPENDIX II

WAGES

Year	Carpenters			Tylers		Thatchers	
	Rogers'[169] Average	Rogers' Highest Price	Middlesex Wage	Rogers' Highest Price	Middlesex Wage	Rogers' Average	Middlesex Wage
1273–4	—	—	—	—	—	*2d.*–2⅛*d.*	Edgeware, 2*d.*
1278–9	—	—	—	—	—	2⅝*d.*–2¼*d.*, 3*d.*–4½*d.* (with man)	Edgeware, 4½*d.* (with man)
1300–1	—	—	—	—	—	2½*d.*–2*d.*, 3¼*d.* (with man)	Teddington, 3½*d.* (with man)
1311–12	—	—	—	—	—	2⅝*d.*–3¼*d.*	Teddington, 3*d.*
1314–15	3*d.*–3⅞*d.*	4*d.*–5*d.*	Isleworth, 4*d.* & 5*d.*	5¾*d.*–7*d.* (with help)	Isleworth, 4*d.*	3½*d.*–4*d.*	Isleworth, 4*d.*
1320–1	3¾*d.*	5*d.*	Isleworth, 4*d.*	—	—	2¾*d.*–3½*d.*	Isleworth, 4*d.*
1324–5	3½*d.*	5*d.*	10½*d.* a week	5*d.* (with help)	4*d.* (with man)	3½*d.*	2*d.*
1335–6	3⅜*d.*	4*d.*	Teddington, 3½*d.*	6*d.*–7*d.* (with help)	Teddington, 3*d.*	—	—
1349–50	4⅛*d.*–4¼*d.*	5*d.*–7*d.*	Teddington, 4*d.*	—	—	3⅞*d.*–3¼*d.*, 5*d.*–6*d.* (with man)	Paddington, 9*d.* (with man)
1350–1	4¼*d.*–3⅜*d.*	7*d.*–4*d.*	Teddington, 6*d.*	—	—	—	—
1351–2	4*d.*	9*d.* (with man)	Isleworth, 6*d.* Teddington, 6*d.* & 4*d.*	4*d.*	Isleworth, 7*d.* (with boy)	3*d.*–3½*d.*, 6⅜*d.* (with man)	Isleworth, 7*d.* (with boy) Teddington, 3½*d.*
1384–5	5*d.*–4¾*d.*	5*d.*–6*d.*	Isleworth, 6*d.*	—	—	4*d.*	Isleworth, 4*d.*
1407–8	4¼*d.*–5¾*d.*	5½*d.*–6*d.*	Sutton, 5*d.* (without food)	—	—	4*d.*–5¼*d.*	Sutton, 5*d.* (without food)
1433–4	5½*d.*–6*d.*	6*d.*–8½*d.*	Harmondsworth, 6*d.*	—	—	—	—
1434–5	5¾*d.*	8½*d.*	Sawyer, 6*d.* Carpenter, 5*d.*	—	—	—	—
1439–40	6*d.*–5¾*d.*	7½*d.*–7*d.*	6*d.*	6*d.*–8*d.*	6*d.*	5*d.*	—

[169] *Hist. of Agric. and Prices*, i and iv.

WAGES (*continued*)

Year	Helps and Women		Carters and Ploughmen		Thrashing		—
	Rogers' Average	Middlesex Wage	Rogers' Highest Price	Middlesex Wage	Rogers' Highest Price	Middlesex Wage	
1273–4 .	½d.	Edgeware, 1½d.	—	—	—	—	Edgeware, Messor, 4s.6½d.
1274–5 .	1¾d.	Teddington, Daye, 3s. 6d.	—	Teddington, Ploughman, 6s. and 5s.	1½d. 2½d.	Teddington, Barley, 1½d. Wheat, 2½d.	Teddington, Herdsman, 4s. 6d.
1278–9 .	—	Edgeware, 3d.	—		3d. 1½d.	Edgeware, Wheat, 3d. Barley, 1d.	
1300–1 .	½d. to 1d.	Teddington, Daye, 3s. 6d.	—	Teddington, Ploughman, 6s. Fugator, 5s.	1½d. 3d.	Teddington, Barley, 1½d. Wheat, 2½d.	Teddington, Herdsman, 4s. 6d.
1311–12 .	1¼d. to 1⅜d.	Teddington, Daye, 3s. 6d.	—	Teddington, Ploughman, 6s. Fugator, 5s.	—	—	Teddington, Herdsman, 4s. 6d.
1314–15 .	1⅜d.	Isleworth, Help, 2d. & 1½d. Women, 1½d.	—	—	—	Isleworth, Wheat, 3d. Oats, 1d.	—
1320–1 .	1¼d. to 1⅜d.	Isleworth, Help, 1½d. Labourer, 2d.	—	—	4d. 1½d.	Isleworth, Wheat, 3d. Oats, 1d.	—
1324–5 .	1d.	Woman help, 1d.	—	—	3d. 1d.	Wheat, 3d. Oats, 1d.	—
1335–6 .	1d. to 1½d.	Teddington, Daye, 2s.	—	Teddington, Tentor, 6s. Fugator, 5s. Carter, 4s. 6d.	—	—	—
1349–50 .	1¾d.	Teddington, Daye, 4s. Paddington, Poultry-maid, 5s.	—	Teddington, Ploughm'n, 11s. Carter, 11s. Herdsman, 11s. Paddington, Ploughm'n, 11s.	5½d. 2½d.	Teddington, Wheat, 4d. Paddington, Wheat, 6d. Oats, 2d.	*After Black Death* Serjeant, 13s. 4d. per ann.
1350–1 .	2⅛d.	Teddington, Daye, 4s. Labourer, 3d.	—	Teddington, Tentor, 11s. Fugator, 10s. Carter, 10s.	4½d. 3d.	Teddington, Wheat, 4d. Barley, 3d.	Teddington, Herdsman, 10s.
1351–2 .	1¾d. to 1⅞d.	Isleworth, Woman, 2d. Teddington, Daye, 4s Woman, 2d. Labourer, 3d.	—	Teddington, Tentor, 7s. Fugator, 7s. Carter, 7s.	2d. 4½d. 3d.	Isleworth, Oats, 2d Teddington, Wheat, 4d. Barley, 3d.	*After Statute of Labourers* Swineherd, 6s. 8d.

WAGES (continued)

Year	Helps and Women		Carters and Ploughmen		Thrashing		—
	Rogers' Average	Middlesex Wage	Rogers' Highest Price	Middlesex Wage	Rogers' Highest Price	Middlesex Wage	
1376–7 .	—	—	—	—	—	Totenhale, Wheat, 4d. Oats, 2d.	—
1384–5 .	2d.	Isleworth, Labourer, 3d. and 4d.	—	—	—	Isleworth, Barley, 3d.	Bailiff, 20s.
1385–6 .	2d. to 2⅛d.	Workman, 4d.	—	—	4d.	Wheat, 3d.	—
1388–9 .	2d. to 2½d.	3d.(without food)	—	Ploughman, 8s., 6s., 5s. Carter, 13s. 4d.	—	Wheat, 4d.	Swineherd, 6s.
1407–8 .	3d.	Haymakers, men and women, 3d.	—	Ploughman, 16s. Carter, 16s. Second plough-man, 13s. 4d. Third plough-man, 9s.	—	—	Bailiff, 40s.
1433–4 .	3d.	Harmondsworth, Daye, 5s.	—	Harmondsworth, Ploughm'n,16s. 13s. 4d. Carter, 16s.	3¾d. to 4½d. 2¾d. to 3d.	Wheat, 4½d. Barley, 3½d.	Reaper, 16s. Swineherd, 10s. Bailiff, 40s.
1434–5 .	3d.	Help, 4d.	—	—	—	—	—
1439–40 .	3d. to 4d.	Help, 4d. and 5d.	—	—	—	—	Bailiff, 53s. 4d Foresters, 50s.

ASSESSMENT OF WAGES FOR THE COUNTY OF MIDDLESEX, CHARLES II

Artificers by the year, £10 12s. ; second sort, £6 8s. Husbandmen, carters, and drivers : First sort, £8 ; second sort, £6 ; third sort, £4. Women servants, £4, £3, and £2.

DAY WAGES

Carpenters . . . . . {
Winter . . { With food, 12d. and 10d.
Without food, 2s. and 20d.
Summer . { With food, 1s. 6d. and 1s.
Without food, 2s. 6d. and 2s.

Tylers . . . . . . {
Winter . . { With food, 1s. and 10d.
Without food, 2s. and 1s. 8d.
Summer . { With food, 1s 6d. and 1s.
Without food, 2s. 6d. and 2s.

Thatchers . . . . . {
Winter . . { With food, 8d. and 6d.
Without food, 1s. 6d. and 1s. 4d.
Summer . . { With food, 12d. and 9d.
Without food, 2s. and 1s. 6d.

REPORTS TO BOARD OF AGRICULTURE, 1794

Labourers, 1s. 6d. to 1s. 8d. a day ; handy workmen near London, 2s. winter and summer. Thrashing barley and oats, 2s. 6d. a quarter ; wheat, 4s. Common labourers by the week, 12s. to 8s. ; 15s. at harvest time. Women, 5s. and 6s.

PRICES

Year	Oxen		Cows		Sheep	
	Rogers' Average	Middlesex Price	Rogers' Average	Middlesex Price	Rogers' Average	Middlesex Price
1268 . .	—	—	6s. 8d.	With calf, 8s. 11d.	—	—
1269 . .	10s. 0½d.	10s.	6s.	7s. 9d.–10s.	—	—
1275 . .	—	—	—	—	—	1s. 10d.; ewe, 2s. 6d.
1300 . .	—	—	8s. 0¼d.	With calf, 8s.	—	—
1311 . .	14s. 5½d.	9s. 9d.–13s. 4d.	—	—	—	—
1314 . .	—	—	10s. 2½d.	With calf, 13s.	—	—
1321 . .	—	—	—	—	—	12d.
1325 . .	15s. 1¾d.	8s.–5s. 6¼d.	10s. 10¾d.	6s. 8d. & 5s. 8¾d.	—	10d.
1344 . .	12s. 8½d.	16s. 6½d.	9s. 3½d.	10s.	—	2s.
1350 . .	9s. 8d.	8s.–18s. 6d.	9s. 8½d.	7s.–10s. 1d.	—	—
1353 . .	14s. 3d.	13s. 4d.	—	—	—	—
1364 . .	16s. 8d.	10s. 6d.	—	—	—	1s. 8d.–2s.
1389 . .	—	13s. 4d.	—	9s.; with calf, 10s. 6d.	—	—
1408 . .	13s. 5½d.	13s. 4½d.	—	—	—	—
1434 . .	15s.	12s. 4d.	—	8s.; with calf, 11s.	2s. 4d.	12d.

Year	Pigs		Horses		Poultry	
	Rogers' Average	Middlesex Price	Rogers' Average	Middlesex Price	Rogers' Average	Middlesex Price
1269 .	—	—	12s. 0¼d.	Affri, 6s.–12s.	—	—
1275 .	3s. 3¼d.	3s.; hog, 2s. 4d.	—	—	—	Goose, 3½d.
1300 .	2s. 6d.	2s. 3½., 2s. 6d.	—	—	—	Eggs, 4d. per 100; goose, 3½d.; hen, 2d.
1302 .	—	—	9s. 6¼d.	Affri, 16s.	—	Goose, 3½d.; capon, 3d.
1311 .	4s. 1d.	3s. 1d.	—	—	—	Goose, 3½d.
1314 .	—	—	—	Cart. 6s.	—	—
1325 .	3s. 1¾d. 3s. 11¾d. 3s. 8d	1s. 6d.–2s. Sow, 2s.–2s. 6d. Boar, 2s.–3s. 4d.	16s. 6d.	Cart 10s.–5s.	—	Duck, 2d.; goose, 2d.; capon, 2d.; hen, 1½d.
1336 .	—	—	—	—	—	Hen, 2d.; goose, 3½d.
1344 .	—	—	16s. 8d. 9s. 4½d.	Cart. 23s. Affri, 13s.	—	—
1350 .	Pig, 2s. 7d. Boar, 3s. 2d.	Boar, 3s. 6d. Pig, 2s. 6d. and 2s.	—	—	—	Capon, 3d.; hen, 2d.; goose, 2½d.
1353 .	—	—	—	Affri, 12s.	—	Capon, 4d.
1364 .	—	—	—	—	—	Goose, 4d.; eggs, 12 for 1d.
1389 .	—	2s. 6d.	—	—	—	—
1408 .	—	—	—	—	4d.	Capon, 4d.; pullet, 1½d.
1434 .	3s. 4d.	2s.	—	—	Hen, 2d. Goose, 4d.	Goose, 4d.; hen, 2d.; eggs, 5d. per 100

PRICES (*continued*)

Year	Wheat		Oats		Barley		Salt (per bushel)
	Rogers' Average	Middlesex Price	Rogers' Average	Middlesex Price	Rogers' Average	Middlesex Price	
1268 .	5s. 3⅜d.	1s. 10d., 2s. 5d., 4s.	—	—	—	—	—
1269 .	—	—	1s. 7¼d.	2s. 4d.–2s. 11d.	—	—	4d.
1275 .	5s. 0⅞d.	8s. 8d.	2s. 2½d.	6s. 8d.	—	—	5d.
1300 .	4s. 9d.	5s. 6d.	1s. 11⅜d.	1s. 4d.	3s. 8½d.	3s. 4d.	4d.
1302 .	4s. 11⅞d.	4s. 8d.	2s. 1⅜d.	1s. 4d.–2s.	3s. 4⅞d.	4s.	6d.–8d.
1311 .	—	—	—	—	—	—	5d.
1314 .	—	—	2s. 8¾d.	3s.	5s. 4d.	4s. 10d.	4½d.
1321 .	—	—	4s. 0¾d.	2s.	—	—	7d.
1325 .	5s. 8⅞d.	6s. 8d.	2s. 1d.	1s. 10d.	3s. 8½d.	4s.–6s.	7d.
1344 .	—	—	—	—	—	—	1s. 2d.
1350 .	8s. 3⅛d.	6s. and 6s. 8d.	3s. 8d.	2s.–4s.	6s. 4d.	5s.	8d.
1353 .	4s. 2½d.	10s.	2s. 3⅞d.	2s. 8d.	—	—	1s. 6d.
1364 .	7s. 5⅜d.	10s. 8d.	2s. 8⅝d.	2s.	4s. 2¼d.	6s. 8d.	—
1389 .	5s. 5⅜d.	4s.	—	—	3s. 0⅜d.	2s. 8d.	—
1408 .	7s. 3¼d.	10s. 2d., 10s., 8s. 8d.	—	—	4s. 4¾d.	5s.	8d.
1434 .	5s. 4½d.	6s. 8d.	1s. 11½d.	2s.	2s. 10d.	5s. 4d.	7d.

Year	
1275 . .	Wool, 2s. 4d. per st. (92 fells = 13 st.)
1300 . .	Wool, 2s. 3½d. per st. (119 fells = 15 st.)
1311 . .	Wool, 2s. 2d. per st. (83 fells = 14½ st.)
1321 . .	Salmon, 2s. 8d.
1325 . .	Keep of prior, 3s. weekly; his attendant monk, 1s. 6d.; price of donkey, 5s.
1336 . .	Wool fells, 5d. each.
1353 . .	Wool fells, 3d. each; 1½d. represents cost of daily keep of workman.

Rents in Middlesex vary a good deal from holding to holding, but the most usual rent for one virgate is 5s. (4s.–7s. 6d.) and for half a virgate 2s. 6d. (2s.) from the time of Henry III to Henry VI.

APPENDIX III

INCLOSURE ACTS IN MIDDLESEX, 1702–1876

Ruislip, 1769.
Laleham, 1774.
Enfield Chase, 1777.
Ickenham, 1780.
Stanwell, 1789.
Hillingdon and Cowley, three fields, 1795.
Feltham, Sunbury, and Hanworth, 1798, 1799, 1800, and 1801 (39, 40 & 41 Geo. III, cap. 51 & 146).
Teddington, 1799, 883 acres.
Edmonton, 1800, 1,231 acres.
Enfield Common and Common Fields, 1801, 3,540 acres (41 Geo. III, cap. 143).
Harrow, 1802–3 (43 Geo. III, cap. 43).
Ruislip Common, 1804 (44 Geo. III, cap. 45).
Harmondsworth Common, 1805, 3,000 acres (45 Geo. III, cap. 176).
Chiswick, extinction of Common, 1806 (46 Geo. III, cap. 111).
Harrow, 1805–6 (46 Geo. III, cap. 33).
Ashford Common, 1809, 1,200 acres (49 Geo. III, cap. 17).
Hayes Common, 1809, 2,000 acres (49 Geo. III, cap. 151).
Harlington, 1810 (50 Geo. III, cap. 33).
Finchley Common, 1811, 900 acres (51 Geo. III, cap. 23).
Hampton Common, 1811 (51 Geo. III, cap. 138).
Harefield and Moor Hall Common, 1811, 700 acres (51 Geo. III, cap. 66).
Hillingdon, 1811–12, 1,400 acres (52 Geo. III, cap. 28).
Littleton, 1811.
East Bedfont and Hatton Common, 1813, 1,300 acres [170] (53 Geo. III, cap. 172).
Hornsey Common, 1813, 400 acres (53 Geo. III, cap. 7).
Isleworth, Heston and Twickenham Common, 1813, 7,870 acres (53 Geo. III, cap. 174).
Laleham, 1813 (53 Geo. III, cap. 25).
Hanwell Common, 1813, 350 acres (53 Geo. III, cap. 6).
Great Stanmore Common, 1813, 216 acres (53 Geo. III, cap. 11).
Greenford Common, 1814, 640 acres (55 Geo. III, cap. 5).
Chiswick, 1814, 40 acres (54 Geo. III, cap. 69).
Willesden, 1814, 560 acres (55 Geo. III, cap. 49).
Harmondsworth, 1815 (56 Geo. III, cap. 72).
Cranford Common, 1818, 395 acres (private) (58 Geo. III, cap. 50).
Heston, 1818 (58 Geo. III, cap. 10).
Harlington Common, 1819, 820 acres
West Drayton Common, 1824 (5 Geo. IV, cap. 44).
Northolt Common, 1825 (6 Geo. IV, cap. 59).

[170] Dr. Slater states the area inclosed at 1,100 acres.

APPENDIX IV

TABLE OF POPULATION, 1801 TO 1901

Introductory Notes

AREA

The county taken in this table is that existing subsequently to 7 & 8 Vict., chap. 61 (1844). By this Act detached parts of counties, which had already for parliamentary purposes been amalgamated with the county by which they were surrounded or with which the detached part had the longest common boundary (2 & 3 Wm. IV, chap. 64—1832), were annexed to the same county for all purposes ; some exceptions were, however, permitted.

By the same Act (7 & 8 Vict., chap. 61) the detached parts of counties, transferred to other counties, were also annexed to the hundred, ward, wapentake, &c. by which they were wholly or mostly surrounded, or to which they next adjoined, in the counties to which they were transferred. The hundreds, &c. in this table are also given as existing subsequently to this Act.

As is well known, the famous statute of Queen Elizabeth for the relief of the poor took the then-existing ecclesiastical parish as the unit for Poor Law relief. This continued for some centuries with but few modifications; notably by an Act passed in the thirteenth year of Charles II's reign which permitted townships and villages to maintain their own poor. This permission was necessary owing to the large size of some of the parishes, especially in the north of England.

In 1801 the parish for rating purposes (now known as the civil parish, i.e. 'an area for which a separate poor rate is or can be made, or for which a separate overseer is or can be appointed') was in most cases co-extensive with the ecclesiastical parish of the same name ; but already there were numerous townships and villages rated separately for the relief of the poor, and also there were many places scattered up and down the country, known as extra-parochial places, which paid no rates at all. Further, many parishes had detached parts entirely surrounded by another parish or parishes.

Parliament first turned its attention to extra-parochial places, and by an Act (20 Vict., chap. 19—1857) it was laid down (*a*) that all extra-parochial places entered separately in the 1851 census returns are to be deemed civil parishes, (*b*) that in any other place being, or being reputed to be, extra-parochial, overseers of the poor may be appointed, and (*c*) that where, however, owners and occupiers of two-thirds in value of the land of any such place desire its annexation to an adjoining civil parish, it may be so added with the consent of the said parish. This Act was not found entirely to fulfil its object, so by a further Act (31 & 32 Vict., chap. 122—1868) it was enacted that every such place remaining on 25 December, 1868, should be added to the parish with which it had the longest common boundary.

The next thing to be dealt with was the question of detached parts of civil parishes, which was done by the Divided Parishes Acts of 1876, 1879, and 1882. The last, which amended the one of 1876, provides that every detached part of an entirely extra-metropolitan parish which is entirely surrounded by another parish becomes transferred to this latter for civil purposes, or if the population exceeds 300 persons it may be made a separate parish. These Acts also gave power to add detached parts surrounded by more than one parish to one or more of the surrounding parishes, and also to amalgamate entire parishes with one or more parishes. Under the 1879 Act it was not necessary for the area dealt with to be entirely detached. These Acts also declared that every part added to a parish in another county becomes part of that county.

Then came the Local Government Act, 1888, which permits the alteration of civil parish boundaries and the amalgamation of civil parishes by Local Government Board orders. It also created the administrative counties. The Local Government Act of 1894 enacts that where a civil parish is partly in a rural district and partly in an urban district each part shall become a separate civil parish ; and also that where a civil parish is situated in more than one urban district each part shall become a separate civil parish, unless the county council otherwise direct. Meanwhile, the ecclesiastical parishes had been altered and new ones created under entirely different Acts, which cannot be entered into here, as the table treats of the ancient parishes in their civil aspect.

POPULATION

The first census of England was taken in 1801, and was very little more than a counting of the population in each parish (or place), excluding all persons, such as soldiers, sailors, &c., who formed no part of its ordinary population. It was the *de facto* population (i.e. the population actually resident at a particular time) and not the *de jure* (i.e. the population really belonging to any particular place at a particular time). This principle has been sustained throughout the censuses.

The Army at home (including militia), the men of the Royal Navy ashore, and the registered seamen ashore were not included in the population of the places where they happened to be, at the time of the census, until 1841. The men of the Royal Navy and other persons on board vessels (naval or mercantile) in home ports were first included in the population of those places in 1851. Others temporarily present, such as gipsies, persons in barges, &c. were included in 1841 and perhaps earlier.

GENERAL

Up to and including 1831 the returns were mainly made by the overseers of the poor and more than one day was allowed for the enumeration, but the 1841–1901 returns were made under the superintendence of the registration officers and the enumeration was to be completed in one day. The Householder's Schedule was first used in 1841. The exact dates of the censuses are as follows :—

10 March, 1801	30 May, 1831	8 April, 1861	6 April, 1891
27 May, 1811	7 June, 1841	3 April, 1871	1 April, 1901
28 May, 1821	31 March, 1851	4 April, 1881	

NOTES EXPLANATORY OF THE TABLE

This table gives the population of the ancient county and arranges the parishes, &c. under the hundred or other sub-division to which they belong, but there is no doubt that the constitution of hundreds, &c. was in some cases doubtful.

In the main the table follows the arrangement in the 1841 census volume.

The table gives the population and area of each parish, &c. as it existed in 1801, as far as possible.

The areas are those supplied by the Ordnance Survey Department, except in the case of those marked 'e,' which are only estimates. The area includes inland water (if any), but not tidal water or foreshore.

† after the name of a civil parish indicates that the parish was affected by the operation of the Divided Parishes Acts, but the Registrar-General failed to obtain particulars of every such change. The changes which escaped notification were, however, probably small in area and with little, if any, population. Considerable difficulty was experienced both in 1891 and 1901 in tracing the results of changes effected in civil parishes under the provisions of these Acts ; by the Registrar-General's courtesy, however, reference has been permitted to certain records of formerly detached parts of parishes, which has made it possible approximately to ascertain the population in 1901 of parishes as constituted prior to such alterations, though the figures in many instances must be regarded as partly estimates.

* after the name of a parish (or place) indicates that such parish (or place) contains a union workhouse which was in use in (or before) 1851 and was still in use in 1901.

‡ after the name of a parish (or place) indicates that the ecclesiastical parish of the same name at the 1901 census is co-extensive with such parish (or place).

o in the table indicates that there is no population on the area in question.

— in the table indicates that no population can be ascertained.

The word 'chapelry' seems often to have been used as an equivalent for 'township' in 1841, which census volume has been adopted as the standard for names and descriptions of areas.

The figures in italics in the table relate to the area and population of such sub-divisions of ancient parishes as chapelries, townships, and hamlets.

TABLE OF POPULATION

1801—1901

—	Acre-age	1801	1811	1821	1831	1841	1851	1861	1871	1881	1891	1901
Ancient or Geographical County [1]	181,320	818,129	953,774	1,144,531	1,358,130	1,574,416	1,886,576	2,206,485	2,539,765	2,920,485	3,251,671	3,585,323

PARISH	Acre-age	1801	1811	1821	1831	1841	1851	1861	1871	1881	1891	1901
Edmonton Hundred												
Edmonton †	7,483	5,093	6,824	7,900	8,192	9,027	9,708	10,930	13,860	23,463	36,351	61,892
Enfield †	12,653	5,881	6,636	8,227	8,812	9,367	9,453	12,424	16,054	19,104	31,811	43,042
Hadley, or Monken Hadley †	641	584	718	926	979	945	1,003	1,053	978	1,160	1,294	1,389
Mimms, South §	6,386	1,698	1,628	1,906	2,010	2,760	2,825	3,238	3,571	4,002	5,785	7,402
Tottenham	4,642	3,629	4,771	5,812	6,937	8,584	9,120	13,240	22,869	46,456	97,174	136,774
Elthorne Hundred												
Brentford, New [2] ‡	217	1,443	1,733	2,036	2,085	2,174	2,063	1,995	2,043	2,138	2,069	2,029
Cowley †	306	214	382	349	315	392	344	371	491	498	525	601
Cranford ‡	737	212	267	288	377	370	437	530	557	503	507	488
Drayton, West ‡	878	515	555	608	662	802	906	951	984	1,009	1,118	1,246
Greenford † ‡ §	2,078	359	345	415	477	588	507	557	578	538	511	647
Hanwell [2][3] ‡	1,067	817	803	977	1,213	1,469	1,547	2,687	3,766	5,178	6,139	10,438
Harefield ‡	4,621	951	1,079	1,228	1,285	1,516	1,498	1,567	1,579	1,503	1,867	2,008
Harlington ‡	1,465	363	461	472	648	841	872	1,159	1,296	1,538	1,542	1,690
Harmondsworth ‡	3,307	879	926	1,076	1,276	1,330	1,307	1,385	1,584	1,812	1,914	1,971
Hayes ‡	3,311	1,026	1,252	1,530	1,575	2,076	2,076	2,650	2,654	2,891	2,651	2,594
Norwood Precinct [4]	2,461	697	875	1,124	1,320	2,385	2,693	4,484	5,882	6,681	7,627	12,499
Hillingdon :—	4,944	3,894	4,663	5,636	6,885	9,246	9,588	10,758	11,601	12,641	13,776	14,895
Hillingdon * † §	*4,845*	*1,783*	*2,252*	*2,886*	*3,842*	*6,027*	*6,352*	*7,522*	*8,237*	*9,295*	*10,622*	*11,832*
Uxbridge Chap. † ‡	*99*	*2,111*	*2,411*	*2,750*	*3,043*	*3,219*	*3,236*	*3,236*	*3,364*	*3,346*	*3,154*	*3,063*
Ickenham †	1,458	213	257	281	297	396	364	351	386	376	368	329
Northolt † ‡ §	2,230	336	392	455	447	653	614	658	479	496	538	589
Perivale ‡	633	28	37	25	32	46	32	48	33	34	55	60
Ruislip	6,585	1,012	1,239	1,343	1,197	1,413	1,392	1,365	1,482	1,455	1,836	3,566
Gore Hundred												
Edgeware ‡	2,090	412	543	551	591	659	765	705	655	816	864	868
Harrow-on-the-Hill §	10,027	2,485	2,813	3,017	3,861	4,627	4,951	5,525	8,537	10,277	12,988	22,157
Hendon * §	8,382	1,955	2,589	3,100	3,110	3,327	3,333	4,544	6,972	10,484	15,843	22,450
Kingsbury	1,829	209	328	360	463	536	606	509	622	759	581	757
Pinner [5] §	3,782	761	1,078	1,076	1,270	1,331	1,310	1,849	2,332	2,519	2,727	3,366
Stanmore, Great ‡	1,484	722	840	990	1,144	1,177	1,180	1,318	1,355	1,312	1,473	1,827
Stanmore, Little ‡	1,591	424	547	712	876	830	811	891	818	862	926	1,069

[1] *Ancient or Geographical County.*—The County as defined by the Act 7 & 8 Vict., cap. 61. The population figures exclude (1) in 1821, 526 Militiamen; (2) in 1831, 200 Militiamen; and (3) in 1841, 2,220 Police on duty. (See also note to Willesden.)

[2] *New Brentford* appears to be a Township of *Hanwell Ancient Parish.*

[3] *Hanwell.*—The Central London District Workhouse School was established in this Parish between 1851 and 1861.

[4] *Norwood Precinct.*—The boundary was not accurately known in 1831.

[5] *Pinner.*—The Commercial Travellers' School was established in this Parish between 1851 and 1861.

TABLE OF POPULATION, 1801—1901 (continued)

PARISH	Acre-age	1801	1811	1821	1831	1841	1851	1861	1871	1881	1891	1901
Isleworth Hundred												
Heston	3,823	1,782	2,251	2,810	3,407	4,071	5,202	7,096	8,432	9,754	10,389	11,690
Isleworth* . . .	3,150	4,346	4,661	5,269	5,590	6,614	7,007	8,437	11,498	12,973	15,884	19,874
Twickenham . .	2,421	3,138	3,757	4,206	4,571	5,208	6,254	8,077	10,533	12,479	16,027	20,991
Ossulstone Hundred— Finsbury Division												
Charterhouse Extra Par.	10·3	249	162	144	164	185	277	255	271	161	136	140
Clerkenwell 6 . .	380	23,396	30,537	39,105	47,634	56,756	64,778	65,681	65,380	69,076	66,216	64,077
Finchley	3,384	1,503	1,292	2,349	3,210	3,664	4,120	4,937	7,146	11,191	16,647	22,126
Friern Barnet 7 †	1,304	432	487	534	615	849	974	3,344	4,347	6,424	9,173	11,566
Hornsey 6 † . .	3,039	2,716	3,349	4,122	4,856	5,937	7,135	11,082	19,357	37,078	61,097	87,626
Islington	3,109	10,212	15,065	22,417	37,316	55,690	95,329	155,341	213,778	282,865	319,143	335,238
Old Artillery Ground Liberty Extra Par.	5·3	1,428	1,385	1,487	1,411	1,558	1,972	2,168	2,467	2,516	2,138	2,098
St. Botolph Aldersgate (part of) 8:—												
Glasshouse Yard Liberty	5·6	1,221	1,343	1,358	1,312	1,415	1,476	1,455	1,232	931	779	741
St. Luke	237	26,881	32,545	40,876	46,642	49,829	54,055	57,073	54,995	46,849	42,440	37,443
St. Sepulchre (part of) 8	19	3,768	4,224	4,740	4,769	4,801	4,832	4,609	2,888	2,392	1,972	1,503
Stoke Newington .	638	1,462	2,149	2,670	3,480	4,490	4,840	6,608	9,841	22,781	30,936	34,293
Ossulstone Hundred— Holborn Division												
Hampstead . . .	2,248	4,343	5,483	7,263	8,588	10,093	11,986	19,106	32,281	45,452	68,416	82,329
Paddington . . .	1,251	1,881	4,609	6,476	14,540	25,173	46,305	75,784	96,813	107,218	118,054	127,557
St. Andrew Holborn (the part above the Bars) 9	76	22,205	23,972	26,492	27,334	21,438	23,355	22,384	23,096	28,874	26,228	23,683
St. George the Martyr	36					7,897	8,763	9,867	10,397			
Saffron Hill, Hatton Garden, Ely Rents, and Ely Place Liberty 10 ‡	32	7,781	7,482	9,270	9,745	9,455	8,728	7,148	5,907	3,980	4,506	3,396
St. Giles in the Fields †	123	28,764	34,672	51,793	36,432	37,311	37,407	36,684	35,703	28,701	23,087	20,332
St. George Bloomsbury	121	7,738	13,864		16,475	16,981	16,807	17,392	17,853	16,681	16,695	14,202
St. Marylebone . .	1,506	63,982	75,624	96,040	122,206	138,164	157,696	161,680	159,254	154,910	142,404	132,295
St. Pancras † . .	2,672	31,779	46,333	71,838	103,548	129,735	166,956	198,788	221,465	236,258	234,379	234,912
The Liberty of the Rolls Extra Par.	11	2,409	2,620	2,737	2,682	2,557	2,567	2,274	1,757	546	421	258
The Savoy Precinct 10a ‡	6·6	320	287	222	431	414	372	380	365	245	201	166

6 *Clerkenwell.*—A detached part was wrongly included in the return for *Hornsey Parish*, 1801-1831. This detached area only contained 48 persons in 1841.

7 *Friern Barnet.*—Colney Hatch Lunatic Asylum established between 1851 and 1861.

8 *St. Sepulchre and St. Botolph Aldersgate Ancient Parishes* are situated in Ossulstone Hundred—Finsbury Division and in London City—Without the Walls.

9 *St. Andrew Holborn Ancient Parish* is situated in (A) Ossulstone Hundred—Holborn Division, (B) London City—Without the Walls, and (c) the Inns of Court and Chancery.

10 *Saffron Hill, &c.*—The 1821 increase attributed partly to the absence of the fear of being compelled to serve in the Militia.

10a See note 36, *post.*

TABLE OF POPULATION, 1801—1901 (continued)

PARISH	Acre-age	1801	1811	1821	1831	1841	1851	1861	1871	1881	1891	1901
Ossulstone Hundred—Kensington Division												
Acton	2,305	1,425	1,674	1,929	2,453	2,665	2,582	3,151	8,306	17,126	24,206	37,703
Chelsea	794	11,604	18,262	26,860	32,371	39,896	56,185	63,104	70,738	88,128	96,253	95,086
Chiswick † . . .	1,216	3,235	3,892	4,236	4,994	5,811	6,303	6,505	8,508	15,663	21,344	28,513
Ealing †	3,850	5,035	5,361	6,608	7,783	8,407	9,828	11,963	18,189	25,748	36,267	47,510
Fulham [11]	1,701	4,428	5,903	6,492	7,317	9,319	11,886	15,539	23,350	42,900	91,639	137,249
Hammersmith [11] :—	2,286	5,600	7,393	8,809	10,222	13,453	17,760	24,519	42,691	71,939	97,239	111,970
Hammersmith .	2,101	—	—	—	—	9,888	13,293	19,104	36,029	64,349	88,653	102,474
Hammersmith, St. Peter Chapl.	185	—	—	—	—	3,565	4,467	5,415	6,662	7,590	8,586	9,496
Kensington . . .	2,188	8,556	10,886	14,428	20,902	26,834	44,053	70,108	120,299	163,151	166,308	173,073
Twyford Abbey Extra Par.	281	8	10	33	43	27	21	18	47	75	60	87
Willesden [12] § . .	4,383	751	1,169	1,413	1,876	2,930	2,939	3,879	15,869	27,453	61,057	114,582
Ossulstone Hundred—Tower Division												
Bethnal Green . .	755	22,310	33,619	45,676	62,018	74,088	90,193	105,101	120,104	126,961	129,132	129,727
Bow, or Stratford-le-Bow	565	2,101	2,259	2,349	3,371	4,626	6,989	11,590	26,055	37,074	40,365	42,181
Bromley	610	1,684	3,581	4,360	4,846	6,154	11,789	24,077	41,710	64,359	70,000	68,371
Hackney	3,299	12,730	16,771	22,494	31,047	37,771	53,589	76,687	115,110	163,681	198,606	218,998
Holy Trinity Minories	4	644	602	680	508	579	572	420	417	449	301	41
Limehouse :—	244	4,678	7,386	9,805	15,695	21,121	24,561	29,108	29,919	32,041	32,202	32,538
Limehouse . .	244	4,678	7,386	9,805	15,695	19,337	22,782	27,161	29,919	32,041	32,202	32,538
Ratcliff Hamlet (part of) [13]	—	—	—	—	—	1,784	1,779	1,947	—	—	—	—
Norton Folgate Liberty Extra Par.	10	1,752	1,716	1,896	1,918	1,674	1,771	1,873	1,550	1,528	1,449	1,622
Poplar [14]	1,158	4,493	7,708	12,223	16,849	20,342	28,384	43,529	48,611	55,077	56,383	58,334
St. Botolph without Aldgate, or East Smithfield Liberty [15]	34	6,153	5,265	6,429	3,453	3,627	4,163	4,000	3,812	2,883	2,971	3,051
St. George in the East	244	21,170	26,917	32,528	38,505	41,350	48,376	48,891	48,052	47,157	45,795	49,068
St. Katharine by the Tower Precinct [15]	14	2,652	2,706	2,624	72	96	517	208	241	104	182	76
Shadwell [16] . . .	68	8,828	9,855	9,557	9,544	10,060	11,702	8,499	8,230	8,170	8,123	8,633
Shoreditch . . .	648	34,766	43,930	52,966	68,564	83,432	109,257	129,364	127,164	126,591	124,009	117,706
Spitalfields . . .	73	15,091	16,200	18,650	17,949	20,436	20,960	20,593	20,783	21,340	22,859	24,192
Stepney [14] :—	830	20,767	27,491	36,940	51,023	63,723	80,218	98,836	120,383	132,393	133,823	140,532
Mile End New Town Hamlet	42	5,253	6,028	7,091	7,384	8,325	10,183	10,845	11,100	10,673	11,303	13,157
Mile End Old Town Hamlet	677	9,848	14,465	22,876	33,898	45,308	56,602	73,064	93,152	105,613	107,592	112,565
Ratcliff Hamlet (part of) [13]	111	5,666	6,998	6,973	9,741	10,090	13,433	14,927	16,131	16,107	14,928	14,810
Tower of London Extra Par.	22	—	417	463	433	1,107	954	783	1,021	928	868	736
Old Tower Without Precinct	6	563	775	205	280	310	819	626	308	233	65	43
Wapping [16] . . .	41	5,889	3,313	3,078	3,564	4,108	4,477	4,038	3,410	2,225	2,123	2,125
Whitechapel [17] . .	170	23,666	27,578	29,407	30,733	34,053	37,848	37,454	34,874	30,709	32,326	33,640

[11] *Hammersmith Parish* created out of *Fulham Ancient Parish* in 1834 by Act of Parliament.

[12] *Willesden.*—The 1811 figures are an estimate.

[13] *Ratcliff Hamlet* is situated in *Limehouse* and *Stepney Parishes.*—The entire area and population, 1801-1831 and 1871-1901, are shown in Stepney Parish.

[14] *Poplar Parish* created out of *Stepney Ancient Parish* about 1817 by Act of Parliament.

[15] *East Smithfield and St. Katharine by the Tower.*—The decline in 1831 of the population in these two places is attributed to the formation of the St. Katharine Docks between 1821 and 1831.

[16] *Shadwell and Wapping.*—Many houses were demolished in these two Parishes between 1851 and 1861 in order to construct a new dock.

[17] *Whitechapel.*—A small part, containing only 22 persons in 1901, is situated in the City of London—Without the Walls; none shown there.

TABLE OF POPULATION, 1801—1901 (*continued*)

Parish	Acre-age	1801	1811	1821	1831	1841	1851	1861	1871	1881	1891	1901
Spelthorne Hundred												
Ashford ‡ . . .	1,402	264	266	331	458	524	497	784	1,019	1,484	2,700	4,816
Bedfont, East ‡ .	1,926	456	577	771	968	982	1,035	1,150	1,288	1,452	1,815	2,131
Feltham ‡ . . .	1,790	620	703	962	924	1,029	1,109	1,837	2,748	2,909	3,661	4,534
Hampton :—	3,350	2,515	2,754	3,549	3,992	4,711	4,802	5,355	6,122	6,940	8,200	9,419
Hampton . . .	2,036	1,722	1,984	2,288	2,529	3,097	3,134	3,361	3,915	4,776	5,822	6,813
Hampton Wick Hamlet ‡	1,314	793	770	1,261	1,463	1,614	1,668	1,994	2,207	2,164	2,378	2,606
Hanworth ‡ . . .	1,373	334	533	552	671	751	790	763	867	1,040	1,309	2,159
Laleham ‡ . . .	1,301	372	481	499	588	612	637	613	567	544	504	500
Littleton ‡ . . .	1,037	147	130	149	134	111	106	111	165	126	99	320
Shepperton ‡ . .	1,492	731	751	782	847	858	807	849	1,126	1,285	1,299	1,810
Staines	1,843	1,750	2,042	1,957	2,486	2,487	2,577	2,749	3,659	4,628	5,060	6,049
Stanwell * . . .	3,999	893	1,032	1,225	1,386	1,495	1,723	1,714	1,955	2,156	2,383	2,849
Sunbury	2,659	1,447	1,655	1,777	1,863	1,828	2,076	2,332	3,368	4,297	4,099	4,544
Teddington § . .	1,214	699	732	863	895	1,199	1,146	1,183	4,063	6,599	10,052	14,037
London City— Within the Walls												
Allhallows Barking ‡	11·2	2,087	1,777	1,664	1,761	1,924	2,001	1,679	1,065	716	447	326
Allhallows, Bread Street	2·6	430	345	320	336	263	251	95	90	50	24	15
Allhallows the Great	7·7	572	502	526	588	672	700	603	187	29	37	39
Allhallows the Less	3·3	244	179	98	154	181	130	79	69	63	43	44
Allhallows, Honey Lane	1·0	175	161	137	189	155	150	65	51	32	22	33
Allhallows, Lombard Street	2·9	679	620	580	596	516	456	415	259	169	68	80
Allhallows, London Wall ‡	8·5	1,552	1,601	1,677	1,861	1,620	2,070	1,999	805	535	183	164
Allhallows Staining	4·1	714	623	577	577	502	512	358	243	175	128	121
Christ Church, Newgate Street [18]	12·2	2,818	2,744	2,737	2,622	2,446	2,541	1,975	1,899	1,359	958	999
Holy Trinity the Less	1·8	558	513	502	443	633	691	553	190	63	40	57
St. Alban, Wood Street	3·4	682	621	631	582	479	424	276	345	176	167	209
St. Alphage, Sion College ‡	4·2	1,008	1,009	1,206	1,087	976	919	699	274	31	66	29
St. Andrew Hubbard	2·0	376	333	287	354	331	342	205	139	89	46	41
St. Andrew Undershaft, with St. Mary Axe ‡	9·3	1,307	1,068	1,161	1,080	1,163	1,181	1,071	580	327	218	157
St. Andrew by the Wardrobe	6·6	900	709	690	756	750	680	682	351	175	170	116
St. Anne and St. Agnes Aldersgate [18a]	2·7	952	392	561	421	513	459	362	229	158	24	21
St. Anne, Blackfriars	12·3	3,071	2,609	2,938	2,622	2,846	3,029	2,615	1,381	943	728	487
St. Antholin	2·6	363	367	365	356	357	305	263	74	31	59	62
St. Augustine Watling Street	1·8	333	247	307	311	289	273	110	110	151	76	20
St. Bartholomew by the Royal Exchange	4·1	560	398	339	345	307	254	236	181	199	155	112
St. Benet Fink . .	2·9	539	526	511	459	383	314	213	165	126	72	53
St. Benet Gracechurch	1·9	429	358	290	348	333	294	278	113	51	52	52
St. Benet, Paul's Walk	5·4	620	636	552	612	588	663	537	105	73	65	31
St. Benet Sherehog	1·1	186	152	142	180	145	144	114	32	24	35	39

[18] *Christ Church, Newgate Street*, includes Christ's Hospital School.   [18a] See note 35, *post*

TABLE OF POPULATION, 1801—1901 (*continued*)

PARISH	Acre-age	1801	1811	1821	1831	1841	1851	1861	1871	1881	1891	1901
London City—Within the Walls (cont.)												
St. Botolph Billingsgate	2·6	196	176	191	207	278	341	222	154	99	133	44
St. Christopher le Stock	2·8	133	89	84	72	16	45	23	45	38	34	24
St. Clement Eastcheap	1·8	352	262	273	256	236	233	198	111	86	66	79
St. Dionis Backchurch	4·7	868	755	791	810	806	746	534	350	211	161	112
St. Dunstan in the East ‡	11·8	1,613	1,249	1,155	1,157	1,010	1,025	971	669	442	395	294
St. Edmund the King and Martyr	2·4	477	452	442	382	391	440	333	153	106	105	93
St. Ethelburga ‡ .	3·3	599	564	704	665	669	693	606	315	199	158	100
t. Faith the Virgin	5·6	964	942	999	841	781	853	761	606	403	314	201
St. Gabriel Fenchurch Street	2·8	509	408	343	355	386	274	178	125	111	88	75
St. George Botolph Lane	1·3	254	215	215	229	235	225	217	162	96	35	24
St. Gregory by St. Paul's	11·4	1,634	1,444	1,468	1,456	1,444	1,428	1,154	896	730	515	512
St. Helen Bishopsgate	7·1	655	652	696	692	659	674	558	404	289	251	177
St. James Duke Street	3·2	851	823	732	805	964	827	851	747	622	359	187
St. James Garlickhithe	3·3	595	594	473	637	520	627	461	391	222	146	69
St. John the Baptist Walbrook	1·9	412	369	417	411	367	249	132	97	57	73	72
St. John the Evangelist	0·8	125	118	86	106	108	99	27	51	5	18	2
St. John Zachary	2·2	507	408	322	241	183	156	132	127	115	109	46
St. Katharine Coleman ‡	6·2	732	716	712	650	606	547	444	317	277	237	136
St. Katharine Cree	9·2	1,727	1,471	1,814	1,718	1,740	1,905	1,794	1,291	858	445	178
St. Lawrence Jewry [19]	5·7	800	1,039	702	756	625	526	410	214	162	187	298
St. Laurence Pountney	2·9	355	337	352	372	381	314	233	131	94	80	29
St. Leonard Eastcheap	1·4	304	290	307	110	137	152	111	93	50	32	42
St. Leonard Foster Lane [19a]	2·5	905	197	377	220	331	305	297	42	27	23	29
St. Magnus . . .	3·4	289	248	227	113	239	300	197	262	169	136	172
St. Margaret Lothbury	3·9	569	327	331	252	189	191	164	90	124	92	65
St. Margaret Moses	1·6	265	241	149	199	250	249	137	53	55	32	39
St. Margaret, Fish Street Hill	2·0	365	346	344	167	266	305	317	165	106	68	87
St. Margaret Pattens	1·6	221	159	185	181	167	169	103	104	67	28	46
St. Martin Ironmonger Lane	1·1	192	189	132	218	198	181	185	179	137	103	71
St. Martin Ludgate	4·8	1,229	1,199	1,200	1,185	1,255	1,246	1,080	730	247	158	175
St. Martin Orgar .	2·7	393	290	350	367	353	324	296	212	152	150	105
St. Martin Outwich	3·2	326	236	252	245	135	174	165	137	132	102	63
St. Martin Vintry [20]	4·4	543	356	205	226	288	300	244	118	107	87	79
St. Mary Abchurch	2·6	549	511	505	501	526	273	264	191	142	144	114
St. Mary Aldermanbury ‡	4·4	822	743	883	789	751	687	443	308	168	102	69
St. Mary Aldermary	2·4	562	472	429	507	494	511	232	154	121	139	115

[19] The return for *St. Lawrence Jewry* includes the population of *St. Mary Magdalen, Milk Street*, in 1811.

[19a] See note 35, *post*.

[20] *St. Martin Vintry.*—Many houses demolished in this Parish between 1811 and 1821 in order to give access to the new Southwark Bridge.

TABLE OF POPULATION, 1801—1901 (*continued*)

PARISH	Acre-age	1801	1811	1821	1831	1841	1851	1861	1871	1881	1891	1901
London City— Within the Walls (cont.)												
St. Mary le Bow .	2·7	468	363	368	376	346	363	317	170	130	129	118
St. Mary Bothaw .	1·9	236	233	225	253	257	194	161	146	101	99	125
St. Mary Cole-church	1·6	304	276	275	274	238	225	164	99	36	20	29
St. Mary at Hill .	4·2	762	696	818	773	987	812	738	477	206	127	150
St. Mary Magda-len, Old Fish Street	2·4	521	711	721	762	783	890	732	354	224	83	42
St. Mary Magdalen Milk Street [20a]	1·7	207	—	300	288	207	193	125	84	54	39	18
St. Mary Mount-haw [21]	1·0	366	357	358	434	378	406	474	0	3	14	20
St. Mary Somer-set	3·6	459	289	270	374	375	394	271	200	74	82	33
St. Mary Staining	1·3	239	224	221	309	268	202	161	38	33	36	15
St. Mary Wool-church Haw	2·3	270	229	206	247	150	125	102	89	29	71	68
St Mary Wool-noth	2·6	551	457	511	414	317	328	291	242	290	137	109
St. Matthew Friday Street	1·4	209	196	228	225	160	164	167	70	84	67	38
St. Michael Bassi-shaw	5·8	747	652	714	661	687	616	501	357	215	127	90
St. Michael Corn-hill ‡	3·6	691	603	492	508	454	491	371	254	227	198	162
St. Michael Crooked Lane [22]	3·1	618	523	576	327	329	443	323	222	127	94	78
St. Michael Queen-hithe	3·7	827	739	716	773	647	761	548	267	189	67	26
St. Michael le Querne	1·6	390	317	252	248	212	134	74	71	70	38	67
St. Michael Pater-noster Royal	2·1	307	219	181	198	251	171	169	90	101	56	38
St. Michael Wood Street	2·0	574	435	433	404	328	286	214	156	139	58	65
St. Mildred Bread Street	1·5	281	322	329	302	351	310	86	46	21	21	32
St. Mildred Poultry	2·5	504	302	271	285	280	319	257	115	36	56	57
St. Nicholas Acons	1·5	275	264	180	228	194	221	168	144	116	67	71
St. Nicholas Cole Abbey	1·6	257	178	228	209	254	379	230	104	53	13	56
St. Nicholas Olave	1·4	324	264	350	372	431	533	355	167	94	111	91
St. Olave Hart Street, with St. Nicholas - in - the-Shambles	10·3	1,216	1,030	1,012	1,041	816	893	757	363	255	236	184
St.Olave Old Jewry	2·5	301	236	239	213	168	177	143	121	91	83	85
St. Olave Silver Street	3·3	1,078	1,131	1,135	711	972	948	527	49	82	38	35
St. Pancras Soper Lane	1·2	217	153	190	168	162	177	76	107	55	60	34
St. Peter Cornhill‡	6·0	1,003	860	731	729	656	656	533	418	196	162	108
St. Peter Paul's Wharf	2·5	353	370	346	354	341	383	410	107	19	37	16
St. Peter le Poor .	9·3	867	638	576	546	559	562	540	438	404	270	266
St. Peter West-cheap	1·6	335	271	266	226	227	209	148	67	22	16	24
St. Stephen Cole-man Street ‡	26·7	3,225	2,957	3,062	4,014	3,699	3,936	3,324	2,647	1,799	1,038	540
St. Stephen Wal-brook	2·8	340	289	278	281	322	312	300	147	103	89	79
St. Swithin Lon-don Stone	3·0	474	428	508	486	389	333	297	200	142	118	120

[20a] See note 19, *ante*.

[21] *St. Mary Mounthaw.*—All the houses in this Parish, except two uninhabited ones, were pulled down between 1861 and 1871 in order to form Queen Victoria Street.

[22] *St. Michael Crooked Lane.*—The Church and 35 houses were demolished between 1821 and 1831 in order to improve the access to the new London Bridge.

TABLE OF POPULATION, 1801—1901 (*continued*)

Parish	Acreage	1801	1811	1821	1831	1841	1851	1861	1871	1881	1891	1901
London City— Within the Walls (cont.)												
St. Thomas the Apostle	2·4	566	483	565	531	648	369	112	112	76	122	139
St. Vedast Foster Lane	2·5	423	412	398	496	427	410	278	224	184	139	82
London City— Without the Walls.												
St. Andrew, Holborn below the Bars [22a] [23] [26]	20·7	5,511	5,741	6,234	5,570	5,966	5,965	6,337	3,818	2,883	2,546	1,365
St. Bartholomew the Great ‡	8·9	2,645	2,769	2,931	2,923	3,414	3,499	3,426	3,114	2.373	1,843	1,441
St. Bartholomew the Less ‡ [24]	4·2	952	843	823	863	744	827	849	747	819	847	869
St. Botolph Aldersgate (part of) [24a]	19·9	4,161	4,135	4,003	3,994	4,491	4,745	4,744	3,512	2,399	1,670	826
St. Botolph, Aldgate [25]	38·7	8,689	8,297	9,067	9,615	9,525	11,325	9,421	8,433	6,269	5,866	4,653
St. Botolph without Bishopsgate ‡	44·5	10,314	9,184	10,140	10,256	10,969	12,499	11,569	6,107	4,905	3,078	1,660
St. Bride :—	34·2	7,531	7,462	7,731	7,316	6,655	6,569	6,070	4,563	3,516	2,676	1,918
St. Bride [23] . .	28·9	7,078	7,003	7,288	6,860	6,126	6,039	5,660	4,095	3,001	2,208	1,528
Bridewell Hospital and Precinct Chapelry	5·3	453	459	443	456	529	530	410	468	515	468	390
St. Dunstan in the West [28]	13·4	3,021	3,239	3,549	3,443	3,266	2,887	2,511	2,316	1,584	1,058	775
St. Giles without Cripplegate ‡	42·6	11,446	11,704	13,038	13,134	13,255	14,361	13,498	8,894	3,863	2,090	1,052
St. Sepulchre (the part without Newgate) [24a]	35·5	8,092	8,724	8,271	7,710	8,524	8,620	7,475	3,701	2,166	1,754	1,160
Whitefriars Precinct Extra Par.	8·5	783	929	1,247	1,302	1,294	1,230	1,155	965	467	393	170
Inns of Court and Chancery												
Barnard's Inn (in St. Andrew Holborn) [22a] [26]	0·6	37	44	—	—	39	32	69	62	53	59	5
Clement's Inn (in St. Clement Danes) [27]	—	140	—	—	—	143	112	85	—	—	—	—
Clifford's Inn, Extra Par. [28]	—	113	111	101	—	27	38	—	—	—	—	—
Furnival's Inn, Extra Par. [29]	1	80	—	100	160	213	164	202	115	155	121	0
Gray's Inn, Extra Par.	11·5	289	344	208	324	325	366	308	361	328	253	232
Inner Temple, Extra Par.	11·5	485	460	405	288	278	162	148	116	156	96	127

[22a] See note 9, *ante*

[23] *St. Andrew, Holborn below the Bars* and *St. Bride.*—Many houses were pulled down between 1821 and 1831 in order to erect Farringdon Market.

[24] *St. Bartholomew the Less* comprises only St. Bartholomew's Hospital in 1901.

[24a] See note 8, *ante*.

[25] *St. Botolph, Aldgate.*—This Parish is partly Within the Walls, but none is shown there.

[26] *Barnard's Inn* was returned with *St. Andrew, Holborn below the Bars* in 1821 and 1831.

[27] *St. Clement Danes Ancient Parish* is situated in (A) Ossulstone Hundred—Holborn Division, (B) the City and Liberty of Westminster, and (C) the Inns of Court and Chancery. The entire area is shown in the City and Liberty of Westminster, including that of *New Inn and Clement's Inn;* the populations of these two Inns are included there in 1811–1831 and 1871–1901. The population of New Inn is also included there in 1801. No part of this Parish is shown in Ossulstone Hundred—Holborn Division.

[28] *Clifford's Inn* and *Serjeants' Inn* (Chancery Lane).—The areas of these Inns and their populations, 1831 and 1861–1901, are included in those of *St. Dunstan in the West Parish.*

[29] *Furnival's Inn* was returned with *St. Andrew Holborn Parish* in 1811.

TABLE OF POPULATION, 1801—1901 (continued)

Parish	Acre-age	1801	1811	1821	1831	1841	1851	1861	1871	1881	1891	1901
Lincoln's Inn (part of), Extra Par. [30]	8	179	242	268	142	115	79	47	40	16	27	47
Middle Temple, Extra Par.	5·4	382	423	298	195	229	124	81	93	95	95	107
New Inn, Extra Par. [30a]	—	—	—	—	—	46	30	30	—	—	—	—
Serjeants' Inn, Chancery Lane, Extra Par. [30b]	—	22	28	31		5	5					
Serjeants' Inn, Fleet Street, Extra Par.	0·6	113	78	94	104	81	74	75	73	49	50	48
Staple Inn, Extra Par.	1·0	67	66	41	58	32	57	42	41	38	21	12
Thavies Inn, Extra Par.	0·8	—	—	—	—	175	155	185	237	121	109	85
Westminster (City and Liberty)												
St. Anne Soho . .	53	11,637	12,288	15,215	15,600	16,480	17,335	17,426	17,562	16,608	12,317	11,493
St. Clement Danes [30a] [36]	55	12,861	13,706	14,763	15,442	15,459	15,550	15,477	11,503	10,280	8,492	6,010
St. George Hanover Square [34] [37]	1,117	38,440	41,687	46,384	58,209	66,736	73,458	88,066	89,988	89,573	78,364	76,734
St. James Westminster	163	34,462	34,093	33,819	37,053	37,426	36,406	35,326	33,619	29,941	24,995	21,588
St. John the Evangelist [31]	210	8,375	10,615	16,835	22,648	26,223	34,295	37,483	38,478	35,496	34,106 }	} 50,559
St. Margaret [32] [37] .	603	17,508	19,027	22,387	25,344	30,258	30,942	30,407	27,572	24,430	21,433 }	
St. Martin in the Fields [32] [33] [37]	286	25,752	26,585	28,252	23,732	24,917	24,461	22,689	21,238	17,508	14,616	11,596
Buckingham Palace (the Palace Proper), Extra Par. [34]	—	—	—	—	—	99	125	40	40	—	—	—
St. James's Palace, Extra Par. [33]	—	—	—	—	—	174	179					
St. Martin le Grand Liberty [35]	—	—	688	0	0	0	0	0	0	0	0	0
St. Mary le Strand [36] ‡	14	2,178	2,021	2,273	2,462	2,520	2,517	2,072	2,007	1,989	1,549	494
St. Paul Covent Garden ‡	26	4,992	5,304	5,834	5,203	5,718	5,810	5,154	4,376	2,919	2,142	1,692
The Close of the Collegiate Church of St. Peter, Extra Par.	10	—	175	181	185	231	372	323	209	249	235	231
Verge of the Palaces of St. James and Whitehall [32] [37]	—	1,685	249	641	238	—	—	—	—	—	—	—

[80] *Lincoln's Inn.*—The remainder was not Extra Parochial, neither was it shown separately in the Census Returns.

[80a] See note 27, *ante.*   [80b] See note 28, *ante.*

[81] *Westminster, St. John the Evangelist.*—Millbank Penitentiary was built in this parish between 1811 and 1821.

[82] The population of Whitehall and Privy Gardens was returned in 1801 and 1821 with the *Verge of the Palaces of St. James and Whitehall,* in 1831 in *St. Martin in the Fields,* and in 1811 and 1841-1901 in *Westminster, St. Margaret.* The area is included in the last Parish. This area seems to have claimed to be Extra Parochial; the population in 1811 was 347.

[83] *St. Martin in the Fields* includes the area and the population, 1801-1831 and 1861-1901, of *St. James's Palace.*

[84] *St. George Hanover Square,* includes the area and the population, 1881-1901, of *Buckingham Palace (the Palace Proper).*

[85] *St. Martin le Grand Liberty* is locally situated in the Parishes of *St. Anne and St. Agnes, Aldersgate,* and *St. Leonard, Foster Lane* (both in London City—Within the Walls), where its area is included. Its population was apparently included in that of St. Leonard in 1801. The Liberty was added to the City of London under the Act for erecting the new Post Office (55 George III, cap. 91), under which Act part of the new Post Office was erected upon it, covering its entire area.

[86] The population of the Duchy of Lancaster Liberty is entirely shown in *St. Mary le Strand Parish* 1801-1831. From 1841-1901 the population is rightly divided among *St. Mary le Strand, St. Clement Danes,* and *the Precinct of the Savoy.* Its area is also divided between these. The Liberty contained 410 persons in 1831.

[87] *The Verge of the Palaces of St. James and Whitehall.*—The population, 1841-1901, is divided between *St. Martin in the Fields, St. George Hanover Square,* and *St. Margaret Westminster Parishes.* The area is also divided among these three Parishes.

General Notes

1. The Populations in 1841 of the Parishes (or Places) marked thus § were markedly increased by the presence of temporary residents, such as haymakers.

2. The following Urban Districts are co-extensive at the Census of 1901 with one or more places mentioned in the Table :—

Urban District	Place
Finchley	Finchley Parish (Ossulstone Hundred—Finsbury Division)
Friern Barnet	Friern Barnet Parish (Ossulstone Hundred—Finsbury Division)
Hampton	Hampton Township (Spelthorne Hundred)
Hampton Wick	Hampton Wick Hamlet (Spelthorne Hundred)
Hanwell	Hanwell Parish (Elthorne Hundred)
Hendon	Hendon Parish (Gore Hundred)
Kingsbury	Kingsbury Parish (Gore Hundred)
Sunbury-on-Thames	Sunbury Parish (Spelthorne Hundred)
Teddington	Teddington Parish (Spelthorne Hundred)
Twickenham	Twickenham Parish (Isleworth Hundred)

INDUSTRIES

INTRODUCTION

BEFORE entering into a detailed relation of the industries of Middlesex it will be well to look at the characteristic features of the county. A glance at the map reveals its somewhat compact shape, with rivers on three boundaries, and an irregular range of hills on the north.

As regards its history, Middlesex has been for centuries an appanage of London ; and its natural resources have been more or less at the service of the inhabitants of the metropolis. A closer topographical inspection shows further that all the highways radiate from London, and that there are no important cross-roads whatever. There are five so-called market-towns, but none of them are of high rank, unless Uxbridge should claim to be so. Except that Brentford and Staines are upon the same road, and that Brentford connects with Uxbridge by a branch of that main road, there is no special connexion between any two of them as members of the same community. Of cross-roads those worth naming are : traces of an old highway from Kingston (Surrey) through Uxbridge to the north-west ; traces of a very ancient way from Brentford to Harrow and beyond ; and perhaps a road joining Enfield with Barnet (Hertfordshire). Every other track tends directly to the metropolis.

Even little more than a century ago the condition of the turnpike roads near London was very unsatisfactory, in spite of the large sums of money available for cleansing and repair. The road from Hadley through South Mimms was insufferably bad, and disgraceful to the trustees. The Edgware road was no better, the mud being 4 in. deep after every heavy rain in summer, and 9 in. all the winter. The menders never thought of scraping it, but laid fresh gravel on the sloppy surface ; the first cart cut it into ruts, and so it remained all the year round. The Uxbridge road was even worse; and during the winter 1797–8 there was only one passable track, and that less than 6 ft.

wide and usually 8 in. deep in fluid mud. The rest of the road on either side was covered with adhesive mire from 1 ft. to 1½ ft. deep. And it must be remembered that the road from Tyburn to Uxbridge was supposed to have more broad-wheeled wagons pass over it than any other in the county ; they naturally monopolized the fairly traversable 8 in. of mud, and forced light vehicles and horsemen into the bordering quagmire. During that winter, remarks an indignant sufferer,[1] 'The only labourers to be seen on the road were those of a neighbouring gentleman, and they were employed in carting the footpath into his inclosures.' The road from Hyde Park Corner through Brentford and Hounslow was equally filthy in winter, though the king often travelled along it several times a week. It is rather curious that the parish highways were sometimes much better : 'hard and clean in every sort of weather, so much so, that gentlemen may ride along them, even directly after rain, and scarcely receive a splash.' At the present day the main roads out of London, and many of the by-roads also, are well looked after, and furnish little occasion for reasonable complaint.

The main roads, it may be said, have for the most part existed on their present sites for long ages past. Where they have been altered, the cause of displacement has been sometimes local necessity or caprice, and sometimes national interest. One example (of those few which have been investigated) will be an interesting illustration of the point. The great road to the north of London, passing to the eastward of old St. Pancras Church, along what is now the Hornsey Road, went over Muswell Hill and by Colney Hatch to Whetstone. This proved so deep and miry in winter 'that it was refused of wayfaring men and carriers, in regard whereof it was agreed betweene the Bishop of London and the Countrie that a newe waie shoulde bee layde forth through the said Bishops parks,

[1] Middleton, *View of Agric. of Midd.* 395 et seq.

beginning at Highgate Hill to leade directly to Whetstone.'[2] The old road to Highgate was doubtless but a communication along the ridge to Hampstead, with little more than local value. The augmentation of the toll revenue at Highgate must have benefited greatly by the change. But the time came at last, when 'way-faring men and carriers' were not the only classes to be served by the new highway. Coaches and carriages found it an arduous affair to cross the hill, and at length, after much protest and waiting for redress, it was determined to improve the road by diverting it to the right upon a lower level. This was in 1812. At first a tunnel was projected, about 300 yds. in length. After about half of it was constructed, the whole fell in early one morning, luckily before the workmen were on duty. It was then determined to revise the plan. Operations were resumed with a deep open cutting, an archway to be thrown over at the point where the road is traversed by the Hornsey Lane. The road was completed, and opened for traffic on 21 August 1813, and proved very welcome as an easier route to the north.[3] The acclivity was still considerable, and in actual distance only 100 yds. or so were saved, but it has well justified the enterprise of the promoters. The archway was of stone with enormous brick supports and a stone balustrade, and had the merit of being rather ornamental when approached from either side. It is now superseded by an iron bridge, on bolder lines, more suitable to the needs of a busier generation.

The decrease of traffic on the Middlesex roads after 1840 was never so marked as on some of the great trade routes in more rural counties; and any falling-off has been regained within the last decade owing to the development of electric tramways, and the heavy motor goods-services of various companies. Both of these systems, in fact, are now vigorous competitors with the suburban railway lines. Owing, however, to the position of London at its heart, few counties are so well supplied as Middlesex with railroad facilities, since the national trunk lines radiate from the capital as a centre ; the latest to acquire a terminus within the metropolitan area being the Great Central Railway at Marylebone. The construction of the electric tubes and their gradual extension to the suburbs has also, within the last few years, introduced a further element of competition as regards passenger traffic. The tramways,

the omnibus companies, and the older railways have all been affected, though in different degrees. The loss of suburban traffic has been the main factor in suggesting the project for amalgamating the three great lines of the Great Northern, Great Eastern, and Great Central which is under consideration.

The county of Middlesex has the advantage of extensive means of water-carriage. Before the railways came, this advantage was more apparent than it is now when the value of time, in speedy dispatch and removal, is more fully appreciated. To begin with, the entire eastern and southern borders of the county are provided with navigable rivers, in the Thames and the Lea, while the Grand Junction Canal and its offshoots supply the needs of the county from Uxbridge in the west to several parts of the metropolis. The first canalization of the River Lea was undertaken about the year 1770, at a period when such measures were in their infancy, or were being undertaken with timidity. During the remaining years of the 18th century more ambitious efforts were made. A great many useful canals were formed throughout the kingdom, some of which have become disused through the influence of railway enterprise. Among those which remain in operation, and are to some extent prosperous, the Lea and Stort Navigation and the Grand Junction Canal may be included. They are almost a necessity to the localities they serve, and their proprietors may be congratulated on their dividends.

The Grand Junction Canal, with its direct and uninterrupted communications with Staffordshire, Warwickshire, and Lancashire, enters the county at Uxbridge on the western outskirts of the town. Its course is through the levels of Cowley, West Drayton, and Southall, at a nearly uniform elevation above the ordnance datum of 100 ft. In the last-named parish a short series of locks brings it to the level of the River Brent, which is from this point canalized until it reaches the Thames at Brentford. It is significant of the importance of this canal to the traffic for which it was designed that a short branch of the Great Western Railway runs nearly parallel, from Southall to Brentford, without seriously diminishing the prosperity of the canal.

The success of the Grand Junction Canal naturally led to extensions of the principle. It was determined to make a supplementary cutting in order to bring navigation to the West End of London, and an Act of Parliament was obtained for extending the canal to Paddington. At the end of the 18th

---

[2] John Norden, *Speculum Brit.* (1723), 15.
[3] E. W. Brayley, *Lond. and Midd.* x (4), 223.

century Paddington was a rural hamlet, thinly populated, one of those almost unnoticed places that lie apart from the highways. A spirited life was put into the place when the new canal was opened in 1801 ; warehouses were built, dwelling-houses sprang up around, and by the day of opening Paddington had become a suburb. Great expectations were formed of its future ; the first day was kept with festivity, and inaugurated by an aquatic procession.

The Paddington Canal begins with a junction at Bull's Bridge, on the River Cran, north of Cranford, pursuing thence a winding course, without locks, by Northolt, Greenford, Alperton, and Kensal Green ; an ideal country for canal-constructors. The success of the enterprise was immediate. Traders had found a new and excellent route to and from the Midlands. Passage-boats with merchandise went daily to Uxbridge. Twice a week during the summer months other boats with passenger accommodation went backwards and forwards, and as late as the year 1853 a Sunday traffic of pleasure trips to Greenford Green was largely patronized.[4]

In 1812 a further extension was proposed and soon carried into effect. Under the name of the Regent's Canal, a cut was made round the entire metropolis to the River Thames, near Limehouse. There are many locks and bridges, and two tunnels, one under Maida Hill, and another of considerable length at Islington. There is a dock with large dépôts and warehouses in the City Road, besides a substantial dock at Limehouse.[5] The canal has been of immense benefit to the eastern and north-eastern districts of London. Miles of warehouses and yards occupy now the space of the green fields that existed at the period of its construction. Few undertakings of the kind have been justified so signally in their results.

In olden times there was one harbour in the very heart of the City of London, at the mouth of the Fleet River, which was navigable at least as far as Holborn. A mention of Fleet Hithe, in an old record,[6] is enough

to establish the former existence of a tiny port near Blackfriars. Besides this, on the extreme eastern boundary of the county there was some sort of harbour at the mouth of the River Lea.

The extension of the canal system naturally incited the commercial and engineering classes to fresh efforts for the convenience of navigation. Docks were now wanted, and not many years elapsed before several spacious docks were given to the metropolis. Dock extension has never since these times ceased to be demanded. Indeed the need for remedial measures has long become urgent, and it is to be hoped that the Act of 1908 establishing the new 'Port of London Authority'[7] will afford a much-needed relief, and stop the serious decline in the trade of the port.

The West India Docks were the earliest of such enterprises, at least in the county of Middlesex. They were begun in July 1800 and took something over two years in construction. A good feature of the undertaking was the making a water-way across the Isle of Dogs, thus avoiding a long bend of the river. The West Indian trade at this time had grown enormously. Shippers were rather tired of waterside wharves, with their lack of warehouse room, and lighterage was increasingly troublesome and expensive. The first stone of the docks was laid in the presence of a great assemblage of merchants and shipowners, headed by William Pitt and Lord Chancellor Loughborough. The enthusiasm of that day was well justified when the work was done. The docks were occupied, and the new warehouses speedily filled with sugar, rare woods, and other staple products of the West. The saving to the mercantile community was immediate and permanent, and the revenue is understood to have benefited no less. Confidence in the docking system was established. A few years saw the completion of the London Docks (1805), the East India Docks (1806), St. Katharine's Dock (1828). Since those days dock extension has proceeded with intermittent but steady steps outside the boundary of our county.

The River Thames, after all, has a practical utility to which no combination of artificial water-courses can aspire. It is a perfect highway ; and in its course of about 43 miles as the southern boundary of the county from Staines Bridge to the mouth of the River Lea, affords a prodigious water-supply, beside all the possible conveniences offered by water-side premises. As to actual traffic upon its surface, the Thames was, until the middle of the

[4] Personal recollections kindly supplied by Mr. E. Smith.

[5] Brayley, op. cit. x (4), 163.

[6] In the third folio (recto) of the ancient book known as *Liber A. sive Pilosus*, containing the ancient evidences of the Dean and Chapter of St. Paul's, is a Process of Recognition of the reign of Henry I which states that stone ships or barges belonging to the dean and chapter unshipped their lading at Fleet Hithe, and that the owners complained of a toll levied upon them. W. J. Pinks, *Clerkenwell*, 377.

[7] Stat. 8 Edw. VII, cap. 68.

19th century, a most important and lively artery for the purpose either of business or pleasure. The existing steps, wharves, and water-lanes are as old as anything on the river, and betoken a habit of passing to and fro by water, even if our chronicles did not testify to the prevalence of the waterman's calling. The rise of steam-navigation did not materially affect the waterman; it is rather the haste engendered by a busier age which has rendered the pursuit of his calling less lucrative. The first steamer that usurped the pleasure side of his trade was the *Endeavour*, which plied to Richmond in the year 1830. By 1842 the passenger traffic by steamers had grown enormously. In the summer of that year there were no fewer than four steamboat companies making a profitable traffic on the Thames.[8] But, as in the case of the Paddington barge above mentioned, these things lost their popularity when speed, alike in pleasure and business, was the urgent demand of a rising generation.

The government of the river was originally in the hands of the Corporation of London, whose jurisdiction was limited to the lower part, beginning at Staines Bridge. This lasted until the year 1857, when the Thames Conservancy Board was created by Act of Parliament. Later legislation gave the Thames Conservancy power over the whole length of the river, besides a distance of five miles up all its tributaries. The duties of the board include the maintenance of weirs, locks, &c., prevention of pollution by sewage, regulations as to fishing and pleasure-traffic, care of the towing-path (which is continuous from Putney upwards), dredging, and the general control of the disposition of the water.

Middlesex is wholly within the Thames basin; so that every spring within the county finds its way into one or other of the northern tributaries of the river. Of these, the Colne skirts the western boundary of the county, receiving no less than five important affluents at or near Uxbridge; near Staines it pours a good volume of water into the Thames, besides forming a separate channel which finds its way to Hampton Court. The Cran, rising in the higher levels near Harrow, and augmented by the Yeading brooks, passes through Cranford to Twickenham and Isleworth. The Brent, the stream of which is arrested by a large reservoir constructed by the Canal Company, meets the Thames at Brentford. Several small bourns flowed into the Thames in ancient times, which have long since been converted into artificial lakes

or suffered to become mere drains. The Lea is a contributory from Bedfordshire and Hertfordshire, fed in its course by numerous springs, and by storm-waters from several rivulets. It is fairly certain that the Lea once flowed with a more powerful stream, and was a good natural water-way along the entire eastern boundary of Middlesex.

There has been a good deal of vicissitude in the process of bridging the Thames. Before the present fine bridge at Staines was built there was a succession of failures. A bridge existed here in very ancient days. There is repeated mention of a bridge at Staines in old records. The wooden one existing towards the end of the 18th century was at last condemned, and an Act of Parliament obtained for rebuilding. A stone bridge was forthwith put in hand, and opened for traffic in 1797. But this was found to be insecure, and it had to be taken down. A cast-iron bridge followed, and in its turn failed. A third attempt was made, with a low arch of cast iron supported on wooden piles; but this in turn was at length condemned. George Rennie then undertook the construction, and the result was the handsome bridge now standing. It was opened in 1832, with much state, the ceremony being attended by William IV and his queen.

Chertsey Bridge is a substantial structure in stone, opened in 1785. It is hardly equal to modern needs, with the increased speed and size of modern traffic. A bridge was raised at Walton, an eccentric-looking structure in wood and brick, which required alteration and repair from time to time. The central arch fell in 1859, and a new bridge was opened in 1863, a rather ugly but more convenient structure. Hampton Court Bridge was built in 1865, in place of a wooden structure erected in 1750. Kingston Bridge is one of the handsomest on the river. It replaced a wooden one several centuries old, and was opened in 1828. This bridge now has a strain on its accommodation, and is fated to be altered if not entirely superseded. On account of the busy population in and around the town, Richmond Bridge is likewise becoming inadequate to the wants of the neighbourhood. It was built in the year 1777. Half a mile lower down is the foot-bridge and lock, opened 19 May 1894. The shallowness of the stream hereabouts prompted a design which should hold up the tide at half-ebb, and always provide sufficient water for navigation. The plan was quite successful, and added a new triumph to the arts of modern bridge-building.

The new bridge at Kew, inaugurated by King Edward VII in 1905, is a great

---

[8] *Illus. Lond. News*, 1842.

ornament to the river, and an immense improvement upon the old one of 1789. That was of stone and brick, but it became unfit for modern usage. The next bridge is at Hammersmith, on the suspension principle, opened in 1827. It has served its purpose, and is highly attractive in appearance; but it is destined to make room for a heavier structure, in view of modern needs. Fulham Bridge is a very fine modern one, suitable to the needs of an immense traffic. It was completed in 1885, replacing one of quaint-looking appearance which dated from 1729. At Wandsworth an iron lattice bridge was opened in 1873. Battersea Bridge is one of the best and handsomest on the river, raised in place of an old wooden structure dating back two centuries and a half. Below this are two handsome suspension bridges, which were rendered necessary by the extension of London suburbs on this side.

The new Vauxhall Bridge, opened in 1906, represents all that is complete in modern bridge-building, being spacious, elegant, and substantial, yet less expensive than its predecessor, which cost nearly £300,000. This older bridge had lasted only from the year 1816. The suspension bridge at Lambeth was opened in 1862, but is already considered defective as far as concerns the upper works. The splendid iron bridge at Westminster was opened in 1860–2 after a long period of obstruction of the water-way by its half-ruined predecessor of 1750. This latter had been injured at the foundations through the increased scour of the river caused chiefly by the demolition of old London Bridge. Near Charing Cross a suspension-bridge was raised in 1842, named after Hungerford Market, which has since been superseded by a railway bridge with accompanying footway. Waterloo Bridge is still in some respects one of the finest in the world, and was built some two years after the date of the celebrated battle.

The remaining bridges are in London proper. The Blackfriars Bridge of 1760 was an excellent work; but it suffered like its neighbour from the stronger scour of recent years. Its successor was finished in 1869, and has lately been widened to provide tramway accommodation. Southwark Bridge was built 1813–19.[9] The new London Bridge is slightly to the west of the site of a wooden structure of Saxon times, which had several successors. The first stone was laid in 1825. Half a million pounds were

expended on the work, which was finished in 1831 and opened in state by William IV. The congestion of traffic was relieved in 1904 by widening the bridge to allow of four lines of vehicles, the centre being reserved for light carts and passenger conveyances. Finally, the Tower Bridge, one of the great triumphs of modern engineering, was completed in 1894.

The natural water supply of Middlesex is copious. Some parts of the county are better served than others. Until the invention of artesian wells, there was both difficulty and expense in reaching water, because of the thick deposit of clay beneath the surface. The numerous springs which rise from northern declivities supply every district of the county. When these rivulets failed from drought, it was formerly of great concern to have deep wells for occasional supply. But well-sinking was a serious affair in the London Clay. There is record of a well at Paddington, where the workmen had to go to a depth of 300 ft. before reaching water. Another well at Holloway, dug early in the 19th century, required an excavation of 172 ft. It is matter of wonder that a system of storage was never resorted to. At Ruislip, and at the head waters of the Brent, near Hendon, are large reservoirs which were provided for the wants of the Canal Company. Similar constructions, for domestic and other purposes, might have been of immense utility in some districts. Doubtless the question of initial expense hindered resort to this sort of economy.

In selecting for detailed treatment the more prominent industries, due weight has been given to the following among other considerations :—(1) The importance of the industry from its national character; (2) its historical interest; (3) its first appearance in this country; and (4) its being principally carried on in Middlesex. But a number of trades, some of which merit more attention, must for lack of room be allowed only a cursory notice in this introduction.

It may be convenient to turn our attention in the first place to the trades of East London and Hackney, where the proportion of the population engaged in manufacturing industries is exceptionally large. It shows a percentage of 39·95, whilst that of all London is 28·38, and that of the whole of England 30·7. Out of this army of workers we shall treat here principally of those engaged in home occupations.

Tailoring is one of the chief industries, and is carried on in some 900 workshops of Jewish contractors, and by home workers both for West End and City firms. 'The Jewish

---

[9] A scheme is on foot for rebuilding Southwark Bridge or improving its gradients and approaches; also for building a new bridge near St. Paul's.

coat-making industry is practically concentrated within an area of less than one square mile, comprising the whole of Whitechapel, a small piece of Mile End, and a part of St. George's-in-the-East.'[10] Here is congregated a compact Jewish community of from 30,000 to 40,000 persons of all nationalities. Yiddish is the language of the streets, and Hebrew announcements are everywhere to be seen. The work of the English journeyman cannot be equalled, but the conditions of his home workshop are too often deplorable. Excellent work is also produced in the Jewish workshop, together with inferior work of every grade down to the 'slops' manufactured for the export trade. The existence of the lowest trade is dependent on the presence of a class of workers such as Jews and women, with an indefinitely low standard of life. Domestic workshops are most numerous in the eastern portion of Mile End Old Town ; Stepney and Poplar are the centres of the slop, trouser, and juvenile trade.

In point of numbers, bootmaking is an equally important East End industry, and is rapidly growing in extent, especially in the districts of Shoreditch and Bethnal Green, where it gives occupation to a considerable fraction of the population.[11] Under the old system of bootmaking, the various workmen engaged for bespoke work were the last-maker, the clicker, who cut out the material for the 'uppers,' the closer, who sewed the upper or top portion, and the maker, who fitted on the sole or heel. Last-making is now almost a separate business, and it is becoming increasingly the custom to make uppers in a factory in wholesale quantity. In the hand-made bespoke work, the labour of the closer was largely done in the home, generally with the help of the wife and daughters of the family. Since the introduction of sewing-machines, many closers have left the trade and no one is learning it. The machine-made bespoke work is constructed with ready-made uppers from the provinces, and completed by makers working, at home or in associated workshops, on the fitted last. In the ready-made wholesale trade the organization is more complex, as cheapness is an indispensable element. A complete machine-sewn boot passes through the hands of twenty different workers. The work of clickers and rough-stuff cutters is usually done in the factory in London, whilst lasters, closers, and sole-sewers are out-workers. The manufac-

tories in London vary considerably in extent. There are the large makers who turn out 10,000 and more pairs a week, and the chamber-masters who chiefly employ members of their own family and whose weekly output is limited to a few gross. Then we reach the lowest level, that of the owner of a couple of rooms, who cuts his uppers, gets his wife and daughter to close them, and lasts and finishes the boots himself. Owing principally to the conditions resulting from the restrictions imposed by the Trade Union wage-standard, the work is being driven from London to Northampton.

Shirt-making is largely carried on by women in East London ; both shirts and underclothing requiring good handiwork are made in several middle-class London suburbs. The shirt machinists who take work home belong to various grades of the social scale. Many are widows who are partly assisted by their relatives or by the parish. Some are young ladies who work for pocket money for a mere trifle, and so lower the standard of payment. Other causes of low wages are incapacity (many of the workers being feeble or inexperienced), sub-contract, and the indifference to the quality of work on the part of the consumer. Tie-making is carried on partly in factories and partly in the home. There is much sub-contracting, and prices paid for labour greatly vary, although the rate of payment is higher than that for shirts.

In umbrella-making, the covers and the frames are made in factories, and are then put together in dozens and given out to the home-workers. There are also small umbrella-makers in the East End who supply shops in the neighbourhood ; they buy sticks and frames, and their families are all employed in the actual umbrella manufacture.

Corsets and stays are principally made in provincial towns, but there are a few factories in the East End. Several small stay-makers have workshops of their own, employing a few hands besides the members of their families, and a few hundred women do work at home for the factories.

The fur-trade is, with very few exceptions, in Jewish hands, both in the City and in the East End. The City furriers have part of the work done at their own warehouses ; but most of them give out the sewing to be done by home-workers. The fur-sewing is most disagreeable and unhealthy, besides being the worst paid of any industry carried on in East London workshops.

The box-making industry gives employment largely to women. Fancy boxes are made almost entirely on the premises of the manufacturer, but much of the work in plain boxes

---

[10] The writer has to acknowledge his indebtedness to the splendid survey of this subject in Booth's *Life and Labour in Lond.*

[11] Charles Booth, op. cit. (Ser. 1), iv, 69.

is done by out-door hands at home. The cardboard is cut by men, and then made up by women and girls. Skill is required; and a girl does not become a good hand at plain work under two years, whilst for fancy work three years' training is required. Matchbox making requires no previous training, and is the lowest in the scale of the industries of the poor. It is the last resort of the destitute, and the employment of children of the earliest age. A child can earn 1d. an hour, and few women can earn more than 1¾d. an hour.

Brush-making is carried on principally in factories, very few of which give out work. The work is fairly regular, and requires a combination of skill and honesty. The lighter parts of the work are performed by women, and shorter hours on the whole prevail in this trade than in most others.

Match-making is a notable industry of East London, in which over one thousand women and girls are employed. The match girls have successfully combined to promote their interests, and make each other's cause their own. They form clubs among themselves for buying clothes and feathers, seven or eight paying 1s. a week, and drawing lots to decide who shall have the money each week. Their prolonged strike in July 1888 resulted in the formation of a Trade Union, the largest in England composed of women and girls. By improvements in the manufacture, the quantity of phosphorus employed has been very greatly reduced, and a considerable diminution in the terrible disease *necrosis* has consequently resulted.

In the confectionery factories, the manufacture of jam, preserves, pickles, and even sweets, is in greater part performed by men, women only being employed for labelling, packing, &c. The employment is of an irregular kind, only a certain number of the better hands being kept on permanently.

Among other industries which deserve more than a passing notice is that of cap-making. Here the factory system is driving the small workshops out of the field. The largest factory employs 600 girls, and the work is very laborious, although fairly well paid.

Artificial flowers are made in Hoxton and De Beauvoir Town, as well as by a few workers in the East End. This is a season trade, and subject also to much irregularity from the caprices of fashion.

Feather-curling, although fluctuating with changes of fashion, gives fairly regular employment to a large number of girls in East and North-East London.

The industries which supply man's everyday wants have the same characteristics more or less in every locality. Among beverages, the manufacture of aerated and mineral waters is carried on by many firms such as Perrier, Idris & Co., Schweppes Ltd., and John G. Webb & Co.

Turning to solid food it is a noticeable feature of the present day that the wants of residents and visitors of all classes of society were never so well provided for as by the various hotels, restaurants, bread and dairy companies, and people's cafés which now abound. In this great improvement the metropolis has certainly led the way. Of sauce and pickle manufacturers there are two well-known firms in Middlesex, John Burgess and Son, and Crosse & Blackwell. In its vinegar works the metropolis until lately took the lead, and among the principal firms were those of Champion & Co., in Old Street, and Henry Sarson and Sons, City Road.

Middlesex was formerly noted for its extensive distilleries; the duty paid by English distilleries for the year ending 5 January 1833 was £1,420,525 10s., which was nearly £100,000 above that paid in Scotland, but below that in Ireland.[12] Of the total duty paid in England, two firms in the metropolis contributed together more than one-fourth, viz., O. H. Smith and R. Carrington of Thames Bank £201,287 5s., and T. and G. Smith of Whitechapel £207,559 2s. 6d. This industry is still extensively carried on in Middlesex, but almost wholly within the metropolitan district.

There are maltsters at Brentford, Chiswick, Isleworth, Staines, and many other localities. Malting seems to have been carried on at Enfield to a considerable extent at an early period. In the latter half of the 15th century it is recorded[13] that John Hunnesdon of 'Endefeld' sought to recover £8 13s. 10d. from Robert Trott of Southwark, brewer, who 'hath used wekely to bye malt by the space of many yeres of your seid besecher,' and who it seems never settled in full for the same. 'At some tyme ther hath remayned unpayed for 2 or 3 quarters of malt, at som tyme 4 or 5, at som tyme mor,' until at length Hunnesdon's patience was exhausted. Other Middlesex maltsters (of the same period) of whom record exists are William Hall of 'Endfeld,'[14] Henry Wynn of Enfield,[15] and William Barley of 'Enffelde.'[16]

Hat-making was formerly a great Middlesex industry, but has of late years shrunk to very small proportions in the metropolis. The manufacture of felt hats was introduced early in the reign of Henry VIII; while in 1530

[12] *Commissioners of Excise Enq. Rep.* vii, 1834–5, p. 229.
[13] Early Chan. Proc. bdle. 60, no. 97.
[14] Ibid. bdle. 64, no. 189.   [15] Ibid. no. 110
[16] Ibid. bdle. 86, no. 47.

letters of denization were granted to Martin Johnson from Guelders,[17] 'strawen hat maker, otherwise splyter hat maker.'

Norden mentions a copper and brass mill at Isleworth between that place and Horton, where the metal was wrought, melted, and forged from ore which came from Somerset. 'Manie artificiall deuises,' he says, 'are there to be noted in the performance of the worke.'[18] These works formed the subject of a lengthy dispute between John Brode and Sir Richard Martin, Lord Mayor of London in 1593, which came before the Privy Council in 1596.[19] The manufacture carried on was that of 'lattin and battry,' the metals being produced chiefly in an unwrought state, although the term 'battry' was usually applied to brass or copper vessels and chiefly those for culinary and table use. Brode in his petition states that the metal was procured from a mixture of copper and calamine ore by a process employed by one Christopher Shutz, who had 'great cunning and experience' in its use. In 1565 Shutz, with a partner, William Humphrey, obtained an exclusive licence to search, dig for, and use calamine stone. These partners, as Brode alleged, although they brought over divers strangers, did not bring anything to pass, 'and so gave yt over as not fecible.' The project then, he says, continued without hope for nineteen years, when he in partnership with others leased the privilege for fourteen years at a yearly rent of £50. During the period of his lease his expenditure upon the works at Isleworth had amounted to £3,500, and he claimed to have brought the undertaking by his study and labour to a state of perfection. He is now (1596) threatened with forfeiture of his lease and seizure of his 'stuffe and tooles' for non-payment of rent. He prays that his tools and metal may not be seized, as he is willing and able to pay, and not personally defaulting; he is equally prepared to buy out his partners or that they should buy him out. Sir Richard Martin in his reply states that he, Andrew Palmer, and Humphrey Michell, were persuaded to become Brode's partners by his statement that he could perfectly produce 'commixed copper,' and that it would bring in £1,000 a year. The alderman then agreed to defray the charges of the first year, amounting to about £3,000, and each of the other partners contributed £800, so that Brode's statement that he had paid £3,500 was not true. Brode was allowed

by the partners £50 a year to direct the works, but this he must have taken out of capital, as no profit was made. He would not divulge the secret (if it existed) either to his partners or to the Mines Corporation, although that company offered him and Palmer on such condition a further lease of seven years. Shutz and Humphrey's 'privilege' had meanwhile been acquired by the Mines Corporation. Brode in his rejoinder gives some curious information about the works. He asserts that Shutz and Humphrey did not succeed in perfecting their discovery, although they had from 20 to 30 tons of calamine stone from Worle Hill in Somerset conveyed to Tintern Abbey, where it was experimented upon without success by one Hinckins, a stranger whom they employed. He denies Sir Richard's account of the financial side of the transactions, and reaffirms his previous statement. The co-partners employed one John Dickson, coppersmith of London, to 'melte and batter out 20,000 wt. of copper and make it into plates and make the same malleable.' Dickson failed, but he the said Brode performed the task, and also refined 43 tons of Barbary copper, and brought it into plates, 'an act perfected never before by any Englishman.' About eight years since, Sir Richard Martin and Michell withdrew from the partnership and received the whole of their stock back again and £238 more in copper, plates, and kettles. The 'lattin' works were also attempted, but nothing brought to pass; by expending his own money Brode has brought these to perfection. On 17 April 1596 the Mineral and Battry Company petitioned Lord Burghley[20] to order Brode to supply their new lessees with materials at reasonable rates. They state that the patent granted in 7 Elizabeth to Shutz and Humphrey was for making 'lattyn, battrye, castworke, and wyre.' In 10 Elizabeth the patent was acquired by their company then incorporated, which consisted of thirty-six shareholders, among whom were the Duke of Norfolk, the Lord Treasurer, Lord Cobham, and others. The company pursued the work for a time, and then took up wire-work and other work under another patent. In 24 Elizabeth they granted a lease of their battery works for 150 years at £50 a year to John Brode and his partners, who built the works at Isleworth, Brode having sole management with £50 a year for his pains. Brode caused great loss to his partners, refused to divulge his secret, and now refused to pay the rent. The company then by judicial order made his lease void, and granted a new

[17] W. Page, *Denizations and Naturalizations* (Huguenot Soc.), p. xlvii.
[18] *Speculum Britanniae* (ed. 1723), 41.
[19] Lansd. MS. 81, fol. 1.

[20] Ibid. fol. 2–3.

INDUSTRIES

lease of twenty-one years to others at £100 rent for the first year and £400 yearly after. They conclude by stating that Brode has secured the supply of calamine and will not supply it to the new lessees. The petition is signed by Sir Julius Caesar, Sir Richard Martin, Thomas Caesar, William Bond, Richard Martin, jnr., and others. The company and Sir Richard Martin were also in controversy in 1596 with Richard Hanbery and Edmund Wheler.[21] How these disputes ended does not appear. Lysons wrote in 1795,[22] 'these copper-mills still exist, being situated at Baberbridge; they belong to the Duke of Northumberland, and are rented by the incorporated Society of the Mines Royal.'

Although cutlery as a trade has long since left the metropolis, the making of surgical instruments is a branch which still continues to flourish in this county, and to produce some highly-skilled workmen. Among the principal Middlesex firms are Down Bros., Ltd., St. Thomas's Street, S.E.; Allen and Hanbury's, Ltd., Wigmore Street; and John Weiss & Son, Ltd., now of Oxford Street, but originally established in the Strand in 1787.

In its highest and most costly form goldsmiths' and silversmiths' work is largely carried on in Middlesex by firms of high standing.

Soap-manufacture is an old established Middlesex industry. From the report of the Excise Commissioners for 1835[23] it appears that whilst the total amount of duty paid for all England was £1,418,832 4s., fifty-five firms in London contributed no less a portion than £378,175 13s. 6¼d. Ten of these firms paid over £10,000 each. One of the oldest firms in Middlesex is that of D. & W. Gibbs, Ltd., whose premises, known as the City Soap Works, are in Wapping. The business was established in 1712, and was subsequently acquired by David Gibbs, whose grandsons are now directors of the company. Until 1889 the manufactory was in Milton Street, Cripplegate; but that building being destroyed by fire, the firm purchased the business of Paton and Charles at Wapping together with that of Sharp Brothers. The works cover 2½ acres of ground, and employ 200 hands, excluding the clerical and travelling staff, numbering about fifty. The firm holds patents for many specialities in soap. Other important Middlesex firms are A. F. Pears & Co., who have large works at Isleworth; Osborne Bauer and Cheseman of Golden Square; and T. D. Rowe & Co., and Wylie & Co., both of Brentford.

Although the London streets have much improved in cleanliness, the art of the shoe-black has long been a necessity, and blacking has always been an important Middlesex industry, the firm of Day and Martin being one of its chief representatives.

In the metropolis, with its concentration of public and private boards and institutions, its ever-increasing population, and the rebuilding and repairs of existing property, there is always so much work for builders that the building trade is one of the most important of its industrial groups. Brick and tile-making is extensively carried on, more especially on the outer fringe of the London districts. It seems probable that bricks and coarse tiles have been made in Middlesex from an early period. Late in the 15th century we hear of John Maier and Agnes his wife making tiles for William Code of Harlesden Green at the rate of 11d. per 1,000.[24]

There are floorcloth and linoleum factories at Staines (Linoleum Manufacturing Co.), Edmonton (Ridley, Whitley & Co.), and Ponders End (Corticene Floor Covering Co.).

Ever since Robert Barron of Hoxton took out a patent[25] for a lock 'far more secure than any hitherto made,' the locksmiths and safe-makers of Middlesex have done their best to provide secure keeping for the great wealth of the metropolis. Some of the principal firms in Middlesex are Bramah & Co., New Bond Street; C. H. Griffiths & Sons, Bethnal Green; Ratner Safe Co., Ltd., Bromley-by-Bow; and John Tann, Old Ford.

London being distant from the coalfields, manufactures in iron are carried on to a small extent only. Copper is worked largely in Middlesex, and so is lead; both metals being so malleable and ductile that their manufacture can be effected with much less heat than iron requires. The extensive lead-smelting works of the old firm, Locke, Lancaster and Johnson & Sons, Ltd., are situated at Poplar, Limehouse, and Millwall.

Gas-tar works form an important feature of the East London Industries. The works of Messrs. Burt, Boulton, and Haywood for the distillation of gas-tar occupied in 1876 about 17 acres at Prince Regent's Wharf, Silvertown; and another 2 acres at Millwall. Gas tar produces by distillation four valuable substances: naphtha, creosote oil, anthracene, and pitch. But still more valuable products are the series of aniline dyes, the discovery of which forms one of the greatest triumphs of modern chemistry. In another department

[21] Lansd. MS. 81, fol. 4–7.
[22] *Environs of Lond.* iii, 122.
[23] *Rep.* xvii, 64.
[24] Early Chan. Proc. bdle. 150, no. 82.
[25] No. 1200, 31 Oct. 1778.

of these large works the making of creosote railway sleepers was carried on upon an extensive scale.[26]

Many leading firms of manufacturing chemists have extensive works in Middlesex. At Southall are the premises of W. Houlder, Son & Co.; at Poplar are F. Allen & Sons; at Ponder's End, T. Morson & Son; at Hounslow, Parke, Davis & Co.; at West Drayton, Alfred White & Sons; in the City Road, Stafford Allen & Sons; at Limehouse, Chapman & Messel; and at Hackney Wick, W. C. Barnes & Co., Ltd., and E. Beanes & Co. At the works of Carless, Capel & Leonard, at Hackney Wick, the various products of petroleum are manufactured on a large scale, and oil-refining is well represented by Fenner, Alder & Co. of Millwall; Hubbuck & Co. of Ratcliff; and the Union Oil and Cake Mills at Limehouse. Compressed and liquid gases are produced by Coxeter & Son at Seaton Street, N.W.; and the British Oxygen Company manufacture oxygen at Westminster.

Paint, colour, and varnish manufacturers are represented by D. Anderson & Son of Old Ford, and Denton & Jutsum of Bow Common; Louis Berger & Son of Homerton, and Duggan, Neel, & McColm, Ltd., of Millwall. Of makers of electrical appliances we can only mention the Jandus Arc Lamp and Electrical Company, of Holloway. Among the drug manufacturers are Allen & Hanbury of Bethnal Green, and Burgoyne & Burbidges of Mile End New Town. The manufacture of perfumery is represented by Hovenden & Sons of City Road, and W. J. Bush & Co. of Hackney. That of celluloid is carried on by Frederick Hill & Co., at Kingsland.

There are extensive powder-mills in the parish of Twickenham, 2 miles from Hounslow, generally known as the Hounslow Powder Mills; also at East Bedfont.

Among the decayed industries of Middlesex is that of sugar-refining, which at one time was an important trade in the east of London. We learn from Stow that 'about the year 1544 refining of sugar was first used in England. Then there were but two sugar-houses; and their profit was but very little, by reason there were so many sugar bakers in Antwerp, and sugar came from thence better cheap than it could be afforded at London; and for the space of twenty years together those two sugar-houses served the whole realm, both to the commendation and profit of them that undertook the same.'[27]

Sugar undergoes but little manufacture after it reaches our shores. The business of the sugar refiner, or sugar baker as he has been wrongly termed, is that of preparing from the common brown 'moist' the white conical lumps or loaves of crystallized sugar, familiarly known as lump sugar. This used to be carried on in the neighbourhood of Goodman's Fields, the factories being congregated within a circle of half-a-mile radius immediately eastward of Aldgate.[28] The chief supply of English sugar came formerly from the West Indies, where the sugar-cane was cultivated to a vast extent. Its preparation for shipment involved three stages: it was first a juice expressed from the cane, then a syrup from which the impurities had been removed, and lastly a brown granulated substance from which a considerable portion of molasses or uncrystallizable sugar had been separated. The ponderous hogsheads which used to be seen forty or fifty years ago outside the shops of the retail grocers contained moist sugar, somewhat resembling that imported by the refiner, but with a finer and softer grain. This sugar, well known to the housewife in those days as 'sevenpenny or eightpenny moist,' had various shades of brown colour, according to its quality. This was caused by the presence of molasses to a greater or less extent, but the sugar was largely consumed in the condition in which it arrived from the producing country, this being possible, and even pleasant, with the sweet and fragrant cane muscavadoes. Loaf sugar (which was a luxury in the fifties, even to the middle classes) and other sugars of fine quality were obtained by purifying still further the sugar of commerce, the object of the refiner being to expel the molasses together with other impurities which still remained in the sugar as imported. The factories for sugar refining were of special construction, the chief object being to obtain a large extent of flooring. Hence the buildings were lofty, containing a large number of stories, and being lighted by numerous small windows. The interior presented a peculiar appearance arising from the small height of the rooms compared with their great extent. As a precaution against fire, rendered necessary by the inflammable nature of sugar, the refineries were largely constructed of iron, stone, and brick. The great increase in the use of beetroot sugar made no difference to the operations of the refiner. The hogsheads of sugar or the bags of beet were emptied on an

---

[26] Crory, *East London Industries* (1876), 25.
[27] *Survey*, 1720, bk. v, 244.

[28] Among the tenants of the Cutlers' Company on their Houndsditch estates were many who rented melting houses between 1584 and 1598, the period for which the information is available.

upper floor, and then discharged in shoots to a lower floor to be melted in the 'blow-ups'; these were cast-iron tanks fitted with mechanical stirrers and steam pipes for heating the water. The solution, called 'liquor,' was brought to a certain degree of gravity (25 to 33 deg. Baumé) and then filtered through twilled cotton bags, encased in a meshing of hemp. The syrup was next decolorized by being passed through beds of animal charcoal, inclosed in cisterns to a depth of from 30 ft. to 50 ft., the sugar being then discharged into tanks. It was then boiled in vacuum pans, and variously treated afterwards according to the nature of the finished sugar required. To make sugar loaves, small crystals only were formed in the pan, and the granular magma was poured into steam-jacketed open pans, and raised to a temperature of about 180 to 190 deg. Fahr., which liquefied the grains. The hot solution was then cast into conical moulds of the shape of the loaves, where it crystallized into a solid mass. A plug at the bottom of the mould was then opened to allow the syrup containing coloured and other impurities to drain away. This process was assisted by pouring into the cone successive doses of saturated syrup, ending with a syrup of pure colourless sugar. The syrup which drained from the loaves was sold as golden syrup; the liquor which obstinately remained in the interstices being driven out by suction or centrifugal action; the loaf was then rounded off, papered, and placed in a stove for drying.

The art of dyeing textile fabrics and leather had been practised from an early period in different parts of England, and much woad from Toulouse, and madder and scarlet dye from Italy, were imported by Florentine and Genoese merchants. So great, however, was the skill of the Continental dyers that much English cloth was from the 14th to the 16th century sent abroad to be dyed and finished. During the Tudor and Stuart periods improved methods of dyeing were introduced into this country. John Baptist Semyn,[29] a Genoese dwelling in Southwark, the king's dyer, was made a denizen in 1533. In the same reign several foreign leather dyers settled in or near London, and James Tybault, who took out letters of denization in 1544, describes himself as 'a leather dyer after the Spanish dyeing.' He had been then eighteen years in England. In 1561 Stiata Cavalcaunti, a Florentine, obtained a licence to be the sole

importer of indigo into England, where it was then apparently unknown as a dyeing agent, though it had been employed at a much earlier time in Italy. It did not, however, come into general use, and was quite a novelty in England sixteen years later.[30] In 1567 Peter de Croix[31] offered to set up the 'feate of dying and dressing of clothis after the manna of Flaunders.' In a return of aliens[32] in 1568 he is described as a Frenchman 'who goeth to the Frentche church,' while in a house crowded with refugees in St. Magnus parish we hear of 'Francis Tybbold dyer, borne in Ipar, in Flanders, and goeth to the Dutch churche; he paith no rent.' With the immigration of Protestant refugees foreign dyers of silk, leather, and cloth increased in numbers in and about the city of London; but the most important enterprise undertaken by a dyer of foreign origin belongs to the next century when Dr. Johannes Sibertus Kuffler of Leyden, who had married a daughter of the famous Dutch chemist Drebbel, set up a scarlet-dye house at Bow, probably putting to practical use improved methods learnt from his father-in-law. The scarlet he obtained soon became known as 'Bow dye.' Further improvements in dyeing cloth were made by Bauer, a Fleming who came to England in 1667.[33]

Gun-making and the manufacture of small arms is an important industry of the county. The Royal Small Arms Factory at Enfield was built in 1855–6 at a cost of £150,000; and has a station (Enfield Lock) on the Great Eastern Railway. The buildings form three sides of a quadrangle, and, with the testing ranges, cover an area of about 5 acres. The new magazine rifle is now made instead of the Martini-Henri, and machine-guns and swords are also manufactured. About four thousand rifles can be turned out weekly. At Edmonton are the ammunition works of Ely Brothers, Ltd. This industry is under the control of the Gunmakers' Company, the only livery company whose hall is situated outside the boundaries of the City of London. As compared with the majority of City gilds the Gunmakers' Company is quite a modern institution, not having been incorporated until the reign of Charles I. Under the charter of this sovereign, dated 14 March 1637, power was given to the company to prove and mark all gun-barrels made in London, which the

[29] W. Page, *Denizations and Naturalizations* (Huguenot Soc.), p. xliii et seq.

[30] Lansd. MS. 24, fol. 156.
[31] Ibid. 9, fol. 208.
[32] Kirk, *Returns of Aliens* (Huguenot Soc.), iii, 370 et seq.
[33] J. S. Burn, *Hist. Foreign Refugees*, 259.

makers were obliged to bring to the company's proof-house for such purpose. The authority of the company over the trade was confirmed by the Act of 53 George III, cap. 115, (1813), and by subsequent amending statutes. The last of these Acts, under which the company now exercises its powers, was passed in 1868, 31–2 Victoria, cap. 113. The proof-house is in Commercial Road East, and serves the company for the purposes of a hall. In one of the principal apartments is a fine trophy of arms. Apart from its trade duties and privileges the company exercises all the functions of an ordinary livery company. It is governed by a master and two wardens, chosen annually from the members of the court of assistants, and has a clerk, proof-master, beadle, and other officials. The company, in common with the other City gilds, makes liberal grants from its income to pensioners and general philanthropic objects.

The Thames near the metropolis was once the seat of a flourishing trade in shipbuilding, which has now almost become extinct. In April 1594 Peter Hills of Redrith (Rotherhithe) received a tally for 431 crowns, value 5s. each, as the queen's gift towards his charges in building three new ships.[34] The number of shipwrights employed in the metropolis shows a rapid decrease in the census returns. The number in 1861 was 8,300; in 1871, 6,200; in 1881, 5,300; and in 1891, 2,300; this last return being little more than one-fourth of those counted in 1861.[35] The finest vessels in the East India trade were made in the Thames shipbuilding yards, but this valuable industry is being gradu-

ally lost to the metropolis. In August 1907 it was announced that Yarrow's yard at Millwall would be entirely closed within twelve months, and the business removed to Scotstoun on the Clyde.[36] This well-known firm of marine and mechanical engineers was established in 1864, and their premises at Poplar covered 12 acres of ground at the river side. Here they had given employment to hundreds of artisans in East London during the last fifty years. Their speciality was torpedo boats, torpedo-boat destroyers, vessels of shallow draught for military and trading purposes, and the 'Yarrow' water-tube boilers. They especially succeeded in the construction of high-speed naval craft, which they supplied both to the British and to foreign governments. The firm was incorporated as a limited company in 1897. Another well-known firm of shipbuilders below bridge is the Thames Iron Works, whose extensive premises are at Canning Town, on the side of the River Lea. At Chiswick there are the large engineering and steam-launch building works of Thorneycroft & Co., equally famous with Searle & Sons, their old competitors on the Surrey shore.

The control of all Middlesex industries within a radius varying from three to ten or more miles from the metropolis lay, in former times, with the City authorities ultimately, and more directly with the companies controlling the various trades. This authority still exists in some industries—the goldsmiths and stationers, for example. But it fell generally into disuse towards the close of the 18th century.

SILK-WEAVING

The origin of this important industry as located in Spitalfields dates from the revocation of the Edict of Nantes by Louis XIV in 1685, when the French Protestants, driven by persecution from their own country, took refuge in England in large numbers. Long before this, however, silk-weavers from abroad had settled in England, and during the reign of Henry VIII a considerable number of silk-workers, principally from Rouen, made their homes in this country. During the reign of Elizabeth, French and Flemish refugees had crowded into England, but do not appear to have settled in Spitalfields and Bethnal Green,

which were at that time mere country hamlets.

A great body of the refugees of 1685 occupied a large district which is usually called Spitalfields, but which includes also large portions of Bethnal Green, Shoreditch, Whitechapel, and Mile End New Town. The great majority brought with them little beyond the knowledge of their occupations, and being in great necessity, subscriptions for their immediate relief were procured to a large amount by means of the King's Briefs. On 16 April 1687 an Order in Council prescribed a fresh general collection in England, Scotland, and Ireland. The amount thus obtained was about £200,000, which formed a fund known

---

[34] Cal. S.P. Dom. 1591–4, p. 480.
[35] Booth, Life and Labour of the People of London: Industries, i, 178.

[36] Daily Telegraph, 23 Aug. 1907.

as the Royal Bounty. A lay French committee composed of the chiefs of the immigration was entrusted with the annual distribution of a sum of £16,000 amongst the poor refugees and their descendants. A second committee composed of ecclesiastics under the direction of the Archbishop of Canterbury, the Bishop of London, and the Lord Chancellor, was formed for dividing amongst the distressed pastors and their churches an annual sum of £1,718 drawn from the public treasury.[1]

From the first report of the French committee, dated December 1687 and published in the following year, it appears that 13,050 French refugees were settled in London, the greater part of whom were probably located in Spitalfields. The editor of Stow's *Survey of London* pays a high tribute to the character and industry of the refugees. Speaking of Spitalfields he writes:[2] 'Here they have found quiet and security, and settled themselves in their several trades and occupations; weavers especially. Whereby God's blessing surely is not only brought upon the parish by receiving poor strangers, but also a great advantage hath accrued to the whole nation by the rich manufactures of weaving silks and stuffs and camlets, which art they brought along with them. And this benefit also to the neighbourhood, that these strangers may serve for patterns of thrift, honesty, industry, and sobriety as well.'

The principal source of information as to the Spitalfields weavers themselves is contained in the registers of the various Huguenot churches to which they belonged. A cluster of eleven of these congregations existed[3] from the latter part of the 17th century to the beginning of the 19th, in Spitalfields, Shoreditch, Petticoat Lane, and Wapping.

The registers of one of these churches, that known as 'La Patente,' which after various migrations settled in Brown's Lane near Spitalfields Market, have been printed by the Huguenot Society.[4] They extend from 1689 to 1786, when the congregation was merged in the London Walloon Church, and show that the French population of the district consisted very largely of silk weavers and their allied trades. A great preponderance of

weavers over those engaged in other trades is found in the settlements of foreign refugees; and the editor, Mr. William Minet,[5] suggests in explanation that the new religion may have spread specially among the men of this trade.

The strangers were skilled weavers from Lyons and Tours, who set up their looms in Spitalfields and there manufactured in large quantities lustrings, velvets, brocades, satins, very strong silks known as paduasoys, watered silks, black and coloured mantuas, ducapes, watered tabies, and stuffs of mingled silk and cotton—all of the highest excellence, which previously could only be procured from the famous looms of France. The refugees soon taught the people of Spitalfields to produce these and other goods of the finest quality for themselves, and their pupils soon equalled and even excelled their teachers. Weiss says[6] that the figured silks which proceeded from the London manufactories were due almost exclusively to the skill and industry of three refugees, Lauson, Mariscot, and Monceaux.

The artist who supplied the designs was another refugee named Beaudoin. A common workman named Mongeorge brought them the secret recently discovered at Lyons, of giving lustre to silk taffeta: this enabled Spitalfields to obtain a large share of the trade for which Lyons had long been famous. Up to that time large quantities of black lustrings specially made for English use, and known as English taffetas, had been annually imported from France. The manufacture of lustrings and alamode silks, then articles in general use, was rapidly brought by the Spitalfield weavers to a state of great excellence, and the persons engaged in this industry were, in 1692, incorporated by charter under the name of the Royal Lustring Company.[7] The company then procured the passing of an Act prohibiting the importation of foreign lustrings and alamodes, alleging as a ground for passing such a restriction in their favour that the manufacture of these articles in England had now reached a greater degree of perfection than was obtained by foreigners.

An anonymous writer in 1695,[8] who declaims against the tricks of stock-jobbers and the great number of joint-stock trading companies, makes exception in favour of (among other undertakings) the Royal Lustring Company, which he says has 'throve,

---

[1] For an exhaustive account of the sums raised for the relief of foreign Protestant refugees and the distribution of the amount, see an article by W. A. Shaw, in *Engl. Hist. Rev.* (1894), ix, 662–83.

[2] Stow, *Surv. of Lond.* bk. iv, 48.

[3] Burn, *Hist. Protestant Refugees in Engl.* (1846), 159–80.

[4] *Publications*, xi (1898).

[5] Ibid. p. xx.

[6] Charles Weiss, *Hist. of French Protestant Refugees* (1854), 253.

[7] G. R. Porter, 'Treatise on the Silk Manufacture,' *Lardner's Cab. Cycl.* (1831), 60–1.

[8] *Angliae Tutamen, or the safety of Engl.* 31.

and will so long as they keep the stock-jobbers from breaking in upon them.' In spite of its prohibition the importation of French goods still continued, and for its greater protection the company received a confirmation of their charter by Act of Parliament in 1698,[9] and an important extension of their powers and privileges. The sole right 'of making, dressing and lustrating of plain and black alamodes, renforcez, and lustrings' in England and Wales was granted to them for fourteen years. Before the expiration of its charter, however, a change in the public taste had set in, fabrics of a different texture had become fashionable, and the company lost all its money and was finally broken up.

The weavers in 1713[10] presented a petition to Parliament against the commercial treaty with France, in which they stated 'that by the encouragement of the Crown and of divers Acts of Parliament, the silk manufacture is come to be above twenty times as great as it was in the year 1664, and that all sorts of as good black and coloured silks, gold and silver stuffs and ribands, are now made here as in France. The black silk for hoods and scarfs, not made here above twenty-five years ago, hath amounted annually to above £300,000 for several years past, which before were imported from France. Which increase of the silk manufacture hath caused an increase of our exportation of woollen goods to Turkey, Italy &c.'

The silk industry received a great impetus from the exertions of Sir Thomas Lombe, who introduced from Italy the process of organzining (or preparing for the weaver) raw silk by machinery, for which he was granted a patent in 1718. When his patent ran out in 1732 he applied for a renewal on the grounds that it was owing to his ingenuity that silk was now 5s. a pound cheaper in England. Such outcry, however, was raised by the cotton manufacturers and others, who wished to use his apparatus, that Parliament refused the renewal, but voted him £14,000 as compensation.

In 1718 also a certain John Apletree conceived the notion of rendering England independent of importing Italian raw silk by a system of silkworm farming upon an extensive scale. A patent was granted him, and he issued a prospectus inviting the public to subscribe to the amount of a million pounds. A plantation of silkworms was actually made in Chelsea walled park. The apparatus included an evaporating stove and 'a certain

engine called the Egg Cheste.'[11] But the English climate not being suitable for silkworm farming, the experiment soon proved a complete failure.

The Spitalfields industry now advanced with great rapidity; but foreign competition, in spite of prohibitory legislation, continued to increase, and was much encouraged by the preference shown to French materials and fashions over those of native design. On the other hand, the tide of fashion in France set with at least equal strength in favour of English goods.[12]

The growing fashion for wearing Indian calicoes and printed linen was the cause of serious disturbances in 1719.[13] On 13 June a mob of about 4,000 Spitalfields weavers paraded the streets of the City attacking all females whom they could find wearing Indian calicoes or linens, and sousing them with ink, aqua fortis, and other fluids. The Lord Mayor obtained the assistance of the Trained Bands to suppress the rioters, two of whom were secured by the Horse Grenadiers and lodged in the Marshalsea Prison. As soon as the Guards left, the mob re-assembled, the weavers tearing all the calico gowns they could meet with. The troops were hurried back from Whitehall, and new arrests were made. The weavers then attempted to rescue their comrades, and were not deterred by volleys of blank cartridge fired by the soldiers; one of the troops then fired ball, wounding three persons. The next day four of the mob were committed to Newgate for rioting, and on Sunday night two more were sent there for felony in tearing the gown off the back of one Mrs. Beckett.[14]

In 1721 the manufacture of silk in England had increased in value to £700,000 more than formerly.[15] It is described as 'one of the most considerable branches of the manufactures of this kingdom' in an Act passed in the same year for the encouragement of this industry.[16] This Act granted on the exportation of wrought fabrics a drawback, or repayment of part of the duties exacted, on the importation of the raw material, which was practically equivalent to a bounty. The high duties on foreign silk led to smuggling on a most extensive scale. French writers estimate the average exportation of silks from France to England from 1688 to 1741 at about

[9] *Stat. of the Realm*, vii, 428.
[10] S. W. Beck, *Draper's Dict.* 309.

[11] H. D. Traill, *Social Engl.* v, 148–9; T. F. Croker, *Walk fr. Lond. to Fulham* (1860), 90–1.
[12] Porter, op. cit. 63.
[13] William C. Sydney, *Engl. and the English*, ii, 195.
[14] *Orig. Weekly Journ.* 20 June, 1719.
[15] C. King, *Brit. Merchant* (1721), ii, 220.
[16] Stat. 8 Geo. I, cap. 15.

12,500,000 francs or £500,000 a year in value.

In the rebellion of 1745 the silk manufacturers of Spitalfields were especially prominent in loyally supporting the throne; they waited personally upon the king and assured him of their unswerving loyalty and readiness to take up arms in his cause if need required. Each firm had endeavoured to induce their workpeople to give a like promise, and the total number of men which Spitalfields thus offered to furnish was 2,919. The address to King George [17] presented by Mr. Alderman Baker is followed by a list of the manufacturers' names, against each of which is placed the number of workmen 'who have been engaged by their masters to take up arms when called thereto by His Majesty in defence of his person and government,' amounting to 2,919 as above. The list includes eighty-four masters, the greater proportion of whom bear French names.

In 1763 attempts were made to check the prevalence of smuggling, and the silk mercers of the metropolis are said to have recalled their orders for foreign goods. It appears, however, from an inquiry made by a Committee of the Privy Council appointed in 1766 that smuggling was then carried on to a greater extent than ever, and that 7,072 looms were out of employment. Riots broke out in the beginning of October 1763, when several thousand journeymen assembled in Spitalfields and broke open the house of one of the masters. They destroyed his looms, cut to pieces much valuable silk, carried his effigy in a cart through the neighbourhood and afterwards burnt it, hung in chains from a gibbet.[18]

Although the English silks were now considered to be superior to those of foreign make, the latter found a ready market in England, and their importation caused great excitement among the weavers, who petitioned Parliament to impose double duties upon all foreign wrought silks. Their petition not being granted, the London weavers went to the House of Commons on 10 January 1764 'with drums beating and banners flying,' to demand the total prohibition of foreign silks.[19] This was the day of the opening of Parliament, and its members were besieged by the weavers with tales of the great distress which had fallen upon them and their families. Some relief was afforded by Parliament [20] by lowering the import duty on raw silk and prohibiting the importation of

silk ribbons, stockings, and gloves. The dealers in foreign silks also undertook to countermand all their orders for foreign silks, and a contribution was made for the immediate relief of the sufferers. By these means the weavers were for the time appeased, and the only violence committed was that of breaking the windows of some mercers who dealt in French silks.

The agitation was increased rather than suppressed by these concessions, and an Act was passed in 1765 [21] declaring it to be felony and punishable with death to break into any house or shop with intent maliciously to damage or destroy any silk goods in the process of manufacture. This was occasioned by an outbreak on 6 May when a mob of 5,000 weavers from Spitalfields [22] armed with bludgeons and pickaxes marched to the residence of one of the Cabinet Ministers in Bloomsbury Square, and having paraded their grievances marched away threatening to return if they did not receive speedy redress. Next day serious rioting began, and to the end of the month kept London in such a state of general alarm that the citizens were compelled to enrol themselves for military duty. 'Monday night,' says a contemporary newspaper,[23] 'the guards were doubled at Bedford House, and in each street leading thereto were placed six or seven of the Horse Guards, who continued till yesterday at ten with their swords drawn. A strong party of Albemarle's Dragoons took post in Tottenham Court Road, and patrols of them were sent off towards Islington and Marylebone, and the other environs on that side of the town; the Duke of Bedford's new road by Baltimore House was opened, when every hour a patrol came that way to and round Bloomsbury to see that all was well.' In 1767 [24] the 'culters,' as they were called, again became rioters, breaking into workshops, cutting the work off the looms, and dangerously wounding several who endeavoured to arrest their progress; similar outbreaks occurred in 1768 and 1769.

These outbreaks and those which soon afterwards followed were caused by the bitter disputes between the journeymen and master weavers on the subject of wages. Their differences gave rise to the famous 'Spitalfields Acts' of 1773, 1792, and 1811.[25] The first Act empowered the aldermen of London and the magistrates of Middlesex to settle in

[17] *Proc. Huguenot Soc.* ii, 453–6.
[18] *Gent. Mag.* xxxiii, 514–15.
[19] Knight, *Lond.* ii, 394; Porter, op. cit. 66–7.
[20] Stat. 5 Geo. III, cap. 29, 48.

[21] Porter, op. cit. 68.
[22] Sydney, *Engl. and the English,* ii, 197.
[23] *Lloyd's Evening Post,* 22 May 1765.
[24] Sydney, loc. cit.
[25] Knight, *Lond.* ii, 394–5.

quarter sessions the wages of journeymen silk weavers. Penalties were inflicted upon such masters as gave and upon such journeymen as received or demanded either more or less than should be thus settled by authority, and silk weavers were prohibited from having more than two apprentices at one time. The Act of 1792 included those weavers who worked upon silk mixed with other materials, and that of 1811 extended the provisions to female weavers. The 'Spitalfields Acts' continued in force until 1824 ;[26] and their effect can only be described as disastrous. They were passed to get rid of an evil, but they originated an evil of a different kind ; they were intended to protect both masters and men from unjust exactions on either part, but they only brought about a paralysis of the Spitalfields trade which would have ended in its utter ruin but for their repeal. But, as the effects of the Acts did not immediately manifest themselves, they were at first exceedingly popular. After 1785, however, the substitution of cottons in the place of silk gave a severe check to the manufacture, and the weavers then began to discover the real nature of the Spitalfields Acts. Being forbidden to work at reduced wages they were totally thrown out of employment, so that in 1793 upwards of 4,000 Spitalfields looms were quite idle. In 1798 the trade began to revive, and continued to extend slowly till 1815 and 1816, when the Spitalfields weavers were involved in sufferings far more extensive and severe than at any former period.[27] At a public meeting held at the Mansion House on 26 November 1816, for the relief of the Spitalfields weavers, the secretary stated that two-thirds of them were without employment and without the means of support, that 'some had deserted their houses in despair unable to endure the sight of their starving families, and many pined under languishing diseases brought on by the want of food and clothing.' At the same meeting Sir T. Fowell Buxton stated that the distress among the silk weavers was so intense that 'it partook of the nature of a pestilence which spreads its contagion around and devastates an entire district.'

The repeal of these Acts was largely brought about by a petition presented to the House of Commons on 9 May 1823. The petitioners stated [28] that 'these Acts by not permitting the masters to reward such of their workmen as exhibit superior skill and ingenuity, but compelling them to pay an equal price for all work whether well or ill performed, have materially retarded the progress of improvement and repressed industry and emulation.' In consequence of an order from the magistrates that silk made by machinery should be paid for at the same rate as that made by hand, few improvements could be introduced, and 'the London silk-loom with a trifling exception remains in the same state as at its original introduction into this country by the French refugees.' [29] On the effect of this important legislation McCulloch remarks : [30]

The monopoly which the manufacturers had hitherto enjoyed, though incomplete, had had sufficient influence to render inventions and discoveries of comparatively rare occurrence in the silk trade ; but the Spitalfields Act extinguished every germ of improvement. Parliament in its wisdom having seen fit to enact that a manufacturer should be obliged to pay as much for work done by the best machinery as if it were done by hand, it would have been folly to have thought of attempting anything new. It is not, however, to be denied that Macclesfield, Norwich, Manchester, Paisley, &c., are under obligations to this Act. Had it extended to the whole kingdom it would have totally extirpated the manufacture ; but being confined to Middlesex it gradually drove the most valuable branches from Spitalfields to places where the rate of wages was determined by the competition of the parties, on the principle of mutual interest and compromised advantage.

During the continuance of the Acts there was in the Spitalfields district no medium between the full regulation prices and the total absence of employment, and the repeal of this restrictive legislation gave immediate relief to the local industry. The introduction at this time of the loom invented by Jacquard,[31] a straw-hat manufacturer at Lyons, for the manufacture of figured silks, largely helped to restore the falling fortune of the Spitalfields trade. The elaborate brocades which were previously made at Spitalfields [32] were produced only by the most skilful among the craft, who bestowed upon them an immense amount of labour. The most beautiful products of the Jacquard loom are executed by workmen possessing only the ordinary amount of skill, whilst the labour attendant upon the actual weaving is but little more than that required for making the plainest goods. In 1846 the figure weavers of Spitalfields engaged in the production, by the aid of a Jacquard loom, of a piece of silk which was to surpass everything hitherto made in England, and to rival a masterpiece of the Lyons weavers pro-

[26] Repealed by 5 Geo. IV, cap. 66.
[27] McCulloch, *Dict. of Commerce* (1882), 1279.
[28] Knight, op. cit. ii, 395.

[29] Porter, op. cit. 78.
[30] *Dict. of Commerce* (1882), 1279.
[31] Thos. R. Ashenhurst, *Weaving* (1893), 61.
[32] Porter, op. cit. 245.

duced in the previous year. The subject of the design was partly allegorical, introducing Neptune, Mars, Time, Honour, and Harmony, with medallion portraits of English naval and military heroes, and figures of Queen Victoria and Prince Albert.[33]

In the evidence taken before a committee of the House of Commons on the silk trade in 1831–2 it was stated that the population of the districts in which the Spitalfields weavers resided could not be less at that time than 100,000, of whom 50,000 were entirely dependent on the silk manufacture, and the remaining moiety more or less dependent indirectly. The number of looms at this period[34] varied from 14,000 to 17,000 (including 100 Jacquard looms), and of these about 4,000 to 5,000 were generally unemployed in times of depression. As there were on an average, children included, about thrice as many operatives as looms, it is clear that during stagnation of trade not less than from 10,000 to 15,000 persons would be reduced to a state of non-employment and destitution.[35] An excellent account of the condition of the silk trade, written in 1868, will be found in *Once a Week*.[36] From the census of 1901 it appears that the number of silk weavers in the various processes of the trade in the entire county of London reached only 548, of whom 48 were employers. The relations between the employer and the operative deserve a passing notice. The manufacturer procures his thrown 'organzine' and 'tram' either from the throwster or from the silk importers, and selects the silk necessary to execute any particular order. The weaver goes to the house or shop of his employer and receives a sufficient quantity of the material, which he takes home to his own dwelling and weaves at his own looms or sometimes at looms supplied by the manufacturer, being paid at a certain rate per ell. In a report to the Poor Law Commissioners in 1837 Dr. Kay thus describes the methods of work of a weaver and his family :—

A weaver has generally two looms, one for his wife and another for himself, and as his family increases the children are set to work at six or seven years of age to quill silk ; at nine or ten years to pick silk ; and at the age of twelve or thirteen (according to the size of the child) he is put to the loom to weave. A child very soon learns to weave a plain silk fabric, so as to become a proficient in that branch ; a weaver has thus not unfrequently four looms on which members of his own family are employed. On a Jacquard loom a weaver can earn 25*s*. a week on an average[37] ; on a velvet or rich plain silk-loom from 16*s*. to 20*s*. per week ; and on a plain silk-loom from 12*s*. to 14*s*. ; excepting when the silk is bad and requires much cleaning, when his earnings are reduced to 10*s*. per week ; and on one or two very inferior fabrics 8*s*. a week only are sometimes earned, though the earnings are reported to be seldom so low on these coarse fabrics. On the occurrence of a commercial crisis the loss of work occurs first among the least skilful operatives, who are discharged from work.

Porter in his *Treatise on the Silk Manufacture* gives a pleasing picture of the home life of a Spitalfields weaver and of his happy and prosperous condition ; but a writer in Knight's *London*[38] paints in much more sober colours the condition of a weaver and his family.[39] Each account is taken from personal observation, and the difference is probably to be explained by the state of trade at the time of the visit, and the class of workman visited. The houses occupied by the weavers are constructed for the special convenience of their trade, having in the upper stories wide, lattice-like windows which run across almost the whole frontage of the house. These 'lights' are absolutely necessary in order to throw a strong light on every part of the looms, which are usually placed directly under them. Many of the roofs present a strange appearance, having ingenious bird-traps of various kinds and large bird cages, the weavers having long been famed for their skill in snaring song-birds. They used largely to supply the home market with linnets, goldfinches, chaffinches, greenfinches, and other song birds which they caught by trained 'call-birds' and other devices in the fields of north and east London. The treaty with France in 1860 which allowed French silks to come in duty free, found Great Britain and Ireland unable to compete with France, and in a short time the trade dwindled immensely with disastrous results to Spitalfields and other centres.

The progress of the decay of the Spitalfields silk trade from 1860 onwards and the recent attempted revival of its silk brocade industry are well treated in an interesting article by Lasenby Liberty contributed in 1893 to the *Studio* on 'Spitalfields Brocades.'[40]

---

[33] *Penny Mag.* (1841), x, 478.
[34] Badnall, *A View of the Silk Trade* (1828), 93.
[35] Hogg, *Weekly Instructor*, 1854 (new ser.), ii, 38.
[36] Vol. xviii, 228, 250, 276.

[37] For the best kind of work weavers have been paid as much as 15*s*. a day. Knight, *Lond.* ii, 396 note. See also *Eclectic Mag.* 1851, xxiii, 268.
[38] Vol. ii, 397.
[39] See also for the darker side of the picture, Dr. Hector Gavin, *Sanitary Ramblings* (1848), 42 ; Hogg, *Instructor* (Ser. 2), ii, 96.
[40] *Studio*, i, 20–4.

TAPESTRY

Both Henry VIII and Elizabeth kept a staff of tapestry workers or arras-makers, of which the chief members were usually of foreign birth.[1] Amongst the adherents of the Dutch Church in 1550 were Hendryck Moreels, 'tapitsier,' and Roelandt de Mets, living in St. Martin's-le-Grand, and the first of these is probably the 'Henrhicus Moreels[2] tapestarius in opere Reginae' of a return of 1561. Another of the queen's workers at this time was John Celot, and the names of several other tapestry-makers are to be found in later returns of the reign of Elizabeth, living for the most part within the limits of the City of London.

A small tapestry manufactory was set up at Fulham by some Walloon refugees at the end of the 17th century. The parish register of burials[3] records the name of 'William King, Clarke at the Manufactori' in 1699, and that of 'Richard fflower, a weaver, from the Manufactori' in 1700.

Early in the next century another attempt was made to introduce the manufacture of tapestry into Middlesex. James Christopher Le Blon, a Fleming by birth and a mezzotint engraver by profession, some time subsequently to 1732 'set up a project for copying cartoons in tapestry, and made some very fine drawings for that purpose. Houses were built and looms erected in the Mulberry-ground at Chelsea (see p. 134 ante), but either the expense was precipitated too fast or contributions did not arrive fast enough', and the enterprise proved a failure.[4] Le Blon is said to have died in a hospital at Paris in 1740.

A more noted manufactory for weaving carpets and tapestries was started by Peter Parisot, a Frenchman domiciled in England, in 1753. Parisot's undertaking is described by himself in a scarce little book entitled *An account of the new manufacture of Tapestry after the manner of that at the Gobelins ; and of Carpets after the manner of that at Chaillot &c. now undertaken at Fulham, by Mr. Peter Parisot*, 1753.

Parisot had engaged some workmen from Chaillot whom at first he employed at Paddington, but afterwards removed to Fulham, where this manufacture had already been established. Here he procured spacious accommodation for his business and for instructing young persons of both sexes in the arts of drawing, weaving, dyeing, and other branches of the work. In his book Parisot speaks of the patronage of the Duke of Cumberland, who gave him great financial help ; other members of the Royal family, including the Princess Dowager of Wales, also supported the work.[5] His goods however were too expensive, and the manufacture soon declined. George Bubb Dodington the diarist, who lived at Fulham, records a visit he paid to this factory on 8th March 1753 :—'We went to see the manufacture of tapestry from France, now set up at Fulham by the Duke. The work both of the gobelins and of chaillot, called savonnerie, is very fine, but very dear.'[6]

According to Giuseppe Baretti, Parisot was a renegade priest, once a noted Capuchin, whose real name was Père Norbert, and his failure was due to his own shortcomings as a spendthrift.[7] Within three years of its establishment the Fulham manufactory, which was chiefly devoted to the production of velvet pile carpets, had to close its doors. Parisot left Fulham for Exeter in 1753, and on 12 January 1756 his whole stock was sold off. The highest price reached at the sale was £64 1s., given for 'a magnificent large carpet 18 ft. by 13 ft. of a most elegant and beautiful design'. A catalogue of the collection consisting of four small pages (the only known copy) is in the British Museum.

The various items mentioned in this catalogue[8] show clearly the nature of Parisot's business. Amongst the fire-screens after the manner of the Gobelins one bore a representation of a 'landscape with two doves billing,' another a 'Chinese pheasant with a green parrot and a butterfly,' and others, such fables as 'the Monkey and the Cat', 'the Fox and the Crane' and 'the Bear and the Bees.' Amongst the stock also were chairs similarly adorned ; one 'large seat for a chair, depicting in the background a range of hills at a distant view, and a fountain in the middle ; the border of which is ornamented with flowers.' Cotton-work after the manner of the manu-

---

[1] W. Page, *Denizations and Naturalizations* (Huguenot Soc.), p. l.
[2] Kirk, *Returns of Aliens* (Huguenot Soc.), i, 205 et seq. and 274.
[3] C. J. Feret, *Fulham Old and New* (1900), 85.
[4] Walpole, *Cat. of Engravers* (1794), 178

[5] Lysons, *Environs of Lond.* (1795), ii, 400 ; *Gent. Mag.* 1754, p. 385.
[6] Dodington, *Diary* (4th ed. 1809), 199.
[7] Feret, op. cit. 87–8.
[8] Brit. Mus. pressmark, $\frac{7805.e.89}{55}$

factory at Rouen in imitation of needlework was represented by large pieces with birds and flowers. Besides these there were also fire-screens, chairs, and velvet carpets after the manner of the velvet manufactory of Chaillot with similar designs. Three of the carpets had been worked by Parisot's apprentices, 'natives of England,' as a note on the catalogue informs us.

Another 17th-century factory of which no information appears to exist was set up in Soho Fields, the site of Soho Square.[9]

CABINET-MAKING AND WOOD-CARVING

Horace Walpole mentions among the artists in woodwork of the Tudor period Lawrence Truber, a carver, and Humphrey Cooke, master carpenter of the new buildings at the Savoy.[1] Another workman in this art is met with in the reign of Henry VIII, one William Grene the king's coffer maker,[2] who received £6 18s. 'for making of a coffer covered with fustyan of Naples, and being full of drawers and boxes lined with red and grene sarcynet to put in stones of divers sorts'. There is ample evidence that many foreign wood-carvers and cabinet-makers were working in London in the 16th century. In 1540 foreign joiners[3] are found in East Smithfield. Ten years later the roll of the Dutch Church[4] records a large number of Flemish 'schryn-makers' and 'kistmakers' living in the City, Southwark, and St. Giles. In 1567 in the Ward of Bridge Without[5] alone there were at least twenty-four foreign joiners and carpenters, and many later instances might be cited. Indeed in 1582–3 so serious had become the competition of the strangers that the Joiners' Company returned a list of 100 foreigners exercising this craft, and declared[6] :

The Master and Wardens of the Companye of Joyners never licensed nor admitted any of the persons hereunder expressed to use their said trade, yett they, dwelling somme in Westminster, somme in Sainct Katherins, and somme in Sowthworke, do use the sayd occupacion, and have joyned themselves togeather and have sued the joyners these tenne yeres in the lawe and procured to be spent above £400 only to thend to worck in London as fullye as a freeman may doe, to the utter undoing of a great number of freemen joyners, mere Englishemen, who are all sowayes [sic] ready for any service for her Majestie, this Realme and Citie of London.

The greatest master of the school of Eng-lish wood-carving was Grinling Gibbons, who flourished in the latter part of the 17th and in the early 18th century. He was of English parentage but born in Holland, and was brought by Evelyn under the notice of Charles II, who gave him an appointment in the Board of Works. He afterwards lived in Belle Sauvage Court, Ludgate Hill. Here he carved so delicately a pot of flowers for his window sill, that the leaves shook with the vibration caused by the coaches as they rumbled through the yard. His finest work is at Petworth House, Sussex, but the choir stalls at St. Paul's Cathedral afford an excellent example of his style. He died on 3 August 1721 at his house in Bow Street, Covent Garden. His followers built up a school of architectural carvers whose beautiful work abounds in old London buildings, such as the court-room at Stationers' Hall, the vestry of the church of St. Lawrence Jewry, &c., the traditions of which continued down to the last century.

With the reign of William and Mary marquetry furniture became the fashion in the form of bandy-legged chairs, secrétaires or bureaux, long clock-cases, &c., that afforded surfaces available for such decoration. This art had not previously been practised in England, specimens being procured by importation chiefly from Italy. The leaves and other figures composing the pattern were cut out of dyed woods, shading being given by means of hot sand.[7] George Ethrington was a London maker of this work about the year 1665.[8] Many London cabinet-makers subsequently engaged in this manufacture, and a national style was developed. Another style of decoration known as Boule (from its inventor André Charles Boule, born in 1642) shared with marquetry the favour of the public. This was a kind of veneered work usually composed of tortoiseshell and thin brass. Sir William Chambers, the celebrated architect (1725–96), published a book of designs of Chinese furniture, dresses, &c., in 1757, and largely employed the best artists in wood-carving for the decoration of his interiors. John Wilton, one

[9] J. H. Pollen, *Anct. and Modern Furniture in the South Kensington Museum* (1874), Introd. cxxxix.
[1] *Works* (1798), iii, 87.
[2] N. H. Nicolas, *Privy Purse Exp. of Hen. VIII*, index, s.v. 'coffer', p. 311.
[3] Kirk, *Returns of Aliens*, i, 22 et seq.
[4] Ibid. i, 202 et seq. [5] Ibid. i, 342 et seq.
[6] Ibid. ii, 312.

[7] Tomlinson, *Cycl.* (1866), ii, 133.
[8] F. J. Britten, *Old Clocks*, 320.

of his *protégés*, was born in London in 1722, and studied abroad for many years, returning to England in 1757 with Sir William Chambers. He was employed in designing carriage and furniture decorations, and painted the royal state coach now in use. John Baptist Cipriani and Angelica Kauffman, painters of the same period, did much decorative work for Chambers, Adam, Chippendale, and other furniture designers ; Cipriani decorated Carlton House.

Thomas Chippendale, the son and father of furniture makers, exercised the same trade in London in the latter half of the 18th century. He published in 1758–9 a book of designs of furniture of every kind.[9] He used mahogany as a material instead of oak, and brought that wood into general use. His designs are distinguished for their fine architectural mouldings, and his workmanship is admirable. In his gilt-work he is specially celebrated for his frames, which are in the French style, and cut with great freedom and delicacy. He also designed Chinese scenes in his gilt-work, following the taste introduced by Sir William Chambers. Another of his published works was intituled *The Gentleman and Cabinet-maker's Director*, a collection of designs of household furniture ; of this a third edition appeared in 1762.

Matthew Lock, a London carver and gilder, with whom was associated a cabinet-maker named H. Copeland, published a book of furniture designs, undated, but probably of the year 1743.[10] At the exhibition of 1862 a collection of his original drawings and those of Chippendale was shown. The accompanying notes gave the names of his workmen, their wages, &c., in 1743, from which it appears that 5s. a day was the sum earned by a wood-carver at that time. Lock belonged to and left behind him a talented school of wood-carvers.

The brothers Robert and James Adam are known to fame chiefly as architects who greatly improved street architecture in London, and as architects to King George III. Having obtained from the Duke of St. Albans' estate a lease for 100 years of Durham Yard, they built the terrace known as the Adelphi on ground largely reclaimed from the Thames. Robert and James Adam rank also as the most important designers of furniture of their day, adapting a suitable and harmonious system of decoration to the houses which they built.

An explanation of the general principles which they adopted is afforded by the published plates of Derby House, Grosvenor Square, now destroyed. The brothers Adam designed fireplaces, steel grate fronts, sideboards, and other articles of furniture, which are much sought after at the present day by those who follow the prevailing fancy for antique furniture. Robert Adam published, in 1773, a volume of illustrations of the buildings, room decoration, furniture, &c., designed by him, which was reprinted in 1823. A. Heppelwhite, a cabinet-maker of this period, trading with his assistants as Heppelwhite & Co., published in 1789 a complete set of designs for all sorts of reception-room and bedroom furniture. These mahogany chairs, library tables, desks and bureaux, continued in fashion during the early years of the next century, as did also the lighter objects in satinwood painted with various decorations.

The work of Thomas Sheraton, another cabinet-maker, is still in high repute for its admirable workmanship, which unites lightness and strength. The specimens of his work seem to resist the ravages of time, being made of wood well-seasoned and admirably put together. Sheraton was the author of a complete dictionary of his trade,[11] and of a *Cabinet-maker's Drawing-book*.[12]

Throughout the 18th century the work of upholsterers in England was much influenced by the designs of the brothers Adam, Chippendale, Sheraton, and Pergolesi. They evince regard for general utility and comfort, combined with skill and delicacy in design and sound workmanship.

Mr. J. Hungerford Pollen, in his *Ancient and Modern Furniture in the South Kensington Museum*,[13] says: 'Only the most meagre notices are to be found of the artists to whom we owe the designs of modern furniture . . . of the furniture makers who attained such eminence during the last [18th] century very little is known.' A principal reason for this is to be found in the fact that for a hundred and fifty years after the Renaissance furniture design was so closely associated with architecture that it almost ceased to exist as a separate art. The woodwork of rooms and the character of their furniture followed the style of architecture employed for the building ; the ornamental chimney-pieces, &c., were mostly designed by the architects themselves, and fashioned by excellent artist workmen of whom no record has been preserved.

---

[9] Chippendale, *Ornaments and interior decorations in the old French style.*

[10] *Collection of ornamental designs applicable to the decoration of rooms in the style of Louis XIV.* Another book by Lock, *A book of ornaments, drawn and engraved by M. L.*, was republished by John Weale in 1858–9.

[11] *The Cabinet Dictionary* (1803).

[12] Published in 1793–4.

[13] 1874, Introd. p. ccxviii.

During the last century inspiration was obtained from many eminent artists, of whom it is unnecessary to mention more than A. W. Pugin, H. Shaw, Owen Jones, William Morris, William Burges, and C. L. Eastlake. Among the firms which have honestly endeavoured to lead and improve public taste in furniture and have gained a high reputation for the quality of their work are Gillow's, Jeffrey, Jackson & Graham, Crace, Shoolbred, and Trollope & Sons. The list might be considerably increased.

With regard to the system of production, valuable information is afforded in Charles Booth's *Life and Labour of the People in London.*[14] The districts comprise Shoreditch, Bethnal Green, Hackney, and the Tower Hamlets. The Curtain Road district in Shoreditch is the chief market of the trade and the centre of its distribution. 'From the East-end workshops,' says Mr. Booth, 'produce goes out of every description, from the richly inlaid cabinet that may be sold for £100 or the carved chair that can be made to pass as rare " antique " workmanship, down to the gypsy tables that the maker sells for 9s. a dozen or the cheap bedroom suites and duchesse tables that are now flooding the market.'[15]

The producers fall into four main groups. The first class, that of the factories, forms but an insignificant portion of the trade, there being not more than three or four large factories with elaborate machinery, where from about 50 to 190 men are employed. They supply the large dealers in the Tottenham Court Road, in the provinces, or in the colonies. The second class, that of the larger workshops, comprises shops in which from 15 to 25 men are generally employed. Here the best East-end furniture is made, but the number of first-class shops is very small, many good firms having been obliged to give up altogether in recent years through the prevailing demand for cheapness. In the third class are the small makers, masters who employ from 4 to 8 men in small workshops, either built behind the house or away from it, sometimes even in the houses themselves. 'As a general rule the larger shops turn out the better work. But even among the small men excellent work is done, in the same way that large shops often turn out cheap and inferior goods.'[16] These small men sell at the nearest market, that is, the Curtain Road and its district; here they can be sure of getting cash, whilst the West-end shops and the provincial trade take credit, which the small maker can rarely afford to give. In a fourth class are the independent workers. These are mostly found among the turners, carvers, fret-cutters, and sawyers, and are not a large class. Other special classes described by Mr. Booth are chair makers, looking-glass frame makers, carvers, french polishers, and upholsterers.

POTTERY

The most famous of Middlesex industries is certainly its pottery, but few traces can be found of any local manufacture before the 17th century. Down to the latter half of that century English home-made pottery was of a very rude kind, and consisted chiefly of common domestic vessels,[1] such as large coarse dishes, tygs, pitchers, bowls, cups, and other similar articles. Vessels of stoneware of greater durability and more artistic workmanship were imported from abroad. Among these were the bellarmines or grey-beards and ale-pots, which were largely imported from Germany and Flanders.

In 1570 two potters,[2] named Jasper Andries and Jacob Janson, who had settled in Norwich in 1567, 'removed to London, and in a petition to Queen Elizabeth asserted that they were the first that brought in and exercised the said science in this realm, and were at great charges before they could find materials in this realm. They besought her, in recompense of their great cost and charges, that she would grant them house room in or without the liberties of London by the water side.' A similar petition was preferred to the queen by one William Simpson,[3] who also asked for the sole licence to import stone pots from Cologne. Patents were granted in 1626 to Thomas Rous (or Ruis) and Abraham Cullyn of London,[4] merchants, and in 1636 to David Ramsey, esq. for making stone pots, but nothing is known of any use which they made of the privileges granted to them.

---

[14] (1902) Ser. 1, iv, 157 et seq.
[15] Ibid. 163.
[16] Ibid. 174.
[1] Llewellyn Jewitt, *Ceramic Art* (1878), i, 89.
[2] Stow, *Surv. of Lond.* bk. v, 240-1.
[3] Lansd. MS. 108, fol. 60; Jewitt, op. cit. i, 90.
[4] *Cal. S.P. Dom.* 1625-6, p. 575.

FULHAM STONEWARE

It was not until the beginning of the reign of Charles II that the secret of this manufacture was discovered in England, and the credit of the discovery belongs to John Dwight of Fulham. Dr. Plot, writing in 1677,[5] says :

The ingenious John Dwight, formerly M.A. of Christ Church College, Oxon., hath discovered the mystery of the Stone or Cologne wares (such as D'Alva bottles, jugs, noggins) heretofore made only in Germany, and by the Dutch brought over into England in great quantities, and hath set up a manufacture of the same, which (by methods and contrivances of his own, altogether unlike those used by the Germans) in three or four years' time he hath brought it to a greater perfection than it has attained where it hath been used for many ages, insomuch that the Company of Glass-Sellers, London, who are the dealers for that commodity, have contracted with the inventor to buy only of his English manufacture, and refuse the foreign.

Dwight, who is said to have been a native of Oxfordshire, took his Oxford degree of B.C.L. in 1661, and afterwards became secretary to Bryan Walton, Bishop of Chester, and his episcopal successors Henry Ferne and Joseph Hall. After a long series of trials and experiments upon the properties of clays and mineral products as materials for porcelain and stoneware, he obtained, in April 1671, a patent for his discoveries.[6] In his petition he claimed to have 'discovered[7] the mistery of transparent earthenware comonly knowne by the name of porcelaine or China and Persian ware, as alsoe the misterie of the Stone ware vulgarly called Cologne ware.' As regards his first claim, Professor Church[8] admits that Dwight 'did make some approach to success in producing a body which if not porcelain is distinctly porcellanous.'

Dwight's experiments and researches into the properties of various clays and their proper treatment for the production of china ware must have extended over a considerable number of years before he took the patent for his 'discovery' in 1671. An interesting confirmation of his claim occurs in a periodical work, entitled *A Collection for the Improvement of Husbandry and Trade*, by a contemporary writer, John Houghton, who was a Fellow of the Royal Society.[9] He is speaking (12 January 1693–4) of the tobacco-pipe clays, 'gotten at or nigh Pool, a port town in Dorsetshire, and there dug in square pieces, of the bigness of about half a hundredweight each ; from thence

'tis brought to London, and sold in peaceable times at about eighteen shillings a ton, but now in this time of war is worth about three-and-twenty shillings.' He proceeds : 'This sort of clay, as I hinted formerly, is used to clay sugar and the best sort of mugs are made with it, and the ingenious Mr. Dwight of Fulham tells me that 'tis the same earth China-ware is made of, and 'tis made not by lying long in the earth but in the fire ; and if it were worth while, we may make as good China here as any is in the world. And so for this time farewell clay.' In another letter,[10] dated 13 March 1695–6, he writes :—

Of China-ware I see but little imported in the year 1694, I presume by reason of the war and our bad luck at sea. There came only from Spain certain, and from India certain twice. 'Tis a curious manufacture and deserves to be encourag'd here, which without doubt money would do, and Mr. Dwoit of Fulham has done it, and can again in anything that is flat. But the difficulty is that if a hollow dish be made, it must be burnt so much, that the heat of the fire will make the sides fall. He tells me that our clay will very well do it, the main skill is in managing the fire. By my consent, the man that would bring it to perfection should have for his encouragement 1,000*l.* from the Publick, tho' I help'd to pay a tax towards it.

Dwight's discovery seems to have stopped short at the practical point, the time and expense involved in the manufacture proving totally unremunerative. Mr. L. M. Solon,[11] however, after a careful analysis of all the evidence, including the recipes and memoranda contained in two little books in Dwight's own hand, concludes that he got no further than making transparent specimens of his stoneware by casting it thin and firing it hard.

His claim to the discovery of the composition of stoneware is beyond question. Dwight's stoneware vessels were equal if not superior to those imported from Germany, and very soon superseded them. A list of his wares is given in the specification of his second patent granted in 1684 for a further term of fourteen years. This description is as follows:—
'Severall new manufactures of earthenwares called by the names of white gorges, marbled porcellane vessels, statues, and figures, and fine stone gorges and vessells, never before made in England or elsewhere.'

Mr. Solon, in his work above quoted,[12] pays the following high tribute to Dwight's skill and genius :—'To him must be attributed the foundation of an important industry;

[5] *Nat. Hist. Oxon.* (2nd ed. 1705), 255.
[6] *Cal. S.P. Dom.* 1671–2, p. 420.   [7] Ibid. 335.
[8] *Engl. Earthenware* (1904), 44.
[9] Houghton, op. cit. iv, no. 76.

[10] Ibid. viii, no. 189.
[11] *The Art of the Old English Potter* (ed. 2, 1885), 32–5.   [12] Ibid. 31.

by his unremitting researches and their practical application, he not only found the means of supplying in large quantities the daily wants of the people with an article superior to anything that had ever been known before, but besides, by the exercise of his refined taste and uncommon skill, he raised his craft to a high level; nothing among the masterpieces of ceramic art of all other countries can excel the beauty of Dwight's brown stone-ware figures, either of design, modelling, or fineness of material.'

Very little is known of Dwight's personal history; the facts are few and somewhat obscure. Professor Church [13] conjectures 1637 or 1638 as the year of his birth, and states that his eldest child John was born at Chester in 1662. In the patent which he obtained in 1671 Dwight states that he has set up at Fulham a manufactory, but in 1683 when his son George matriculated at Oxford he is described as ' of the city of Chester.' The year following, his second patent describes him as a manufacturer at Fulham, whilst in 1687 and 1689 in the matriculation entries of his sons Samuel and Philip he is styled John Dwight of Wigan. It is not till the matriculation of his son Edmund in 1692 that the university register gives his address as Fulham. Professor Church [14] states that this child was born at Fulham in 1676. He also says that ' until 1665 Dwight lived at Chester, but before the end of 1668 he moved to Wigan; some time between March 1671 and August 1676 he settled at Fulham.'

This does not, however, agree with the statements in the matriculation registers. A more probable explanation is that Dwight opened his factory at Fulham before he left Chester and carried it on whilst still living there and at Wigan. He may have had friends or relatives in Middlesex, as a family of that name was living at Sudbury near Harrow in 1637. Lysons states [15] that Mr. William Dwight in that year gave 40s. per annum out of his lands at Sudbury to the poor of Harrow. John Dwight died [16] at Fulham in 1703, and was buried there on 13 October. His widow Lydia was buried at Fulham on 3 November 1709.

Dwight had the habit of hiding money, and left memoranda in his note-books of places, such as holes in the fireplace, holes in the furnace, &c., where packets of guineas were concealed. He also buried specimens of his stoneware which were found during some excava-

tions for new buildings at the Fulham factory in a vaulted chamber or cellar which had been firmly walled up. The objects thus discovered were chiefly bellarmines and ale-jugs, identical in form with those imported from Cologne. Another authentic collection of examples from the Fulham works, which had been kept by the family, was sold to Mr. Baylis of Prior's Bank about the year 1862. These pieces were shortly afterwards disposed of to Mr. C. W. Reynolds, and finally dispersed by auction at Christie's in 1871.

The two collections have afforded valuable criteria for assigning to the Fulham factory specimens of stoneware about which collectors previously were in considerable doubt. The Baylis-Reynolds collection also revealed the high artistic merit of Dwight's pottery, the variety of his productions, and the great perfection to which he had brought the potter's art, both in the manipulation and in the employment of enamel colours for decoration. The collection contained twenty-eight specimens which had been carefully preserved by members of the Dwight family, and kept as heirlooms from the time of their manufacture. The most interesting piece, and probably the earliest in date, is a beautiful half-length figure in hard stoneware of the artist's little daughter, inscribed 'Lydia Dwight, dyd March the 3rd, 1762.' The child lies upon a pillow with eyes closed, her hands clasping to her breast a bouquet of flowers, and a broad lace band over her forehead. The figure, evidently modelled after death, exhibits, as Mr. Solon well remarks, 'the loving care of a bereaved father in the reproduction of the features and the minute perfection with which the accessories, such as flowers and lace, are treated.' This beautiful work was purchased for £150 at the Reynolds sale, and is now in the Victoria and Albert Museum. Another figure, also at South Kensington, was bought at the Reynolds sale for £30, and is believed to represent Lydia Dwight; she is figured standing, wrapped in a shroud, with a skull at her feet. The fine life-size statue of Prince Rupert, now in the British Museum, was bought at the Reynolds sale for thirty-eight guineas, and is a magnificent specimen of modelling. The ' Meleager,' also in the British Museum, and the ' Jupiter' in the Liverpool Museum, are declared by Mr. Solon to be worthy of an Italian artist of the Renaissance. Other specimens in the collection [17] were a life-size bust of Charles II, smaller busts of Charles II

[13] A. H. Church, op. cit. 46.   [14] Ibid. 44.
[15] *Environs of Lond.* (1795), ii, 582–3.
[16] Church, op. cit. 47.

[17] An account of his collection before its purchase by Mr. Reynolds was contributed by Mr. Baylis to the *Art Journ.* Oct. 1862, p. 204.

and Catherine of Braganza, others of James II and his queen Mary, full-length figures of Flora and Minerva, a sportsman in the costume of the reign of Charles II, a girl holding flowers with two lambs by her side, and five stoneware statuettes (in imitation of bronze) of Jupiter, Mars, Neptune, Meleager, and Saturn. Speaking of the above collection of pieces, Mr. Burton remarks [18]:—'It is still more remarkable to find a series of figures displaying such finished modelling, perfect proportion, and breadth of treatment. Finer artistic work than this, in clay, has never been produced in this country, and the knowledge, taste, and skill shown in their production fully entitle Dwight to be reckoned among the great potters of Europe.'

The characteristics of Dwight's pottery have been described as follows [19] :—

The Fulham stone-ware, in imitation of that of Cologne, is of exceedingly hard and close texture, very compact and sonorous and usually of a grey colour, ornamented with a brilliant blue enamel, in bands, leaves, and flowers. The stalks have frequently four or more lines running parallel, as though drawn with a flat notched stick on the moist clay ; the flowers, as well as the outlines, are raised, and painted a purple or marone colour, sometimes with small ornaments of flowers and cherubs' heads, and medallions of kings and queens of England in front, with Latin names and titles, and initials of Charles II, William III, William and Mary, Anne, and George I. The forms are mugs, jugs, butterpots, cylindrical or barrel-shaped, &c. ; the jugs are spherical, with straight narrow necks, frequently mounted in pewter, and raised medallions in front with the letters CR WR AR GR, &c. These were in very common use, and superseded the Bellarmines and longbeards of Cologne manufacture.

The quality of hardness which distinguishes stoneware from other kinds of pottery is imparted to it, says Professor Church, [20] partly by the nature and proportions of the materials used in making the body or paste, partly by the temperature at which it is fired. The salt-glaze employed for European stoneware is formed on the ware itself and in part out of its constituents. It is produced by throwing into the kiln moist common salt towards the end of the firing when the pieces have acquired a very high temperature. The salt is volatilized, and reacting with the water-vapour present is decomposed into hydro-chloric acid gas, which escapes, and into soda, which attacking and combining with the silica of the clay in the body, forms with it a hard glass or glaze of silicate of soda, in which a little alumina is also always present. This was the two-fold secret which Dwight at length succeeded in discovering. His note-books [21] contain many curious recipes for the composition of his various pastes or 'cleys' which were the results of his numerous and laborious experiments. Large extracts from these memoranda have been published. [22] There is a tradition in the family [23] that besides concealing the vessels found in the bricked-up chamber, Dwight buried all his models, tools, and moulds connected with the finer branches of his manufactory in some secret place on the premises at Fulham, observing that the production of such matters was expensive and unremunerative ; and that his successors might not be tempted to perpetuate this part of the business he put it out of their power by concealing the means. Search has often been made for these hidden treasures, but hitherto without success.

For a long time after Dwight's death his descendants continued to manufacture the same sort of jugs and mugs. In a private collection there is a flip-can of historical interest, which once belonged to the original of Defoe's Robinson Crusoe. It is inscribed 'Alexander Silkirke. This is my one. When you take me on bord of ship, Pray fill me full of punch or flipp, Fulham.' It is said to have been made for Selkirk in or about 1703. In cottages along the Thames bank have been found many large tankards with the names of well-known public houses. Some of the jugs have hunting scenes and others bear decorations of a loyal or political character. For example, a mug with a medallion portrait of Queen Anne, supported by two beefeaters, is inscribed round the top, 'Drink to the pious memory of good Queen Anne, 1729.'

John Dwight had five sons, but it is not known whether all of them survived him or which was his successor in business. Some writers say he was succeeded by his son Dr. Samuel Dwight, who died in November 1737 ; the *Gentleman's Magazine*, [24] in his

---

[18] W. Burton, *Hist. of Engl. Earthenware* (1904), 43.

[19] W. Chaffers, *Marks and Monograms on Pottery and Porcelain* (ed. 7, 1886), 805.

[20] A. H. Church in *Some Minor Arts as practised in Engl.* (1894), 33.

[21] These were found by Lady Charlotte Schreiber in 1869 on a visit to the Fulham Potteries. A manuscript copy made by her is in the British Museum, but the original note-books have disappeared.

[22] Chaffers, op. cit. 808–9.

[23] *Art Journ.* 1862, p. 204.

[24] *Gent. Mag.* 1737, p. 702.

obituary notice, after mentioning his authorship of 'several curious treatises on physic,' states that 'he was the first that found out the secret to colour earthenware like china.' He is said to have practised in his profession as a physician, and wrote some Latin medical treatises between 1722 and 1731. It is possible that he was a partner only, and that the business was carried on jointly with another brother. The male descendants seem to have disappeared by the end of the 18th century.

Lysons, who wrote in 1795,[25] says, 'These manufactures are still carried on at Fulham by Mr. White, a descendant in the female line of the first proprietor. Mr. White's father, who married one of the Dwight family (a niece of Dr. Dwight, vicar of Fulham), obtained a premium anno 1761 from the Society for the Encouragement of Arts &c., for making crucibles of British materials.' The niece of Dr. Dwight above mentioned was probably the Margaret Dwight who with her partner, Thomas Warland, became bankrupt in 1746.[26]

William White, whom she is said to have married, described as 'of Fulham in the county of Middlesex, potter,' took out a patent in 1762 for the manufacture of 'white crucibles or melting potts made of British materials, and never before made in England or elsewhere and which I have lately sett up at Fulham aforesaid.'

The earliest dated piece of Fulham stoneware known to exist is in the collection of Mr. J. E. Hodgkin. It is a mug ornamented with a ship and figure of a shipwright caulking the seams of a hull, and bearing an inscription in script, 'Robert Asslet London Street 1721.' Another specimen of quaint design, belonging to Mr. H. C. Moffat, is a large mug with pewter mount ; its decoration consists of a centre medallion representing Hogarth's 'Midnight modern conversation,' another medallion bearing the Butchers' Arms of Hereford, and the inscription 'Waller Vaughan of Hereford, His mug must not be brock, 1740.'

Speaking of the later history of this manufactory Chaffers says—[27]

In Mr. Llewellynn Jewitt's sale there was a gallon flipcan of stoneware with strongly hinged

cover of the same material and a grated spout. It was ornamented with raised borders and figures of a woman milling, a church in the distance, a hunting scene, Hope, Peace, and other figures ; with a well-modelled head on the spout, marked at the bottom in letters scratched into the soft clay 'W. J. White fecit Dec. 8, 1800.' On the heart-shaped termination of the handle is 'W. W. 1800.' In 1813 the manufactory was in the hands of Mr. White, a son of the above, and the articles then made were chiefly stoneware jars, pots, jugs, &c. The Fulham works remained in the family until 1862, when the last Mr. White died, and he was succeeded by Messrs. MacIntosh and Clements ; but in consequence of the death of the leading partner, the works were disposed of to Mr. C. J. C. Bailey, the present proprietor, in 1864. This gentleman has made considerable alterations and fitted up a quantity of machinery with a view of facilitating the manufacture and extending the business.

Writing in 1883 Jewitt speaks [28] very highly of the improvements introduced by Mr. Bailey. The output in stoneware included all the usual domestic vessels, besides sanitary and chemical appliances of various kinds. In addition, works of art of a high order in stoneware, terra-cotta, china, and other materials were produced, thus restoring the ancient reputation of the firm. For the stoneware department the services of M. Cazin, formerly director of the school of art at Tours, were engaged. A cannette in his own collection bearing the artist's name, "CAZIN, 1872, STUDY," Jewitt praises as remarkably good.[29] Also another example made expressly for him, which bears an admirably modelled armorial medallion and other incised and relief ornaments, with the date 1873, and artist's name, C. CAZIN, also incised. The coloured stone or 'sgraffito' ware has a high repute, and Mr. Bailey in 1872 received a medal at the Dublin Exhibition for his stoneware and terra-cotta. In the latter ware were produced vases, statues, architectural enrichments, chimney shafts, stoves, &c., of very good quality and of admirable design, Mr. Martin, sculptor, having been engaged as modeller and designer, and giving to some of the productions the name of Martin ware. The manufacture of chinaware was added during the year 1873, with the aid of good workmen and of Mr. E. Bennet and Mr. Hopkinson as artists. As the beginning of a new manufacture which had done much to establish a fresh fame for Fulham, Jewitt thus describes the composition of the ware : [30] 'The body is made from Dwight's original recipe, the very body of

[25] *Environs of Lond.* (1795), ii, 400.

[26] *Gent. Mag.* 1746, p. 45. Prof. Church considers that Margaret was the widow of Dr. Samuel Dwight, and that their only daughter Lydia was married to Thomas Warland, her mother's partner, and after his death to William White.

[27] Chaffers, op. cit. 811.

[28] *Ceramic Art* (1883), 91.

[29] Ibid.   [30] Ibid. 92.

which the first chinaware made in England was produced, and therefore the "Fulham china" of to-day has an historical interest attached to it which is possessed by no other.' The business has since passed into other hands and is now the property of the Fulham Pottery and Cheavin Filter Company, Limited.

A factory of stoneware, galley-pots, mugs, pans, dishes, &c., was carried on by James Ruel at Sandford House, Sand End, King's Road, Fulham. The undertaking proved unsuccessful, and in 1798 the factory and stock in trade were advertised for sale by auction by order of the sheriff, but were disposed of previously by private contract.

The pottery of William de Morgan & Co. has since 1888 been carried on at Fulham. The business was started in 1870 by Mr. William de Morgan, who began by decorating tiles and pots in Fitzroy Square. Removing afterwards to Chelsea, he continued to paint Dutch pottery, and that made by Stiff & Co. of Lambeth and by Staffordshire potters; whilst at Chelsea he built an oven, and engaged in the practical business of a potter. On removing to Fulham in 1888, he entered into partnership with Mr. Halsey Ricardo, a new pottery was built, and the wares stamped 'W. de Morgan & Co., Sands End Pottery, Fulham, S.W.,' and with a small floral device surmounted with the initials DM. The output of this firm also includes lustre ware, an imitation of the Hispano-Moresco work of the 15th and 16th centuries, and pottery decorated in the Persian style and with Dutch scenes.

At Southall is a small pottery carried on by the four brothers Martin, with an office in Brownlow Street, Holborn, for the sale of their wares.[31] The founder of the firm was Robert Wallace Martin, a Royal Academy student, and pupil of Alexander Munro the sculptor, who revived in this country the glazed stoneware of the 16th and 17th centuries. After an unsuccessful co-operation with Mr. Bailey, who was then proprietor of the Fulham Pottery, Martin entered into partnership in the early seventies with his three brothers, Charles Douglas, Walter Fraser, and Edwin Bruce. This ware, which is greatly appreciated by connoisseurs, is the outcome of a long series of experiments with clays and colours and methods of firing them. A special feature with the makers is that the decoration of a specimen is never repeated, so that each piece is in its way a unique example of the handiwork of the potter. The style varies greatly from the classical to the gro-

tesque, and the colouring is frequently as original as the decoration, which is incised, modelled, or carved. The mark consists of the name and address of the firm, with the month and year of production, incised in cursive lettering.

BOW PORCELAIN

The origin of the porcelain manufacture at Bow is very obscure. The first reliable notice of it is the patent[1] applied for on 6 December 1744 by 'Edward Heylin in the parish of Bow in the county of Middlesex, merchant, and Thomas Frye of the parish of West Ham in the county of Essex, painter.' The specification, enrolled 5 April 1745, is 'for a new method of manufacturing a certain mineral, whereby a ware might be made of the same nature or kind, and equal to, if not exceeding in goodness and beauty, china or porcelain ware imported from abroad. The material is an earth, the produce of the Cherokee nation in America, called by the natives *unaker*.' The specification proceeds to give a detailed account of the composition of the porcelain and the mode of its manufacture. It seems probable that the description given was purposely vague, and that porcelain was not made in any quantity, if at all, under this patent; the object of the patentees may have been to protect the use of substances of which they had no practical experience. Mr. William Burton[2] gives an analysis of the ware described in Heylin and Frye's patent, and arrives at the conclusion that 'not only were the proportions of Heylin and Frye entirely wrong, but their "frit"[3] was useless for its supposed purpose.' The Cherokee clay or 'unaker' is said to have been brought to England by a traveller who recognized its similarity to the 'kaolin,' or china clay, of the Chinese. Some information concerning this man is given by William Cookworthy of Plymouth, who afterwards discovered in Cornwall the materials, china stone (petuntse) and china clay (kaolin), from which true porcelain is made. Writing to a friend in 1745, Cookworthy says—[4]

I had lately with me the person who has discovered the china earth. He had with him several samples of the china ware which I think were equal to the Asiatic. It was found on the back of Virginia, where he was in quest of mines,

[31] Chaffers, *Marks and Monograms* (ed. 9, revised by Frederick Litchfield, 1900), 882-3.

[1] W. Burton, *Porcelain*, 59 et seq.
[2] *Hist. of English Porcelain* (1902), 10.
[3] The glassy substance used with the clay to form the paste or body of the ware.
[4] Chaffers, *Marks and Monograms* (ed. 9, 1900), 887.

and having read Du Halde, he discovered both the petunze and kaolin. It is this latter earth which he says is essential to the success of the manufacture. He is gone for a cargo of it, having bought from the Indians the whole country where it rises. They can import it for £13 per ton, and by that means afford their china as cheap as common stoneware.

Another patent was applied for by Frye on 17 November 1748, and the specification was enrolled 17 March 1749. This was for the manufacture of 'porcelain ware' from totally different materials, and the wording of this patent was even more obscure than that of the first. The substance for which protection was claimed was a 'virgin earth' produced by calcining animals, vegetables, and fossils, 'but some in greater quantity than others, as all animal substances, all fossils of the calcareous kind, as chalk, limestone, &c.'[5]

Thomas Frye was born near Dublin in 1710, and in early life came to London, where he followed the profession of an artist. He painted for the Saddlers' Company the full-length portrait of Frederick Prince of Wales preserved in their hall, which he also engraved and published in 1741. He became manager of the Bow works probably from their commencement, but after fifteen years' exposure to the furnaces his health gave way and he retired in 1759. After staying for a year in Wales, he returned to London and resumed his occupation as an engraver, publishing a series of life-size portraits in mezzotint, by which he is best known to the world at large. Frye died of consumption on 2 April 1762, and is described in his epitaph as 'the inventor and first manufacturer of porcelain in England.' His two daughters assisted him in painting the china at Bow until their marriage. One of them, who married a Mr. Willcox, was employed by Josiah Wedgwood at Etruria in painting figure-subjects from 1759 to 1776, the year of her death. Heylin and Frye do not appear to have had a factory of their own, but probably carried on their experiments at a factory already existing at Bow, having first secured the services of a well-skilled workman whose name has not been preserved, and who may have been the real inventor of English porcelain. Of Heylin nothing is known except that he was a merchant at Bow, and his name disappears from the second patent, taken out in 1749. In the following year Frye no longer appears as a principal, but as a manager to another firm. Some valuable information concerning the Bow factory is given in a col-lection of memoranda, diaries, and notebooks, formerly belonging to Lady Charlotte Schreiber,[6] which includes a diary of John Bowcocke, who was employed in the works as a commercial manager and traveller. These state that Messrs. Crowther and Weatherby were proprietors of the Bow manufactory, and that Thomas Frye acted as their works manager. Their works were known as 'New Canton,' and though situated on the Essex side of the River Lea, close to Bow Bridge, were commonly described as the Bow China Works and were so styled by the proprietors. About 1758 the firm reached its highest point of success. The memoranda above mentioned state that in that year three hundred person were employed, ninety of whom were painters, all living under one roof. An account of the business returns for a period of five years shows that the cash receipts, which were £6,573 in 1750–1, increased steadily from year to year, and had reached £11,229 in 1755. The total amount of sales in 1754 realized £18,115. The firm had a retail shop in Cornhill and a warehouse at St. Katharine's near the Tower.[7] Among the artists whom they employed were some of considerable repute. J. T. Smith records the following conversation between Nollekens the sculptor and a dealer in works of art named Panton Betew, from whom he wished to obtain a model of a boy by Fiamingo by way of exchange :—[8]

Nollekens. Do you still buy broken silver? I have some odd sleeve-buttons, and Mrs. Nollekens wants to get rid of a chased watch-case by old Moser, one that he made when he used to model for the Bow manufactory.
Betew. Ay, I know there were many very clever things produced there; what very curious heads for canes they made at that manufactory! I think Crowther was the proprietor's name. There were some clever men who modelled for the Bow concern, and they produced several spirited figures: Quin in Falstaff; Garrick in Richard; Frederick, Duke of Cumberland, striding triumphantly over the Pretender, who is begging quarter of him; John Wilkes, and so forth.
Nollekens. Mr. Moser, who was the keeper of our Academy, modelled several things for them; he was a chaser originally.

George Michael Moser, who died in 1783, was the head of his profession as a gold-chaser,

[5] Chaffers, op. cit. 888.
[6] Extensive extracts from these MSS. are given in Chaffers, *Marks and Monograms* (1900), 894 et seq.
[7] They appear in *Kent's Dir.* from 1753 to 1763 as Weatherby and Crowther, potters, St. Katharine's, near the Tower.
[8] *Nollekens and his Times* (1894), 175–6.

medallist, and enameller; he was one of the founders of the Royal Academy, and its first keeper. John Bacon, the famous sculptor, who was in his youth a pupil of Crisp, a modeller of porcelain, is also said to have designed figures and groups for the Bow works. Some of the finest specimens of Bow china have a small 'B' impressed in the paste below, this being the mark of John Bacon. The best known of these are the male and female cooks.[9]

To obtain a supply of good artists the proprietors advertised in newspapers which had a circulation in the Potteries district. The following advertisement appeared in November 1753 in *Aris's Birmingham Gazette*: 'This is to give notice to all painters in the blue and white potting way and enamellers on china ware, that by applying at the counting-house at the china-house near Bow, they may meet with employment and proper encouragement according to their merit; likewise painters brought up in the snuff-box way, japanning, fan-painting, &c., may have an opportunity of trial, wherein if they succeed, they shall have due encouragement. N.B. At the same house a person is wanted who can model small figures in clay neatly.'

The production of the factory was not limited to objects of a highly decorative character only, but included also vessels for domestic use. The first sale by auction of articles in stock advertised in the *Public Advertiser* of 17 April 1757 included not only 'services for deserts &c. exquisitely painted in enamel,' but also 'a large assortment of the most useful china in lots, for the use of gentlemen's kitchens, private families, taverns, &c.' In the same year (1757) a West-end warehouse was opened, announced thus by the firm: 'For the convenience of the nobility and gentry, their warehouse on the Terrace in St. James's Street is constantly supplied with everything new, where it is sold as at Cornhill, with the real price marked on each piece without abatement.' The new branch did not succeed, and was closed the next year (1758), the entire stock being sold by auction.

The partnership continued till the death of Weatherby, at his house on Tower Hill, on 15 October 1762, and Crowther became bankrupt in the following year, and is described as 'John Crowther, of Cornhill, chinaman.' Three sales of his effects by order of the assignees took place, viz., on 12 March 1764 and following days, at the Bow warehouse in Cornhill; on 19 May 1764; and at the great

exhibition-room in Spring Gardens on 30 May 1764. The last sale consisted 'of a large quantity of the finest porcelain, chosen out of the stock in curious figures, girandoles, and branches for chimney-pieces, finely decorated with figures and flowers, &c., dishes, compotiers, &c.; beautiful desserts of the fine old partridge and wheatsheaf patterns, a quantity of knife and fork handles, some neatly mounted, and a variety of other porcelain.'

Crowther seems to have carried on the business again after his bankruptcy, but it never regained its former prosperity. There are plates of Bow ware marked 'Robert Crowther 1770,' probably made for some relative, and in the *London Directory* from 1770 to 1775 it is stated that John Crowther of the Bow China Works had a warehouse at 28 St. Paul's Churchyard. The business must have dwindled down into insignificance, for in 1776 it was sold for a small sum to William Duesbury, and all the moulds and implements were transferred to Derby. Duesbury had between 1751 and 1753 worked in London as an enameller to various firms of potters, including the Bow factory.[10] From a memorandum left by Thomas Craft,[11] an artist at the Bow factory, it appears that Crowther was elected an inmate of Morden College, Blackheath, where he was still alive in 1790.

Great difficulties exist in distinguishing specimens of Bow china from the productions of Chelsea and other factories, but towards the end of 1867 a discovery made on the site of the old works brought to light some very useful information as to the characteristics of the ware. During some drainage operations at the match factory of Messrs. Bell & Black at Bell Road, St. Leonard's Street, Bromley-by-Bow, the foundations of one of the kilns were discovered, with a large quantity of 'wasters' and fragments of broken pottery. The houses close by are still called China Row. Some of these specimens, which came into the possession of Lady Charlotte Schreiber, were chemically tested by Professor A. H. Church, who found that bone-ash was an almost constant ingredient in their composition.[12] This refuted the opinion, until then generally held, that Josiah Spode the younger first introduced the use of bone-ash into the composition of English porcelain about the

[9] W. Burton, op. cit. 72.

[10] *Marks and Monograms.* See extracts from his 'work-book' in W. Bemrose, *Bow, Chelsea, and Derby Porcelain* (1898), 9 et seq.

[11] Printed in W. Chaffers, *Marks and Monograms* (1908), 892–3.

[12] A. H. Church, *Engl. Porcelain* (1904), 36.

years 1797–1800. The fragments [13] also gave information as to methods of ornamentation employed at Bow. Some are decorated in blue with Chinese landscapes, flowers, figures, birds, and branches of willow leaves; others are portions of services with the favourite decoration of the *prunus* or may-flower, and there are several perfect moulds for stamping these flowers. The extensive collection includes milkpots, cups, cans, saucers, open-work baskets, octagon plates, knife-handles, cup-handles, lion's-paw feet, and small pots for colour or rouge; but none of the fragments has any mark, except the name 'Norman,' which is marked in pencil on one of the cups. Some are broken pieces of decorated ware, such as sweetmeat dishes, figures of dogs, large bowls, and a man kneeling and supporting a shell with both hands; of the last-named design a pair of figures is known to exist. Although transfer printing is not found in any of the above pieces, it was adopted both under and over the glaze at an early period in the Bow works.[14]

An undoubted specimen of this ware is an inkstand, now in private possession, painted with the well-known Bow pattern of the *prunus*, and inscribed on the upper surface 'Made at New Canton 1750.' Another similar specimen, of a year later and not so fine, came into the Jermyn Street collection. Of undoubted genuineness is the interesting 'Craft' bowl in the British Museum already mentioned, with its accompanying memorandum, dated 1790 :—

This bowl was made at the Bow China Manufactory at Stratford-le-Bow, Essex, about the year 1760, and painted there by me Thomas Craft, my cipher is in the bottom; it is painted in what we used to call the old Japan taste, a taste at that time much esteemed by the then Duke of Argyle; there is nearly two pennyworth of gold, about 15s. I had it in hand, at different times, about three months; about two weeks' time was bestowed upon it. It could not have been manufactured for less than £4. There is not its similitude. . . .

Other pieces which may safely be assigned to Bow are a white tureen in the Victoria and Albert Museum, decorated with the *prunus* pattern in high relief. The ware is mostly of great thickness, but extremely translucent in its thinner parts, through which the transmitted light appears somewhat yellowish. A dessert dish in the same museum is in the form of a scallop shell. The centre

is decorated with a quail and wheatsheaf pattern, often mentioned as the 'partridge pattern' in the note-books of John Bowcock of Bow. Among other examples in this museum are vases, sauce-boats, knife-handles, an inkstand, and several figures. Many undoubted specimens of Bow ware, comprising statuettes, plates, vases, and other pieces richly ornamented, are contained in the Schreiber collection, some of which are figured by Solon,[15] and by Burton and Bemrose in their works already quoted. The figures of H. Woodward as 'a fine gentleman,' and Kitty Clive as Mrs. Riot, though often attributed to Bow, were certainly made at Chelsea; but the fine figure of Britannia with a medallion of George II is considered to have been made at Bow.

Many of the Bow figures and groups were made for use, and have at their back near the base a square hole for holding a metal stem to support branches for candlesticks; sometimes there is a round hole beneath the base for riveting the metal stem. This feature is peculiar to the Bow pottery, and serves to distinguish it from that of Chelsea. The earliest productions at Bow were decorated (like Thomas Craft's bowl) in the Japanese style, which suited the fashionable taste of the day; but since both the Bow and Chelsea factories borrowed from Oriental and Continental sources, they no doubt also copied favourite subjects and patterns from each other. This makes it the more difficult to determine with certainty the products of each factory. The *prunus* decoration has already been referred to; the blue and white porcelain is also typical, and was largely employed for the more useful articles. A little teapot in the British Museum, with its embossed vine ornament in white, and the angler's rod in a delicate greyish blue, is marked T F, and appears to have been the work of Thomas Frye. The 'sprigged' pieces so frequently mentioned in Bowcock's memoranda are generally white, decorated with modelled ornaments separately made in a mould and applied to the surface of the ware whilst it was in a clay state. The earlier figures are seldom more than 4 or 5 in. high, and are placed on simple flat stands; but these were soon replaced by more elaborate stands designed in the favourite rococo style of the period. The largest figure supposed to have been made at Bow is the 'Farnese Flora,' 18¼ in. high, in the Schreiber collection at South Kensington, which is said to have been modelled by John Bacon. In the British Museum are some examples of Chinese

---

[13] These are illustrated by Chaffers, op. cit. 909–11.

[14] This interesting 'find' is now in the Victoria and Albert Museum.

[15] *Old Engl. Porcelain* (1903), 32, 34, 40.

porcelain painted at Bow. The use of colours in enamelling sometimes serves to distinguish Bow ware from that of Chelsea; the enamelling of the latter was artistically superior, and introduced the rich blue, pea-green, and turquoise, which were not employed at Bow with equal effect. Three distinctive colours were in use at Bow, but not with satisfactory result. These were an enamel sealing-wax red, badly compounded and wanting in gloss; a cold opaque enamel blue, often used for touching up parts of dresses; and a gold purple, which in thin washes becomes of a pale mauve-pink hue, and is far from pleasant. Other points of difference between the products of the two factories are given by Burton.[16]

The use of printing for decorative purposes was largely practised at Bow. There seems no foundation for the statement that pieces were sent to Liverpool to be printed by Sadler and Green. The great majority of specimens consist of table ware with houses and groups of figures printed in outline and washed in with strong enamel colours—purple, blue, yellow, and green. The large figure of Britannia in the British Museum has a robe and stand decorated in printed outline carefully touched in with colour.

Many marks have been attributed to Bow, of which a list, figured and described, is given by Chaffers.[17] The commonest is the anchor and dagger in red enamel; the italic capital *B* is rarely found. The shell sweetmeat stands are rarely marked. The monogram of Thomas Frye, in capitals, sometimes in italic and sometimes reversed, occurs on some pieces. These must be attributed to an early period of the Bow works, and were probably painted by Thomas Frye himself.

CHELSEA PORCELAIN

The founder of the Chelsea pottery and the date of its origin cannot be traced. The earliest information is derived from a white cream jug supported by two goats and having a bee in its natural size placed on the front. Several specimens exist which bear the maker's mark, a triangle, scratched in the clay, and one of them is inscribed in incised cursive characters 'Chelsea 1745.' The workmanship of these pieces is of high merit, and leads to the conclusion that the factory had been established for some time, or that (as has been said [1]) the pieces were the production of some French workmen brought over from the factories of St. Cloud or Chantilly. Some curious information as to the early history of the enterprise is furnished by Simeon Shaw: [2]

Carlos Simpson, sixty-three years of age, 1817, was born at Chelsea; to which place his father, Aaron Simpson, went in 1747, along with Thomas Lawton, slip maker, Samuel Parr, turner, Richard Meir, fireman, and John Astbury, painter, all of Hot Lane; Carlos Wedgwood, of the Stocks, a good thrower; Thomas Ward and several others, of Burslem, to work at the Chelsea china manufactory. They soon ascertained that they were the principal workmen, on whose exertions all the excellence of the porcelain must depend, they then resolved to commence business on their own account at Chelsea, and were in some degree successful; but at length, owing to disagreement among themselves, they abandoned it and returned to Burslem.

No other information exists in support of this statement or concerning the factory said to have been set up by the Burslem workmen. R. Campbell,[3] writing in 1747, says: 'Of late we have made some attempts to make porcelain or china-ware after the manner it is done in China and Dresden; there is a house at Greenwich and another at Chelsea where the undertakers have been for some time trying to imitate that beautiful manufacture.' The probability that the Chelsea industry was at the first in the hands of French workmen is confirmed by information gathered by Mr. J. E. Nightingale [4] from newspapers of the period. It also appears, from the mention of a French chapel in an advertisement of property, that a French colony existed at Chelsea. In the *London Evening Post* of 19 December 1749 a freehold messuage is advertised to be sold in 'Great China Row, Chelsea,' inquiries to be made of Mr. Brown 'over against the French Chapel in Chelsea.'

From advertisements which appeared in 1750 it appears that the works had then existed for some time. The *General Advertiser* of 4 December 1750 announces a sale by auction of a 'Closet of fine Old Japan China' in which is included 'curious Dresden and Chelsea figures.' This is the first allusion which Mr. Nightingale has found to any English porcelain in an *auction* sale. In the same year rival advertisements appeared of the old and new proprietors of the Chelsea factory. The *Daily Advertiser* of 15 May 1750 contains the following:

Chelsea Porcelaine. The Publick is hereby informed that the Sale-Warehouse at the Manufactory

[16] *Hist. of Engl. Porcelain*, 73.
[17] *Marks and Monograms* (1900), 903–7.
[1] Burton, *Hist. of Engl. Porcelain* (1902), 9.
[2] *Hist. of Staffs. Potteries* (1829), 167.
[3] *The London Tradesman* (ed. 3), 186.
[4] *Contributions towards the Hist. of Early Engl. Porcelain* (1881), 5 et seq.

there will from henceforward be constantly open, and that new Productions are daily produced, and brought into the Sale-Room. And the Publick may be assured, that no Pains will be spared to extend this manufacture to as great a Variety as possible, either for Use or Ornament. Note, the Quality and Gentry may be assured, that I am not concern'd in any Shape whatsoever with the Goods expos'd to Sale in St. James's Street, called the Chelsea China Warehouse. N. Sprimont.

An advertisement in reply to the above is in the *General Advertiser* of 29 January 1750 (old style) :

Chelsea China Warehouse. Seeing it frequently advertised, that the Proprietor of *Chelsea Porcelaine* is not concerned in any shape whatsoever in the Goods exposed to Sale in St. James's-street, called *The Chelsea China Warehouse*, in common justice to N. Sprimont (who signed the Advertisement) as well as myself, I think it incumbent, publickly to declare to the Nobility, Gentry, &c., that my China Warehouse is not supply'd by any other Person than *Mr. Charles Gouyn*, late Proprietor and Chief Manager of the Chelsea-House, who continues to supply me with the most curious Goods of that Manufacture, as well useful as ornamental, and which I dispose of at very reasonable Rates. S. Stables, Chelsea China Warehouse, St. James's-street, Jan. 17th, 1750.

From these two advertisements, which comprise the earliest information obtainable respecting the proprietors, it appears that the business was shortly before 1750 in the hands of Charles Gouyn. It then passed to Nicholas Sprimont, but Gouyn set up a rival warehouse in St. James's Street, Chelsea, which does not seem to have lasted long, as no further mention of it has been found. The names of both proprietors declare their foreign origin,[5] but Nicholas Sprimont had long lived in London as a silversmith, residing in Compton Street, Soho. His name was entered at Goldsmiths' Hall on 25 January 1742, when he duly registered his mark, which was *NS* in italics with a star above. His silver work is chiefly remarkable for its representation in relief of coral, rockwork, crawfish, and reptiles. Among the earliest specimens of Chelsea ware are the crawfish salts in the British Museum, which are undoubtedly the work of Sprimont. Chaffers quotes [6] a statement from a workman named Mason who was employed at Chelsea and whose son worked many years at the Wor-

cester manufactory. The statement is to the effect that he joined the factory about the year 1751, and that it was first started by the Duke of Cumberland and Sir Everard Faulkner, the sole management being entrusted to a foreigner named Sprimont. He proceeds : 'I think Sir Everard died about 1755,[7] much reduced in circumstances, when Mr. Sprimont became sole proprietor, and having amassed a fortune he travelled about England, and the manufactory was shut up about two years ; for he neither would let it or carry it on himself.' After working at Bow for a short time Mason returned to Chelsea, where he remained till the works were purchased by Duesbury, with whom he went to Derby 'about the year 1763.' The story has some additional support, and there is a further link to connect the Duke of Cumberland with the undertaking, in the beautifully-modelled bust of him which was produced at the works ; the bust is of plain white glazed porcelain, and represents the duke bareheaded with a cuirass on his breast. Alexander Stephens, a reputable writer and resident at Chelsea, where he died in 1821, speaks [8] of the Duke of Cumberland and Sir R. Faulkner as *patrons* of Chelsea china. He adds that the ware 'was a long time in such repute as to be sold by auction, and as a set was purchased as soon as baked, dealers were surrounding the door for that purpose.' The same writer tells us, on the authority of a foreman of the Chelsea factory who had become an inmate of St. Luke's workhouse, that Dr. Johnson thought he could improve the manufacture of china, and obtained permission to bake specimens of his manufacture in the Chelsea ovens. 'He was accordingly accustomed to go down with his housekeeper about twice a week, and staid the whole day, she carrying a basket of provisions along with her. The doctor . . . had free access to the oven and superintended the whole process, but completely failed, both as to composition and baking, for his materials always yielded to the intensity of the heat, while those of the company came out of the furnace perfect and complete.'

The site of the factory has been located at the west side of the river end of Lawrence Street.[9] Faulkner says [10] it was at the corner

---

[5] Prof. Church regards both names as Flemish, but M. Rouquet, who lived in England thirty years and must therefore have known Sprimont, speaks of him as a clever French artist who supervised the works, whilst a wealthy personage undertook the expense; *L'état des arts en Angleterre*, Paris (1755), 143.

[6] *Marks and Monograms* (1900), 913–14.

Sir Everard Faulkner died at Bath in November 1758, and his Chelsea porcelain, which included several 'of the most admired productions of that manufactory,' was sold by auction in the Haymarket in February 1759.

[8] 'Stephensiana,' no. 1, *Monthly Mag.* (1821), lii, 231.

[9] Church, *Engl. Porcelain* (1904), 19.

[10] *Hist. of Chelsea* (1829), i, 272.

of Justice Walk, a portion of the river frontage running east from Lawrence Street to Church Street, and that it 'occupied the houses to the upper end of the street,' i.e. Lawrence Street. Part of the works was situated in Cheyne Row West, where large quantities of broken figures and bases were found during some excavations in 1843. Some time between 1750 and 1754 a warehouse was opened in Pall Mall for the sale of the Chelsea ware, and by February 1757 the warehouse had removed to Piccadilly. There is in the British Museum [11] a memorial (written after 1752) from 'the undertaker of the Chelsea porcelain,' who complains of the smuggling of Dresden porcelain into England. He states that he sold last winter to the value of £3,500, and employed one hundred persons. Writing in 1750 Jonas Hanway [12] says, 'It is with great satisfaction that I observe the manufactories of Bow, Chelsea, and Stepney [13] have made such a considerable progress ; on the other hand it is equally a subject of horror to see so many shops in the streets of London supplied with the porcelain of Dresden, though it is importable only under oath of being for private use and *not* for sale.'

A public sale of the ware by auction was held in March and April 1754 at St. James's, Haymarket, and lasted fourteen days. 'The undertaker of this manufactory, having at a very great expense brought it to that perfection as to be allowed superior to any other attempts made in that way,' hopes for the encouragement of the public, 'more particularly as he is determined to submit the value entirely to their generosity, and likewise that he will positively not open his warehouses, nor exhibit any article to sale after this till next year.' A further sale, however, of five days took place in November–December following, confined to small and fancy objects, such as snuff-boxes, smelling-bottles, trinkets for watches, and knife-handles. These articles were 'in lots suitable for jewellers, goldsmiths, toy-shops, china-shops, cutlers, and workmen in those branches of business.' The second annual sale took place on 10 March 1755 and fifteen following days, and among the goods mentioned is 'a most magnificent and superbe lustre.' This is probably a lustre similar to that made for the Duke of Cumberland, described by Mrs. Delany,[13a] who visited

the duke's lodge at Windsor in June 1757. Here she saw a closet decorated in gold and green with shelves filled with china, 'in the middle hangs a lustre of Chelsea china that cost six hundred pounds and is really beautiful.' None of the catalogues of the earliest sales have survived, but that of the next sale, held on 29 March 1756 and fifteen following days, has been reprinted by Mr. Raphael W. Read,[14] and gives a valuable account of the output of the manufactory. There was then a great popular demand for china. A retail dealer at 'Mr. Foy's china shop opposite the King's Palace' advertises in March 1756 'upwards of one hundred thousand pieces of china ware,' including Old Japan, Dresden, and Chelsea porcelain. Much of Sprimont's best ware went abroad, as appears from the catalogue of a sale advertised in April 1756 of the stock of Laumas and Rolyat, Lisbon merchants, which included 'one hundred double dozen of Chelsea knives and forks, silver-mounted.'

A crisis now occurred in the undertaking : Sprimont was taken ill, and announced by advertisement in February 1757 that though the manufactory had been much retarded, 'several curious things' had been finished and would be sold at the Piccadilly warehouse. The annual spring sales were resumed in 1759, and continued in 1760 and 1761. The close of the advertisement in 1761 ran thus :— 'The proprietor, N. Sprimont, after many years' intense application has brought this manufactory to its present perfection ; but as his indisposition will not permit him to carry it on much longer, he takes the liberty to assure the nobility, gentry, and others, that next year will be the last sale he will offer to the public.' The sale was deferred till March 1763, when Sprimont announced that on account of his lameness the manufactory itself would shortly be disposed of. Another announcement of the intended sale of the stock and plant was made in January 1764, 'as Mr. Sprimont, the sole possessor of this rare porcelain secret, is advised to go to the German Spaw.' No sale appears to have taken place, and another sale (the last of the regular spring auctions) was held in March. It included what was probably a replica of the magnificent dessert service in mazarine blue and gold presented by the king and queen to the Duke of Mecklenburg, as it is described as 'the same as the royal pattern which was sold for £1,150.' At a sale of specimens of all the English porcelain manufactories at the

---

[11] Lansd. MS. 829, fol. 4.

[12] *Travels* (1753), iv, 228. Quoted by Walter F. Tiffin, *Chronograph of Bow, Chelsea, and Derby Porcelain Manufactories*, 5–6.

[13] Of the Stepney porcelain works no information has as yet been found.

[13a] *Life and Corres.* (Ser. 1), iii, 462.

[14] *Reprint of the original catalogue of the Chelsea Porcelain Manufactory.* Privately printed. Salisbury (1880).

INDUSTRIES

Exhibition room, Spring Gardens, in July 1766, Chelsea dessert services were priced at from £17 to £150 the set.

M. P. J. Groslet,[15] who visited London in April 1765, speaks of the Chelsea manufactory as having just then fallen, and says he had heard that the county of Cornwall furnished the clay proper for making the porcelain.

The output from the factory now dwindled down to very small dimensions, but had not ceased in March 1768, when a dealer named Jones announced [16] for disposal porcelain 'even still brought from that noble manufactory.' Writing in April 1769 to Bentley, who was then at Liverpool, Josiah Wedgwood tells him 'the Chelsea moulds, models, &c., are to be sold . . . there's an immense amount of fine things.' From a later letter in July it appears that Wedgwood wished to purchase some of the plant, but was not prepared to buy the whole.[17] In May 1769 Sprimont announced a further sale of Chelsea porcelain, 'he having entirely left off making the same,' and made another unsuccessful effort to dispose by auction of the plant of his factory. In the following autumn Sprimont's connexion with the works ceased, and a hurried sale of the remaining stock took place in February 1770. In the catalogue of the sale of his pictures in March 1771 Sprimont is described as 'the late proprietor of the Chelsea porcelain manufactory who is retired into the country.' The business was bought by William Duesbury, probably early in 1770. Bemrose gives particulars [18] of the various leases of the site of the works in Lawrence Street, from which it appears that Sprimont held a lease for fourteen years, dated 3 March 1759, and on 15 August 1769 re-leased it to James Cox, who again leased the property on 9 February 1770 to William Duesbury and John Heath. Duesbury obtained a further lease on 25 March 1773 for seven years, being then no longer in partnership with Heath. On the expiration of his new lease in 1780 he took a lease for a single year, after which he leased the premises for three years more. In 1784 he gave up the property and finally closed the works.

On Sprimont's retirement the first purchaser of the works was James Cox, who on 17 August 1769 gave £600 for the mills, kilns, shops, warehouses, and all their contents in the premises at Lawrence Street. Cox being unable to carry on the business sold it within a few months, at a trifling profit, to Duesbury. Sprimont's managing foreman was Francis Thomas, who died just after his master's retirement. A lawsuit then arose between Duesbury and Burnsall the auctioneer, Thomas's executor, it being alleged that Thomas had concealed 'a great quantity of finished and unfinished porcelain to the amount of several hundred pounds.' The list of this porcelain is of value, as it shows the nature of the ware made prior to 1769.[19] Sprimont seems to have contemplated, or actually entered into, a partnership with Matthew Boulton for the sale of porcelain vases mounted with ormolu, but did not regain his health, and died in 1771. His artistic tastes are shown in his gallery of pictures which was sold by Mr. Christie in the same year.

William Duesbury was born on 7 September 1725, and as his work-book shows was working as an enameller in London in 1751. He afterwards worked at Longton Hall, and settled at Derby in 1755-6, when with the financial help of the Heaths, the Derby bankers, he purchased the site of the Derby Porcelain Works. By his ability, integrity, and indefatigable diligence, he became the proprietor of four factories, Bow, Chelsea, Longton Hall, and Derby, and at his death in 1786 was probably the largest manufacturer of porcelain of his time in England.

When the Chelsea business passed into Duesbury's hands the auction sales were resumed. The first was on 17 April 1771 and the three following days, the next in 1773, and then after an interval of four years they continued annually until 1785. The ware was announced sometimes as Derby and Chelsea, and sometimes as Chelsea alone; and specimens of the various wares were on permanent view at the warehouse in Bedford Street, Covent Garden.

Some particulars of the Chelsea factory are given in a conversation between Nollekens the sculptor and P. Betew, an art dealer :—[20]

Betew. Chelsea was another place for china.

Nollekens. Do you know where that factory stood ?

Betew. Why, it stood upon the site of Lord Dartery's house, just beyond the bridge.

Nollekens. My father worked for them at one time.

Betew. Yes, and Sir James Thornhill designed for them. Mr. Walpole at Strawberry Hill has a dozen plates by Sir James which he purchased at Mrs. Hogarth's sale in Leicester Square. Paul Ferg painted for them.

Betew proceeded to ascribe the failure of these works to the refusal of the Chinese to

[15] *Londres* (1770), iii, 37–8.
[16] J. E. Nightingale, op. cit. 26.
[17] Eliza Meteyard, *Life of Wedgwood*, ii, 120.
[18] *Bow, Chelsea, and Derby Porcelain*, 20–31.
[19] Ibid. 45–8.
[20] J. T. Smith, *Nollekens and his Times* (1894), 177.

allow any longer the importation of china clay into this country as ballast. Thornhill could not have designed for the Chelsea works, for he died in 1734, several years before their establishment ; and the plates spoken of by Betew were of blue and white delf painted by Thornhill with the twelve signs of the zodiac in August 1711.

The Chelsea ware, as far as regards the composition of its body or paste, groups itself naturally into two divisions. The first in- cludes the earliest productions down to 1756 or 1757. These are generally characterized[21] by an ivory-white or wax-white hue, and by considerable translucency, much glassy frit being employed in the paste, both glaze and body being very soft. The pieces, owing to this softness, were often distorted in firing, and resemble the porcelain of St. Cloud in the richness of their texture and tone. These early specimens were frequently left white, and their decoration consists almost exclusively of sprays of flowers and leaves, butterflies and other insects, with portions of the modelled ornament very simply lined in colours, and occasionally in gold. The decoration was not always executed at the Chelsea factory. Parcels of white ware, glazed but not decorated, were frequently sold to artists who painted them in enamel colours to suit the requirements of dealers. William Duesbury, as appears from his work-book already mentioned,[22] decorated in this way pieces of ware from Chelsea, Bow, and other factories. Burton[23] has classified the produc- tions of the early period under eight heads :—

1. White pieces, of which the goat and bee cream-jug and the craw-fish salts are examples.
2. Pieces with Oriental decoration : square and hexagonal cups, saucers, plates, and dishes in the Japanese style. The decora- tion is often in blue under-glaze in imitation of the Chinese pieces, or in red and gold on the glaze after the style of Japan.
3. Leaf dishes. These are generally decorated with a brown or pink-lined edge, and have the veins of the leaves touched in with the same colour. Little sprays of flowers, leaves and insects are scattered over the surface.
4. Vessels, for table use or ornament, of fantastic shape : tureens, dishes, sauce-boats, &c., modelled and coloured to represent animals, fruit, vegetables, birds, and fish.
5. Handles for knives and forks. These were produced in great variety.

6. Porcelain trinkets and toys. The famous Chelsea trinkets comprised a charming series of small, delicately-modelled figures, bouquets, animals, groups and single heads, intended to be mounted in gold, and worn on chains. These made their appearance in the first period, but continuing in great demand were produced down to the close of the factory.
7. Statuettes and groups of figures. Chel- sea was famous for these from an early period. The simpler groups and figures, slightly decorated and with very little gold, were prob- ably produced first. These early figures in- clude the bust of the Duke of Cumberland, figures emblematical of the Continents, the Seasons, the Senses, and the monkey orchestra. With these must be classed the birds perched on stumps and enamelled in naturalistic colours, of which there are many fine ex- amples in the Schreiber bequest.
8. Green enamel decoration. Pieces of this class were produced during the early years, but at a later date also. On a perfectly white ground, landscapes, often with ruins, were finely outlined in purple, and then a very glossy green enamel was thickly washed over the scene. Dishes, plates, and particularly toilet sets, were frequently decor- ated in this way. The exquisite scent-bottles which appear in the sale catalogues of 1754 and 1756 frequently bear French inscriptions (sometimes incorrectly spelt), and were long mistaken for productions of the Sèvres manu- factory.

The productions of the latter period of the works have two important characteristics, the presence of bone-ash in the paste, and the extensive use of rich coloured grounds with lavish gold decoration. In 1759 the works took a new development in striking contrast to the two preceding years, when through Spri- mont's illness the output first slackened and then almost ceased. New experiments were now made, and the use of bone-ash produced a body mixture which was more manageable and therefore less costly in practice. The first departure from the simplicity of the early style is the introduction of a rich mazarine- blue ground, a few examples of which appear in the sale catalogue of 1756. Other ground colours soon appeared, and were often em- ployed to cover the main body of the vase or dish, a space being left white to receive painted floral or figure subjects. Pea-green and turquoise-blue were invented at Chelsea in 1758 or 1759, and the claret for which the factory became so famous in 1759 also. This colour was imitated at Dresden and at Sèvres ; the Rose-Pompadour, which was the

[21] Church, op. cit. 24.
[22] W. Bemrose, op. cit., has published in facsimile several pages of the work-book of William Dues- bury, dated 1751–3.
[23] *Hist. Engl. Porcelain*, 40–3.

INDUSTRIES

pride of Sèvres, appears in a Chelsea catalogue of 1771. These colours were enamelled—that is applied over the fired glaze—differing from the blue under-glaze of the earlier period. The gilding of the latter period is far superior to that of any other contemporary English porcelain, but came at last to be so lavishly used as to destroy all artistic effect. The style of decoration was entirely altered; instead of the simple use of flowers, birds or insects, carelessly thrown over their surface, the pieces of this later period are richly decorated with brilliant colours, ambitious paintings and excessive gildings. The form of the pieces also underwent a change. Large and elaborate vases in extravagant rococo style, but exhibiting the highest technical skill, were produced in great numbers, and the subjects painted on their panels now owed their entire inspiration to the school of Watteau, Boucher, and other French artists. The statuettes of this later period were larger and more important than the earlier works, and many of them were modelled by Roubiliac, who lived in England from 1744 to 1762. Some of his works have an R impressed on the paste, but

many are not so distinguished. The following may safely be considered as from his design: 'The Music Lesson' in the Victoria and Albert Museum; 'Shakespeare'; 'Apollo and the Muses'; 'The Four Seasons'; and a group of a man playing a hurdy-gurdy and a lady teaching a dog to dance.

The use of raised flowers grew in this later period to an extraordinary excess. This form of decoration began with festoons and wreaths of flowers on the shoulders of vases or hanging down their sides; then little figures were made in combination with flowers and foliage; and finally elaborate boscage pieces were produced, of which 'The Music Lesson' is an excellent example. The earliest mark of Chelsea ware was an incised triangle, but this is seldom found and may have been only a workman's mark. The most general Chelsea mark is an anchor. In its earliest form the anchor is found in low relief upon an embossed ground. At a later date the anchor was drawn by the enameller or gilder, usually in red, but also in purple and sometimes in gilt; occasionally in later pieces two gold anchors occur side by side.

GLASS

One of the earliest known references to the purchase of glass in Middlesex is contained in a writ issued by Edward III, dated 28 March 1350.[1] It recites that John de Lincoln, master for the works in the King's Chapel in the Palace of Westminster, and John Geddyng had been appointed jointly and severally to provide, procure, and buy in the counties of Surrey, Sussex, Kent, Middlesex [and twenty-three others], in the most convenient places, as much glass as should be necessary for the said chapel; and also to provide workmen, glaziers, &c. A similar writ dated 20 March 1351[2] gives the like commission to John de Bampton and John de Geddyng. The expense rolls give full details of the wages paid to the glaziers and other workmen from 20 June 25 Edw. III, to 5 December 26 Edw. III.[3] Master John de Chester was paid 7s. a week for working on the drawings of several images for the glass windows, and was assisted by five master glaziers working on similar drawings at 1s. a day each. Other painters on glass received 7d. a day each, glaziers who cut and joined glass for the

windows were paid 6d. a day, and workmen who were apparently labourers had 4d. or 4½d. a day. Thomas de Dadyngton and Robert Yerdesle, who ground the colours, were also paid at the rate of 4½d.; and white, blue, azure, and red glass was bought by the 'pondus' and conveyed from London to Westminster. Other examples of window-glass both pictorial and heraldic in religious and secular buildings throughout the country show how great an advance had been made by this art in England by the middle of the 14th century.

We meet with some interesting information concerning a Middlesex glass-house in 1447, when the executors of Richard de Beauchamp, Earl of Warwick, who died in 1439, were engaging the services of various artificers for the construction of the magnificent Beauchamp Chapel in St. Mary's Church, Warwick, as a last resting-place for the earl. The contract for glazing the windows was assigned to a Westminster glazier in the following terms:—[4]

John Prudde of Westminster glasier, 23 Junii 25 H. 6, covenanteth &c. to glase all the windows

[1] Pat. 24 Edw. III, pt. i, m. 26 d.
[2] *Abbrev. Rot. Orig.* (Rec. Com.), ii, 217b.
[3] J. T. Smith, *Antiq. of Westm.* (1807), 191-6.
[4] Dugdale, *Antiq. of Warw.* (ed. 2, 1730), 446

155

in the new chapell in Warwick, with Glasse beyond the Seas, and with no Glasse of England ; and that in the finest wise, with the best, cleanest, and strongest glasse of beyond the Sea that may be had in England, and of the finest colours of blew, yellow, red, purpurl, sanguine, and violet, and of all other colours that shall be most necessary, and best to make rich and embellish the matters, Images, and stories [histories] that shall be delivered and appointed by the said Executors by patterns in paper, afterwards to be newly traced and pictured by another Painter in rich colour at the charges of the said Glasier. All which proportions the said John Prudde must make perfectly to fine, glase, eneylin it, and finely and strongly set it in lead and souder, as well as any Glasse is in England. Of white Glasse, green Glasse, black Glasse, he shall put in as little as shall be needfull for the shewing and setting forth of the matters, Images, and storyes, and the said Glasier shall take charge of the same Glasse, wrought and to be brought to Warwick, and set up there in the windows of the said Chapell ; the Executors paying to the said Glasier for every foot of Glasse ijs. and so for the whole xcjli. js. xd.

For some alterations Prudde received a further payment of 'xiijli. vjs. ivd.' These comprised some additions ' for our Lady, and Scripture of the marriage of the Earle . . . the same to be set forth in Glasse in most fine and curious colours.' Some information as to the relative cost of English and foreign glass appears in 'The reporte of John Bote, glassyer,'[5] which gives his charges for work done in 1485 at Cold Harbour, the famous London mansion fronting the Thames. The prices of the various kinds of glass were : Dutch, $4\frac{1}{2}d$. a foot ; Venice, 5d. ; Normandy, 6d. ; English, 1d. ; it is probable that the English glass was of smaller size.

Macpherson,[6] quoting from *The Present state of England, anno* 1683, says, ' The fine flint glass, little inferior to that of Venice, was first made in the Savoy House in the Strand ; ' nothing beyond this statement is known respecting this supposed manufactory. Other unsuccessful attempts made in Tudor times to set up the manufacture will come more conveniently for notice under London.

Another of these pioneers was one Cornelius de Lannoy who came from the Netherlands towards the end of 1564 and set up a workshop in Somerset House.[7] He was subsidized by the English Government, and undertook to introduce improvements and instruct English workmen in the glass-makers' art as practised in his own country. A letter from Armagill Waade to Cecil[8] of 7 August 1565 states that Lannoy could not find suitable materials in England, and that the potters could not 'make one pot to content him. They know not howe to seasson their stuff to make the same to susteyne the force of his great fyres.' He was forced to send to Antwerp ' for new provisyons of glasses, his old being spent.' The English workmen made no progress in learning the art, perhaps through the want of the proper materials ; ' all our glasse makers cannot facyon him one glasse tho' he stoode by to teach them.' Lannoy received £150 for 'provisyons,' £30 on his arrival in England, and £30 a quarter, the first payment being for the quarter ending 25 March 1565. The queen and her council were, like the heads of most other countries, very desirous of promoting the glass manufacture, but Lannoy's enterprise proved unsuccessful. He was also an alchemist, and made persistent attempts to induce the queen to take up his schemes for transmuting base metals into gold.[9]

Among the French Protestant refugees who fled from their country after the massacre of St. Bartholomew in 1572 were some who brought with them the art of glass-making. One of these families of French glass-makers named Bigoe, Bagoe, or Bagg, has been traced by Hallen[10] in various parts of England and Ireland. In 1623 Abraham Bigoe had a glass-house at Ratcliff and another in the isle of Purbeck. He was probably the founder of the firm mentioned by Lysons in his account of the parish of Stepney published in 1795.[11] Among the industries of the hamlet of Ratcliff he includes ' Bowles's celebrated manufacture of window glass, established by the great-grandfather of the present proprietor, who is said to have been the first to manufacture crown glass in this kingdom.' Lysons adds, ' it has certainly been brought to its present improved state by his family.'

The number of glass-houses in England in 1696 is said to have been eighty-eight,[12] but how many of these were in Middlesex cannot be ascertained.

An important discovery in glass manufacture made by Thomas Tilston, a merchant of London, early in the reign of Charles II, gave London glass a great reputation both here and

---

[5] Lansd. MS. no. 59, art. 76 ; quoted by T. Hudson Turner, *Dom. Archit.* 78.

[6] *Ann. of Commerce* (1805), ii, 122.

[7] *Denizations and Naturalizations* (Huguenot Soc.), p. xlvi.

[8] S.P. Dom. Eliz. xxxvii, 3.

[9] Ibid. *passim*.

[10] A. W. C. Hallen, *French 'Gentlemen Glassmakers,' in Engl. and Scotl.* 8.

[11] *Environs of Lond.* iii, 473.

[12] John Houghton, *Coll. for Improvement of Trade and Commerce* (1727), ii, 48.

abroad. After many fruitless experiments it was found that by reducing the proportion of lime and adding a small quantity of litharge or oxide of lead a brilliant and practically colourless glass was obtained, which was not only more fusible but brighter and clearer than the old glass. This became known as English flint glass, and Tilston, who made the discovery, applied for and obtained a grant of the whole use and benefit of his invention.[13] The fine qualities of this new glass struck a severe blow at the Bohemian colourless glass, which had itself beaten Venetian glass out of the field.[14] Its superiority lay in its great density, which in some cases exceeded that of the diamond; the English cut glass rivalled the diamond in the production of prismatic displays. In 1713 English cut glass began to appear on the Continent. In 1760, on the authority of M. Gerspach, a French writer, England practically supplied the whole of France with glass. It is strange that so few specimens of this important art and so little information concerning it have survived. The earliest known piece of English cut glass is one bearing the monogram of Frederick Prince of Wales, which must therefore be dated between 1729 and 1751. The best period of this industry is between 1750 and 1790, and it began to decay early in the 19th century. Mr. Powell marks three stages of progress: the first, in which cutting is subservient to form, lasted to about 1790; the second, in which the claims of form and cutting are equally balanced, continued till about 1810; and the third, not yet terminated, in which form has largely given way to cutting. The softness and high refractive power of their glass proved a snare to English cutters, who to please the public strove after still greater dazzling prismatic effects. For this, deeper cutting and thicker material became necessary, and the glass produced bristled with prismatic pyramids which effectually destroyed all beauty of form.

No other records of glass-makers in London outside the City walls are met with until 1760, when William Riccards, merchant, and Richard Russell, glass-maker, both of Whitechapel, obtained a patent[15] for fourteen years for a new method of making pots and building furnaces for crown glass, plate glass, and all sorts of green glass.

William Tassie, who is best known by his wax medallion-portraits, invented a white enamel composition which he used for reproductions of gems. This was a vitreous paste, the method of preparing which he kept secret; his place of business was from 1772 to 1777 in Compton Street, Soho, and from 1778 to 1791 at 20 Leicester Fields (Leicester Square). A manufactory for the production of plate-glass by blowing, the last of its kind, existed in East Smithfield almost down to 1830, before it gave way to the powerful competition of the British Cast Plate Glass Manufacturers.[16]

The Banks collection of tradesmen's cards in the Print Room of the British Museum has notices of the following firms:—Price, Sherrard Street, St. James's, 1779-89; Stanfield & Co., successors to Orpin, 481 Strand, 1785; Hancock, Shepherd & Rixon, 1 Cockspur Street, 1808. Two makers of stained glass also occur:—Baker's Patent Manufactory, 25 Marsham Street, Westminster, 1792; and William Collins, 227 Strand, near Temple Bar, 1815.

A minor glass industry was carried on by small workers in Bethnal Green and Shoreditch up to about forty years ago. This was the manufacture of glass beads for exportation to native tribes in Africa. Hartshorne,[17] writing in 1897, says:—'They bought their coloured glass canes from the glass-makers and melted them at a jet, dropping the metal upon a copper wire coated with whitening, the wire being turned during the process, and when cold the beads would slip off. The men were, however, so careless and unpunctual that the trade came to an end.'

Mirror-making is carried on as part of the cabinet-maker's trade, which involves among other operations that of glass-bevelling. The glass, having been made of right size and shape by the cutter, is passed to the beveller, who first presses the edge of the glass against an iron grinding-mill, or wheel, upon which a mixture of sand and water continually plays. The next process is to submit the glass to a revolving stone, upon which water trickles; this removes the roughness left by the first operation. The final polish is then given by a wooden wheel covered with polishing material. The shape workers, who produce curves and other elaborate shapes with their bevelling, are highly-skilled workmen. The glass then goes to the 'sider,' who cleans and prepares it for silvering. It is then turned into a mirror by the silverer, by the application of silver reduced by admixture with

[13] *Cal. S.P. Dom.* 1663-4, p. 266.
[14] See quotations from Peligot and Gerspach, French writers on glass, in a paper on 'Cut Glass,' by Harry Powell; *Journ. Soc. of Arts,* June 1906.
[15] No. 744, 12 May 1760.

[16] Porter, 'Treatise on Glass,' *Lardner's Cab. Cycl,* 195.
[17] *Old Engl. Glasses* (1897), 106 n.

various chemicals. By substituting this process for the use of quicksilver, which formerly prevailed, silvering has now become as little dangerous as any other branch of the trade. When the cost of plate-glass became so much reduced, and the use of mirrors in all kinds of furniture increased, the trade grew considerably; but during quite recent years, although the price of glass has still continued to fall, the London trade has remained stationary.[18]

Our English glass at the present day suffers much from the competition of French and Belgian glass.[19] The foreign glass is not only cheaper to produce, wages being lower where it is made than in this country, but it is said to be purer and whiter in colour, because of some superiority in the material available.

Through the exertions of Dr. Salviati, a native of Venice, the old glass industry of Murano has been successfully revived, and a London company (known as the Venice and Murano Glass & Mosaic Company, Ltd.) was formed in 1870 for the sale of its goods. One department is the manufacture of enamel mosaics, an excellent example of which may be seen in the mosaic decorations of St. Paul's Cathedral. The firm also largely produces table glass of artistic design and fine quality.

It remains to speak very briefly of artists in stained glass. Some excellent work has been done by firms of the present day. Much of the painted glass produced by Messrs. Cottier & Co., of Grafton Street, is extremely fine, both in design and colour. Messrs. James Powell & Sons, of South Kensington and Bayswater, whose principal works are at Whitefriars, have supplied six windows for St. James's Church, Marylebone. Messrs. Clayton & Bell, of Regent Street, have placed some good windows in Ely Cathedral; and Messrs. Heaton, Butler & Bayne, of Garrick Street, have also executed very fine work.

CLOCK AND WATCH-MAKING

The early history of the clock and watch trade in London is very obscure. Very little is known about the early clockmakers, and had it not been for the custom of marking the works of each watch with the name of its maker, our knowledge would have been still more scanty. The obligation of stamping all gold and silver cases at Goldsmiths' Hall affords some statistics of the number of watches produced in England, but not of the hands employed in their manufacture. A contributor to Knight's *London*,[1] writing in 1842, estimates the average annual number of watches which passed through Goldsmiths' Hall at 14,000 gold and 85,000 silver. This estimate is much below that given in the report of a committee of the House of Commons made in 1818, which gives the number of watches stamped at Goldsmiths' Hall in 1796 as 191,678. This latter number, which includes both gold and silver watches, has never been equalled before or since, and probably included large numbers of the inferior watches with forged makers' names which were then flooding the country.

The principal makers mostly congregated in the City of London, but many settled at the West End in the neighbourhood of the Court, so that Middlesex had its fair share of the prominent craftsmen of the metropolis.

In Soho there was an important settlement of French watchmakers, skilled operatives driven over by the Huguenot persecution. Since the beginning of the 18th century Clerkenwell has been the great centre of the working members of the trade. Many streets were almost wholly occupied by workmen engaged in the various subdivisions of the trade, such as 'escapement maker,' 'engine turner,' 'fusee cutter,' 'springer,' 'secret-springer,' 'finisher,' 'joint finisher,' &c.

An early reference to clockmaking in Middlesex relates to the clockmaker or clock-mender of Westminster Abbey in 1469, one Harcourt, who was employed also by Sir John Paston. Writing in the spring of that year, Sir John mentions two clocks which he had left for repair in Harcourt's hands, one of which was 'My Lordys Archebysshopis.'[2]

Some of the most skilled clockmakers employed in England during the 16th century were foreigners. Nicholas Cratzer or Craczer,[3] a German astronomer, was 'deviser of the King's (Hen. VIII) horloges,' and lived thirty years in England. He was a Bavarian, born in 1487. Six French craftsmen were imported in the time of Henry VIII to make a clock for Nonsuch Palace. Nicholas Oursiau, Frenchman and denizen, was clockmaker to both Queen Mary and Queen Elizabeth, and constructed the old turret clock at Hampton

[18] Charles Booth, *Life and Labour of the People of Lond.* (Ser. 2), i, 189.
[19] Ibid. i, 189 n.
[1] Knight, *Lond.* iii, 142.
[2] *Paston Letters* (ed. 1900), ii, 393.
[3] F. J Britten, *Old Clocks*, 45.

Court.[4] He as well as his two assistants Laurence Daunton of the French Church and Peter Doute of the Dutch Church, are returned as living in Westminster in 1568.

One of the earliest Middlesex clockmakers whose work has survived is Bartholomew Newsam, who lived in the Strand near Somerset House. In 1568 he obtained from the Crown a lease of these premises for thirty years, and lived to occupy them to within five years of the expiration of the term. In 1572 he obtained the reversion of the office of Clockmaker to the Queen, and in 1590 he succeeded to that office on the death of Nicholas Urseau or Oursiau. Newsam had, prior to 1582, been clock-keeper to the queen, and on 4 June 1583 received under privy seal 32s. 8d. for 'mending of clocks during the past year.' He did not long enjoy his double office, but died in 1593. His will, executed in 1586, contains some interesting bequests. He leaves to John Newsam, clockmaker, of York, various tools, including his 'best vice save one, a beckhorne to stand upon borde, a great fore hammer, and two hand hammers.' The rest of his tools he gave to his son Edward, 'with condition he became a clockmaker as I am,' if not, the said tools were to be sold. His bequests to friends included 'a sonne dyall of copper gylte,' 'one cristall jewell with a watch in it, garnished with gould,' 'one watch clocke in a silken purse,' 'a sonne dyall to stand uppon a post in his garden,' and 'a chamber clocke of fyve markes price.' The British Museum has a striking clock by Newsam, which is a masterpiece of construction. The case is of brass, gilt and engraved, about 2½ in. square and 6½ in. high, with an ornamental dome and perforated top. The clock has a verge escapement; its workmanship is unusually fine for the period, and is remarkably free from subsequent interference. An illustration of a fine casket by Bartholomew Newsam is given in *Archaeologia*, vol. 55.

Holborn and its neighbourhood was for over two centuries a favourite locality for horological craftsmen. Jeffery Bailey, who was admitted to the freedom of the Clockmakers' Company in 1648, and served as master in 1674, was a maker of lantern clocks 'at ye Turn Style in Holborn.'

Edward East, watchmaker to Charles I, was in business at first in Pall Mall, near the Tennis Court. He afterwards removed to Fleet Street, and later still to the Strand, as in the *London Gazette* for 22–26 January, 1690,

he is described as 'Mr. East at the Sun, outside Temple Bar.' His watches were held in high repute, and were often used by Charles II as stakes at games of tennis in the Mall. Sir Thomas Herbert relates in his *Memoirs*,[5] that having failed to call the king at an early hour His Majesty ordered him to be supplied with a gold alarm-watch, 'which, as there may be cause, shall awake you.' A watch was accordingly procured by the Earl of Pembroke from Mr. East his watchmaker in Fleet Street. East was a member of the Clockmakers' Company, and one of the ten original assistants named in its charter of incorporation. After serving the office of warden, he was twice elected master, in 1645 and again in 1652. In 1647 he also served the office of treasurer of the company, an office of which he was the unique occupant. In 1693, probably not long before his death, he gave £100 to the company for the benefit of the poor. A very large silver alarum clock-watch by East which Charles I kept at his bedside, and gave to Mr., afterwards Sir Thomas, Herbert on 30 January 1649, when on his way to execution at Whitehall, is still in private possession. It is a beautiful piece of work, and has been frequently illustrated; the dial and back are finely decorated with pierced work. This may be the 'Watch and a Larum of gould' for which East received 'fortie pounds' from the Receiver-General on 23 June 1649,[6] the watch having been supplied 'for the late King's use the xviith of January last.' Another fine example of an 'Eduardus East' is in the British Museum; it is an octangular crystal-cased watch made about the year 1640, and has a recumbent female figure engraved on the dial. The Ashmolean Museum at Oxford possesses a gold watch by East in the form of a melon. Other specimens of this maker known to exist are a watch with tortoise-shell case, in the British Museum, dating from about 1640; another in the Victoria and Albert Museum; two examples in the Guildhall Museum, one a watch movement and the other a silver watch in oval hunting case with crystal centre; and two clock-watches in finely-pierced silver cases, in private possession.

Jeremy East, a contemporary and probably a relative of Edward East, was admitted to the freedom of the Clockmakers' Company in 1641. Two specimens of his workmanship are described by Britten.[7] One is a superb and very early example of English work, a watch in an hexagonal crystal case with gilt

[4] W. Page, *Denizations and Naturalizations* (Huguenot Soc.), p. xliii.

[5] (1813), 148.
[6] Britten, *Old Clocks and Watches*, 167–8.
[7] Ibid. 112, 402.

brass mountings; the plate is inscribed 'Jeremie East, Londini,' and the work is not later than 1600. The other is a small oval watch with a plain silver dial and one hand; its date is about 1610. East was living in 1656, when he joined with some other freemen of the Clockmakers' Company in a petition to the Lord Mayor respecting certain disputes as to the management of the company.

Another skilled maker of this period was William Clay, who appears to have been in business from 1646 to 1670, but of whom very little is known. An engraved metal dial, very fine for this early period, and denoting the minutes in a peculiar way, bears the inscription, 'William Clay, King's Street, Westminster.' Clay took part in the disputes which occurred in the Clockmakers' Company in 1656, and was probably the maker of a watch presented by Cromwell to Colonel Bagnell at the siege of Clonmel.

Of somewhat earlier date was Richard Harris, who is said to have constructed a turret clock with a pendulum for the church of St. Paul, Covent Garden, which was afterwards destroyed by fire. An inscription on an engraved plate in the old vestry-room states that 'The clock fixed in the tower of the said church was the first long pendulum clock in Europe, invented and made by Richard Harris of London, although the honour of the invention was assumed by Vincenzio Galilei, A.D. 1649, and also by Huygens in 1657.'

Richard Bowen, a London maker whose address is not known, but who was in business in the earlier half of the 17th century, was one of the first makers of a keyless watch. In the *London Gazette* for 10–13 January 1686, there is an advertisement, ' Lost, a watch in black shagreen studded case with a glass in it, having only one Motion and Time pointing to the Hour on the Dial Plate, the spring being wound up without a key, and it opening contrary to all other watches. R. Bowen, Londini, fecit, on the black plate.' Another watch by Bowen is said to have been given by Charles I in 1647, while at Carisbrooke, to Colonel Hammond. It is a large silver watch with two cases, the outer one chased and engraved with a border of flowers and the figure of the king praying, and the words: 'And what I sai to you I sai unto all, Watch.'

Among the numerous French Protestant refugees who settled in Soho towards the close of the 17th century were the Debaufres, a family of very skilful French watchmakers. Peter Debaufre, who was in business in Church Street, Soho, from 1686 to 1720, was admitted into the Clockmakers' Company in 1689, and in 1704, in conjunction with Nicholas Facio

and Jacob Debaufre, was granted a patent for the application of jewels to the pivot holes of watches and clocks. A few months later the patentees applied to Parliament for permission to extend the term of their patent, but the Bill was opposed by the Clockmakers' Company[8] on what appears to have been insufficient grounds, and was defeated. In 1704 the firm announced by advertisement that jewelled watches were to be seen at their shop; a watch bearing the name 'Debauffre' is in the Victoria and Albert Museum. Peter Debaufre also devised a dead-beat or 'club-footed' verge escapement which was adopted with some alterations by several other makers. James Debaufre became connected with the business in 1712 and carried it on at Church Street, Soho, until 1750.

Another successful Huguenot firm was that of the De Charmes. Simon De Charmes, who was driven over here by the persecution about the year 1688, was admitted as a clockmaker in 1691 and built Grove Hall, Hammersmith, in 1730. The house was occupied by his son David, who lived there till his death in 1783,[9] and succeeded his father in the business.

Jonathan Lowndes, who was in business in Pall Mall between 1680 and 1700, was a celebrated maker of his day.

Christopher Pinchbeck, son of the inventor of the 'Pinchbeck' alloy, carried on a successful business in Cockspur Street, and is described as clockmaker to the king. In 1766 he is said to have procured for George III the first pocket watch made with a compensation curb. He was elected an honorary freeman of the Clockmakers' Company in 1781, and died in 1783 at the age of seventy-three.

The Perigals were a family of celebrated horologists from which three firms originated. Francis Perigal, the founder, was established from 1740 at the Royal Exchange, where he was succeeded by his son and grandson. Another Francis (1770–94), who was watchmaker to the king, settled in New Bond Street and was succeeded by Perigal & Duterran, 'Watchmakers to His Majesty,' from 1810 to 1840. Another branch of the family established itself in Coventry Street as John Perigal (1770–1800), and Perigal & Browne (1794–1800).

Charles Haley (1770–1800), of Wigmore Street, who was admitted to the honorary freedom of the Clockmakers' Company in 1781, was a celebrated maker, and a patentee of a remontoire escapement for chronometers.[10]

---

[8] Britten, *Old Clocks and Watches*, 351.
[9] T. Faulkner, *Hist. of Fulham* (1813), 349.
[10] No. 2,132, 17 Aug. 1796.

He was one of the experts appointed by the Parliamentary Committee in 1793 to report on Mudge's chronometers. The firm afterwards became Haley and Milner (1800–15), Haley and Son (1832), and James Grohe (1834–42).

Other prominent makers of this period were James Short (1740–70), who sent to the Royal Society in 1752 an interesting letter on compensated pendulums; John Bittleston (1765–94), of High Holborn, the maker of a very curious astronomical watch; Thomas Best (1770–94), of Red Lion Street, a maker of musical clocks and watches; Francis Magniac (1770–94) of St. John's Square, Clerkenwell, a maker of complicated clocks and automata; James Smith (1776–94) of Jermyn Street, clockmaker to George III; and William Hughes (1769–94) of High Holborn, a maker of musical clocks and clocks of curious mechanism.

John Harrison, one of the most famous of English clockmakers, was born in 1693 near Pontefract in Yorkshire. For several years he followed his father's trade as a carpenter, and, having a great taste for mechanical pursuits, gave much of his attention to the improvement of clocks and watches. The family removed to Barrow in Lincolnshire in 1700, and here Harrison made his first attempts at clockmaking. One of his earliest efforts, a clock with wheels and pinions of wood, bears his signature and the date 1713. Another long-case clock by him is in the Victoria and Albert Museum, and a similar specimen is in the Guildhall Museum. He was then attracted by the reward of £20,000 offered by Parliament for the construction of a time-keeper of sufficient accuracy to ascertain the longitude at sea within half a degree. He invented a form of recoil escapement known as the 'grasshopper,' and also succeeded in constructing his famous 'gridiron' pendulum in which the effects of heat and cold in lengthening and shortening the pendulum were neutralized by the use of two metals having different ratios of expansion. These he brought to London in 1728, with drawings of his proposed time-keeper for submission to the Board of Longitude. On the advice of George Graham, the celebrated watch-maker, Harrison delayed submitting his designs until he had constructed his time-keeper and tested its capabilities. After spending seven more years in experiments, he returned to London in 1735, bringing with him his timepiece, and resided in Orange Street, Red Lion Square. His work received the highest approval of Halley, Graham, and other fellows of the Royal Society, and on

their recommendation he was allowed in 1736 to proceed with it to Lisbon in a king's ship. During the voyage he was able to correct the reckoning to within a degree and a half, and the Board of Longitude gave him £500 as an encouragement to proceed with his experiments. He finished another timepiece in 1739, and afterwards a third; this procured him in 1749 the medal annually awarded by the Royal Society for the most useful discovery. His last timepiece was smaller, and he now resolved to abandon the heavy framing and wheels which he used in his earlier attempts. In 1759 he perfected his celebrated 'watch,' which, after being tested in two voyages, to Jamaica in 1761–2, and to Barbadoes in 1764, at length obtained for him the full reward offered by government. Harrison's watch and the three timepieces which preceded it are still preserved at the Royal Observatory at Greenwich. A duplicate of the fourth watch which secured for him the government reward was purchased by the Clockmakers' Company in 1891 for £105, and is exhibited with other chronometers in their museum at the Guildhall. It was at one time in the Shandon Collection, and bears the hall-mark of 1768–9.[11] He died on 24 March 1776 at his house in Red Lion Square, and was buried in the south-west corner of Hampstead churchyard. His tomb, which was restored by the Clockmakers' Company in 1880, contains a long inscription recording the merits of his inventions.[12] There is an engraved portrait by Reading of 'Longitude Harrison' in the *European Magazine*, and another by Tassaert was published in Knight's *Portrait Gallery*.

Another inventor of improvements in the chronometer was Thomas Earnshaw, who was born at Ashton-under-Lyne in 1749. After serving his apprenticeship to a watch-maker, he came to London and worked for some time as a finisher of verge and cylinder watches; he also taught himself watch-jewelling and cylinder-escapement making, making use of ruby cylinders and steel wheels. Earnshaw worked for John Brockbank, Thomas Wright of the Poultry, and other makers, and in 1781 improved the chronometer escapement by using a spring detent instead of the pivot form employed by the French makers. After showing a watch with his new device to Brockbank, it was agreed that Wright should patent it, but the latter kept the watch for a year to observe its going, and did not

[11] *Cat. of the Mus. of the Clockmakers' Company* (1902), 46.
[12] S. E. Atkins and W. H. Overall, *Hist. of the Clockmakers' Co.* (1881), 179–80.

procure the patent till 1783. Meanwhile John Arnold had registered a patent specification claiming the device as his own invention; this embittered Earnshaw's feelings towards Brockbank, whom he accused of having divulged his plan to Arnold. In 1795 Earnshaw set up in business for himself at 119, High Holborn, one door east of what is now Southampton Row. In 1801 he was awarded £500 by the Board of Longitude on account of his inventions, and in 1803 a further sum of £2,500. This did not, however, satisfy him, and in 1808 he issued 'An appeal to the Public,' in which he urged his claim to higher consideration. He died at Chenies Street in 1829, but the business was carried on by his son Thomas in Holborn, and afterwards at 87, Fenchurch Street. There is a portrait of Earnshaw engraved by Bullin from a painting by Sir Martin Archer Shee, R.A.

Benjamin Gray, who was in business in Pall Mall, was the founder of a celebrated firm of watchmakers. He was clockmaker to George II, and several specimens of his work between 1730 and 1758 are in the Guildhall Museum. Gray was joined in partnership by Justin Vulliamy, who settled in London about 1730. Vulliamy was of Swiss origin, and the first of a line of well-known makers of that name; he married the daughter of Benjamin Gray, and succeeded him in his business in Pall Mall. The watches made by this firm were of very fine quality: one of them fetched £120 15s. when the Hawkins Collection was dispersed by auction in 1895. This beautiful example had an outer case of gold and crystal and a diamond thumb-piece to press back the locking spring, the inner case being enamelled in colours with a garden scene. Justin Vulliamy was succeeded by his son Benjamin, who was in favour with George III, and much consulted by the king on mechanical subjects, especially in connexion with Kew Observatory. Benjamin Lewis Vulliamy, the next head of the firm, was born in 1780, and obtained a high reputation for the exactness and excellent finish of his work, both in clocks and watches. Until his death in 1854, the office of clockmaker to the reigning sovereign continued to be held by members of the Vulliamy family. The royal palaces contain many fine clocks made by the Vulliamys. At Windsor Castle, on the mantelpiece of the royal dining-room, is a clock by Justin Vulliamy, and in the presence chamber is another clock by the firm inclosed in a marble case which forms part of a mantelpiece designed by J. Bacon, R.A. Among the public timekeepers made by B. L. Vulliamy were the large

clock at the old Post Office, St. Martin's-le-Grand, and one at Christ Church, Oxford. Vulliamy was the author of several pamphlets on the art of clock-making; one of them being on the construction of the dead-beat escapement. He was a very active member of the Company of Clockmakers, of which he was five times master; in recognition of his services to them, the company presented him with a piece of plate in 1849.

There is a fine long-clock by Richard Vick, in a handsome Chippendale case, at Windsor Castle. Vick, who carried on business in the Strand, was master of the Clockmakers' Company in 1729, and is the maker of a repeating watch inscribed 'Richard Vick, watchmaker to his late Majesty.' Among the celebrated Clerkenwell makers the firm of Thwaites occupies an honourable place. Ainsworth Thwaites, who was in business in Rosoman Street between 1740 and 1780, made the Horse Guards clock in 1756, and a handsome long-clock about 1770 for the East India Company which is now in the India Office. He was succeeded as head of the firm by John Thwaites, who was master of the Clockmakers' Company in 1815, 1819, and 1820, and presented the company with a notable timekeeper by Henry Sully. He remained at the head of the firm from 1780 to 1816, when the firm became Thwaites & Reed, and so remained until 1842.

Stephen Rimbault was a maker of high reputation between the years 1760 and 1781, and carried on business in Great St. Andrew's Street, St. Giles's. He particularly excelled in clocks with mechanical figures dancing or working on the dials, and other complicated time-pieces; a musical clock made by Rimbault in 1780, which plays six tunes on eleven bells, is illustrated by Britten. John Zoffany, R.A., in his early days was Rimbault's decorative assistant, and his services no doubt helped largely to establish this maker's reputation.

Thomas Grignion, the first of a celebrated family of clockmakers, is stated in the inscription of St. Paul's, Covent Garden, already quoted, to have brought to perfection in 1740 'the horizontal principle in watches and the dead beat in clocks,' and to have made 'the time-piece in the pediment at the end of this parish church, destroyed by fire A.D. 1795.' A new turret clock with bells was made for the church in 1797 by Thomas Grignion the younger. The firm started at the 'King's Arms and Dial' in Great Russell Street, Covent Garden, with Daniel and Thomas Grignion as partners, who described themselves as finishers to the late Daniel Quare.

One of their watches, a fine repeater with beautifully enamelled case, is of about the year 1730, and another in the Dunn Gardner collection has the hall-mark of 1748. Thomas Grignion junior, who succeeded as head of the firm, was born in 1713 and died in 1784; a watch by him, in a *repoussé* case, is in the Victoria and Albert Museum. In 1775 the firm was styled Grignion & Son, and a third Thomas Grignion was at the head of it between 1800 and 1825.

Eardley Norton was a well-known Clerkenwell maker living at 49, St. John Street, and celebrated for his musical and astronomical clocks and watches. In 1771 he patented (No. 987) 'a clock which strikes the hours and parts upon a principle entirely new, and a watch which repeats the hours and parts, so concisely contrived and disposed as to admit of being conveniently contained not only in a watch, but also in its appendage, such as a key, seal, or trinket.' An astronomical clock with four dials made by Norton for George III is in Buckingham Palace. He was in business from 1770 to 1794, and was succeeded by Gravell & Tolkein (1794–1820), William Gravell & Son (1820–50), and Robert Rolfe (1850).

A Swiss watchmaker of eminent ability, Josiah Emery, came to England and settled in London, carrying on business at 33, Cockspur Street, Charing Cross, between 1770 and 1805. Emery was one of the earliest makers to adopt Mudge's invention of the lever escapement, and having made a watch on this principle for Count Bruhl, which proved a most satisfactory timekeeper, he decided to continue its use. In his evidence before the House of Commons Committee appointed to consider Mudge's claims to the government reward he said that he had made thirty-two or thirty-three such watches, and that his price for them was £150 each. Emery was presented with the honorary freedom of the Clockmakers' Company on 2 April 1781; there is a watch by him with ruby cylinder, helical balance spring, and compensation curb, in the Guildhall Museum.

Louis Recordon, who succeeded Emery, was in business for himself in 1780 at Greek Street, Soho. In that year he patented a pedometer-winding for watches,[13] a contrivance by which the motion of the wearer's body is utilized for winding. Recordon lived until 1810, and the business next passed into the hands of Peter Des Granges, who retired in 1842, when his shop and its goodwill was acquired by Edward John Dent.

[13] 18 Mar. 1780, no. 1249.

John Leroux was a maker of high repute who was settled between 1760 and 1800 at 8, Charing Cross. He was admitted to the honorary freedom of the Clockmakers' Company in 1781, and there is a fine watch by him dated 1785 in the Guildhall Museum.

Space will only allow of very brief mention of makers of note in the 19th century. James Tregent (1770–1804), a celebrated French maker who settled in London, first in the Strand and afterwards in Cranbourne Street, was watchmaker to the Prince of Wales, and intimate with Garrick, Sheridan, and other celebrities of the stage. Joseph Anthony Berollas (1800–30), of Denmark Street, St. Giles's, and afterwards of Coppice Row, Clerkenwell, was an ingenious maker. In 1808[14] he patented a repeater, in 1810[15] a warning watch, and in 1827[16] an alarum watch and pumping keyless arrangement. William Anthony (? 1764–1844) was one of the most expert watchmakers of his day, and specimens of his work are highly prized; his place of business was in Red Lion Street, St. John's Square. William Hardy (1800–30) was a skilful maker, living in Coppice Row, Coldbath Square, Clerkenwell. He devised, among other inventions, an escapement for clocks, which obtained a gold medal and prize of fifty guineas from the Society of Arts. A firm of well-known makers, which continued for about one hundred years at the same address, was started by Robert Storer in 1743 at 11, Berkeley Court, Clerkenwell. Walter Storer, great-grandson of the founder of the firm, retired about 1840 and died at Olney in 1865.[17]

Among the principal chronometer makers within the county of Middlesex two present-day firms, those of Barwise and Frodsham, require special mention. The first-named firm was founded by John Barwise in 1790 at St. Martin's Lane, and was afterwards removed to 3, Bury Street, St. James's. The *British Press* of 18 February 1811 describes an attack made by highwaymen on John Barwise whilst on his way to Dulwich. Barwise was associated in 1841 with Alex. Bain in a patent for electric clocks.[18] The present firm holds patents for a wristband watch and other inventions.

[14] No. 3174, 31 Oct.   [15] No. 3342, 26 May.
[16] No. 5489, 28 Apr. ; no. 5586, 13 Dec.
[17] The writer has to express his great indebtedness to Mr. F. J. Britten's admirable and exhaustive work, *Old Clocks and Watches*, and gratefully acknowledges that author's kindness in personally affording him information.
[18] No. 8783, 11 Jan.

The family of Frodsham has produced several highly skilled chronometer and watchmakers. William Frodsham, of Kingsgate Street, Red Lion Square, received the honorary freedom of the Clockmakers' Company in 1781, and attested the value of Earnshaw's improvements in 1804. He took his son into partnership in 1790, and died in 1806, when the business was continued by John Frodsham until 1814. William James Frodsham, another member of this family, started in Change Alley, was a fellow of the Royal Society, and was some time in partnership with William Parkinson; he died in 1850, and left four sons who were brought up to the trade. One of them, John, was in business with his son in Gracechurch Street from 1825 to 1842. Charles, another of the sons of W. J. Frodsham, was the founder of the present firm of Charles Frodsham & Co. He lived from 1810 to 1871, and started business in 1842 at 7, Finsbury Pavement, and in the following year succeeded John R. Arnold at 84, Strand. He conducted many experiments to investigate the principles of the compensation balance and the balance spring, and wrote many papers on technical subjects; he also invented many improvements which still exist in chronometers and watches. He was succeeded by his son, H. M. Frodsham, in 1871, and the firm became a limited company in 1893. They gained the Admiralty prize of £170 for excellence of marine chronometers.

English watches were highly esteemed at the end of the 18th century, but about this time a swarm of worthless timepieces bearing the forged names of eminent London makers swamped the best markets and inflicted a great blow upon the high reputation of English work. The Swiss took advantage of this to drive us out of the foreign markets, and much distress was caused among operatives in the trade, which led in 1816 to the appointment of a Parliamentary Committee on the petition of the watchmakers of London and Coventry. The Swiss makers still continue, with the Americans, to be our most formidable rivals in the production of cheap watches, although their work will not compare in accuracy with the more costly watches produced by English makers. The necessity for the frequent repair of these foreign time-keepers has given employment to an increasing number of the less skilful members of the trade in this country.

Little has been done in England to synchronize our public clocks, and London is in this respect still much behind other great cities. A system of magnetic clocks devised by Sir Charles Wheatstone is at work at the Royal Institution and other places. A single motor clock upon this principle will govern sixty or seventy indicating clocks, the maintaining power being supplied by magneto-electric currents. A clock in the Royal Observatory, Greenwich, distributes the time to clocks in a few London centres, but the general adoption of this much-needed system, though often talked about, seems as far off as ever.

This is not the place to trace the progress of the art of watchmaking in England, which comes more suitably in the portion of this work to be specially devoted to the City of London, the most notable improvements in the art having been made by Tompion, Graham, Mudge, and other eminent London makers. Early in the reign of Charles I, when the Clockmakers' Company was incorporated (1632), the City of London was certainly the centre of British clock and watchmaking. Clerkenwell next became the head quarters of the trade, and maintained its supremacy as long as verge watches continued in use. Soon after the invention of the lever escapement by Mudge in 1750, the movement-making was transferred to Lancashire. Here in 1866 the movements were made in Wycherley's factory by machinery in eight standard sizes, the different parts for thousands of movements being perfectly interchangeable. The movement when received by the manufacturer is usually first sent to the dial-maker to be fitted with a dial. The watch then passes through the hands of various subsidiary makers in the following order :—The escapement maker—with whom is associated the wheel-cutter and the pallet-maker, the jeweller, the finisher, and the fusee-cutter. The stop-work is then added, and (when necessary) the keyless work fitted. The case-maker, balance-maker, and hand-maker then add their work, and the examiner fits the movement to the case and puts on the hands. A work of great skill and delicacy remains, the introduction of the balance-spring. The screws of the balance require adjustment with the greatest care in order that the watch may keep time at temperatures ranging from 40 deg. to 90 deg.

The principal development of watchmaking in recent years is the application of machinery. This was attempted in London by the British Watch Company, established in 1843, at 75, Dean Street, Soho, to manufacture watches with duplicating tools invented by P. F. Ingold. An excellent watch was designed and several were made, but the incorporation of the company was successfully opposed by the ' trade,' and the undertaking consequently failed. In America the attempt to cheapen the cost of production has met with greater success. The pioneer of the movement was Aaron L. Denison, who after several preliminary attempts started a factory in 1851 at Roxbury, Massachusetts.[19] The enterprise passed through many vicissitudes before financial success and a satisfactory standard of manufacture were attained. It was not until 1860 that a dividend of 5 per cent. was declared by the American Watch Company, this being the first dividend declared by any watch factory in America. In 1900 the Waltham Watch Company produced 2,500 watches per day, and employed 1,400 women and 500 men. By the abolition of the fusee and chain a very great reduction was brought about in the number of pieces. In England the most expensive watches contain from one hundred and fifty to over a thousand pieces ; the modern short-wind watch consists of forty-seven machine-made parts.

Whilst the efforts of foreign manufacturers have been almost wholly devoted to cheapening the cost of watches, it is satisfactory to note that in England the attainment of a high quality of workmanship continues to be a great object with our principal makers. A great help in this direction has been afforded by the trials instituted at Kew Observatory in 1884, under the auspices of the Royal Society, and now carried out by the National Physical Laboratory. Three classes of certificate are granted, known respectively as A, B, and C, the test for A being especially severe. Watches that obtain eighty or more out of a total of 100 marks are classed as ' especially good,' and in spite of the severity of the tests applied the number of watches which gain this distinction has a noticeable tendency to increase.

BELL-FOUNDERS[1]

The earliest bell-founders of the metropolis are met with towards the end of the 13th century, and the trade was located near the City's eastern boundary, being chiefly connected with the parishes of St. Andrew Cornhill (now Undershaft), and St. Botolph Aldgate. The Reformation brought disaster to the craft of the bell-founders, but it is not until after the great change of religion that foundries are met with in Middlesex. From Aldgate the trade extended to the neighbouring district of Whitechapel, where Robert Mot established a business on the north side of the High Street where Tewkesbury Court now is, which after nearly three and a half centuries still exists in a flourishing state. The earliest known bell from his foundry is one bearing his name and the date 1575, formerly at Danbury in Essex. Other bells cast by him still exist at Banstead, Chertsey, Merstham, and elsewhere ; and in London the sanctus bells at St. Andrew's Holborn, and St. Clement Danes, and four of the six bells of St. Andrew Undershaft, three of which are dated 1597, and the fourth 1600. Two of the fine bells at Westminster Abbey, the third and fifth, are also Mot's work, and bear the inscription in black letter :—

CAMPANIS PATREM LAUDATE SONANTIBUS ALTUM
GABRIELL GOOD MAN WESTMON' DECANUS

Both are dated, one 1598 and the other 1583, and their lettering is very elaborate. Mot was in business for about thirty years ; many of his bells have been recast, but eighty still remain. They frequently bear his circular stamp containing the letters I.H.S., his own initials, a crown, and three bells, and are almost always dated. Most of the bells bear the inscription in black letter, 'Robertus mot me fecit,' in which he invariably spells his surname with a small *m*.

There are two petitions[2] from Mot in November 1577 to Lord Burghley, praying for the payment of debts of £10 10s. and £5 5s. due to him for eight years past from Henry Howard, esq. He complains[3] that 'your said poor orator is greatly impoverished and come into decay, and is likely every day to be arrested for such debts as he oweth.' His petition for payment of the larger sum was repeated on 7 June 1578, and again on the same date in conjunction with two other creditors of Howard. The petition was apparently hopeless ; Howard, who was the son of Viscount Bindon, was overwhelmed with debt ,and abundant evidence of his ill-conduct exists in the State Papers of this period.

---

[19] H. G. Abbott, *Watch Factories of America* (1888), 13 ; *Ency. Brit.* (ed. 10), xxxiii, 763.

[1] The writer is much indebted to Mr. H. B. Walters, M.A., F.S.A., for kindly placing at his disposal the result of his researches on this subject embodied in his paper on ' London Church Bells and Bell Founders,' contributed to the *Transactions of the St. Paul's Ecclesiological Soc.*

[2] *Cal. S.P. Dom.* 1547–80, pp. 568, 591, 593.

[3] A. D. Tyssen, *Ch. Bells of Suss.* (1864), 20.

Mot died in 1608,[4] and was succeeded in business by Joseph Carter, who was a bell-founder at Reading from 1579 to 1610. He was in business in London in 1606, apparently at the Whitechapel Foundry, of which his son William became manager. The elder Carter died in 1610, and very few of his bells are known; there is one at Walton on Thames dated 1608,[5] and one formerly belonged to Allhallows Staining, but is now melted down. William Carter succeeded his father in business, but only lived to carry it on for nine years. The inscriptions on his bells are in Gothic capitals, the alphabet being regarded by some as identical with that used by the Brasyers, Norwich founders of the 15th century.[6] Some of the younger Carter's bells have the private mark (a trefoil) of his foreman, Thomas Bartlett, who succeeded him as proprietor in 1619.

The Bartlett family remained at the head of the Whitechapel foundry to the close of the 17th century, and worthily maintained its reputation. Many of Thomas Bartlett's bells remain, although most of those which he cast for City churches must have perished in the Great Fire. One, however—that of St. Margaret Pattens, set up in 1624—survived even that catastrophe, although the church lay within the doomed district. Another of his bells, a very fine specimen, which has survived is the Curfew bell, still rung nightly in the chapel of the Charterhouse. This was cast in 1631, and bears the arms and initials of Thomas Sutton, the famous founder of that institution. Thomas Bartlett died in or before the year 1632, and his son Anthony being apparently only a child the business was carried on during the next eight years by John Clifton, whose bells are chiefly found in south-west Essex. They did not bear the trade mark of the Whitechapel foundry until 1640; a bell at Lambourne, Essex, marked with that date and the initials A. B., seems to show that young Anthony had then advanced in age sufficiently to take charge of the business. He began his career at an unfortunate time, when the church was laid low and church requisites were destroyed instead of being purchased or renewed. But he survived this gloomy period in spite of the vigorous competition of a famous City firm. The revival of Church life at the Restoration, and the repair of the ravages caused by the terrible conflagration, brought a welcome change to the fortunes of the head of the Whitechapel foundry, and examples of Anthony Bartlett's work remain at St. Edmund Lombard Street, St. George Botolph Lane (recently united with St. Mary at Hill), and St. Olave Hart Street. The bells at the latter church, which escaped the Fire, are dated 1662. Anthony died in 1676 and was succeeded by his son James, who was a member of the Founders' Company, becoming a liveryman in 1677, and serving as under-warden in 1691 and upper-warden in 1695. He supplied many of the bells required for Wren's new churches, four at Christ Church Southwark, dated 1700, and four at Richmond, Surrey, dated 1680. One of the latter has the following somewhat boastful inscription :—

LAMBERT MADE ME WEAK, NOT FIT TO RING,
BUT BARTLET AMONGST THE REST HATH MADE ME SING.

On the death of James Bartlett in January 1700–1 the Whitechapel foundry passed into the hands of Richard Phelps, who was born at Avebury, Wiltshire. He continued at the head of the firm for thirty-seven years, during which time the business grew to be the most successful in the kingdom. His bells are met with in many different localities, and among his best work are the peals at St. Michael Cornhill, St. Magnus, Allhallows Lombard Street, and St. Andrew Holborn. His inscriptions are much longer, if not more intelligent, than those of his predecessors. The following appears on the tenth bell of St. Michael Cornhill :—

TO PRAYER WE DO CALL ST. MICHAEL'S PEOPLE ALL
WE HONOUR TO THE KING AND IOY TO BRIDES DO SING
TRIUMPHS WE LOUDLY TELL AND RING THE DEAD
    MAN'S KNELL.

Phelps is chiefly known as the founder of the great hour-bell of St. Paul's, which now hangs in the south-west tower of the cathedral and bears the inscription : 'RICHARD PHELPS MADE ME 1716.' It weighs 5 tons 4 cwt., and its diameter is 6 ft. 10⅝ in. ; this bell is only used for tolling the hour, and for tolling at the death and funeral of a member of the royal family, the Bishop of London, the Dean of the Cathedral, or the Lord Mayor. The larger part of the metal of which it is made belonged to the bell formerly hanging in the clock-tower opposite Westminster Hall and known first as 'Edward,' after the Confessor, and afterwards as 'Great Tom'; the price paid for it was £3,025 17s. 6d.[7] St. Paul's

[4] A. D. Tyssen, *Ch. Bells of Suss.* (1864), 35.
[5] J. C. L. Stahlschmidt, *Surr. Bells and Lond. Bell-founders* (1884), 94–5.
[6] Ibid. 95 ; cf. Tyssen, op. cit. 36.

[7] Harl. MS. 6824, fol. 31. An engraving with particulars of this bell is in the *Antiq. Repertory*, i, 11 ; ii, 162.

received in 1877 the gift of a new ring of twelve bells cast by Messrs. Taylor of Loughborough, and 'Great Paul' by the same firm, weighing 17 tons, was safely hung in the north-west tower in May 1882.

The latest bell bearing Phelps's name is the priests' bell at St. George's Southwark, inscribed : R. PHELPS 1738 T. LESTER FECIT. Phelps died in 1738, and the order for this bell was completed by his foreman Thomas Lester, to whom he bequeathed his business and the lease of the foundry. Lester removed the business from Essex Street to the premises which it has continued to occupy until now at 32 and 34, Whitechapel Road. His first peal was cast for Shoreditch parish church in 1739 and the commission greatly pleased him. The tenor bell of St. Mary-le-Bow, which weighs 53 cwt. 24 lb., was cast by Phelps and Lester in 1738, nine others by Lester and Pack in 1762, and two trebles (increasing the peal to twelve) by the successors of the firm in 1881.[8] In the same year (1738) the tenor at Westminster Abbey, which once belonged to St. Michael's Cornhill, was recast by the firm. Lester's management, however, was not successful, and the fortunes of the foundry were at a low ebb until 1752, when he took into partnership Thomas Pack, who appears to have been his foreman. The partnership of Lester and Pack was more prosperous, and was marked by several changes in the style of lettering on the bells and the extensive use of rhyming couplets. One instance of the latter will suffice, taken from the treble at Ingatestone, Essex :—

THE FOUNDER HE HAS PLAY'D HIS PART WHICH SHEWS
HIM MASTER OF HIS ART
SO HANG ME WELL AND RING ME TRUE AND I WILL
SING YOUR PRAISES DUE.

In the decoration of their bells they used various ornamental devices, one of which, consisting of alternate loops and V-shaped terminations, became known as the Whitechapel pattern and lasted till 1835. They also introduced the practice of inscribing each bell with its weight. Lester died in 1769, when his nephew William Chapman was taken into partnership, and the firm continued as Pack and Chapman until the death of Thomas Pack in 1781. Chapman then took into partnership William Mears, whom, as a young man, he had for some time employed and taught the business, and who had afterwards set up in business for himself.[9] On the death of Chapman in 1784 Mears re-

mained sole partner until 1789, when he retired, leaving the foundry in the hands of his son Thomas Mears.[10] It is interesting to note, as Mr. Walters points out, that the name of Mears has been connected with the firm for 125 years, although the last representative died in 1873.

The Whitechapel foundry became at this time the most famous foundry in England,[11] Dobson's foundry at Downham Market, Norfolk, having been fused into it, as well as the Gloucester foundry, which was incorporated in 1732. The old foundry at Gloucester had existed for centuries. 'John of Gloster' was a bell-founder there in the 13th century ; but it came chiefly into note under the Rudhall family in the 18th century.

Thomas Mears was at the head of the business until 1810, taking his son Thomas into partnership in 1806. The fine peal of bells at the parish church of St. Dunstan, Stepney, was cast by this firm in 1806. Thomas Mears the younger succeeded in 1810 and remained sole head until 1843, when the firm became Charles and George Mears and so continued until 1857. On the death of Charles Mears in that year the style of the firm was altered to George Mears and Co. The famous Big Ben which strikes the hours in the Clock Tower of the Houses of Parliament was recast by George Mears from a design by Mr. Denison (afterwards Lord Grimthorpe) in 1858. The bell weighs 13 tons 10 cwt. 3 qrs. 15 lb. and took the place of one weighing $16\frac{1}{2}$ tons cast by John Warner and Sons in 1856, which was unfortunately cracked whilst being exhibited to the public before being mounted in the Clock Tower. In 1863 George Mears took as his partner Robert Stainbank, and the firm became known as Mears and Stainbank. On the death of Mears in 1873 Stainbank was the sole proprietor. He died in 1883, and was succeeded by Arthur Silva Lawson, on whose death in 1904 the business passed into the hands of Arthur Hughes, its present proprietor.

There were some minor Middlesex founders. Thomas Swain, who was born at West Bedfont in the county, succeeded in 1739 as executor and residuary legatee to the business of Robert Catlin, a founder in St. Andrew's Holborn. Swain removed the foundry to Longford near West Drayton ; besides the peal at Thames Ditton, several bells cast by

---

[8] H. B. Walters, op. cit. 20.
[9] A. D. Tyssen, op. cit. 41.

[10] Stahlschmidt (*Ch. Bells o, Surr.* 105) says that William Mears took his son Thomas into partnership in 1787, the partnership lasting till 1791
[11] Ellacombe, *Ch. Bells of Devon* (1872), 9, 62.

him are to be found in Surrey and Sussex. Another founder was Thomas Janeway, who left the Whitechapel firm to set up in business for himself at Chelsea. He was fairly successful, and his bells dating from 1763 to 1785 include those of old Chelsea Church, Kensington, Edgware, and Hornsey, peals of eight at Battersea and Blechingley, and many other bells in Surrey and Sussex.[12] His business, like that of Thomas Swain, does not appear to have continued after his death.

Robert Patrick married Sarah Oliver, granddaughter of Thomas Lester of the Whitechapel Foundry,[13] and started an opposition business in Whitechapel, being some time in partnership with one Osborn of Downham, Norfolk. He cast the bells of St. John at Hackney and St. Botolph Bishopsgate, and the peal of eight at Reigate, which bear the date 1784. C. Oliver, a bell-founder in Bethnal Green, cast a peal of bells for the church of Worth, Sussex, in 1844.

BREWING

In the Middle Ages when ale was the general drink of all classes, brewing was a necessary and often domestic industry, and few records of local courts are without some reference to its regulation. When, however, brewing became an extensive trade, and especially after the gradual change of taste which substituted hopped beer for the old English ale, we have few notices of any interest relating to brewing in rural Middlesex until comparatively modern times, though, as hereafter mentioned, a number of breweries are known to have existed near the river bank east of the Tower as early as the 15th century and perhaps before. The history of the licensing and regulation of ale houses belongs rather to Social and Economic History. William Hucks, who represented Wallingford in Parliament, was a well-known brewer of the 18th century. He was brewer to King George I, and paid that sovereign the doubtful honour of setting up his statue on the summit of the steeple of St. George's Church, Bloomsbury. This occasioned the following satirical quatrain :—

The King of Great Britain was reckon'd before
  The head of the Church by all good Christian people,
But his brewer has added still one title more
  To the rest, and has made him the head of the steeple.

William Hucks was one of the principal inhabitants of the parish of St. Giles in the Fields, and of the new parish of St. George Bloomsbury, formed out of it in the year 1731.[1] He filled various parochial offices from 1689 to the separation of the parishes, was receiver of the subscriptions for building the workhouse, and took an active part in rebuilding St.

Giles's Church. Parton attributes to him the well-known anecdote of the interview of King Lewis XV with the ' chevalier de malt ' which is generally associated with Humphrey Parsons the East Smithfield brewer.[2]

On his death on 4 November 1740, he was succeeded by his son Robert Hucks. The site of the brewery is not known, but it appears to have been near the junction of Shaftesbury Avenue and Charing Cross Road. Mottley, who wrote (under the pseudonym of Robert Seymour) a *Survey of London*, published in 1735, gives a list of the streets and lanes in St. Giles's parish.[3] Among those included in ' the first part of the old town ' are ' Brown's Gardens and therein Two Brewers Yard.' This is probably the site of the brewery, and the surrounding localities point to its position as indicated above.

The firm appears from the following note in the *Annual Register* for 1758,[4] to have had a branch establishment in Pall Mall : ' 30th May. At a store-cellar in Pall Mall, Mrs. Hucks's cooper, and a chairman who went down after him, were both suffocated as supposed by the steam of 40 butts of unstopped beer.' In the beer tax returns of 1760 ' Huck ' occupies a position eighth on the list with an output of 28,615 barrels.[5]

Hucks had a brother, also a brewer, in partnership with Smith Meggot, whose business was in Stoney Lane, Southwark, the firm being recorded in Kent's *London Directory* of 1738 as Hucks and Meggott.

The Black Eagle Brewery at Spitalfields of Messrs. Truman, Hanbury, Buxton & Co., Ltd., is one of the oldest in London and covers an area of over 6 acres. The founder was one Thomas Bucknall, who in 1669 erected a

[12] Tyssen, *Ch. Bells of Suss.* 43.   [13] Ibid. 40.
[1] John Parton, *Some Acct. of the Par. of St. Giles in the Fields* (1822), 392–3.
[2] See *post*, p. 172.
[3] Op. cit. ii, 767.   [4] Op. cit. 96.
[5] Alfred Barnard, *Noted Breweries*, i, 209.

brewhouse on 'Lolsworth Field at Spittle-hope,' an estate then belonging to Sir William Wheler, bart. The business passed in 1694 into the hands of Joseph Truman the elder, the property consisting of six messuages and one brewhouse.[6] The remainder of the Wheler estate was built upon and covered with streets, and part of this property has since been acquired by the firm for the extension of their premises. Joseph Truman was a successful business man, and in 1716 took into partnership Joseph Truman, jun., Alud Denne, and others. He died in 1719, and a curious document of that date is in the firm's possession described as 'An inventory of the goods, chattels, and credits of Joseph Truman, which since his death have come into the hands, possession and knowledge of Benjamin Truman, Daniel Cooper, and the executors named in the will of Joseph Truman.'[7] Benjamin Truman who was an executor of Joseph Truman, sen., joined the firm in 1722. An anecdote which exhibits his shrewdness as a business man is told by J. P. Malcolm.[8] On the birth of the Duchess of Brunswick, granddaughter of George II, in August 1737, the Prince of Wales ordered four loads of faggots and a number of tar barrels to be burnt before Carlton House to celebrate the event, and directed the brewer of his household to place four barrels of beer near the bonfire for the use of those who chose to partake of the beverage. The beer proved to be of inferior quality and the people threw it into each other's faces and the barrels into the fire. The prince remedied the matter on the following night by ordering a fresh quantity of beer from another brewer. This was supplied by Truman, who took care that it should be of the best, thus earning for himself considerable popularity.

Another early document possessed by the firm, dated 1739, is endorsed, 'A "rest"[8a] taken and general account stated of all debts and credits, and also of the malt, hoppes, coales, beer in the several store cellers and brewhouse, with all the other goods, utensells as affixt, used and employ'd in the brewing trade carried on by Benjamin Truman, John Denne, Francis Cooper, and the surviving executors of Alud Denne, at their brewhouse and several warehouses, situated in Brick Lane, in the parish of Christchurch, in the county of Middlesex.' At this time the brewery was very extensive, and had on its books 296 publicans, one of whom was the second partner in the firm, Alud Denne. The business greatly prospered under the management of Benjamin Truman, who was knighted by George III on his accession in recognition of his loyalty in contributing to the voluntary loans raised to carry on the various foreign wars. Sir Benjamin was a man of refined taste and a lover of the arts; his portrait by Gainsborough is preserved in the board-room, formerly the drawing-room, of the house in Brick Lane. Sir Benjamin Truman died 20 March 1780, and left a daughter, his only child, whose two grandsons (Sir Benjamin's great-grandchildren), John Freeman Villebois and Henry Villebois, succeeded to his interest in the business. The Hanbury family now became connected with the firm, Sampson Hanbury becoming a partner in 1780, and being joined later by his brother Osgood Hanbury. The brothers belonged to an old Essex family, their father, Osgood Hanbury, having a seat at Holfield Grange. Sampson Hanbury was greatly devoted to agriculture and a keen sportsman. He was an excellent man of business, and is said to have excelled all his clerks in his knowledge of book-keeping. His brother Osgood took a less active part in the business, devoting himself more to country life and the management of his Essex estate. Anna, the sister of Sampson Hanbury, married Thomas Fowell Buxton, of Earls Colne, Essex, and their son, Thomas Fowell Buxton, born in 1786, entered the service of his uncles at the brewery in 1808, at first as an assistant and three years afterwards as a partner. The young man had had a brilliant career at Trinity College, Dublin, and soon after his admission as a partner, the seniors, struck with his capability and energy, entrusted him with the responsible task of reorganizing the entire system on which the brewery was conducted. This he accomplished with great success, overcoming objections from the senior officials with great firmness and tact. Among other measures of reform, he resolved to remedy the state of gross ignorance which prevailed among the workmen. He dealt with this in a summary method, by calling the men together and threatening to discharge at the end of six weeks everyone who could not read and write. He gave them a schoolmaster and other means of instruction and fixed a day for examination, when he was gratified to find that he had not to send away a single man. He was also very careful to prevent the servants of the firm from working on Sunday. Mr. Buxton

[6] Alf. Barnard, *Noted Breweries* (1889), i, 173 et seq.
[7] Ibid. 174.
[8] *Manners and Customs of Lond. in 18th century* (1810), i, 314.
[8a] This term (in its old meaning of 'balance') is still employed by the firm, the annual stock-taking being called the 'Rest-day.'

entered Parliament in 1818, and distinguished himself there by his efforts in the cause of philanthropy and in the reform of our judicial and penal systems. The great work of his life and the cause which lay nearest to his heart was that in which he was associated with William Wilberforce—the abolition of slavery in the dominions of Great Britain. In 1816, when almost the whole population of Spitalfields was on the verge of starvation, a meeting was called at the Mansion House, and Buxton delivered a forcible speech. He narrated the results of his personal investigations; the large sum of £43,369 was raised at the meeting, and an extensive and well-organized system of relief was established. He was for twenty years the representative of Weymouth in Parliament, and was made a baronet in 1841. He did not live long to enjoy his honours, but died in 1845, worn out by his great labours in public and private life.

Mr. Osgood Hanbury was succeeded by his son Robert, who was born in 1796 and entered the firm in 1820. He possessed great business abilities, and when Mr. Buxton's Parliamentary duties withdrew him from the active management of the brewery, the superintendence and control of the business passed entirely into his hands. Amongst other alterations which he carried out was the institution of the ale department, an example speedily followed by other London breweries. One of Mr. Hanbury's sons, Mr. Charles Addington Hanbury, became a member of the firm, and a son of the last-named, Mr. John M. Hanbury, is a director. The Pryor family became connected with the brewery in 1816, when Messrs. T. M. Pryor and Robert Pryor, who were owners of the Shoreditch brewery, and came from an old Hertfordshire family, joined the firm. Mr. Robert Pryor died in 1839, having the previous year introduced his nephew, Mr. Arthur Pryor, who became a partner and succeeded him in his duties. Mr. Arthur Pryor died in September 1904; two of his sons, Mr. Arthur Vickris Pryor and Mr. Robert Pryor, became directors. Mr. A. V. Pryor is now the head of the company's brewery at Burton-on-Trent, but Mr. Robert Pryor died in July 1905.

The premises in Spitalfields are of enormous extent. At the entrance to the brewery yard is the weighbridge, where the van-loads of malt as they arrive from the railway are easily unloaded by one man, who tips the sacks over the tail of the van into a bin or receiver. From this receptacle the malt is conveyed to the top of the brewery, where it is screened, and then passed along one of two Archimedean screws which deliver the grain into the malt-bins. The malt stores adjoin the brewhouse on its western side, and are contained within a building 200 ft. long, 30 ft. wide, and 60 ft. high; this great storehouse is divided off into twenty-one bins, each of which holds from 500 qrs. to 1,200 qrs. of malt. When required for use the malt is conveyed by screws to crushing-mills erected on a gallery in the brewhouse, supported on massive columns and girders. Eight pairs of rolls or cylinders are employed, each having its own screening machinery, and being fitted with dust destroyers; these rollers are driven by the main engine or by another of 30 h.p. on the same floor, and crush over 100 qrs. of malt per hour. The malt is bruised or crushed sufficiently to detach the husk from the grain, so that the latter may be easily reached by the water and the whole of its valuable qualities extracted. The grinding accomplished, the bruised malt or grist is next conveyed by large copper tubes to the elevators into the six grist cases at the top of the building, each of which contains 160 qrs. The next process is that known as mashing, and the water used for this purpose is obtained from a well bored to a depth of 850 ft. For 200 ft. it has a diameter of 8 ft.; here the chalk of the London basin was reached, and the curious discovery made of a bed of oysters 18 in. thick, and probably extending for a great distance, as a similar bed was afterwards found on sinking a well at Stratford. A bore-pipe of 12 in. diameter carries the well down to its full depth of 850 ft. Good water, hard and free from organic matter, is indispensable to the manufacture of good beer. The object of the process of mashing is to mix the malt with water at such a temperature as shall not only extract the saccharine matter existing in the malt, but shall also change the still unconverted starch into grape sugar. The appliances for this process at Truman's brewery are said to be among the finest in England. There are six mash-tuns having a total capacity of 700 qrs.; each is provided with a Steel's mashing-machine and other modern contrivances, and has a copper cover lifted up by springs and pulleys. The mash-tuns are supported by circular iron frames raised on stout iron columns to enable the mashmen to get beneath the tuns. The wort is drawn off into a copper receiver by means of several pipes running from different parts of the mash-tun; each of these is fitted with a trap top to enable the brewer to test the strength of the liquor from every part of the tun. The furnaces employed for heating the boilers were fitted with Jucke's smoke-consuming contrivances in 1848. Mr. Fraser, who introduced their use into the brewery, was so satisfied with their efficiency that he read a paper before the Society of Arts strongly recommending Jucke's furnaces for general use. For this he received a letter of thanks from Lord Palmerston, the Home Secretary, who also referred to his paper in reply to a deputation which waited upon him in reference to the smoke nuisance.[9] Whilst the wort is in the coppers the hops are added, the whole being boiled under a slight pressure. The storage-room for hops is an apartment 200 ft. long by 50 ft. broad, and darkened to keep away the light from the delicate hops, of which some 3,000 pockets are kept ready for use.

When the wort has boiled the necessary time it runs into the hop-back to settle. The ale hop-back is a square vessel with a copper lining and gun-metal plates at the bottom to retain the hops when the wort is drawn off into the coolers. The porter hop-back is of similar construction. The cooling is hastened by refrigerators in the room beneath, these refrigerators being supplied with water which has come from two ice machines. The next process is that of fermentation, which is carried on in a splendid room below, the floor of which is constructed entirely of slate. It is known as the 'Havelock Room,' having been built at the time of the Indian Mutiny, and is shaped like the letter L with dimensions of 210 ft. and 132 ft. Here are contained fermenting vessels of slate and wood, each provided with a copper parachute for skimming yeast, communicating with the yeast tanks below. Each of the vessels holds from 120 to 190 barrels and contains an attemporator to raise or lower the temperature of the gyle at pleasure. This contrivance consists of a series of pipes fixed within the tun and having its inlet and outlet on the outside ; by this means it is possible to run hot or cold water through the pipes at any hour. The object of the natural process which we know as fermentation is to convert the saccharine matter into alcohol, this requiring the most careful attention on the brewer's part. To obtain a quick and regular fermentation yeast, or barm as it is sometimes called, is employed, and this must be perfectly fresh and healthy. The appearance of a 'gyle' of beer in the earlier stages of fermentation is very beautiful.[10] At first the surface is covered with a thick white foam which within a few hours curls itself into a variety of fantastic shapes. As the froth rises higher it presents the appearance of jagged rocks of snowy whiteness. Then

the froth becomes viscid and the whole surface subsides. The operation of cleansing next follows, and consists of removing the yeast from the beer in order to stop the fermentation. This is performed in another large apartment called 'King's College,' which contains ten cleansing batches holding together 3,000 barrels, all fitted with copper parachutes. A series of cleansing batches each measuring 18 ft. by 11 ft. is also fitted up in 'Long Acre.' This was once a long street, dividing two extensive blocks of buildings, extending nearly a sixth of a mile, which was roofed and inclosed at each end by the firm many years ago, and is now the longest building in the brewery.

On the ground floor is a spacious room paved with stone containing a large number of shallow yeast tanks or batches. These receive the yeast from the copper parachutes above, and are kept cool by means of a false bottom in each vessel, through which a stream of cold water is constantly running. The extent of the cellars in the basement is enormous. They are divided off into great main avenues which appear of endless length, and these are intersected by others branching in all directions.

The main brewhouse, in which most of the operations which we have described above are carried on, is a fine structure. A glance at its fine roof, the spacious galleries which surround it, and the massive columns which support its various stages, shows how successful the architect has been in producing so excellent a combination of utility and beauty. The vat-houses and racking rooms open out of one another and occupy an area of $1\frac{1}{2}$ acres. One of the largest of these storehouses was first opened on the 9th of November 1841, when the workmen had a dinner in honour of the event. Whilst they sat at table word was brought that an heir was born to the English throne, whereupon the largest vat was named the 'Prince of Wales,' its name with the date being painted on it. On a visit which he paid to the brewery, the Prince (his late Majesty King Edward VII) drank a glass of stout from this vat, whose age was identical with his own. To reach the top of these huge vats metal staircases are fixed to the wall in certain places ; the view from above is remarkable, and affords an idea which no words can describe of the vast capacity of these gigantic receptacles.

Space does not permit to speak of the cooperage, sign-writing, and many other departments which are on a similar extensive scale, the firm having from a very early period made all the wooden vessels and utensils

[9] Barnard, *Noted Breweries*, i, 192.
[10] *Ency. Brit.* (ed. 9), iv, 275.

required for the brewery. From a printed return for the beer tax made in 1760,[11] a copy of which is in the firm's possession, Truman's Brewery appears third on the list of London brewers, with 60,140 barrels, but they are not placed among the six principal ale brewers in London in 1806–7. In a return of porter brewed in 1813–14 they stand third on the list of London brewers, with 145,141 barrels. In 1886–7 they were second among their competitors, having brewed in London and Burton 500,000 barrels.

In the residence attached to the brewery, which was in former days occupied by members of the firm, is the historic dining-room, the scene of many a famous banquet graced by distinguished company. One of the most notable of these convivialities was that described as the 'cabinet dinner' in the *Memoirs of Sir Thomas Fowell Buxton*.[12] In June 1831 several members of the government and other gentlemen came to look over the brewery in Spitalfields and afterwards dined there with Mr. Buxton, professedly on beef-steaks cooked in one of the furnaces. The company included the Premier Earl Grey, Brougham Lord Chancellor, the Duke of Richmond, Lord Shaftesbury and others, making twenty-three in all. Brougham astonished everyone by his versatility and the accuracy and extent of his knowledge, being equally at home in discussing Paley's *Moral Philosophy*, the construction of machinery, and the points of a horse. Since 1873 Messrs. Truman, Hanbury, and Buxton have carried on a large brewery of pale ale at Burton in addition to their London establishment. In recent years a great demand has arisen for beer in bottle, and to meet this Messrs. Truman & Co. have established an extensive bottling department. The partnership business was converted into a company in 1889, with a share capital of £1,215,000. The present directors are Messrs. E. U. Buxton, A. V. Pryor, J. H. Buxton, J. M. Hanbury, Gerald Buxton, H. F. Buxton, J. A. Pryor, and Anthony Buxton.

Stow[13] says that St. Katharine's, a district on the Thames bank east of the Tower of London, 'was famous for brewhouses in ancient times. One Geffrey Gate in K. Henry VII his days spoiled the brewhouses at St. Katharines twice ; either for brewing too much to their customers beyond the sea, or for putting too much water into the beer of their customers that they served on this side

the sea, or for both.' In the year 1492 John Merchant, a Fleming, was licensed by the same king to export fifty tuns of ale called Berré. Pennant[14] says : ' Below St. Catherine's on the riverside stood the great breweries or Bere House as it is called in the map published in the first volume of the *Civitates Orbis*.' This was the public brewhouse where the citizens of London could bring their malt and other materials, and for a fee paid to the government brew therein their own ales. Pennant also states that the demand from foreign parts for English beer increased to a high degree and that in the reign of Queen Elizabeth 500 'tons' were exported at one time.

The Red Lion Brewery, which stands on the site of the ancient Beer House, can be traced back to the 16th century. In 1705 the brewery belonged to Alderman Humphrey Parsons,[15] who was elected alderman of Portsoken Ward in 1721, served as sheriff in the following year, and was Lord Mayor in 1730 and again in 1740. The following anecdote is told of him in a contemporary journal :—On one occasion, during his mayoralty, he went out riding with a hunting party which included Louis XV and his suite. He was exceedingly well mounted, and, contrary to the etiquette observed in the French Court, outstripped the rest of the company, and was first in at the death. The king, observing this, inquired the name of the stranger, and was indignantly informed that he was ' un chevalier de malte.' On receiving this information the king entered into conversation with Mr. Parsons and asked the price of his horse. Bowing in the most courtly style, the 'chevalier' replied that his horse was beyond any price other than His Majesty's acceptance. In due time the horse was accepted by the king, and from thenceforward Chevalier Parsons had the exclusive honour and privilege of supplying the French Court with his far-famed porter. In the year 1802 the brewery came into the hands of the Hoare family, and since that time has descended from father to son without changing hands. The Red Lion Brewery is of considerable extent, consisting of a large range of buildings facing the River Thames, and covers 3 acres of ground.

The brewhouse is situated in Lower East Smithfield and has a convenient wharf at the river side. The malthouse is the most ancient part of the premises, with its cross-beams and joists of enormous thickness and curious old staircases with broad landings and quaint turnings ; the elevator or 'Jacob's

---

[11] Quoted Barnard, op. cit. 209.
[21] Ibid. 210.   [13] *Surv.* (1720), bk. ii, 8.
[14] *Hist. of Lond.* (ed. 4, 1805), 265.
[15] Barnard, op. cit. iii, 53–4.

ladder' in this building is said to be a hundred years old, but does its work to-day as well as ever. Like many other London breweries, the Red Lion Brewery is supplied with the purest water by means of a well of great depth sunk on the premises. This well has a diameter of 5 ft. to the depth of 100 ft., below which it is carried by two bore-holes, of 12 and 9 in. diameter respectively, 300 ft. down to the chalk. A further supply of water is obtained from the London Clay by other wells of less depth which are only used in summer, when the Thames water is not cold enough for supplying the refrigerators. Up to the beginning of the 19th century, says Mr. Barnard,[16] the peculiar flavour of porter hitherto thought inimitable gave rise to an opinion that no other than Thames water was calculated to produce good porter. This opinion became so general that not only in the United Kingdom but in the world at large, wherever porter was known and prized as a beverage, the genuine brew was considered as locally confined to London. Here, in the oldest brewery in London, Thames water was never used, the supply from the wells being considered superior for mashing and for preserving the intrinsic quality of the beverage. It is a well known fact that up to quite recently the London brewers were not quite agreed among themselves on the process of brewing porter, each pursuing a different road to the same object, and all pretending to some secret with which the others were supposed to be unacquainted.

The brewing of porter is not now confined to London, but is carried on in various parts of the United Kingdom with great success, particularly in Ireland, though Mr. Barnard, speaking from personal experience, has not met with a brew of porter or stout superior to that of Messrs. Hoare in the three kingdoms. One of the storage cellars, 48 yds. long and containing a series of twenty bricked vaults, is said to have been built in the time of Elizabeth. Another, in which the finest stouts are stored and matured, has been known as 'Old London' from time immemorial. The returns already quoted for the year 1760 give the output of this brewery in the time of Lady Parsons as 34,098 barrels, which places it sixth in rank among the principal London brewhouses, and just above that of Thrale the famous Southwark brewer. The brewery is now conducted under the style of Hoare & Co., Ltd.

A small brewhouse existed about the year 1730 on the east side of High Street, Shore-ditch, which deserves mention from the interest attaching to its proprietor. This was one Ralph Harwood, who is said to have invented porter. In Curtain Road, Shoreditch, a public house, known as the 'Blue Last,' formerly displayed a board inscribed, 'The house where porter was first sold.' The beer-drinkers in the early part of the 18th century had the choice of three beverages, known as ale, beer, and 'twopenny.' Those who preferred a combination of any two of these would ask for 'half and half,' whilst some would favour a mixture of all three, and call for a pot of three threads or three thirds. The drawer could only supply this compound by drawing from three different casks—a wasteful and inconvenient process. To meet this growing taste it occurred to Ralph Harwood to brew a liquor which should combine in itself the virtues and flavours of the 'three threads'—ale, beer, and twopenny. And so was produced a drink which he called 'Entire,' or 'Entire Butts.' This completely met the public taste, and the beverage has never since lost its popularity.

Another famous Middlesex brewery of early date was the Griffin Brewery, in Liquorpond Street, now known as Clerkenwell Road. The locality is one of much interest ; close by are Gray's Inn Road and Hatton Garden, and in Brooke Street, near the brewery, the poet Chatterton brought his life to its sad end. The buildings, which covered upwards of 4 acres, extended from the north end of Gray's Inn Lane, across Leather Lane, to Hatton Garden. The business was established some time in the 17th century, and was always noted for its black beer or porter. In 1809 the firm dissolved partnership, Mr. Meux acquiring a business for himself in Tottenham Court Road, and Mr. A. Reid retaining possession of the old brewhouse in Liquorpond Street. Various distinguished persons from time to time visited the brewery, among them the Emperor Napoleon III, who showed his appreciation of the firm's famous stout by emptying a tankard.

Pennant[17] gives statistics of the barrels of strong beer brewed by the chief porter brewers of London in 1786-7, in which Richard Meux, who then owned the Griffin Brewery, figures ninth on the list with an output of 49,651 barrels. The same writer, speaking of this brewhouse as it existed in his day, says[18] :—

The sight of a great London brewhouse exhibits a magnificence unspeakable. The vessels evince the extent of the trade. Mr. Meux of Liquorpond

---

[16] Op. cit. iii, 58.

[17] Thos. Pennant, op. cit. 266.　[18] Ibid. 267.

Street, Gray's Inn Lane, can show twenty-four tuns, containing in all 35,000 barrels. In the present year he has built a vessel 60 feet in diameter, 176 feet in circumference, and 23 feet in height. It cost £5,000 in building, and contains from ten to twelve thousand barrels of beer, valued at about £20,000. A dinner was given to 200 people at the bottom, and 200 more joined the company to drink success to the vat.

Another vat of even greater dimensions was, about the time that Pennant wrote, constructed by this firm in their no. 3 store. This was called the 'X.Y.Z.,' and exceeded in size all similar vessels constructed before or since ; its capacity was for 20,000 barrels of porter, and it cost £10,000. At that time the London porter brewers strove in rivalry for the possession of the largest vat. These enormous receptacles were afterwards disused, their places being taken by about five thousand casks of ale. A plentiful supply of water was obtained from two wells and from the New River Company, being pumped for storage into four large reservoirs on the roofs of the buildings. In the fermenting rooms were four huge rounds, the largest of which contained 56,700 gallons, besides two smaller ones. Two of these vessels were regarded as being the largest of their kind in London, and rose 12 ft. above the floor.

A well-furnished library was provided by the firm for the use of their staff of officials and workmen. This was founded in 1860, but the new building containing it, known as the Griffin Library House, was built in 1883. In June 1898 this brewery was amalgamated with the Stag Brewery of Messrs. Watney & Co., the buildings in Clerkenwell Road being pulled down.

The Woodyard Brewery, of Castle Street, Long Acre, situated midway between the City and the West End of London, took its name from the original occupation of Thomas Shackle, a dealer in timber, who founded it in 1740. Shackle is said to have delivered his beer in small casks with his wood, and by his energy and diligence to have built up a valuable business. He was succeeded by a Mr. Gyfford, of whom no further record remains, but at the beginning of the 19th century the brewery was acquired by Mr. Harvey Christian Combe, who was remarkable for his energy and great business ability. He became Lord Mayor in 1799, and was returned five times as the City's representative in Parliament. Alderman Combe was a man of liberal tastes, fond of good company, and quick at repartee. A dinner which he gave on 7 June 1807 became known as the Royal Brewhouse Dinner, and was widely talked of in all parts of London. From a newspaper report of the time we learn that the company included the Duke and Duchess of York, the Duke or Cambridge, the Earl of Lauderdale, Lord Erskine, Sheridan, Stepney, and others, who were received by the alderman and his family and conducted to an upper floor of the brewhouse, where a table was prepared for their reception furnished only with such requisites as the brewhouse could supply. The tablecloth was a hop-sack nailed to the table, the plates were wooden trenchers, with wooden bowls for salads, wooden salt-cellars, bone spoons, and Tunbridge-ware pepper-castors. The provisions consisted of rump steaks cooked by the brewhouse stoker, and served in a new malt-shovel covered with a tin lid, porter being the only beverage. After an inspection of the brewery the company were taken by the alderman to his house in Great Russell Street, where they were entertained with a second course and dessert which included every delicacy of the season.

The business was largely increased under the management of Mr. Combe, who expended a considerable sum in the repair and rebuilding of the brewery premises. On his death in 1832 the brewery passed to his son, Mr. Harvey Combe, and his brother-in-law, Mr. Delafield, by whom the premises were still further enlarged. Mr. Harvey Combe, who was a great sportsman and well-known as the master of the Berkeley Hounds, died unmarried in 1858. He was succeeded by his two nephews, Messrs. R. H. and Charles Combe, Mr. Joseph Bonsor and his two sons, and Mr. John Spicer. Under the management of these partners the brewhouse property was still further extended, and ultimately covered more than 4 acres. The premises comprised three extensive blocks of buildings, the first being the brewhouse quadrangle, offices, and fermenting rooms ; the second, malt stores, other fermenting rooms, and cellars ; the third, stables, dray-sheds, and general stores. The water, or 'liquor' as the brewers term it, required for brewing purposes was supplied in part by the New River Company and partly by three deep wells sunk by the firm upon the premises. The cooperage department, in which casks were both constructed and repaired, was on an extensive scale. The brewery employed about four hundred and fifty hands, and the annual output exceeded 500,000 barrels. In June 1898 this business was also acquired by Messrs. Watney & Co.

The Horse Shoe Brewery of Messrs. Meux & Co. at the junction of Tottenham Court Road and Oxford Street forms a picturesque object in an old print of the

INDUSTRIES

'Entrance to London from Tottenham Court Road.' It was founded by a Mr. Blackburn, and was from the days of George III famous for its black beer. The brewery was purchased by Mr. (afterwards Sir Henry) Meux when he retired from the famous firm in Liquorpond Street, of which he was the principal partner. This gentleman, who was very prominent in his day and a cousin of Lord Brougham, was made a baronet by William IV in 1831. The great porter vat of this brewery, which was one of the sights of London, was 22 ft. high and contained 3,555 barrels, sufficient to supply more than a million persons with a pint of beer each. A terrible catastrophe occurred in 1814, caused by the bursting of this huge vat owing to the insecurity and defective state of some of its hoops. The brewery was then surrounded by a multitude of small tenements which were crowded with tenants of the poorer classes. Many of these houses were flooded by porter, and some of them collapsed with fatal results ; no less than eight persons died from drowning, injury, poisoning by the porter fumes, or drunkenness. The loss to the firm was also most serious, and threatened their existence ; but an application to Parliament procured for them the return by the excise commissioners of the duty paid upon the lost liquor. The retail department of the brewery, known as the 'Horse Shoe' tap, is now converted into a restaurant and hotel, but was formerly a comfortable inn and place of refreshment patronized by tradesmen and well-to-do people in the district. It was also early in the last century a favourite place of call for farmers and porters, who refreshed themselves with the porter for which the house was celebrated.

This firm supplied with Meux's porter most of the old-fashioned inns in the western suburbs of London, of which the 'Watering House' at Knightsbridge was a typical example. The house was a quaint, comfortable little structure where gentlemen's horses and grooms were put up, and farmers and graziers resorted. In front was a stone bench where porters might rest themselves or place their loads. The malt used in this brewery is specially manufactured for the firm and shipped to their wharf in Grosvenor Road, Pimlico, from whence it is conveyed to the brewery in their own wagons. Messrs. Meux have long been famed for their porter—a beverage which is said to take its name from the partiality shown to it by porters. It began to be generally brewed by the London brewers about the year 1722, and was then sold at 23s. per barrel. From this price it gradually rose to 30s., which it reached in 1799, when in consequence of the increase in price of both malt and hops porter was raised to 35s. per barrel, and was retailed at 4d. a quart instead of 3d. as heretofore. Since 1872 Messrs. Meux & Co. have brewed ales to meet the public demand for that beverage ; they had previously brewed stout and porter only, and for many years were the only brewers in London who did not brew ales. The firm is now styled Meux's Brewery Co., Ltd.

On the borders of the City of London, but within the parish of St. Luke's, is Whitbread's brewery in Chiswell Street. The business was established in 1742 by Samuel Whitbread, son of a yeoman possessed of a small estate in Cardington, Bedfordshire. He first set up as a brewer in Old Street, but these premises soon became too confined, and in 1750 Mr. Whitbread purchased a brewery in Chiswell Street, which had been established for over fifty years. The business rapidly grew, and in 1760 had reached the position of the second largest brewery in London, with an annual output of nearly 64,000 barrels. Pennant gives a list,[19] taken from a newspaper of his day, of the chief porter brewers of London and the barrels of strong beer they brewed for the year 1786-7. In this list Whitbread stands first with 150,280 barrels ; the number of breweries is twenty-four, and the total quantity of beer amounts to 1,176,856 barrels. The number of breweries had largely decreased in 1796, when there were not more than twelve of first-rate importance, Whitbread still heading the list with 202,000 barrels. This brewery was one of the first to take advantage of the introduction of steam power, and in 1785 set up a sun and planet engine, supplied by the firm of which the celebrated James Watt was a partner. This engine, originally of 35, was increased to 70 horse-power in 1795, and until the year 1887 was still in use at the brewery. It is now exhibited in the Victoria Museum, South Australia, and bears an inscription recounting its history. In 1787 King George III and Queen Charlotte, attracted by the fame of this brewery, paid a visit of inspection, when the king entered minutely into the details of the various processes, and took care not to overlook any department. The royal visit forms the subject of a lengthy humorous poem by Peter Pindar (Dr. Wolcot), who, speaking of the king's conversation, says his Majesty

Asked a thousand questions with a laugh
Before poor Whitbread comprehended half.

[19] *Some Account of Lond.* (ed. 4, 1805), 266.

After the brewery had been inspected the king and queen were entertained by their host at a sumptuous banquet.

Whitbread represented Derby in Parliament, and in 1795, after acquiring a large fortune, he purchased Lord Torrington's estate at Southill in his native county. He was a man of strict religious principle, and of a benevolent disposition ; his portrait by Sir Joshua Reynolds is in the hall of the Brewers' Company. To this company he left various charities for the relief of decayed master brewers and of poor freemen (or widows of freemen) of the Brewers' Company. On the death of his father in 1796 Samuel Whitbread the younger succeeded him as head of the brewery with which he had been connected for the previous ten years, and from 1799 the business was conducted under the style of Whitbread & Co. The younger Whitbread is best known as a keen politician and supporter of Fox and the Whigs. He obtained more leisure for his parliamentary work by taking partners into his business, which continued to increase considerably. In 1806 Whitbread & Co. ranked fourth among the London brewers, brewing 101,311 barrels. In the following ten years the business more than doubled itself, the quantity of beer brewed in 1815 reaching 261,018 barrels. In 1834 ale-brewing was commenced here, porter and stout only having previously been brewed. Mr. Whitbread the politician left two sons, the younger of whom was M.P. for Middlesex for several years and died in 1879. Mr. Samuel Whitbread, grandson of the politician, represented Bedford in Parliament from 1852 to 1895, and was a Lord of the Admiralty from 1859 to 1863. Although situated so closely on the confines of the City of London, where land is of such high value, the brewery of Messrs. Whitbread is fitted up with every necessary for carrying on their business under the most approved conditions, and with the help of the latest inventions and improvements.

The Swan Brewery, Fulham, dates from the early part of the 18th century, when it started in a very humble way at Walham Green, and was afterwards successively owned by John Stocken, William Chambers, and Sidney Milnes Hawkes, all well-known members of the trade. The following advertisement appeared in the *London Evening Post* from Tuesday, 26 August, to Thursday, 28 August 1740 :—' To be lett, and enter'd on immediately for the remainder of a term of about eight years to come. A very convenient and well-accustom'd Brew House at Walham Green, in the parish of Fulham, with the malt-house, dwelling-house, and all manner of useful offices thereto belonging, and also four acres of hop-ground lying behind the same. For further particulars, &c.'

In 1746 Henry Temple of St. George's Hanover Square, was admitted to ' two pieces of customary land at Wansdon's Green,' on one of which was erected a messuage 'known by the name or sign of the White Swan.' He shortly afterwards surrendered the property to John Carwell.[20] Nothing more is known of the Swan Brewery until its great development by Oliver Stocken, who acquired the business in 1769. He came from an ancient family, a branch of which was settled at Linton, Cambridgeshire, where Richard Stocken, the grandfather of Oliver Stocken the brewer, was buried on 19 March 1714–15.[21] Young Oliver came to seek his fortune in London and first settled himself at a small ale-house at Walham Green. He afterwards purchased the Swan Brewery and converted it into a flourishing business, which he continued to manage until his death in 1808. The brewery then passed into the hands of his sons William and John, the latter of whom died in 1820, leaving William the sole proprietor. William Stocken, who died in 1824, was succeeded by his son Oliver Thomas Joseph Stocken, who was then only twenty-four. Under his management the business again greatly developed until his unfortunate failure in 1840, when the brewery passed by public auction into the hands of Mr. William Chambers, Stocken's son-in-law. About the year 1852 Mr. Sidney Milnes Hawkes bought the brewery, and two years later sold it to the Right Hon. Sir James Stansfeld. The firm became known later as Messrs. Stansfeld & Co., Ltd.

In the days of the Stockens, the Swan Brewery had a wide and justly-earned celebrity ; among its aristocratic patrons were George IV, the Duke of York, and the Prince of Saxe-Coburg. The Old Swan tap in connexion with the brewery developed eventually into a well-known tavern, and remained in the hands of the Stockens until the year 1840. Included within the brewhouse property was Wendon or Wandon House, a fine old mansion which faced Walham Green. This building, known also as 'Dowlers,' from the name of a tenant, John Dowbeler, was the manor-house of Wendon, and had been the abode of many families of note. To an old price

---

[20] C. J. Feret, *Fulham Old and New* (1900), ii, 217.
[21] Particulars of the family and a pedigree are given by Feret, op. cit. ii, 218, 220.

list issued by the firm early in the 19th century is attached a pictorial frontispiece which shows the quaint and comfortable-looking inn (with its recreation ground and gardens) which was then attached to the brewery. In 1880 the old buildings of the brewery were required for improvements, but the proprietors secured another site close adjoining and consisting of 3 acres, on which to build their new premises. The new brewery was designed with considerable attention to architectural effect, a result very rarely attained or even possible in buildings devoted to this trade. The walls are built of red bricks with Corsehill stone dressings, and the roofs are covered with Broseley tiles; the interior arrangement of the brewery is notable for its extreme simplicity. The main supply of water is from a well sunk on the premises to a depth of 450 ft.; for the first 30 ft. it is inclosed in iron cylinders, 7 ft. in diameter, which are sunk into the London clay and prevent any contamination by surface water. One of the special features of this brewery is its well-appointed chemical laboratory fitted with every apparatus necessary for the examination of malt and all other brewing materials. The Swan Brewery, though not ranking among the largest metropolitan breweries, is notable for its excellent design, cleanliness, and completeness in every detail.

The Stag Brewery at Pimlico, of Messrs. Watney & Co., arose from small beginnings. In the first half of the 18th century it consisted of some few buildings attached to a small brewhouse standing in the midst of green fields and far away from any habitations. The site now covered by Messrs. Watney & Co.'s premises is one of great interest. It formerly was part of St. James's Palace, being occupied by the royal mews, which were removed when Buckingham House became a royal palace. Underneath the cooperage of the brewery runs the King's Pond watercourse, a stream which issues from the lake in St. James's Park. In 1782 this lake was simply a marshy pond surrounded by a green pasture for cows, whose milk was disposed of on the spot. In 1820 no one dared to set out for London from that quarter at night, as Pimlico was infested with footpads. So late, too, as 1859 there stood, on the site now covered by the brewery yard, Pimlico House, with its pleasure grounds extending beyond the confines of the present Victoria Street. In 1763 an old plan of the estate shows the brewery situated on its town side amidst a cluster of tea gardens, and places of amusement famous for dancing, concerts, and firework displays. Close by was St. Peter's Chapel,

of which the notorious Dr. Dodd was incumbent, and within the brewery gates was the residence of Richard Heberr the accomplished scholar, and owner of perhaps the most famous private library ever known.

At the close of the 17th century the brewery belonged to a Mr. Green, of whom nothing definite is known; nearly a century later, in 1786, the proprietor was one Matthew Wiggins, who two years afterwards disposed of it to Edward Moore and John Elliot. This Mr. Elliot, who was an active man of liberal education, built Pimlico House, already mentioned, and used it as his town residence. He was prominently connected with public affairs in the city of Westminster, where he was held in high esteem. Sir John Call joined the firm in 1792, and somewhat later Mr. Elliot was succeeded by his son J. Lettsom Elliot. The latter took into partnership Mr. James Watney of Wandsworth in 1837, and himself retired in 1856 in favour of Mr. Watney's two sons, James and Norman. From this time the firm consisted solely of members of the Watney family until the year 1884, when Mr. James Watney, the head of the firm, died, and the business was turned into a private limited company. The fame of the Pimlico Stag ales began to spread early in the 18th century, and in 1830 the business had developed into a great and important brewery, taking rank among the first-class breweries of London.

As may be expected, the buildings are on an extensive scale. The malt stores contain fifteen iron bins, four of which rise from the ground level to the top of the building. The largest has a capacity of 5,300 quarters, and the smallest holds 1,200 quarters. The mashing-room is a fine apartment 200 ft. long and 110 ft. broad, and its arrangements are unique in their completeness. On the right hand is the malt department, on the left the cooling and refrigerating rooms, at the end the fermenting department, carried on in another series of rooms. All is so arranged that each process follows the other, almost under the eye of the head brewer, whose private office is on the same level, and situated to the right of the entrance into the hall. The Stag Brewery employs upwards of 600 hands, for whom model dwellings abutting on the brewery premises have been built by the firm, the occupants forming quite a colony among themselves. Attached to the dwellings are a club-room, library, and bagatelle-room, for purposes of recreation. In June 1898 Messrs. Watney acquired the two celebrated breweries of Messrs. Combe, Delafield & Co. and Messrs. Reid & Co. The premises of the Stag Brewery have had extensive development : a new fermenting-room has been added, one of the pontoon rooms is now fitted with dropping tanks, a large bottling department has been established in a separate building, and new cooperage works are in course of construction. The firm also possesses a fine laboratory, a model brewery for experiments, and improved and extensive stabling.

The Anchor Brewery of Messrs. Charrington & Co. is situated on the north side of Mile End Road, occupying the frontage between Cleveland Street and St. Peter's Road. The earliest record of the firm is in 1743, when the brewery belonged to Messrs. Wastfield and Moss, of whom nothing further is known. About the year 1766 Mr. John Charrington purchased Mr. Wastfield's share of the business, and the firm became Charrington & Moss. John Charrington was a son of the vicar of Aldenham, Herts., and was the first of his family to enter upon business pursuits. Mr. Moss soon afterwards retired, and the brewery then remained wholly in the possession of the Charrington family until the year 1833. The business rapidly increased, and in 1806 ranked second among the ale breweries in London, the output for that year being 15,556 barrels.

There were two Nicholas Charringtons connected with the firm, one of whom died in 1827, and was succeeded by his sons Edward and Spencer ; the other died in 1859 at the advanced age of eighty-three, and was succeeded by his sons Charles and Frederick. Mr. Head, of the firm of Stewart & Head of Stratford, became a partner in the brewery in 1833, and introduced the brewing of porter and stout ; previous to this Messrs. Charrington had been ale brewers only. They now gradually dropped their large private and family trade and devoted themselves entirely to supplying licensed victuallers. From this time the business was exclusively a trade brewery, and the name of Charrington became one of the most familiar in London. In consequence of the rapid increase of the business it was necessary in the year 1871 to establish an ale brewery at Burton-on-Trent to supply the demands of their customers for that class of beer. On the death of Mr. Frederick Charrington in 1873 and of Mr. Charles Charrington in 1877, they were succeeded by their sons, Mr. John Douglas Charrington and Mr. Charles E. N. Charrington. Mr. Head, who

had during his partnership for nearly fifty years taken a responsible part in the management of the business, died universally regretted. His sound judgement and great experience gained for him much reputation among the London brewers as a high authority upon all matters connected with the brewing trade. Mr. Head had no son to succeed him, and the firm once more consisted of the Charrington family only until 1884, when Mr. George C. Croft was admitted into partnership. A severe loss was sustained by the firm in 1888, when Mr. Edward Charrington, the senior partner, who had for fifty-seven years been a member of the firm, died at Burys Court, Reigate. He was a man of great gentleness and affability, and a warm supporter of every philanthropic movement in the east of London. After the death of Mr. Edward Charrington Mr. Spencer Charrington, who represented in Parliament the Mile End division of the Tower Hamlets, became the head of the firm. The business was turned into a limited liability company in 1897, and Colonel F. Charrington is the present chairman of the board of directors. Every attention is paid by the firm to the needs and comforts of their numerous staff ; there are several houses for the higher officials, and a long row of excellent cottages for the most deserving of the workmen. The malt required in the breweries is made by the firm themselves at Norwich and other places in the eastern counties, under the superintendence of a member of the firm and the head brewer, by whom the various maltings are periodically visited. Among the special features of this great brewery, whose operations are carried on upon a vast scale, is a well-appointed experimental or model brewery, which is excellently adapted for the various scientific experiments conducted in it from time to time.

The Albion Brewery of Messrs. Mann, Crossman & Paulin lies on the north side of Whitechapel Road, at its junction with Mile End Road. Just at this spot formerly stood the Mile End turnpike gate, and adjoining the brewery is the 'Blind Beggar' public house, which commemorates the legend associated with the neighbouring parish of Bethnal Green.

Local breweries on a more or less extensive scale exist at Brentford, Uxbridge, Great Stanmore, Staines, Chiswick, Isleworth, Twickenham, and Hounslow, among other places in this county.

INDUSTRIES

TOBACCO

Tobacco is said to have been introduced into this country in 1586 ; it was placed under a duty of 2*d.* a pound in Elizabeth's reign. The duty on Virginian tobacco was raised to 6*s.* 10*d.* by James I. Under this sovereign the industry became a monopoly, and the Virginia planters were limited to an export of 100 lb. a year. Tobacco is said to have been first smoked at the 'Pied Bull' at Islington, and the number of tobacconists' shops in London in 1614 is estimated by Barnaby Rich as over 7,000.[1] In the MS. notes left by Sir Henry Oglander of Nunwell in the Isle of Wight he records among other expenses in the year 1626, 'for eight ounces of tobacco five shillings'; this was procured for him in London. Tobacco was also sold by apothecaries,[2] and prescribed as a drug; it came into very general use for this purpose during the time of the Great Plague.

What we call smoking was then termed 'drinking' tobacco, the smoke being inhaled and allowed to escape through the nose. An anonymous writer in 1636, speaking of dissolute persons who spend most of their time at taverns, says : [3] 'Men will not stand upon it to *drink* either wine or *tobacco* with them who are more fit for Bridewell.'

The signs of tobacconists' shops in the 18th century generally consisted of a large wooden figure of a black Indian, wearing a crown of tobacco leaves and a kilt of the same material. He was usually placed at the side of the door, above which hung three rolls, also cut in wood. The decorated cards or shop-bills of tradesmen at this period were often designed by artists of repute. Hogarth in his early days designed one for 'Richard Lee at ye Golden Tobacco-Roll in Panton Street near Leicester Fields,' which much resembles his *Modern Midnight Conversation.* Another curious tobacconist's sign consists of three hands issuing from an arm ; the first holding snuff, the second a pipe, and the third a quid of tobacco ; attached to this are the lines :—

We three are engaged in one cause ;
I snuffs, I smokes, and I chaws.

This distich is sometimes found on painted signs, beneath figures of a Scotchman, a Dutchman, and a sailor.

The manufacture of tobacco is carried on very largely in East London and Hackney, which contain seventy-six factories for the production of tobacco, cigars, cigarettes, and snuff. In all London there are about one hundred and eighty factories in this trade, and in the whole of England, the metropolis included, there are about four hundred and thirty, so that in the number of its tobacco factories East London occupies a conspicuous position. The cigars produced in English factories are known as British cigars, and vary considerably in price and quality. Those made by the best firms are infinitely superior to some of the lower grades of imported Havanas. The importation of sham Havanas from Belgium and other countries has been checked by the 'Merchandise Marks Act,' but the British manufacturer suffers severely from the competition of cheap Mexican cigars.

The process of manufacture begins with 'liquoring,' in which the leaf is treated with pure water to render it soft and pliant for the hands of the 'stripper.' The process of 'stripping' consists in stripping the leaf by taking out its midrib. The leaf when stripped is handed to the 'cigar-maker,' and in this branch of the trade many female hands are employed.[4]

Tobacco as distinct from cigars is also largely manufactured in East London, but fewer hands are employed in its preparation by reason of the extensive use of machinery. After undergoing the process of 'liquoring' and 'stripping,' the leaf is, in the case of cut tobacco, handed over to the machine-men. It is next passed on to the 'stovers,' who first place it on a steam-pan to separate the fibres, and then on a fire-pan to make it fit for keeping and to improve its smoking quality. The final process is that of 'cooling,' where a current of cold air is passed through it to drive off the moisture. By other processes are produced the varieties known as 'roll' or 'spun' tobacco, and 'cake' or 'plug.'

The manufacture of snuff involves various complicated processes, which space will not permit us to describe. The ingredients consist largely of the shreds, stalks, and other leavings resulting from the processes above mentioned.

Some thirty years ago the London tobacco manufacturers comprised, it is estimated, about one-fourth of the whole of the manufacturers in England. Some old firms still exist, as that of Richard Lloyd & Sons, of Clerkenwell Road, which has been in existence for over two centuries.

[1] *The Honestie of this Age*, 26.
[2] Dekker, *Gull's Horn-book.* Quoted by F. W. Fairholt. *Tobacco, its History*, &c. (1859), 49, 56.
[3] *Vox civitatis, or London's Complaint against her Children in the Country* (1636).
[4] Booth, *Life and Labour of the People in London* (1902), (Ser. 1), iv, 225.

MUSICAL INSTRUMENTS

The manufacture of musical instruments dates back to a remote antiquity. They were constantly in use by minstrels at feasts and pageants, and in religious services and ceremonies. At the pageant exhibited at Westminster Hall in 1502 on the occasion of an entertainment given to Catherine of Spain we read[1] that 'twelve ladies had claricordis, claricymballs, and such other.' Henry VIII and both of his daughters were skilful players upon the chief instruments of music in use in their day. London makers in the 16th century helped to supply the demands of the Continent, although musical imports from abroad were also considerable. In a little book entitled 'The rates of the Custome House, both inwarde and outwarde, very necessary for all merchants to knowe, Imprinted at London by Rycharde Kele, 1545,' will be found 'clarycordes the payre 2s., harp strynges the boxe 10s., lute strynges called mynikins the groce 22d., orgons the payre ut sint in valore, wyer for clarycordes the pound 4d., virginales the payer 3s. 4d.' Very few particulars of early makers exist. In April 1530 one William Lewes received £3 for two 'payer of virginalls' supplied to the king at Greenwich, £3 for two pair 'brought to the More,' and 20s. for 'a little payer.' In February 1531 Lewes received a further sum of £8 6s. 8d. for five pair of virginals supplied to his royal patron.[2] Nothing is known of Lewes, but in the *Privy Purse expenses of the Princess Mary*,[3] among various payments connected with instruction of the princess in the virginals are sums 'geven to one Cowts [or Cots] of London for mendyng of my ladys grace Virginalls at soundry tymes.' Several 'pairs' of virginals which once belonged to Queen Elizabeth are described by Dr. Rimbault, who wrote in 1860,[4] as existing in his time ; that of chief interest is an instrument purchased at Lord Spencer Chichester's sale in 1805.

Some at least of the early musical instrument makers settled in London were certainly born beyond the seas, as, for example, William Treasurer, returned as 'virginall-maker Doucheman' in 1568.[5] Three years after it was reported[6] that he had been fifty years in England. His 'servant' or apprentice, Jasper Blanckart, may have succeeded to his business, for he is found in Aldgate Ward in 1582–3 as a virginal-maker.[7] Other foreign virginal makers were clearly religious refugees,[8] as 'Lodewyke Tyves' in 1568, while in 1582–3 we hear[9] of 'Polle Fyeld and Marie his wief ; he was borne at Loven, in England 3 yeares at September last and came for religion ; he ys a sojourner with John James, a virginall-maker, no denizon and of the Duche churche.' Foreign lute and harp-string makers are also not uncommon, as Norde Pallarum a Sicilian[10] (1568), Audrian Daniell a Hollander (1571), and two Antwerp men, Joyce Vanderoke and Peter Wellence (1571).

Two celebrated virginal-makers in the latter half of the 17th century were John Loosemore and Stephen Keen. A fine instrument bearing Loosemore's name and the date 1655 is stated by Rimbault to be in private possession.[11] There is an advertisement of Keen at the end of Playford's *Introduction to the Skill of Musick*, 1672, stating that 'Mr. Stephen Keen, Maker of Harpsycons and Virginals, dwelleth now in Threadneadle Street, at the sign of the Virginal, who maketh them exactly good, both for sound and substance.' Keen was in business from 1685 to 1716.

The instruments above-mentioned all possessed key-boards, and were early precursors of the pianoforte. The clavier, or key-board, invented at the close of the 11th century, was at first applied to the organ, but was probably soon adapted to stringed instruments. One of the earliest of these was the clavicytherium—a small oblong box with the strings arranged in the form of a half triangle. The strings were of catgut, and were sounded by quill plectra rudely fastened to the ends of the keys. The clavichord or clarichord was a much superior instrument, in the shape of a small square pianoforte, but without frame or legs. The strings were of brass, and the action consisted simply of a piece of brass pin wire placed vertically at a point where it could be struck or pressed against its proper string. The virginal introduced a new plan of striking the strings by small quills attached to minute springs fitted

---

[1] *Antiq. Repertory*, ii, 310.
[2] *Privy Purse exp. of Hen. VIII* (ed. Nicolas, 1827), 37.
[3] Ed. by Fred. Madden, 1831, pp. 20, 46.
[4] *The Pianoforte*, 58.
[5] Kirk, *Returns of Aliens* (Huguenot Soc.), iii, 344.

[6] Ibid. i, 413.　　[7] Ibid. i, 413 ; ii, 304.
[8] Ibid. iii, 345.　　[9] Ibid. ii, 81.
[10] Ibid. iii, 413 ; ii, 100 ; i, 463 ; ii, 114.
[11] *The Pianoforte*, 64, &c.

in the upper part of small flat pieces of wood termed *jacks*. These jacks were perpendicular to the keys, and when after striking the string the jack had made its escape it fell in such a way as to be able at will to reproduce the sound anew. The strings of the virginal were of metal instead of catgut. The spinet was of similar construction, differing only in its shape, which was that of a harp laid in a horizontal position. The chief London makers of the spinet and harpsichord in the first three-quarters of the 17th century were the Hitchcocks and Haywards, fathers and sons. John Hitchcock made spinets with a compass of five octaves; some are known bearing dates between 1620 and 1640. Charles Haward or Hayward is also mentioned as a celebrated maker in 1672.[12] Hayward lived in Aldgate, and was patronized by Samuel Pepys.

Another celebrated maker was Joseph Baudin; a spinet by him, which belonged to Dr. Rimbault, has the inscription: 'Josephus Baudin, Londini, fecit 1723.' Another maker named Player is said to have made spinets with quarter tones.[13] In Hogarth's 'Rake's Progress' is a harpsichord by Mahoon, who was harpsichord maker to his Majesty and also a maker of spinets. Baker Harris was another eminent maker in the latter half of the 18th century; one of his spinets with white keys and dated 1776 was seen by Dr. Rimbault in 1858. Spinets ceased to be made in London or elsewhere, according to Mr. A. J. Hipkins,[14] in 1784.

A more important instrument than any of those yet described was the harpsichord, which held during the 16th, 17th, and 18th centuries a position similar to that of the grand pianoforte, an instrument which it also resembled in shape. It was used in the orchestra as an accompanying instrument from the time of the first opera and the first oratorio in the year 1600, and continued to be a favourite with musicians down to the times of Handel and Bach. The action of the harpsichord was simply a key and a jack, the latter consisting of a piece of pear-wood with a small movable tongue of holly through which crow-quills or points of hard leather were passed to touch the string when the jack was in action. The larger harpsichords had two rows of keys and three strings to each note; of the latter, two were tuned in unison and the third sounded an octave higher.

Like the rest of the minor key-board instruments, the harpsichord was of Italian origin, the name being an English equivalent of *arpicordo*; but the Italian workmanship was inferior, and the finest examples of early harpsichords were made by the Ruckers family of Antwerp. Four members of this family acquired great reputation for their work from 1579 to the middle of the following century. Their instruments lasted long, and were sometimes expensively decorated a hundred years after they had been made. Many Ruckers harpsichords survived and fetched high prices until nearly the end of the 18th century, one being sold in 1770 for 3,000 francs, or £120. When the Ruckers family passed away the makers of London and Paris succeeded to their reputation. Tabel, a Fleming of whom very little is known, came over to this country and settled in London, bringing with him the influence of the Ruckers school. A harpsichord made by Tabel is possessed by Helena, Countess of Radnor, and bears the inscription 'Hermanus Tabel fecit Londini, 1721.' Harpsichords had, however, been made in London in the 17th century by the spinet-makers, the Hitchcocks, Hayward, and Keene; only one harpsichord by John Hitchcock is now known to exist, but spinets by the above makers are still occasionally met with in old country mansions. Another early maker was Johannes Asard, one of whose instruments is dated 1622.[15]

John Playford, the well-known music publisher who kept a shop in the Inner Temple near the church door, advertised in the second book of his *Select Ayres and Dialogues*, folio, 1669:—'If any person desire to be furnished with good new virginals and harpsicons, if they send to Mr. Playford's shop, they may be furnished at reasonable rates to their content.' Mace, writing in 1676,[16] gives a curious account of the pedal harpsichord, and mentions the price of these instruments, which was ordinarily £20, though two were bought by Sir Robert Bolles for £30 and £50 respectively.

John Harris, son of the celebrated organ-builder Renatus Harris, who was a maker of organs, harpsichords, and spinets in Red Lion Street, Holborn, claimed to have taken out the first patent[17] in this country for an improvement in the construction of the harpsichord. His invention is described in his printed advertisement, a copy of which is preserved in the Chetham Library, Manchester.[18] On a harpsichord with two sets of

---

[12] Salmon, *Vindication of an Essay* (1672), 68.
[13] A. Warren, *Tonometer* (1725), 7.
[14] Edw. F. Rimbault, op. cit. 72.

[15] Ibid. 401.
[16] Mace, *Musick's Monument*, 235.
[17] 22 Oct. 1730, no. 521.
[18] J. O. Halliwell, *Coll. of Broadsides*, no. 830; Rimbault, *Pianoforte*, 86.

strings, by his invention, 'may be performed either one unison or two, or two unisons and an octave together ; and the fortes or pianos, or loud or soft, or the contrary, may be executed as quick as thought ; and double basses may be also expressed by touching single keys.' Harris was joined in partnership by John Byfield, and the firm built an organ in 1729 for Shrewsbury, and in 1740 one for Doncaster which cost £525.

William Barton, of whom nothing further is known, was granted a patent[19] for improving the tone and durability of harpsichords by using 'pens of silver, brass, steel, and other sorts of metall' in place of 'crow and raven quills of which they are now made.' The reputation of London makers of musical instruments now stood very high, especially abroad, and continued until the close of the century. It was much enhanced by several foreigners who found their way to this country and started business in London. Dr. Burney, in an account of his travels in Germany,[20] writes :—'The Germans work much better out of their own country than in it, if we may judge by the harpsichords of Kirkman and Shudi, the pianofortes of Backers, and the organs of Snetzler, which far surpass in goodness all the keyed instruments that I met with in my tour through Germany.'

Rutgerus (or Roger) Plenius, one of these German makers, lived in South Audley Street, Grosvenor Square, 'ye King's Arms being over ye Door,' and in 1741 put forth a curious printed advertisement[21] in which he claims to have made 'more than twenty essential improvements' in the harpsichord, and sets forth the merits of his 'new invented musical instrument called a Lyrichord.' An advertisement in the *Public Advertiser* of 12 June 1755 states that his lyrichord was 'to be seen and heard 'till sold' daily from 11 till 2 'at the Golden Ball opposite the little south door of St. Paul's, in St. Paul's Church-yard, for half a crown each person.' Plenius and his invention are last met with in an auction sale on 11 February 1772 at Christie's in Pall Mall, when fifteen harpsichords, several 'with double and single bass pedals, being the stock in trade of Frederick Naubauer, harpsichord maker,' were advertised to be sold, together with a lyrichord 'made by the famous Rutgerus Plenius.' This instrument was intended to imitate bow stringed instruments, and was played upon by means of a keyboard and a treadle ;

the strings of wire and gut were set vibrating by rotating wheels, the keys when pressed down forming the contact. Plenius took out two patents, one dated 30 December 1741,[22] for various improvements in harpsichords, spinets, &c. ; the second, dated 10 July 1745,[23] specifies among other improvements a 'Welch harp' stop which he worked by a pedal. Plenius was the first to make a pianoforte in England.[24]

During the 18th century Tabel's pupils Burckhardt Tschudi or Burkat Shudi, and Jacob Kirkman became famous as eminent makers. Shudi, who was the founder of the firm of Broadwood, was of noble parentage in Switzerland and born 13 March 1702. He came to England in 1718 as a simple journeyman joiner, and became, like his fellow workman Kirkman, a foreman in Tabel's London workshop. About 1728 he set up for himself in Meard Street, Dean Street, Soho. In 1742 he removed to 33, Great Pulteney Street, and took for his sign the Plume of Feathers to indicate his patronage by Frederick Prince of Wales. His new shop was well chosen, being then situated in the most fashionable part of London and close to the Court at St. James's Palace. Shudi was fortunate in obtaining the patronage of Handel ; and the making of harpsichords, and their tuning and repair especially, being a lucrative business, he soon became wealthy. The harpsichord made by him which once belonged to Queen Charlotte and is now in Windsor Castle bears the date 1740. It has a 'lute' stop which, like the pedal, was an English invention of the 17th century. Shudi is said to have presented a harpsichord to Frederick the Great, whom he greatly admired and considered to be the leader of the Protestant cause, after the capture of Prague in 1744. A picture which was formerly in one of the rooms at Great Pulteney Street is said to represent Shudi, in the company of his wife and their two children, engaged in tuning this identical instrument. The picture is reproduced as a frontispiece to Dr. Rimbault's *History of the Pianoforte*. Frederick afterwards (in 1766) ordered from Shudi two double harpsichords for his new palace at Potsdam, where they still remain. One of these is described by Burney[25] as a magnificent instrument which cost 200 gns., 'the hinges, pedals, and frame are of silver, the case is inlaid, and the front is of tortoiseshell.' The Potsdam harpsichords were made with

[19] 17 Dec. 1730, no. 525.
[20] *Present State of Music in Germany* (1773), ii, 146.
[21] Halliwell Coll. no. 772, in Chet. Lib. ; Rimbault, *Pianoforte*, 87–8.
[22] No. 581.   [23] No. 613.
[24] A. J. Hipkins, *Musical Instruments*, 94.
[25] *Present State of Music in Germany*, ii, 145.

Shudi's Venetian swell, which he afterwards patented.[26] Roger Plenius had in 1750 devised a swell imitated from the organ, which consisted of gradually raising or lowering by a pedal movement a portion of the top or cover of the harpsichord. Shudi improved upon this by a swell on the principle of the venetian blind.

John Broadwood, who had married Shudi's daughter Barbara, was taken into partnership by his father-in-law. A harpsichord exists dated 1770, with the names of Shudi and Broadwood as makers, but Shudi made harpsichords alone after that date. About 1772 he retired to a house in Charlotte Street, leaving the business in the hands of his son-in-law; he died on 19 August 1773. His son, the younger Burkat Shudi, then joined John Broadwood in partnership until 1782, when he retired; he died in 1803. A list of thirteen existing harpsichords made by this firm is given in Grove's *Dictionary of Music.*[27] The price of a single harpsichord about 1770 ranged from thirty-five to fifty guineas, that of a double harpsichord with swell was eighty guineas.

Tabel's other pupil, Jacob Kirchmann or Kirkman, obtained a success and reputation as a harpsichord maker quite equal to that of his eminent rival Shudi. A curious story is told by Burney of Kirkman's rapid courtship of Tabel's widow, whom he wooed and married in one morning, just a month after her husband's death. With the widow he secured also the business and the stock-in-trade. Kirkman was of high repute not only as a maker but also as a musician. He was organist of St. George's, Hanover Square, and the author of several compositions for the organ and the pianoforte which he published himself at the sign of the 'King's Arms' in Broad Street, Carnaby Market (now Broad Street, Soho). The rivalry of the two makers extended to their patrons, King George favouring Kirkman and the Prince of Wales, who was notoriously on ill terms with his royal father, patronizing Shudi. Burney relates another anecdote of Kirkman, by which he is said to have retrieved his fortunes when ruin threatened him through a sudden freak of fashion. The guitar suddenly rose into favour among ladies of fashion, who sold their harpsichords for what they would fetch. Kirkman bought them up at a nominal price, and succeeded in stopping the rage for the new favourite by giving a large number of guitars

to girls in milliners' shops and ballad-singers in the streets whom he taught to strum an accompaniment. This had the effect of disgusting the fashionable ladies, whose favour soon returned to the more costly harpsichord. Kirkman died in 1778 and left a fortune of nearly £200,000; he had no children, but was succeeded in business by his nephew Abraham, whose son Joseph followed him. Harpsichords were made by this firm so late as 1798, which date appears on an instrument also with the name 'Josephus Kirckman.'

In the hands of Tabel and his pupils Shudi and Kirkman the harpsichord reached its highest point of excellence in compass, tone, and power. The increase of power was obtained chiefly by the greater length of Shudi and Kirkman's harpsichords, which measured nearly 9 ft., whilst those of Ruckers were from 6 ft. to 7½ ft. long. Kirkman added a pedal to raise a portion of the top or cover. Both makers used two pedals; one for the swell, the other by an external lever mechanism to shut off the octave and one of the unison registers, leaving the player with both hands free. The English makers did not adopt the practice of decorating the cases with beautiful paintings, a practice which caused many fine Flemish harpsichords to be broken up when out of repair.

Many contrivances were invented by English harpsichord makers to produce sonority of tone and do away with the jarring noise of the quills plucking the string, but it must suffice to mention here the improvements effected by John Joseph Merlin. He was born at Huys in the Low Countries in 1735, and came to England in the suite of the Spanish ambassador in 1760. For several years he was director of Cox's Museum in Spring Gardens, where in 1768 he exhibited many of his curious inventions. He afterwards exhibited at his own museum in Princes Street, Hanover Square,[28] a great variety of musical instruments and remarkable pieces of mechanism designed and constructed by himself. In 1774[29] he took out a patent for an improved harpsichord, in which he is described as a mathematical instrument maker living in Little Queen Ann Street, Marylebone. His patent was for a 'compound harpsichord in which, besides the jacks with quills, a set of hammers of the nature of those used in the kind of harpsichords called pianoforte are introduced in such a manner that either may be played separately or both together at the pleasure of the performer, and for adding the aforesaid

[26] See specification, 13 Apr. 1769, of patent granted 18 Dec. 1768, no. 947.
[27] 1883, iii, 490.

[28] Busby, *Concert Room Anecdotes*, ii, 137.
[29] 12 Jan. 1774, no. 1081.

hammers to an harpsichord of the common kind already made so as to render it such compound harpsichord.' Merlin effected another improvement in harpsichords in 1775. The larger instruments had ordinarily two rows of keys and three strings to each note, two of the strings being in unison and the third sounding an octave higher. Merlin abolished the latter and replaced it by another unison string which left the tone equally full and rendered the instrument less liable to get out of tune, the octave stop being very susceptible to atmospheric influences. He died in May 1804, and the 'celebrated musical instruments invented and manufactured' by him were sold by auction on 21 July 1837.

The Pianoforte.—The manufacture of pianofortes is an industry for which London has been long and justly famed. The origin of the invention has caused much controversy, but it is now generally conceded that the inventor of this beautiful instrument was Bartolomeo Cristofori, a harpsichord maker of Florence and custodian of the musical instruments of Prince Ferdinand dei Medici; he had in 1709 made four pianofortes in Florence, where they were seen by Scipione Maffei. The invention is described by Maffei [30] in the *Giornale de Litterati d'Italia*, 1711, and the idea seems also to have been independently arrived at by two other musicians, viz. :— Marius, a French manufacturer, who in 1716 submitted his instruments to the Académie des Sciences, and Christopher Gottlieb Schröter, a German musician, who constructed a model of a pianoforte at Dresden in 1717. Two instruments made by Cristofori still exist; one dated 1720 in the Metropolitan Museum of New York, the other dated 1726 in the private museum of the Signori Kraus at Florence. The invention constituted a vast improvement upon the action of the harpsichord, which was the immediate precursor of the pianoforte. This was done by substituting for the quills formerly used leather-covered hammers to strike the strings. By this means the jarring noise of the old instrument described by Dr. Burney as a 'scratch with a sound at the end of it' gave place to a clear, precise, and delicate tone until then unknown. The great invention lay dormant in Italy, but was taken up in Germany, where Gottfried Silbermann, after some unsuccessful attempts, made a pianoforte which gained the unstinted praise of J. S. Bach; Frederick the Great also ordered some of Silbermann's instruments for his palace at

Potsdam. Other famous German makers were Johann Andreas Stein of Augsburg, Johann Gottfried Hildebrand, and Johann Andreas Streicher. In France the chief manufacturers and inventors were Sebastian Erard and Ignace Pleyel.

The earliest pianos were horizontal and wing-shaped like the harpsichord, the oblong or 'square' of clavichord shape is said to have been invented by Frederici, the celebrated organ builder of Gera. The first piano seen in England was made, Burney tells us, in Rome by Father Wood, an English monk. This was copied by Roger Plenius, but without any attempt to place the enterprise on a commercial basis. Another German, Johannes Zumpe, who is said to have worked for Shudi the harpsichord maker, was more successful. At his manufactory in Princes Street, Hanover Square, he made small square pianos of very sweet tone, similar in shape and size to a virginal. These, from their low price and convenient size, soon became so popular that there was hardly a house in the kingdom where a keyed instrument had ever had admission but was supplied with one of them, and there was nearly as great a call for them in France as in England.[31] The oldest Zumpe piano known bears the date 1766 and is now owned by Messrs. Broadwood. Johann Pohlmann, another German maker in London, helped also to supply the demand, and his instruments also became widely known, although greatly inferior in quality to those of Zumpe. The action which Zumpe adopted or invented was simple and easy, and is said by some to have been suggested by the Rev. William Mason, composer, poet, and friend of the poet Gray. Zumpe had a partner named Meyer in 1778, and was joined by Buntlebart in 1784; after realizing a handsome fortune he returned to Germany to end his days in retirement.

The list of early German makers of the pianoforte in London is, however, not yet complete. A maker named Victor, resident in London, made several improvements in the instrument. He was followed by Americus Backers, who calls himself on one of his pianos which still exists, 'Americus Backers, factor et inventor, Jermyn Street, London 1776.' Backers had been in the employ of Silbermann of Neuberg, and is described by Burney as a harpsichord maker of second rank, who constructed several pianofortes, and improved the mechanism in some particulars, 'but the tone, with all the delicacy of Schroeter's touch, lost the spirit of the

[30] *Venice*, v, 144. Reprinted and trans. by Rimbault, *Pianoforte*, 95-102.

[31] Charles Burney in *Abraham Rees's Cyclopaedia*, art. 'Harpsichord.'

harpsichord and gained nothing in sweetness.'[32] He was, however, the inventor of what became known as the 'English action.'

In 1759 John Sebastian Bach came to London, and after his arrival 'all the harpsichord makers in this country tried their mechanical powers on pianofortes, but the first attempts were always on the large size.'[33]

In 1767 the pianoforte was introduced on the stage of Covent Garden Theatre as a new instrument. In a play bill for a performance of 'The Beggar's Opera,' on Saturday 16 May 1767, it is announced that at the 'end of Act 1, Miss Brickler will sing a favourite song from Judith, accompanied by Mr. Dibdin on a new instrument called piano-forte.'

It is time now to trace the further fortunes of the famous house of John Broadwood & Sons, founded as we have already seen by Burkat Shudi. John Broadwood, the first of that name connected with the firm, was born at Cockburn's Path in Scotland in 1732. He was a carpenter by trade and was employed by Shudi in his harpsichord manufactory in 1761. He was a partner of his father-in-law, the elder Shudi, and also of Shudi's son. From 1782 to 1795 he was sole partner in the firm of Shudi and Broadwood ; at the latter date, by the admission of his son James Shudi Broadwood as a partner, the firm became John Broadwood & Son, and lastly by taking into partnership another son, Thomas, in 1807, the style of the firm was John Broadwood & Sons. The firm began to make pianos in 1773, the construction followed being that of Zumpe, but in 1780 John Broadwood produced a square piano of his own design for which he was granted a patent in 1783.[34] By this invention he remodelled the case, placing the wrest-plank which carried the tuning-pins along the back, besides effecting other improvements, all of which became generally adopted. John Broadwood died in 1812 at the age of eighty-one years ; there exists a mezzotint portrait of him by Harrison and Say. The firm was continued by his son James Shudi Broadwood, who lived from 1772 to 1851 ; he was the first to use bracing or tension bars of iron or steel placed above the strings. This was to strengthen the wrest-plank, which had been so seriously weakened by the extension of the compass of his pianos, introduced in 1804, that the treble sank in pitch more rapidly than the rest of the instrument. The experiment, which was noted in the firm's work-books of that date, was repeated in 1818, and the

method is now universally adopted. Henry Fowler Broadwood, grandson of the founder, was a member of the firm from 1811 to 1893. Henry John Tschudi Broadwood, great-grandson of John Broadwood, patentee of the 'Barless' grand piano, is a director of John Broadwood & Sons, Ltd., a private company established in October 1901. In 1904 the business was removed from its original quarters in Pulteney Street to larger premises at the corner of Conduit Street and Hanover Square. The earliest account book of this firm is lost, but later accounts show that between 1771 and 1851 no fewer than 103,750 pianos were produced from their workshops.

Robert Stodart of Wardour Street, Soho, who founded another well-known firm, is variously described as pupil and fellow-workman of John Broadwood. Stodart succeeded Backers in business, and jointly with Broadwood developed to a high degree the 'English action' of Backers. Stodart himself took out a patent in 1777 for 'a *grand* forte piano with an octave swell, and to produce various fine tones, together or separate, at the option of the performer.'[35] This firm became subsequently known as John, William, and Matthew Stodart, and on 29 January 1795 William took out a patent[36] for his 'upright grand pianoforte of the form of a bookcase.' They exhibited at the Great Exhibition of 1851 as 'Stodart & Son.'

The early history of the great firm of Kirkman has been treated of above. Jacob the founder was succeeded by his nephew Abraham, in whose time the manufacture of pianos was first begun by the firm. Following Abraham Kirkman were two Josephs, his son and grandson ; the latter died in 1877 at the advanced age of eighty-seven years. His second son, Henry, who pre-deceased him, greatly extended the business, which in 1896 was amalgamated with that of the Collards. The firm is described in 1794 as Kirkman & Son, harpsichord makers, 19, Broad Street, Carnaby Market. Later on, and for many years, their show rooms were in Soho Square.

An interesting list of harpsichord and pianoforte makers in London at the end of the 18th century is given by Rimbault ;[37] it is taken from the *Musical Directory* for the year 1794. The thirteen makers mentioned include Shudi & Broadwood, Kirkman & Son, Stodart, and Buntlebart & Sievers (successors of Zumpe). Three other firms, those of Beck, Corrie, and Ganer, were in business in Broad

[32] Burney in *Rees's Cyclopaedia*, art. 'Harpsichord.'
[33] Ibid.
[34] 15 Nov. 1783, no. 1,379.
[35] 21 Nov. 1777, no. 1,172.
[36] No. 2,028.
[37] Rimbault, op cit. 147.

Street, Carnaby Market. The six remaining makers were Done of 30, Chancery Lane, Elwick of Long Acre, Hancock of Parliament Street, Houston & Co. of Great Marlborough Street, Longman & Broderip of Cheapside, the Haymarket, and Tottenham Court Road, and Pether of Oxford Street.

The business of Longman & Broderip, of Cheapside, was taken over and reorganized by Muzio Clementi between 1798 and 1801. His most important colleague in the 19th century was F. W. Collard, whose name is connected with many improvements in the pianos produced by the firm, which is now known as Collard & Collard, of Cheapside and Grosvenor Square. Rimbault gives a list of 106 patents by various makers between 1774 and 1851 [38] which includes the names of every London manufacturer of high reputation. The pianoforte had a long struggle to fight its way to general appreciation. It was neglected in Italy, the land of its birth, and made slow progress in France and Germany. In England it long suffered neglect until the elder Broadwood, by constructing its mechanism in a superior style, was the first to show the superiority of this instrument over the harpsichord. The continental musicians still clung to the harpsichord after popular taste in England had decidedly pronounced for its rival the pianoforte. As the instrument came more and more into general use, rival makers were incessant in their efforts to improve it in power and quality of tone and in delicacy and effectiveness of touch. These improvements were effected chiefly by enlarging the instrument generally, by extending the scale and increasing the weight of the strings, by correspondingly strengthening the framework, and by improving the mechanism of the action.

The first pianoforte constructed in France was made in 1777 by Sebastian Erard, who became famous as an English maker. He took refuge in London during the Terror, and took out patents between 1794 and 1810 for improvements in harps and pianofortes,[39] in which he is described as a musical instrument maker of Great Marlborough Street. He returned to Paris in 1796 and made there his first grand piano, using the English action, which he continued to employ until 1808. He died on 5 August 1831, and the business was continued by his nephew Pierre, who took out six English patents between 1821 and 1850.

This celebrated firm ceased to manufacture pianofortes in London in 1890.

In 1811 Robert Wornum the younger, of Princes Street, Hanover Square, patented [40] his improvements of the 'upright' pianoforte, which he afterwards more fully developed in his 'Cottage' and 'Piccolo' instruments. He was a man of remarkable ingenuity, whose improvements rapidly spread both in this country and abroad. Other patents were granted to him in 11 July 1820, 4 September 1826, and 14 January 1829,[41] in which his address is given as Wigmore Street, Cavendish Square. His last patent is dated 3 August 1842,[42] when he was living in Store Street, Bedford Square.

Another inventor of great skill to whom the pianoforte is indebted for many great improvements was William Southwell, a Dublin maker of musical instruments, who was in business in Lad Lane, London, when he took out his first patent on 18 October 1794.[43] He was living in Broad Court, St. Martin-in-the-Fields on 8 November 1798 when he took out a further patent; [44] and on 8 April 1807, when he patented his 'Cabinet' pianoforte,[45] he had returned to Dublin. His next two patents [46] are dated 4 March 1811 and 5 April 1821, when he was in business in Gresse Street, Rathbone Place. His name (or that of his son) occurs in a much later patent[47] of 24 August 1837, when he was living at 5, Winchester Row, New Road, Middlesex.

A notable invention made by James Thom and William Allen, workmen in his employ, was brought out by Stodart in a patent dated 15 January 1820.[48] It consisted of a compensating system for grand pianos and a new method of bracing by metallic tubes. This paved the way for many later devices, such as the introduction of steel tension bars, metal bracings of various kinds, and steel string plates; all these had for their object the strengthening of the instrument to enable it to bear the enormous strain from the increasing weight and tension of the strings. Erard's patent for his 'repetition action' in 1821 effected a great improvement in the mechanism for the perfection of touch, which was still further perfected by the patent of John Hopkinson of Oxford Street for his 'repetition and tremolo action' granted to him on 3 June 1851.[49]

[38] Rimbault, op. cit. 150–7.

[39] 17 Oct. 1794, no. 2,016; 16 June 1801, no. 2,502; 24 Sept. 1808, no. 3,170; 2 May, 1810, no. 3,332.

[40] 26 Mar. 1811, no. 3,419.
[41] No. 4,460, 5,348, and 5,678.
[42] No. 9,262.   [43] No. 2,017.
[44] No. 2,264.   [45] No. 3,029.
[46] No. 3,403 and 4,546.
[47] No. 7,424.   [48] No. 4,431.
[49] No. 13,652.

INDUSTRIES

The principle of division of labour is adopted to a large extent in pianoforte making in order to ensure the utmost precision of detail. Rimbault gives a list [50] of over forty different workmen, each of whom, with his assistants, is exclusively engaged in a special branch of the manufacture. At the Great Exhibition of 1851 the exhibitors of pianofortes included thirty manufacturers in London and six from provincial towns.

The founder of the firm of John Brinsmead & Sons was John Brinsmead, who was born at Wear Gifford, North Devonshire, on 13 October 1814. He began business at 35, Windmill Street, Tottenham Court Road, in 1836, removing in 1841 to Charlotte Street, Fitzroy Square; he took out a patent [51] in 1862 for improved mechanism in grand and upright pianos, 'producing a perfect check, great power, and quick repetition.' On taking his sons into partnership in 1863 the firm removed to 18, Wigmore Street, Cavendish Square, their present warehouse; and between 1868 and 1879 John Brinsmead took out three further patents. [52] For his meritorious exhibits at the Paris Exhibition of 1868 he received from the French government the cross of the Legion of Honour. Thomas James Brinsmead, a member of the firm, was granted a patent on 21 May 1881, [53] and Edgar William, his younger brother, and author of *The History of the Pianoforte* (Cassell, 1868; Novello, 1879), also patented some further improvements on 4 December 1883. [54] The firm became a limited company in January 1900.

Reed Instruments.—Messrs. H. Potter & Co. are a firm of high standing in the metropolis; eminent musical instrument makers of this family are met with from the 18th century to the present day. Richard Potter, who is said by Captain Day to have been the grandfather of the famous Cipriani Potter, [55] made flutes in London before 1774 with the then newly-invented keys for f♮, g♯, and b♭. On 28 October 1785 a patent (no. 1,499) was granted to Richard Potter for improvements in the German flute. These consisted of a graduated tuning slide, graduated cork, and metal plugs. Four concert flutes by this maker were exhibited at the Royal Military Exhibition of 1890, one is illustrated in the catalogue, [56] and another gives Potter's address as Johnson's Court. In his patent he is described as of Pemberton Row (Gough Square) in the City of London, and this is the address also (no. 5) of William Henry Potter, flute maker, in the patent for improvements in the flute which he took out on 28 May 1808 (no. 3,136). An 18th-century tabor-pipe bears the inscription 'Henry Potter 2 Bridge Street Westminster,' but is probably before that maker's time. [57] The Hon. Artillery Company possess a key bugle, presented to their light infantry in 1828, which is stamped 'Potter King Street Westminster.' [58] Messrs. H. Potter & Co., who have for many years occupied their present premises at 30, Charing Cross, are contractors to the government for army instruments and large exporters to our colonies and to distant foreign countries. A branch of the firm was founded in 1860 and carried on under the style of George Potter & Co.

William Bainbridge, who devised several improvements in musical instruments, was living in Little Queen Street in 1803 when he patented a device for more easily fingering the 'flageolet or English flute.' [59] In 1807 he was in business as a musical instrument maker in Holborn and patented further improvements in the flute. [60] About this date he was joined by Wood, and flageolets with the makers' stamp 'Bainbridge and Wood, 35 Holborn Hill' are described in Day's *Catalogue*. [61]

Brass Instruments.—Messrs. Rudall, Carte & Co. claim to be (with Messrs. Köhler) the oldest manufacturers of brass instruments in this country. The founder of the firm was Mr. Kramer or Cramer, who came over from Hanover in 1746 to take the post of bandmaster to King George II and established a music business. [62] Cramer subsequently took Thomas Key into partnership; a bassoon of late 18th or early 19th century is stamped 'Cramer and Key London Pall Mall,' and a clarionet of early 19th century bears the mark 'Cramer London.' [63] On another clarionet to which no date is ascribed the firm appears as 'Cramer & Son London 20 Pall Mall,' [64] and on two serpents occur 'Key and Co. 1820' and 'T. Key 20 Charing Cross' (date about 1830). [65] Rose states that Key had a

---

[50] *Pianoforte*, 213–14.
[51] 11 Feb. 1862, no. 358.
[52] 6 Mar. 1868, no. 774; 18 Mar. 1879, no. 1,060; 16 Aug. 1881, no. 3,557.
[53] No. 2,232.　　　[54] No. 5,635.
[55] C. Russell Day, *Cat. of Musical Instruments at Roy. Mil. Exhib.* Lond. 1891, p. 25.

[56] Pl. 1, fig. H, and pp. 32–3.
[57] Ibid. 14.　　　[58] Ibid. 173.
[59] No. 2,693, 1 Apr. 1803.
[60] No. 3,043, 14 May 1807.　　[61] pp. 17, 19.
[62] Algernon Rose, *Talks with Bandsmen* (1897), 102.
[63] Day, op. cit. 78, 114.
[64] Ibid. 127.　　　[65] Ibid. 163–4.

workshop in High Holborn,[66] and that he made there in 1809 for the 2nd Life Guards the first circular bass tuba with rotary action used in this country. The firm next appears as Rudall and Rose of 15, Piazza, Covent Garden (about 1830),[67] and on 27 November 1832 a patent for improvements in constructing flutes was granted to George Rudall and John Mitchell Rose (no. 6,338). About 1844 their address was 1, Tavistock Street, Covent Garden,[68] and in a patent granted to Rose on 6 September 1847 (no. 11,853) they are described as of Southampton Street; this patent was taken out by Rose on behalf of Boehm for improvements in the 'cylinder flute.' The firm was now joined by Richard Carte, a professor of music residing at 38, Southampton Street, who is so described in a patent for improvements in flutes, clarionets, hautboys and bassoons registered on 7 March 1850.[69] Carte was an inventor of great skill and enterprise, and in the following year constructed a flute which became known as Carte's '1851 flute.' This procured him the award of a prize medal at the Exhibition of 1851, the object of his invention being to 'design a mechanism which should retain the open keys . . . of Boehm's flute, and yet secure a greater facility of fingering.' This flute is described and illustrated in Day's *Catalogue*.[70] The firm now adopted the style of Rudall, Rose, Carte & Co., and in a patent (no. 245) taken out by Carte on 9 February 1858 for his well-known improvements in clarionets [71] their address is given as 20, Charing Cross. Other important inventions by members of this firm were secured by patents on 4 October 1859 (no. 2,248), 3 December 1860 (no. 2,967),[72] 5 December 1866 (no. 3,208), and 5 June 1875 (no. 2,071). Their latest style is Rudall, Carte & Co., and the final removal of their premises was to 23, Berners Street.[73]

The Violin.—The violin in its present form is about three centuries old. In the second half of the 16th century Cremona was the chief centre of manufacture and owed its reputation to the Amati family, and especially to the brothers Antonio and Girolamo Amati. This reputation was carried well into the 18th century by Antonio Stradivari, who brought the Cremona violin to its utmost perfection. London also has for some centuries been famous for the manufacture of

stringed instruments. The makers of the viol were very numerous, as that instrument was universally popular, and the names of many in the 16th and 17th centuries are given by Sir George Grove.[74]

The violin proper, although known in England as early as the reign of Elizabeth, was generally associated for many years after with popular merry-making, but became more highly esteemed amongst musicians when Charles II introduced his band of twenty-four violins, and thus gave a lead to fashion. The information,[75] however, which has come down to us with reference to the early London and Middlesex makers is very meagre, and it is difficult to determine whether they belong to Middlesex, the City, or Southwark. Three 17th century makers who are traditionally associated as partners were Thomas Urquhart, Edward Pamphilon, and one Pemberton, whose Christian name is uncertain. Indeed, it has even been suggested that the late date of 1680 assigned to Pemberton may be incorrect, and that he was in fact the J.P. of 1578 who made the instrument presented to the Earl of Leicester by Queen Elizabeth. Urquhart was probably an immigrant from beyond the Border, and his violins are said to be of unusual merit for the period at which he worked. From Urquhart Pamphilon may have learnt his craft, though his instruments, which are strong in wood, with a clear and penetrating tone, hardly reached the high standard of his supposed master.

Daniel Parker, who was still working in 1714–15, may be regarded as the last of the primitive school of English makers. Both in outline and model his instruments show an advance, and their tone is clear and strong. He seems, however, to have used a spirit varnish of a brickdust red colour, and very thickly laid on, which is in strong contrast to the pleasant oil varnish of Urquhart.

During the first half of the 18th century the London and Middlesex makers were largely under the influence of Stainer or Steiner, the well-known German maker.

John Barrett, contemporary with the London maker Nathaniel Crosse, was a strictly Middlesex maker, whose place of business lay at the 'Harp and Crown,' in Piccadilly. His violins are of a long and high model, tending to the Amati pattern, but with distinct traces of the influence of Steiner.

In the work of Peter Wamsley some modification of the outline and model of John

[66] Rose, loc. cit.
[67] Day, op. cit. 40.
[68] Ibid. 42.
[69] No. 12,996.
[70] Day, op. cit. 46, 47.
[71] Ibid. 104–5.
[72] Ibid. 195.
[73] *Whitaker's Red Bk. of Commerce* (1906), 346.
[74] *Dict. of Music*, ii, 163.
[75] See Sandys & Forster, *Hist. of the Violin*, 253 et seq.

INDUSTRIES

Barrett is apparent. The characteristic fault of his instruments, and especially the violoncellos, is that they are often worked too thin, and in consequence the tone is apt to suffer. His earlier labels bear the address of the 'Golden Harp,' in Piccadilly, the later of the 'Harp and Hautboy,' Piccadilly. Peter Wamsley was succeeded in business by his pupil Thomas Smith. In neither quality of tone nor varnish can his violoncellos compare with those of his master. Two apprentices of Smith, John Norris and Robert Barnes, were partners for a time in Windmill Street (1785) and Coventry Street (1794). Henry Jay, a maker of Long Acre (1746) and Windmill Street (1768) may, however, be mentioned as a neat and careful craftsman, who won repute for the kits he made for dancing-masters. Richard Duke, the elder, also gained a considerable name during the last half of the 18th century. At one time he lived in Red Lion Street, Holborn. His workmanship followed the Steiner pattern, and the tone of his violins was clear and silvery.

In 1741 the name of William Hill is first met with as a maker in Poland Street, near Broad Street, in Carnaby Market. He used a beautiful oil varnish of a transparent yellow colour. His brother, Joseph Hill, lived in Dover Street, Piccadilly, then at the 'Harp and Flute,' in the Haymarket, (where his house was burnt out with all his stock), and after that in Newington, to the south of the Thames. The work of these two brothers has remarkable affinities with that of Edmund Aireton, who at an advanced age was living in Hog Lane, Soho, as late as 1805. Aireton made inferior as well as high-class instruments, and his violins and tenors were built on the pattern of Stradivari.

John Edward, or old John, Betts and his nephew, Ned Betts, were Lincolnshire men, and both pupils of Richard Duke. The older man was a better dealer than maker, his nephew had more original ability, but both of them, as well as the Fendts, whom John Betts employed, were specially skilled in imitating the Italian and old English makers.

One of the most famous of the 18th-century makers has still to be mentioned, William Forster,[76] generally known as 'Old Forster,' to distinguish him from his son. Born in Cumberland in 1739 he came to London as a young man of twenty or twenty-one, and after working in the City set up for himself in St. Martin's Lane, from which he removed to 348 Strand, probably about 1784 or 1785.

By 1781 he had gained the patronage of the Duke of Cumberland, and his instruments had become celebrated for the 'original varnish' to which he refers in his labels. His earlier instruments were after the Steiner pattern. About 1772 he adopted the Amati outline, though his first work in this manner lacks the elegance and delicacy which he achieved later. His violas and violoncellos were the most highly esteemed, though some of his violins reached a high standard. Henry Hill remarks of his 'amber-coloured violoncellos' that 'they are renowned for mellowness, a volume and power of tone, equalled by few, surpassed by none.' William Forster died at his son's house, York Street, Westminster, in 1808.

The last period of the London school dates from 1790 to 1840, when the influence of Stradivari and Joseph Guarnieri became predominant. Some Middlesex makers belong to this period. John Furber, 1810–45, worked for J. Betts of the Royal Exchange, and afterwards for himself at Brick Lane, Old Street; his instruments are copied from both the Amati and the Stradivari patterns. Samuel Gilkes, a pupil of Charles Harris of Ratcliff Highway, was born in 1787 and died in 1827. He worked as journeyman with William Forster the younger, and afterwards was in business for himself at James Street, Buckingham Gate; his better-class work was excellent. John Carter, of Wych Street, worked chiefly for Betts, but produced some violins on his own account of good quality. Henry Lockey Hill, 1774–1835, was the son of a violin maker, and a pupil of his father and of John Betts. He then became with his brothers partner in his father's firm, and by his talent and fine workmanship largely helped to make the name of Hill famous. He was succeeded by his even more celebrated son William Ebsworth Hill (1817–95), and the latter by his four sons, William Henry, Arthur Frederick, Alfred Ebsworth, and Walter Edgar. These gentlemen now constitute the firm of Hill and Sons, whose reputation is world-wide, and has been still further enhanced by the publication of several valuable works, including a life of Stradivari.

The abolition of the import duty on violins from abroad and the large number of violins of old makers upon the market, which were more in demand than new ones, ruined the English manufacture, and but few firms have survived. Whether the trade is destined to revive the future only can show.

The Organ.—As early [77] as the year 1528

[76] See Sandys & Forster, *Hist. of the Violin,* 296 et seq.

[77] W. Page, *Denizations and Naturalizations* (Huguenot Soc.), 132, and cf. Kirk, op. cit. i, 159, 413.

we hear of John de John, a foreign organ-maker in London, and from the Subsidy Roll of 1549 it is clear that William Tresourer, born in Germany, but at that time living in the parish of Christ Church, Newgate, made organs as well as virginals. The year 1644 was a fatal one for organs and for the art of organ-building in this country. On the 4 January in that year an ordinance of the Lords and Commons assembled in Parliament was published for the speedy demolishing of organs and other so-called superstitious objects. Very few of the old organs in our cathedrals, collegiate churches, and chapels escaped. Organ-building must have practically ceased in England, and it was not till some fifty or sixty years after the Restoration that organs became common in the parish churches.[78]

To remedy the scarcity of native work-men (Dr. Burney tells us[79]), 'it was thought expedient to invite foreign builders of known abilities to settle among us; and the premiums offered on this occasion brought over the two celebrated workmen Smith and Harris.'

Renatus Harris, the famous organ-builder, and his rival Bernard Schmidt, better known as Father Smith, both lived in the City of London, but John Harris, a son of Renatus, set up in business in Red Lion Street, Holborn. In March 1738 he contracted to build 'a good tuneful and compleat organ' for the parish church of Doncaster at a cost of £525. He appears to have been in partnership with John Byfield, who married his daughter; the firm must have enjoyed a great reputation, as they built organs (among others) for Grantham Church, Lincolnshire; St. Mary Redcliffe, Bristol; and two churches in the City of London, viz., St. Alban's Wood Street, and St. Bartholomew Exchange. Christopher Schrider, who built the organ of Westminster Abbey in 1730, and those of the Chapel Royal, St. James's (1710), St. Mary Abbot's, Kensington (1716), and St. Martin in the Fields (1726), probably lived at Westminster. He was a workman employed by Father Smith, whose daughter he married in 1708. He succeeded Smith in his business after the latter's death, and in 1710 became also organ-builder to the Chapels Royal. He died in or before 1754, when his son Christopher held the appointment of king's organ-maker in succession to his father.[80]

Richard Bridge, a builder of high reputation, is said to have been employed as a workman by the younger Harris, and was probably in business in Hand Court, Holborn, in 1748. Nothing further is known of his biography except that he died before 1776. Between 1730 and 1757 or later he built many fine organs for churches in the Metropolis; among these were St. Paul's Deptford; Christ Church Spitalfields (one of the largest parish church organs in London); St. Bartholomew the Great; St. Anne's Limehouse, and the parish churches of Shoreditch and Paddington.

To meet the great demand for organs which arose early in the 18th century, when so many new churches were being erected, and to prevent the employment of incompetent persons, the three great makers of that time undertook jointly to supply instruments of good quality at a moderate cost. The makers uniting in this strong combination were Byfield, Jordan, and Bridge, who built the organ for Great Yarmouth Church in 1733. John Byfield, junior, of whom no personal particulars can be found, has been treated by most writers only as a partner or assistant to his father, but Rimbault has shown[81] that the younger Byfield was a builder of note on his own account, and gives a list of eighteen organs constructed by him between 1750 and 1771, including those of St. Botolph's Bishops-gate; Christ Church Cathedral, Dublin; St. John's College, Oxford; Drury Lane Theatre; the chapel of Greenwich Hospital; the theatre, Oxford; and St. Mary's Islington.

Messrs. William Hill & Son of York Road, Islington, take their origin as a firm from the celebrated John Snetzler, who was one of the most famous of our early English organ builders. He was born at Passau in Germany about 1710, and after gaining a reputation in his own country came over to England. Here the excellence of his work and the novelty of some of his methods soon procured him many commissions, and Dr. Rimbault gives a list of thirty-five organs built by him, most of them between 1741 and 1780. Among them were Chesterfield, Derbyshire; Finchley, Edmonton, and Hackney, Middlesex; St. Mary's Hall; Beverley Minster; Leatherhead and Richmond, Surrey; Leeds Parish Church; St. Martin's Leicester; St. Clements, Lombard Street; the German Lutheran Chapel in the Savoy, and Buckingham Palace, the last-named being now in the German Chapel, St. James's. One of his noblest organs was that for King's

---

[78] G. A. Audsley, *Art of Organ-building* (1905), i, 74.

[79] Burney, *Hist. of Music* (1789), iii, 436.

[80] Edward and John Chamberlayne, *Mag. Brit. Notitia* (1755), pt. ii, bk. iii, 110.

[81] Edw. J. Hopkins and F. Rimbault, *Hist. of the Organ* (1877), 145.

Lynn, Norfolk, where the churchwardens inquired what their old organ would be worth if repaired. His reply was, 'If they would lay out a hundred pounds upon it, perhaps it would be worth fifty.' Snetzler lived to an advanced age and died at the end of the 18th or the beginning of the 19th century. Having realized a competent income he returned to his native country to settle for the remainder of his life. He had, however, become too much of a Londoner to live elsewhere, and the attractions of London porter and London living proved so great as to compel him to return and spend the rest of his days in the Metropolis.

Snetzler was succeeded in 1780 by his foreman Ohrmann, who took W. Nutt into partnership in 1790. Thomas Elliott next joined the firm, but appears in 1794[82] as in business by himself at 10, Sutton Street, Soho, and one of six organ-builders then carrying on their trade in London. Elliott took into partnership in 1825 William Hill of Lincolnshire, who had married his daughter, and was the inventor of a pattern of viola da gamba which became extensively used. On the death of Elliott in 1832 Hill remained alone till 1837, when he was joined by Frederic Davison, who shortly afterwards retired to become a partner of John Gray. Thomas Hill then joined the firm, which became Hill & Son, and William Hill died 18 December 1870. He will long be remembered for having in conjunction with Dr. Gauntlett introduced the C C compass into this country. The present partners of the firm are A. G. Hill and W. Hill. The firm has built, amongst many others, organs for Westminster Abbey, 1884, Ely, Worcester, and Manchester Cathedrals, Birmingham and Melbourne Town Halls, St. Peter's Cornhill, and All Saints' Margaret Street. One of the present partners, Mr. Arthur George Hill, is the author of a valuable work on *Organ-cases and Organs of the Middle Ages and Renaissance*, published in 1883.

The firm of Bishop & Son of 20, Upper Gloucester Place, London, N.W., was established about the end of the 18th century by James C. Bishop, and has always had a high reputation for excellent workmanship. The invention of the double-acting composition pedal, the clarabella stop, and the anti-concussion valve is to be placed to the credit of the founder of this firm. Among the finest specimens of their work are the organs of St. Giles's Camberwell; St. James's Piccadilly; the Brompton Oratory; Jesus College, Cambridge;

and those of Bombay Cathedral and Town Hall. After the death of J. C. Bishop the style of the firm successively became Bishop, Son & Starr; Bishop, Starr & Richardson; Bishop & Starr; and Bishop & Son. Mr. C. K. K. Bishop is the author of *Notes on Church Organs*, published in 1873.

Messrs. Gray & Davison are a London firm of long standing and high reputation. Robert Gray established an organ factory in London in 1774, and was succeeded by William Gray, who died in 1820. John Gray then became head of the firm, which became in 1837–8 John Gray & Son; shortly afterwards Frederic Davison was received into partnership, when the style of the firm was altered to Gray & Davison. John Gray died in 1849, but the style of the firm continued, their premises in London being at 6, Pratt Street, N.W.; they have also a factory at Liverpool. Among the many fine organs built by this famous firm are those of the Crystal Palace; St. Paul's Wilton Place; St. Pancras; Magdalen College, Oxford; and the Town Halls of Bolton, Leeds, and Glasgow. The Keraulophon stop was invented by the firm in 1843.

Samuel Green, who appears to have been a London maker, was born in 1740, and died at Isleworth 14 September 1796. He is said by Rimbault[83] to have been a partner of the younger Byfield, and to have probably learned his trade in the workshops of Byfield, Bridge & Jordan. Green was organ-builder to George III, and much patronized by the king. The royal favour brought him much business, but little financial benefit; although he was so long at the head of his profession he yet scarcely obtained a moderate competency, and died a poor man. Green was a true artist, and his zeal for the mechanical improvement of the organ consumed a great part of his time in experiment and research which brought him little or no emolument. The organs built by Green possess a peculiar sweetness and delicacy of tone entirely original, and probably in this he has never been excelled. There is a list of fifty organs of his construction taken from his own account book and printed in the *Gentleman's Magazine*.[84] It contains no less than twelve cathedral and collegiate organs, including that of Canterbury Cathedral, eleven London organs, including several City churches and Freemasons' Hall, and twenty-seven others built for the country or abroad.

Crang & Hancock were a London firm established in the last quarter of the 18th

---

[82] *Musical Directory* (1794). See Hopkins and Rimbault, *Organ*, 156.

[83] Hopkins & Rimbault, *Hist. of the Organ*, 150.
[84] June 1814, pp. 543–4.

century. John Crang came from Devonshire and joined in partnership with Hancock, a good voicer of reeds. Hancock added new reeds to many of Father Smith's organs, and Crang was chiefly occupied in turning the old echoes into swells. Among the organs thus treated by the firm were those of St. Paul's Cathedral, St. Peter's Cornhill, and St. Clement Danes. There were two Hancocks, James and John, who with John Crang were employed in repairing the organ of Maidstone Church between 1755 and 1790. In some particulars taken from the churchwardens' accounts published by Mr. W. B. Gilbert,[85] 'Mr. Hancock,' who is described as 'organ-builder of Wych Street, London,' is stated to have died suddenly near Maidstone in January 1792. James Hancock was living in 1820, and perhaps some years later. The following are some of the organs built by this firm :— St. John's Horsleydown, 1770 ; Barnstaple Church, 1772 ; Chelmsford, Essex, 1772 ; St. George the Martyr Queen's Square, 1773; St. Vedast Foster Lane, 1780 ; and Brompton Chapel.

John Avery, whose work was held in high reputation, was in business at this time in the churchyard of St. Margaret's Westminster. No other particulars of his life are known. His organs were built between the years 1775 and 1808 ; in the latter year he died whilst constructing the organ of Carlisle Cathedral. The list includes the following: Croydon, Surrey, 1794, which he considered his best work ; Sevenoaks, Kent, 1798 ; Winchester Cathedral, 1799 ; Christ Church Bath, 1800; St. Margaret's Westminster, 1804 ; King's College Chapel, Cambridge, 1804 ; in which he incorporated portions of Dallam's earlier work and the case made by Chapman & Hartop in 1606 ; and Carlisle Cathedral, 1808.

Henry Willis, one of the greatest of English organ-builders, was born on 27 April 1821, and was articled in 1835 to John Gray. In 1847 he rebuilt the organ of Gloucester Cathedral with the then unusual compass of twenty-nine notes in the pedals. In a patent[86] which he took out on 28 August 1851 for 'improvements in the construction of organs,' he is described as of Manchester Street, but on 9 March 1868, when another patent[87] was granted him, his address is given as Rochester Terrace, Camden Road. He obtained much fame at the Exhibition of 1851 for the large organ which he exhibited there, and this led to his receiving the commission to build the organ for St. George's Hall, Liverpool, which so greatly enhanced his reputation. For the Exhibition of 1862 he made another organ, which became the nucleus of that of the Alexandra Palace, unfortunately destroyed by fire on 9 June 1873. He next built the splendid organ at the Royal Albert Hall, which for its size, and the efficiency of its pneumatic, mechanical, and acoustic qualities, shares the high reputation procured for him by his second Alexandra Palace organ, which was opened in 1875. The improvements in organ-construction which he effected in 1851 comprise the application of an improved exhausting valve to the pneumatic lever, the application of pneumatic levers in a compound form, and the invention of a movement for facilitating the drawing of stops, singly or in combination. Sir George Grove[88] thus estimates the work of this celebrated maker :—'Mr. Willis has always been a scientific organ-builder, and his organs are distinguished for their excellent "engineering," clever contrivances, and first-rate workmanship, as much as for their brilliancy, force of tone, and orchestral character.' Willis died in 1905. Besides his principal works already mentioned he also built or renewed the organs of nearly half the English cathedrals, besides those of numerous halls, colleges, churches, &c.

George England, a notable builder, flourished between the years 1740 and 1788, and is stated to have married the daughter of his contemporary, Richard Bridge. He built the following among many other fine instruments: —St. Stephen's Walbrook (1760) ; Gravesend, Kent (1764) ; St. Michael's Queenhithe (1779); St. Mary's Aldermary (1781);[89] St. Alphege Greenwich ; and Dulwich College Chapel. The last organ, built in 1760, cost £260, together with the old instrument by Father Smith, which England took in part payment. In 1887 the organ was restored on the advice of Dr. Hopkins, who pronounced it to be a magnificent specimen of England's work, and well worthy of reverent and thorough restoration. An illustration of this organ is given in J. W. Hinton's *Organ Construction*.[90] George England was succeeded by his son, G. P. England, at Stephen Street, Rathbone Place, who carried on the business until 1814, and built twenty-two organs between 1788 and 1812. The list of these

[85] *Mem. of the Collegiate Ch. of Maidstone* (1866), 216–17.
[86] No. 13,538.   [87] No. 812.

[88] *Dict. of Music* (ed. 1), iv, 460.
[89] The last two in conjunction with Hugh Russell. An organ builder of that name in Theobald's Road is one of the six named in the *Musical Dir.* for 1794 ; Hopkins & Rimbault, op. cit. 156.
[90] 1900, pl. iii, 54.

taken from England's own account book[91] includes St. James's Clerkenwell; St. Margaret's Lothbury; Gainsborough, Lincolnshire; Sheffield Parish Church; and Richmond, Yorkshire. The Englands' business was taken over by their apprentice, Joseph William Walker, in 1819,[92] or according to another account in 1828.[93] Walker started in Museum Street, and removed in 1838 to 27, Francis Street, Tottenham Court Road, where the business is still carried on. Walker died in 1870, and was succeeded by his four sons, whom he had previously taken into partnership, the style of the firm being changed to J. W. Walker & Sons. The high reputation of the firm is shown by the large number of important organs which have come from their works, including those of York Minster; Exeter Hall; St. Margaret's Westminster; Bow Church, Cheapside; the Royal College of Music, South Kensington; and Sandringham Church.

The firm of Flight and Kelly, organ builders of Exeter Change, Strand, is one of the six London makers recorded in the *Musical Directory* of 1794.[94] Nothing further is known of John Kelly, but Benjamin Flight was succeeded by his son, also named Benjamin (born in 1767), who commenced business about 1800 in partnership with Joseph Robson, in Lisle Street, Leicester Square, under the style of Flight and Robson. They afterwards removed to St. Martin's Lane, where they constructed and for many years publicly exhibited the Apollonicon, a large chamber organ of peculiar construction, comprising both keyboards and barrels. They had previously exhibited a smaller instrument made for Viscount Kirkwall, and in consequence of its popularity they designed one of larger dimensions in 1812 which occupied five years and cost £10,000 in its construction and perfecting. For nearly a quarter of a century after its completion in

1817, an exhibition of its mechanical powers was daily given. The performance of the overture to 'Oberon' has been especially recorded as a notable triumph of mechanical skill and ingenuity, every note of the score being rendered as accurately as though executed by a fine orchestra. Flight also perfected and gave practical form to the invention of an improved form of bellows by which a supply of steady wind is maintained.[95] The partnership was dissolved in 1832, after which Robson's share of the business was bought by Gray and Davison, whilst Flight in conjunction with his son J. Flight, who had long actively assisted him, carried on business in St. Martin's Lane as Flight and Son. Benjamin Flight died in 1847, Robson in 1876, and J. Flight in 1890 at Strathblaine Road, Clapham Junction.

The firm of Bevington and Sons was founded about the beginning of the 19th century by Henry Bevington, who was apprenticed to Ohrmann and Nutt, successors to the famous Snetzler. The present members of the firm are Henry and Martin Bevington, sons of the founder, who are in business in Rose Street, Soho. The organs of St. Martin's in the Fields, the Foundling Hospital, and St. Patrick's Cathedral, Dublin, were built by this firm. The firm of Bryceson Brothers was founded in 1796 by Henry Bryceson, and carries on business at St. Thomas's Hall, Highbury. The principal organs which they have built are those for the great Concert Hall, Brighton; the Pro-Cathedral, Kensington; St. Michael's Cornhill; and St. Peter and St. Paul, Cork. Many equally famous builders had their works within the City of London. Such were, among early makers, the Dallams and the Jordans; the last-named were the inventors of the Swell Organ, which they first introduced in 1712 in the famous organ of St. Magnus London Bridge.

COACH-MAKING

The earliest coaches were of necessity heavy and clumsy in their design, as the terrible condition of even the most frequented highways of the City prohibited the use of lighter vehicles. For this reason the Thames was for many centuries London's great highway, and the waterman down to the beginning of the 19th

century was the serious competitor of the coach and fly-man. The London coach-building trade took up its quarters from an early period principally in the western part of the City. When once introduced the trade grew apace, as it soon became the correct thing for people of fashion to have their own coach. The art of coach-building gave great scope

---

[91] Hopkins and Rimbault, *The Organ*, 155.
[92] Grove, *Dict. of Music* (ed. 1), iv, 376.
[93] *Who's Who in Business*, 1906.
[94] Hopkins and Rimbault, op. cit. 156.

[95] This invention is ascribed to Cummins, whose name appears as residing at Pentonville, in the *Musical Dir.* (1794).

for talent, ingenuity, and taste in devising a safe, comfortable, shapely, and artistically decorated conveyance. For the decoration of the panels the services of artists of the highest rank were engaged. Smirke, the Royal Academician, served his time to Bromley the heraldic carriage painter of Lincoln's Inn Fields. Monamy, the marine painter of the latter part of the 18th century, painted the carriage of the ill-fated Admiral Byng; and Charles Cotton, R.A., decorated coaches with armorial bearings.[1]

Hackney coaches came into use in 1605. At first they stood about in the yards of the principal inns, but in 1634 Captain Bailey [2] 'created according to his ability some four hackney coaches, put his men in livery and appointed them to stand at the "Maypole" in the Strand,' where St. Mary's Church now is. A patent (No. 3) was granted to Edward Knapp on 7 January 1625 'for hanging the bodies of carriages by springs of steel;' another patent (No. 244) was taken out by John Bellingham on 7 January 1685 'for making square window glasses for chaises and coaches.' On 13 May 1740 John Tull was granted a patent (No. 570) for a sedan-chair fixed on a wheel carriage for horse draught. Many years earlier (in 1691) John Green obtained a patent for coach springs, but these did not come into general use until the latter half of the 18th century.

William Felton, coach-maker, of 36, Leather Lane, Holborn, in his *Treatise on Carriages*, published in 1794, says ' the principal improvements that have been made in carriages for these last twenty years are originally the invention of Mr. John Hatchett of Long Acre, whose taste in building has greatly contributed to the increase of their numbers, and enhancement of their value. To him every coach maker is highly indebted, as at present they seldom build without copying his designs.' The famous state-coach of the Irish Lord Chancellor was built in 1790 either by this firm or by that of Baxter.[3]

In 1769 T. Hunt received sixty guineas from the Society of Arts for improvements in tyring wheels. The well-known firm of Barker & Co. possesses drawings of coaches built for the Duke of Bedford and others between 1780 and 1800. At a later time their customers included Count D'Orsay, Lord

Chesterfield, and Charles Dickens. The most famous coach-builders in London in 1815 were Rowley, Mansell, and Cook, a large firm in Liquorpond Street, Windus in Bishopsgate Street, Barker in Chandos Street, Hatchett of Long Acre, Houlditch and Hawkins, and Luke Hopkinson of Holborn.

Great improvements in the manufacture of English carriages were made in 1820 by Samuel Hobson. He reduced the height of the wheels, lengthened the coach body and hung it lower, substituting a double step to the door instead of a three-step ladder. Hobson traded in the firm of Barker and Co. of Chandos Street and later rose to be a partner. About the year 1815 he set up for himself in Long Acre, and removed later to the large premises previously occupied by Messrs. Hatchett. In his improvements he was assisted by his experience gained at Messrs. Barker's, and his methods were copied in turn by the principal members of the trade, in the same way that he had copied his predecessor, Mr. Hatchett, in 1780.

James Bennett, of Finsbury, was the inventor of a two-wheeled carriage called the Dennett, which was a great improvement on the whisky or gig of 1790. — Tilbury, the originator of an easy vehicle known by that name, was also the builder of the 'Stanhope,' under the superintendence of the Hon. Fitzroy Stanhope, brother of Lord Petersham.

The dog-cart dates from the beginning of the 19th century, one variety being known as the Whitechapel. This became the favourite vehicle of the commercial travellers, to whom about 1830 one coach factory in London supplied several hundreds of these vehicles at an annual rental. The introduction of railways gave the commercial traveller a more expeditious method of showing his samples, and the chief users of the dog-cart have since been the tradesman and the farmer.

David Davies, of Albany Street, and afterwards of Wigmore Street, was a coach-builder of considerable inventive faculties. Among many other of his inventions was the Pilentum phaeton, which he designed about the year 1834. The Pilentum was an open carriage with the doorway very near the ground, built of different sizes, to carry four or six persons, and adapted for one or two horses. He is also the reputed inventor of the cab phaeton, which was soon generally adopted as a popular pleasure carriage. This became a fashionable conveyance not only in England, but also on the Continent, until 1850, about which time it came into use as a hackney carriage, and so lost favour with the gentry. It

---

[1] J. H. Pollen, *Anct. and Modern furniture in the S. Kens. Mus.* (1874), Introd.

[2] From a letter written by Lord Strafford in 1634. Quoted by Sir W. Gilbey, *Early Carriages*, 27.

[3] G. A. Thrupp, *Hist. of the Art of Coach-Building* (1876), 89.

has since come once more into fashion under the name of the victoria.

Another old firm of coach-builders is that of Messrs. Peters, of George Street, Portman Square, whose mail phaetons were noted as long ago as 1836 for their steadiness on rough roads. The year 1838 marks an important epoch in the annals of coach-building, the coronation of Queen Victoria having occasioned a larger number of court-dress carriages than had ever previously been seen in London. About this time Luke Hopkinson, a celebrated coach-maker in Holborn, introduced the briska landau, which led with subsequent improvements to the popular landau of the present day.[4]

— Robinson, of Mount Street, built the first vehicle in the shape of the present brougham in 1839. This was made for Lord Brougham, from whom it took its name; other makers soon followed, and the brougham quickly came into general use.

The first omnibus was started in London on 4 July 1829 by John Shillibeer, who had been for a short time a coach-maker in Paris. The omnibuses were drawn by three horses, and ran at a fare of 1s. from the 'Yorkshire Stingo,' in the Marylebone Road, near the bottom of Lisson Grove, to the Bank. The London General Omnibus Company was founded in 1856. Mr. Shanks, of Great Queen Street, was a very famous builder of four-in-hand coaches and sporting vehicles. The business was wound up within the last few years after the death of the proprietor. Other firms of note in Middlesex are Fountain of Enfield, Carpenter and Co., Staines, and Wilkinson, of Uxbridge. Within the metropolitan area are Cook and Holdway, of Halkin Place; Corben and Sons, Great Queen Street; Laurie and Marner, Ltd., Oxford Street; Holland, Oxford Street; Gill, Chilworth Street, Hyde Park; C. S. Windover and Co., Ltd., Long Acre; and Thomas Worges and Co., Palace Street, S.W.

The motor-car industry, of which this country has now secured a share, has some representative firms in Middlesex. The Napier Company have works at Acton, where the Napier cars, for which S. F. Edge, Ltd., are agents, are made. Clement Talbot, Ltd., of Ladbroke Grove, are also manufacturers. The chief Middlesex makers of motor bodies are Barker and Co., Ltd., Chandos Street; Mulliners Ltd., Long Acre; Cole and Son, Kensington High Street and Hammersmith; and H. S. Mulliner, Brook Street and Bedford Park.[5]

PAPER

The earliest attempt at paper-making in England was made by John Tate, the younger, mayor of London in 1496, who erected a paper mill in the neighbouring county of Hertford. This mill furnished the paper for a book entitled *Bartholomaeus Anglicus de proprietatibus rerum*, printed by Wynkyn de Worde in 1495 (?), as we learn from the eighth verse of the 'Prohemium' :—

And John Tate the yonger Ioye mote he broke
Whiche late hath in Englande doo make this paper
    thynne
That now in our Englyssh this boke is prynted
    Inne.

Many subsequent attempts were, however, made before the art was successfully established in this country. Between 1574 and 1576 another eminent London citizen, Sir Thomas Gresham, set up a paper mill on his estate at Osterley Park, Middlesex. This mill formed the subject of an Exchequer inquiry to determine whether it had encroached on the queen's highway or injured the queen's mills.[1] This inquiry took place in 1584, and from the evidence of the witnesses examined it appears that Gresham's mill stood on the river Brent, 'nere Cruxewell's forde,' that it was erected about thirteen years previously, and that it was a corn-mill when first erected. Not long before his death in 1579 Gresham 'ioyned a paper myll thervnto and yet vsed the same myll a corne myll still, and all vnder one roufe and dryven by one streame.'[2] Norden, writing in 1593, fourteen years after Gresham's death, states that his mills (for paper, oil, and corn), were then 'decaied, a corne mill excepted.'[3] Had his life been spared there is little doubt that the great com-

[4] Mr. George N. Hooper, to whom I am indebted for much information, is of opinion that landaus were introduced into England by Charles Lucas Birch of Great Queen Street, Long Acre, or by William Birch.

[5] The writer has to acknowledge information kindly supplied by Mr. C. Cooper, jun., editor of the *Coach Builders' Art Journ.*
[1] Exch. Dep. by Com. Hil. 26 Eliz. no. 6.
[2] Ibid. Trin. 2.
[3] *Speculum Brit.* (1723), 37.

mercial genius of Sir Thomas Gresham would have made out of this beginning a flourishing industry for our country.

Richard Tottel, or Tottyll, a printer in the City of London, appears next as a paper manufacturer. In a petition addressed in 1585 (?) to Lord Burghley he says that twelve years before he, with some partners, agreed to set up a paper mill, but his companions left the undertaking, on the ground that the project had twice or thrice been attempted before, but without success. He was resolved to persevere and complained of the hindrance of Frenchmen, 'who buy up all our rags.' He prays that the exportation of rags from this country may be prohibited, and that a site for a paper mill may be granted him with sole privilege for thirty years of making paper in England.[4] Tottel seems to have had no better success than his predecessors. A German named Spilman, or Spielman, who erected a paper mill at Dartford in 1588, was more successful, and is said to have been knighted by Queen Elizabeth in recognition of this national service.[5] A recurrence of the plague in 1636–7 led to a correspondence between Peter Heywood, a Westminster justice of the peace, and Lord Keeper Coventry. Heywood urged the necessity of seizing the rags sold at rag shops in Clerkenwell, St. Giles's Cripplegate, Shoreditch, Whitechapel, Stepney, and St. Katharine's, to prevent their being sold to make paper.[6] One of the offending paper makers was William Bushee, who had set up a mill in Middlesex midway between Hounslow and East Bedfont. On 8 December 1636 he was summoned to the Middlesex Sessions 'for grindinge ragges in his paper-mill that came from London, whereby one of his servantes became infected with the plague.'[7] The popular alarm seems to have stopped the mills from working, and the privy council ordered the local authorities to give help to the workpeople thrown out of their employment. This produced an indignant petition from the inhabitants of Middlesex and Bucks who lived in the neighbourhood of the mills. The correspondence provides us with some useful facts. There were at least four paper mills in this district: that of William Bushee, one of Edmond Phipps at Horton, one probably belonging to Richard West at Poyle, and the mill at Colnbrook,

which may have been held by Henry Harris. The petitioners complained that the landlords by converting their corn mills into paper mills advanced their rents from £10 and £15 to £100 and £150 per annum, that the paper-makers brought many indigent persons into their parishes whom they ought to maintain, and their workmen had double wages in comparison with other labourers and might well save, that the paper made was so 'unuseful' that it would bear no ink on one side, and was sold at dearer rates than formerly. For these and other reasons the petitioners, so far from consenting to the paper-makers, desire if possible that their mills may be suppressed or removed further off.[8]

In spite of these and other attempts in various parts of the country to manufacture paper, the greater part of the paper used in England, and certainly that of finer quality, was imported from abroad. In 1675 a patent[9] was granted to Eustace Burneby for 'making all sorts of white paper for the use of writing and printing, being a new manufacture never practised in any our kingdomes or dominions.' Burneby must have had some success, for three years later a book was presented to the king,[10] 'being printed upon English paper and made within five miles of Windsor by Eustace Burneby, esq. who was the first Englishman that brought it into England, attested by Henry Million, who was overseer in the making of this royal manufacture.' Burneby's mill is said to have been at Stanwell, Middlesex, but its success was short-lived.

The Craftsman (No. 910) records that William III granted certain Huguenot refugees, Biscoe and others, a patent for establishing paper manufactories, but that the undertaking was not successful. In 1713 Thomas Watkin, a stationer in London, brought the art of manufacturing paper to great perfection, in consequence of which numerous paper mills were established in England.[11]

On 17 September 1787 Samuel Hooper, a bookseller and stationer of St. Giles-in-the-Fields, patented[12] 'a new method of making or manufacturing printing paper particularly for copper-plate printing.' Hooper is said also to have produced, in 1790, paper of various qualities from leather cuttings and

[4] S.P. Dom. Eliz. clxxxv, 69.
[5] Lewis Evans, *Anct. Papermaking* (1896), 6.
[6] S.P. Dom. Chas. I, cccxxxi, 31.
[7] *Midd. Sess. Rolls* (Midd. Co. Rec. Soc.), iii, 167.

[8] Rhys Jenkins, 'Paper-making in England, 1588–1680' in *Lib. Assoc. Rec.* Nov. 1900, p. 584.
[9] 21 Jan. 1675, no. 178.
[10] *Paper and Paper-making Chronology* (1875), 21.
[11] Matthias Koops, *Historical Account of Substances used to describe Events and to convey Ideas* (1801), 225–6.
[12] No. 1622.

refuse paper.[13] Other inventions for bleaching rags for paper were registered by Hector Campbell on 28 November 1792 (No. 1,922) and by John Bigg on 28 February 1795 (No. 2,040).

In 1804 Henry and Sealy Fourdrinier, stationers and paper manufacturers of London, erected their first paper-making machine at Boxmoor, Herts. This, with many improvements by subsequent inventors, continued to be for many years the principal type of paper-making machinery. The excise returns for 1835 [14] show that seventy London manufacturers of stained paper paid a total duty of £35,012 9s. 7d., while the total for all England was £49,746 8s.

Wall Papers.—The manufacture of paper hangings in England is said to have begun about 1746, when it was started by Potter of Manchester. Paper-staining as an industry has long been carried on in Old Ford. About the beginning of the 19th century the founders of the firm of John Allan & Son came up from their native county of Elgin in Scotland and settled in the East of London. Here they created a large business which in 1876 employed 150 hands and produced wall paper of every kind, suitable for the cottage, the mansion, or the palace.[15] There is no industry in which the influence of the artistic revival in England has been more apparent than in this manufacture. Among the firms who have taken a prominent part in the production of paper hangings of good quality are those of Jeffrey & Co., Morris & Co., and Crace. There are more than twenty other trades connected with the paper industry. Among the more important paper-makers in Middlesex at the present day are the Colnbrook Paper Mills, Ltd., Poyle Mill, Colnbrook; Isaac Warwick & Co., Wraysbury Mill, near Staines; the Patent Impermeable Millboard Co., Ltd., Sunbury Common; and the West Drayton Millboard Co., Ltd.

PRINTING

The City of Westminster enjoys the honour of being the place where a printing press was first set up in this country.

Of William Caxton it is unnecessary to speak at length. Sprung from an old Kentish family, he was born, probably in London, about the year 1422, and was afterwards apprenticed to Robert Large, an eminent member of the Mercers' Company, and Lord Mayor. On the expiration of his indentures, in 1446, he went to Bruges, where he engaged in business and became the Governor of the Company of Merchant Adventurers. In March 1468–9 he began an English translation, 'as a preventive against idlenes' (he tells us) of the *Recuyell of the Historyes of Troye*, which he continued at Ghent, and finished at Cologne, in 1471. The book being in great demand Caxton set himself to learn the newly-discovered art of printing in order to multiply copies. The *Recuyell* probably appeared in 1474, and was the first book printed in English. Caxton learnt the art of printing from Colard Mansion, who set up a press at Bruges about 1473. He left Bruges in 1476 and returned to England.

Caxton's claim to be the first English printer has been opposed by some older writers, who considered that Oxford was the first seat of printing in England. It is now generally agreed that Oxford's claim to have had a press in 1468 cannot be sustained, and rests only on a typographical blunder in the printing of a date. Caxton's first printed works were small treatises and short poems by Lydgate and Chaucer; many of these are probably lost; his first dated book is *The Dictes and Sayinges of the Philosophers*, printed in 1477. The chief work from his press was *The Golden Legend*, a large folio volume illustrated with rude woodcuts, and containing the lives of the English saints. His press was set up in the Almonry at Westminster, where the Guards' Memorial now stands.

Caxton remained a parishioner of St. Margaret's until his death in 1491. The parish accounts for 1490–2 state that 6s. 8d. was paid for four torches 'atte burreying of Wylliam Caxton,' and '6d. for the belle atte same burreying.' A memorial tablet was erected to his memory in 1820 by the Roxburghe Club, and in 1883 a stained glass window was also set up in his honour by the London printers and publishers. Caxton's life was a busy one. To his work as a translator we are indebted for twenty-one books from the French and one from the Dutch; besides

[13] J. Munsell, *Chronology* (1870), 43.
[14] *Excise Commissioners' Rep.* xiv, 44–5.
[15] Crory, *East Lond. Industries*, 17.

which he printed nearly eighty books, some of which passed through more than one large edition. William Blades his biographer sums up his character as that of a pious, diligent, and educated man, who without aiming very high led the life of an honest and useful merchant.

Caxton's successor was Wynkyn de Worde, who came to England with him, as a youth, and continued as his workman and chief assistant. He remained at Westminster after his master's death and finished the *Canterbury Tales* and Hilton's *Seale of Perfection*, which had been begun by Caxton. In 1496 he removed to the sign of the 'Sun' in Fleet Street, and printed as many as 488 books between 1493 and 1534. He was, like Caxton, a man of learning, and introduced many improvements in the art of printing as practised in England. He founded his own types, which were of beautiful design, and his books are noted for the excellence of their press-work. He was the first printer who introduced the Roman letter into England, and made use of it to distinguish anything remarkable.

Richard Pynson, like Wynkyn de Worde, was a workman or 'servant' of Caxton, and afterwards set up a press of his own at Temple Bar. He was King's Printer to Henry VIII, from whom he received a grant of £4 annually during life. In this grant, which is dated 27 September 1515, he is styled 'Richard Pynson, *Esquire*, our Printer.' Pynson used this title of 'Esquire' in the colophon of his *Statuta*, etc. His known productions number 210, and his types are clear and good; but his press work is hardly equal to that of De Worde. His first dated book was *Dives and Pauper*, printed in 1493, and he continued to print until 1529 or 1531. In his later books he describes himself as living at the sign of the 'George,' in Fleet Street, beside the church.

One other early printer contributes to the fame of Westminster as the cradle of the English press. Julian Notary is believed by Ames to have printed in France before he came to this country. His name is associated with that of John Barbier as printer of the Salisbury Missal which Ames believed to have been printed on the Continent. His first residence in England, as stated on the colophons of his earliest books, was in King Street, Westminster, but about 1503 he removed to a house with the sign of the 'Three Kings,' in the parish of St. Clement Danes, without Temple Bar. In 1515 the colophon to *The Cronycle of England* shows that he had removed to a house with the same sign in St. Paul's Churchyard, at the west door of the Cathedral, by the Bishop of London's Palace. He is known to have printed twenty-three books, the earliest of which is dated 20 December 1498, and the latest 1520. Notary used two devices, which also appear upon his bindings, and will be described in the following section of this article.

London printing soon left its first home. Caxton's successors migrated to Fleet Street, and the entire body of printers with hardly an exception set up their presses within the City, where the trade remained almost exclusively for over two centuries. Professor Arber's list of London printers for the year 1556 reveals the curious fact that of the 32 booksellers and printers then living in London no less than 15 lived in St. Paul's Churchyard, 5 others in close proximity, 8 in Fleet Street, 2 in Lombard Street, 1 in Aldersgate, and another in a locality unknown.

As a result of an examination of London printed books from the time of Caxton to the year 1556 it appears probable that only three presses existed during that period outside the City of London besides those of Caxton and his immediate successors.[1] The three printers were William Follingham or Follington, who printed for Richard Banks in 1544 at Holy Well in Shoreditch; Hill, who printed between 1548 and 1553 at St. John's Street, Clerkenwell; and Robert Wyer, 1527–50, whose press was ' in the byshop of Norwytche rentes, besyde charyng crosse.'

Wyer was one of the most prolific of the English printers of the 16th century. Many of his books are without date, and of a fugitive and popular character. His printing for the most part is exceedingly poor, but some of his books in 'foreign secretary Gothic' and ' large lower case Gothic' types are very well executed.

The printing trade was kept under strict control by the state, a control exercised chiefly through the Archbishop of Canterbury and the Stationers' Company. This company made an order on 9 May 1615 limiting the number of presses in the City of London to nineteen. Similar, but for the most part ineffectual, attempts were made from time to time to stop the natural growth of the art of printing. In a list of printers in England who in 1649–50 entered into recognizances not to print seditious books, among sixty-seven names, only one Middlesex printer is found—William Bentley of Finsbury.[2] In 1666, the year of the Great

[1] C. Welch, *Literary Associations of St. Paul's* (1891), 77 et seq.
[2] *Bibliographica*, ii, 225.

Fire, the entire number of working printers in and about London was stated to be 140, but how many of them were working outside the City does not appear.[3] From another list in 1724 we have a more complete view of the printing trade of the metropolis.[4] The list was prepared by Samuel Negus, a printer, who distinguished printers according to their religious and political principles. The number of printers is 75, of whom 15 have addresses outside the City. Of these 6 lived in St. John's Lane, 2 in Goswell Street, 2 in or near the Savoy, 2 in Lincoln's Inn Fields, and the 3 others in Covent Garden, Bloomsbury, and Without Temple Bar.

The only printer of note in Negus's list living outside the City is Woodfall, 'Without Temple Bar.' An anonymous contributor to *Notes and Queries*[5] gives some valuable notes drawn from the ledgers of Henry Woodfall between the years 1734 and 1737. On 15 December 1735 he charged Bernard Lintot as follows :—

	£	s.	d.
Printing the first volume of Mr. Pope's Works, Cr. Long Primer, 8vo, 3000 (and 75 fine), @ £2 2s. per sheet, 14 sheets and a half	30	09	0
Title in red and black	1	1	0
Paid for 2 reams and ¼ of writing demy	2	16	3

He also printed Pope's *Iliad* for Henry Lintot in 1736 at a cost of £143 17s., described as 'demy, Long Primer and Brevier, No. 2000 in 6 vols. 68 sheets & ½ @ £2 2s. per sheet.' Woodfall's customers included also Robert Dodsley, Lawton Gilliver, and Andrew Millar. For the latter he printed Thomson's poems ; 250 8vo. copies of *Spring*, in October 1734, and in the following January the 1st part of *Liberty* in a cr. 8vo. edition of 3,000 and 250 'fine copies.' *The Seasons* was issued on 9 June 1744 in octavo. There were 1,500 errata in the work, and a special charge of £2 4s. was made for 'divers and repeated alterations.'

In 1731 Edward Cave, who had followed many employments, purchased a small printing-office at St. John's Gate, Clerkenwell. Here he printed and published the *Gentleman's Magazine*, the first number of which appeared in January 1730–1.

One of the most useful enterprises of the brilliant Horace Walpole was the private printing-press which he set up on 4 August 1757 at Strawberry Hill, his villa at Twickenham. In his letter of this date to Sir Horace Mann he says, 'I am turned printer, and have converted a little cottage into a printing office.' He began with two *Odes* of Gray, printed by William Robinson, who did not remain long in his employment. His next work was Paul Hentzner's interesting *Journey into England*, a small edition of 220 copies. In April 1758 appeared the two volumes of his *Catalogue o Royal and Noble Authors*, of which a second edition, not printed at Strawberry Hill, was called for before the end of the year. Writing in 1760 he says, 'I have been plagued with a succession of bad printers ; ' this hindered the production of his edition of *Lucan*. It was published in January 1761, and in the following year appeared the first and second volumes of *Anecdotes of Painting in England*, with plates and portraits, and the imprint 'Printed by Thomas Farmer at Strawberry Hill, MDCCLXII.' Then another difficulty arose with the printers, and the third volume, published in 1763, had no printer's name in the imprint. The fourth volume, not issued till 1780, bears the name of Thomas Kirgate, who seems to have been taken on in 1772, and held his post until Walpole's death. Between 1764 and 1768 the Strawberry Press was idle, but in the latter year Walpole printed 200 copies of a French play entitled *Cornélie Vestale Tragédie*, and from that time to 1789 he continued to print at intervals, his chief productions being *Mémoires du Comte de Grammont*, 1772, of which only 100 copies were printed, twenty-five of which went to Paris ; *The Sleep Walker*, a comedy in two acts, 1778 ; *A Description of the villa of Mr. Horace Walpole*, 1784, of which 200 copies were printed ; and *Hieroglyphic Tales*, 1785.

A private printing office was carried on by the notorious John Wilkes at his house in Great George Street, Westminster,[6] where he produced two works in 1763 and a few copies of the third volume of the *North Briton*. He is said to have employed Thomas Farmer, who had also assisted Horace Walpole at Strawberry Hill.[7]

One of the few firms of renown in later times outside the City of London is that of Gilbert & Rivington. John Rivington, fourth son of John Rivington the publisher, and descendant of Charles Rivington of the

---

[3] *The case and proposals of the free Journeymen Printers in and about London.*

[4] *A compleat and private list of all the Printing-houses in and about the Cities of London and Westminster*, 1724, printed by William Bowyer.

[5] First series, xi, 377, 418.

[6] C. H. Timperley, *Ency. of Lit. and Typog. Anecdote*, 710–11.

[7] H. R. Plomer, *Short Hist. of Engl. Printing*, 280.

"Bible and Crown," Paternoster Row, succeeded to the business of James Emonson, printer, in St. John's Square, Clerkenwell. Rivington died in 1785, and his widow then continued the business, taking John Marshall into partnership in 1786. The firm became noted for their fine series of the classical authors. After many changes the business passed into the hands of Richard Gilbert, who in 1830 entered into partnership with William Rivington, great-grandson of the first Charles Rivington ; the firm then became and has since continued to be known as Gilbert & Rivington.[8] The business has since 1881 been converted into a limited liability company, and the firm has a high reputation for its oriental printing.[8a]

The well-known firm of Nichols, of Parliament Street, Westminster, was founded and long continued in the City of London, and does not come under notice here. The old firm of Charles Whittingham & Co., though on the borders of our county, also properly belongs to London, having started in Fetter Lane, and being now established in Took's Court, Chancery Lane.

The story of the Kelmscott Press is a fascinating page in the annals of 19th-century printing. In May 1891 Mr. William Morris the poet set up a private press in the Upper Mall, Hammersmith, where he printed a small quarto book entitled *The Story of the Glittering Plain*. This was soon followed by a three-volume reprint of Caxton's *Golden Legend*, illustrated with splendid woodcuts from the designs of Sir Edward Burne-Jones. Together with those completed by his executors after his death, Morris printed in all fifty-three books in sixty-five volumes, including the magnificent *Chaucer*. By his tasteful combination of artistic borders, initials, and illustrations, with beautiful paper, Morris showed the world how the book as a whole might be made a thing of beauty, and his influence upon book-production will certainly be long-lived.

The local presses of Middlesex[9] are not important and cannot be treated of at length. At Ratcliff, John Storye[10] printed in (?) 1585 *A breviat or table for the better observance of fish days*. William Bentley printed Bibles at Finsbury in 1646, 1648, 1651, and later. Thomas Newcomb printed the *London Gazette* in the Savoy from 1665 to 1668. In other places in Middlesex the earliest known products of the press date from the 18th century. A few instances may suffice. Thomas Davis printed in Whitechapel in 1706. Whitehead's *Satires* were printed at Islington, 'near the Three Pumps,' in 1748. T. Lake was a printer at Uxbridge in 1774. Printing was carried on at Chelsea in 1772.[11]

Type Founding.—Closely allied to the art of printing is that of type-founding. Modern type-founding was first successfully established in England at Caslon's foundry in Chiswell Street, close upon the City's border. Caxton seems to have imported from abroad some at least of the type which he used in printing. His immediate successors, Wynkyn de Worde and Pynson, may have used their own types, and Pynson is thought to have supplied other printers with type, but of this there is no direct evidence.[12] John Day in 1567 cast the type for the works published by Archbishop Parker in Anglo-Saxon. After this date type-founding languished here for nearly two centuries. English type had a poor repute, and the best continued to be imported from Holland. In 1637, by a decree of the Star Chamber, type-foundries in England were limited to four, each of which was allowed to have two apprentices and no more. William Caslon, founder of the existing letterfoundry in Chiswell Street, was born in 1692. He first turned his attention to type-founding in 1740, when he was engaged by the Christian Knowledge Society to make the punches for a fount of Arabic type for printing the Psalms and New Testament in that language. This decided him to follow type-founding as a distinct trade, and he established his foundry in Chiswell Street, his first punches being cut with his own hands. This foundry became the parent house of type-founding in England, and the excellence of Caslon's workmanship soon drove Dutch types from the English market. William Caslon died in 1766, and the firm was then continued by William his son, who died in 1778, Elizabeth Caslon, who died in 1809, and Henry William Caslon, who died in 1874.[13] The business is now conducted by a limited company under the style of H. W. Caslon & Co. Limited.

[8] E. C. Bigmore and Chas. W. H. Wyman, *Bibliography of Printing*, ii, 263.

[8a] The firm is now amalgamated with that of Wm. Clowes & Sons, Ltd.

[9] See W. H. Alnutt, ' English Provincial Presses,' *Bibliographica*, ii, 23, 150, 276.

[10] *Cal. S.P. Dom.* 1581–90, p. 299.

[11] Rev. Hen. Cotton, *Typog. Gaz.* 43, 318.

[12] William Blades, *Life of Caxton* (1882), 104.

[13] *Caslon's Quarterly Circular*, July 1877.

BOOKBINDING

The art of binding flourished in England from a very early period, and in the 12th century[1] English binders were in advance of all foreign workers in this craft. Several distinct schools of binding of this period may be traced, by the beautiful examples of their work which have survived, to certain important towns and religious houses; of chief interest among these were the schools of London, Durham, and Winchester. The decoration of the book covers consisted of very small stamps, delicately cut and arranged in formal patterns of infinite variety. The design frequently consists of a parallelogram, the lines of which are formed by dies, the centre being filled with circles and segments of circles, these being characteristic of English work. The 13th and 14th centuries do not mark any distinct progress in English binding, and very few examples of that period have survived, but the excessive use of dies appears to have decreased.

There is an early example of the *panel* stamp on a loose binding in the library of Westminster Abbey. The covers are tooled at their edges with small tools, and in the centre is a twice-repeated stamp with the arms presumably of Edward IV.[2]

With the invention of printing, binding became much more in request. The binding of the earliest English printed books differed in a very marked way from that of the manuscripts which they gradually superseded. The latter had reached a point of great excellence in 1476-7, when Caxton produced his first book printed at Westminster, and their bindings were correspondingly rich, ornamented with enamels, carved ivory, and other materials of the most costly kind. But printed books had at first a very sober covering of plain leather, calf or deerskin, and sometimes of parchment. The covers were wooden boards and the backs were of leather, which was also drawn wholly or partly over the wooden covers, the latter being usually fitted with clasps. A short title is often found written on the fore-edge, the book being placed on the shelf with the fore-edge displayed to view. The bindings of books printed by Caxton, and perhaps bound in his workshop, have a simple decoration composed of straight lines variously arranged, and sometimes inclosing impressions of small stamps made up into a simple pattern. Caxton's successors produced a more ambitious style of decoration by the use of large heraldic stamps.

After his death in 1491 these stamps were used by Wynkyn de Worde until the beginning of the 16th century; some of them were used even later by the stationer Henry Jacobi. Wynkyn de Worde also used a small stamp of the Royal Arms. This style was distinctly English, for though heraldic decoration was employed by contemporary foreign binders, the designs were produced in quite a different way, either in cut or tooled leather. Where the printer was his own binder his device or initials are often found on the binding as well as on the printed page of the book.

The Royal coat-of-arms used by the early London printers for their bindings was the same during the reigns of Henry VII and Henry VIII, except for a difference in the supporters. The dragon and greyhound borne by both sovereigns were changed in 1528 by Henry VIII, who adopted the lion for his dexter and the dragon for his sinister supporter, leaving out the greyhound. The Tudor rose which so frequently occurs on these early bindings was the proudest emblem of the House of Tudor, and used by all its sovereigns. It was adopted by Henry VII on his marriage with Elizabeth of York, and consisted of a double rose with petals of red and white, signifying the union of the houses of York and Lancaster, whose conflicts had desolated England for so many years. Associated with the Royal coat-of-arms the cross of St. George and the arms of the City of London are frequently found upon the same stamp. The City arms indicates that the binder was a citizen, and when this was not the case the citizen shield was replaced by some other device. The panel of the Royal arms was used by many English binders who are only known by their initials; a certain 'G. G.' discarded the more usual supporters and replaced them by two angels.

Wynkyn de Worde employed latterly binders from the Low Countries resident in England; among them was J. Gaver, who was one of the executors to his will, and was probably connected with the large family of Gavere, binders in the Low Countries.

Most of the early printers bound their own books. Richard Pynson, Caxton's pupil, pro-

[1] W. H. J. Weale, 'Lectures on Engl. Bookbinding in the Reigns of Henry VII and Henry VIII,' *Journ. Soc. of Arts*, 26 Feb. 1889.

[2] Sarah T. Prideaux, *Hist. Sketch of Bookbinding* (1893), 16.

duced some highly decorated designs. The British Museum possesses a little volume of *Abridgements of the Statutes* printed and bound by him in 1499.[3] The book is bound in wooden boards covered with sheepskin, and shows indications of having been fitted with two clasps of leather. The cover is decorated on the obverse with the monogram R.P. on a shield, supported by two figures and surmounted by a helmet with mantling bearing a fillet and crest of a bird; in the sky are nine stars, and below the shield are a flower and leaf. Surrounding this central design is a handsome floral border, having in each of the two upper corners a bird, and between them a man shooting, probably with a cross-bow. At the base are a figure of the Madonna, and another of a female saint, each crowned and having an aureole, and near the lower right-hand corner is the bust of a king crowned and bearing a sceptre. On the reverse is a similar plan of decoration, the central panel in this case having in the centre a double rose, surrounded by a decorative arrangement of vine leaves, grapes, and tendrils. The border is a graceful pattern of flowers and leaves, and has an arabesque at each corner.

Another early printer and binder was Julian Notary, who worked first at Westminster, and afterwards in the City between the years 1498 and 1520. Many books bound by Notary are decorated with two handsome stamps; one such volume, not from his own press, but from that of Jean Petit of Paris, is in the British Museum. It is a copy of Cicero's *Tusculan Disputations*, printed in January 1509, which formerly belonged to Henry VIII. It is bound in wooden boards, covered with leather, sewn on leather bands, and has remains of leather clasps with brass fastenings. The front cover has the arms of Henry VIII, the three fleurs de lis of France quartered with the three lions of England, with the dragon and greyhound as supporters. In the upper part the shield of St. George and the arms of the City of London, with the sun, moon, and stars; the lower part is decorated with plants of elementary design. The back cover has a similar design with the substitution of a large Tudor rose inclosed by two ribands borne by angels for the Royal coat-of-arms. In the base are the initials I.N. of the binder, and his curious device with the initials repeated in the lower part of it. On larger books bound by Julian Notary both these stamps are sometimes found on the same cover divided by a long panel bearing the initials L.R. and R.L. tied

together respectively by a cord, and the Tudor emblems of the pomegranate, rose, portcullis, and lion. The portcullis was used to signify the descent of the Tudors from the House of Beaufort, and is said to represent the castle of De Beaufort at Anjou.

Before the time of Elizabeth the only leather used for binding was brown calf and sheep, the only other materials with very rare exceptions being vellum and velvet. Morocco was not employed until the reign of Elizabeth or that of James I.

English bindings of the 16th and 17th centuries are classified by Miss Prideaux as follows[4] :—1. Those in material other than leather, and often decorated with enamels and gold and silver pierced and engraved; 2. Stamped vellum and calf bindings; 3. The Venetian-Lyonese work; 4. Occasional specimens of French Grolier work, very frequent ones of the French semis, and some very good imitations of the delicate Le Gascon, done between 1660 and 1720, the most frequently imitated of all French work; 5. The cottage ornamented bindings, the one distinctively English style belonging to the 17th century.

Although the names of some English binders are known, it is impossible to connect many books with their names. Robert Barker and James Norton were binders to James I, and Eliot and Chapman bound 'in the Harleian style' for Robert Harley, first Earl of Oxford.[5] Other binders of the period were Thomas Hollis and his successor Thomas Brand. Among the French emigrant binders were the Comte de Caumont, Comte de Clermont de Lodeve, Vicomte Gauthier de Brecy, and Du Lau, the friend and bookseller of Chateaubriand.[6]

The work of Roger Payne in the latter half of the 18th century marks an era in English bookbinding, which had since the beginning of that century fallen to a low ebb. Payne was born at Windsor in 1739, and after a short service with Pote, the Eton bookseller, came to London in 1766, and entered the employment of Thomas Osborne, the bookseller, in Gray's Inn. A few years later he set up in business for himself as a bookbinder, near Leicester Square. Here he was joined by his brother Thomas, who attended to the 'forwarding' part of the business, whilst Roger devoted himself wholly to the 'finishing.' His great artistic talents placed him easily at the head of all the binders of his day, and procured him a number of distinguished patrons, among whom were Earl

[3] C. J. Davenport, 'Early London Bookbinders,' *The Queen*, 20 June 1891.

[4] *Hist. Sketch of Bookbinding*, 110.
[5] Prideaux, op. cit. 27.   [6] Ibid. 128.

Spencer, the Duke of Devonshire, Colonel Stanley, and the Rev. Clayton Mordaunt Cracherode. The brothers did not long continue their partnership, and on the departure of Thomas Payne, Roger took as a fellow-worker Richard Wier, whose wife was a clever mender and restorer of old books. The new partnership had one serious drawback, both Payne and Wier being addicted to strong drink; this led to frequent quarrels, and at last to separation. During his association with Wier some of Payne's finest bindings were executed, and they are all characteristically English. Dibdin [7] gives a sad picture of the condition to which Payne was brought by his intemperance. 'His appearance bespoke either squalid wretchedness or a foolish and fierce indifference to the received opinions of mankind. His hair was unkempt, his visage elongated, his attire wretched, and the interior of his workshop—where, like the Turk, he would "bear no brother near his throne"—harmonized not too justly with the general character and appearance of its owner. With the greatest possible display of humility in speech and in writing, he united quite the spirit of quixotic independence.' Payne died in Duke's Court, St. Martin's Lane, on 20 November 1797, and was buried in the churchyard of St. Martin-in-the-Fields, at the expense of his friend Thomas Payne, the bookseller. To this friend, who was not a relative, he was indebted for his first start in business on his own account, and for his support during the last eight years of his life.

As an artist in binding Payne certainly shows signs of the influence of Samuel Mearn, who was the English court binder towards the end of the 17th century, but his genius enabled him to originate a style which was quite his own. The covers of his books usually bear a simple design, whilst the backs are elaborately decorated. His bindings also combine elegance and strength, the sheets of the books being often sewn with silk, and the backs lined with leather to give them additional strength. The centre of his covers is usually left vacant, but among the specimens of his work in the Cracherode collection at the British Museum many examples are found in which the centre of the board is embellished with the beautiful and delicately-engraved Cracherode coat-of-arms. The decoration which he generally employed for his covers consisted of a rectangular line as a border ornamented with beautiful and very delicately stamped corners, and angle-pieces of decorative work. Occasionally he adds ornamental designs which fill or nearly fill the space between the outer edge of the book and the inner panel. Payne's decorative devices are made up chiefly of small stamps, somewhat resembling those of Mearn, interspersed with minute dots, stars, and circles. The stamps he most commonly used were crescents, stars, acorns, running vines, and leaves. To each of his bindings he attached a bill describing the design and the ornaments used, written in a most quaint and precise style. Many of these bills are still preserved in the volumes whose bindings they describe. Payne took considerable care in choosing his leather, usually selecting russia or straight-grained morocco of a dark blue, bright red, or olive colour. The olive morocco which he sometimes used being perhaps the most perfect binding material that is procurable for receiving the impression of a gold stamp. Samuel Mearn and his son Charles, who were binders to Charles II, lived in Little Britain.[8]

Exigencies of space will only admit of a brief summary of the masters of the art in modern times. Among the later binders of the 18th century were a little colony of Germans—Baumgarten, Benedict, Walther, Staggemeier, Kalthoeber—who continued the traditions of Robert Payne. Charles Herring, a binder of repute, chiefly worked in Payne's style. The excellence of the work of these binders was largely inspired by John Mackinlay, for whom Payne worked before his death. John Whitaker introduced the Etruscan style in which designs from the decoration of Etruscan vases were copied in colours by means of acids instead of in gold. Charles Lewis, in conjunction with Staggemeier, bound most of the Althorp books, and also those for Beckford at Fonthill. Dibdin, who was a great admirer of Lewis's work, says, 'He united the taste of Roger Payne with a freedom of forwarding and squareness of finish peculiar to himself.' Lewis was assisted by Clarke, famous for his tree-marbled calf in binding the library of the Rev. Theodore Williams. Bedford, who has been regarded as the best of all English binders in forwarding, did much important work for Mr. Huth. Of the binders of to-day among the first-class firms who carry on the traditions of the past, that of Mr. Joseph W. Zaehnsdorf is specially well known.

---

[7] *Bibliographical Decameron* (1817), ii, 506–18.

[8] An excellent account of Mearn by Mr. Cyril Davenport will be found in *Bibliographica*, iii, 129 et seq.

AGRICULTURE

THE agriculture of Middlesex has always been of special interest, though the county is small. The fact that it included London as a market for its produce was a stimulus to agriculture as an industry; while the physical features of the district lent themselves to good husbandry.

The climate is equable, the July isotherm being 64 degrees, and that of January 40 degrees, while the mean of the whole year is 50 degrees on the higher ground north of London, and 51 degrees in the Thames Valley. Rainfall varies much more considerably than is usually recognized; thus in 1905, 27·83 in. fell at Hadley in the north of the county, while only 19·50 fell at Hampton in the south-west.[1] The explanation of this is twofold: parts of the county are much better wooded than others, and the whole north is much more hilly than the south.

The area of Middlesex returned in the census of 1901 was 178,606 acres; in 1906 the area under 'all crops, including woods, fruit and gardens,' was 94,067 acres. In 1806 the area under agriculture was reckoned at 136,000 acres, and there were 2,591 acres of commons. It has been remarked that

> these cannot very well be exact returns of area because roads and steeps at cross ways are not returned in any uniform manner, and water areas are also left very much to fancy, some street conveyancers adhering to the old definition of ponds as 'land covered by water,' and including them in the land acreage, while house agents, despite their natural interest in magnifying the property, more usually return the area exclusive of water. Wayside ponds are reckoned by some surveyors as part of the road; by others they are not so reckoned.

This caveat seems worth entering, though it will not account for any very material proportion of the difference of 84,539 acres between the total and the agricultural area. 'Bricks and mortar,' together with private gardens, account for much, perhaps most, of it.

The county is well watered by the rivers Lea, Thames, Brent, and Colne. The soil is fertile; it varies from clay and strong loam to sand and gravel. The following estimate, taken from 'Foot's View of the Agriculture of Middlesex,' reported to the Board of Agriculture in 1794,

---

[1] *Symons's Meteorological Magazine*, vol. xli; H. R. Mill, *The Rainfall of* 1905.

will show the variations in soil, many of which have since been lost sight of amidst the progress of building :—

1. Hundred of Edmonton, including South Mimms, Enfield, Edmonton, Tottenham. The soil is clay and strong loam, with some gravel.
2. Hundred of Gore, including Hendon, Harrow, Edgeware, Stanmore, Wembley. The soil is stiff clay, with a little gravelly loam.
3. Hundred of Ossulstone, including
    (a) Barnet, Finchley, Highgate, Hornsey, Hampstead, Willesden. The soil is clay, mixed with gravel and loam.
    (b) Stoke Newington, Clapton, Hackney, Bethnal Green, Stepney. The soil is rich and mellow, and at Hackney there is some strong loam-like clay, called brick-earth.
    (c) Islington, Pancras, Paddington. The soil is gravelly loam, with a little clay.
    (d) Kensington, Brompton, Chelsea, Fulham, Chiswick. The soil varies from strong to sandy loam, mixed with sand and gravel, some black and fertile, some sharp and white. Chiswick has some pure surface gravel.
    (e) Acton and Ealing. The soil is gravel, like that of Chiswick, with loam and clay in parts.
4. Hundred of Isleworth, including Isleworth, Twickenham, Teddington, &c., on the Thames, and the district round Heston. The soil includes hazel loam, rich and mellow, also strong loam and a little light gravel.
5. Hundred of Elthorne. The soil varies from strong loam, with gravel, to light loam.
6. Hundred of Spelthorne. The soil includes light loam, lean gravel, and strong loam.[2]

Lysons gives much the same information in his detailed view of sixteen parishes of about a hundred years ago, but his account is less comprehensive than that of Foot.

Some account of the early agricultural history of Middlesex has been given in another article, but we may cite in this place a short description of the county as it appeared to Norden,[3] the well-known surveyor of the days of Elizabeth and her successor.

> Myddlesex is a small Shire, in length not twentie myles, in circuite (as it were by the ring) not about (sic above) 70 myles, yet for the fertilitie thereof, it may compare with any other shire : for the soyle is excellent, fat and fertile and full of profite : it yeeldeth corne and graine, not onelie in aboundance, but most excellente good wheate, especiallie about *Heston*, which place may be called *Granarium tritici regalis*, for the singularitie of the corne. The vaine of this especiall corne seemeth to extend from *Heston* to *Harrow* on the hill, betweene which as in the mid way, is *Perivale*, more truely *Purevale*. In which vale is also *Northold*, *Southold*, *Norcote*, *Gerneford*, *Hayes*, &c. And it seemeth to extend to Pynner, though with some alteration of the soile. It may be noted also how nature has exalted *Harrow* on the hill, which seemeth to make ostentation of its scituation in the *Purevale*, from whence, towardes the time of Harvest, a man may beholde the fields round about, so sweetely to address themselves, to the siccle, and sith, with such comfortable aboundaunce, of all kinde of graine, that the husbandman which waiteth for the fruits of his labours, cannot but clap his hands, for joy, to see this vale, so to laugh and sing.
>
> Yet doth not this so fruitefull soyle yeeld comfort, to the way-fairing man in the wintertime, by reason of the claiesh nature of soyle ; which after it hath tasted the Autumne showers, waxeth both dyrtie and deepe : But unto the countrie swaine it is as a sweete and pleasant garden, in regard of his hope of future profite, for :—
>
>> The deepe, and dirtie loathsome soyle,
>> Yeelds golden gaine, to painfull toyle.
>
> The industrious and painefull husbandman will refuse a pallace, to droyle in these golden puddles.[4]

[2] Peter Foot, *Gen. View of Agric. of Midd.* 9.
[3] *Speculum Britanniae.*   [4] John Norden, op. cit. pt. i, p. 11.

AGRICULTURE

Norden evidently wishes by these words to urge the inhabitants to take fuller advantage of these favourable circumstances. With this intention, he adds :—

> This part of Myddlesex may for fertilitie compare with *Tandeane*, in the west part of *Somersetshire*. But that Tandeane, farre surpasseth it for sundrie fruites, and commodities, which this countrie might also yeeld, were it to the like imployed : but it seemeth they onely covet to maintaine their auncient course of life, and observe the husbandrie of their fathers, without adding anything to their greater profite.

In mentioning orchards he seems to regard them as indicating a pastime rather than a serious pursuit ; thus, in describing the larger houses, he says that they are 'invironed with Orchards of sundrie delicate fruites.'[5] He afterwards adds a list of 'Cities, Townes, Hamlets, Villages, and howses of name within Middelsex ;'[6] and says of Greenford, 'A very fertile place of corne standing in the *purevale*.'[7] Heston, however, was pre-eminent in fertility ; it was

> A most fertyle place of wheate yet not so much to be commended for the quantitie, as for the qualitie, for the wheat is most pure, accompted the purest in manie shires. And therefore Queene Elizabeth hath the most part of her provision from that place for manchet for her Highnes owne diet, as is reported.[8]

Michael Drayton, again, in his *Polyolbion* introduces Perivale 'vaunting her rich estate.'

> Why should I not be coy and of my beauties nice,
> Since this my goodly grain is held of greatest price?
> No manchet can so well the courtly palate please,
> As that made of the meal fetch'd from my fertile leaze.
> Their finest of that kind, compared with my wheat,
> For whiteness of the bread doth look like common cheat.
> What barley is there found, whose fair and bearded ear
> Makes stouter English ale, or stronger English beer?
> The oat, the bean and pease, with me but pulses are ;
> The coarse and browner rye, no more than fitch and tare.

And further the poet notices her 'sure abode near goodly London,' the ready mart for all her 'fruitful store.'

In the Tudor period[9] rural Middlesex—especially Islington and the neighbouring parishes—was called upon to supply much of the milk, cream, and cheese required in London. A curious illustration of this fact appears in the introduction at the famous festivities at Kenilworth in 1575 of a minstrel from Islington who in mock heroic style celebrated the praises of his 'worshipful village,' and gravely described and explained as the arms of Islington 'On a Field Argent, a fess tenny three platez between three mylk tankerds proper,' while the scroll or badge was to be 'Lac, Caseus Infans that is goode milke and yonge cheez.'

Agricultural activity was at its height in the county in the eighteenth century, and the beginning of the nineteenth. In addition

[5] John Norden, op. cit. pt. i, p. 12.   [6] Ibid. 15.   [7] Ibid. 21.
[8] Ibid. 25.   [9] Lewis, *Hist. of Islington*, 15 et seq.

to evidence of a more general character, there are three full accounts of the agricultural conditions of Middlesex at this time. These are reports on the subject, addressed to the Board of Agriculture, and issued within a few years of each other. That by Thomas Baird appeared in 1793, Peter Foot's in 1794, and John Middleton's in 1797, with a second edition ten years later. They contain much the same information, though in different form. Foot describes fully the extent of cultivation, and the methods used. In his map it will be seen that crops occupy considerably less than half the area of the county. They lie in the west and south-west ; also in the north-east with scattered districts elsewhere. The rest of the county, with the exception of a few woods and parks, consists of meadows, pasture, and nursery-gardens. The latter are situated on the left bank of the Thames, in a continuous line from Teddington to London, while some extend immediately north-east of London to Islington. The total area of Middlesex is estimated at 240 square miles, or 217,600 acres.

After describing the nature and variations of the soil Foot gives an account of the 'garden ground.' [10] He considers it well cultivated, and in describing how the lands are dressed he adds :—' To this manure, and care of sowing seeds, the kitchen-gardeners who supply the markets at Spitalfields, who cultivate in general on a light black soil owe their celebrity in the article of lettuces.' [11] Near Chelsea, the work of farmer and kitchen-gardener was often combined ; thus peas, turnips, and coleworts were grown in succession on the same ground. Fruit was successful, and much care was given to grafting. Certain nurseries (e.g. those of Mile End, Hammersmith, Hackney, and Dalston) were famous for their adoption of foreign plants ; Isleworth was noted for strawberries. Foot himself thought that the vine could be cultivated with advantage. He was also sanguine about the proposed cultivation of plants for dyes, as a substitute for madder : a certain species of common bed-straw was chosen for this purpose, and at the time much was hoped from the result of the experiment.

The next subject treated by this author is the system of husbandry then pursued by the farmers of Middlesex. He points out that all success must depend upon that rotation of crops which will get as much as possible out of the land, but which yet will not injure its productiveness. The following account shows the general system and how it varied in different districts :—

I.—South Mimms :—

    (a) On the clay.
        (1) summer fallow ;   (3) beans, pease, or oats ;
        (2) wheat ;   (4) summer fallow.
    (b) On the better soil.
        (1) turnips on summer fallows ;   (3) clover fed or mown ;
        (2) barley with broad clover;   (4) wheat on clover lay, with one ploughing.

[10] Peter Foot, *Gen. View of Agric. of Midd.* 11.   [11] Ibid. 12.

AGRICULTURE

II.—District round Norwood, Hayes, &c. :—

    (a) In the common fields :

        (1) fallow;   (2) wheat ;   (3) barley or oats, with clover.

    (b) In the inclosed lands :

        (1) wheat ;   (2) barley and clover ;   (3) turnips.

III.—Fulham :—

    (1) barley ;   (4) wheat ;

    (2) coleworts (off in March) ;   (5) turnips or tares (manuring well after the

    (3) potatoes (off in October);   barley).

IV.—Edmonton :—

    (1) potatoes ;   (4) oats, tares, pease or beans—to be

    (2) wheat;   gathered ;

    (3) turnips on wheat stubbles ;   (5) wheat (manuring well).

V.—Heston :—

    (1) wheat ;   (4) turnips ;

    (2) barley with clover, mown twice ; (5) wheat.

    (3) pease or beans to be gathered ;

VI.—Harmondsworth :—

    (1) clover, well dressed with coal ashes ;

    (2) pease, beans, or tares ;

    (3) wheat, then turnips on the stubbles, fed off ;

    (4) barley;   (5) oats.

VII.—Chiswick :—

    (1) vetches for spring seed, or pease, or beans, to be gathered green ;

    (2) turnips (good on inclosed land) sold straight to London cowkeepers ;

    (3) wheat ;   (4) barley or oats.

        (manuring before pulse, wheat, and barley).

  A better course here would be :—

    (1) pulse ;   (3) oats or barley, with clover;

    (2) turnips ;   (4) wheat (manuring well before pulse).

  This would exhaust the soil less, but the cultivators are bound by the Lammas tenure not to have any clover.[12]

We notice here three main points of interest, viz., the decline of fallow ; the restrictions of the Lammas tenure ; and the fertility of Heston, which still kept up the high reputation which it possessed in the sixteenth century. Thus Foot says :

> The lands about Heston are chiefly of a strong loam, and celebrated for producing the finest wheat in the county ; the skin is thin, the corn full and bold, and the flower white, or, as the millers term it, fair.[13]

The barley of Middlesex, especially that of Chelsea, Fulham, and Chiswick, was also ' distinguished for its good quality, and has been much sought after for seed ' ;[14] it was the ' whitest, most thin skinned, and mellowest barley in England.'[15] Foot deplores that this fine barley was being supplanted by vegetables grown for the London market, but this was doubtless because the demands of a large city make variety above all things necessary.

[12] Peter Foot, *Gen. View of Agric. of Midd.* 20.   [13] Ibid. 22.   [13] Ibid. 24.   [15] Ibid. 24.

The importance and methods of manuring the land are then discussed. The carriage of the manure by water or land, rather than the manure itself, formed one of the most costly items in the farmer's expenditure. The burden could only be decreased, not by neglecting to dress the land, but by feeding cattle on arable fields. The expense fell chiefly on the gardeners, who were obliged to apply manure more frequently than the farmers.[16]

Foot, with most of the writers of his time, condemns the system of commons as wasteful in agriculture.[17] In this connexion he describes at some length the agricultural conditions of Enfield Chase, part of which had just been inclosed. Even after a short time, and in spite of the difficulties of changing cultivation, the results, he thinks, had been favourable, thus :—

> South Mimms inclosure is also part of Enfield Chace, and consists of nearly 1,000 acres. In its open state it was supposed not to have yielded the parish at large more than two shillings an acre per annum, but since its inclosure it is worth on an average fifteen shillings an acre.
>
> It is at present in tillage ; but in a few years it may be converted to grass, which will give it an increased value of at least five shillings an acre.[18]

Drainage had been much required on these new inclosures ; 'the common shoulder-draining spade and scoop have been used with great success.'[19] In clearing the land also various methods had been used. Paring and burning were done by some, while others said that this process destroyed the pabulum for future plants. Foot adds that 'marle is one of the most valuable manures upon the Chace.'[20] In many cases, owing to want of experience, the best methods had not been followed, but even then inclosures had been found more profitable than the common lands where rights were abused and the land over-burdened.

Foot goes on to say that 'hay-making in Middlesex is carried on by a process peculiar to the county.'[21] He describes it in detail :—

> On the first day the grass was mown before 9 a.m., tedded, broken up as much as possible, and well turned by mid-day. It was then raked into wind-rows and made into small cocks. On the second day the grass mown after 9 a.m. on the first day was tedded, while all grass mown before 9 a.m. on this day was treated as before. Meanwhile the cocks already made were shaken into straddles or separate plats of five or six yards square, and the spaces, if any, were raked clean. The plats were turned first, then the second day's mowing—all before the dinner hour. After that the straddles were raked into double wind-rows, and the grass into single wind-rows ; the hay was cocked into bastard or medium cocks, and the grass cocked as on the first day. On the third day the same order was pursued as before. Medium cocks were spread into straddles, then turned ; grass cocks and grass were also turned before 1 p.m. If fine, the medium cocks of yesterday could now be carried. The second day's hay was then made into double wind-rows, and the grass into single wind-rows. The first day's hay was made into large cocks with a fork, and the rakings put on the top of each cock. The hay in double wind-rows was made into medium cocks, and the grass in single wind-rows was made into small cocks. The hay in the large cocks could then be carried, and the medium cocks could be made into large cocks, the grass cocks into medium cocks, and the grass (tedded that morning) into small cocks. On the fourth day the hay was put into stacks, 'well tucked and thatched.'

[16] Peter Foot, *Gen. View of Agric. of Midd.* 26.   [17] Ibid. 30.
[18] Ibid. 55.   [19] Ibid. 42.   [20] Ibid. 53.   [21] Ibid. 55.

AGRICULTURE

It was important to keep a good proportion in numbers between the mowers and the haymakers, so that this sequence of operations could be strictly maintained. The process was made as systematic as possible, from grass, single wind-rows, small cocks, straddles, double wind-rows, medium cocks, straddles again, large cocks—to the stacks [22] themselves. Apparently this method was followed with good results, as hay at this period was found profitable in Middlesex, and the area used for hay was increasing.

Horses were not bred in the county, but were bought at fairs, and the standard required was a high one.

> The draught-horses in general, in possession of the brewers and carmen, are as to strength and figure, scarcely to be equalled. The brewers' and carmen's horses are fed with grains, clover, chaff, and beans; racked with rye-grass, and clover, and broad clover hay of the best quality; and in summer it is not uncommon to feed them with green tares and clover. Many of the saddle and coach horses are bred in Yorkshire, and brought up from thence and from other counties by the dealers. These horses are fed with meadow hay only.[23]

Foot considered Middlesex to be less noted for sheep than for horses; 6,000 were kept on Hounslow Heath, but with this exception the numbers were small. The hay-farmers round Hendon and Barnet allowed sheep and cattle to feed on their after-grass at so much per head. There is a long account of experiments in breeding Spanish sheep which might produce as fine a cloth as that imported. In raising lambs under cover for the butcher, ewes were obtained from Dorset.[24]

Oxen were sometimes used for draught or the plough, a custom which this author (unlike some others of the time) looked upon as likely to prevail. He says, ' Five oxen are used to draw a wagon on the road, one in the shafts, and four in pairs, with collars or holsters, and head-stalls. At plough two pair are used; at dung-cart three oxen only are used.' [25] Calves were raised in the western parts of the county, but not to any great extent.

Before going on to the subject of cow-keeping and dairies, Foot now returns to the subject of commons. He describes the common meadows [26] and their capabilities. Those near the Lea were under Lammas tenure, which did not admit of ' any general system ' of cultivation. They were let for 25s. per acre, but if inclosed the rent would have been 40s. per acre. The meadows near the Thames from Fulham to Chiswick and Staines were much flooded, and the rushes made it difficult to get good hay there. They were also too flat for ordinary drainage, and therefore became soft. The meadows on the banks of the Colne were more fertile, and here the drainage was better.

The common arable lands are said to be ' at present in a good course of husbandry ' [27]; though if inclosed they might have been made more profitable.

[22] 'There are no hay-stacks when finished that are so well secured and nicely formed as those in Middlesex'; ibid. 57.
[23] Ibid. 59.
[24] Ibid. 60 et seq.
[25] Ibid. 67.
[26] Ibid. 69 et seq.
[27] Ibid. 72.

Farm buildings were well constructed and in good repair on the whole, as they would naturally be in a county where agriculture produced good returns. The only defect pointed out here by Foot is the fact that they were in inaccessible situations, especially on the common arable lands.[28] Round Harrow, Hendon, and Finchley there were large hay barns, holding from 50 to 100 loads of hay each.[29]

The report of the agricultural instruments [30] is not so satisfactory; evidently improvements in implements were not readily adopted by the farmers. The common wooden swing-plough was the one in general use; the Hertfordshire wheel-plough being used for summer fallowing. The harrows varied in weight from one-horse to four-horse carriage; they had rollers of wood and iron of equal capacity. Carts with iron arms were more used than wagons. The improved plough and cultivator invented by the Rev. James Coke had been tried by few.

The subject of dairy-farming was one of growing importance, and the number of cows was very large, compared with that in neighbouring counties. Foot gives the numbers as follows :—

Tothill Fields and Knightsbridge	205
Edgeware Road	550
Paddington, Tottenham Court Road, Battle Bridge, Gray's Inn Lane, Bagnigge Wells, Islington .	3,950
Hoxton	150
Mile End	406
Ratcliff	205
Limehouse	180
Poplar	70
Hackney	600
Bow	100
Bethnal Green	200
Bromley	160
Shoreditch and Kingsland	200

These, with 224 odd cows, made a total of 7,200.[31]

The best milch cows, kept for supplying London with milk, were bred in Yorkshire, Lancashire, and Staffordshire. They were bought at three years old, costing from eight guineas to £14 each. They either came straight to the purchasers from the northern counties, or were bought at the fairs and markets of Barnet, Islington, and other places. The food and shelter of these cows was a matter of systematic routine, in which apparently an absolutely uniform method was followed.[32] Foot summarizes their productiveness as follows :—Each cow on an average gave eight quarts a day, for 365 days, i.e. 2,920 quarts, which at 1¾d. per quart comes to £21 5s. This represents the price given by retailers. Consumers paid 3d. per quart, and the retailers got the difference, as profit. He adds that this may over-rate profit as 'When the families leave London, the cow-keepers do not find a ready sale for all their milk; and in this case they generally set the unsold milk for cream, of which they make fresh butter for the London markets,

[28] Peter Foot, *Gen. View of Agric. of Midd.* 79. [29] Ibid. 57.
[30] Ibid. 75 et seq.   [31] Ibid. 80.   [32] Ibid. 82.

and give their butter-milk to the hogs.'[33]   The author refers to Arthur Young's investigations in dairy-farming; he evidently regards it as a subject of interest, increasing in proportion to the increase of London itself, since dairy-farming requires a near and a constant market.

Foot closes his account with words of advice;[34] he points out the importance of hedges in making the new inclosures. These should not be made of 'wild-quick,'[35] such as the poor use, but 'quicks ought to be had from the nursery-men,'[36] having been already twice transplanted.

Middleton's *View of the Agriculture of Middlesex* [addressed to the Board of Agriculture, 1797; 2nd Edition, 1807] covers much the same ground as Foot's, though it is far more voluminous, and touches on many irrelevant subjects. He describes the agricultural conditions of Middlesex as most favourable, and is therefore all the more anxious to point out defects in cultivation. Thus he says:—'The plough in general use throughout this county is a swing one of the most clumsy construction,'[37] and 'I do not know of any instance of Mr. Ducket's simple, cheap, and effectual drill being used in this county.'[38]   He also is opposed to the waste in common land, which he defines as the 'uncultivated soil of this county, capable of receiving improvement,'[39] consisting as it did of 'about 8,700 acres, or one-twentieth part of the whole quantity.'[40]   In the same way he finds that trees grow well, but are 'scandalously' pollarded,[41] and that hedges are badly constructed, being 'generally full of live wood.'[42] According to his computation the land was 'not producing wheat sufficient to supply one-sixtieth part of the inhabitants with bread,'[43] in spite of its fertility. Heston is again highly spoken of, the soil there being 'a most productive loam, possessing that most happy medium of texture which fits it alike for the production of every kind of corn, pulse, and root, and its staple is five or six feet in depth, on a bed of gravel.'[44]

Middleton gives a detailed account of the corn harvest. In the case of wheat it began in the first week of August, and became general in three weeks. Reaping was done by 'a toothless hook, of about twice the weight of a common sickle.'[45]   The reaper struck within two or three inches of the ground; he collected the sheaves separately, and then bound ten together in a shock: this was called bagging or fagging.[46] Thrashing was usually done by the flail; though the author points out that mills were coming into more general use, in spite of the fact that in them the corn became more bruised.[47]   He considers barley to be particularly productive in this county; thus:—

> Two sorts of spring barley are usually grown.   On rich land, the sprat or battledore barley, which produces a short tapering straw, is mostly sown, owing to its being less liable to fall to the ground than the other sorts.   The common spring barley, containing two rows of grain in the ear, is sown in every case when the soil is not so rich as to endanger losing the crop.[48]

[33] Peter Foot, *Gen. View of Agric. of Midd.* 85.   [34] Ibid. 86 et seq.   [35] Ibid. 88.
[36] Ibid. 87.   [37] John Middleton, *View of the Agric. of Midd.* 99.
[38] Ibid. 107.   [39] Ibid. 114.   [40] Ibid. 114.
[41] Ibid. 344 et seq.   [42] Ibid. 150.   [43] Ibid. 158.
[44] Ibid. 186 note.   [45] Ibid. 216.   [46] Ibid. 216.
[47] Ibid. 217–8.   [48] Ibid. 234–5.

Barley was mown by scythes, 'previously furnished with a bow or cradle, to collect the corn together, and keep it from scattering.' [49] Unusually heavy crops were bound into sheaves and set up in stocks ; but the average ones were arranged in swaths, then raked into rows, and carted for stack or barn.[50] The produce of wheat was reckoned by Middleton to be from ten to over forty bushels per acre ; that of barley, from fifteen to seventy-five bushels.[51]

He describes the other crops, and urges such a system of rotation 'as shall support cattle on arable land all the year round.'[52] But, except in matters of detail, he adds little information to that given by Foot, whom he sometimes quotes. Both writers agree on two subjects, viz. the wastefulness of commons, and the excellence of the hay-making. 'This branch of the rural art has, by the farmers of Middlesex, been brought to a degree of perfection altogether unequalled by any other part of the kingdom.' [53]

The kitchen gardens between Westminster and Chelsea, with the nursery grounds for fruit, shrubs, and flowers at Chelsea, Brompton, Kensington, Hackney, Dalston, Bow, Mile End, are described as flourishing.[54] The author deplores the neglect of drainage [55] as well as of paring and burning,[56] this neglect being due to want of enterprise rather than to ignorance. In discussing the use of oxen for field labour, he says :—' Upon the whole, I am of opinion that the very few advantages which oxen possess, are not by any means of such consideration as to compensate for the damage which their being used would do upon some kinds of land.' [57]

The uniformly profitable character of agriculture from 1801 to 1815 gave to rural Middlesex an immense impetus which, thanks to the rapid growth of metropolitan population, was in no way lost from 1815 to 1845. The Free Trade movement was vehemently fought in Middlesex, the rural parts of which gravitated to Conservatism in the middle Victorian era after two centuries of a Puritan and then Whig cast.

But, for reasons which lie outside the scope of this article, Free Trade did not produce bad results for agriculture between 1846 and 1873, and the famous new *Domesday Book* of the latter year reveals decided prosperity. In the parish of Ickenham 981 acres of agricultural land were bringing in £2,235 a year, and 122 acres at Hoddesdon, £650 a year. Small holdings even in very minor rural places yielded a good rent, as for instance 10 acres at South Mimms £71 a year, 3 acres at Ruislip £38 a year, and 6 acres at Cranford £38 a year. In the market gardening region we find at Isleworth, Brentford, Chiswick, Acton, and Hammersmith a total area of 66 acres bringing in £445 a year, while dairy meadows in Finchley, Edmonton, Wood Green, and Southgate yielded £414 a year from 41 acres. The riparian parishes of Teddington, Shepperton, Sunbury, Staines, and Laleham were acquiring

[49] John Middleton, *View of the Agric. of Midd.* 236.
[50] Ibid. 236.
[51] Ibid. 219, 237.
[52] Ibid. 220, &c.
[53] Ibid. 309.
[54] Ibid. 330, 338.
[55] Ibid. 364
[56] Ibid. 366.
[57] Ibid. 482.

agricultural value as appanage lands to wealthy men's estates; in these five parishes 665 acres of land otherwise agricultural, but really used for the most part for rich men's pleasure, brought in £3,320 a year.

Coming to modern agriculture in its fullest sense of contemporary record and comparisons within living memory we shall find it most advantageous to take the figures for 1876 and for 1906. Those for 1876 because they are the earliest available at an exact interval in decades and because those of 1873 (the earliest published) show no vital difference. The reason for taking the figures in 1906 is manifest: they are the latest published.

The total area in Middlesex under all kinds of crops thus compares :—

1876 . . . . 117,493 acres
1906 . . . . 94,067 „

The decline in these figures, which include grass as a crop, is serious, and if we could clearly distinguish how much is due to a decline in agriculture generally and how much is simply the result of residential uses increasing we should get a very fair measure of how far agriculture as a whole is losing ground. But this is just what we do not seem able to get at, and the figures must needs blend. A residential occupier of means, for instance, will usually keep some private meadows as grass.

The area under wheat shows the following change :—

1876 . . . . 8,096 acres
1906 . . . . 2,264 „

This is a disastrous and altogether discouraging return. The London market takes, roughly speaking, the produce of 25,000 acres every week, and there is no part of Middlesex from which a cart cannot carry wheat to Mark Lane within four hours of sober going, such as befits the cart. The greater area of Middlesex may regard the distance as one of two hours' journey. The whole riparian district from Isleworth to Staines has water-borne traffic, which is far cheaper than either road or rail. Soil and climate suit wheat over at least the moiety of the county, and, as we see, as recently as 1876 some 8,096 acres were devoted to its cultivation. The inevitable conclusion seems to be that the average price of wheat from 1876 to 1906 did not make it a profitable crop to grow even under circumstances in the main favourable. The difficulties of sending produce to market which so often modify the situation in other counties have not here prevailed ; the uncertainty of market demand which so often discourages production does not apply where at hand we have an exchange placing for actual food wants nearly five million quarters of bread-stuffs annually. One may even add that the demand for bran and middlings would be more constant in Middlesex than in an average district.

The area under barley is thus returned :—

1876 . . . . 2,405 acres
1906 . . . . 358 „

This practical wiping out of barley as a Middlesex crop is wholly deplorable, for the area devoted to it was never excessive, and consisted of the less heavy soils on which it did well. Of the moderate area in 1876, 2,405 acres, it may be said with fair safety that not a single acre was of unfit land. That the cultivation of barley in Middlesex has been all but wholly abandoned is therefore a very evil sign. The farmers who have given it up were not incompetent ; the prices ruling since 1876 have made it unprofitable.

Oats are thus returned :—

1876	5,293 acres
1906	2,317 „

Long-stricken wheat and all but eliminated barley cultivation will have prepared readers for even worse figures for oats than those which we are now printing. The decline is very serious, but it leaves oats in the position of the leading cereal crop of the county. The large demand for good heavy English oats for good horses kept in London is probably the reason why the decline has not been greater than that actually recorded.

Rye has not been largely cultivated in Middlesex since the great war with France, when the universal desire to grow wheat was born of a belief that the whole country was likely to find itself on short commons and that wheat 'went further' than rye. There is no great difference in point of fact, the ideas of 1794 being exaggerated. Still, there is some difference, rye weighs a little less to the quarter as a rule and yields a little less to the acre. Areas devoted to it in Middlesex are :—

1876	341 acres
1906	141 „

Seeing the extreme usefulness of rye as a crop which can be fed off in the green state if food for stock runs short or allowed to ripen into grain which is 'safe' for say 24s. per quarter, seeing, too, that its straw is of high quality and in constant demand the rye area ought to reverse the figures of the thirty past years and revert to a good figure.

Areas under beans are :—

1876	1,383 acres
1906	651 „

The bean crop is a capricious one, but Middlesex is a county where it should do well. Foreign production has declined so materially for the past five years that prices are steadily advancing. Farmers to be 'in the movement' should grow more beans.

Peas are returned as follows :—

1876	1,833 acres
1906	1,058 „

The fall in peas may be due to a too exclusive cultivation of maple and dun sorts which seldom fetch a very adequate sum at Mark Lane. High-class peas pay well, but this branch of agriculture touches on market gardening, and will probably produce its most paying results in the hands of those who understand the kitchen garden.

Potatoes have a large and steady sale in London, but Middlesex has never cultivated the crop so freely as might have been expected. Acres have thus varied :—

1876	2,814 acres
1906	1,873 „

Early potatoes from the Scilly and Channel Islands, the Canary Islands, and Portugal have been inimical to high-value cultivation in Middlesex, and the main potato crop may safely be left to shires less fortunately situated than the privileged little district within five and twenty miles of the Borough market.

Roots, such as turnips, swedes, mangolds, carrots, cabbages, kohl-rabi and rape, were in 1876 thus returned :—

Turnips and swedes	2,010 acres
Mangolds	1,985 „
Carrots	100 „
All other roots	1,203 „
	5,298 „

The returns of 1906 show a somewhat different division :—

Turnips and swedes	475 acres
Mangolds	1,190 „
Cabbages	1,637 „
Kohl-rabi	22 „
Rape	18 „
	3,342 „

Carrots appear to have lost their special market. Why turnips and swedes have gone out of favour so much faster than mangolds is a little difficult to determine. The cultivation of cabbages has evidently increased materially, for ' all other roots etc.' in 1876 represented a much smaller figure than cabbages by themselves stand for now. Kohl-rabi wins favour very slowly. It is a hard root and not easy eating for cattle even when sliced. The net decline in roots doubtless corresponds to some degree with the large decline in the number of sheep kept within the county.

Tares, lucerne, and ' other green crops except clover and grass ' were returned in 1876 at 5,503 acres, while 674 acres were in bare fallow. In 1906 some 515 acres were under tares and 106 acres were devoted to lucerne. The decline in tares is curious, for in 1906 the price was seldom under 40s. per quarter, and in 1905 it was for some months at 60s. per quarter. The soil of Middlesex is by no means unfriendly to this crop. The cultivation of lucerne cannot be exactly estimated, because in a hot, dry season the grower makes money, in a wet or chill year he loses heavily. Lucerne cultivation is a speculation in weather futures.

Pasture pure and simple was thus represented in 1876 :—

Rotation	4,902 acres
Permanent	<u>78,933</u> ,,
	<u>83,835</u> ,,

In 1906 the figures were :—

Rotation	1,552 acres
Permanent	<u>69,769</u> ,,
	<u>71,321</u> ,,

The declining area of rotation pastures is peculiarly discouraging, for such pastures are nearly always a sign of progressive and scientific agriculture.

The number of horses kept in Middlesex has been returned as follows :—

1876	6,015
1906	6,042

There is an extraordinary stability about these figures, thirty years having made no appreciable modification in the total. The number of well-to-do private residents who keep horses has probably increased, that of farmers keeping ordinary cart-horses diminished, and the two changes may be taken to balance each other. Middlesex has never been a horse-breeding county, and it is not likely to become one. The increased use of steam machinery on go-ahead farms has told against the number of horses kept.

Cattle are thus returned :—

1876	26,460
1906	17,499

These figures are smaller than would have been expected, for they include the large herds of dairy cattle kept by Sir George Barham and other dairy kings, and they also comprise the beautiful if more or less fancy cattle kept by noble and wealthy residents like the owners of Osterley and Gunnersbury and Syon Parks. The number of cattle kept for non-dairy purposes has almost certainly retrograded very fast. Yet London every Christmas gives orders for many thousand tons of prime beef.

Of sheep the number before 1870 probably exceeded 40,000, but from about 1871 the keeping of sheep in Middlesex tended to decline. In 1876 the number was 36,770. The returns for 1906 were :—

Ewes	3,860
Lambs	4,503
Others	<u>6,520</u>
	<u>14,883</u>

The revival of sheep-breeding, which is in progress in England generally, has thus far failed to touch this county, although it is in close contact with a market always willing to give a good price for good mutton. Any of the Down breeds will flourish in Middlesex.

AGRICULTURE

Of pigs the returns are as follows :—

1876	12,352
1906	16,272

This is an interesting return. The small owners who are a feature of the county evidently tend to keep pigs, and the fact that the figures for swine have increased while those for cattle and sheep have diminished is one which the critic can hardly fail to associate with the fact that in Middlesex the average agricultural holding is a third smaller than for the kingdom as a whole.

In the *Report* of the Royal Commission on Agricultural Depression, 1897, Middlesex is included among the Eastern Counties, in ' the arable section,' but it is not mentioned separately. Certain causes of the general depression affect this county, such as foreign competition and the fall in the prices of farm produce. On the other hand, high railway rates do not constitute a grievance, and ' land in proximity to favoured markets has maintained or even increased its value.'

The following special and very valuable return was issued in December last, and gives the number of agricultural holdings in the county :—

Class 1	588	Petty occupiers (under 5 acres)
„ 2	1,008	Small „ („ 50 „)
„ 3	465	Medium „ („ 300 „)
„ 4	42	Large „ (over „ „)
Total	2,103	agricultural holdings.

The average size of agricultural holdings in Middlesex is 44·7 acres against 63·2 acres for Great Britain. It is only half that of the average holding in the neighbouring county to the north, Hertford, and it is eleven acres less than in the county across the Thames, Surrey. The number of large holdings is curiously limited, for, the great estate holders' home farms being omitted, the number of actual working tenant farmers holding 300 acres and upwards must be extremely small. What is it, in a county still under primogeniture, which makes this division ? It seems to be that property divided into several lots (the ideal unit is seen to be 44 acres in Middlesex) sells better than larger undivided properties. What keeps an owner from offering 440 acres in ten separate lots elsewhere is the fear that some may remain on hand, but in Middlesex the land appears promptly to be taken up, and of course the rent of 44 acres would almost anywhere exceed the rent of 440 acres divided by ten.

Percentages of acres under agriculture in Middlesex are as follows :—

Arable	16·5	per cent.
Grass	47·5	„ „
Woods	2·7	„ „
Commons	·1	„ „
	66·8	„ „
Non-agricultural	33·2	„ „
	100	„ „

The heaths, like that of Hounslow, appear under the heading of non-agricultural land ; the small area of commons described as agricultural consists of agricultural inclosures as in Bushey Park, where the public are by no means allowed to roam over all the public or quasi-public land. The large area of non-agricultural land is mainly a consequence of the extension and expansion of London.

In 1873 there were in Middlesex some 11,881 landowners and the average rent was £135 13s. a year from 11 acres, 3 roods, and 32 perches. Land therefore brought in a little over £11 per acre, and if we capitalize freeholds at 30 years' purchase, had an average value of about £340 an acre. There were, however, only 1,263 farmers and country gentlemen, the remaining owners possessing less than 10 acres apiece. Large estates, over 100 acres, numbered 276. The largest landowner was the earl of Strafford, who held 4,436 acres.

The owners of a thousand acres and over were as follows :—F. D. Cater, esq., Enfield, 1,364 acres; All Souls College, Oxford, 1,814 acres; Christ Church, Oxford, 1,132 acres ; King's College, Cambridge, 1,097 acres ; the Crown, 2,383 acres ; F. H. Deane, esq., Ruislip, 1,449 acres ; the earl of Jersey, 1,982 acres ; the Lady Delpierre, Greenford, 1,051 acres ; the duchy of Lancaster, 2,273 acres ; the Church (Ecclesiastical Commissioners), 1,309 acres ; D. A. Hamborough, esq,, Ventnor, 1,252 acres; the earl of Strafford, Barnet, 4,436 acres; Sir C. Mill, Hillingdon, 2,710 acres ; C. Newdigate, esq., Warwick, 1,492 acres ; the Lord Northwick, London, 1,260 acres ; General Wood, Littleton, 1,572 acres ; here we have sixteen owners of 28,576 acres, or 1,786 acres each.

There is great and obvious need of a new Domesday Book. Since 1873 the changes have been many, and it would be a very useful thing if with every third census a return of landed and agricultural properties was secured according to the precedent of 1873.

Shorthorns are professionally bred and sold by Mr. George Taylor of Cranford. He is a great upholder of the Bates strain, which he regards as producing deep milkers of the very first quality. Such famous prize animals as Beau Sabreur 74094, Melody, and Barrington Duchess 31st might in 1906 be seen on his farm. The last-named had an extraordinary record, winning the first prize inspection, first prize milking, first prize Shorthorn Society, and prize for best pure-bred animal at the Islington Dairy Show in October, 1906. This was the only time she was shown. Beau Sabreur is a stud bull with a splendid record, and other stud bulls are Drumcree, Rowbury, and Kirk Charm. Seeing the great success of Mr. Taylor at Cranford it is somewhat surprising that Shorthorn breeding does not develop faster in the county.

Channel Islands cattle are kept by all the chief landowners for dairy purposes, but there is not such strict observance of purity of strain as might be expected. The very best places, such as Osterley and Syon, are an exception to this remark. No flocks of sheep or herds of pigs are professionally bred for sale in Middlesex, but excellent Down sheep may be seen on the leading farms, and the best breeds of pigs are kept. Horse-breeding is but little carried on in Middlesex, yet in no county can finer dray horses be seen, or finer carriage horses. Here we have the advantage of population ; the brewer is sure to have the best heavy horses by emulation with a neighbouring brewery, and the county gentry are numerous enough and wealthy enough to be healthily critical of each others' horses.

A very interesting poultry establishment at Lower Edmonton is kept by Mr. Bowater of Bury Hall, who not only supplies birds to many poultry keepers within the county, but ships to foreign countries. His fowls are chiefly the Cochin China cross-breds known as Orpingtons, from their first specific differentiation on Mr. Cook's farm, Tower House, Orpington. The Aylesbury duck does as well in Middlesex as in the adjacent county of its home, and Mr. Bowater has also had much success with Toulouse geese. His prosperity is of good promise for advanced and scientific poultry keeping in Middlesex generally.

A few old agricultural words still surviving in rural Middlesex are 'farren' for half an acre, 'fale' for marshy land, and 'fat' for eight bushels, the modern quarter. The word 'ever' as a substantive is also heard, and means a sort of meadow. In Devonshire the word is in full use for rye-grass, but the writer has been unable to fix a like definite meaning in Middlesex. Old labourers evidently use the word with reference to the general aspect of the grass. 'Fagging' is the term applied to the use of the smaller scythe, but this implement is not called a fag as we might expect.

FORESTRY

THE Domesday Survey affords conclusive evidence of the widespread and considerable character of the woods of Middlesex in the eleventh century, up to the very gates of the city of London. Woodland was of such great value that it was always entered on the survey of a manor. It was not only an invaluable material for building purposes and a necessity as fuel, but the acorns and beech-mast were of the greatest worth for the sustenance of the pigs. In some counties the Domesday Commissioners endeavoured to estimate the extent of the wood in each manor by means of measurement, but more often, as in the case of Middlesex, by the number of swine that the wood would support in the time of pannage or autumn feeding. Such returns can, after all, only supply quite a rough estimate as to the extent of a wood, for its pannage value would depend on the nature and density of the trees. Occasionally in other counties there is entry of a *silva infructuosa*, by which is meant a wood where timber other than oak or beech prevailed, such, say, as ash, which would be useless as far as swine were concerned. The swine-supporting properties of the majority of the Middlesex manors were, however, sufficiently large to betoken a most unusual amount of woodland throughout this small county as compared with the large majority of such divisions. The following list of all the manors that had pannage woods, coupled with the size of the herds of swine they could support, is of interest as showing the distribution of the woods of Middlesex :—

Manor	Swine	Manor	Swine
Edmonton	2,000	Northolt	200
Enfield	2,000	Kensington	200
Harrow	2,000	Westminster	200
Stanmore	1,600	Twyford	150
Ruislip	1,500	'Slanestaple'	150
Fulham	1,450	Tottenhall	150
Stepney	1,220	Harlesden	100
Harefield	1,200	Hampstead	100
Kingsbury	1,200	Stanwell	100
Hendon	1,000	Lisson Green	100
Hillingdon	1,000	Chelsea	60
Tottenham	500	Tollington	60
Willesden	500	Hanwell	50
Harmondsworth	500	Tyburn	50
Isleworth	500	Elthorne	50
Colham	400	Cowley	40
Hayes	400	Staines	30
Greenford	300	Dawley	15
Ickenham	270		

It therefore follows that the woods in Middlesex at this date provided autumn feeding for a vast herd of upwards of 20,000 swine.

On four manors mention is made of wood sufficient for hedging purposes (*nemus ad sepes faciendas*), namely Harlesden, Cranford, St. Pancras, and part of Ossulstone. At Enfield mention is made of a park belonging to Geoffrey de Mandeville, and at Ruislip there was a park for wild game (*ferarum silvaticarum*).

Throughout the Domesday Survey vineyards are mentioned in thirty-eight places; six of these occur in Middlesex, namely at Kensington, Holborn, Staines, Kempton, Colham, and Harmondsworth.

In the often-cited account of 'the most noble city of London,' written in the reign of Henry II by William Fitz Stephen, a monk of Canterbury, occurs the following passage : 'On the north side, too, are fields for pasture, and a delightful plain of meadow-land, interspersed with flowing streams, on which stand mills whose clack is very pleasing to the ear. Close by lies an immense forest, in which are densely wooded thickets, the coverts of game, red and fallow deer, boars and wild bulls.'[1]

A blunder in statement, as well as in date, made by Stow in his *Survey of London* as first printed in 1598, and repeated in all subsequent editions, has led many a writer on Middlesex and London astray. Stow's statement is to the effect that : 'The 2d. of King Henry III the forest in Middlesex and the warren of Staines were disafforested ; since the which time the suburbs about London hath been also mightily increased with buildings.'[2]

There is, on the contrary, no proof whatever of there ever having been a royal forest in Middlesex, at all events in Norman days. The crown lands were very small, and two of the great wooded districts of the county, Enfield with its park, and Harrow, were in the respective hands of Geoffrey de Mandeville and the archbishop of Canterbury.

There was, however, a royal warren extant as early as the reign of Henry II at Staines,[3] to which certain forest rights pertained ; it extended from Staines to Hounslow.[4] On 28 March, 1227, a charter was granted to the prior and brethren of St. John of Jerusalem, permitting them to have unlawed dogs to guard their house in Hamtonet, which was within the king's warren of Staines—wherein the sisters of the order dwelt—and also to have unlawed dogs to guard their sheepfolds at the same place, and this without any interference from the foresters or warreners of Staines.[5] Close letters to this effect were dispatched on 10 April.[6]

The value, however, of such a grant was but of short duration, for on 18 August of the same year the king granted a charter, addressed to all the men of Middlesex, to the effect that the warren of Staines was to be no more a warren (*dewarrenata*), and was to be disafforested

---

[1] *Materials for Hist. of Thomas Becket* (Rolls Ser.), iii, 3.   [2] Stow, *Surv. of Lond.* (ed. 1876), 156.
[3] Pipe R. 4 Hen. II.   [4] Camden, *Brit.* (ed. Gough), ii, 3.
[5] Chart R. 11 Hen. III, pt. i, m. 11.   [6] Close, 11 Hen. III, m. 13.

FORESTRY

so that all men might cultivate their lands and inclose their woods therein, without let or hindrance as to vert or venison, etc., from any warrener, forester or justice of the forest.[7]   It was clearly some misreading of this charter that led Stow astray, and hence caused a crop of subsequent errors.

With regard to the warren of mediaeval England, it is well to recollect that the public had a right to hunt wild animals in any uninclosed lands outside forest limits, unless such right had been restricted by some special royal charter or grant.   The word warren was used to denote both the exclusive right of hunting and taking certain wild animals, and also the land over which such right existed.   Grants of free warren over lands or manors outside forests were frequently made by our earlier kings to private individuals and to religious foundations. Such a grant prevented anyone entering on such lands to hunt or take any warrenable animal without the owner's licence, under the very heavy penalty of £10.   No one might, therefore, follow the hunt of hare, fox, or other vermin into warrenable land ; but, strange to say, following the hunt of deer into such land was held to be no trespass, inasmuch as deer were not beasts of the warren.   The beasts of the warren included the hare, rabbit, and fox, and in the fourteenth century (in certain parts) the roe deer ; there were also birds of the warren, including pheasants, partridges, woodcocks, and herons.   Lords of warren had the power of impounding dogs as well as the snares and traps of trespassers.   Royalty had other warrens, apart from forests, in addition to that of Staines, such as the warren of Ashdown, Sussex. It was only in royal warrens that the lawing or mutilating of the forefeet of dogs obtained.[8]

There can scarcely have been timber of any size at Staines in the middle of the thirteenth century, for Henry III, in 1262, gave oaks out of Windsor Forest for the repair of the bridge at Staines.[9]

ENFIELD CHASE

It was at Enfield, in the north-east of the county, bordering on the Essex forest of Waltham, that the woodland of Middlesex chiefly prevailed for several centuries.   A park at Enfield is mentioned, as we have seen, as early as the eleventh century ; and there is a record in 1220 of Henry III obtaining oak shingles from this park to roof certain of the royal houses at Westminster.[10]   Immediately to the north of the town lay an extensive tract of land termed Enfield Chase, which included portions of the adjoining parishes of Edmonton, Hadley, and South Mimms. It extended about 8½ miles from east to west, and from 3½ to 6 miles in width.

A chase was, like a forest, uninclosed, and only defined by metes and bounds ; but it could be held by a subject.   Offences committed

[7] Chart R. 11 Hen. III, pt. 2, m. 5 ; Close, 11 Hen. III, m. 4.
[8] Turner, *Pleas of the Forest*, cxxiii–cxxiv ; Cox, *Royal Forests*, 2–3, 26.
[9] Close, 46 Hen. III, m. 12.   [10] Close, 4 Hen. III, m. 11.

therein were, as a rule, punishable by the common law and not by forest jurisdiction.

In certain ways the chase of Enfield resembled Cranborne Chase (Wiltshire and Dorset), so celebrated in the west of England. Cranborne had its outer and inner bounds, and in like manner there was at Enfield the ancient Great Park (sometimes called le Frith), whilst spreading out from it to the north-east and west was the much larger outer park (*parcus extrinsecus*). In 1324, when Enfield was forfeited to the crown, Edward II ordered Richard Pounz, keeper of Enfield Park, to permit the prior of St. John of Jerusalem at Clerkenwell to take five bucks between Midsummer and Michaelmas, and five does between Michaelmas and Lent, yearly, with archers or dogs at his pleasure, in the outer park, in accordance with the ancient grant of William de Mandeville, earl of Essex. At the same time it was stated that this park had always been held to be a member of the manor of Enfield.[11]

The name 'chase' (as applied to Enfield) first occurs, so far as we are aware, in any public record, on the Close Rolls of 1326, when Richard Pounz, keeper of Enfield Park, petitioned the king and council, stating that Humphrey de Bohun, late earl of Essex, had granted to him for life the custody of the park and chase of his manor of Enfield, receiving yearly 15 quarters of rye and 30s. for wages for himself and his six men keeping the park, but that since the manor was taken into the king's hands on the forfeiture of the earl he had received the rye, but not money.[12]

There are a few entries relative to Enfield Chase among the Domestic State Papers of the reign of Henry VIII. The privy purse expenses of September, 1530, include the payment of 30s. to the ranger and two keepers of 'Endefelde Chace.'[13] The dockets of warrants for the king's signature of the year 1535 contain one to the keepers of Waltham Forest and Enfield Chase for killing a stag and six bucks for the emperor's ambassador.[14]

An elaborate 'Decree for the Comoners of Enfielde chace' was set forth by the crown in 1542. It is stated in the preamble that the decree was called forth by constant complaints not only against his grace's keepers and the chase tenants, but also against the borderers, as to the waste and destruction of the woods and the deer, as well as divers other trespasses and wrongs by them committed. The king, therefore, commanded the earl of Southampton, Chancellor of the Duchy of Lancaster, with certain of the council of the duchy, to view the wood and game, and to report as to the complaints. The result of the report was the drawing up of a series of ordinances arranged under thirty-two heads. The following is an abstract of the more important orders. The tenants to have pannage for swine from Michaelmas to Martinmas; hogs on the chase to be ringed or pegged under a pain of 12d., half to go to the king

---

[11] Close, 18 Edw. II, m. 33. In the Ministers' Accts. (bdle. 1148, No. 17) of the previous year the receipts from Enfield manor, which had just come into the king's hands, are set down at £21.
[12] Close, 19 Edw. II, m. 16. [13] *L. and P. Hen. VIII*, v, 751. [14] Ibid. ix, 217.

and half to the informer ; no hogs in the fence month ; all hogs and swine to bear the owner's as well as the king's mark ; borderers' swine to enter a quarter of a mile and no further ; and no keepers to keep swine, and no foreigner's swine to enter. The master of the game, the ranger, and the bailiffs to have their feewood as before ; no man to sell any of the chase wood to any foreigner or to London ; no tenant or in-habitant to cut any manner of wood for his own use save that assigned him by the woodward ; no 'coates and hogsties' to be allowed in the chase, and such as there are to be pulled down ; horned beasts of two years old and upwards to be marked by the woodward ; and foreigners' beasts found in the chase to be pounded until fine fixed by the steward is paid. The last order but one prohibits any wood-gatherer carrying into the chase any 'bill hooke, hatchett, axe, or any other edge toole what-soever,' under pain of 12d. The final order sets the unusually heavy penalty of 3s. 4d. on any such 'as gather greene boughes to sell to Lon-don oute of any parte of the chace.' [15]

There are also some brief references to the chase during Elizabeth's long reign. In 1575 John Turnpenny and William Killingworth were committed to ward for hunting in Her Majesty's chase of Enfield, but were released on the finding of sureties.[16] In November, 1600, a note was taken of all the deer served by warrant or otherwise out of Enfield Chase, in the west, east, and south bailiwicks ; from the recent audit held at Allhallowtide, 1590–1600, the total number was forty-five bucks and eighteen does.[17]

The timber of the chase is mentioned in a curious petition, pre-sented about 1585 to the queen from John Taylor, asking licence to export 400 tuns of beer annually for twelve years free of custom. The petitioner pleaded that he had served her and her father beyond the seas in the wars, and had received no recompense save thirty loads of wood from Enfield Chase, value 30s.[18]

Norden, writing of Enfield Chase in 1596, says : 'a solitary desert, yet stocked with not less than 3,000 deere.' [19]

During the reign of James I the notices of this royal chase are more frequent. In April, 1603, a report was made to Secretary Cecil as to an assembling of women at White Webbs, on Enfield Chase, to maintain a right that the wood of the chase should not be carried out of Enfield, but burnt in the king's house there, or else given to the poor.[20] In July, 1608, a warrant was issued to pay John West, keeper of the West Baily walk in Enfield Chase, £30 per annum for provision of hay for the deer ;[21] this large amount shows that there was every intention to maintain a considerable stock of fallow deer. In 1611 the king gave assurance under his sign manual in reply to a remonstrance of the knights and gentlemen of Hertfordshire, that he would not disgrace his chase by

[15] Harl. MS. 368, fol. 104–6.   [16] S.P. Dom. Eliz. cvi, 45.
[17] Ibid. cclxxv, 113.   [18] Ibid. Addenda, xxix, 68.
[19] Norden, *Surv. of Midd.* 26.   [20] S.P. Dom. Jas. I, i, 25.
[21] Ibid. xxxv, 4. West died in 1639, whereupon Charles I granted this keepership to Ralph Potter, with a like annual sum for providing hay.

inclosing any more land ; but an agreement was entered into between the king's commissioners and the tenants of the chase for the inclosing of 120 acres.[22]

A warrant for payment of £200 to Sir Robert Wroth and Sir John Brett was signed in November, 1612, to distribute among such tenants as pretended to a right in the waste lands of Enfield Chase, which had been taken in to enlarge Theobalds Park.[23]

William Graves, of East Barnet, entered into an obligation in August, 1616, under pain of £20, to be true and faithful to the keeping of the king's game and venery in His Majesty's chase of Enfield, co. Middlesex.[24] In the following year Sir Nicholas Salter, woodward of the chase, was ordered to deliver trees, with tops and branches, for repairs within the chase.[25]

There was much disorder on the chase during the Commonwealth period, particularly in regard to the killing and snaring of the deer and destruction of the timber. The Council of State wrote to the Earl of Salisbury in June, 1649, to the effect that there could be no better way to repress such disorders than by proceeding against rioters by common law. The chiefest persons were known, and if they were indicted, heavily fined, and the fine speedily levied, they would not, perhaps, hereafter desire venison at so dear a rate. The earl was ordered to proceed against all known offenders at the next sessions or assizes.[26] In the following November the council had to deal with the embezzling of timber trees marked out on Enfield Chase for Admiralty use.[27] A report was presented in 1654 to the effect that there was destruction of wood in Enfield Chase to the value of £2,000 ; the best trees were being felled and the wood sold at very low rates.[28]

On 30 August, 1654, an ordinance was passed for the immediate sale of a third of Enfield Chase, for ready money. From the proceeds of this sale, and of other forest lands in Nottinghamshire and Staffordshire, the arrears of payments to various officers and soldiers were to be liquidated.[29]

A survey made in 1650 showed that the chase had an extent of 7,904 acres, and its value was £4,742 8s. per annum. The deer, whose numbers had greatly diminished during the civil strife, were valued at £150 ; the oak timber, exclusive of 2,500 trees marked for the Navy, at £2,100 ; and the hornbeam and other wood at £12,000.[30]

In the same year as the survey the chase was sold in lots, with the result that a considerable amount was speedily inclosed and houses built thereon. This excited much wrath amongst many of the commoners, resulting in riots attended by destruction of fences and buildings. The riots were eventually suppressed in 1659, by a considerable military force.[31]

[22] S.P. Dom. Jas. I, lxvi, 63, 65, 77.
[24] Ibid. lxxxviii, 47.
[26] S.P. Dom. Commonwealth, ii, 192.
[28] Ibid. lxxi, 63.
[30] Lysons, *Environs of London*, ii, 286.

[23] Ibid. lxxi, 43.
[25] Ibid. xcii, 53.
[27] Ibid. xi, 192.
[29] Ibid. lxxv, 341.
[31] Ct. R. bdle. 94, No. 1371.

FORESTRY

After the Restoration the chase was re-established, much planting done, and deer reintroduced. Among the Court Rolls at the Public Record Office [32] is a large bundle of rolls and papers relative to the manor of Enfield, extending from 1653 to 1716.

As soon as the Restoration was accomplished, the crown received numerous applications for the office of keeper of the different walks of the chase. Captain Thomas Pott was appointed keeper of Westbury walk in August, 1660,[33] and in October Captain William Barker obtained the like office in the South Baily Walk.[34] Samuel Norris, keeper of the East Walk, petitioned for continuance for life in his place, to which he had been ordained twenty-four years ago, having served the crown for thirty years, but had been turned out by the usurper, and was then disturbed by Mr. Hall, who pretended a patent from His Majesty. Norris eventually gained his request, and Hall's appointment was revoked.[35]

Charles Lord Gerard was appointed ranger and chief keeper of the chase and park of Enfield in 1660, inasmuch as the Earl of Salisbury, the late holder of those offices, forfeited the same by the destruction of the wood and deer, and by suffering the buildings to go to decay.[36]

Not long after the Restoration, the tenants and inhabitants of the manor of Enfield petitioned for leave to bring in a bill to Parliament to inclose their common fields, raising a tax of 20s. an acre for a fund to set the poor to work; they alleged that 200 or 300 poor families removed thither and built cottages on the chase during the troubles, and were gaining a livelihood by destroying and selling the wood.[37]

An effort was made in January, 1662, to restock the chase with deer. A warrant was issued to the 'Masters of the Buck Hounds and of the Toils' to take such deer from the parks of the Earl of Essex, Mrs. Sadler, Mr. Butler, and Sir Henry Blunt as they shall direct, and convey them to Enfield Chase or elsewhere as ordered by Lord Gerard.[38]

At the court leet of 11 June, 1679, there were several presentments for vert offences on the chase. William Sherwood of South Mimms was fined 20s. for cutting and carrying away bushes and furze out of Enfield Chase at several times; two other offenders were fined 6s. 8d. each for cutting and carrying away underwood; two others, 3s. 4d. each; and William Ducke 5s. for carrying off young trees.

The records of a court baron of 1689 are exceptionally interesting as supplying a customary of the chases. The jury presented that the tenants and inhabitants of Enfield, among other things, claimed to find an able person to drive the chase for taking up strays thereupon after warning given by the woodward and bailiff of the manor; also the right to take bushes in the chase to fence their grounds within the parish, by appointment with the woodward, at the price of 8d. a load;

[32] Hodson and Ford, *Hist. of Enfield*, 36–7; S.P. Dom. Commonwealth, cciii, 362, 368.
[33] S.P. Dom. Chas. II, xi, 105.   [34] Ibid. xix, 81.
[35] Ibid. xiii, 15.   See also xliv, 38; xlviii, 82; and xcviii, 46.
[36] Ibid. xxxv, 57; xlvi, 6.   [37] Ibid. xxii, 153.   [38] Ibid. xlix, 32.

also the right to take bushes, stakes, and heather, without appointment with the woodward or keeper of the chase, for the fences bordering on the chase, without paying anything for the same.

The jury further presented that the tenants of the manor from time out of mind had all trees standing and adjoining so near their grounds that a horse and a pack could not go between; that the copyholders had sufficient timber allowed them for repairing their houses out of the chase if they had none within their own ground; that the copyholders and all lawful commoners had clay, gravel, and fern for their necessary uses; that the tenants, time out of mind, received a load of the wood on St. George's Day, being the view day, for their pains, which the keepers felled yearly on the chase for the browse of the deer; also so much of the browse wood as should be necessary for their fuel at the old accustomed price of 8*d*.; also decayed and 'doted' trees at 2*s*. the load; also rotten wood, crabs, acorns, and the roots of felled trees for necessary fuel without payment; and that the commoners might turn out what cattle they thought fit, without stint, on the chase. Moreover timber had to be provided from the chase for public bridges and for rails within the manor. The tenants by custom received annually from the steward a buck and a doe in their respective seasons. Another interesting custom was that all tenants were permitted to plant trees for the safeguarding of their houses, and that they and their heirs were entitled to the lop of such trees as they had planted.

The largest oak then standing on the chase was felled in 1766; the bole measured 30 ft. long and contained about three tons of timber; the diameter of the butt end was 3 ft. The price was only £10.

Reverting to the more general consideration of the wooded parks of the county, Sexton's map of 1575 shows two parks and the chase of Enfield, as well as the parks of 'Mariburne' (Marylebone) and Hyde. Norden's survey of the county, 1596, is full of praise of the noble and well-timbered parks of Middlesex, and enumerates ten that belonged to Her Majesty, namely St. James's, Hyde, Marylebone, Hunsworth, 'Hemton,' Hampton Court (2), Enfield (2), and Twickenham; the last, however, of these had been recently disparked.[39]

With regard to the two parks of Enfield, the one was the ancient Great Park or Frith, the *parcus intrinsecus* from which the outer bounds of the chase radiated. The survey of 1650, the results of which so far as the chase was concerned have already been cited, gave the area of the park as 553 acres, 74 of which were in the parish of Edmonton; the oaks numbered 1,246, exclusive of 397 marked for the Navy; and the hornbeam and other trees 508. The other was the new or Little Park adjoining Enfield House (taken out of the chase), which was conveyed to the Crown by the Earl of Rutland. It was here that the children of Henry VIII, Edward and Elizabeth, long resided. This park, of 375 acres, was sold by Charles I in 1641 to the Earl of Pembroke.[40]

[39] Norden, *Surv. of Midd.* (ed. 1723), 14.
[40] Lysons, *Environs of Lond.* ii, 291, 297; Shirley, *Deer Parks*, 55.

FORESTRY

HYDE PARK

Hyde Park, which was cultivated ground known as the manor of Eia at the time of the Domesday Survey, was in the hands of subjects from the days of the Conqueror to those of Henry VIII. The latter king in 1532 effected an exchange of lands with the abbot and convent of Westminster, whereby the monks secured the early dissolved priory lands of Poughley, Berkshire, in exchange for about 100 acres in Westminster which were formed into St. James's Park. In 1536 Henry VIII gave the abbey the lands of the priory of Hurley, Berkshire, in exchange for the manors of Eyebury, Eabury or Ebury (which included the part afterwards known as Hyde Park), Neyte, and Toddington. There is no doubt that the king wanted these manors, so closely adjacent to his palace of Westminster, for hunting purposes. The manor of Hyde was speedily inclosed and made a park, with sufficiently high fences to restrain the deer with which it was stocked. [41]

The transference to the king of the 'sayte, sayle, circuyte, and procyncte of the manor of Hyde' is recited at length in an Act passed for the purpose of assuring to the crown this manor and the other adjacent property of the abbey of Westminster. [42] Hyde Park was then of much greater extent, for it included the portion taken to add to Kensington Gardens, as well as a good deal of land now built over at Hyde Park Corner ; it comprised about 620 acres instead of the 361 acres of the present day. Special keepers were speedily assigned to it ; payments made to two keepers of 'Hide Park,' named Edward Free and George Roper, occur in the King's Accounts of 1544. [43] The two keepers occupied separate lodges, the one on the site of Apsley House, and the other in the centre of the park in a building long known as the Old Lodge, which was pulled down when the Serpentine was formed. [44]

The park was used as a hunting-ground in the reigns of Edward VI, Mary, Elizabeth, and James I. In June, 1550, the boy king here entertained a special embassy from France, who had crossed the seas to obtain the ratification of the treaty ceding Boulogne for 400,000 crowns. A letter from the lords of the council to the English ambassador at Paris says, 'Upon Tuesday the king's Majesty had them on hunting in Hyde Park, and that night they supped with his Highness in the Privy Chamber.' [45]

Queen Elizabeth was also ready to entertain her guests, after like fashion, with sport in Hyde Park. The Talbot Papers, in a letter from Gilbert Talbot to the Earl of Shrewsbury in February, 1578, record the entertainment offered to Count Casimir, son of the Elector Palatine :—

> My Lord of Leicester also hath given him dyvers other thynges, as geldynges, hawks and hounds, crosse-bowes, &c. . . . for he delyghteth greatly in huntynge and can chouse his wynter deere very well. He kylled a barren doe with his pece this other daye in Hyde Parke from amongst ccc other deere. [46]

[41] Ashton, *Hyde Park, from Domesday to Date* (1896), 1–8.   [42] *Stat. of Realm*, 28 Hen. VIII, cap. 49.
[43] *L. and P. Hen. VII!*, xix (1), 368.   [44] Larwood, *The Story of the Lond. Parks*, i, 9.
[45] Tytler, *Edw. VI and Mary*, i, 288.   [46] Lodge, *Illus. of Brit. Hist.* ii, 205.

In 1553 Roger was succeeded in the keepership by Francis Nevell, who held it singlehanded for twenty-one years. His actual fee was only 4*d.* a day, but the patent of appointment secured for him pasture rights for twelve cows, one bull, and six oxen, together with certain other profits accruing to the office. In 1574 Queen Elizabeth appointed Henry Carey, first Lord Hunsdon, an associate keeper with Nevell ; he was to receive the like sum of 4*d.* a day and all the herbage, pannage, and browsewood for the deer. At the death of Nevell he was to be sole keeper at 8*d.* a day. During Nevell's keepership, namely, in 1570, forty acres of land on the Knightsbridge side were added to the park and railed in, the grass therein being reserved to be mown for hay for the deer in winter. Nevell died before Lord Hunsdon, and when the latter died, in 1596, he was succeeded by his fourth son, Sir Edward Carey, in the office of keeper of Hyde Park at 8*d.* a day and without any associate. The chief lodge and mansion, with the herbage and pannage attached to it, was reserved for his mother, the Lady Anne Hunsdon. Sir Edward Carey was succeeded in the keepership in 1607 by Robert Cecil, Earl of Salisbury. Cecil had a colleague assigned him in 1610 in Sir Walter Cope, with benefit of survivorship. Sir Walter Cope, Master of the Wards and Chamberlain to the Exchequer, was a considerable landowner in Kensington ; he built the centre portion and turrets of Holland House. On Lord Salisbury's death in 1612, Sir Walter surrendered the keepership of Hyde Park in favour of his son-in-law, Sir Henry Rich, who was subsequently created Earl of Holland, and beheaded by the Parliament in 1649.[47]

The accounts of the Board of Works for 1582 contain the entry of a payment when the Duke of Anjou and his court were in England, 'for making of two new standings in Marybone (Regent's Park) and Hyde Park, for the Queen's Majesty and the noblemen of France to see the hunting.'[48] Norden, writing in 1596, alludes to the 'princely stands' that he noted in Hyde Park.[49]

The deer of this park were well-maintained during the reign of James I. In a 1607 list of nine royal parks, out of each of which four bucks were to be taken, the parks of Hyde, Enfield Chase, Richmond, and Hampton are included. A letter of the king in the following year states that he was pleased to bestow upon the ambassadors of France, Spain, Venice, and the States of the Low Countries, certain bucks for their sport during the time of his absence on progress, and to permit them to come to the parks (Hyde Park being one) and kill a brace of bucks with hounds or bow if they should think fit. At the same time James gave directions for the bestowing of a brace of bucks on the farmers of the Customs and the tellers of the Exchequer ; to find this supply a brace each were to be taken, *inter alia*, from the parks of Hyde and Enfield Chase, and from the Little Park of Enfield.[50]

[47] Larwood, *The Story of the London Parks*, i, 10–15.   [48] Ashton, *Hyde Park*, 10.
[49] Norden, *Survey of Midd. and Herts.* 19.
[50] S.P. Dom. Jas. I, xxxix, 41, 73.

FORESTRY

A distribution of fat venison, made by order of Charles I in 1639 to the foreign ambassadors, included three bucks to the French ambassador, one of which came from Hyde Park.[51]

In the reign of James I Westminster Palace was supplied with water from springs in Hyde Park ; a grant was made by the king in 1617 to the Earl of Suffolk of liberty to have a small pipe for the conveyance of water to Suffolk House inserted in the main pipe from Hyde Park to Westminster Palace.[52]

In the same year the crown granted to one Hector Johnson, for service to the Electress Palatine, a lease of the waste ground called Hay Hill, near Hyde Park, and of another plot near Hyde Park Corner, with power to build thereon.[53]

In 1619 the park was the scene of a serious poaching affray, when two or three poachers were caught shooting the deer at night. They were executed at Hyde Park Gate ; even a poor labourer who had been hired to hold their dogs for 16d. shared their fate.[54]

The deer of Marylebone Park suffered much from great rains in the winter of 1624–5 ; on 12 January a warrant was issued to the keepers of Hyde Park to cause three brace of bucks to be taken and conveyed to Marylebone on that account. At the same time another warrant was served on the master of the toils to cause the toils (nets) to be sent to Hyde Park for that service.[55]

Londoners may be thankful to Charles I for the initiation of one great boon, namely, the opening of Hyde Park as a pleasure ground to the public, an act of grace which was not extorted by any pressure. The exact date of this concession is not known, but it was certainly before 1635. On 23 April of that year two Leicestershire gentlemen, John Prettyman and John Havers, agreed to run a match with their horses for £100 each, between the hours of 9 and 10 in the forenoon. They were to start 'at the upper lodge and to run the usual way from thence over the lower bridge unto the ending place at the Park Gate.' The words ' usual way ' show that races were at this date common on this course. A comedy produced in 1637 by James Shirley, under the title ' Hyde Park,' has a race as the principal incident. The author states that this play was written at the suggestion of Henry, Earl of Holland, the keeper, and that he had been ' made happy by his smile when it was presented after a long silence upon first opening of the park.' From this play it is obvious that considerable crowds gathered at this period to see the horse-racing and other sports in the park. One of the episodes is a foot-race. A milkmaid goes round amongst the people crying ' Milk of a red cow,' whilst the more fashionable company partake of syllabub laced with sack. Other parts of the play show the rural character of much of the park ; birds are singing ' on every tree,' whilst the nightingale and the cuckoo obtain particular mention.[56]

[51] Cox, *Royal Forests*, 78.
[52] S.P. Dom. Jas. I, xc, 123.   Three years later the dean and chapter of Westminster obtained a like permission.   [53] Ibid. 142.   [54] Ibid. cx, 133, 149.
[55] Ibid. clxxxi, 48.   [56] Larwood, *The Story of the London Parks*, 21–3.

Charles I took special care of the Hyde Park deer; he revoked the various warrants of his father granting water from the springs to particular inhabitants and for the general use of the city of Westminster, by writ of King's Bench, on complaint of the keepers that the ponds were so drained that there was not water enough for the deer, notwithstanding that the inhabitants stated by petition that they knew the ponds to be full.[57]

At the beginning of the Civil War, when fortune appeared to be favouring the Royalists, London was alarmed, and in March, 1643, Parliament ordered that the City and its immediate suburbs should be surrounded by a great earthen rampart, with bastions and redoubts. The work was begun with much energy in the following May, and included a large square fort, with four bastions, on the site of the present Hamilton Place, Piccadilly, which was at that date within the extreme limits of the park on that side.[58] The fort at Hyde Park Corner stood for four years; it was demolished in 1647, by order of Parliament, as there was no further dread of attack. A guard was also established in 1643 at the north-east corner of the park, to keep a close watch on all those taking the Oxford Road, and several important arrests were made within its precincts.

The park suffered much from the excitement of the times. The House of Commons ordered in 1643

> that the officers and soldiers at the courts of guard be required not to permit any to cut down trees or wood in Hyde Park, and not to suffer any such persons as go out to the works to cut wood in the park, or to bring any from thence but by warrant from the committee appointed for that ordinance.[59]

The committee referred to in this order was one recently appointed

> in regard of the extraordinary want of fuel, to see to the cutting down of the under-wood within sixty miles of London in the king's and queen's parks, as well as in those belonging to any bishops, prebendaries, deans or chapters, and to distribute the same among the poor.[60]

In 1645, when Puritanism was at its height, orders were given

> that Hyde Park and Spring Gardens should be kept shut, and no person allowed to go into any of those places on the Lord's day, fast and thanksgiving days, and hereof those that have the keeping of the said places are to take notice and see this order obeyed, as they will answer to the contrary at their uttermost peril.[61]

Several events of importance occurred within the precincts of Hyde Park during the Commonwealth strife. On 6 August, 1647, the Parliamentary forces under Fairfax, between whom and the Common Council of London there had been serious ill feeling, which was now allayed, marched three deep into Westminster on their way to the City with laurel branches in their hats; and in Hyde Park they were formally

---

[57] Larwood, *The Story of the London Parks*, 18.
[58] *Perfect Diurnal*, 24 Apr.–1 May, 1643; Gardiner, *Hist. of the Great Civil War*, i, 52, 98. See the plan of these fortifications in Maitland, *Hist. of Lond.* i, 369.
[59] *Commons' Journ.* iii, 267.   [60] *Weekly Acct.* 4 Oct. 1643.   [61] *Lords' Journ.* vii.

FORESTRY

received and welcomed by the lord mayor and aldermen on horse-back.[62] In December of the following year, Lord Essex and Colonel Lambert encamped with their forces in this park; and it was here also that Cromwell, on 9 May, 1649, reviewed his regiment of Ironsides, together with Fairfax's regiment of horse, and made his memorable appeal to the Levellers.[63]

A great military pageant was held in the park on 31 May, 1650, to celebrate the return of Oliver Cromwell from the terrible wars in Ireland. The Protector was met on Hounslow Heath by members of Parliament and officers of the army, and as he passed through Hyde Park on his way to Whitehall, the great guns fired salutes, and Colonel Backstead's regiment fired a volley.[64]

Soon after the execution of Charles I, Hyde Park was seized by the state as part of the crown lands. A survey was taken in 1652, when the park's area was declared to be 620 acres of the annual value of £894 13s. 8d., and the timber was valued at the great sum of £4,779 19s. 6d., and the deer at £300. The park was divided into lots and sold to various purchasers, producing the sum of £17,068 6s. 8d., including the deer and the timber;[65] and to this sum the wood and underwood[66] contributed £5,099 19s. 6d.

But although much of the park was now in private hands, it continued to be frequented. In the year following the sale, Evelyn wrote in his diary, under 11 April: 'I went to take the air in Hyde Park, where every coach was made to pay a shilling, and horse sixpence, by the sordid fellow who had purchased it of the State, as they were called.'[67]

The park was by no means all gloom under the Commonwealth. A letter-writer of the time states that on May-day, 1654:

> Great resorts came to Hyde Park, many hundreds of coaches and gallants in attire, but most shameful powder'd hair men, and painted and spotted women. Some men played with a silver ball and some took other recreation. But his Highness the Lord Protector was not hither, nor any of the Lords of the Council, but were busy about the great affairs of the Commonwealth.[68]

The Protector, however, was present on that May-day, and appeared keenly to enjoy the sports, as we learn from another source. In company with many of his Privy Council he watched a great hurling match by fifty Cornish gentlemen against fifty others. 'The ball they played withal was silver, and designed for that party which did win the goal.'[69]

Later in the same year, namely on 29 September, Cromwell went into Hyde Park to enjoy a small picnic dinner under the trees with Secretary Thurloe, and attended by a few servants. Afterwards he

[62] Rushworth, *Hist. Coll.* vii, 756.
[64] Larwood, *Story of the Lond. Parks*, i, 34–5.
[66] Rutton, 'Making of Kensington Gardens' in *Home Counties Mag.* vi, 149.
[67] Evelyn, *Diary*, i, 284.
[69] *Moderate Intell.* 26 Apr.–4 May, 1654.

[63] *Perfect Occurrences*, 4–11 May, 1649.
[65] Lysons, *Environs of Lond.* ii, 182.
[68] *Gen. Proc. of Parl.* 27 Apr.–4 May, 1654.

desired to try a fine new team of six grey horses which the Earl of Oldenburg had lately sent him. Cromwell drove with success for some time, but using the whip too freely, he lost control of the team, which plunging threw him off the box on to the pole, 'dragging him by the foot for some time so that a pistol went off in his pocket to the amazement of men.' As a result of this accident, he was let blood and confined to his house for several days.[70]

The Protector's life was subsequently again endangered in Hyde Park from a very different cause. During the trial of Miles Sindercombe for shooting at Cromwell at Shepherd's Bush in February, 1656, it was deposed by one of his accomplices that

> They [the conspirators] went out several times for the purpose of shooting him, and having received notice from one of the Troope of his Highness's Lifeguards that he would be in the Park on a certain day, they went thither heavily armed, and that the hinges of the Park gate were filed in in order to facilitate their escape. . . . That when his Highness rode into the Park he alighted and speaking to Cecill asked whose horse that was he rode upon, Sindercombe being then outside the Park ; that Cecill was then ready to have done it, but doubted the fleetness of his horse, he having a cold.[71]

Another incident of a very different kind that happened in the park during the Commonwealth is recorded by Evelyn, after a very terse fashion, as occurring on 20 May, 1658. He says : 'I went to a coach race in Hyde Park, and collationed in Spring Garden.'[72]

In April, 1660, some six weeks before the recall of Charles II, towards which General Monk was so assiduously scheming, a great review of the trained bands and their auxiliaries was held in Hyde Park, when a force of about 20,000 men marched past a 'spacious fabric' in the centre of the Park, wherein the lord mayor, the court of aldermen, and the Commissioners for the Militia were seated in state.[73] On May-day the park was crowded with a gay throng in anticipation of the coming return of the monarchy, and on 29 May occurred the triumphant entry of the long-banished king. Ere the year closed Charles II held a review in Hyde Park of 20,000 of the re-modelled trained bands and of 800 cavalry.[74]

The references to the gaiety of Hyde Park during the reign of Charles II, particularly on May-day, by the diarists Evelyn and Pepys are far too numerous for citation.

It must not, however, be supposed that the fashionable folk of the time were in the habit of taking the air throughout the whole or any considerable part of the park. There was an inner circle in the centre of its northern half known as the 'Ring,' round which it was the custom to ride and drive. Sometimes this circle was known as the 'Tour,' a term cited by Pepys. The origin of this Ring is unknown, but it has been conjectured that it was a remnant of the gardens attached to the old Banqueting House.[75]

[70] Carlyle, *Cromwell*, iv, 22–3.
[72] *Diary*, i, 327.
[74] Stow, *Survey* (Strype's ed.), iii, 572.

[71] *Mercurius Politicus*, 15–21 Jan. 1657.
[73] *Mercurius Politicus*, 19–26 Apr. 1660.
[75] Larwood, *Story of the Lond. Parks*, 58–9.

FORESTRY

Hyde Park, at the Restoration, was included among the resumed crown lands. It was replenished with deer and surrounded with a brick wall in the place of the former pales. This wall stood until 1726, when a new and higher wall, 8 ft. on the outside, was erected. Iron railings were first introduced in 1828.[76]

In June, 1660, Charles II granted the custody of Hyde Park to his youngest brother, the Duke of Gloucester, at a salary of 8d. a day,[77] but he died of the small pox within a few months of his appointment, and in September Colonel John Hamilton, who gave his name to Hamilton Place, was appointed in his stead.[77]

The purchaser of the Kensington division of the Park, at the sale of 1652, was one John Tracey, who gave £3,906 7s. 6d. for the lot, including the timber. In September, 1660, Tracey petitioned the crown, begging to be allowed to retain two houses which he had built on the road at Knightsbridge to save him from ruin. He stated that he had been for thirty-eight years a merchant in the United Provinces, and returning in 1652, ignorant of affairs, was induced to buy part of the crown lands in Hyde Park, but he had not cut down the timber and had never been engaged in hostilities.[78] In 1662 Charles II consented to dispark certain portions of the park, at the Kensington end, in favour of Solicitor-general Finch.[79]

In April, 1664, a grant was made by the crown to James Hamilton, park ranger, and to John Birch, auditor of excise, of 55 acres of land on the borders of Hyde Park, to be planted with apple trees for apples or cider, reserving a right of way from Westminster to Kensington, on condition of their inclosing and planting the ground at their own expense, paying a rental of £5, and giving half the apples or the cider for the use of the king's household. The apples were to consist chiefly of golden pippins and redstreaks.[80]

The custom of charging for the admission of coaches and horsemen to Hyde Park, introduced during the Commonwealth, was continued to a large extent when the park was resumed by the crown. James Hamilton, the ranger, was ordered, in April, 1664, to water the passage from the gate to where the coaches resorted in the park, to avoid the annoyance of dust, the expense to be borne by a charge of 6d. on each coach ; at the same time he was instructed to prevent all horses entering the park save such as have gentlemen or livery servants on them.[81]

Many particulars might be given as to the use of Hyde Park during the centuries following the Restoration, such as military reviews, royal birthday celebrations, robberies, duels, or executions—but such details can readily be found in various well-known works on London.

A number of deer remained in the park until the year 1831 ; but they never roamed at large throughout the park after the Restoration, being penned off in a large inclosure in the north-west corner, termed Buckdean

[76] Larwood, *Story of the Lond. Parks*, 73.
[77] S.P. Dom. Chas. II, v, 75.
[78] Ibid. xvii, 64.
[79] Ibid. lii, 13, 114.
[80] Pat. 16 Chas. II, pt. 18, m. 7 ; S.P. Dom. Chas. II, xcvii, 23.
[81] S.P. Dom. Chas. II, xcvii, 63.

Hill or the Deer Paddock. The last known occasion of royal sport in the park occurred on 9 September, 1768, as recorded in *The Public Advertiser* of 12 September :—

> Same day, their Serene Highnesses the two Princes of Saxe Gotha, and many other Foreigners of Distinction, together with a great number of our own Nobility and Gentry, attended the Diversion of Deer Shooting in Hyde Park, which continued all the Evening until Dark, when one was at last killed, after being shot at ten Times. What rendered it so difficult to kill him was the Hardship of getting him from among the Deer; and no other was allowed to be shot but this one : Several wagers were won and lost upon this Occasion.

There is one great feature of Hyde Park which ought not to be passed over in silence, for it has added so materially to its beauties and to the enjoyment of its frequenters for nearly two centuries; we allude to the great piece of water known as the Serpentine. Queen Caroline, in 1730, conceived the idea of improving the appearance of both Hyde Park and Kensington Gardens, by draining the various pools and by increasing the volume of the little stream of Westbourne—which came down from Hampstead and flowed sluggishly through the park to the Thames, and widening it into a lake of some forty acres. This lake was named the Serpentine, or the Serpentine River ; its outline has been considerably straightened from time to time since its first formation. The operations then conducted were officially termed the 'laying the Six Ponds in Hyde Park into one.' Mr. Rutton's recent diligence [82] has brought to light full details as to cost and nature of this undertaking. A highly interesting feature was the care taken in the transplanting of trees, as shown by the following items :—

> For grubbing up in several places and drawing up upon the hill out of the way of the water line 105 large Oaks, Elms, and Willows at 4*d.* each, £21.
>
> For grubbing up several small Oaks in the Grove, £3 10*s.*
>
> For 900 Cube yards of Earth dug and carted to the south side of the Ponds to fill up a line for the planting of 20 large Elms at 9*d.* per yard, £33 15*s.*
>
> For the charge of taking up the said 20 Elms, with large balls, and carrying them from the several parts to the place of planting, in doing of which and setting each was used generally 18 horses and 60 men making up large stools to place them in, and making up the pans several times after they were broke down by the carts and horses, at £2 10*s.* per tree, £50.
>
> For Watering Cart to water the trees at 5*s.* a day, and for a Labourer attending the same at 20*d.* a day for 152 days between the beginning of April and the 20th day of November, 1731, £50 13*s.* 4*d.*
>
> For charges about the 20 large Elms new planted, viz., to Joseph Banister for a new sledge for drawing the trees, and repairing it, £3 4*s.*; William Watkins for smiths work in mending and repairing the Chains, 28*s.*; Henry Skene, carpenter, for Oak Boxes for the trees and Deals and in taking 'em up, £35 3*s.* 8*d.* And to Mark Collberd for Ropes, Wax, Pitch, Tallow, Oakham, Straw, &c., used about the Trees, and for Hayseed to sow the Slopes, £8 19*s.* 7*d.* In all as by Bills and Receipts, £48 15*s.* 3*d.*

The total expenditure incurred in making the Serpentine amounted to £4,755 19*s.* 7*d.*

Five years later it was found necessary to strengthen the dam at Knightsbridge, and to improve the outlet of the water, the total cost of

---

[82] Rutton, 'The Making of the Serpentine,' *Home Counties Mag.* (1903), v, 81–91, 183–95.

which amounted to £2,606 13s. Rennie's bridge across the Serpentine was erected at a great cost (said in a letter to the *Times* to be £100,000) in 1826. Eight years after the building of the bridge, namely in 1834, occurred the change in the source from which the water was drawn. The old brook of Westbourne had become befouled with sewage, and brought much filth into the Serpentine; the stream was therefore turned into a large culvert and since that date the water has been supplied from a changing and complex system of waterworks.

The Round Pond of Kensington Gardens was first supplied with water in 1728.[83]

ST. JAMES'S PARK

The origin of St. James's Park, in 1532, has already been stated. Henry VIII stocked it with deer, and their numbers were well maintained throughout the century. A foreign visitor in 1598 wrote of St. James's Park: 'In this park is great plenty of deer.'[84] It is generally stated that Charles II added 36 acres, gained by purchase, to its area: but it is more correct to call this addition, which ran up into Piccadilly, the Green Park, though at first styled 'Upper St. James's Park.' This small park was inclosed with a brick wall in 1667.[85]

The deer of St. James's Park disappeared about the beginning of the Commonwealth trouble, but in 1652 when Hyde Park was sold, the House of Commons ordered that 'James's Park' should be spared and restocked with deer from the parks of Hampton and Bushey.[86]

Evelyn, writing in 1665, says that he noted in St. James's Park 'deer of several countries, white spotted like leopards, antelopes, an elk, red deer, roebucks and staggs.'[87] In Kip's view of St. James's, taken in 1714, deer are shown in a park beyond the Mall.

The present area of St. James's Park is 93 acres, and of the Green Park 52¾ acres.

KENSINGTON GARDENS

The origin of Kensington Gardens, with the present area of 274½ acres, has given rise to much dispute and to a multiplicity of erroneous statements. The fact is, as has already been stated, that Charles II in 1662 disparked certain parts of Hyde Park at the Kensington end, in favour of Secretary Finch, who afterwards became earl of Nottingham. William III, however, bought back Nottingham House with its extensive grounds in 1689, making it his favourite London residence. Hence it became known as Kensington Palace.

The difficulties as to the story of the founding of Kensington Gardens have recently been much simplified by the researches of Mr. Rutton.[88] He points out that the area of Hyde Park apportioned to be sold in 1652 was 621·83 acres, but the acreage to-day (including the Serpentine) is

[83] Rutton, 'The Making of the Serpentine,' *Home Counties Mag.* (1903), v, 81 et seq. and 183 et seq.
[84] Hentzner, *Travels*, 34.   [85] Larwood, *Lond. Parks*, ii, 25–6.
[86] Ibid. 78–9.   [87] Evelyn, *Memoirs*, i, 356.
[88] Rutton, 'The Making of Kensington Gardens,' *Home Counties Mag.* (1904), vi, 145–59, 222–31

368·44. The park has therefore only lost 253·39 acres, and as its boundaries north, east, and south are nearly the same as formerly, the loss must necessarily therefore have chiefly occurred on the western or Kensington side. As at the sale of 1652 the Kensington portion (the largest of the five divisions) comprised 177·36 acres, Mr. Rutton, from his study of accounts and particulars at the Record Office, concludes that Queen Anne caused about 100 acres to be appropriated from the park for the Palace Gardens, and that George I was responsible for annexing most of the remainder, which could not have exceeded 150 acres.[89] Queen Caroline's own contributory work to Kensington Gardens seems to have been confined to the completion of the work left unfinished by George I, though she has been credited by Lysons and Faulkner with having filched some 200 or 300 acres from Hyde Park.

It was probably, however, Queen Caroline who caused the stately Broad Walk to be laid out, in its final form, as a gravelled road, 60 ft. wide, between four rows of elms; but as Mr. Rutton points out,[90] Queen Anne seems to have been its originator.

The elm is more especially the tree of Kensington Gardens than of any other of our London Parks; at least ninety per cent. of the Kensington trees being of that species. It has been said that several of the giant elms of Kensington Gardens and Hyde Park are 350 years old. But the best judges are sceptical as to this; it is probable that very few of even the most carefully tended English elms attain to an age of more than two centuries. The elm is an essentially dangerous tree, both on account of its liability to be blown over through the roots spreading over the surface of the soil (instead of penetrating deeply like the oak), and because of the great brittleness of the wood, which causes the occasional sudden falling of large boughs. A young woman lost her life in Kensington Gardens in 1906 through the latter cause. Hence a very careful survey of the timber was made, and a large number of the veteran elms were pollarded during the winter of 1906–7.[91]

MARYLEBONE OR REGENT'S PARK

In 1541, when Henry VIII was busily engaged in extending his hunting grounds in the immediate vicinity of London, he acquired divers lands belonging to the prebendal manor of Rugmere for the enlarging of 'Marybone Park in the county of Middlesex,' in lieu of which land the king secured the parsonage of Throwley, Kent, to the prebendary and his successors by a private Act of Parliament of that year.[92] In 1544 the king

[89] In fact it may have been less, as a triangular slip of Hyde Park covering 22 acres was taken into Kensington Gardens in 1872. Mr. Rutton's final conclusion is that 231·39 acres were taken from the park by Queen Anne and George I, and that in all probability about 66·36 acres were originally attached to the palace, having been purchased by William III. *Home Counties Mag.* vi, 226 n.

[90] *Home Counties Mag.* vi, 227.

[91] A child was killed in these gardens on 1 May, 1903, through the blowing over of an elm tree during a slight gale.

[92] Davies, 'The Prebendal Manor of Rugmere,' in *Home Counties Mag.* iv, 24; *L. and P. Hen. VIII,* xv, 217.

secured further lands in the same district, exchanging the manor of Tyburn for other property with Thomas Hobson. The district of Marylebone or Tyburn used to be well-wooded, and included a considerable park.[93]

Queen Mary in 1554 gave orders for the five or six hundred acres which formed Marylebone Park to be disparked; but this order must have been revoked or disregarded, for it was certainly used as a hunting ground by Queen Elizabeth.[94] In 1582 an entry in the accounts of the Board of Works records a payment 'for making of two new standings in Marybone and Hyde Park for the Queens Majesty and the noblemen of France to see the hunting.'[95] This was on the occasion of the visit to England of the duke of Anjou, Elizabeth's suitor, with a considerable train of the French nobility. During the winter of 1600–1 Marylebone Park provided good sport for the ambassador from Russia and other Muscovites; they rode to 'Marybone Park' and there hunted at their pleasure.[96]

When James I, in 1611, granted the manor of Marylebone to Mr. Forset the park was reserved. It continued in the possession of the crown until 1646, when it was granted to Sir George Strode and John Wandsford as security for a debt of £2,318 11s. 9d. incurred in providing ammunition and other military stores for the Royalists. It was sold by the Commonwealth for £13,215, including £130 for the deer (of which there were 124 of all sorts) and £1,779 for timber, exclusive of 2,976 trees which were reserved for the navy. The park must therefore have been magnificently wooded in its prime. At the Restoration Strode and Wansford were reinstated and held the park until the debt was paid. No attempt, however, was made to form it again into a single park, or to restock it with deer. Various crown leases fell in during the Regency, and the old lands of Marylebone Park began to be laid out in 1812 on an elaborate scale by Mr. Nash, and have henceforth been known by the name of Regent's Park.[97] Regent's Park, with Primrose Hill, covers an area of 274½ acres.

At the dissolution of the monasteries Henry VIII founded the brief-lived bishopric of Westminster, assigning the county of Middlesex to it for a diocese, and bestowing on it a part of the lands of the dissolved abbey, of which the manor and advowson of Hampstead formed part. At this time there is evidence that a considerable part of the woods of Hampstead as well as of Highgate and Hornsey were in full vigour, and harboured game other than deer. A proclamation was issued by Henry VIII shortly before his death, that

> noe person interrupt the King's game of hare, partridge, pheasant and heron preserved in and about his house at his palace of Westminster for his own disport and pastime; that is to saye, from his said palace of Westminster to St. Gyles in the Fields, and from thence to Islington to or Lady of the Oke, to Highgate, to Hornsey Parke, to Hamsted Heath, and from thence to his said palace of Westminster to be preserved and kept for his owne disport, pleasure and recreation.[98]

[93] Nichols, *Queen Eliz. Progresses.*   [94] *Arch.* xviii, 180.   [95] Ashton, *Hyde Park,* 10.
[96] Ibid.   [97] Clinch, *Marylebone and St. Pancras* (1890), 5, 6, 48, 50.
[98] White, *Hampstead and its Associations,* 24.

The woods of Hampstead continued to flourish during the reigns of Edward VI and his two sisters, reaching on the east to the village now known as Kentish Town, and spreading on the west by Belsize and past the Adelaide road to St. John's Wood. With King James Hampstead was a favourite hunting ground ; the plateau on the West Heath, known as King's Hill, is said to be the place whence that king was wont to see the hounds throw off.[99]

The district of St. John's Wood was so called after its former possessors, the English priors of St. John of Jerusalem, who had their head quarters at Clerkenwell. These woodlands were originally known as Great St. John's Wood, to distinguish them from a Little St. John's Wood at Highbury.[100]

The Order of Hospitallers or Knights of St. John was suppressed by Henry VIII in 1540. Great St. John's Wood was then for a time entrusted to the keepership of John Conway. Certain papers among the Forest Accounts at the Public Record Office for 1541–2 show that the wood had been well maintained by the priory authorities, and that large quantities of timber and underwood were immediately sold when it came into the hands of the crown :—

> Accont of John Conway Esq[101] late keeper of the same Woode Aswell of and for all suche woodes and underwoodes there by hym solde By the vertue of ij severall warrauntes beneth specified to hym in that bihalf directed Anno Regni Regis Hen. 8 328 and also for certeyne lodes of wood in the same yere delyued forthe of the said wood to the kinges Ma[ies] use, as of all and all mano[r] of paym[ts] costes and expences by the foresaid John Conway had made paid and employed the foresaid xxxii[d] yere in and about the making carryage and fensyng. And also for the making of new gates w[thin] the said wood As hereafter pertyclarly within the same accompt more playnely aperithe
>
> 50 lodes of polewood and talwood to the Earl of Sussex by warrant of 14 July 2/2 a lode   108/4
>
> 298 lodes of underwood called bushe baven[102] sold to divers persons 14d. a lode under warrant of 19 July   £17 7s. 8d.
>
> 50 lodes of like bushe baven sold to Geffrey P'st of Westminster by warrant above at 13¾d. a lode lesse in the holl 2½d.   57s. 6d.
>
> Of £30 2s. 4d. comyng and rysinge of and for the price of 278 lodes of pole wood and talwood fallen and cut downe within the saide wood not receyved for that the said 278 lodes were delyured forthe of the said wood to the keper of the palice of Westmynster, to the kinges Heignes use as the foresaid John Conway sayethe.
>
> Sum of the lodes sold 398   Talwood 50
> of the money £25 8s. 6d.   and Baven 348

At the foot of the account Conway desired to be allowed £9 4s. 8d. for the making up all this wood into 554 loads at 4d. a load ; stating that he also found additional 722 loads 'made and there lying before the dissoluetion of the said late priorye.' He further asked payment of £11 11s. 8d. for the carriage of 278 loads of wood to the palace of Westminster at 10d. a load ; £2 18s. 11d. for making and fencing 527 perches of new hedge in and about the said wood for the protection

[99] White, *Hampstead and its Associations*, 27.
[100] Walford, *Old and New Lond.* v, 248.   [101] Exch. Acct. R. bdle. 148, No. 32.
[102] A baven was a faggot of brushwood bound with a single withe.

of the 'sprynge'[103] there ; 7s. for repairing and making of three gates in the fence of the wood ; and £3 in the name of his fee for the keeping of the wood for a year and a half.

The various warrants to John Conway, authorizing sales to Lady Sussex and others during his time of keepership, are also extant.[104]

In June, 1542, Sir Henry Knyvett, gentleman of the Privy Chamber, was appointed keeper of the wood 'called Seynt Johns Woode beside the parish of St. Giles in the Feilds near London.'[105]

Sad as has been the loss of woods and timber owing to the waves of population that have swept over so much of this district, it is permissible to rejoice not only in the preservation of the heath itself, and many a clump of ancient elms or blossoming chestnuts, but also in the fact that there has been of late years such a judicious expenditure on tree-planting by local authorities in roads and elsewhere. As long ago as 1888 the following trees, mostly of new planting, were under the care of the then vestry authorities : 987 limes, 557 planes, 285 elms, 161 sycamores, 155 chestnuts, 66 poplars, 27 ash trees, 16 wych-elms, 4 beech trees, and from one to three specimens of ailantus, acacia, maple, oak, willow and birch, a solitary pear-tree, a yew tree, and a mountain ash ; making a total of 2,273 trees.[106] Since that date, the amount of public planting has proceeded apace under the County Council.

Parliament Hill and Fields, consisting of 267¼ acres, adjoin Hampstead Heath, and are now included in that great open space ; they were acquired for the public in 1889.

Waterlow Park, 26 acres, on the southern slope of Highgate Hill, was presented to the council for use as a public park by Sir Sydney Waterlow in 1889. The park is rugged in contour, and well timbered with old cedars and various forest trees.

At Highgate there is still a tract of pleasant woodland, termed Highgate Woods, extending over about 150 acres, and divided into two parts by the Muswell Hill road. The eastern portion, of about 55 acres, which used to be known as Churchyard Bottom Wood, was opened to the public by the Duchess of Albany in 1898, and renamed Queen's Wood. Down the steep side of the hill leading to the Lea valley there are dense thickets of hazel and other underwood, whilst small poplars, ashes, alders, and hornbeams rise in places above the tangle. The western half, 96 acres in extent, known as Gravel Pit Wood, was presented in 1886 by the Ecclesiastical Commissioners to the Common Council of the City of London for the use of the public. The trees are larger than in the other section, and include a curious avenue of pollarded hornbeams.

The grounds in the centre of Lincoln's Inn Fields were secured by the London County Council in 1894 for the sum of £12,000. They are well wooded, and possess some unusually fine plane trees.

Clissold Park, Stoke Newington, 54½ acres, was acquired for the public from the Ecclesiastical Commissioners at a cost of over £90,000 ;

[103] i.e. new shoots springing up from the old stools.
[105] Aug. Bks. ccxxxv, fol. 68b.
[104] Exch. Accts. K.R. bdle. 148, No. 33.
[106] Baines, *Rec. of Hampstead*, 110.

it was opened in 1889. It contains a wealth of well-arranged trees, both ancient and modern. There is also a small deer inclosure.

Finsbury Park, 115 acres, which was opened to the public in 1869, lies on the south-east side of the parish of Hornsey. It is well-wooded in parts, and includes a portion of the site of old Hornsey Wood. Hornsey Wood was within the ancient deer park of Hornsey that belonged to the bishops of London.

One of the latest additions to London's parks, acquired by the County Council, is Springfield Park, Clapton, 32½ acres, which was purchased in 1904 for £37,237. The ground is very finely timbered, and overlooks the River Lea.

Wormwood (formerly Wormholt) Scrubbs, in the north-west suburbs of London, is a common of 193 acres, purchased by the War Office and transferred to the Metropolitan Board of Works in 1879, reserving a certain part for military purposes when required. A belt of trees now marks the division between the military ground and that to which the public have the exclusive right. Its former bare appearance has of late years been greatly improved by the planting of many hundreds of trees.

Ravenscourt Park, 32½ acres, at the western end of Hammersmith, was acquired for the public in 1887; its principal feature is a noble avenue of stately elms.

The grounds of Fulham Palace first became famous in the time of Bishop Grindal (1559–70), who was a great gardener. According to Fuller, the tamarisk was brought into this country by the bishop about 1560 :—

> It was brought over by Bishop Grindal out of Switzerland (where *he was in exile* under Queen Mary) and planted in his garden at Fulham, where the scite being moist and fenny well complied with the nature of this plant, which since is removed and thriveth well in many other places yet it groweth not up to be timber, as in Arabia, though often to that substance that cups of great size are made thereof.[107]

To Bishop Aylmer belongs the discredit of destroying a great number of elms in the Fulham grounds. It is stated by Aubrey that ' the bishop of London did cutt downe a noble crowd of trees at Fulham. The Lord Chancellor told him that he was a good expounder of darke places.'[108] An information was laid against him for cutting down timber that belonged to the see, and he was restrained from doing so by order of the council; the information was laid by one Litchfield, a court musician, whom the bishop had annoyed by refusing to give him twenty timber trees. Strype, however, defends the bishop against the charge of any considerable felling of the elms about the palace. There seems to have been a certain amount of clearing after a visit from Elizabeth, as the queen complained that her lodgings there were kept from all good prospects by the thickness of the trees.[109]

The grounds of Fulham attained to great and deserved celebrity in the days of Bishop Compton, (1675–1713) ; there was probably at that

---

[107] Fuller, *Worthies*, 35.
[108] Aubrey, *Brief Lives*, i, 74
[109] Feret, *Fulham Old and New*, iii, 129.

period no other place in England where so much attention was paid to arboriculture. Evelyn in his diary, under date 11 October, 1681, writes : 'I went to Fulham to visit the Bishop of London in whose garden I saw the *Sedum arborescens* in flower, which was exceedingly beautiful.'[110] Compton took infinite pains to obtain hardy exotic trees from North America ; he was the first to introduce American maples, acacias, magnolias, hickories, and other trees into English gardens and plantations. Ray, the distinguished naturalist, visited the Fulham grounds in 1687, and set forth a long Latin list of tulip trees and other rarities which were then flourishing.[111]

Compton's successor, Bishop Robinson (1713–23), did not share his tastes, and to his disgrace permitted his gardener to make merchandise of whatever trees and shrubs would bear transplanting.[112] Fortunately, however, many of the earlier planted trees were far too well rooted to be removed. In 1751 that great botanist, Sir William Watson, visited Fulham, and reported to the Royal Society on the remnants of Bishop Compton's work. A catalogue of the exotic trees then remaining was drawn up, which included the silver fir, the Norway maple, the cedar of Lebanon, the Virginia cedar, the red horse-chestnut, the Virginia sumach, the arbutus, and a variety of flowering maples and evergreen oaks ; many of them were considered to be the largest of their kind then growing in Europe.[113]

Daniel Lysons made another careful survey of the trees in the Fulham grounds in 1793, when he found eleven trees that had been planted by Bishop Compton still flourishing. An ash-leaf maple, planted in 1688, to the west of the house, had a girth of 6 ft. 4 in., and a height of 45 ft. ; the black walnut tree on the east lawn, 'a most magnificent tree,' had a girth of 11 ft. 2 in., and a height of 70 ft. ; the cluster pine, in the nuns' walk, 10 ft. girth, and 80 ft. height ; and the cork tree on the south lawn, 10 ft. 10 in. girth, and 45 ft. height. The other trees were two three-thorned acacias, an ilex, a white oak, a scarlet-flowered maple, an upright cypress, and a Virginia red cedar. Lysons also noted a cedar planted in 1683, and an avenue of limes near the porter's lodge, which were probably planted by Compton about 1688.[114]

Most of the veterans mentioned in the lists of Watson and Lysons have disappeared. The white oak perished in a gale in 1877 ; and a large part of the black walnut was blown down in 1881. Bishops Blomfield, Tait, and Jackson all took much interest in the grounds, and planted a variety of exotic trees. In Mr. Feret's pages there is a full account of the more recent plantings, and of the present condition of the older and larger trees. The trees with the greatest girth at a height of 3 ft. from the ground are a common elm, 19 ft. 8 in. ; a black walnut, 17 ft. 3 in. ; a plane tree, 16 ft. 10 in. ; and a beech, 13 ft. 10 in. All that now exists of the trees of Compton's planting appear to be the

---

[110] Evelyn, *Diary and Corresp.* ii, 159.
[112] Lysons, *Environs of Lond.* ii, 349.
[114] Lysons, *Environs of Lond.* ii, 351–2.
[111] Ray, *Historia Plantarum*, ii, 1798.
[113] *Philosophical Trans.* xlvii, 241.

battered remnants of the cork tree in the angle where the Tait chapel joins the south block, and of the black walnut on the lawn at the east front of the palace.[115] In the Warren, the name of a large grazing field to the north of the palace, are several fine old elm and walnut trees. Bishop Porteus (1787–1809) described the Warren as 'surrounded by a magnificent belt of lofty elms.' The palace grounds have been considerably curtailed by the formation of a small public park on the river side. The idea of giving this strip of land to the public was carried out by Bishop Temple, but it originated with his predecessor.

Leaving the suburbs of London, some attention must be paid to the parks in other parts of Middlesex. The most important of these is Hampton Court, with the adjunct of Bushey Park. In early days Hampton was an open tract forming part of the famous Hounslow Heath. Some of the thorns in Bushey Park, and a few of the magnificent old oaks in the Home Park, were probably remnants of the district in its original state. In the thirteenth century the manor of Hampton Court was purchased by the Knights Hospitallers. Cardinal Wolsey obtained a ninety-nine years' lease of it from the Order, at a rental of £50, in 1514. On the fall of Wolsey in 1530, Hampton Court was taken possession of by Henry VIII, and speedily became one of his favourite residences. Here he was able to indulge to the full in his passionate attachment to hunting, hawking, shooting, and other outdoor sports. On coming into possession Henry found his property consisted of two main divisions, that now called Bushey Park, and the Home Park, which were separated by the Kingston Road. The king or Wolsey partly inclosed these parks by brick walls. These inclosures, though affording every facility for shooting and coursing, were not of sufficient size to serve for deer hunting. Thereupon the king proceeded to acquire by purchase or exchange all the manors adjacent to Hampton Court, on both sides of the Thames, and by an Act of Parliament of 1539 united them into an honour, that is a seigneury of several manors held under one baron or lord paramount, and 'the King shall have therein a chase and free chase and warren, for all beasts of venery and fowls of warren which shall be called Hampton Court Chase.'[116] This new chase of Hampton lay on the Surrey side of the river, and included East and West Moulsey, Walton, Esher, Weybridge, and part of Cobham. It was inclosed within a high wooden fence, and well supplied with deer. On the accession of Edward VI local complaints of damage by the deer came to a head, the pales and deer were removed, and the shortlived chase came to an end.

A Commonwealth survey of Hampton, in 1652, shows that by that time the Home Park had been divided into two parts, known respectively as the House Park and Hampton Court Course, which were distinct from the part now known as Bushey Park, then divided into the Hare Warren, the Middle Park and Bushey Park. The grounds and parks were much

---

[115] Feret, *Fulham Old and New* (1900), iii, 134–7.
[116] Statutes at large, 31 Hen. VIII, cap. v.

FORESTRY

appreciated by Oliver Cromwell. Soon after the Restoration Charles II not only put the gardens into thorough order, but laid out the Home Park in its present form, planting the great avenues of lime trees that radiated from the centre of the east front of the palace. William and Mary effected many changes in the planting of this park.[117]

Bushey Park has an area of 994 acres, exclusive of the stud paddocks of an additional hundred acres. These paddocks are divided from the park proper by a brick wall, but are in reality a part of Bushey Park; they are under the separate management of the 'Master of the Horse.' The herd of fallow deer has been recently much reduced, and now numbers about four hundred and fifty. In 1900 part of the Bushey herd was transferred to the Home Park, the average number there being about one hundred and fifty. The red deer of Bushey Park have averaged forty-five for the last few years.[118] Bushey Park has much noble timber, but is chiefly celebrated for its splendid avenue of chestnuts, which is 56 yds. wide, and a mile and 40 yds. long. The Home Park has an area of 752 acres, and is splendidly timbered in parts, many of the trees being fine specimens of limes.

The only other parks in Middlesex where deer are now to be found, besides those of Bushey and Hampton Court, and a few in the inclosure of Clissold Park, are Victoria Park and Grovelands, Southgate. In Victoria Park is a small herd of from eight to a dozen fallow deer, introduced in 1893 or 1894.[118a] Southgate takes its name from having been the southern entrance to Enfield Chase. Grovelands is the seat of Mr. J. V. Taylor; the well-planted park is 150 acres, whilst the park and adjoining woods are together 310 acres. The number of fallow deer is now about one hundred, nearly fifty were lost in the winter of 1905–6. They are not really an old herd, being the progeny of a pair given to Mr. Taylor's grandfather in 1840. There are many very finely grown oaks; including several that have girths, 3 ft. from the ground, varying from 15 ft. 10 in. to 14 ft. 7 in. One of them has a spread of branches of 105 ft. A remarkable feature of the woods on this estate is the fact that the common heather or ling grows luxuriantly, though never seen elsewhere in the neighbourhood; this seems to point to the land being part of the old waste.[119]

The largest oak in this district, known as the Minchenden oak, is at Arno's Grove, Southgate. It is said to have the widest spread of branches of any English oak. This oak, then termed the Chandos oak, is figured in Strutt's *Sylvia*, and also in Loudon's *Arboretum*. The latter gives the branch-spread as having a diameter of 118 ft., and the girth, one foot from the ground, as 18 ft. 3 in.[120]

Broomfield House, Southgate, was an old hunting-lodge used by James I; it is surrounded by park-like grounds of 80 acres.

[117] Law, *Hist. of Hampton Court*, 3 vols. *passim*.
[118] From information kindly supplied by Mr. Halliday, Park Superintendent, in Jan. 1907.
[118a] From information kindly supplied by the Park Superintendent.
[119] From information kindly supplied by Mr. Taylor.
[120] Loudon, *Arboretum*, iii, 1763.

At Enfield, opposite the parish church, are the remains of old Enfield House. In the grounds the fine historic cedar tree, one of the first planted in England, is still standing. It was planted by Dr. Robert Uvedale, a celebrated botanist, who was master of the Enfield Grammar School in the time of Charles II.

White Webbs Park, of about three hundred acres, on the borders of Hertfordshire, is beautiful and well-wooded, and retains traces of the ancient chase. Forty Hall has another park of about the like area, which contains many old forest trees, and is also part of the former extensive chase. Trent Park, on the western border of Enfield parish, is a third great tract of the ancient chase, preserved by being inclosed. It was given by George III to his favourite physician, Sir Richard Jebb. The park, which is undulating and well-wooded in parts, covers an area of about one thousand acres.

In the south-west of the county, near to Hampton, were the two adjacent hunting-parks of Hanworth and Kempton. The manor and park of the former were purchased by Henry VIII. Camden calls Hanworth a small royal seat ; Henry made it the scene of many of his sporting pleasures.[121] Towards the end of his reign Hanworth Park was settled in dower on Queen Katherine Parr, who frequently resided there after the king's death, with her second husband, Sir Thomas Seymour, and the young Princess Elizabeth.[122] Elizabeth, as queen, visited Hanworth in 1578, and again in September, 1600, when she hunted in the park.[123] Hanworth Park at the present day consists of 207 acres, and is extensively wooded.

Kempton Park, in Sunbury parish, on the Thames, was granted by Charles I in 1631 to Sir Robert Killigrew, vice-chamberlain to the queen. The manor and park of Kempton, as well as the manor and park of Hanworth, had been granted for eighty years without rent to Sir Robert's father by Queen Elizabeth. In consideration of the expense which the petitioner had bestowed in maintaining the game in Kempton Park, he prayed for a grant in fee of the said manor and park at a rent of £18 1s. 0½d. The prayer was granted, on the expiration of Queen Elizabeth's lease, at the rental named, provided that he maintained ' the park stocked with 300 deer for his Majesty's disport.'[124] There were deer in Kempton Park up to about 1835.[125] The park comprises about 500 acres, 300 of which are now leased to the Kempton Park Race-Course Company.

Other private parks of Middlesex which are noteworthy and more or less well-timbered, are Osterley park, 500 acres ; Bentley Priory, 250 acres ; Wrotham Park, 286 acres ; Gunnersbury Park, 100 acres ; Harefield Place, 60 acres ; and Ruislip Park, 40 acres. Twickenham Park was sold in lots in 1805.[126]

---

[121] Camden, *Britannia* (ed. Gough), ii, 2. [122] Lysons, *Midd. Parishes*, 94.
[123] Nichols, *Queen Elizabeth's Progresses*, iii, 513–14.
[124] S.P. Dom. Chas. I, cc, 30 ; ccii, 29.
[125] Shirley, *Deer Parks*, 56.
[126] Lysons, *Environs of Lond.* ii, 775.

FORESTRY

The Board of Agriculture in 1793 brought out a report on the agricultural condition of Middlesex.[127] Reference is made to the inclosure of Enfield Chase in 1779, and it is stated that from two to three thousand acres still remained 'unimproved.'

> In regard to Enfield Chase it is to be observed that though the cottagers are much in want of small fields of inclosed land, yet so much attached are they to their idle system of keeping a few half starved cattle on the chase, often to the ruin of themselves and their families, without the smallest advantage accruing to the public, that they constantly oppose any inclosure.

In the following year a further report was put forth by the Board, edited by Peter Foot, a land surveyor, containing various additional particulars. An interesting section relative to fruit trees shows how considerable was the culture of 'peaches, nectarines, apricots, vines, apples, cherries, pears, plums, quince, medlars and filberts,' by the nurserymen round London. As to vines, the gardener of Mr. John James of Hammersmith, in 1778, made a quantity of good wine from English-grown grapes. Shortly afterwards he made wine from his well-trained vines in the proportion of 100 gallons to 100 yards of wall. Mr. Foot adds, 'I am persuaded that, from Hammersmith to Staines, vineyards might be made at little expense, if a small premium were given to adventurers and no tax laid upon them for some years.'

Mr. Foot sets out full and interesting particulars as to Enfield Chase and its inclosure. He describes the ground of the Chase as having been covered with trees; the oak found a ready sale, but the beech did not repay the woodman's labour. The grubbing up of the roots proved to be more costly than was expected. The result was that the ground, though rapidly cleared of its wood, lay for the most part in an uncultivated state for several years.

From Fulham to Staines the banks of the Thames are reported as profitably employed in the cultivation of the willow. Three distinct species are named, the *Salix vitallina* or yellow willow, the *Salix amygdalina* or almond-leaved willow, and the *Salix viminalis* or osier willow. The two last-named were chiefly used by basket and corn-sieve makers, and the first by nursery-men for binding packages of trees, shrubs, etc. Mr. Foot did not supply any special information as to the woodlands.

In 1797 the Board of Agriculture were responsible for the issue of a far more comprehensive work on Middlesex, based on the two earlier reports, a much extended second edition of which, consisting of a stout octavo volume of about seven hundred pages, appeared in 1807.[128] The sixth chapter deals with commons and inclosures. The great commons of that time were Hounslow Heath and Finchley Common, on the latter of which there were several thousands of pollarded oaks and hornbeams. In commenting on the common fields of Harrow and Pinner it is noted that oak and elm grew with equal health throughout the whole of

[127] Thomas Baird, *General View of the Agric. of the County of Midd.*
[128] John Middleton, land surveyor, *View of the Agric. of Midd.* (ed. 2, 1807).

this district. The elm abounded in the hedgerows, eight trees were numbered in twenty feet. As to Enfield Chase and parish there had been a further inclosure in 1803, not confined to the 1,500 acres of waste-land, but also embracing 2,746 acres of common fields, and 794 acres of marsh-land. For four years before this second inclosure the parish had annually cut down a considerable number of oaks in aid of the poor rates. The timber had been generally felled, except what Dr. Wilkinson had preserved (some 80 acres) in the neighbourhood of White Webbs.

The tenth chapter discusses ' copses, woods, plantations, hedgerows and osiers.' Mr. Middleton states that the copses and woods of Middle-sex had been decreasing for ages, and expected that in a few centuries more they would be annihilated. He mentions, however, some acres thus occupied on the northern slopes of Hampstead and Highgate hills ; 100 acres on the east side of Finchley Common ; and 2,000 acres on the north-west side of Ruislip. The hills about Copthall and Hornsey were then appropriated to the scythe, though a few years before they were covered with wood. Mr. Middleton was by no means distressed at the disappearance of woodland, for he regarded the woods and copses of Middlesex as ' nurseries for thieves,' and also ' the occasion of many mur-ders and robberies.' He was also strongly of opinion, emphasizing the statement by the use of italics, that ' every acre of this county ought to be appropriated to the production of more valuable crops than timber and underwood.' It was his opinion in 1807 that there was only an area in Middlesex of 3,000 acres bearing copse, plantation, or forest timber.

Just a century has elapsed since the issue of this singular report, so adverse to any form of woodland, by the then Board of Agriculture. Better opinions happily now prevail.

The attention given to arboriculture during the last quarter of a century has resulted in a gratifying and steadily growing increase in the woodlands of England and Wales. Notwithstanding the great growth of population, and, therefore, of the building area of Middlesex, it is as pleasant as it is surprising that this small county well maintains its share in this advance in proportion to its size. In Middlesex the total acreage of woods and plantations in 1888 was 2,545 acres ; in 1891 it had grown to 3,036 ; and in 1895 to 3,656. The detailed returns made up to 5 June 1905, show a steady rise in the last decade, for the total acreage of woods was then 3,968. This total is usefully divided into coppice, 1,590 acres (by which term is meant woods cut periodically and repro-ducing themselves by stool shoots) ; plantations, 98 acres, covering lands planted or replanted within the last ten years ; and other woods 2,280 acres.

Nor does this growth of 1,000 acres of pure woodlands in a century by any means exhaust the marvellous improvement effected in Middlesex in the way of tree-culture.

So far as the growth of timber, both forest and ornamental, is con-cerned, apart from that which is included in woodland returns, the improve-

FORESTRY

ment immediately round London is more marked and decided than in any other part of the kingdom. By far the greater portion of this improvement is due to the continuous and spirited action of the London County Council. Under the rule of the Council, since its first formation in 1889, the public parks and open spaces of London, all more or less well-timbered, have grown, in round numbers, from 2,500 to 5,000 acres. Of this total, 2,746¼ acres are in Middlesex. And in addition to all this there has of late years been a vast amount of tree planting and tree tending accomplished in streets and roads and by the side of the highway. For every tree standing in Middlesex in 1807 there are probably at least three in 1907.

SPORT ANCIENT AND MODERN

INTRODUCTION

THOUGH Middlesex still occupies a prominent position with respect to pastimes such as rowing, cricket, football, polo, tennis, and archery — the last-named three of which originated in it—the higher forms of sport formerly pursued in the county may be said to have now become, practically, subjects of archaeological interest.

As in other counties, the pursuit of 'the nobler beasts of venery, such as the stag, the wolf, and the boar,' which, to quote a well-known writer of the last century, 'gradually faded away upon the increase of population and the advancement of agriculture,'[1] was for a time replaced by 'the noble science' of fox-hunting, which was introduced into Middlesex very soon after its first adoption as a popular form of sport in England. The increase of population and the advancement of agriculture were both, however, from the first materially accelerated by the fact that Middlesex is not only the smallest county in England, except Rutland, but also the original seat of the English capital, and, owing to the recent rapid expansion within its limits of the largest city in the world, both fox-hunting and covert shooting have now shared the fate of the older forms of the chase. At the beginning of the nineteenth century Middlesex was a purely agricultural county.[2] In 1801 it was possible to walk from Hadley through Enfield Chase, Epping and Hainault Forests without leaving the turf or losing sight of forest scenery ; and, in addition to a wide extent of pasture land which rendered

it eminently suitable for a hunting country,[3] the county comprised Hounslow Heath and Finchley Common ; Harrow Weald Common and eight other commons in the parish of Harrow ; Uxbridge Moor and five other commons in the parishes of Uxbridge and Hillingdon ; Ruislip, Sunbury, and Hanwell Commons, and Wormwood Scrubbs.[4] In the present year of grace Hadley Woods, Hadley Common, and the 'Rough Lot' in Trent Park are the only remains of Enfield Chase, and such of the few commons as remain have been reduced to insignificant dimensions. At the census of 1901 the population, which in 1801 was only 70,000, had increased to 798,736, or over eleven-fold during the century, the increase during the last decade being 45·8 per cent. ;[5] and of the total extent of 149,668 statute acres within the county 88,105 acres are comprised in urban districts.[6] Of the twelve principal estates within the rural districts there is only one of 1,000 acres—Trent Park, belonging to Mr. A. F. Benson—and one of 500 acres —Osterley Park, belonging to the Earl of Jersey ; while of the remaining ten, eight are between 100 and 300 acres, and the other two are under 100 acres in extent. Covert shooting has thus ceased to be of any practical

---

[1] Scrutator, Horses and Hounds (ed. 1858), 63.

[2] Cf. Lysons, Environs of London (1792) ; J. A. Cooke, Topographical and Statistical Survey of the County of Middlesex (1819) ; and Brayley, London and Middlesex (1810), passim.

[3] Cf. Hon. G. C. Grantley Berkeley, Reminiscences of a Huntsman (ed. 1895), 49–50 ; and 'Brooksby,' The Hunting Counties of England (1878), 115. Though the first edition of Mr. Grantley Berkeley's book was published in 1854, cultivation had then considerably increased and the expansion of London had begun.

[4] Topographical and Statistical Description of Middlesex, 101.

[5] Census for Middlesex, 1901. Accts. and P. 1902, cxx (ed. 1211), i, ii.

[6] Ibid.

importance,[7] and though a small fringe of country on its northern border is still occasionally hunted from adjacent counties, Middlesex no longer possesses any hunt of its own. It was, however, not till the middle of the last century that these inevitable results of the growth of London began to make themselves seriously felt; and, owing probably to the fact that Middlesex has never possessed any towns of importance, its woodlands, commons, and pastures continued for many centuries prior to that date to afford to its inhabitants ample facilities for sport.

It is stated by Fitz Stephen, a monk of Canterbury, who in the reign of Henry II wrote a description of London and its environs,[8] that 'many citizens do take delight in birds, as sparrow-hawks, gos-hawks, &c., and in dogs to sport in the woody coverts, for they were privileged to hunt in *Middlesex*, in Hertfordshire, in all the Chilterns, and in Kent as low down as Crag Water'; and also that beyond the open meadows and pasture lands on the north side of the city was a great forest 'in whose woody coverts lurked the stag, the hind, the wild boar, and the bull.'[9] These animals were hunted with hounds on horseback or stalked on foot, and shot with the bow, but the term 'hunting' also included coursing with greyhounds and hawking.[10]

The citizens of London appear to have possessed this privilege from the earliest times, for, in a charter obtained from him early in the twelfth century, Henry I grants 'to my citizens of London to hold Middlesex to farm for three hundred pounds upon accompt to them and their heirs,' and that they 'may have their chases to hunt *as well and truly as their ancestors have had*, that is to say in Chiltre, *in Middlesex*, and in Surrey.'[11] This charter was confirmed by that of Henry II, granted probably some twenty years[12] later; by the first charter of Richard I, dated 23 April 1194;[13] the first charter of King John,

dated 17 June 1199;[14] and by the fourth charter of Henry III, dated 16 May 1227, which expressly states that 'we do grant them that they may have hunting wheresoever they had in the time of King Henry our grandfather and King Henry our great-grandfather.'[15] In the same year Henry III still further augmented these rights of hunting by a charter of 18 August granting 'to all men in the county of Middlesex that the Warren of Stanes shall be no more a warren [dewarrenata], and shall be disafforested'[16]— a concession which, while throwing open the warren for purposes of agriculture to such as were disposed to 'cultivate their lands and assart their woods therein,' provided a new hunting ground for the public, who had the right of hunting animals *ferae naturae* in all uninclosed lands except those subject to the forest laws or to some restriction upon hunting arising from a royal grant.[17]

There is no evidence with respect to the extent of the Warren of Staines, but as a grant of 11 Henry III to the prior and brethren of St. John of Jerusalem, apparently made just before it was disafforested,[18] shows that it included the manor of Hampton, and as Hampton itself then formed part of Hounslow Heath,[19] it must have comprised the greater portion of the south-western extremity of Middlesex.

Though styled a 'warren' it differed from ordinary warrens in being subject to the forest laws—a fact which would seem to imply that it must have contained '*beasts of forest*'—the red and the fallow deer, the roe, and the wild boar—in addition to '*beasts and fowls of warren*'—the hare, the coney, the fox, the pheasant, and the partridge—and that it must practically therefore have been a forest.[20] The

[14] Ibid. 12.

[15] *Historical Charters of the City of London;* cf. *Cal. Chart. R.* i, 24.

[16] *Cal. Chart. R.* i, 56, and cf. ii, 477.

[17] Turner, *Select Pleas of the Forest* (Selden Soc.), cxxiii.

[18] *Cal. Chart. R.* i, 30. The charter granted the order leave 'to keep their dogs unlawed in their House in Hamtonet in the King's Warren of Stanes,' for guarding the house 'in which the Sisters of the said Order do dwell,' and also for guarding their sheep-folds.

[19] Ernest Law, *The History of Hampton Court Palace* (2nd ed. 1890), i, 415.

[20] *Select Pleas of the Forest,* x, cxiv, cxxviii, cxxix. Cf. John Manwood, *Treatise of the Lawes of the Forest,* 1615, where the author makes a distinction between 'beasts of forest' and 'beasts of chace' which, however, in Mr. Turner's opinion is not good in law (see *Select Pleas of the Forest,* cxiv). The roe ceased to be a beast of forest in the

[7] The number of persons employed as gamekeepers in the census of 1901 was 60.

[8] Stephanides, Descriptio nobili formae civitatis Londinii, first published in Stow's *Survey of London* (q.v.) (ed. Strype), ii, App. I, 9.

[9] Ibid. 9, 11, 12, 15.

[10] Strutt, *Sports and Pastimes* (ed. 1903), Introd.; Sir T. Elyot, *The Governour,* 104, 192; Cecil, *Records of the Chase,* 8, 12, 15.

[11] Birch, *Historical Charters and Constitutional Documents of the City of London.* The date of this charter is uncertain, but is placed by the author between 1100 and 1129.

[12] Ibid. Between 1138 and 1162.

[13] Ibid. 8.

'great forest' to the north of London mentioned in the description of the City by Fitz Stephen, alluded to above, probably extended as far as the royal forests of Essex on the east, and the woodlands of Herts and Bucks on the north and west; but it was not in the thirteenth century a forest in the strict legal sense of the term, which denoted a definite tract of land within which a particular body of law was enforced, having for its object the perservation of certain animals *ferae naturae*.[21] Though certain portions of these lands were from time to time aliened to subjects by various sovereigns, most of them were the property of the Crown, and it is stated by the learned editor of the *Select Pleas of the Forest* that, with the exception of the Warren of Staines, 'there was certainly no forest in Middlesex in the thirteenth, and probably none in the twelfth century.'[22]

There were numerous manors in Middlesex[23]—there were as many as six manors in the parish of Edmonton[24] and the same number in that of Enfield[25]—which during this period must have been well stocked with game. The lords of several of these manors enjoyed the right of free warren, the grant of which prohibited any person from entering the lands of the grantee, or hunting or taking any beasts or fowls of warren, 'without his licence or will,' though it did not entitle him to prevent other people from entering his warren in pursuit of deer.[26] It is curious to find among grants of this description—the right conveyed by which was not appurtenant to the land, and was usually limited by the king to the demesne lands of his subjects[27]—one made by Edward I in 1291 'to Richard Bishop of London and his successors of free warren in

all his lands of *Stebenhythe* (Stepney) and *Hackney*.'[28] Another made by Henry III on 22 March 1245 to Hamo Papelowe confers a similar right with respect to 'the demesne lands of the manors of Barve (Barron) in Suffolk and *Newton* (*Stoke Newington*) in Middlesex';[29] and after the change of ownership of the latter manor a fresh grant of free warren in it was made by Edward I on 10 May 1286 to the Order of St. John of Jerusalem.[30] Free warren in the manor of 'Acton under the wood,' the lesser of the two manors in Acton parish, was granted to the dean and chapter of St. Paul's by Edward II in 1316;[31] and the calendar of Charter Rolls contains similar grants in the manor of *Edelmeton* (*Edmonton*) to William de Say in 1245,[32] to Henry de Lacy, Earl of Lincoln, in the manors of *Eggeware* (*Edgware*) *Cowele* (*Cowley*) in 1294;[33] to Bartholomew Peche in the last-named manor and that of *Ikenham* (*Ickenham*) in 1252 ;[34] and in the same year to the Abbot of Bec in the manor of *Risselip* (*Ruislip*),[35] and James de Aldethelly in that of '*Halewyke*.'[36]

The confirmation, on 8 June 1280, of a charter of Henry III, granting to the Order of St. John of Jerusalem free warren in the demesne lands of the manor of Hampton[37] shows that the proprietary rights attaching to it remained unaffected by the disafforesting of the Warren of Staines. In the early part of the sixteenth century it was acquired by Cardinal Wolsey, who, after the completion of Hampton Court Palace, hunted there with Henry VIII;[38] and after the king had taken possession of it this part of the warren became a royal hunting preserve.

The manor, the boundaries of which were conterminous with those of the parish, was about 3,000 acres in extent, and originally consisted of the Home Park, lying to the east, and Bushey Park, lying to the north of the Kingston Road.[39]

Henry VIII, who was devoted to shooting, hawking, and all other kinds of sport, caused these two parks to be well stocked with deer and other game, and subdivided Bushey Park by brick walls into three equal divisions—the

---

fourteenth century owing to a decision in the Court of King's Bench, 13 Edw. III, which decided that it was a beast of warren on the ground that it drove away the other deer (*Select Pleas*, xxi).

[21] *Select Pleas*, ix.

[22] Ibid. viii.

[23] At Acton (two), Ealing, Edgware, Stanmore, Willesden, Neasden, Harlesden, East Twyford, Hanworth, Hampton, Twickenham, Uxbridge, Cowley, Ickenham, Ruislip, Staines, 'Halewyke,' Newington, Stepney, Hackney, Kempton, &c. Some of these are mentioned in Domesday Book.

[24] Lysons, *Environs of London*, 209.

[25] Ibid. and Ford, *Hist. of Enfield*, 70, 71, 92, 93. A conveyance of the manor of Worcesters in Enfield Parish (executed 4 July 1616) to Sir Nicholas Raynton shows that this manor contained 'ye piece of land called ye Warren and ye close or park called Little Park.'

[26] *Select Pleas of the Forest*, cxxiii, and cf. cxxviii and cxxix.

[27] Ibid. cxxv.

[28] 9 Edw. I, *Cal. Chart. R.* ii, 383.

[29] 27 Hen. III, *Cal. Chart. R.* i, 282.

[30] 14 Edw. I, *Cal. Chart. R.* ii, 337.

[31] Chart. R. 9 Edw. II, no. 31 ; cf. Lysons, *Environs of London*, 3.

[32] 22 Hen. III, *Cal. Chart. R.* i, 282.

[33] 22 Edw. I, *Cal. Chart. R.* ii, 436.

[34] 37 Hen. III, *Cal. Chart. R.* i, 409.

[35] Ibid.   [36] Ibid.

[37] 34 Hen. III, *Cal. Chart. R.* ii, 226.

[38] Law, *Hist. of Hampton Court*, i, 91.

[39] Ibid. 4, 5

Hare Warren on the east, the Upper Park on the west, and the Middle Park between them—and the Home Park into The Course, adjoining the Kingston Road, and the Home Park proper, which was bounded on the west and south by the Thames.[40] These inclosures, however, though well adapted for coursing or shooting, did not afford the king sufficient scope for his favourite sport of stag-hunting, and he therefore acquired by purchase or exchange the manors of Hanworth, Kempton, Feltham, and Teddington in Middlesex, together with those of East and West Molesey and some ten others on the Surrey side of the Thames,[41] and by an Act of Parliament passed in 1509[42] erected them into an honour or seignory of several manors under a single lord paramount. Of this honour it was provided that 'the manor of Hampton Court shall henceforth be the chief capital place or part.'[43] Its creation by statute gave it an importance and dignity superior to that attaching to an ordinary feudal manor,[44] and with the exception of a brief interval during the Interregnum it continued to be a favourite hunting seat of the Crown until the end of the eighteenth century.

Queen Elizabeth, who inherited her father's love of stag-hunting, frequently hunted at Hampton Court and shot the deer with her own bow.[45] James I, who was an equally ardent but more timorous sportsman, was a still more constant visitor, and shared the sport with his consort Anne of Denmark, who by a random shot on one occasion killed one of the king's favourite hounds—an accident which greatly excited his anger till he learnt who had caused it, when he is said to have immediately pardoned the royal offender.[46] He so improved the parks and stocked them so well with deer that a visit to Hampton Court came to be recognized as one of the duties of all travellers, and especially amongst foreigners of distinction.[47] Its reputation in this respect must, however, for a time have been somewhat impaired by the results of the Civil War, since in a Parliamentary Survey of 1653 that was made just before its sale, in

which the total area of the property irrespective of the ground occupied by the palace and gardens is stated as 1,607 acres, the number of deer is returned as 228, which were valued at £1 per head.[48] That it was not entirely denuded of game is, however, evident from an entry of 4 January 1657–8 in the Middlesex County Records with respect to a charge against John Hare, husbandman, Hugh Clerke, fisherman, and John Durdin, victualler of 'Tuddington,' of

taking and destroying seventy hares, with cordes and other instruments; nigh unto the hare warren of the Lord Protector within the Honour of Hampton Court in the said County.[49]

It was probably restocked after the Restoration, though neither Charles II nor his brother James seems to have been much addicted to the chase, and the absence of any references to the higher forms of sport in the diaries both of Pepys and Evelyn seems to justify the supposition that these were somewhat out of fashion during their reigns. After the Restoration, however, we find William III frequently pursuing his favourite pastime of coursing, then still called 'hunting,' at Hampton Court up to within a short period of his death; and on one occasion he writes to Portland that he had two days before 'taken a stag to forest with the Prince of Denmark's pack,' and 'had a pretty good run as far as this villainous country will permit.'[50] Queen Anne, who seems to have been as fond of hunting as she was of racing,[51] also constantly hunted there, following the chase, according to a description in Swift's journal to Stella, in a chaise with one horse 'which she drives herself and drives furiously like Jehu.' On another occasion she is said by the dean to have hunted the stag till four o'clock in the afternoon, and to have covered no less than forty miles in her chaise.[52] Both of her immediate successors fully maintained the traditions of the honour of Hampton Court, and George II was so fond of stag-hunting and coursing that he did not relinquish them even in summer, and it was only when the

---

[40] Law, *Hist. of Hampton Court*, i, 135, 212, and App. F. vii, 7.

[41] These included Walton, Weybridge, Esher, Oatlands, and Sandown; *Hist. of Hampton Court*, i, 212, 213.

[42] 31 Hen. VIII, cap. 5 (*Stat. of the Realm*, iii).

[43] Law, *Hist. of Hampton Court*, i, 212, 213.

[44] Ibid.

[45] Evelyn Shirley, *Some Account of English Deer Parks*, 40.

[46] Law, *Hist. of Hampton Court*, ii, 73, 74.

[47] Ibid. 62.

[48] Aug. Off. Parl. Surv. 32.

[49] *Midd. County Rec.* iii, 65.

[50] Law, *Hist. of Hampton Court*, iii, 103, 159, 160, 163.

[51] Cf. J. P. Hore, *Hist. of the Royal Buckhounds* (1893), 226, 249.

[52] Law, *Hist. of Hampton Court*, iii, 188. It must be added that the queen was obliged to adopt this mode of hunting by attacks of gout, and in her younger days followed the hounds on horseback; Hore, op. cit. 228.

palace ceased to be a royal residence that sport in the parks was finally abandoned.[53]

Somewhat similar, though of a less eventful character, is the history of another notable royal hunting domain which was of much greater extent than the honour of Hampton Court. Enfield Chase, one of the earliest references to which is in a record of 1236,[54] is stated by Camden to have been 'an extensive tract of land formerly covered with trees' and 'famous for deer hunting,' which had passed from the possession of the Mandevilles to the Bohuns and then to the Duchy of Lancaster.[55]

Queen Elizabeth, who for a time resided at Enfield House, hunted in Enfield Chase. That her subjects sometimes endeavoured to follow her example without her permission is shown by the conviction on 23 May 1574 of William Padye, 'gentleman,' of Hadley, and a 'husbandman' and a 'yeoman' of South Mimms for breaking into the Chase and killing 'unam damam'[56]; on 27 July of the same year Henry Lawrence of Hadley was found guilty of a similar offence.[57] The inclosure of 500 acres of the Chase in Theobalds Park was made by James I. That Theobalds continued, however, for some years after to be regarded as still part of the Chase is shown by a true bill returned 4 August 1845 against three yeomen of Enfield for

entering with bows and arrows and other apparatus for hunting, and without licence, the King's park . . . used for the preservation of deer and commonly called Theobalds Parke in Enfield

and 'killing and taking away two stags worth £5.'[58] Fond as he was of Theobalds, James I frequently hunted in Enfield Chase— as he is represented as doing in Sir Walter Scott's *Fortunes of Nigel*—and, as in the case of Hampton Court Honour, he took care that it should be abundantly stocked with deer.[59] In his reign we find Philip Hammond of London, 'gentleman,' charged on 6 March 1610 with 'shootynge in a piece on His Majesty's Chase,'[60] and in 1649, the year before the Parliamentary Survey, there are two

convictions, on 15 and 18 July, recorded for entering the Chase and killing deer 'with guns charged with gunpowder and bullets.'[61] The later history of the Chase cannot be narrated here, but some reference to it will be found in the article on Forestry.

In addition to the Chase in the north-eastern and the honour of Hampton in the south-eastern extremity of the county, Middlesex possessed an exceptional number of parks —inclosed tracts of land for the creation of which by a subject a licence, though unnecessary during the Plantagenet reigns, was always required under the Tudor and Stuart dynasties. The beasts *ferae naturae*, almost exclusively deer, contained in them were the private property of the owner. Some reference to the more important of these parks will be found elsewhere in these volumes; but it may be noted that they comprised Hyde Park, though there was probably little or no hunting in it after the Restoration, as we find Pepys and Evelyn both alluding to the park as famous for horse, and foot, and coach races.[62] That deer were maintained there during the seventeenth century is, however, evident from a report of the Surveyor-General of Woods to the Lords of the Treasury on 11 June 1695, with respect to repairs in Hyde Park costing £425 19s. 2½d., and £200 for hay for the deer and for the salaries of the under-keepers,[63] and there appear to have been still some remaining there in the early part of the nineteenth century.[64]

It is noteworthy, having regard to the number and extent of the royal preserves, that the cases dealing with 'breaking into and entering' mentioned in the Middlesex County Records, which extend from the accession of Queen Elizabeth to the Restoration, are so few; and also that, with the exception of an offence in 1576 at Osterley Park, the object of which seems to have been firewood rather than game,[65] they should all relate to royal parks. During the whole of this period there appear to be only two records with respect to similar offences in connexion with the property of private individuals. One of these is in 1569, when Mathew Vincent of Ickenham, 'not having lands, tenements or rents or service to value of 40s.,' is convicted of

[53] Law, *Hist. of Hampton Court*, iii, 220, 241; and cf. Lord Ribblesdale, *The Queen's Hounds and Stag-hunting Recollections*, 29, 30.

[54] Chart. R. 19 Edw. II, m. 16; Lysons, *Environs of Lond.* 280.

[55] Cf. W. Robinson, *Hist. and Antiq. of Enfield*, (1823), 175-6.

[56] *Midd. County Rec.* 1, 187.   [57] Ibid. 188.

[58] Ibid. iii, 93, 94.

[59] Robinson, *Hist. of Enfield*, 197; cf. Nichols, *Progresses of James I*, ii, 101.

[60] Ibid. ii, 62.

[61] Ibid. iii, 190, 191.

[62] *Memoirs and Diary of Samuel Pepys, F.R.S.* (ed. by Lord Braybrooke), i, 131; *Evelyn's Diary and Correspondence* (ed. 1902), i, 345; Henry B. Wheatley, *Lond. Past and Present*, ii, 250.

[63] *Cal. of Treasury Papers*, 1557-1696, xxiii, 447.

[64] Shirley, *Deer Parks*, 56.

[65] *Midd. Co. Rec.* i, 198.

' keeping and using dogs for coursing, nets, ferrets, and dogs for chasing by scent,' and, 'in company with others, breaking into the free warren of the earl of Darbie at Hillington, county Middlesex, and hunting the rabbits of the said earl.' [66] The other case, dated 29 December 1613, records the acceptance of recognizances of the total value of £60 from 'Alexander Cottrell of London, merchant taylor,' and two others for his appearance at the next sessions of the peace ' to answer for breaking into my Lord of London's grounds at Fulham within his moat nere his dwelling house there to kill and take his conies.' [67] It is rather curious that these two cases, and that with respect to Hampton Court during the Interregnum already mentioned,[68] are the only three that deal with rabbits in the whole series.

Not less notable is the entire absence of any cases relating to deer-stealing or poaching in the Middlesex County Records throughout the reigns of Charles II and his brother James. This may perhaps in a measure be accounted for by the very large number of cases with respect to treason, recusancy, and non-attendance at public worship that these records contain, which can have left the justices little leisure for dealing with offences of any other description. It is also, doubtless, partly due to the fact that—with the exception of 'the sons or heirs apparent of an esquire or other person of higher degree, and the owners or keepers of forests, parks, chases, or warrens, being stocked with deer or conies for their necessary use '—it was illegal for any person ' to have or keep for himself or any other person any guns, bows, greyhounds, setting dogs, ferrets, nets, gins, snares, or any other engines for the taking of game,' unless he was possessed of landed property of the clear yearly value of £100 a year, or leases for ninety-nine years or more of the clear yearly value of £150 a year.[69] At the close of the seventeenth century all the royal parks of Middlesex, with the exception of the two in Hampton Court Honour and Hyde Park, which had ceased to be used for hunting, had,

as has been shown, been disparked. During the next hundred years the bulk of the manors to which the right of free warren had attached began one by one to disappear before the advance of London, and in spite of the Game Laws, which continued in force till the reign of William IV, the area available for sport became gradually restricted to the northern portions of the county. Its impending disappearance in the first quarter of the nineteenth century is indicated by the *Reminiscences of a Huntsman* by the Hon. George Grantley Berkeley, who, with his brother Moreton, preserved the game at the family seat at Cranford during the years 1824–36. 'For the size of the covers and estate,' he says

no place had such a stock of pheasants and hares. It is but 1,000 acres in all, on the outside of which Brentford, Isleworth, Twickenham and indeed London furnished a certified set of marauders to destroy all living things that did not return home to our covers before 1 September. At break of day on 1 September for an hour there was a running fire, indeed,

' A squadron's charge each tenant's heart dismayed,
  On every cover fired a bold brigade.'

To remedy this evil, we drove the outskirts in so soon as the gathering of the corn would permit us ; and the 1 September I always went forth and began to bag every hare and partridge I could get near at break of day.[70]

According to a parliamentary return of the number of convictions under the Game Laws in separate counties of England and Wales for the year 1869 issued on 7 March 1870, which appears to be the last published on the subject, 131 out of a total of 10,335 were in Middlesex, as against 90 in Surrey, 260 in Kent, 302 in Herts, and 310 in Essex.[71] Of these 131 convictions, however, only four were for night poaching and the remaining 127 for trespassing in the day time in pursuit of game ; and this total must therefore presumably be regarded rather as a criterion of the number and audacity of the poaching fraternity in London and the suburbs than of the extent of preservation or the supply of game.

---

[66] *Midd. Co. Rec.* i, 67.
[67] Ibid. ii, 176. [68] *Ante.*
[69] 22 & 23 Chas. II, cap. 25 § 3. Cf. Stephen's *Commentaries*, iv, 577, and Thornhill's *Sporting Directory*, 131, where there is an elaborate examination of the meaning of the term ' esquire.'

[70] Hon. G. C. Grantley Berkeley, *Reminiscences of a Huntsman* (new ed. 1897), 11. The first edition was published in 1854.
[71] *Accounts and Papers* (1870), lvii, 105.

HUNTING

FOXHOUNDS

The only pack of foxhounds to which Middlesex can lay claim is the original Old Berkeley Hunt, which ceased to hunt the county more than half a century ago and is now divided into the Old Berkeley East and the Old Berkeley West, whose kennels are at Chorleywood in Hertfordshire and at Hazelmere Park, High Wycombe, respectively.

The original Old Berkeley Hunt was formed by Frederick Augustus, fifth Lord Berkeley, who adopted orange yellow or 'tawny' coats for it in commemoration of the fact—stated by Smith in his MS. history of the Berkeley family—that 'a former Lord Berkeley' kept thirty huntsmen in 'tawny coats' and his hounds at the village of Charing, now Charing Cross in the centre of London, and hunted in the vicinity.[1] It was not so called, however, till after Lord Berkeley's death in 1810, when this name was given to it in memory of its founder by Mr. Harvey Combe, who succeeded him as master, and for a similar reason retained the Berkeley livery.[2]

The country hunted by Lord Berkeley has probably never been exceeded in extent, though authorities differ as to its exact limits. 'Nimrod' in his *Hunting Tours*, written in 1835, says that it extended from Scratch Wood, seven miles from London and then part of Wormwood Scrubbs, to Cirencester, a distance of upwards of eighty miles; while 'Cecil,' writing in 1854, makes Scratch Wood five miles from London, and says that the Old Berkeley country extended to beyond Thornbury in Gloucestershire.[3] Mr. George Grantley Berkeley, whose *Reminiscences of a Huntsman* was also published in 1854, says that his father 'used to hunt all the country from Kensington Gardens to Berkeley Castle and Bristol,' and his opinion as regards Kensington appears to be confirmed by the statement made to him by old Tom Oldaker, Lord Berkeley's huntsman, that he had while with his father once 'found a fox in Scratch Wood and lost him in rough ground and cover in Kensington.'[4] There were kennels at Cranford and at Nettlebed near Henley on Thames, and another, Grantley Berkeley believed, at Gerrards Cross in Buckinghamshire. 'Where else the hounds used to put up in that wide stretch of country,' he adds, 'I know not, but I suppose occasionally at inns.'[5]

At the time 'Nimrod' wrote, the subscription to the Old Berkeley did not exceed £700 per annum, the remainder being made up by Mr. Harvey Combe and Mr. Marjoribanks. Six hunters and a hack were provided for a given annual sum by Mr. Tilbury for Henry and Robert Oldaker, the sons of Lord Berkeley's old huntsman, who were respectively huntsman and whipper-in to Mr. Harvey Combe, 'but they are never at a loss for a horse, for Mr. Harvey Combe always has a good stud.'[6] There seems to have been no very distinctive character in the Old Berkeley pack, owing to the fact that Tom Oldaker had not bred hounds for many years past but trusted to drafts to keep up his kennel—a defect which his son Henry did his best to remedy. The hounds were however

very steady . . . very true to the line and with a scent pretty sure of their fox . . . I saw [says Nimrod] no fault in the condition of the Old Berkeley hounds, taking into consideration the great extent of country they travel over, the frequent change of kennel, and the very wet weather to which they are exposed.[7]

The sale of this pack at Hyde Park Corner in 1842 is described by Mr. Robert Vyner in his *Notitia Venatica* as the 'most remarkable ever known.'

The lots sold were thirteen in number, making 127 hounds, exclusive of whelps; their produce was 6,511 guineas, or upwards of £100 per couple. It was Mr. Osbaldeston's old pack that realised this enormous sum. It had been sold conditionally some years earlier to Mr. Harvey Combe, and upon Mr. Combe's relinquishing the Old Berkeley country where these hounds had been hunting they were sent to Mr. Tattersall's to be sold by auction. Report says it was a fictitious sale; whether it was or not it gave employment to gentlemen of the long robe, there being some previous agreement between Mr. Osbaldeston and Mr. Combe relative to the price the hounds *might fetch* if sold at the time when Mr. Combe chose to part with them.[8]

[1] *Reminiscences of a Huntsman*, 25.
[2] Cecil, *Records of the Chase*, 32, 33; *Reminiscences of a Huntsman*, 25.
[3] *Records of the Chase*, 32, 33.
[4] *Reminiscences of a Huntsman*, 25, 26.
[5] Ibid.
[6] Nimrod, *Hunting Tours*, 125; cf. *Records of the Chase*, 53.   [7] Ibid. 197.
[8] Robert Vyner, *Notitia Venatica, a Treatise on Fox Hunting* (6th ed.), 22, 23.

As time went on the Old Berkeley were obliged, Brooksby tells us, to abstain from advertising their meets

in order to avoid the pressure of a swarm of nondescripts who, starting from every suburb in London, were glad to make a meet of foxhounds their excuse for a holiday on hackney or wagonette, overwhelming the whole procedure by their presence and irritating farmers and landowners, to the great injury of the hunt.[9]

At that time there was still in the Harrow district 'a small stretch of as good grass as is to be ridden over in England,' but it was yearly being narrowed by 'the advancing waste of bricks and mortar' and the increase in the value of land arising from the spread of London westward.[10] As in the case of Mr. Grantley Berkeley's staghounds, these conditions proved eventually fatal to the continuance of the Old Berkeley Hunt under its old conditions and resulted in its division into the two packs which still maintain its traditions in neighbouring counties.

STAGHOUNDS

The place of honour as regards antiquity among the staghounds of Middlesex must be assigned to the Lord Mayor's hounds, which may be regarded as a development of the ancient privileges with respect to hunting of the citizens of London which were confirmed by Henry I in the charter already referred to.[11]

It is evident from references to 'The Common Hunt,' or huntsman of the corporation, contained in the Liber Albus, that these hounds were a recognized institution in the fifteenth century, when John Courtenay was elected to the post;[12] and in later times, according to tradition, its meets were frequently held in Lincoln's Inn Fields, St. James's, and Mayfair.[13] According to an account given of the chief officers of the City by Maitland in his *History of London*, written in 1756, the chief business of the Common Hunt

is to take care of the Pack of Hounds belonging to the Mayor and Citizens, and to attend them in

Hunting when they please. This Officer's House allowed him is in Finsbury Fields. He has a yearly Allowance besides Perquisites. He is to attend the Lord Mayor on set days. This officer is Michael Lally, Esquire.[14]

It is interesting to compare this account with that given by Mr. Loftie of this official in 1891. In describing the City banquets he says :

Behind the Lord Mayor stands the 'Common Hunt,' an officer in a sporting costume with a jockey cap, all that is left of the old privileges of the citizens granted to them by Henry I to hunt in Middlesex and Surrey and as far away as the Chiltern Hills.[15]

In the reign of George I, 'riding on horseback and hunting with my Lord Mayor's hounds when the Common Hunt goes out' was, according to Strype, one of the favourite amusements of Londoners. At the close of this reign and for some years in the succeeding one the Common Hunt was Mr. Cruttenden, appointed to the office in September 1723. Among those who hunted with the pack was Sir Francis Child, who is described by Mr. Hore in his *History of the Royal Buckhounds* as 'fairly rivalling' in the hunting field Alderman Humphrey Parsons, the most notable of the metropolitan patrons of the Royal Hunt, whose reputation as an intrepid rider 'extended to every part of Europe wherever hunting men might chance to congregate.'[16] Sir Francis Child, as may be inferred from this description, also hunted sometimes with the Royal Buckhounds, and during the reigns of the first two Georges the Lord Mayor's hounds must have suffered in popularity from the predilection shown for the former by

merchant princes of the City, the lawyers, the doctors, the clergy, and the rich, though humble, bagman, mounted on the now obsolete 'nag' on which he travelled on business thoughts intent throughout the land.[17]

They were moreover gradually driven from Middlesex by the extension of London, and Epping Forest, formerly only occasionally

---

[9] Brooksby, *Hunting Counties of England*, 114, 115.
[10] Ibid. 115. [11] *Ante*, p. 254.
[12] Liber Albus, Bk. iv, 485.
[13] *Hunting* (Badminton Library), 17. The pack has been sometimes erroneously described as 'the Common Hunt,' of which the Lord Mayor was *ex officio* the master ; Ibid ; Lord Ribblesdale, *The Queen's Hounds and Staghunting Recollections*.

[14] Op. cit. 1027 ; cf. a similar account in Chamberlain's *Hist. and Surv. of the Cities of Lond. and Westm.* (written in 1770), 440.
[15] W. J. Loftie, *Lond. City*, 117.
[16] Op. cit. 264. Alderman Parsons was twice Lord Mayor of London.
[17] *Hist. of the Royal Buckhounds*, 264 ; cf. *The Queen's Hounds and Staghunting Recollections*, 29, 30.

visited, eventually became the only country hunted by them.[18]

In addition to the Lord Mayor's hounds, Middlesex has at different dates possessed two other packs of staghounds, both of which were formed by the enterprise of well-known sportsmen. One of these, the kennels of which were at Cranford, was formed in 1824 by the Hon. George Grantley Berkeley, who was for a time assisted by Mr. Wombwell. The hounds consisted of thirty couple, almost all bred at Berkeley Castle, and among them were two given to Mr. Grantley Berkeley by Mr. Villebois—Batchelor and Blunder—the portrait of the latter of which by Cooper appeared in the *New Sporting Magazine*.[18a] The deer were sent from Berkeley Castle and from Hampstead Lodge by Lord Craven, and at the close of the hunting season all that survived were sent back again to Berkeley Castle, where five months amongst their fellows undid the effects of artificial maintenance and restored their running. They were thus, in Mr. Grantley Berkeley's opinion, superior to the generality of those from the Royal kennels, which were from season to season kept in a paddock.[18b]

Mr. Berkeley's hounds hunted twice a week,[18c] the central portion of the country hunted being the Harrow Weald, and amongst those who regularly attended the meets were Lord Cardigan, Col. Thomas Wood and Col. Standen, both of the Guards, Mr. Smith of Hanwell, Mr. Peyton, Mr. Charles Tollemache, Col. Parker of the Life Guards, and Lord Alvanley.[19]

Owing to the proximity of London the runs were sometimes attended with amusing incidents, such as one in which the stag eventually headed for Hounslow, Isleworth, Twickenham, and Brentford. Of this run Lord Alvanley is said to have given the following description :

Devilish good run ; but the asparagus beds went awfully heavy and the grass all through was up to one's hocks ; the only thing wanted was a landing net, for the deer got into the Thames and Berkeley had not the means to get him ashore.[20]

On another occasion the stag was run to bay in Lady Mary Hussey's drawing-room at Hillingdon ; and on a third it entered the kitchen of a house, the wrathful owner of which said in reply to Grantley Berkeley's apologies :

Your stag, sir, not content with walking through every office has been here, sir, here in my drawing room, sir, whence he proceeded upstairs to the nursery, and damn me, sir, he's now in Mrs. ——'s boudoir.[21]

One of the oddest scenes, however, caused by the vagaries of the stag, occurred when, after entering London by Regent's Park, a fine one covered with foam and stained with blood, and followed by two couple of hounds, one morning ran up the steps of No. 1 Montague Street, Russell Square. The efforts of Grantley Berkeley to persuade two young ladies who were looking out of the window to allow the stag to enter the hall in order to ensure his capture were rudely interrupted by their father, who, to the amusement of the other members of the hunt and the large crowd that had assembled, told him that if he did not instantly take ' his animal away ' he would ' send for the beadle.' The stag was eventually captured by the aid of some friendly butcher boys.[22]

Mr. Grantley Berkeley maintained the sport for twelve years, but the difficulty of doing so was materially increased towards the close of this period by the number of men that hunted with him, the populous character of the country, and the opposition of the farmers, whose principal crop, hay, suffered considerably from the damage done by the hunt.[23]

Inclosure after inclosure went on, heath and common vanished, villas sprang up where gravel pits used to be . . . and babies cries were heard on sites that in my remembrance were only waked by the prettier whistle of the plover.[24]

The farmers refused to be pacified by

a dinner suggested by Messrs. Norton of Uxbridge, coursing to all who kept or could borrow greyhounds, and shooting, with presents of game and occasionally venison.

An action brought against him by a farmer named Barker, who was represented by Scarlett as counsel, ended, in spite of his defence by Brougham, in a verdict for the plaintiff for £100 damages ; and this, coupled with an offer at this time of the mastership of the Oakley Hunt, determined Mr. Grantley Berkeley to give up his pack in 1836.

[18] *The Queen's Hounds*, 29. An account of a run with the Lord Mayor's hounds is given in *The Sporting Magazine* for 1795. The hunt was ridiculed by Tom D'Urfey in his *Pills to purge Melancholy ;* but as late as 1822 we find the editor of *Bell's Life* writing that ' the cockney hunts are not to be laughed at or despised by clod-hopping squires who each thinks that he knows more about the thing than anyone else.' 21 April, 1822.

[18a] *Reminiscences of a Huntsman*, 26, 27, 30.

[18b] Ibid. 30, 48.   [18c] Ibid. 29.

[19] Ibid. 27, 28, 30, 44, 45.   [20] Ibid. 45, 46.

[21] Ibid. 57.   [22] Ibid. 46, 47.

[23] Ibid. 49, 50, 51.   [24] Ibid. 53.

In 1885 Col. Sir Alfred Plantagenet Frederick Charles Somerset, K.C.B., on relinquishing the mastership of the Hertford Foxhounds, started a pack of staghounds at Enfield, the kennels of which were at his seat of Enfield Court. In commemoration of the fact that the Enfield country had not been hunted since the days of Queen Elizabeth they were named the Enfield Chase Staghounds, and the dress adopted was that of the Elizabethan era —namely, a red coat with blue lapels and gold buttons, yellow vest and cap.

Sir Alfred Somerset retained the mastership till 1899, when he was obliged by ill-health to relinquish it. The kennels were then removed by his successor, Mr. Hartridge, to Barnet. On the retirement of Mr. Hartridge the increase of building led to their transfer to High Canons, near Shenley in Hertfordshire, the residence of the next master, Mr. W. Walker. In 1910 Mr. D. D. Bulger became master ; and hounds were kennelled at Pursley near Shenley. The hunt can therefore no longer be regarded as being in Middlesex, though a portion of the county—round Potters Bar and on to Enfield—is occasionally hunted.[25]

There are 23 couples of hounds. The hunting days are Tuesday and (usually) Saturday, the most convenient places for attending the meets being Hatfield, St. Albans, and Barnet. The master is also secretary of the hunt, the whipper-in of which is C. Strickland.

HARRIERS

In the last quarter of the last century Mr. Westbrooke of Cranford is stated by Mr. Grantley Berkeley to have kept by subscription a pack of harriers. His elder brother, the Hon. Moreton Berkeley, afterwards sixth Earl of Berkeley, acted as whipper-in, and on Mr. Westbrooke's resignation, the two brothers appear to have kept up this pack for a time. The country hunted comprised Hownslow Heath, Harlington Common, Hampton Common, and occasionally West End in the Harrow country.[27]

There is an allusion to a pack of harriers in a *History of Hampton* by Ripley, published in 1868, which had then ceased to exist, but no details are given as to the date either of its formation or dissolution.

Middlesex was formerly frequently, and is still occasionally, hunted by hunts belonging to the adjacent counties, such as the Hertfordshire, the Old Berkeley East, and the Royal Buckhounds.

Among the places indicated on a chart of the meets of the last-named hunt, contained in Lord Ribblesdale's *The Queen's Hounds*, are Uxbridge, Southall, Hayes, Cranford, and Bedfont, and he quotes a graphic description of a run given by Lord Colville in 1868, in which his late Majesty King Edward, then Prince of Wales, took part. On this occasion the stag ran from Denham Court, past Pinner, and straight over Harrow Hill into what are known as the Duck Paddle Fields, and thence to Wormwood Scrubbs. It was eventually taken at Paddington Goods Station and the hunt accompanied the Prince of Wales to Marlborough House, riding through Hyde Park and Constitution Hill in hunting dress.[28]

COURSING

It has been mentioned that Henry VIII when subdividing the Home Park and Bushey Park at Hampton converted portions of them into the course, 144 acres, and the hare warren, 380 acres in extent, and that he and several other sovereigns, and notably William III, with whom it was a favourite pastime, were greatly addicted to coursing, then called hunting.[26] In modern times the Home Park was used by two coursing societies, the Amicable and the Speltham, which were eventually amalgamated into the South of England Coursing Club.[29] The sport, which had considerably declined in 1899, has, however, now been abandoned, and the Home Park is occupied by a golf club.

[25] The writer is indebted for these particulars to the courtesy of Col. Sir A. P. Somerset, the founder, and Mr. W. Walker, master, in 1908, of the hunt.
[26] Aug. Off. Parl. Surv. 32. See *ante*, p. 256.

[27] *Reminiscences of a Huntsman*, 18.
[28] *The Queen's Hounds and Staghunting Recollections*, 147.
[29] *Coursing* (Badminton Library), 225.

SPORT ANCIENT AND MODERN

RACING

The earliest mention of racing in connexion with Middlesex is the statement of Fitz Stephen, in his description of London, that horses were then usually exposed for sale at Smithfield, and that the merits of hackneys and charging horses were generally tested by matching them against each other.[1] In the opinion of so high an authority as Nimrod, the monk of Canterbury gives 'a very animated description of the start and finish of a horse-race.'[1a] Such matches must have been common from the earliest times, for 'running horses' are mentioned as items of the royal expenditure as early as King John's reign and in those of the first four Edwards and of Henry VIII.[2]

Strutt tells us that in Elizabeth's reign races were called 'bell courses' because the prize was a silver bell. In proof that it was then pursued without any idea of gambling he quotes a Puritan writer of the period, who, while denouncing 'cards, dice, vain plays, interludes, and other idle pastimes,' speaks of horse-racing as 'yielding goodly exercise.'[3] But by the close of the seventeenth century we find Burton speaking of 'gentlemen galloping out of their fortunes by means of races.'[4] During the interval public race meetings were first established in the reign of James I, and one of the earliest of these was held at Theobalds in Enfield Chase, the prize being a golden bell, and it was not till after the Restoration, when the gambling referred to by Burton most probably had begun, that these bells were converted into cups.[5] In the following reign, horse-races were run in the Ring in Hyde Park;[6] but they appear from an allusion to them in *A Jovial Crew*, a comedy by Richard Broome, written in 1650,[7] to have been combined with foot-races, one of which Pepys witnessed in 1660,[8] and in the time of Cromwell and Charles II with coach races.[9] At the close of the next century we

also find a description of 'matches' and sweepstakes races in Hyde Park in the *Sporting Magazine* for 7 February 1796.

Queen Anne, whom Mr. Hore describes in his *History of the Royal Buckhounds* as being 'every inch a sportsman,'[9a] encouraged horse-racing[10] and ran horses in her own name;[11] and her husband, Prince George of Denmark, seems to have taken interest in the breeding of horses.[12]

One of the first acts of her reign was to expend £686 in fencing the meadows adjoining the barge walk in the Home Park at Hampton Court in order to preserve 'Her Majesty's studd there from being killed or drowned.'[13] The royal stud here alluded to, the paddocks of which lay, until its final dispersion a few years ago, behind the brick walls on either side of the road separating Bushey Park from the Home Park, had already existed in the reign of William III,[14] and its development during the reigns of Queen Anne and her successors may be said to be the most important event in the history of horse-racing in Middlesex.

The efficiency of the stud seems to have been fairly maintained throughout the first three reigns of the Hanoverian dynasty.[15] The Treasury Papers for 1724-5 contain the statement of the 'case of Richard Marshall, Esq., Studd Master, in regard to his allowance for keeping the Studd,' showing the terms on which he had kept it 'during the time of King William, the Prince of Denmark, Queen Anne, and his present Majesty (George I),' and the loss he had sustained since the grant by the House of Commons of the park and meadows to the Duke of Somerset 'by reason of the great quantity of hay' which he had been forced to buy instead of that which he had formerly obtained from the meadows.[16] He appears from this to have received eventu-

---

[1] Stow, *Surv. of Lond.* (ed. Strype), ii, App. I, 10, 13.

[1a] Nimrod, *The Turf*, 8.   [2] Ibid.

[3] Strutt, *Sports and Pastimes* (ed. 1903), 36.

[4] *Anatomy of Melancholy*, (Ed. 1893) ii, 174.

[5] Strutt, *Sports and Pastimes* (ed. 1903), 36.

[6] Ibid.

[7] *The Turf*, 11 ; *London Past and Present*, ii, 250.

[8] *Memoirs of Samuel Pepys* (ed. Lord Braybrooke), i, 131.

[9] Evelyn, *Diary* (ed. 1902), i, 345. Cf. *London Past and Present*, 250. Among the curiosities of racing in Middlesex is a swimming race between

two horses from Tyler's Ferry to the Bridge in Hackney Marsh on 13 August 1737, described in Robinson's *Hist. and Antiq. of Hackney*, the winner of which came in two lengths ahead.

[9a] J. P. Hore, *Hist. of the Royal Buckhounds*, 225.

[10] *Records of the Chase*, 26.

[11] Law, *Hist. of Hampton Ct.* iii, 334.

[12] Ibid.

[13] *Treas. Papers*, lxxx, 130, 6 July, 1702, and lxxxv, 89, 16 July, 1703; cf. Law, *Hist. of Hampton Ct.* iii, 172-3.

[14] Law, *Hist. of Hampton Ct.* iii, 334.

[15] Ibid. iii, 334, 335.

[16] *Cal. Treas. Papers*, cclii, 326, no. 29, 3 Mar. 1724-5.

ally a 'reasonable allowance' above 'the annual allowance of £184 10s. for each stallion, mare, and colt, and servant;' while a warrant of 2 July 1730 authorizes the passing of the accounts of Richard, Earl of Stafford, manager of the stud, the extraordinary expenses of which appear to have amounted to £10,000.[17]

The real founder of the royal stud, however, was George IV, who built the paddocks, and, while Prince of Wales, had already established a stud there for breeding riding-horses of pure blood. This was, however, sold on his accession to the throne, when the stables temporarily passed into the hands of the Duke of York, who kept a stud of his own there for breeding race-horses. On the sale of the stock of the latter at Tattersall's on his death in 1827, George IV retained possession of the paddocks for breeding his own race-horses. He devoted considerable sums to raising the royal stud to the highest state of efficiency and improving the stabling and paddocks. These, at the time of their abandonment, were forty-three in number, varying in size from three to five acres each,[18] seventeen being in the Home and twenty-six in Bushey Park. The king had as many as thirty-three brood mares, while particular regard was always paid, according to Nimrod, in the Hampton Court stud to what is termed 'stout blood'; and there were in his stables towards the end of his reign Waterloo out of a Trumpeter mare; Tranby out of an Orville; Ranter out of a Benninborough; and The Colonel out of a Delpini mare.[19] The Colonel won the Champagne Stakes at Doncaster in 1827. Two other good horses that the king owned were Fleur de Lis and Ziganee. Fleur de Lis won the Doncaster Cup in 1826, and the Goodwood Cup in two successive years—in 1829, carrying 9 st. 3 lb., and in 1830 when he had 6 lb. more.

William IV, who, though anxious to maintain and improve the stud, was absolutely ignorant of the subject, left its management entirely in the hands of Colonel Wemyss and his stud groom. It was supplemented during his reign by four Arabian stallions—two of which were presented to him by the king of Oude and two by the Imaum of Muscat—and by the following English stallions :—Actaeon by Scud out of Diana by Stamford, Cain by Paulowitz, and Rubric by St. Patrick out of Slight by Selim, the two latter being hired for the use of the stud. On King William's death in 1837 the entire stud, consisting of 43 brood mares, 5 stallions, and 31 foals, was sold under the hammer for 15,692 guineas—a proceeding much resented in sporting circles on account of the opportunity it afforded to foreigners of making valuable purchases of thoroughbred stock. The objectors, were, however, somewhat appeased by the giving of additional King's Plates. After an interval, during which Mr. Charles Greville and General, then Colonel, Peel—who enjoyed the privilege until he sold off all his stock except the stallion Orlando, winner of the Derby of 1844, were permitted to occupy the paddocks with their breeding stocks, her late Majesty, Queen Victoria, consented on the advice of the Prince Consort to the formation of the nucleus of the present royal stud in 1851. Mr. Greville was allowed to remain in part possession of the paddocks, while the queen's managers were Major Groves and Mr. Lewis, assisted by Mr. W. Goodman as veterinary surgeon.[20] In the days of George IV and William IV the yearlings in the royal stud were sold at Tattersall's on the Monday in Epsom week and generally realized an average of from £150 to £200.[21] During the reign of her late Majesty, Queen Victoria, these prices steadily rose. The sales of the queen's yearlings were held in the week after Ascot week in one of the paddocks in Bushey Park, and always attracted large numbers of gentlemen interested in horse-breeding and most of the celebrities of the racing world. The prices obtained indicate that the royal stud at Hampton Court has produced some of the most valuable race-horses in the world. In the sale of 1889 28 yearlings realized 11,745 guineas, an average of 430 guineas apiece, Sainfoin (by Springfield out of Landon), winner of the Derby of 1890, being sold for 550 guineas to Mr. John Porter, the Kingsclere trainer, while a bay colt by Hampton fetched 3,000 guineas. At the sale on 20 June 1890, 12 fillies and 8 colts were sold for a little over 14,000 guineas, an average of 700 guineas each, while the Duke of Westminster gave 1,350 guineas for a bay filly by Hampshire out of Gallantry; Lord Randolph Churchill gave 1,750 guineas for a bay colt by Springfield out of Lady Binks; and a sister of Memoir (winner of the Oaks and a Hampton Court yearling) was sold to Lord Marcus

---

[17] *Cal. of Treas. Books and Papers,* i, 323. See too another warrant as to the order of accounts (no. 502).
[18] Law, *Hist. of Hampton Ct.* 334–5.
[19] Nimrod, *The Turf* (ed. 1901), 17.

[20] Law, *Hist. of Hampton Ct.* iii, 335–6.
[21] Nimrod, *The Turf,* 16, 17. The author refers to a list of prices given in the June number of the *New Sporting Magazine* for 1886

Beresford, for Baron Hirsch, for 5,500 guineas, the largest price ever given for a yearling.[22]

The first race meeting under modern conditions held in Middlesex appears to be the Enfield Races, established in 1788, and held on the marshes at the bottom of Green Street, when two £50 plates were run for on 23 and 24 September.[23] There are notices of these meetings in the October numbers of the *Sporting Magazine* for 1794–5, and also in the September number for 1796, and one with respect to them is given as late as 1822 in *Bell's Life*,[24] when the date had been changed to 9 and 10 October. 'The company' is there described as being 'by no means so numerous or fashionable as we could have desired,' and this seems to have been almost the last of the meetings which, after several attempts to continue them, were eventually discontinued on account of the decline of local interest.[25] The second of these meetings (1 September 1790) is noteworthy on account of the arrest during the races of the notorious pickpocket, George Borough, who after undergoing seven years' transportation became chief of the police at Paramatta in Australia, and composed, for the opening of one of the Sydney theatres, the well known lines:

True patriots all, for, be it understood,
We left our country for our country's good.[26]

Among the meetings enumerated in Baily's *Turf Guide* for 1864 is one at Harrow, but this seems to be the only record of its existence. There appear to have been also races at Ealing, the course being a piece of rough common, now converted into an allotment ground. Ealing races are described in the *Annals of Ealing* as having been 'always of a simple character and anything but popular with the majority of the inhabitants.'

There are at present two race meetings held in Middlesex.

Of these the older and more important is that of Kempton Park, established in 1889, when the value of the Royal Stakes was £9,500.

The fixtures for 1910 are :—

Spring Meeting in March, one day; Jubilee Meeting in May, two days; First Summer Meeting in June, one day; Second Summer Meeting in August, two days; September Meeting, one day; and October Meeting, two days.

The winners of the most important race, the Kempton Jubilee Handicap, during the last eight years have been :

1902, Royal George .	4 yrs.	6 st.	9 lb.
1903, Ypsilanti . .	5 yrs.	8 st.	1 lb.
1904, Ypsilanti . .	6 yrs.	9 st.	5 lb.
1905, Ambition . .	4 yrs.	7 st.	1 lb.
1906, Donnetta . .	6 yrs.	8 st.	1 lb.
1907, Polar Star . .	3 yrs.	7 st.	12 lb.
1908, Hayden . .	4 yrs.	6 st.	12 lb.
1909, Ebor . . .	4 yrs.	7 st.	7 lb.

In 1910 the important Jubilee meeting was abandoned on account of the death of his late Majesty, King Edward VII.

The other is that at Alexandra Park, the first meeting at which was held on 30 June 1888. The meeting is now under the management of the Middlesex County Racing Club, which was established in 1897, and the Committee of Election and Stewards are Lord Alington, Captain J. G. R. Homfray, Lord Lurgan, and F. Luscombe, esq.

The fixtures for 1910 are :

April, two days; Saturday after Newmarket, 1 July; Saturday after Goodwood; Saturday after Doncaster, September; Saturday after Newmarket, 1 October.

POLO

Polo was initiated in England at a match played at Hounslow between the 10th Hussars, who introduced the game into the country from India, and the 9th Lancers. Middlesex therefore may claim the credit of having been mainly instrumental in bringing the game into notice, and the county has ever since maintained the leading position it thus acquired.[1]

The Polo Club was formed in 1872, and for the next two years all the important matches were played at Lillie Bridge, but in 1874 the area of play was transferred to Hurlingham.[2] The Hurlingham Polo Committee has ever since been accepted as the ruling authority with respect to the game,[3] and by its new rules the original size of polo grounds, which was 300 by 200 yds., has been altered to 300 by 160 yds.[4] After the establishment of the County Polo Association in 1901 and

[22] Law, *Hist. of Hampton Ct.* iii, 338–9.
[23] Robinson, *Hist. and Antiq. of Enfield*, 23–4.
[24] *Bell's Life*, 13 Oct. 1822.
[25] Robinson, *Hist. of Enfield*, 24; Ford, *Enfield*, 108.
[26] Ibid. Borough (whose real name was Waldron) was transported for stealing a gold watch belonging to Mr. Henry Hare Townsend of Bruce Castle.

[1] *Polo and Riding* (Badminton Library), 254–6.
[2] Ibid. 256.   [3] Ibid. 357.   [4] Ibid. 285.

of the Army Polo Committee in 1902 the Hurlingham Polo Committee was reconstituted on a more representative basis, and now includes three members from the County Polo Association, two from the Army Polo Committee, and one each from the Ranelagh and Roehampton Clubs.[5]

In 1886 a team sent by the Hurlingham Club won the cup offered by the American polo players for competition at Newport, U.S.A.[6]

Among the most notable players have been Captain F. Herbert, Mr. Kenyon Slaney, Mr. E. H. Baldock, Mr. Algernon Peyton, 11th Hussars, Mr. (now Captain) Wyndham-Quinn, 16th Lancers, Mr. W. Ince Anderson, Col. Duncombe and Mr. Miller ;[7] while Mr. J. R. and Mr. W. H. Walker are not only brilliant players but also breeders of polo ponies.[8]

The Wembley Park Polo Club, recently founded, is the only other club in Middlesex.

SHOOTING

As has been mentioned, shooting in Middlesex, owing to the absence of any large estates and the small amount of game preservation, is not of sufficient importance to require a detailed notice. An exception must, however, be made in the case of one form of this sport with respect to which the county, though not the originating centre, has long occupied a prominent position, namely, pigeon shooting.

In the early days of pigeon shooting, which came into vogue about 1790,[9] 'The Old Hatte,' at Ealing—an inn three centuries old—[10] appears to have been the chief rendezvous for the sport in Middlesex.[11] Its head quarters, however, till the middle of the last century, were at the Red House Club at Battersea, which was frequented among others by Lord Winchilsea, Lord Huntingfield, Sir Richard Sutton, Mr. Osbaldeston and Captain Ross, who won the club cup, value 200 guineas, in 1828 and in 1829. As late as 1840 it is described in Colburn's *Kalendar of Amusements* as taking ' the lead in the quantity and quality of this sport.' [12]

The system of handicapping appears, however, to have been then unknown and it was not until 1856, six years after the closing of the Red House Club, that it was introduced by Mr. Frank Heathcote, in order to place good and bad shots on something like an equality.[13] It was adopted in some matches shot at Purdey's grounds at Willesden, the

handicap running from 30 to 24 yds., and subsequently at the Old Hornsey Wood House.[14] Among the most noted shots of those days was General Bullock Hall, of Six Mile Bottom near Newmarket. He then commanded the 1st Life Guards, among whose officers were Lord Leconfield, Mr. R. de Winton, Captain (now General) Bateson, and several other shots almost equally good. A match for a large sum of money, shot at Hornsey Wood during this period, between General Bateson and Sir F. Mullock, at twenty-five birds each, 25 yds. rise, and won by the former, attracted an immense attendance, over twenty coaches being on the ground.[15]

A fresh impetus was given to the sport by the foundation in 1860, by Lord Stormont and other well-known shots, of the Gun Club, where many of the most important developments in the science of gun-making have been tested. Among the most celebrated matches at the club were those between Dr. Carver, the well-known American shot, and Lord Walsingham, and between the former and Mr. Heygate, and those in which Capt. Bogardus, another famous American marksman, shot against Mr. Dudley Ward and against Captain Shelley.[16]

A few years after the establishment of the Gun Club the spread of London northward obliged Mr. Frank Heathcote to abandon the Old Hornsey Wood House, and in 1867 he rented the Hurlingham Estate at Fulham for £700 a year. This action was followed shortly afterwards by the formation of the Hurlingham Club, which purchased the property for £20,000. It achieved such

[5] *Polo and Riding* (Badminton Library), 357, 359, 360.

[6] *Polo* (Badminton Library), 279–80.

[7] Ibid. 256–7.

[8] Ibid. 340.

[9] Lord Walsingham and Sir Ralph Payne-Gallwey, *Shooting* (Badminton Library), 343.

[10] Edith Jackson, *Annals of Ealing.*

[11] *Shooting* (Badminton Library), 356.

[12] *Chambers's Encyclopedia* (ed. 1901), Art. 'Pigeon Shooting.'

[13] Ibid.

[14] *Shooting* (Badminton Library), 343.

[15] Ibid. Another notable match at Hornsey Wood was that between Lord Aveland and Mr. Reginald Cholmondley.

[16] *Shooting* (Badminton Library), 343–4.

success under the management of the Hon. D. J. Monson that for several years prior to 1891 it had its full complement of 1,500 members under the presidency of his late Majesty, King Edward, then Prince of Wales. Of these, however, only 200 were shooting members, many of whom took no part in pigeon shooting. The sport therefore gradually ceased to be carried on under the favourable conditions it had enjoyed at Hornsey Wood and the Gun Club, and owing to the greater popularity of polo, it has now been driven from the scene where it may be said to have attained its zenith.

The best shots at Hurlingham and the Gun Club during recent years have been Lord Hill, Lord de Grey, Captain Shelley, Mr. Berkeley Lucy, Mr. Dudley Ward, Mr. Aubrey Coventry, Captain Aubrey Pullen, Mr. H. J. Roberts, and Lord de Clifford.[17]

ANGLING

The fishing rivers of Middlesex are the Thames, the Lea, the Colne, and the Brent, none of which, however, rises in the county. The Thames first touches Middlesex at Staines, and from that point to Shepperton the river forms part of the western boundary of the county; and is its southern boundary from Shepperton to Bromley in Essex, where it is entered by the Lea, which from this point northwards to Waltham forms the eastern boundary of Middlesex.

As the Thames appears to have been from time immemorial tidal as well as navigable up to Richmond,[1] there has always been a public right of fishery in its waters up to that point; but in early times this right was limited by the existence of private fisheries created by the crown prior to the passing of Magna Charta which put an end to such grants. In Domesday Book eleven manors in Middlesex are returned as leasing several fisheries, the owners of which had an exclusive right to all the fish therein, and of these manors three—Staines, Shepperton (Scepertone) and Hampton (Hamntone)—were situated on the non-tidal, and two, Isleworth (Gestleworde) and Fulham (Fuleham) on the tidal waters of the Thames. It also appears from the confirmation by Henry III in 1225 of various charters granted to 'the Charity of St. Mary Merton and the canons there in the county of Surrey' that this order had rights of fishery at Brentford, as it provides, *inter alia*, that 'no one shall in future fish before the weir of the said canons in Brainford, or more than was wont to be done in the time of the king's ancestors.'[2] The king's water bailiff and conservator, however, claimed a 'fee draught' or right to take a net down the Thames through all the private fisheries once a year, a right which appears to have been exercised as late as 1820.[3]

The injury both to fishery and navigation resulting from the number of weirs, kiddles and other fixed engines with which fishery was carried on in mediaeval times led to the enactment in Magna Charta,[4] repeated in subsequent statutes,[5] that 'all weirs shall henceforth be entirely put down on the Thames and Medway and throughout all England except on the sea coast,' and in the fifteenth century we find similar legislation with respect to fixed nets. A statute of 1423[6] prohibits the fastening of 'nets and other engines called trinks and all other nets which be fastened continually day and night by a certain time of year to great posts, boats, and anchors overthwart the river of Thames and other rivers of the realm,' as causing 'as great and more destruction of the brood and fry of fish and disturbance of the common passage of vessels' as the weirs and kiddles. It therefore enacts that nets should only be used by drawing and pulling hem by hem as other fishers do with other nets; but it may be noted that this restriction is followed by a proviso 'saving always to every of the king's liege people, their right, title, and inheritance in their fishings in the said water.'[7] In 1393 the conservancy of fishery in the Thames from Staines downwards, and also in the Medway, was entrusted to the Lord Mayor of London by the statute of 17 Richard II, which provided for the appointment of justices of

[3] *Hist. and Law of Fisheries*, 81. This right was also exercised on the Avon in Sussex and the Frome in Dorset and possibly in other rivers.
[4] 9 Hen. III (1225).
[5] 21 Ric. II, cap. 19, (1397); 1 Hen. IV, cap. 12 (1399), and 4 Hen. IV, cap. 11, &c.
[6] 2 Hen. VI, cap. 15 (1423).
[7] Ibid. Cf. *Hist. and Law of Fisheries*, 171 et seq.

[17] *Shooting* (Badminton Library), 345.
[1] Stewart A. Moore and H. Stewart Moore, *The Hist. and Law of Fisheries*, 101.
[2] *Cal. of Chart.* i, 381.

the peace as conservators for carrying out the statute of Westminster[8]—the first Act which fixes a close time for salmon—and that of 13 Richard II, stat. 1, cap. 19, which, while confirming the former Act, also prohibits the use of nets called 'stalkers' and all other nets or engines 'by which the fry or breed of salmons, lampreys, or other fish may in anywise be taken or destroyed in any of the waters of the realm at any time of the year.'[9] The City of London retained their jurisdiction over the fishery of this portion of the Thames—the limits of which are marked by City Stone at Staines—until the middle of the last century, when it was transferred, together with that relating to the conservancy of navigation, to the Thames Conservancy Board, incorporated by the Thames Conservancy Acts of 1858 and 1864.[10] The powers thus vested in the conservators of making by-laws for regulating and protecting the fishery were confirmed and extended by the Thames Conservancy Act of 1894,[11] appointing the present Conservators of the River Thames.

The fishery in the river is at present regulated by the Thames Fishery by-laws issued by the conservators under the order of council of 1893 which extend and apply to the Thames and the Isis and to 'all creeks, inlets, and bends between Teddington in the county of Middlesex and Gautlet Creek in the county of Kent.'[11a] Above London Bridge only the following instruments and apparatus may be lawfully used in fishing :— Rod and line ; flew or seine nets ; seine or draft nets ; single bley nets ; smelt nets ; flounder nets ; minnow nets ; hand or well nets ; landing nets ; casting or bait nets ; and grig wheels.[12] Below London Bridge such instruments are limited to :— rod and line ; hand lines fished with bait ; trim tram or four beam nets ; and trawl nets.[13] Fixed nets and all devices for catching or hindering fish, spawn, or fry of fish from entering or leaving the river, and the use of spears, and gaffs, except as an accessory in pike-fishing, are prohibited.[14]

The close time for salmon and salmon trout is between 1 September and 31 March ; that for trout and char from 11 September to 31 March ; that for smelts between 25 March and 27 July, and that for lamperns between 1 April and 24 August ; while in the river above London Bridge fishing with rod and line is prohibited from 15 March to June except in the case of rod fishing for trout with an artificial fly or with a spinning or live bait.[15] Fishing—except with rod and line, and by registered fishermen using grig wheels for taking eels in season—is prohibited in stations which have been staked out and marked by the conservators for the preservation and incubation of fish. These stations are at six places on the Surrey side of the river, namely at Richmond, Kingston, Thames Ditton, Walton, Weybridge, and Chertsey,[16] and at the same number in Middlesex, namely, Twickenham, Hampton, Sunbury, Shepperton, Penton Hook, and Staines.

The abundance and variety of fish yielded by the Thames as late as the first quarter of the nineteenth century will be evident from the following list contained in Cooke's *Topographical and Statistical Description of Middlesex* :—

Salmon, flounders, smelt, shad, trout, grayling, perch, carp, tench, barbel, chub, roach, dace, gudgen(*sic*), pike, eels, lamprey, bleak, ruffee, sturgen (*sic*), bass, mullet, turbot, sole, plaice, dab, skate, thornback, halibut, pearl whiting, haddock, oyster, muscles (*sic*), cockles, crab, prawns, red and white shrimps, craw fish, and others.[17]

The existence in the Thames of so many sea fish, and notably of mussels, may sound, perhaps, hardly credible, but the writer has been informed by an octogenarian relative still living that the piles of Old London Bridge were incrusted with mussels and that the water up to that point, then limpid and green in colour, was quite brackish. Within thirty years of the publication of the above list, however, the supply of fish had already begun to diminish and many of the varieties enumerated by Cooke, notably the salmon, had forsaken the river. Hoffland writing of the Thames in his *British Angler's Manual* says :—

Salmon have been driven from the river by the gasworks and steam navigation, not one having been caught to my knowledge during the last twelve or fourteen years ; although many were taken formerly of a peculiarly fine quality within my recollection at Mortlake, Isleworth, and other places. The brandling, salmon pink, or skegger, has also disappeared ; the last salmon I saw taken,

---

[8] 13 Edw. I, stat. 1, cap. 47 (1285).
[9] Cf. *Hist. and Law of Fisheries*, 173–5.
[10] 21 & 22 Vict. cap. 147, and 27 & 28 Vict. cap. 113 ; and cf. the Thames Navigation Act, 1866 (29 & 30 Vict. cap. 89).
[11] 57 & 58 Vict. cap. 187 (Local).
[11a] Bylaw 3.   [12] Bylaw 4.
[13] Bylaw 12.   [14] Bylaws 15–19.

[15] Bylaws 20–5.   [16] Bylaws 26–8.
[17] p. 39. Cooke's work was published in 1819.

in a net, was opposite Twickenham meadow in the year 1818.[18]

Trout he describes as 'few in number but celebrated for their huge size and the excellence of their flavour,' and as being taken from five to fifteen pounds weight; while pike and jack were numerous, and perch, barbel, chub, eels, lampreys, flounders, roach, dace, gudgeon, bleak, pope, ruff, and minnows were abundant in all parts of the Thames from Battersea Bridge upwards, and fine carp and tench were taken in some places, and smelts near London Bridge. Among a list of fishing stations from below London Bridge to Streatley in Berkshire, he mentions in Middlesex, the Wet Docks below London Bridge, Brentford, Isleworth, Twickenham, Teddington, Hampton, Sunbury, Shepperton, Laleham, and Staines.[18a]

It will be observed that of the above stations Brentford, Isleworth, Hampton, Shepperton, and Staines were in ancient days fisheries attached to manors. The noted Hampton station (at which both salmon, the last of which was taken in 1814, and trout were originally very plentiful, while even sturgeon were occasionally caught—the last in 1824) is mentioned in the *Rambler* in 1797 as 'the most famous of all barbel deeps,' and Dr. H. Jepson, one of the founders of The Thames Angling Preservation Society, is stated in Ripley's *History and Topography of Hampton* to have informed the author that he had on several occasions caught over 90 lb. of barbel there before breakfast. Lamperns and jack were also fairly plentiful at Hampton thirty years ago.

Hampton is also notable as being the place where the Thames Angling Preservation Society, to whose efforts and expenditure Thames anglers are indebted for the preservation of the fishery in the river up to Staines, was established at a meeting held at the Bell Inn on 17 March, 1838—more than seventy years ago.[19] The promoters of the movement were Mr. Henry Perkins of Hanworth Park, Mr. C. C. Clarke, and Mr. Edward Jesse of Twickenham, Dr. Henry Jepson and Mr. Richard Kerry of Hampton, Mr. W. Whitbread of Eaton Square, and

Mr. David Crole of Strawberry Hill. Originally formed for the protection of fish from poachers—with respect to which an application was in the first instance made to the then Lord Mayor (Sir John Cowan, bart.), who was at that time one of the Thames conservators[20] —the society eventually extended its operations to restocking the river, and has thus provided thousands of anglers with twenty miles of free water, which furnishes perhaps the finest coarse fishing in England. Among the consignments of fish placed in the river during 1905 were 300 trout, from 10 to 14 in. at Weybridge; 1 ton of roach, dace, bream, and perch about and below Sunbury Lock; 12 cwt. of roach, perch, chub and bream at Chertsey; and about 1 dozen bream, averaging $2\frac{1}{2}$ lb., with a few chub, perch and roach at Walton. Among the patrons of the society may be mentioned the late King Edward and his Majesty King George. The Hon. Harry Lawson, M.A., is the president and Mr. Henry Whitmore Higgins the hon. secretary and hon. treasurer.

The Lea, which, as has been said, forms the eastern boundary of Middlesex, rises at Leagrave Marsh near Luton in Bedfordshire, and flows east-south-east for 10 miles into Hertfordshire and for 16 miles by Hertford to Ware. Thence it flows for 4 miles southwards between Hertfordshire and Essex to the Middlesex border at Waltham Cross, whence its course is 8 miles south-east by Lea Brooke, Old Ford, Bow and Bromley to the Thames at Blackwall.

Two manors on the banks of the Lea are returned in Domesday as having several fisheries—Enfield (Enfelde) and Tottenham (Toteham)—and the river has never ceased to be productive. The fishing above Tottenham at Edmonton and Enfield is referred to by Izaak Walton, who, as he lived the greater part of his life in London where he first became a fisherman and where he wrote *The Compleat Angler,* may be fairly claimed as a Middlesex man.[21] Hoffland, in whose time its course above Limehouse lay through 'a beautiful pastoral country adorned with villages . . . through parks and meadows containing countless herds of cattle and flocks of sheep,' describes the Lea as second only to the Thames in the opinion of London anglers.[22] The river between Stratford and Lea Bridge was then rented and preserved

---

[18] T. C. Hoffland, *The British Angler's Manual, or the Art of Angling in England, Scotland, Wales and Ireland, with some account of the principal rivers, lakes, and trout streams in the United Kingdom.* (New ed. revised and enlarged by Edward Jesse, 1848), 237–8. Hoffland was also an artist of some celebrity.

[18a] Ibid. 238, 248, 263, 265–70.

[19] *The Blue Bk. of the Thames Angling Preservation Soc.* 1906, p. 5.

[20] Ibid.

[21] See the Walton Chronology in the Winchester edition of *The Compleat Angler,* by Mr. George Dewar.

[22] *The British Angler's Manual,* 275.

by Mr. Beresford of the 'White House,' at Homerton, little more than 3 miles from London. He also had the 'Horse and Groom,' a mile above the 'White House,' and the fishery attached to it, and angling in each of these 'subscription waters' was procurable for the payment of half a guinea subscription per annum. Both of these private fisheries are described by Hoffland as abounding in jack and pike, carp, barbel, chub, perch, roach, dace, eels, gudgeon and bleak.[23] 'Above Lea Bridge,' he says, 'a considerable space of the river is free to anglers up to Tottenham Mills, 5 miles from London, where is Tyler's subscription water, and 6 miles farther there is Ford's water.[24]

Hoffland makes no mention of trout, which, if not existent in his day, must have been since introduced into the river, since it is stated in an article in *The Field* of 4 May, 1907, on 'Trout fishing in the Lea,' that 'though not comparable with the Thames, the open or public waters of the Lea are to be by no means despised by the trout angler who has no preserved or private fishery on hand.'

The Colne rises to the south-west of Hatfield in Hertfordshire, running 13 miles south-west past Colney and Watney to Rickmansworth, and entering Middlesex at the north-west extremity flows southward between that county and Bucks past Harefield, Uxbridge —where it divides into several channels forming islands—Cowley, and Colnbrook, to the Thames at Staines. Another arm of the river diverges from its main course at Longford and reaches Staines by Laleham, while another uniting with the Cran—a small stream rising in the high grounds between Pinner and Harrow—flows across Hounslow Heath to Twickenham and Isleworth. Yet another branch runs through Hanworth, Bushey, and Hampton Court parishes.

The manors of West Drayton (Draitone), Harmondsworth (Hermondesworthe), Stanwell (Stanewell), and Harefield (Herefelle) on the Colne are all returned in Domesday as having several fisheries,[25] and other ancient records show that this was also the case as regards those of Cowley (Covele), Denham, and Whitton (Witton) on the same river.[26]

Neither Izaak Walton nor Hoffland refers to the Colne, but it is mentioned by Daniel in his *Rural Sports*, published in 1812, as a good fishing river. The fishing at West Drayton is now preserved by various local angling societies, and is especially abundantly supplied with pike and jack.

The Brent rises near Barnet in Hertfordshire, and entering Middlesex near Finchley flows 16 miles south-west, through the middle of the county, by Hendon, Twyford, and Hanwell, to the Thames at Brentford.

That there was originally fishing in this river is evident from a grant of 1640 by Robert Lee, aliening the manor of East Twyford, 'consisting of 100 acres of arable land, 80 of meadow, 200 of pasture and 50 of wood with *free fishery in the river of Brent*'— a term synonymous with 'several fishery'[27] —to John Hooke and his heirs.[28] The weir at Brentford, already referred to as belonging to the canons of St. Mary Merton,[29] must also presumably have been at the confluence of the Brent with the Thames. Owing, however, to the utilization of the river for the disposal of the drainage of Ealing and adjacent western suburbs it has long ceased to be available for purposes of fishery.

CRICKET

MIDDLESEX COUNTY

The history of county cricket in Middlesex begins in 1863, when it was started at a meeting over which the Hon. Robert Grimston presided, and at which Messrs. J. and V. E. Walker were present. It may be briefly stated that for many years the county club only existed through the munificence of the Walker family, who must be inseparably connected with its history. For a long time the county team suffered from lack of an abiding place. A start was made in Islington in 1863, with R. Thoms as umpire and George Hearne as ground-man, but in 1865 Norris the landlord raised the rent by £50, and in 1869, after further trouble with him, a move was made to Lillie Bridge. There the turf proved bad, and the club was on the verge of dissolution, continuance being carried by one vote at a meeting of thirteen mem-

---

[23] *The British Angler's Manual*, 276, 277.
[24] Ibid. 278.

[25] *Domesday Bk.*; cf. *Hist. and Law of Fisheries*, 403.
[26] *Hist. and Law of Fisheries*, 407, 410, 411, 422.
[27] Ibid. 37, 38.
[28] Pat. 16 Chas. I, pt. 15. Cf. Lysons, *Environs of Lond.* iii, 259, 260.   [29] *Ante*, 267.

bers. Matters somewhat improved in 1871, but no good professionals were engaged. In 1872 another migration was made, this time to Prince's. When the builder invaded that pretty ground, the hospitality of Lord's was accepted, despite the opposition of Mr. I. D. Walker, Mr. P. M. Thornton observing in words that sound strange having regard to modern developments : 'it has yet to be proved that genuine county cricket will attract at Lord's.'

In 1864 Middlesex played their first match against Bucks at Newport Pagnell. The result was a draw. Pooley appeared for Middlesex, and Captain Frederick made the top score. The lobs of Mr. V. E. Walker, dismissing nine for 62 and five for 41, gave the county a victory by an innings over Sussex. The earliest centuries were against M.C.C. with Grundy and Wootton bowling, Tom Hearne scoring 125 and Mr. T. Case 116 towards a total of 411. In the return with Bucks, Middlesex, after being 218 behind, scored 463, and won by 138 runs.

Against Lancashire, with a tie on first innings in 1865, Mr. V. E. Walker claimed all ten wickets in an innings for 104, a feat not again performed for Middlesex until Burton's similar achievement in 1888 against Surrey. The season of 1866 was successful, for Middlesex beat Surrey (scoring over 400 each time), and Lancashire twice, drawing and beating Notts, losing and winning to Cambridge University. In 1867 Middlesex played England, but lost by an innings and 25 runs, Mr. A. Lubbock obtaining 125 and Dr. W. G. Grace 75. There was a tie with Surrey in 1868, for Caesar's benefit.

After this for several years the programme was very restricted. Howitt in 1869 had the excellent analysis of six wickets for 4 runs at the Oval, and T. Hearne six for 12 in the return with Surrey. At Lord's against M.C.C. in 1871, Mr. W. H. Hadow scored 217. In 1874, bowling against Notts, he claimed four for 9 and eight for 35, while in consecutive matches with Notts and Yorkshire in 1875 he captured twenty-three for 227. A sub-committee was that year formed to choose teams—'very difficult owing to the great batting strength.' Among the batsmen may be cited besides the Walkers, Messrs. J. W. Dale, C. E. Green, A. W. T. Daniel, C. F. Buller, C. J. Ottaway, W. H. Hadow, J. J. Sewell, C. I. Thornton, T. Case, and B. B. Cooper. The attack at that period could only be varied between the three Walkers, Messrs. E. Rutter, R. Henderson, C. J. Brune, C. K. Francis, and A. H. Stratford. Middlesex has constantly found its side vary enormously owing to the lack of professionals. As a matter of fact Burton, West, and Mignon were the only bowlers born in the county, T. and J. T. Hearne coming from Bucks, Howitt and Clarke from Notts, Rawlin from Yorkshire, Trott, Phillips, Roche, and Tarrant from Australia. Among others the following amateurs played by qualification : the Hon. Edward and Alfred Lyttelton (born in Worcestershire), Lord George Scott, G. Macgregor and J. G. Walker (Scotland), R. N. and J. Douglas, C. M. Wells and H. B. Chinnery (Surrey), M. E. Pavri (India), Dr. G. Thornton (Yorkshire), C. E. Cobb, C. Robson, F. T. Welman, A. H. Heath, G. W. Hillyard, S. C. Newton, T. S. Pearson, H. Ross, G. Strachan, P. F. Warner, and A. P. Lucas.

In 1876 when Surrey had lost seven men with 100 still needed, Barratt hit splendidly, but when tie was called and the last man in he was easily caught. Mr. I. D. Walker hit Ulyett to square leg out of the Bramall Lane ground in Sheffield. In 1878 the Hon. Edward Lyttelton's 113 for Middlesex was the first century scored against the Australians, and some judges declare this innings was never surpassed except by Mr. G. L. Jessop at the Oval in the last test match of 1902. He was the best bat of the year. Middlesex, it may be mentioned, has on occasion been assisted by notably fine wicket-keepers, to wit, Messrs. Bisset Halliwell, M. Turner (who dismissed nine opponents at Nottingham in 1875), the Hon. Alfred Lyttelton, H. Philipson, F. T. Welman, G. Macgregor, the finest amateur in this department, W. P. Robertson, E. H. Bray, W. S. Bird, and M. W. Payne. The following Middlesex cricketers have appeared in test matches in England : the Hon. Alfred Lyttelton, Sir T. C. O'Brien, Mr. C. T. Studd, Mr. B. J. T. Bosanquet, Mr. P. F. Warner, and J. T. Hearne. The following have gone on tour to Australia in addition to these six : Messrs. A. P. Lucas, A. J. Webbe, C. F. H. Leslie, G. B. Studd, G. F. Vernon, A. E. Stoddart, H. Philipson, and Rawlin.

The bowling of Mr. A. F. J. Ford, who captured thirty-eight for 417, was a pleasing feature of 1879, when in a wet season 476 runs were amassed at Clifton. Mr. C. T. Studd had a capital analysis at the Oval in 1880, four for 6 and three for 24, while Mr. A. F. J. Ford captured six for 42 and seven for 40. During and after 1881 Burton played regularly. He was a steady slow bowler who did an enormous amount of work, being mainly supported by the erratic but effective fast deliveries of Mr. J. Robertson.

Among the features of 1882 was a grand 141 by Mr. C. F. H. Leslie at Nottingham, well supported by Mr. I. D. Walker with 79. The latter batsman, with Mr. A. J. Webbe, put up 130 for first wicket after Surrey had been dismissed for 117. Against Gloucestershire Mr. A. F. J. Ford effected seven catches at short slip. A year later at Clifton Mr. I. D. Walker and the Hon. Alfred Lyttelton added 324 for the second wicket, the latter having the remarkable average of 68. Sir T. C. O'Brien's courageous batting formed the one noteworthy feature of 1884, and in the seven matches in which the Hon. Alfred Lyttelton could not play, the wicket-keeping was put 'in commission.' Disasters in 1885 followed the retirement of Messrs. I. D. Walker, C. T. Studd, and P. J. T. Henery, whilst Messrs. T. S. Pearson, G. E. Vernon, G. B. Studd, A. W. Ridley, and the Hon. Alfred Lyttelton were only seldom available. However, Mr. A. E. Stoddart was at last enlisted from the Hampstead Club, and Mr. S. W. Scott played a notable 135 not out against Gloucestershire. Mr. J. G. Walker in 1886 lent valuable aid, but it was not until 1887 that revival could be noted. Mr. A. J. Webbe showed most remarkable form, averaging 51 for 820 aggregate, playing a great innings of 243 not out in the match against Yorkshire just after his 192 not out against Kent in the Canterbury week. Wet wickets checked the scoring in 1888, Sir T. C. O'Brien, who averaged 53, alone rising superior to the difficulties. Burton had the remarkable analysis of 12·50 for ninety-two wickets, taking all ten for 59 in the first innings of Surrey at the Oval, and three for 19 in the unfinished second effort.

Sir T. C. O'Brien's scoring against Yorkshire in 1889 will never be forgotten. In the first innings 112 were added in less than an hour, Sir Timothy making 92 with Mr. G. F. Vernon, who scored 86. Set to get 280 in three hours and a half Sir T. C. O'Brien, hitting fearlessly, obtained 100 not out, and he and the same colleague made the runs with ten minutes to spare, 151 being added in ninety minutes. Mr. E. A. Nepean showed admirable form with both bat and ball, and Mr. Stoddart played fine cricket. After brilliant victories over Notts, Lancashire, and Gloucester, persistent mediocrity beset the Middlesex cricket of 1890, but an immense advance was to be noticed in 1891 when third place in the championship list was obtained. This great improvement was mainly due to that great and willing bowler J. T. Hearne, whose patience and good length were always remarkable. At Old Trafford he claimed ten Lancashire wickets for 83. Rawlin also played great cricket. In batting Sir T. C. O'Brien continued to show consistent prowess, while Mr. A. E. Stoddart played a magnificent innings of 215 against Lancashire.

The advent of the great wicket-keeper Mr. Gregor Macgregor was a source of material strength in 1892, in which year J. T. Hearne for the second time took 100 wickets in county matches, the only Middlesex bowler who had yet done so. Mr. S. W. Scott displayed an enormous advance in batting, his 244 against Gloucestershire at Lord's being remarkable for an amateur aged 39. Mr. A. E. Stoddart again occupied second place in the averages. In 1893 the county again rose to third position, owing mainly to the fine form of Mr. Stoddart, who scored 1,178 in twenty-five innings, and had the highest county average of the year. In the Notts match at Lord's he took a double century, 195 not out and 124. With Sir T. C. O'Brien he put on 228 in two hours and a half for the first wicket against Surrey. Mr. F. G. J. Ford hit finely, but Hearne and Rawlin found no support with the ball. A similar position was obtained in 1894; but the cricket, apart from the work of the two bowlers, was not up to the standard of the previous summer. This observation equally applies to 1895, although Sir T. C. O'Brien made 202 at Brighton, adding 338 in three hours and a quarter with Mr. R. S. Lucas, who scored 185. Mr. C. M. Wells in August offered some bowling relief, and Mr. J. Douglas strengthened the batting at the same period.

Far better was the form in 1896, when Sir T. C. O'Brien and Mr. A. E. Stoddart time after time played cricket as valuable as it was brilliant, while J. T. Hearne bowled like a hero. His taking of twelve Surrey wickets for 90 was a capital performance. In 1897 the form was less certain, though Mr. F. G. J. Ford gave some extraordinary displays, and Mr. Stoddart, as well as Mr. J. Douglas, when available, was well worth watching. Mr. P. F. Warner, who had long been trying for a place on the side, at last won it, and became at Lord's a singularly useful and enthusiastic bat.

Middlesex had only obtained two successes up to the close of July in 1898, but of the eight matches played in August seven were won and one was drawn, with the result that the county finished a good second to Yorkshire. Hearne, now assisted by Albert Trott, bowled brilliantly, and the Colonial exceeded expectation. Mr. Stoddart averaged 52, his biggest score being 157 on the Aylestone ground. Mr. F. G. J. Ford, in August, obtained no less than 603 runs, while magnificent assistance with the bat and in the field that month came from the brothers Douglas and Mr. C. M. Wells. So well was the standard maintained next summer that the Middlesex side almost won the championship, eleven victories being set against three defeats. Mr. Stoddart and Sir T. C. O'Brien both dropped out, but in August the usual triumvirate of schoolmasters reappeared and Mr. C. M. Wells averaged 81, his great score being 244 against Notts. Mr. Warner batted better than ever before, and Trott not only took 146 wickets for 15, but scored 164 against Yorkshire. It was the victory by an innings and two runs over that team which formed the proudest achievement of Middlesex. Mr. F. G. J. Ford played three great centuries, and Mr. Macgregor as a bat, as wicket-keeper, and as captain was a complete success.

There was a big drop in 1901, though Mr. Stoddart came back for Hearne's benefit and scored a masterly 221 against Somerset. Mr. Bosanquet's play for his double hundred against Leicestershire was electrifying, but Mr. Warner bore the brunt of the batting and Trott of the bowling. Although Middlesex finished second in 1901 there was little brilliancy in the display apart from the fine scoring of Mr. P. F. Warner, though Mr. Bosanquet established himself as Mr. F. G. J. Ford's successor. Disasters came so fast in 1902 that eleventh place only was obtained. Apart from an innings of 180 by Mr. J. Douglas at Leyton, and a creditable victory over Notts, in which Mr. Bosanquet gave his earliest swerve demonstration, there was little to praise.

All-round efficiency accounted for the unexpected fact that Middlesex actually took champion honours in 1903, the only reverse being a tremendous defeat by a margin of 230 at the hands of Yorkshire at Leeds. Messrs. Warner, Beldam, Bosanquet, Moon, and the Douglases formed a formidable batting nucleus. The bowling on paper did not look remarkable, but it was effective. On 14 September the county played a favourable draw with the Rest of England, represented by Lord Hawke and K. S. Ranjitsinhji, with Hayward, Hayes, Tyldesley, Arnold, Hirst, Braund, John Gunn, Rhodes, and Strudwick. In August 1904 the Middlesex side was as good as ever, but previously with unrepresentative elevens they gave only a poor exhibition. The bright feature was the work of Mr. B. J. T. Bosanquet. Against Kent, after making 80, he captured five for 23, and

in the Yorkshire match he took ten for 248, making 141, with Mr. R. E. More adding 128 inside fifty minutes. In each match with Somerset, Mr. G. W. Beldam played a sound century, while Mr. Warner contributed 163 at Nottingham and 106 at the Oval. J. T. Hearne bowled quite in his old style. A lamentable decline was shown in 1905, and blunders in the field prevented the victories of the county from amounting to more than four as against seven defeats. Very occasional success by Mr. Bosanquet alone assisted J. T. Hearne in the attack, while that steady batsman Tarrant enjoyed moderate success. Mr. Bosanquet achieved a double century against Sussex, following it up with eight for 53, but the general form was lifeless. The pertinacious imperturbable skill of Tarrant in every department was the mainstay of the county in the next few years, and in 1907 he proved the best all-round professional in England. Mr. Macgregor kept wicket as finely as ever until he resigned the captaincy to Mr. P. F. Warner.

THE MARYLEBONE CRICKET CLUB

The space at our disposal does not permit of more than a very inadequate mention of this famous club, which is indeed more a national than a county institution. The club virtually was the offshoot of the White Conduit Club dissolved in 1787. Thomas Lord established the first ground that bore his name in Dorset Square. After a temporary residence at North Bank, he opened the present ground in St. John's Wood, the first match played there being M.C.C. against Hertfordshire in 1814. The old pavilion was burnt in 1820. From time to time many alterations and additions have been made.

There are now nearly five thousand members of M.C.C. The administration is in the hands of a president, nominated annually by his predecessor, a treasurer, a committee of sixteen, four of whom retire annually, and a secretary with a subordinate staff. Any alterations in the laws of the game must be approved at a general meeting; and while these laws are implicitly obeyed in England, they form, with some modifications, the rule for cricket in all other parts of the world. Formerly the matches between M.C.C. and Ground and certain counties were of an importance far greater than is at present the case, but the minor matches of the great club are invaluable for popularizing the game.

The match, North against South, has become as obsolete at St. John's Wood as the once famous matches of the All England and United All England elevens. The centenary of M.C.C. was observed in June 1887, when M.C.C. played England; Eighteen Veterans met the Gentlemen of M.C.C.; and a banquet was held at which the Hon. E. Chandos-Leigh, the president of the year, took the chair, among the speakers being Mr. Goschen, the Duke of Abercorn, Lord Bessborough, the Provost of Eton, M. Waddington, Mr. E. Stanhope, Lord George Hamilton, Sir A. L. Smith, Mr. Justice Chitty, and Lord Harris.

THE UNIVERSITY MATCH

Up to the close of 1909 seventy-five university matches have been played, of which Cambridge have won thirty-six and Oxford thirty-one matches; in 1827, 1844, 1888, 1899, 1900, 1901, 1904 and 1909 the matches were drawn. The two largest aggregates, Oxford's 503 and Cambridge's 392, were both obtained in the same match in 1900. The largest individual innings, 172 not out by Mr. J. F. Marsh for Cambridge in 1904, was intrinsically inferior to the 171 of Mr. R. E. Foster for Oxford in 1900. Mr. W. Yardley with 100 and 130 in 1872 for Cambridge is the only cricketer twice to score centuries in this match, but Mr. J. E. Raphael with 130 in 1903 and 99 in 1905 only failed by one run to achieve the same distinction for Oxford. Mr. Eustace Crawley has alone made a 100 both in the Eton and Harrow and Oxford and Cambridge matches. Those who have also scored centuries for Oxford are Messrs. K. J. Key, M. R. Jardine, G. O. Smith, H. K. Foster, F. M. Buckland, V. T. Hill, W. H. Game, A. Eccles, W. H. Patterson, W. Rashleigh, Lord George Scott, C. B. Fry, and C. H. B. Marsham; and for Cambridge Messrs. H. J. Mordaunt, G. B. Studd, E. R. Wilson, S. H. Day, E. C. Streatfeild, C. E. M. Wilson, L. G. Colbeck, W. S. Patterson, C. W. Wright, and H. W. Bainbridge. The most famous finish was in 1870 when Oxford with three wickets to fall wanted only 4 runs to win. Mr. Bourne then caught Mr. Rutter off the second ball of Mr. Cobden's last over, and Messrs. W. A. Stewart and H. A. Belcher were bowled with the next two balls. It was in 1896 that Mr. F. Mitchell provoked an angry demonstration by directing Mr. E. B. Shine to send down no balls to prevent Oxford avoiding the follow on.

GENTLEMEN AND PLAYERS

In seasons when the Australians have not visited England, the fixture at Lord's between Gentlemen and Players has always been regarded as the chief exhibition match in which it was a great honour to be invited to play. Two matches were played in 1806, but the Gentlemen were assisted by Beldham and Lambert. Although in 1819 they played unsupported, in 1820 Howard was introduced. Odds were not given after 1838, since when up to the end of 1909 the Gentlemen have won twenty-eight and the Players thirty-six. The highest individual score is Mr. C. B. Fry's 232 not out in 1903, Dr. W. G. Grace's largest being 169 in 1876, and he is the only cricketer except Hayward who has exceeded the century more than twice at Lord's. The highest for the Players are 163 by J. T. Brown in 1900 and 141 by Braund in 1902. Mr. R. E. Foster scored two hundreds, 102 not out and 136 in the match in 1900, and J. H. King with 104 and 109 not out effected a similar feat in 1904, both on their first appearance in the match. The aggregates exceeding 1,000 are: in 1900, 1,274 for thirty-eight wickets; 1903, 1,218 for twenty-three wickets; 1897, 1,196 runs; 1904, 1,165 for thirty-seven wickets; 1895, 1,156 runs; 1905, 1,149 for thirty-four wickets; 1883, 1,118 for thirty-three wickets; 1901, 1,079 for thirty-six wickets; 1878, 1,066 runs; 1898, 1,059 runs; and 1884, 1,000 for thirty-four wickets. The longest partnership was in 1903, when Messrs. C. B. Fry and A. C. Maclaren added 309 without being separated. In 1900 the Players were set 501 to win, and made them for the loss of eight wickets. The instances of two bowlers being unchanged in the match are W. Lillywhite and James Broadbridge (playing as given men for the Gentlemen) in 1829 and for the Players in 1832; W. Lillywhite and S. Redgate in 1837; Wisden and W. Clarke in 1850; Mr. Matthew Kempson and Sir Frederick Bathurst in 1853; Jackson and Willsher in 1861; Willsher and Tarrant in 1864; and the Hon. F. S. Jackson and Mr. S. M. J. Woods in 1894.

THE AUSTRALIANS AT LORD'S

The first appearance of the Australians at Lord's against M.C.C. and Ground in 1878 was one of the most extraordinary matches ever played. The ground was in a dreadful state, and the Australians in one day defeated a powerful side by nine wickets, dismissing the Club for 33 and 19 Mr. F. R. Spofforth in the first innings took six for 4, including a hat trick, and Mr. H. F. Boyle six for 3 in the second. The Colonials beat Middlesex by 98 runs despite the great century by the Hon. Edward Lyttelton, but were defeated by an innings and 72 runs by the famous Cambridge eleven. The Australians were not seen at Lord's again until 1882. Since that time they have five times met the Gentlemen, winning three times and losing once. In 1906 Mr. W. W. Armstrong scored 248 not out, the third largest innings ever made on the ground in a first-class match.

The Australians were beaten by an innings and 263 runs by the Players in 1890, but won by six wickets in 1893. Against M.C.C. the Australians have won five times, lost six times and had six draws. Middlesex has been met on eleven occasions, but the county has never yet been successful. Ten test matches have been played at Lord's, England being victorious in 1884, 1886, 1890 and 1896, the Australians in 1888, 1899 and 1909, whilst the matches 1893, 1902 and 1905 were unfinished. In 1888 England scored 53, her smallest aggregate in the whole series in this country. Shrewsbury scored 106 in 1893, Mr. A. G. Steel 148 in 1884, Mr. S. E. Gregory 103 in 1896, Mr. V. S. Ransford 143 in 1909, Mr. G. H. S. Trott 143 in 1896, Mr. C. Hill 135 in 1899, Mr. V. Trumper 135 not out in 1899 and Mr. H. Graham 107 in 1893. Gunn's innings of 228 for the Players at Lord's in 1890 is the highest individual innings hit against the Australians in this country.

HARROW SCHOOL CRICKET

Space will not permit adequate treatment of the cricket of Harrow. Unlike Eton, the cricket has not been mainly in charge of masters but of such old Harrovians as the Hon. Robert Grimston, Mr. I. D. Walker, and Mr. A. J. Webbe in conjunction with Mr. M. C. Kemp. The great feature, of course, is the annual match at Lord's with Eton. Of the eighty-three encounters up to 1910, Harrow has won thirty-five and lost thirty-one, seventeen having been drawn, but Harrovians object very strongly to the game

in 1805 (when Lord Byron played) being treated as a regular match between the two schools, contending that it is no more correct to count it than the fixture in 1857 for boys under twenty, which has been rejected.

The centuries scored for Harrow against Eton are, 142 by T. G. O. Cole in 1897, 135 by A. K. Watson in 1885, 124 by J. H. Stogden in 1895, 112 not out by A. W. T. Daniel in 1860, 108 by R. B. Hoare in 1888 and 100 by E. Crawley in 1885, as well as the unparalleled double century in 1907 of M. C. Bird who grandly obtained 100 not out and 131. The largest totals are 388 in 1900, 385 in 1898, 376 in 1901, 326 in 1895 and 324 in 1885.

Winchester only once played at Harrow, in 1837. Harrow had the double satisfaction of winning both matches against Eton and Winchester in 1842.

The following old Harrovians have played in test matches in England :—A. N. Hornby, A. C. Maclaren and the Hon. F. S. Jackson. Old Harrovians who have been to the Antipodes are : A. N. Hornby, F. A. MacKinnon (who was never given his colours), A. C. Maclaren, E. M. Dowson, and M. C. Bird. The following since 1878 have represented the Gentlemen against the Players at Lord's: A. N. Hornby, M. C. Kemp, H. T. Hewett, A. C. Maclaren, the Hon. F. S. Jackson, and E. M. Dowson; while for the Gentlemen against the Australians were selected A. N. Hornby, W. H. Patterson, R. C. Ramsey, M. C. Kemp, and A. C. Maclaren.

Since 1878 the following Old Harrovians have found places in the Oxford eleven: A. Haskett Smith, W. H. Patterson, H. T. Hewet, M. C. Kemp, W. E. Bolitho, A. K. and H. D. Watson, H. J. Wyld, W. S. Medlicot, R. G. Barnes, M. J. Dauglish, D. R. Brandt and K. M. Carlisle. Harrovians in the Cambridge eleven have been P. J. T. Henery, C. D. Buxton, R. C. Ramsey, D. G. Spiro, F. C. C. Rowe, R. Spencer, E. M. Butler, E. Crawley, the Hon. F. S. Jackson, E. M. Dowson, W. P. Robertson, F. B. Wilson, C. H. Eyre, F. J. V. Hopley, E. W. Mann, R. E. H. Bailey and M. Falcon—a list that may well be remembered with pride by anyone reared in the great school on the Hill.

FOOTBALL

Association.—Middlesex has taken a leading part in placing the Association game, the Rugby game and more recently the Amateur Football Association on a constitutional basis. It was in and around London that men first went on playing the various forms of football that they had learnt at school. As nearly every school possessed rules peculiar to itself, varying either to suit its playing area or handed down by tradition, it will easily be understood that the enjoyment of the game was greatly hindered by this lack of uniformity. In 1863 the late Mr. C. W. Alcock and other pioneers of the game of football made strenuous efforts to induce all players to unite under one code. To this end Mr. Alcock and those who played the dribbling, or what is now known as the Association, game were prepared to make certain concessions to those who followed the Rugby or running code.

The first meeting for the purpose was held at the Freemasons' Tavern, 26 October 1863 when the Football Association was formed. The clubs represented were the War Office F. C., the Crusaders, the Forest, Crystal Palace, Kilburn, Barnes and the Rugby clubs of Kensington School, Surbiton, Blackheath, and Percival House. Mr. Arthur Kimber of the Kilburn N.N.'s was elected the first president, Mr. Morley, honorary secretary, and Mr. G. Campbell of Blackheath, treasurer. A further meeting was held on 10 November, when the secretary was empowered to draft an amalgamated code of rules taken from those in vogue at Eton, Westminster, Harrow, Charterhouse, Rugby and Winchester. When the amalgamated code was presented at a subsequent meeting on 1 December concessions to the Rugby section were evident, and at one time it appeared not improbable that the new code would be acceptable to both sections of players. Hacking, then a cherished feature of the Rugby game had, however, been eliminated. The desirability of its retention was vigorously maintained by Mr. Campbell, but his arguments were in vain, and in consequence he and the members of the Rugby clubs decided not to join the Association. From that day to this the two great divisions of the game—Association and Rugby—have remained distinct. The growth of the Association was not at first rapid. By 1868 only twenty clubs, most of which belonged to Middlesex, owned allegiance to it.

In 1867 county football was introduced for the first time when Middlesex on 2 November played a combined team of Kent and Surrey.

The game was keenly contested and resulted in a draw, neither side obtaining a goal. In 1870 the late Mr. C. W. Alcock, who did more towards popularizing Association football than any other man, was elected to the post of secretary, a position he filled for over thirty years. Up to the time of his death in 1907 he continued to take an active part in the administration of the game.

On 20 July 1871 the historic Challenge Cup was instituted and was won by the Wanderers. In early days this team, composed mainly of old public school men resident in London, was a dominating influence in Association football. In the first seven years of the Cup's history this club was successful on five occasions. Mr. C. W. Alcock was the organizer and leading spirit of the Wanderers until, on the formation in London of numerous clubs of old public school men, such as the Old Carthusians, the Old Etonians, and the Old Harrovians, the team was disbanded.

Other London clubs that held the trophy were the Old Etonians (twice) and the Old Carthusians, while the Clapham Rovers, which contained a fair proportion of Middlesex men, won it in 1880. Since the legalization of professionalism all this has been changed, and only once[1] since 1883 has a London club held it or been in the final. In 1883 that famous amateur club, the Corinthians, was formed. The club, whose head quarters are at Queen's Club in West Kensington, is composed of the pick of amateur players. The Corinthians have never entered for the Association Cup, but have contested hundreds of exciting matches with the leading professional teams. A very popular competition in London among the old boys of the various public schools who play the Association game is the Arthur Dunn Cup. This trophy was instituted in 1903 to perpetuate the memory of the Old Etonian whose name it bears, in his day one of the best type of amateur and an international player of note. The final and many of the ties are decided at Queen's Club.

The Old Carthusians are the present holders of the cup, a position they have enjoyed every year since the competition's inception, except in 1907 when the Old Reptonians were successful, while in 1903 the Old Salopians held it jointly with them.

[1] This occurred in 1901, when Tottenham Hotspur, after one drawn game with Sheffield United, subsequently beat the latter.

Another trophy competed for in the metropolitan district is the Sheriff of London's Shield presented by Sir Thomas Dewar during his shrievalty, to be played for by the two leading amateur and professional teams of the year. The proceeds of the match are devoted to deserving London charities.

Lord Kinnaird is president of the Football Association and the secretary is Mr. L. Walls. The Middlesex representative on the committee is Mr. W. W. Heard, who is also secretary of the Middlesex Association. The cup tie competitions in the county comprise the following—Middlesex Senior and Junior, Middlesex Charity, Inter-Hospital, Tottenham Charity, London Senior, Junior, Charity, and London Banks.

The various schools in the county have trained many notable internationals. Westminster heads the list with a dozen players, including N. C. Bailey, who not only captained the English team, but played on no less than eighteen occasions. Harrow ranks next with seven, of whom the late C. W. Alcock will ever be remembered. Mill Hill supplied two distinguished internationals in the brothers Heron, whilst the City of London School furnished S. R. Bastard.

Another far-reaching movement initiated in London has been the formation of the Amateur Football Association. With the great increase of professionalism of recent years in the Association game it was felt that the interests of the amateurs were hardly receiving from the governing body the recognition to which they were entitled, and when in 1907 legislation was brought in threatening the individual freedom of action of the player the amateurs felt that the time had arrived for them to form an association of their own. The Amateur Football Association was accordingly formed with Lord Alverstone as the first president, and H. Hughes-Onslow as secretary. The amateurs of the county are affiliated to the new association.

Rugby.—After the Rugby clubs had decided in 1863 not to join the Football Association, the followers of the running game continued to increase, but no governing body was formed for some years. At that date the most prominent Rugby clubs in the county were Ravenscourt Park, the Harlequins, the Wasps, the Gipsies, Addison, Belsize, Hampstead, the Pirates, the Black Rovers, and the Red Rovers.

The London hospitals also played the Rugby game as well as the following schools :— St. Paul's, Merchant Taylors, Highgate, King's College School, Christ's College Finchley, Godolphin School, Kensington Grammar School, and many smaller seminaries.

In the season of 1870–1 it became evident that the best interest of the sport would be served by placing the Rugby game on a constitutional basis with a uniform code of rules. The movement was confined to the London clubs, and of those represented at a meeting held, 26 January 1871, no less than eleven out of twenty-one belonged to Middlesex. At this meeting the Rugby Union was formed. It is worthy of note that 'hacking,' the elimination of which caused the Rugby men to decline to join the Football Association in 1863, was forbidden by the code drawn up by the newly-formed Union. Middlesex was well represented on the first general committee as well as in the first international match with Scotland, which was played a few weeks after the formation of the governing body.

The head quarters of the Union have always been in Middlesex, and in 1908 its new ground at Twickenham was opened, which will be the centre of the game and all international matches will be played there.

Middlesex was the first of the southern counties to put a football team in the field. On 25 February 1879 they met Yorkshire for the first time and won by 2 goals 2 tries to 2 goals and 1 try. The same season the county also played Surrey, but were defeated by a try. In the succeeding season Middlesex suffered defeat from both Yorkshire and Surrey. On 21 February 1881 Lancashire was met at Manchester for the first time, but the visitors were not a representative side and sustained an easy defeat. In the following season Middlesex engaged the powerful county of Kent for the first time and were defeated by a goal and a try.

In 1887 Middlesex as the strongest county in the south was selected to do battle with Lancashire, the champions of the north, on the occasion of the Charity Festival organized in London jointly by the Rugby Union and the Football Association. A stubbornly contested match resulted in Middlesex, though having the best of the game, being defeated by a try. As a matter of fact Middlesex also gained a try, but the short space marked out between the goal line and the dead-ball line lost them the point. It is worthy of note that his Majesty King Edward VII, then Prince of Wales, was present at the match, and at the conclusion of the game several of the players were brought and introduced to his royal highness. *Causa honoris* we give the names of the Middlesex team :—E. T. Gurdon, A. Rotherham, W. E. Maclagan, C. J. B. Marriott, John Hammond, A. E. Stoddart, W. G. Clibborn, J. H. Roberts,

C. J. Arkle, G. L. Jeffery, G. C. Lindsay, E. S. McEwen, C. Collier, T. Riddell, and A. S. Johnson.

In 1888, the year before the County Championship was officially recognized, Middlesex was without question the strongest Rugby team of the season.

Since the initiation of the County Championship Middlesex has competed each year, and though the county team has never headed the competition, it has generally given a good account of itself. In 1904 in the final Middlesex were only just beaten by Durham by the bare margin of a point. In the season of 1907–8 the county team, as champions of the South-Eastern Division, met Cornwall in the semi-final to decide who should meet Durham for the championship. Cornwall, however, who subsequently defeated Durham in the final, proved the stronger.

Many prominent international players have been associated with Middlesex football; notably E. T. Gurdon, who captained the team for many years, and his brother Charles; the late Alan Rotherham, the most correct half-back of his own or any time, who succeeded Gurdon in the captaincy; C. G. Wade, now Premier of New South Wales; the Hon. H. A. Lawrence; the late John Hammond, who though Yorkshire born, by residence played for the metropolitan county throughout his long career; C. J. B. Marriott, A. E. Stoddart, G. L. Jeffery, and others. Up to 1907 the county received very material assistance from such famous international players as W. E. Maclagan, the late G. C. Lindsay, J. G. McMillan, A. J. Gould, A. F. Harding,

and G. Campbell. In the year mentioned it was thought that the non-inclusion of such players would the better stimulate native talent and the following rule was passed: 'No man possessing an Irish, Scotch, or Welsh International Cap shall be eligible to play in a county championship match.' At the present time Middlesex has more clubs affiliated to the Rugby Union than any other county, and consequently is entitled to two seats in the executive. The present representatives are E. Prescott and W. Williams.

To two Middlesex men, the late Arthur Budd and the late R. S. Whalley, credit is due for the inception of the useful London Referees' Society for supplying referees to all clubs belonging to the society.

Nor have the schools in the county been behind hand in training a considerable number of international players, as the subjoined list will show. Harrow for instance, though still adhering to rules peculiarly its own, has supplied A. N. Hornby, W. E. Openshaw, F. E. Pease, J. T. Gowans, and John Hopley; Mill Hill—J. H. Dewhurst, A. F. Todd, and T. W. Pearson; Christ's College Finchley —C. R. Cleveland, C. H. Coates, the late H. G. Fuller, president of Cambridge University F.C., H. M. Jordan, and W. C. Hutchinson. From St. Paul's School came R. O. Schwarz; from St. John's Wood, A. E. Stoddart, G. L. Jeffery, and J. G. Anderson. Christ's Hospital produced S. Reynolds, and Isleworth College, A. Allport and H. Huth. From Merchant Taylors' came N. C. Fletcher, A. S. and H. H. Taylor; and from the Godolphin School G. Fraser.

GOLF

Golf was first introduced into Middlesex in 1890 by the formation of the Staines and West Middlesex Clubs, which was followed in 1891 by that of the Northwood Club, and during the eighteen years that have since elapsed the game has made rapid progress. The Hillingdon and Finchley Clubs were established in 1892, and the Enfield, Stanmore, Hampstead, and Neasden Clubs in the following year; and the number of clubs in existence, which in 1900 had risen to twenty, is now fifty-one,[1] only four short of that in Surrey, which ranks first among the Home Counties in this respect.

The development of golf in Middlesex has, like that of other sports, been greatly influenced by the growth of London; and this influence, which in the case of field sports has been wholly destructive, has been in the main beneficial to the royal and ancient game. Only *eight* of the fifty-one clubs above mentioned are recruited from the county, and the remaining forty-three are London clubs, the establishment of which has not only promoted a taste for the game amongst Londoners, but by the creation of the links connected with them has also helped to preserve 'open spaces'

[1] This is exclusive of ladies' clubs, of which there are in all twelve, two belonging to the county and twelve London clubs, as to which see *post*. Until 1907 the total number of clubs was fifty-two;

but the Chiswick Golf Club, instituted in 1902, has now succumbed to the long threatened invasion of the builders; see *Golfing Year Bk.* 1905, p. 358, and 1907, p. 393.

from the encroachments of the builder. As, however, only seventeen of these London clubs have links, the same result cannot be claimed in respect of the other twenty-four, which are private clubs connected with the professions, societies, and social clubs, &c., and play, by special arrangement, on the links of other clubs.[2] The oldest of these—the bulk of which have come into existence within the last few years—are the Civil Service and Lloyds, both founded in 1894, and the Chartered Accountants' and the London Insurance Clubs, both founded in 1898. In addition to the three last-named clubs, there are eight others connected with trade and commerce—the Baltic Club, the City Liberal Club, the Chartered Surveyors' Society, the Discount Market Society, the London Metal Exchange Association, the Mark Lane Club, the London Stock Exchange Society, and the Spalding Club for the employés of the firm of Messrs. Spalding Brothers. The law is represented by the Bar Society, the Inns of Court Club, and the London Solicitors' Society; the stage, by the George Edwardes Society and the Green Room Club; and literature by the London Press Society. There is also a Cricketers' Golfing Society, membership of which is confined to players of first and second class counties and university 'blues'; and a London Free Church Ministers' Golfing Society. Lastly there are three clubs connected with Scotland: the Highland Societies Association, the London Lothian Association, and the London Scottish Border Counties Club. Setting aside these private clubs, and taking the county and London clubs together,[3] the total number of golf clubs owning links in Middlesex is twenty-five, nine of which—Northwood, Stanmore, Edgware, Hendon, Finchley, North Middlesex, Enfield, Bush Hill Park (Enfield), and Clayesmore School (Enfield)—may, roughly speaking, be described as situated in the north; five—Muswell Hill, Highgate, Hampstead, Neasden, and Wembley—in the east; seven—St. Quintin's, Acton,

Hanger Hill (Ealing), Ealing, West Middlesex, West Drayton, and Hillingdon (Uxbridge)—in the west; and five—Strawberry Hill, Fulwell, Home Park (Hampton Court), Ashford Manor, and Staines—in the south of the county. The northern and eastern links have the advantage of being situated on the highest land in the county, which in the former case has an altitude of 500 ft., and at Highgate and Hampstead of 450 ft.; while, with the exception of Acton and Hanger Hill, which lie on the slopes of slight elevations, those in the west and south of Middlesex are on level or very slightly undulating ground.

THE NORTHERN LINKS

The Northwood Golf Club, whose course, situated on undulating land not far from Ruislip Park, is one of the best within easy reach of London, was founded in 1891 by Captain Bennett Edwards and Mr. Wright-Nooth. The eighteen-hole course is about $3\frac{1}{4}$ miles round, the length of the holes ranging from 150 to 543 yds. 'Hilly, plentifully supplied with whins and gorse, with several ponds and a stream which has constantly to be negotiated, it is well provided with natural hazards. The greens are beautifully true . . . the eight-hole "death or glory" is by itself worth the journey to Northwood.'[4] Bogey is an easy 81, and the professional and amateur records 70 and 72. The club prizes consist of the Club Challenge Cup, the Coles Shield, the Autumn Cup, the Captain's Prize, and various medals. The best seasons for play are spring and autumn, but the course, which is well drained, is playable all the year. The number of members is limited to 300, with 50 provisional members.

The Stanmore Golf Club, instituted in 1893, has a course of eighteen holes, not far from Bentley Priory on the borders of Hertfordshire, laid out round a high hill from which there is a good view of the surrounding country. The green records are 68 (professional) by H. Vardon, and 71 (amateur) by Mr. M. Copland. There are for competition the President's Gold Medal (scratch), won in 1906 by H. R. Herbert, 77; the Gordon Bowl (holes) and club prizes including the President's and the Vice President's Cup.

Some 4 miles to the east of Stanmore are the links of the Edgware Golf Club, founded in 1906. The eighteen-hole course, 6,000 yds. in circuit, is laid out on the Canons Park Estate, on which a large club-house has been erected.

[2] As, for example, the George Edwardes Society, founded in 1904, for members of the dramatic and musical professions, which plays by special arrangement at Ashford Manor.

[3] The 'county' clubs are:—Ashford Manor, Edgware, Enfield, Bush Hill Park (Enfield), Clayesmore School (Enfield), Staines, Stanmore and Hillingdon (Uxbridge); and the London clubs owning links are Acton, Ealing, Finchley, Fulwell, Hampste. Hanger Hill (Ealing), Hendon, Highgate, Muswell Hill, Neasden, North Middlesex, Northwood, St. Quintin, Strawberry Hill, Wembley, West Drayton, West Middlesex, and Home Park (Hampton Court).

[4] A. J. Lawrie, in *The Golfing Year Bk.* 1907, p. 399.

The Hendon Golf Club, established in 1903, has a course of eighteen holes, varying from 120 to 470 yds., on the east side of the main road from Hendon to Mill Hill ; and 2 miles to the north of this is the Finchley Golf Club, instituted in 1903, the nine-hole course of which is 2,414 yds. in length, the holes ranging from 143 to 443 yds. The hazards are hedges and ditches on pasture land, with some artificial bunkers. The club prizes are a Gold Medal, a Challenge Cup, and monthly medals. Bogey is 76 ; the amateur and professional records being 72 and 68. There is a commodious club-house. Within 2 miles to the north again of this at Friern Barnet is the eighteen-hole course of the North Middlesex Golf Club, established in 1906.

Enfield, the most northerly home of golf in the county, has three clubs. The principal of these, the Enfield Golf Club, instituted in 1893, has a course of eighteen holes, 3 miles 295 yds. round, over the pasture land of the Old Park, with sporting natural hazards, including a winding brook which traverses the links, and numerous artificial bunkers and excellent greens. Bogey is 78, the green records being 73 professional (J. H. Taylor), and 70 amateur (Mr. W. H. Smallwood). Play is possible all through the year, the best months being April and November. There are Whitsuntide, Summer, and Christmas meetings, and the following prizes :— Monthly Gold Medal (handicaps to 14), Monthly Silver Medal (handicaps over 14), finals in October ; Monthly Bogey Competition, final in October; Wyndcroft Bowl (thirty-six holes), Tatler Cup (holes), summer.

The other two Enfield Clubs are the Bush Hill Park Golf Club, with a course of nine holes (circuit 2,800 yds.) ; and the Clayesmore School Golf Club, instituted in 1897, which has also a nine-hole course with a lake as the chief hazard.

THE EASTERN LINKS

Like those in the north, the golf links in the east of the county all lie within easy reach of each other.

The Muswell Hill Golf Club was instituted in 1894. The course of eighteen holes, which is over 3 miles round, is situated between Muswell Hill, Wood Green, and Southgate, on pasture land covering a clay soil, the hazards being trees, ponds, ditches, hedges, hurdles, and artificial bunkers. Bogey is 75, and the record score in a club competition is 67. The prizes are the Quarterly Scratch Cup and a Handicap Cup. The course is playable throughout the year, but the best months are from May to September.

The eighteen-hole course of the Highgate Golf Club, instituted in 1904, is about 3⅓ miles in extent. It adjoins the Bishop's Wood at Highgate and includes the site of the ancient hunting lodge of the Bishops of London. The soil is clay, but the turf is very good and the lies are excellent, the holes being varied and of good length. The course, the hazards of which are artificial sand bunkers, is at its best from May to October, but is well drained and playable all the year round. Bogey is 77, the amateur record is Mr. J. O. Walker's 75, and the professional record by A. Saunders is 70. The prizes consist of a Scratch Medal, Monthly Medal, Captain's Prize, President's Prize (foursome), Reid Cup (quarterly), and Lyle Cup. The club-house has accommodation for ladies as well as men.

The Hampstead Golf Club, founded 1893, has a course of nine holes, with a length of about 2,500 yds., the holes varying from 100 to 420 yds. It is situated at Spaniards Farm, on pasture land with a clay soil, and has artificial hazards only. Play is possible throughout the year, the best months being April to September. Bogey is 78, and the amateur record, held by Mr. G. R. Girdlestone, is 71.

The New Neasden Golf Club was founded in 1893 by Mr. Stanley Clifford. The sporting course of eighteen holes, ranging from 120 to 510 yds., is on pasture land with a clay subsoil, and is nearly 3½ miles (6,120 yds.) in extent. There are numerous natural hazards, such as hedges and ponds, as well as artificial bunkers. The club-house, a fine old mansion, built about 1663, is said to occupy the site of a house mentioned in Domesday Book as the Great Neasden House. Bogey is 79, and the green record, both amateur and professional, held by Mr. A. E. Stoddart and J. Milne, is 75. The prizes include Monthly Medals, Monthly Bogey, Senior and Junior Half-yearly Gold Medals played for in May and October, the Harmsworth Cup (match play), the D. A. Howden Challenge Shield for medal play, and the McCalmont Hill Scratch Trophy, besides various other prizes for foursome competitions, and medal rounds.

The Wembley Golf Club, established in 1896, has an undulating course of eighteen holes, varying from 140 to 430 yds. It has been thoroughly drained and is always dry, and there is a club-house with every convenience. The club prizes include the Smith Cup, the James Cup, the Myer Salver, the Lorne Cup, the Carlton Shield, and the Scratch Medal.

SPORT ANCIENT AND MODERN

THE WESTERN LINKS

The most easterly of the western golf links is the nine-hole course of the St. Quintin's Club, close to Wormwood Scrubbs. The club was instituted in 1894.

The Acton Golf Club, instituted in 1896, has an eighteen-hole course of 5,870 yds. (nearly 3½ miles), laid out by Park, in 1907. The holes range in length from 115 to 465 yds. The ground is old pasture land, and the hazards are ditches, ponds, and various artificial bunkers. The putting greens are very large and good. The club-house is an old-fashioned mansion on the village green of East Acton. Bogey is 78, but owing to the recent opening of the enlarged course no green records are as yet forthcoming. The club prizes comprise monthly medals, several challenge cups, and annual prizes offered by the president, Lord George Hamilton, and the captain. The course is at its best during spring, summer, and autumn, but play is practicable throughout the year.

There are two golf clubs at Ealing—the Ealing Golf Club, instituted in 1898, situated at North Ealing in the Brent valley, near Perivale ; and the Hanger Hill Golf Club, instituted in 1900, the links of which are on the southern slope of the high ground above the town.

The eighteen-hole course of the Ealing Club is a little over 3 miles round, the holes ranging from 110 to 525 yds., and is laid over old pasture land on clay, with subsoil of gravel and brick earth. With the exception of some artificial sand bunkers the hazards are chiefly natural, consisting of the River Brent, ditches, and pits. Play is possible all the year, March to October being the best season. Bogey is 80, the amateur record being Mr. H. H. Hilton's 73, and the professional record 69 by G. Charles. The prizes are the Rothschild Cup, the Record Cup, Bogey and Medal Finals, and numerous annual prizes. The commodious club-house is at 14 and 15, Kent Gardens, close to the first tee and last green.

The course of the Hanger Hill Club also consists of eighteen holes, varying from 105 to 500 yds. The club-house is a fine old mansion situated on Hanger Hill.

The West Middlesex Golf Club, which shares with that of Staines the honour of being the oldest in Middlesex, was instituted in 1890. The course of eighteen holes, varying from 127 to 535 yds., is laid out on land near Hanwell belonging to Lord Jersey, on both sides of the main road from London to Uxbridge, about 8 miles from the Marble Arch. The hazards are gravel pits, ditches, ponds, and the railway, and the going is firm and dry. The record score in a club competition is 74 by Mr. C. T. Bazell. The professional record by C. R. Smith is 68, and the par 70.

The West Drayton Golf Club was founded in 1895 by a few gentlemen living in the neighbourhood, prominent amongst whom was Mr. Ernest Humber. The course of eighteen holes, which is bounded on two sides, and at one point crossed, by the River Colne, was originally laid out by the advice of Mr. Fairlie, but was altered and considerably extended in 1905 under the supervision of J. H. Taylor. It has a total length of rather over 3 miles, the longest hole being 521 and the shortest 125 yds., and traverses pasture land on gravel subsoil. The hazards are the river, ditches, and artificial bunkers. Play is possible all the year round, but is best during the spring, early summer, and autumn. The club house is the old Mill House. Bogey is 80. The amateur record is 72, held by Mr. H. W. Beveridge, and the professional record is Robert Thomson's 66. The prizes are the Fairlie Challenge Medal, the Grimsdale Cup, and the Gairdner Cleek Competition.[6]

The Hillingdon Golf Club, instituted in 1892 by the original trustees—Messrs. C. M. Newton, G. T. Worsley, and C. E. Stevens —has a nine-hole course, which was rearranged in its present form by J. H. Taylor, in the park of Hillingdon House at Uxbridge. The holes vary from 150 to 400 yds. The course lies over pasture land overlying gravel, gravelly loam, and clay, and the hazards are ditches, a stream, and artificial bunkers. Play is possible all the year, but is best during the winter months. Bogey is 39, and the professional record 34. The prizes are a scratch medal and cups, given by Mr. A. N. Gilbey.

THE SOUTHERN LINKS

The Strawberry Hill Golf Club, which was instituted in 1901, has a course of nine holes, varying from 150 to 448 yds., situated about midway between Twickenham and Teddington. Within two miles of this is the eighteen-hole course of the Home Park Golf

---

[6] At a professional match on 5 May 1905, over the West Drayton course, the following records were made :—J. H. Taylor 75, H. Vardon 76, J. Braid 77, W. Thomson 78. In the afternoon, in a four-ball foursome, Vardon and Taylor beat Braid and White by 4 up and 3 to play. Individual scores: Taylor 73, Vardon 75, Braid 75, White 81 ; *The Golfing Year Book*, 1905, p. 476.

Club, in the Home Park at Hampton Court. Here the turf is very fine, and the lies good, and, though somewhat flat, the links, being on gravel soil, are always dry.

The Fulwell Golf Club was originally instituted in 1904; it has been recently extended on the instigation of the hon. secretary, Mr. H. O. Stutchbury. It now has two eighteen-hole courses, opened for play on 19 November 1907, the longer of which is 6,000 and the other 5,000 yds. The shortest holes on each course are 125 yds., the length of the longest on the principal and second courses being respectively 514 and 437 yds. Both courses are laid chiefly over old pasture land on a light gravel soil, where the hazards are principally artificial, with a pond, a stream, and some gorse. They are playable all the winter, but the best months are May and June. Bogey for the principal course is 80, the green records being 71 professional (P. J. Gaudin), and 76 amateur (Mr. E. Gawne). The chief prize is the Tomlinson Challenge Cup, but there are also three monthly medals, and several prizes at the spring and autumn meetings, besides others given by individual members. There are two separate club-houses, for men and for ladies.

The Ashford Manor Golf Club, which is about three-quarters of a mile from Ashford, was founded in 1898. It has an eighteen-hole course of nearly 3½ miles round, which, with the longer course of the same length at Fulwell just mentioned, is the longest in Middlesex; the holes vary from 148 to 461 yds. It is laid over pasture land with a gravel soil, with hedges, ditches, and artificial bunkers as hazards, and is playable throughout the year, being an especially good winter course. The club-house is the old Manor House, which adjoins the links. Bogey is 81, and the record 70 (Mr. H. W. Beveridge). There are spring, summer, and autumn meetings, and prizes consisting of the Captain's, Artists', Wellroth, Hunter, and Mossop cups.[7]

Within 3 miles of the Ashford links is the Staines Golf Club, instituted in 1890. The course, of nine holes, is on Shortwood Common.

LADIES' CLUBS

There are fourteen[8] ladies' golf clubs in Middlesex, three of which—the Enfield and Stanmore Clubs, in the county, and the West Middlesex, amongst London clubs—were founded in 1893. Of the remainder two— the Ashford Manor Club and the Middlesex County Ladies' Club, the latter of which has no links of its own—are county, and the following nine are London clubs : the Muswell Hill Club, instituted in 1894; the Ealing and Hampstead Clubs, instituted in 1895; the Acton and Wembley Clubs, instituted in 1896; the West Drayton and Hanger Hill Clubs, instituted in 1900; and the Fulwell and Highgate Clubs, instituted in 1904. Of these the Stanmore, West Middlesex, Hanger Hill,[9] and Fulwell Clubs have separate courses for ladies, those of the first-named three clubs being of nine holes, while that of the Fulwell Club is an eighteen-hole one 5,000 yds. in extent. The West Middlesex, Fulwell, and Acton Clubs have also separate club-houses for ladies. The other clubs play over the same course as the men; but on the Ealing, Wembley, and West Drayton links the ladies play with shortened tees, and on those at Muswell Hill play only nine holes. The Acton, Ashford Manor, Enfield, Fulwell, Hampstead, Hanger Hill, and Highgate ladies' clubs are all branches of the men's clubs.

In addition to the various golf clubs above noticed, there are two other organizations in connexion with Middlesex golf which require a brief notice.

One of these is the Golfers' Club, Whitehall Court, established in 1893, which admits foreign and colonial as well as town and country members, and has a total membership of 1,000. A challenge shield and other prizes offered by the club are played for annually. The secretary is Col. W. F. Branston.

The other is the Professional Golfers' Association, instituted in 1901, of which the Right Hon. A. J. Balfour, M.P., is president, and Mr. C. E. Melville honorary secretary. A register is kept at the Association offices of situations vacant, and of those in need of employment; and provision is also made, through a benevolent fund, for relieving deserving members by temporary or permanent grants; assistance in cases of sickness, accident, death, and interments and for preventing the lapse of life, accident, or other policies; and for the grant of small annuities to the aged and

---

[7] Ashford Manor won the Middlesex Golf Challenge Trophy on 8 July 1905; *The Golfing Year Book*, 1906, p. 67.

[8] The Neasden Golf Club permits the election of a limited number of ladies as associates, who may play every day except Saturday and Sunday, and for whom separate rooms are assigned in the club-house.

[9] The Hanger Hill Ladies' Club has, however, also the right to play over the men's course on every day except Saturday and Sunday.

incapacitated, and allowances to widows and orphans. A tournament for prizes presented by *The News of the World* is held annually; the winner and runner-up in the competition, held at Richmond in October 1908, were J. H. Taylor and F. Robson.

In concluding this brief notice of Middlesex golf the Editor is glad to take this opportunity of offering his very cordial thanks to the secretaries of the many clubs which have kindly supplied him with information on the subject.

PASTIMES

The four principal pastimes especially associated with Middlesex are Archery, Tennis, Rowing, and Polo, all of which may be said to have originated in the county.[1]

ARCHERY

Owing to the fact that the bow was the principal weapon used both in war and in the chase in mediaeval times, and the consequent necessity for constantly practising its use, archery may be regarded as one of the oldest of our national pastimes. In its modern form this sport originated in London in the last quarter of the eighteenth century.

As the archers formed an important force in every army during the Middle Ages sovereigns endeavoured to make training in the use of the bow obligatory on the whole population. In the thirteenth century every person ' not having a greater interest in land than 100*d*.' was required to have in his possession a bow and arrow, with other arms offensive and defensive, and ' all such as had no possessions but could afford to purchase arms' were required to have a bow with *sharp* arrows if they dwelt without, and one with blunt arrows if resident within the royal forests.[2] In order to prevent the crossbow from in any way superseding the long bow a Statute of 1417 enacted that no one should use the former weapon who was possessed of less than 200 marks a year.[3] Towards the close of the fifteenth century archery had fallen somewhat into decay in spite of enactments of this character, but its practice was revived by Henry VIII, himself a skilful bowman, and an Act was passed soon after his accession, extending the qualification with respect to the use of crossbows to 300 marks, and requiring all his subjects under sixty years of age ' who were not lame, diseased, or maimed, or having any other lawful impediment,' the clergy, judges, &c., excepted, to ' use shooting on the long bow' under penalty on default of 12*d*. per month.[4] Parents were to provide every boy from seven to seventeen years of age with a bow and two arrows, and after seventeen he was to provide himself with a bow and four arrows; and butts for the practice of archery were to be erected in every town. The ' bowyers'— the importance of whose calling is evidenced by the fact that both they and the ' fletchers,' or makers of arrows, were included amongst the old City companies[5]—were required, under a penalty of imprisonment for eight days, to make at least *four* bows of ' elme, wiche, . . . or other wode apt for the same' for every ' ewe bow' which they made. Lastly, in order to prevent other pastimes such as football from interfering with archery prac-

---

[1] Another pastime deserving of a passing notice on account of its being by some regarded as the origin of the modern game of croquet, is that of Mall, a name derived from the French paile-maille, which is described in Skeat's *Etymological Dictionary* as ' a game wherein a round box bowle is with a mallet struck through an arch of iron, and the name of which is preserved in The Mall and Pall Mall.' King Charles, when improving St. James's Park, directed Le Notre, the gardener of Louis XIV, to whom the work was entrusted, to lay out ' a smooth hollow walk enclosed on each side by a border of wood,' and to ' hang an iron hoop at one extremity,' for the purposes of the game. The original Mall as thus constructed was half a mile long and bordered with lime trees. Charles was very fond of the game, and Waller in his poem *St. James's Park* eulogizes his play in the following lines :—

> ' No sooner has touched the flying ball
> But 'tis already more than half the Mall,
> And such a fury from his arm has got
> As from a smoking culverin 'twere shot.'

See Brailey, *Hist. of Middlesex*, iv, 481–2, and Wheatley, *London Past and Present*, ii, 457–6 ; iii, 8.

[2] Strutt, *Sports and Pastimes* (ed. 1903), 63.
[3] 19 Hen. V, cap. 1.
[4] 33 Hen. VIII, cap. 9.
[5] Stow, *Surv. of London* (ed. Strype), ii, bk. v, 217.

tice,[5a] a penalty of 40s. a day was imposed on every person who

> shall for his gain, lucre, or living keep any common house, alley, or place of bowling, coiting, clough, eagles, half-bowls, tennis, dicing tables, or carding, or any other game prohibited by any statute heretofore made or any unlawful new game.[6]

These stringent regulations are intelligible enough in an age when England, like other nations, had always to be fully prepared for war, since, as is pointed out by Colonel Walrond, fully two centuries elapsed after the introduction of hand fire-arms before the bow was finally ousted from its position as the chief weapon of the English soldiers.[7] This, probably, is equally true as regards the bow for the purposes of sport, and supports the view taken by the same authority that the popularity of archery as a sport by no means commenced when the use of the bow in war ceased, but was, on the contrary, greatest when it was most formidable as a military weapon.[8]

We find Sir T. Elyot describing archery in *The Governour*, published in 1531, as 'the principall of all other exercises,' and after praising the long bow as a military weapon, stating that 'there is both profite and pleasure above any other artillery' in its 'seconde utilitie . . . which is killyng of deere, wilde foule, and other game.'[9] *Toxophilus*, a work of Roger Ascham, published fourteen years later and presented to Henry VIII in 1545, is equally eulogistic of its merits. Henry, who is stated by Sir Thomas Elyot to have been an excellent shot,[10] was, like his predecessors, Henry V and Henry VII, very fond of archery, as were also Queen Elizabeth and Charles II;[11] and archery was common in all our early public schools.

At Harrow its practice was encouraged by a bequest establishing annual contests for shooting for a silver arrow, which were continued till 1771, when they were terminated, in spite of vigorous protests, by Dr. Heath.[11a] The extent to which archery was practised by the citizens of London in the sixteenth century is shown by the recital, in a true bill found against John Draney, 'citizen and clothier of London, on 20 January, 1560–1,' for having inclosed 'a certain open field called Stebenhythe Close;' that they had from time immemorial been accustomed, 'without hindrance from any person,' to shoot with bows in the common lands or 'feylds' of 'Stebenhythe' (Stepney), 'Ratclyff,' 'Mylende,' 'Bethnall Grene,' 'Spittlefeylds,' 'Morefeylds,' 'Fynesbury,' and 'Hoggesden;'[12] and evidence of similar rights in other parts of Middlesex is contained in the records of inquests held on deaths accidentally caused by shooting at Hampton,[13] South Mimms,[14] Stepney (two),[15] Matfelon (Whitechapel),[16] and Hendon.[17] Though Shoreditch is not included among the parishes above stated to have possessed common fields its inhabitants must have been keen archers, for one of them was playfully dubbed 'Duke of Shoreditch' by Henry VIII on account of the skill he displayed in a great shooting match at Windsor. At a similar display held at Smithfield during the reign of Elizabeth the same title was assumed by the captain of the archers, while other competitors grandiloquently styled themselves Dukes of Clerkenwell, Islington, Hoxton, and Shadwell, and Earl of St. Pancras.[18] Stow tells us in his *Survey* that in 1498 'all the gardens which had continued time of mind without Moorgate, to wit, about and beyond the Lordship of Fensbary (Finsbury) were destroyed, and of them was made a plain field for archers to shoot in;'[19] while before his time the

---

[5a] Football had already been condemned on this account by Edw. III in 1349. James I in a discourse to Prince Henry on manly accomplishments described it as 'meeter for lameing than for making able.'   [6] 33 Hen. VIII, cap. 9.

[7] C. J. Longman and Col. H. Walrond, *Archery* (Badminton Library), 137–8. Down to the end of the sixteenth century the contest was, he thinks, fairly equal.

[8] *Archery* (Badminton Library), 161. It may be noted in confirmation of this view that Edmund Yorke, when directed by Queen Elizabeth in 1588 to organize the defences of the City, after specifying the number of halberdiers, pikemen, musketeers, and arquebusiers required, adds that *no archers* were to be included, because 'on an alarm the multitude will come *armed with such weapons*' and 'there would be no use in *teaching art what is known by nature*'; Stow, *Surv. of Lond.* (ed. Strype), ii, bk. v, 453.

[9] *The Governour*, 291, 303–5.

[10] Ibid. 297, note *b*.

[11] *Archery* (Badminton Library), 161–2.

[11a] Ibid. 165–6.

[12] *Midd. County Rec.* i, 8. Both James I and Charles II issued commissions to check such inclosures; Stow, *Surv.* (ed. Strype), i, bk. i, 250.

[13] (26 Aug. 11 Eliz.) *Midd. County Rec.* i, 64.

[14] (1 Aug. 3 Eliz.) Ibid. i, 40.

[15] (19 Sept. 8 Eliz. and 4 Sept. 21 Eliz.) Ibid. i, 57, 118.   [16] (26 Sept. 8 Eliz.) Ibid. i, 58.

[17] (12 Oct. 3 Eliz.) Ibid. i, 41.

[18] Stow, *Surv.* (ed. Strype), i, bk. ix, 250.

[19] Ibid. bk. ii, 96, ii; bk. v, 437. In 1628 there were 164 marks in Finsbury Fields, which had dwindled to twenty-one and three butts in 1737. *Archery* (Badminton Library), 167.

mayor, sheriffs, and aldermen used at Bar-
tholomew-tide to 'shoot at the standard for
bow and flight arrows for games' in Finsbury
Fields, 'where the citizens were assembled'
for several days.[20] When he wrote, however,
their practice had become limited to three or
four days after the festival ; [21] and he
frequently laments the decay of archery under
James I and Charles I. The first of the
Stuart kings had indeed, in direct violation
of the Statute of Henry VIII, above mentioned,[22] granted permission in 1620 to
Clement Cottrell, groom porter of his household, to license in London and Westminster
and their suburbs twenty-four bowling alleys
and fourteen tennis courts, besides taverns for
dice and cards, and also a similar licence with
respect to any other game thereafter to be
invented.[23]

Charles II, who was, as has been said,
himself a keen bowman, effected a partial
revival in archery after the Restoration. A
company of 400 archers, under Sir Gilbert
Talbot as colonel and Sir Edward Hungerford
as leutenant-colonel, took part in 'a splendid
and glorious show in Hyde Park' in 1661 ;
and in 1681 the London archers marched to
Hampton Court to shoot before the king
for £30 worth of prizes at eight-score
yards.[24] Archery, appears, however, to
have ceased to be a national sport when the
bow was abandoned as a military weapon,
but prior to this two[25] notable archery
societies had been established in Middlesex in
the sixteenth century, through which the
connexion between ancient and modern
archery has been in some measure preserved.

The first of these was founded by Henry
VIII, who in 1539 by Letters Patent
appointed Sir Christopher Morris, his master
of ordnance, and Arthur Unwyt and Peter
Mewtas, gentlemen of his privy chamber,
'overseers of the science of artillery'—i.e.
long bows, crossbows, &c.[26]—with subordinate 'masters and rulers of the same
science,' and empowered them with their

successors to establish a perpetual corporation
to be called the Fraternity of St. George,
and to admit such persons as they found to be
eligible.[27] This Fraternity of St. George,
the members of which were authorized 'for
pastime's sake to practice shooting at all kinds
of marks, and at the game of popinjay in the
city of London and its suburbs as well as in
other convenient places,' used to practise in
Finsbury Fields.[28] After the abandonment
of the bow in war and the introduction of
firearms, a part of these fields was inclosed
by a wall and used for practice by the gunners
of the Tower, and since the early part of the
nineteenth century has been called the
Artillery Ground, while the Fraternity of
St. George was converted into the Honourable
Artillery Company.[29]

The other society is that of the Finsbury
Archers, which appears to have been founded
by certain members of the Honourable
Artillery Company, who being fond of the
bow practised with it as a pastime after they
had discarded it as a martial weapon,[30] and
it may thus be regarded as indirectly representative of the Fraternity of St. George.
To this society, which is first mentioned in
1590,[31] belongs the honour of having by the
establishment of three several competitions
called the Easter Target, the Whitsuntide Target, and the Eleven Score Target, initiated in
some sense the Grand National Meetings,
which have been held since the institution of
the Grand National Championship in 1844.
Records exist with lists of the captains and
lieutenants of the Easter Targets from 1617
to 1757, and of the Whitsun Targets from
1692 to 1761, and the rules of the Eleven
Score Target, the winners' names of which
are not given, are dated 1761.[32] In 1696 a
bequest of £35, to be divided in prizes, was
left under the will of Elizabeth Shakerley[33]
to the society, which then appears to have
shot in Finsbury Fields. One of the most
notable events in its history was the presentation in 1676 to one of its members, Sir
William Wood, as 'Marshal of the Queen's
Majesty's Regiment of Archers,' of a silver
badge, subscribed for by the officers and others
of the Society of Archers within the cities of
London and Westminster,[34] with an archer

---

[20] Stow, *Surv.* (ed. Strype), i, bk. i, 257.
[21] Ibid.   [22] *Ante*, pp. 283, 284.
[23] Rymer, *Foedera*, vii, 238.
[24] Strutt, *Sports and Pastimes* (ed. 1903).
[25] There was also another ancient society called
'The Ancient Order and Society and Unity of
Prince Arthur and his knights' of which no
records have been preserved. Stow, *Surv.* (ed.
Strype), i, bk. i, 280; *Archery* (Badminton
Library), 167.
[26] Ascham, *Toxophilus* (ed. 1864), 55, says that
'artillery nowadays is taken for two things, guns
and bows.' Cf. The *Governour*, i, 297.

[27] Strutt, op. cit. 44, 46, 57.
[28] Ibid.
[29] Stow, *Surv.* (ed. Strype), i, bk. ii, 96; ii,
bk. v, 457. Cf. Brayley, *Hist. of Midd.* i, 124,
and ii, 153.
[30] *Archery* (Badminton Library), 167-8.
[31] Ibid.   [32] Ibid.
[33] Strutt, op. cit. 57.
[34] *Archery* (Badminton Library), 168.

drawing the long bow embossed thereon, and having the inscription ' Reginae Catherinae Sagitarii,' and the arms of England and Portugal, supported by two bowmen.

In pursuance of a deed executed by Sir William Wood on 6 July, 1691, this badge —now known as the Catherine of Braganza Shield—passed after his death into the custody of the stewards of the society for the time being, and, after the dissolution of the Finsbury Archers, it and other articles belonging to that body were transferred by Mr. Constable, the last captain of the Easter Targets in 1757, to the Royal Toxophilite Society which he joined at its first establishment in 1780.[35]

The Royal Toxophilite Society, the oldest and most important of English archery clubs, was established in 1780 by Sir Ashton Lever, representative of an old Lancashire family and a great sportsman, in conjunction with Mr. Waring, the curator of his museum of collections, who had studied bow-making under Mr. Constable and the survivors of the Finsbury Archers.[36] At its first institution, which marks the revival of archery, the society shot in the grounds of Leicester House which stood in Leicester Square close to the site of the present Empire Theatre.[37] In 1784, however, it obtained leave from the Honourable Artillery Company to shoot in the Artillery Ground, and on 14 July of that year the Earl of Effingham and other members of the latter body subscribed to the rules of the society and formed an Archers' division of the Company, under the captaincy of Lord Effingham. In 1787 H.R.H. the Prince of Wales became patron of the society and sometimes shot with its members. In 1791, when these numbered 168, the society rented grounds in Gower Street near Torrington Square, and it was not until after two successive moves to Highbury, in 1820, and to Westbourne Street, Bayswater, in 1825, that it eventually succeeded, in 1833, in obtaining a lease from the Crown of its present grounds, some 6 acres in extent, at Archer's Lodge in the Inner Circle at Regent's Park.[38]

The position occupied by the Royal Toxophilite Society is, as pointed out by Colonel Walrond, an important one.

It certainly is the leading body of archery, and, though the existence of the Grand National Society prevents its wielding the authority over the sport that is exercised by the M.C.C. over cricket, its influence over archery is great and far reaching.

Its members are scattered all over England, and it is the only society which can really claim to be the nursery of shooting among men, as no society which does not practise the York Round can be looked upon, from an archery point of view, as more than a social gathering.[39]

The high standard that the society has maintained as regards shooting is shown by the fact that since the institution, in 1844, of the Grand National Championship it has only been held by three gentlemen who were not past or present members of the Royal Toxophilite Society.[40]

Most of the Thursdays during the session are Target and Extra Target Days ; and there are Summer and Autumn Handicap Meetings. There is also a Ladies' Day in July when ladies compete, by invitation, for prizes given by members of the society. The club house contains an interesting collection of historical English bows and of those of all other nations, as well as of pictures and relics connected with archery, such as the Catherine of Braganza Shield.[41]

The Archers' Register for 1864 shows the existence of two other archery societies which have since ceased to exist. These were the Enfield Archers, established in 1857, which then had from fifty to seventy members and met in Enfield Old Park ; and the Harrow Archers, with respect to which no details are given.[42] The only other society besides the Royal Toxophilite Society mentioned in the *Archers' Register* for 1906 is the Pinner Archery Society, the date of foundation and membership of which are not recorded.[43]

ROWING

As it is stated in the recital of the first charter of incorporation, granted to the Company of Watermen and Lightermen in 1514 by Henry VIII, that ' it had been a laudable custom and usage tyme out of mind to use the river in barge or wherry boat,'[44] rowing in Middlesex may be said to date from time immemorial, but until the beginning of the

---

[35] *Archery* (Badminton Library), 168–9.
[36] Ibid. 227–8.   [37] Ibid.
[38] Ibid. 230–4.

[39] Ibid. 238. The York Round was first instituted in 1556. It consists of 72 arrows at 100 yds., 48 at 80 yds., and 24 at 60 yds. Ibid. 240.
[40] Ibid. 238.
[41] Cf. *The Archers' Register*, 1906.
[42] Ibid. (1864), 56, 75.
[43] Ibid. (1906), 54.
[44] Humpherus, *Hist. of the Origin and Progress of the Company of Watermen and Lightermen of the River Thames* (1514–1859), i, 212.

nineteenth century it appears to have been entirely professional.

It must not, however, be forgotten that the Thames watermen were the first exponents of the art of rowing,[45] and that amateur oarsmanship is only the development on more scientific lines of the craft from which they derived their livelihood.[46] The oldest rowing fixture on the Thames instituted nearly three centuries ago is the annual race for Doggett's Coat and Badge. The prize is a waterman's coat and silver badge given to be rowed for by six young watermen on the first anniversary of George I, 1 August, 1715, by Thomas Doggett, an eminent actor of Drury Lane, who, at his death in 1722, bequeathed a sum of money for the continuance of the custom.[47] The first regatta is stated in the Badminton volume on *Rowing* [48] to have been rowed in front of Ranelagh Gardens in 1775 'presumably by professionals;' and there is a reference to a similar event on 6 August, 1795, in the *Sporting Magazine* of that year where it is described as 'the contest for the annual wherry given by the Proprietors of Vauxhall by six pairs of oars in three heats.' Coming to the next century, during 1822 we find reports in *Bell's Life* of 'the anniversary of the Grand Aquatic Regatta of the inhabitants of Queenhithe,' when 'a handsome Wherry' and other prizes were contended for on 31 July by 'six of the free watermen belonging to those stairs;' [49] and of a similar contest on 30 June between eight watermen belonging to the Temple Stairs for 'a prize wherry given by the gentlemen of the Inns of Court.' [50] Another report in the same paper during this year [51] is deserving of notice on account of its allusion to amateur oarsmen. It relates to a 'match' on 8 July

between seven pairs of oars for a prize of thirty pounds which was given by 'The gentlemen of the Frederic and the Corsair,' or in other words by the Amateur Rowing Club, which is composed of noblemen and gentlemen nearly the whole of whom are in the Life and Foot Guards.

The course for the first heat of this race was

from Westminster Bridge to the Sun at Battersea round a boat moored off there and back to a boat moored off the Red House ; and for a second heat from Vauxhall Bridge round a boat moored off the Red House and back to a boat moored off White Hall.

The patronage of the Amateur Rowing Club and the fact that the competition was not limited to the watermen of any particular 'Stairs' seems to have made this regatta of exceptional importance, and we are told that 'the river was literally covered with boats and cutters, and the duke of York was present on the Frederic.'

Boating at this period was already beginning to become a popular sport among amateurs. We hear of 'long distance' rows, such as that of 100 miles rowed by 'six gentlemen of the Amicus Cutter Club crew' from Westminster to Gravesend, from Gravesend to Twickenham, and from Twickenham to Westminster in 1821 ; and another in the following year of eighty miles from the Tower Stairs to the Nore Light by eight members of the same club, performed in eighteen hours nineteen minutes with only half an hour's rest.[52] A four composed of officers of the Guards, stroked by the Hon. John Needham, afterwards tenth Viscount Kilmorey, rowed from Oxford to London in a day ; and the Westminster Boys on St. George's Day, 1825, rowed the Challenge to Eton and back, only fourteen of the twenty hours occupied in covering the 115 miles being spent in the boat.[53] Four amateur clubs are known to have been in existence early in the nineteenth century—the Star, the Arrow, the Shark, and the Siren—which rowed races among themselves in six-oared boats, generally over long courses.[54] The members of the Temple seem, too, like the officers of the Guards, to have formed some sort of rowing club, for Mr. Sargeant, in his *Annals of Westminster School*, says that the *Defiance*—the first racing boat which the school put on the river—'in 1818 lowered the unbeaten colours of the Templars.' [55]

It is stated in the *Westminster Water Ledger*, which is probably the oldest contemporary record in existence with respect to rowing on the Thames in London, that the school had

[45] While they practised rowing as a pastime as well as a profession, they could also, as Stow tells us, at the close of the sixteenth century have at any time furnished 20,000 men for the fleet. Numbers of them served both in the Walcheren Expedition in 1809 and in that of Lord Exmouth in 1816. Humpherus, op. cit. iii, 81, 114, 136.

[46] Both Eton and Westminster crews were in early days coached by watermen. *Ency. Brit.* art. 'Rowing' by Edwin D. Brickdale.

[47] Reports of this race are given in the *Sporting Magazine* for August 1795 and *Bell's Life*, August 1822. [48] p. 3.

[49] *Bell's Life* 1822, 183, 4.

[50] Ibid. 143. [51] Ibid. 160.

[52] *Bell's Life* (1822), 159, 160.

[53] Sargeant, *Annals of Westminster School*, 226.

[54] *Rowing* (Badminton Library), 3, 4. *Ency. Brit.* art. 'Rowing' by Edwin Brickdale.

[55] Op. cit. 225.

a boat on the river in 1815.[56] This six-oared boat, the *Fly*, though not apparently built for racing, won a race against the Temple in 1816 and another with the *Defiance*; and two subsequent boats, the *Challenge* and the *Victory*, are said to have never been beaten in the races with London clubs to which the rowing of the school was limited till 1829.[57] It was not until this year that the first race with Eton—previous challenges from which, between 1814 and 1820, Westminster had been prevented by the prejudices of its head masters, Page and Goodenough, from accepting[58]—took place.[59] This—the first recorded amateur race of importance—and two subsequent contests in 1831 and 1835, ended in a victory for Eton. In 1837, however, Westminster had its revenge in a race which is further memorable for the fact that it led to the adoption of pink as the recognized colour of the school, the crew of which had previously, like that of Eton, worn blue and white; and also for the attendance of King William IV, whose rashness in insisting on witnessing the race seriously aggravated the fatal illness from which he was suffering.[60] In 1846 Westminster again beat Eton but was easily defeated in the following year. Under the head-mastership of Liddle, who did not regard rowing with favour, the sport was for a while suppressed.[61] In 1853 the school rowed Leander in a race from Battersea to Putney, losing by a length, and in 1854 it defeated the club in another contest from Vauxhall to Putney.[62]

Among the most noted of the numerous celebrated oarsmen whom Westminster produced were Sir Patrick Colquhoun, winner of the Wingfield Sculls in 1837, Sir Warrington Smyth, and the first Lord Esher.[63] The last named, as W. B. Brett of Caius, rowed in the Cambridge crew which won the first University Boat Race from Westminster to Putney in 1836, and in the following year defeated the Leander Club in a race over the same course.

Leander, the oldest club on the tideway, was founded in 1818 or 1819 by members of the old Star and Arrow Clubs, and was at first limited to sixteen, then to twenty-four and later to thirty-five members, until the removal of this restriction in 1857—which was suggested by the success of the London Club founded in the previous year—converted it into the largest club on the river.[64] In its earlier races it was steered by its waterman, Jim Parish, and it was the first club to lend a helping hand to promising young members of the craft for whose benefit is instituted a coat and badge for scullers.[65] When it rowed Cambridge in 1837, Leander, to quote a description given of that race by Lord Esher, Master of the Rolls, at a dinner in celebration of the fact that four of the appellate judges were old 'varsity oars' was—

a London Club consisting of men who had never been at the University but . . . were recognised throughout England, and perhaps everywhere in the world, as the finest rowers who had up to that time been seen.[66]

In 1831 the club had defeated Oxford in a race rowed from Hambleden Lock to Henley Bridge, but when it lost the match with Cambridge six years later, the members are said by Lord Esher to have been 'verging on being middle aged men.' In 1858 it began to be recruited from both the universities, but it was not until 1875 that it won its first victory at Henley with an eight of one Oxford and seven Cambridge men, stroked by J. H. D. Goldie.[67] Since 1880, when it again won the Grand Challenge with a crew of seven Oxford and one Cambridge oars, stroked by T. C. Edwardes-Moss, there have been only three years when it has not entered at Henley,[68] and between 1898 and 1905 it has won the Grand Challenge Cup seven times. Besides the two just mentioned it has included amongst its famous oarsmen R. H. Labet, C. W. Kent, Guy Nickalls, V. Nickalls, G. D. Rowe and Lord Ampthill. The present captain is Mr. C. B. Johnstone, president of the Cambridge eight which beat Harvard in 1906.

The London Rowing Club and the Thames Rowing Club, which have combined with Leander to raise amateur rowing to its present high standard, have had similarly successful careers, though both of these famous clubs are many years younger. The London was founded by members of the Argonauts Club in 1856, and was the first really large rowing club unlimited in numbers. Within three

[56] *Rowing* (Badminton Library), 5, 6.
[57] *Ann. of Westminster School*, 225; *Ency. Brit.* art. 'Rowing,'
[58] *Ann. of Westminster School*, 225.
[59] Ibid. 238.   [60] Ibid.
[61] Ibid. 248; cf. Markham, *Recollections of a Town Boy at Westminster*, 143.
[62] Ibid. 142.
[63] *Ann. of Westminster School*, 238.

[64] *Rowing* (Badminton Library), 185.
[65] *Ency. Brit.* art. 'Rowing' by Edwin D. Brickdale, and cf. an art. on 'Twelve Famous Clubs' by an Old Blue in the *Daily Telegraph* 20 May 1907.
[66] *Rowing* (Badminton Library), 12.
[67] *Twelve Famous Clubs.*   [68] Ibid.

months of its creation it had 150 members [69] and in the year after its foundation it won the Grand Challenge Cup at Henley with a crew composed of Ireland (bow), Potter, Schlosel, Nottidge, Paine, Farrar, Casamajor, and H. H. Playford (stroke).[70] It has been prominently associated with every advance in rowing except the keelless eight, and was the first to introduce the sliding seat in 1872 at Henley.[71] It has won the Grand Challenge Cup at Henley twelve times, the Stewards fifteen times and the Goblets eleven times. Among its most celebrated members may be named F. and H. H. Playford, J. Nottidge, J. Paine, A. A. Casamajor, W. Stout, and F. S. Gulston, the last named of whom won the Grand Challenge for London five times, the Stewards Fours ten times, and the Pairs five times.[72] The captain for 1907 is Mr. R. B. Freeman.

The Thames Rowing Club, started under the name of the City of London Boat Club, was instituted as a pleasure-boat club in 1861, but soon became a serious rival to the London.[73] Since its first appearance at Henley in 1870 it has won the Grand Challenge four times, the Stewards six times, and the Goblets three times, and has comprised among its noted oars, A. J. Lowe, R. H. Foster, J. A. M. Rolleston, W. L. Slater, W. H. Eyre, J. A. Drake Smith, B. W. Looker, D. Brown, and J. Hastie.[74]

In 1879 the Thames and London Rowing Clubs co-operated in establishing the Metropolitan, now the Amateur Rowing Association, which has combined the various Metropolitan Clubs under one flag for promoting the interests of amateur oarsmanship.[75]

Among the remaining Middlesex clubs, the Twickenham Rowing Club was founded in 1860, the same year as the Thames, and thus shares with it the honour of being the third oldest club on the river. It won its first regatta prize four years later by securing the Junior Fours at the Walton-on-Thames regatta but did not make its first appearance at Henley till 1879 when a crew, coached by the late J. H. D. Goldie, won the Thames Cup which it also secured in 1881 and 1884. In 1883, when the club was strengthened by the accession of D. E. Brown, J. Lowndes, E. Buck and G. E. Roberts from Hertford College, Oxford, and later by that of L. Frere, it rowed in the final for the Grand Challenge Cup, but

was beaten by London. It also succeeded in getting into the final for the same event during the two following years, but was defeated by London in 1884, and by Jesus College, Cambridge, in 1885. During recent years it has won the Junior Eights at Molesey Regatta in 1904, the Walton Eights, and the Junior Eights at Staines Regatta in 1905, and the Walton Eights and Walton Junior Eights at Walton, and the Coronation Cup at Kingston Regatta in 1906. The Diamond Sculls were won for the club five times in succession by J. Lowndes, from 1878 to 1883. The captain of the club is Mr. T. S. Grant.[76]

In addition to the above there are five other Middlesex rowing clubs:—The Kensington, founded 1873, the North London about the same date; and the Auriol, founded 1887, at Hammersmith; the Anglian, founded 1887, at Strand on the Green; and the Staines Rowing Club, established in 1894. St. Paul's School has also had a boat on the river since 1882, and has fixtures with the Merchant Taylors', Cheltenham, and Winchester Schools, and in 1903 the school won the Junior Eights at Molesey Regatta.[77]

There are annual regattas at Hammersmith, Twickenham, and Staines; but the most important on the tideway is the Metropolitan Regatta, established in 1866, on the initiative of Herbert H. Playford, captain of the London Rowing Club, which is under the sole management of that club.[78] The Wingfield Challenge Sculls—the annual race for the amateur championship of the Thames—was instituted in 1830, and derives its name from the donor of the prize. The course from 1830 to 1848 was from Westminster to Putney, and from 1849 to 1860 from Putney to Kew. Since 1861 the race has been rowed over the championship course from Putney to Mortlake.[79] Since 1897 the race has been won five times—in 1897, 1901, 1905, 1906, and 1908—by T. Blackstaffe of the Vesta Rowing Club,[80] who was also winner of the Diamond Challenge Sculls at Henley; and twice by B. H. Howel—for Cambridge in 1898, and for the Thames Rowing Club in 1899. In 1900 it was won by C. V. Fox of the Brigade of Guards Rowing Club in the

[69] *Rowing* (Badminton Library), 185.
[70] *Twelve Famous Clubs.*
[71] *Rowing* (Badminton Library), 198.
[72] Ibid. 199, 201.
[73] Ibid. 188.   [74] Ibid. 203-4.
[75] Ibid. 189.

[76] The writer is indebted to Mr. T. S. Grant for these particulars. Cf. *Rowing* (Badminton Library), 189-90, and *Twelve Famous Clubs.*
[77] *Rowing* (Badminton Library), 190, and cf. *Twelve Famous Clubs.*
[78] *Rowing* (Badminton Library), 191-2.
[79] Ibid. 131, and App. 331.
[80] The head quarters of the club, which was founded in 1871, are at the 'Feathers,' Wandsworth.

record time of 22 min. 50 sec.; in 1902 by A. H. Choate, London Rowing Club; in 1903 by F. S. Kelly, Leander Rowing Club; in 1904 by St. George Ashe, Thames Rowing Club; in 1907 by J. G. de Edye, and in 1909 by A. A. Stuart, Kingston Rowing Club.

Three international four-oared races have been rowed on the course between Putney and Mortlake; in 1872, when the London Rowing Club beat the Atlanta Boat Club of New York; in 1876, when it beat the Frankfort Rowing Club; and in 1882, when the Thames Rowing Club beat an American crew of somewhat doubtful amateur status.[81] The eight-oared race between Harvard and Cambridge in 1906, won by the Englishmen, was rowed over the same course.

PUNTING

There are punting courses in Middlesex at Staines, Shepperton, and Sunbury.[82]

TENNIS

Though there are allusions to tennis, formerly called 'tenisse' or the 'caitch,' in a ballad to Henry IV, written by Gower in ·1400,[83] and in Shakespeare's Henry V, there are no records of the game in England prior to the sixteenth century. The oldest tennis court in England is that erected by Henry VIII at Hampton Court, between 1515 and 1520.[84]

This court which has been the model for all existing ones appears to have been excellently finished in every detail. There are traces in it of what is termed a *rabat*—a net placed over the end pent-houses—which has not for many years been used in English courts,[85] and the following description given of it by Mr. Law in his *History of Hampton Court* shows the care which was bestowed on its construction:—

Although it is usually supposed by writers on the game of tennis that the courts in England were not glazed till the beginning of this century we find from the old bills that in the tennis court at Hampton Court the windows, which were twelve in number—six on each side—were 'sett with glass' in the year 1550, and over each of them was stretched a wire netting to prevent the glass from being broken by the balls. Each window was divided into three lights, and contained altogether 112 sq. ft. of glass, so that no inconsiderable amount of light was afforded within. At each end of the tennis court still remain 'the new lodgynges by the tennis play' which were built by Henry VIII, and which were doubtless occupied by the master of the court, the markers, servers and others. In these 'lodgings' there are in addition rooms on the ground floor adapted for dressing rooms, and others on the front floor with small windows into the court used by distinguished lookers-on. These and the court itself were connected with the main building of the palace by two passages or galleries, the upper one communicating directly with the old Queen's Gallery.[86]

The privy purse expenses of Henry VIII, who was a frequent and skilful player, contain numerous entries respecting the games he played at this court;[87] and among subsequent royal players there were Prince Henry son of James I,[88] Charles II,[89] and William III.[90] Both Charles II[91] and William III renovated the court,[92] and a bird's-eye view of it as it appeared after its restoration by the latter, engraved by Kip from a drawing by Knyff, is given in the edition of 1720 of *Britannia Illustrata*. Play was continued at the court after the palace had been divided into apartments. George Lambart, the greatest of living players in the last quarter of the nineteenth century, was marker there in 1866, and, on quitting it for the court at Lord's three years later, was succeeded by his younger brother William, who was still playing there in 1878.[93]

In addition to the court or 'close tennys play' at Hampton Court—where there was also an 'open tennys play,' which appears to have been constructed for a game resembling lawn tennis[94]—Henry VIII also built courts both at Whitehall and St. James's Palace.

With regard to that at Whitehall, Stow in his *Survey of London* says that on the right

---

[81] *Rowing* (Badminton Library), 190. The London Rowing Club also beat another American crew of equally doubtful status—the Shoe-wae-cal-meete Club—for the Grand Challenge Cup at Henley in 1878, thus preventing the cup from leaving the country.
[82] Ibid. 281–2.
[83] Strutt, *Sports and Pastimes* (ed. 1903).
[84] Julian Marshall, *The Annals of Tennis* (1878), 36, 86; Law, *History of Hampton Ct.* i, 138.
[85] *Ann. of Tennis*, 36, 39.

[86] *Hist. of Hampton Ct.* i, 139, 140. On the division of the Palace into private apartments the 'Lodgings of the master of the Tennis Court' formed one of the suites. Ibid. iii, 406.
[87] Ibid. i, 138, 139; *Ann. of Tennis*, 55, 56.
[88] *Hist. of Hampton Ct.* ii, 47.
[89] Ibid. 202–3; *Ann. of Tennis*, 88.
[90] *Ann. of Tennis*, 92.
[91] *Hist. of Hampton Ct.* ii, 202, 203.
[92] *Ann. of Tennis*, 75.　　[93] Ibid. 108, 109.
[94] *Hist. of Hampton Ct.* i, 140.

hand, beyond the gallery connecting the two portions of the royal palace at Westminster, were 'divers fayre Tennis Courts, bowling Alleys and Cockpits, all built by King Henry VIII.'[95] Though it is clearly shown in a map of 1658 by Fordham, no traces now exist of this court,[96] while the site of that erected by Henry VIII at St. James's Palace, in which both Henry Prince of Wales and his brother Charles I are recorded to have played,[97] is also unknown.[98] An order was issued 27 July 1649 to 'John Hooke, keeper of the tennis court at St. James's' to deliver the keys to Colonel Thomas Pride ' to enable him to quarter his soldiers there,' and Mr. Marshall suggests that it may have been converted into a sort of guard house or prison.[99] It is, however, referred to as the tennis court at St. James's in a warrant of 19 August, 1729, from the lords of the Treasury to the Clerk of the Pipe with respect to the lease of a piece of ground adjoining it.[100]

Charles II built a new court at Whitehall in 1662—the dimensions of which were taken from that at Hampton Court[101]—which appears to have been commonly called 'Longs,'[102] and an entry of 28 December in that year in Pepys' *Diary* describes a game, which must have been one of the first played there, by the king and Sir A. Slingsby against Lord Suffolk and Lord Chesterfield. 'The king,' he says, 'beat three and lost two sets, they all, and he particularly playing well I thought.'[103] Recording another game on 4 January, 1663, the diarist again says that Charles 'did play very well,' but observes that ' to see how the king's play was extolled without any cause at all was a loathsome sight.'[104] He also mentions 'a great match' at this court, on 2 September, 1667, 'between Prince Rupert and Captain Cooke against Bab May and the elder Chichely, when the king was at the court, and it seems that they are the best players at tennis in the nation.'[105]

In addition to these four royal courts, there were numerous private courts in London during the seventeenth century, nearly all of which

seem to have been on the Middlesex side of the river. In 1620, as has been mentioned in treating of archery,[106] James I granted permission to the groom porter of his household, Clement Cottrell, to license fourteen in London and Westminster,[107] but a list of those in existence in 1615 kept by the clerk of the works at Petworth, quoted by Mr. Marshall in his *Annals of Tennis*,[108] gives—exclusive of the covered and uncovered courts at Whitehall—the following twelve :— Somerset House, Essex House, Fetter Lane, Fleet Street, Blackfriars, Southampton Street (Holborn), Charterhouse, Powles Chaine[108a], Abchurch Lane, St. Laurence Pountney, Crutched Friars and Fenchurch Street.

The last-named court belonged to the Ironmongers' Company, who are shown by Mr. Marshall to have sold tennis balls as early as 1489, and as they were doing so in the twenty-sixth year of the reign of Henry VIII may perhaps have included that sovereign among their customers.[109] Evidence of the site of the court in Southampton Street is furnished by a place called the Tennis Court, on the south side of Holborn in Northumberland Court, Old Southampton Buildings. No traces of the others enumerated in the Petworth list exist.[110] There was, however, another court not included in it, which was built by the Earl of Pembroke's barber, and attached to a gaming house in James Street, Haymarket. This court appears to have been in existence from 1635 to 1866.[111] 'With convenience of situation,' says Mr. Marshall, [112] 'it united great excellence, not only in its proportions but also in the materials of which it was built, the stone of the floor having, as tradition says, been brought from Germany.' Barcella, a noted French player, played in this court in 1802, and in 1829 J. Edmond Barre played Philip Cox there at evens and beat him.[113]

The maintenance of the royal courts at St. James's and Whitehall during the early part of the eighteenth century is shown by references, respectively relating to the lease

[95] Stow, *Surv.* (ed. Strype), vol. ii, bk. vi, 6.
[96] *Ann. of Tennis*, 65, 66.
[97] Ibid. 76, 79, 81.
[98] Ibid. 65, 66.   [99] Ibid. 83 (7).
[100] *Cal. of Treas. Books and Papers*, i, no. 533, p. 133.
[101] *Hist. of Hampton Ct.* ii, 202, 203.
[102] *Ann. of Tennis*, 86.
[103] *Memoirs of Samuel Pepys* (ed. Lord Braybrooke), ii, 136.
[104] Ibid. 138.
[105] Ibid. iii, 348.

[106] *Ante*, p. 290.   [107] Rymer, *Foedera*, xvii, 238.
[108] Op. cit. 79, 80, where their respective dimensions are given.
[108a] Powle's Chaine, i.e. Paul's Chain, an old street near St. Paul's.
[109] *Ann. of Tennis*, 57.
[110] Ibid. 80.
[111] Ibid. 89. It is now numbered 2–6, Orange Street, Leicester Square, and has been converted into a warehouse for Messrs. Simpkin, Marshall, Hamilton, Kent & Co.
[112] Ibid. 90.
[113] Ibid. 102.

and purchase of lands adjoining them, in two treasury warrants of 1729 ;[114] and also by the record of payments of £90 10s. 6d. to Thomas Chaplin ' on his salary of £120 per annum as keeper of the tennis courts,' on 29 April in that year, and of £60 2s. 8d. ' to Charles Fitzroy, esq., keeper of H.M. tennis courts,' on 26 March, 1729, and on 19 August, 1730.[115] The game, however, seems to have then fallen somewhat into decay, and great as its reputation appears to have been, the court in James Street was most probably the sole survivor of the private courts.

It was not until the second quarter of the nineteenth century that there was any revival of interest in the game, and modern tennis must be held to date from the opening of the court at Lord's, the first stone of which was laid by Mr. Benjamin Aislabie on 15 October, 1838.

The dimensions of this court were taken from those of the court in James Street, Haymarket,[116] but it is pointed out by Mr. Marshall that it differs as regards the height of the net from that at Hampton Court and that, in addition to other imperfections, the galleries are all of wrong sizes.[117] Two of the first matches played in it were those between J. Edmond Barre, the celebrated French player, and Peter Tompkins, the Brighton marker, on 10 and 16 July, 1839, in both of which the former—who in the second match gave his opponent half thirty and a bisque—was victorious after a hard contest.[118] Among the most noted players who frequented it in early days were the Hon. C. Ashburton, the Hon. Captain Spencer, Captain Taylor, 6th Carabineers, and Messrs. G. Taylor, W.

Cox, C. Derby, H. Everett, Thorold Murray Crook, H. Clay, and J. M. Heathcote, the amateur champion in 1878.[119] In 1867 a gold and a silver prize for the best and next best amateur of the year, open only to members, was instituted by the Marylebone Club, the winners of which during the following ten years were :—

Gold—1867–77 J. M. Heathcote (every year).

Silver—1867 Julian Marshall.
1868 G. B. Crawley.
1869–73 Hon. C. G. Lyttelton.
1874–75 G. B. Crawley.
1876–77 R. D. Walker.

The winner of the gold prize in 1906 was Mr. Eustace H. Miles, and of the silver prize Major A. Cooper Key.

In addition to the court at Lord's there are two at Prince's—a social club established for the practice of tennis and racquets in 1853—and two at the Queen's Club, West Kensington, which was founded in 1886 for the practice of these games and of lawn tennis.

The match for the amateur championship in tennis, founded in 1889, is played at the Queen's Club. The winners have been :—

Sir Edward Grey 1889, 1891, 1895, 1896, 1898; Mr. F. B. Curtis 1890; Mr. H. F. Crawley 1892, 1893, 1894; Mr. J. B. Gribble 1897; Mr. V. Pennell 1904; Mr. E. H. Miles 1899–1903, 1905, 1906, 1909, 1910; Mr. Jay Gould 1907, 1908.

BOXING

Middlesex has always been the centre of the art of self-defence both for professionals and amateurs. A very large proportion of the champions of both sections have been Londoners or men long located in the metropolis. The first record that we find of public exhibitions and instruction in the art is in 1719 when one Figg, the champion boxer and back-sword player of his time,

opened an amphitheatre near Oxford Street. He also had a boxing booth at Southwark fair and at other similar gatherings. His prowess is commemorated by his pupil, Captain Godfrey, who in his *Treatise upon the useful science of Defence* speaks feelingly of the rugged way in which the preceptor imparted instruction to his pupils.

To Broughton, however, who was champion in 1734, belongs the honour of inventing the horsehair gloves and teaching boxing on scientific lines. His academy was situated in what is now Hanway Street,

[114] *Calendar of Treas. Books and Papers*, i, no. 533, p. 133 ; no. 146, 36.
[115] Ibid. i, 254, 552, 588.
[116] *Ann. of Tennis*, 101.
[117] Ibid. 36. [118] Ibid. 102.
[119] Ibid. 111, 112.

and a copy of his advertisement is here reproduced :

AT BROUGHTON'S NEW
AMPHITHEATRE

Oxford Street
The back of the late Mr. Figg's

On Tuesday next, the 13th instant
Will be exhibited

THE TRUE ART OF BOXING

By the eight famed following men, viz. :—

Abraham Evans	— Allen
— Sweep	Robert Spikes and
— Belas	Harry Gray the clog-
— Glover	maker
— Roger	

The above eight men to be brought on the stage and to be matched according to the approbation of the gentlemen who shall honour them with their Company.

N.B.—There will be BATTLE ROYAL between the NOTED BUCKHORSE

and seven or eight more ; after which there will be several BYE BATTLES by others.

Gentlemen are therefore desired to come by times. The doors open at nine ; the champions mount at eleven.

Broughton was the first to draw up a code of rules for contests, and these rules were revised in 1853 and 1866 by the Pugilistic Association.

Broughton reigned undefeated until 1750, when he accepted the challenge of Slack, the Norfolk champion. Broughton looked upon the affair as a certainty ; he did no training, and actually made Slack a present of ten guineas not to cry off. The match took place at the amphitheatre in Oxford Street, and Broughton's lack of condition lost him the day, his eyes so swelling from Slack's blows that he could not see. The Duke of Cumberland, the victor of Culloden, who was Broughton's backer, was said to have lost 10,000 guineas over the match.

After Slack succeeded champions of varying powers until Mendoza, a Jew from Houndsditch, gained the title in 1792. His battles with 'Gentleman Humphreys' attracted much attention to the art. In 1795 'Gentleman Jackson,' another Londoner, defeated Mendoza. Jackson subsequently at his rooms in Bond Street was instructor to half the nobility, including Lord Byron, the poet. Jackson died 7 October 1845, and a handsome monument was erected to his memory in West Brompton Cemetery.

In 1800 James Belcher of Bristol arrived in London and carried all before him until he was defeated by his fellow townsmen, Pearce and Tom Cribb. Pearce also defeated Gully, afterwards M.P. for Pontefract, for the championship, which Gully subsequently gained in 1808. Tom Cribb (long resident in Panton Street), became a very popular champion by reason of his two tremendous battles with the Herculean black Molyneux. For his second match with the negro he was taken to Scotland and specially trained by Captain Barclay of Urie.

These were the palmy days of the ring, when royalty in the persons of the Prince Regent and his brother the Duke of Clarence were not infrequent attendants at matches. At his coronation George IV engaged twenty of the leading pugilists as pages, and to commemorate their services presented them with a coronation medal, which was raffled for and won by Thomas Belcher.

To Cribb succeeded Thomas Spring, whose establishment, the Castle Inn in Holborn, now the 'Napier,' was long a favourite house of call for country squires and London visitors.

James Ward, a very scientific boxer from East London, gained the championship on Spring's retirement. He lived to the age of 84, and died in 1884. Another Londoner, Burke, a waterman in the Strand, succeeded Ward. In these days minor matches were numerous, and were decided no further away than Paddington, Highgate, Finchley, and Barnet, but when the authorities became more particular the railways and steamboats were utilized to reach spots where interference was unlikely. Caunt, who lived for many years off Regent Street, divided the championship for some years with W. Thompson, the renowned Bendigo of Nottingham, but the champions degenerated greatly in science until the advent of the redoubtable Tom Sayers.

Coming from Sussex at an early age that great fighter settled at Camden Town, and step by step fought his way to the top of the tree. During his career he contested sixteen battles. He only once, when hardly out of his novitiate, suffered defeat, at the hands of the scientific Nathaniel Langham, who, however, declined to meet him a second time. Sayers' height was 5 ft. 8½ in., and his weight 10 st. 6 lb. to 10 st. 12 lb. ; but he took on all comers. With small hands and arms he possessed fine shoulders, with great muscular development, and his hitting was tremendous. He was an excellent judge of distance and of timing his blows, and very active on his feet. He rarely used his right hand until he had got the measure of his opponent, and then brought it into play with such telling effect, that that hand was called his ' auctioneer.'

These qualities, and his indomitable pluck—he never knew when he was beaten—made him the idol of the sporting world. His great battle on 17 April 1860 with the gigantic American Heenan, to whom he conceded $4\frac{1}{2}$ in. in height, 3 stone in weight, and seven years in age, was stopped by the police after two and a half hours' desperate fighting (during two-thirds of which Sayers fought with only one arm, his right, the dreaded 'auctioneer,' having been disabled in the sixth round). Public appreciation of this remarkable exposition of pluck was shown by a presentation of £3,000 collected for Sayers in the House of Commons, on the Stock Exchange, and elsewhere, on the condition that he never fought again. To his untutored mind—he could not tell the time by the clock—this enforced leisure was fatal. Dissipation did its fatal work, and the little warrior who knew no fear lived but five years after his great fight with the American giant. He died at Camden Town 11 November 1865 at the age of 39, and a vast concourse of people attended his funeral in Highgate Cemetery. A fine monument marks his resting-place.

After the retirement of Sayers many clever men appeared, but the rascality of the low hangers-on of the ring quickly drove respectable people from attending matches, and the authorities took action by forbidding railway companies to run special trains. Nevertheless, many finely contested matches were brought off in the 'sixties between Mace, Goss, Travers, King, the brothers Allen, and others. Mace may perhaps be said to be the last of the champions of the old style of boxing, and probably was its most scientific exponent. He visited America and Australia, and carried all before him. King, a native of Stepney, was for years a well-known attendant at race meetings, and died in 1888 worth £54,000. Several attempts have been made to resuscitate bare-fist boxing, and as late as 1886 James Smith, a native of Clerkenwell, gained several victories and was dubbed champion. Since the legalizing of boxing with gloves fist-fighting has died out.

The transition stage between the two styles was the decade from 1870 to 1880. Many of the professors of the old style tried their hands at the new, and not always with success. Those who excelled at the one did not necessarily shine at the other. Even the great Sayers himself was not infrequently worsted with the gloves by men, half a dozen of whom he would have beaten one after another in the same ring with his fists. There were notable exceptions, however; Professor Mullins was never defeated in either style. He is still the most capable instructor of the day, and at his academy in Glasshouse Street has numbered, among his pupils, peers of the realm, men of letters, and even, it is whispered, embryo bishops. After the extinction of the ring, however, gloomy times followed in London for devotees of the art. Owing to the vigilance of the authorities it was at first most difficult to bring off matches with the gloves, and only a limited number of rounds were allowed as legal. Matters, however, gradually improved. Clubs were formed for the encouragement of professional boxing, and leading sporting men retained prominent counsel to prove the legality of boxing with gloves for prizes. The defunct Pelican Club in Gerard Street, which numbered amongst its members men of title and position, took boxing under its protection. Here Peter Jackson, the black champion of Australia, defeated James Smith for the championship, and many other notable matches were decided within its walls. When the Pelican Club ceased to exist the National Sporting Club was opened on 5 March 1891 in Covent Garden, in what had previously been Evans' Supper Rooms, immortalized by Thackeray. The Earl of Lonsdale was elected president of the club, a position which he still holds. This club is not only the head quarters of professional boxing in England, but is the Mecca of boxing champions from all parts of the world. Many hundreds of matches have been decided under its roof, the most famous being that between the two Australians, Peter Jackson and Frank Slavin, while more recently the Canadian T. Burns here defeated 'Gunner' Moir for the championship. The East End of London also has a famous arena called Wonderland, where boxing matches take place all the year through. The entertainment on a Saturday night is quite one of the sights of London.

Before leaving the professional section of boxing we may perhaps mention that a few veterans of old-style boxing may be met with in London, among whom we may name J. Carney; J. Baldock, a fine boxer and better second; and R. Travers, the only surviving opponent of Mace.

Though many fine amateur boxers were to be found in the early days when notable performers were Captain R. Barclay, E. H. Budd, the Hon. Robert Grimston, and Lord Drumlanrig, boxing was not seriously taken up by the mass of amateur athletes till about the time of the demise of the prize ring. In 1866 the eighth Marquess of Queensberry gave his approval to a code of rules drawn up for amateurs, which has ever since gone by his name. He also presented three twenty-five guinea cups for competition by light, middle, and heavy weights. These were boxed for annually at the Old Lillie Bridge grounds at Fulham, under the auspices of the Amateur Athletic Association. In 1882 the cups mysteriously disappeared, and the newly-formed Amateur Boxing Association took over the title of championships for their meetings. These were first held at St. James's Hall, then at Clerkenwell, and more recently, to accommodate the numerous spectators, they have been held at the Alexandra Palace. Competitors are divided into five classes : Bantam weights, 8 st. 4 lb. and under; feather, 9 st. and under ; light, 10 st. and under ; middle, 11 st. 4 lb. and under ; heavy, any weight. A ten-guinea silver cup is presented to the winner in each weight.

Amateur boxing clubs were never more numerous in London than at the present time, some of the better known being the Polytechnic, the Lynn, the Columbia, St. Bride's Institute, Belsize, the Eton Mission, Gainsford, and the German Gymnasium.

The art is also scientifically taught by qualified professors at the great public schools, Harrow, Highgate, and St. Paul's. The students annually compete in the Public School championships, and those from St. Paul's have received from their instructor, Professor Driscoll, such a sound grounding in the grammar of the art, that they have been remarkably successful. To the famous amateurs mentioned above should be added the name of Canon J. J. McCormick, D.D., of St. James', Piccadilly, the Cambridge double 'blue,' who in his university days could hold his own with the scientific Langham and other leading professionals.

THE OLYMPIC GAMES OF LONDON, 1908

The year 1908 is memorable in the annals both of Middlesex and of British sport, for the celebration of the Olympic Games of London—the fourth of a series of similar celebrations, which was initiated by the Games of Athens[1] in 1896, and followed by those of Paris[2] in 1900, and of St. Louis in the United States in 1904.[3] Owing to the large number of entries from twenty-one foreign countries, as well as those of British competitors, amounting in all to some 3,000, the London celebration was by far the largest athletic gathering of which there is any record ;[4] and as the programme comprised over 100 events in connexion with no less than twenty different forms of sport, it also supplied the most comprehensive test of international athletic proficiency which has, probably, ever yet been provided.[5] In addition to this, the historical interest of the Games as the revival in modern form, after an interval of over 1,500 years, of the famous Greek athletic festival was enhanced by the fact that, as the next eighteen celebrations will take place, at intervals of four years, in other countries, nearly three-quarters of a century must elapse before they can again be held in these islands.[6]

[1] See as to the Greek Games, *The Olympic Games,* B.C. 776 *to* A.D. 1896, by Sp. P. Lambros and N. C. Politis, Professor at the University of Athens, published with the sanction and under the patronage of the Central Committee of Athens. Translated from the Greek by C. A. In addition to the learned historical description of the ancient games and the details of the Athens celebration, this work contains, in Part II, an account by M. le Baron Pierre de Coubertin, the prime mover in their revival, of the origin and organization of the modern Olympic Games.

[2] An interesting account of the French Games will be found in an article by Baron Pierre de Coubertin, on 'The Olympian Games,' in the *North American Review* for June 1900, p. 753 et seq.; full records of the results are given in *The Olympic Games of London,* published by *The Sporting Life,* at p. 234, which also gives those of the Athens Games.

[3] Full details of the American Games are given in *The History of the Louisiana Purchase Exposition and the St. Louis World's Fair,* 1904, by Mark Bennett, chap. xvi, 565–73. See, too, as to records of the results, *The Olympic Games of London,* above cited, 234.

[4] *The Times* article on 'The Games of London,' 18 July 1908, p. 18.

[5] Ibid. and cf. an article on 'The Olympic Games,' by a Member of the British Olympic Committee, in *Bailey's Magazine of Sports and Pastimes,* Sept. 1908, p. 215 et seq.

[6] It was originally proposed that the games of 1908 should be held in Rome, and those of 1912 and 1916 probably in Berlin and Stockholm respectively, but, owing to the inability of the Italian representation on the International Olympic Committee to accept this offer, application was made through Lord Desborough—who had been present at the Athens Games in 1896 as one of the British referees—to Great Britain. *The Times* article on 'The Games of London,' 18 July, p. 18.

The Games were held under the auspices of the International Olympic Committee—a body instituted at the Athletic International Congress held in Paris in June 1893. It comprises the representatives of the principal European countries and of the United States, under the presidency of Baron Pierre de Coubertin, the chief originator of the revival of the Olympic Festival.[7] The functions of this committee are, however, mainly limited to the selection of the country in which the games are to be held, and the control of and arrangements for those of London was entrusted entirely to the British Olympic Council, as the sub-committee appointed for the purpose in the country thus selected.[8] Both the chairman and the hon. secretary of the Council—Lord Desborough and the Rev. R. S. de Courcy Laffan—are members of the International Olympic Committee;[9] and its thirty-eight members were respectively appointed by the English governing authority of every sport forming part of the programme, and by such similar authorities in other parts of the United Kingdom as chose and were able to be represented.[10] Captain F. W. Jones acted as assistant secretary, and Mr. W. Henry, hon. secretary Royal Life Saving Society, as Director of the Stadium. The bulk of the extensive and varied work of the Council was distributed amongst four Standing Committees —the Art Committee, responsible for prize and the commemorative medals designed by Mr. Bestwick McKerral; the Finance Committee; the Housing and Entertainment Committee; and the Programme (virtually the Executive) Committee, dealing with all the details of the athletic side of the Games.[11] The management of each branch of the Games was placed entirely in the hands of the association governing that sport in this country, which provided all officials, &c., and was responsible for the proper conduct of the competitions; but, though the representatives of foreign countries took no part in the management unless especially requested to do so in any particular instance, each nation or country competing had the right to appoint three members of a 'comité d'honneur,'[12] through which any protests or objections made by competitors from that nation or country were conveyed to the proper authority.[13]

In a letter of 20 June Lord Desborough

[7] *The Olympic Games*, B.C. 776 to A.D. 1896, pt. ii, 1–8.
[8] Article *North American Review*, June 1900, pt. 8, sup. pp. 803, 804.
[9] *The Olympic Games of London*, 1908. List of members of Council.
[10] *The Times* article on 'The Games of London,' 18 July, p. 18. The following list of members is given in *The Olympic Games of London*, 1908, cit. sup. :—The Lord Montagu of Beaulieu, Automobile Club; Maj.-General the Lord Cheylesmore, C.V.O., chairman of Council National Rifle Association; Sir Lees Knowles, bart., chairman Motor Yacht Club; H. Benjamin, esq., ex-president Amateur Swimming Club; E. A. Biedermann, esq., hon. sec. Tennis and Racquets Association; J. Blair Blair, esq., Scottish Cyclists' Union; T. W. J. Britten, esq., hon. treas. National Cyclists' Union; Michael J. Bulger, esq., M.D., Irish A.A.A.; Guy M. Campbell, esq., F.S.A., Amateur Fencing Association; Lieut.-Colonel C. R. Crosse, sec. National Rifle Association; J. H. Douglas, esq., president Amateur Boxing Association; D. S. Duncan, esq., hon. sec. Scottish A.A.A.; W. Hayes Fisher, esq., president National Skating Association; Major F. Egerton Green, Hurlingham Club; R. G. Gridley, esq., hon. sec. Amateur Rowing Association; F. B. O. Hawes, esq., hon. sec. Lacrosse Union; W. Henry, esq., sec. Royal Life Saving Society; G. Rowland Hill, esq., president Rugby Football Union; Captain A. Hatton, F.S.A., president Amateur Fencing Association; W. J. Leighton, esq., M.B., vice-president Irish A.S.A.; E. Lawrence Levy, esq., hon. sec. Amateur Gymnastic Association; G. R. Mewburn, esq., hon. sec. Lawn Tennis Association; Colonel G. M. Onslow, National Physical Recreation Society; E. J. O'Reilly, esq., Irish Cyclists Association; W. Ryder Richardson, esq., hon. sec. Amateur Golf Championship Committee; G. S. Robertson, esq., Juror at Olympic Games, Athens, 1906; C. Newton Robinson, esq., Yacht Racing Association; A. G. Stoddart, esq., sec. Queen's Club; E. H. Stone, esq., Clay-Bird Shooting Association; A. H. Sutherland, esq., chairman Amateur Wrestling Association; E. Syers, esq., hon. sec. Figure Skating Club; H. M. Tennent, esq., hon. sec. Hockey Association; F. J. Wall, esq., sec. Football Association; Colonel H. Walrond, hon. sec. Royal Toxophilite Society.
[11] *The Times*, 18 July, p. 18.
[12] Ibid. 'Nationality' as a qualification of competition was more strictly defined than in previous games.
[13] " Few greater compliments to English fair play than the delegation to our great associations of the whole judging in these games [says a member of the Council writing in *Bailey's Magazine* for September 1908, p. 216] have ever been paid either by the International Olympic Committee or by any similar body; and the general regulations, approved by the official representatives of every competing nation, are the real basis of the international code of sport authorized by the International Olympic Committee of 1907, which was accepted by the twenty different competing nations, as endorsed by the signed entries of their competitors, and which was translated into French and German and sent to every competitor before the games began."

SPORT ANCIENT AND MODERN

made an appeal through the newspapers for funds to enable the British Olympic Committee to maintain the British reputation for hospitality by arranging a series of social functions, to which all competitors and officials should in turn be invited ; and this was so well supported by the *Daily Mail* and the sporting and general press, that over £10,000 was subscribed for the purpose within a week.[14] On 11 July the athletes were officially welcomed at the Grafton Galleries by Lord Desborough and the Rev. R. S. de Courcy Laffan.[15] A series of banquets, presided over by the former, was given at the Holborn Restaurant to the athletes of different nationalities engaged in the Games,[16] and on 24 July a ball took place at the same place at which 700 ladies and gentlemen from eighteen different countries were present.[17] In addition to these entertainments, the Lord Mayor, on behalf of the City, gave a reception at the Mansion House, which was attended by the members of the International Olympic Committee, the Comité d'Honneur, and the British Olympic Council, and representative athletes from each of the competing countries ;[18] and dinners in honour of the same guests were given by the Government at the Grafton Galleries,[19] by the Fishmongers' Company,[20] and by the Lyceum Club[21] during the same month. The Amateur Swimming Association, Amateur Athletic Association, National Cycling Association, and other kindred bodies also materially aided in furthering the extension of hospitality to the foreign competitors ;[22] and at the close of July a series of entertainments, in which Lord and Lady Desborough, Lord and Lady Michelham, Sir F. Crisp, and the Hon. W. F. D. Smith played a prominent part, were organized in connexion with the Olympic Regatta at Henley.[23]

A British team to compete in the contests for field and track athletics and other kindred sports was, after various trials (beginning on 12 June), finally selected on 12 July, and for this four Middlesex clubs—the Finchley, the Polytechnic, the Highgate Harriers and the London Athletic Club—supplied twenty

members.[24] For this portion—the most popular if not the most important—of the Olympic Games, a Stadium, with sitting accommodation for 70,000, and additional standing room for 20,000 spectators, designed by Mr. Imre Kiralfy, was erected, at a cost of between £60,000 and £70,000, in the grounds of the Franco-British Exhibition at Shepherd's Bush.[25] The centre of the arena was an ellipse of turf, 700 ft. in length and 300 ft. in breadth, encircled by a running track, laid under the superintendence of the Amateur Athletic Association, which was itself encircled by a cycling track ; and a swimming pond, 100 metres long, with a deep space in the middle for high diving and water polo, was also constructed along one side of the arena.[26] On Monday, 13 July, this Stadium was formally opened by his Majesty King Edward,[27] and the Stadium events were continued day by day until 25 July, when the competitions in the following sports were concluded :—athletics, archery, bicycling, fencing, gymnastics, swimming, wrestling, and the Marathon Race (26 miles, 385 yards), the course of which began on the East Lawn of Windsor Castle and ended in the arena of the Stadium. At the close of the contests the prizes were given to the successful competitors by Queen Alexandra.

The Comité d'Honneur was twice called upon to exercise its functions during the progress of these competitions. In the 400-metres flat race between W. Halswelle (Great Britain), and J. C. Carpenter, W. C. Robbins, and J. B. Taylor (United States), Carpenter was disqualified for fouling Halswelle, and the race was declared void and ordered to be run again, when the two Americans, Robbins and Taylor, having failed to appear, Halswelle was given a run over and completed the distance in 50 sec.[28] In the Marathon race J. J. Hayes (United States), who finished in 2 hrs. 55 min. 18⅖ sec., was declared the winner. Dorando Pietri (Italy), who completed the course in 2 hrs. 54 min. 46⅖ sec., and passed the tape about 100 yds. ahead of him, was disqualified on account of assistance given by sympathetic spectators when he fell on the track.[29] On learning of Dorando Pietri's disqualification the queen expressed her intention of presenting him with

---

[14] *The Times*, 22 June, p. 16; *Olympic Games of London*, 227.
[15] Ibid. 227.
[16] *The Times*, 15 July, p. 12 ; *Olympic Games of London*, 227.
[17] *The Times*, 25 July, p. 9 ; *Olympic Games of London*, 228. [18] Ibid. 227.
[19] *The Times*, 25 July, p. 9.
[20] Ibid. 18 July, p. 18.
[21] *Olympic Games of London*, 228.
[22] Ibid. [23] Ibid.

[24] *The Times*, 1 June, p. 14 ; 12 June, p. 11.
[25] Ibid. 22 June, p. 16.
[26] Ibid.
[27] Ibid. 14 July, p. 10.
[28] Ibid. 24 June, p. 9 ; 27 July, p. 10 ; *Olympic Games of London*, 23-8.
[29] *The Times*, 22 July, p. 11 ; 24 July, p. 9 ; *Olympic Games of London*, 66-75.

297

a cup, which he received at the prize-giving on the following day.[30]

In athletics Great Britain won seven out of twenty-seven events, the prize for the tug-of-war going to a Middlesex team, the City of London Police,[31] and three Middlesex men—Webb of Hackney, 2nd both in the 3,500 metres and in the 10-mile walk,[32] Press of Hammersmith, 2nd in catch-as-catch-can wrestling,[33] and Slein of Hammersmith, 2nd in featherweight wrestling—[34] securing four 2nd prizes between them. In cycling Great Britain won five out of seven events, in swimming four out of nine, in archery two out of three, and in wrestling three out of nine; and in the whole Stadium events she secured twenty-three 1st, twenty 2nd, and twelve 3rd prizes as against eighteen 1st, ten 2nd, and eleven 3rd, won by the United States; and five 1st, two 2nd, and six 3rd prizes won by Sweden.[35] With the exception of the 200-metres flat race, all previous Olympic records in track events, and also in the 110 metres hurdles, the hammer and discus throwing, broad, high, and pole jumps, and 'triple' jump were beaten at the London Games.[36]

The competitions in the Stadium had been preceded by those in racquets, in April,[37] at the Queen's Club, West Kensington; in tennis and in lawn tennis (covered courts) at the same place in May; in polo at Hurlingham in June; in lawn tennis (grass courts) at Wimbledon, and in shooting at Bisley, and (in clay-bird shooting) at Uxendon in July. They were followed during the last week of that month by the rowing competitions at Henley, and by the 6, 7, and 8-metres boat events in yachting at Ryde; and in August the 12-metres boat-races, which closed the yachting competitions, were held on the Clyde and motor boat racing on Southampton Water. In October the Games were brought to a conclusion by the competitions in Association football, hockey, and lacrosse, at the Stadium, boxing at the Northampton Institute, Clerkenwell, and skating at Prince's Rink, Knightsbridge.[38]

On the 31st of that month a final official banquet, presided over by Lord Desborough, was given at the Holborn Restaurant to some 400 guests, comprising representatives from France, Germany, Sweden, the United States, Australia, and South Africa.[39]

In the above sports Great Britain won all the events in racquets, lawn tennis, polo, rowing, and yachting, and also six out of fifteen in shooting; and in all the competitions of the Games she won fifty-four 1st, thirty-six 2nd, and twenty-three 3rd prizes, as against twelve 1st, eleven 2nd, and thirteen 3rd, won by the United States; two 1st, five 2nd, and ten 3rd, won by Sweden; and four 1st, six 2nd, and six 3rd won by France; the position of the other nations being as follows :—[40]

	1st	2nd	3rd			1st	2nd	3rd
Canada	4	3	6	Finland	1	1	2
Hungary	3	4	1	Greece	1	2	0
Italy	2	1	0	Russia	0	2	0
Germany	3	4	3	Denmark	0	1	3
Norway	2	3	2	Australasia	0	1	2
S. Africa	1	1	0	Bohemia	0	0	1
Belgium	1	4	1	Austria	0	0	1

The American team, which is described by the writer in *Baily's Magazine*, already cited, as 'the finest team of athletes that has ever visited this country,' some of whom 'proved themselves the finest in the world,'[41] gained five prizes in track and nine in field athletics, and furnished the winner and the third and fourth in the Marathon Race, for which there were seventy-five competitors.[42] Sweden won both the javelin competitions, the high diving, and three of the shooting competitions, and divided the prizes for gymnastics with Italy; while France won first prizes for the tandem cycling 2,000-metres race, continental archery, and the individual and team competitions for the Epée, the other two fencing events for the

---

[30] *Olympic Games of London*, 66–75.
[31] Ibid. 88–91.   [32] Ibid. 60–6.
[33] Ibid. 153–6.   [34] Ibid. 156–7.
[35] Ibid. 229–32. See p. 229 for the positions of the other fifteen counties.
[36] Ibid. 13.
[37] Begun on the 27th of the month.
[38] See art. in *Baily's Magazine* for Sept. cit. sup. 215, and *Olympic Games of London*, passim.

[39] *The Times*, 2 Nov. p. 17.
[40] Art. in *Baily's Magazine*, cit. sup. 217.
[41] Ibid.
[42] *Olympic Games of London*, 13, 70, 71. It is suggested in an interesting criticism of the Marathon Race by the writer in *Baily's Magazine* for Sept., so frequently referred to, that the failure of the English runners, some of whom had beaten the performance of the winners on previous occasions, was due to their forcing the pace at the commencement on an exceptionally sultry day. In 1896 the length of the race which was won by a Greek in 2 hrs. 55 m. 20 sec. was 24 miles 1,500 yds. In the Paris race of 1900, won by a Frenchman in 2 hrs. 59 m. 45 sec., it was 25 m. 402·33 yds. In the St. Louis race of 1904, won by an American in 3 hrs. 28 min. 53 sec., it was 24 miles 2,500 yds. In the 1908 race the course of 26 miles 385 yds. was won in 2 hrs. 55 min. 18⅖ sec., but at a Marathon Race at Athens in 1906 (not Olympic), a course of 26 miles was run by the winner, a Canadian, in under 2 hrs. 52 min. (*Baily's Mag-* Sept. 1908, p. 221, and cf. *Olympic Games of London*, 234–5).

SPORT ANCIENT AND MODERN

sabre being won by Hungary.[43] The following is a list of the 1st Prize Winners (Gold Medallist) in the Games:—[44]

LIST OF FIRST PRIZE WINNERS

I. ATHLETICS (STADIUM)

(1) 100 Metres, R. E. Walker, South Africa
(2) 200 Metres, R. Kerr, Canada
(3) 400 Metres, W. Halswelle, United Kingdom
(4) 800 Metres, M. W. Sheppard, United States
(5) 1,500 Metres, M. W. Sheppard, United States
(6) 110-Metres Hurdles, F. C. Smithson, United States
(7) 400-Metres Hurdles, C. J. Bacon, United States
(8) 3,200-Metres Steeplechase, A. Russell, United Kingdom
(9) Five Miles Race, E. R. Voigt, United Kingdom
(10) Ten-Miles Walk, G. E. Larner, United Kingdom
(11) Marathon Race, J. J. Hayes, United States
(12) Standing Broad Jump, R. C. Ewry, United States
(13) Standing High Jump, R. C. Ewry, United States
(14) Running Broad Jump, F. C. Irons, United States
(15) Running High Jump, H. F. Porter, United States
(16) Hop, Step and Jump, T. J. Ahearne, United Kingdom
(17) Pole Jump, A. C. Gilbert, United States, and E. T. Cooke, United States, tied
(18) Throwing Hammer, J. J. Flanagan, United States
(19) Putting Weight, R. Rose (United States)
(20) Tug-of-War, Great Britain No. 1 Team
(21) Three-Miles Team Race, Great Britain
(22) 3,500-Metre Walk, G. E. Larner, United Kingdom
(23) Discus (Free Style), M. J. Sheridan, United States
(24) Discus (Greek Style), M. J. Sheridan, United States
(25) Javelin (Free Style), E. V. Lemming, Sweden
(26) Javelin (Restricted Style), E. V. Lemming, Sweden
(27) Relay Race, 1,600 Metres, United States

II. ARCHERY (STADIUM)

(28) York Round, W. Dod, United Kingdom
(29) National Round, Miss L. Newall, United Kingdom
(30) 40 Arrows, 50 Metres, M. Grisot, France

III. BICYCLING (STADIUM)

(31) 660 yds. lap, V. L. Johnson, United Kingdom
(32) 1,000 Metres. Declared void
(33) 5,000 Metres, B. Jones, United Kingdom
(34) 20 Kilometres, C. B. Kingsbury, United Kingdom
(35) 100 Kilometres, C. H. Bartlett, United Kingdom
(36) Pursuit Race, Great Britain
(37) 2,000 miles, Tandem, M. Schilles and A. Aufray, France

IV. FENCING (STADIUM)

(38) Epée Individual, Alibert, France
(39) Epée Teams, France
(40) Sabre Individual, Dr. Fuchs, Hungary
(41) Sabre Teams, Hungary

V. GYMNASTICS (STADIUM)

(42) Heptathlon, G. E. Braglia, Italy
(43) Teams, Sweden

VI. LAWN TENNIS (WIMBLEDON AND QUEEN'S CLUB)

(44) Grass Singles (Men), M. J. G. Ritchie, United Kingdom
(45) Grass Doubles (Men), G. W. Hillyard and R. F. Doherty, United Kingdom
(46) Grass Singles (Ladies), Mrs. Lambert Chambers, United Kingdom
(47) Covered Singles (Men), A. W. Gore, United Kingdom
(48) Covered Doubles (Men), A. W. Gore and R. H. Roper Barrett, United Kingdom
(49) Covered Singles (Ladies), Miss Eastlake Smith, United Kingdom

VII. MOTOR BOATS (SOUTHAMPTON WATER)

(50) Class A (Not named), E. B. Thubron, France
(51) Class B, *Gyrinus*, Thorneycroft and Bernard Redwood, United Kingdom
(52) Class C, *Gyrinus*, Thorneycroft and Bernard Redwood, United Kingdom

VIII. POLO (HURLINGHAM)

(53) Winning Team, Great Britain (Roehampton)

IX. RACQUETS (QUEEN'S CLUB, WEST KENSINGTON)

(54) Singles, E. B. Noel, United Kingdom
(55) Doubles, Vane Pennell and J. J. Astor, United Kingdom

[43] *Olympic Games of London*, 230, 233. Sweden also won the Gentlemen's Competition in Skating; *The Times*, 30 Oct. p. 5.
[44] This list is taken from *Baily's Mag.* Sept. 1908, p. 223; cf. that in *Olympic Games of London*, 230–5, and *The Times*, 7 July, p. 10; 26 Oct. p. 14; 30 Oct. p. 5; and 2 Nov. p. 17. For details of the different events, see *The Olympic Games of London*, 13–226, and the reports in *The Times*, 29 July, 29 and 31 Aug., and 5 Oct.– 2 Nov.

X. Shooting (Bisley and Uxendon)

(56) National Rifle Teams, United States
(57) Open Individual Rifles, 1,000 yds., Col. J. K. Millner, United Kingdom
(58) Open Rifle Teams, Norway
(59) Open Individual Rifles, 300 metres, A. Hilgerud, Norway
(60) Miniature Rifle Teams, Great Britain
(61) Individual Miniature Rifles, 50 yds., Great Britain
(62) Miniature Rifles, Disappearing Target, W. K. Styles, United States
(63) Miniature Rifles, Moving Target, J. F. Flemming, United Kingdom
(64) Revolver Teams, United States
(65) Revolver, Individual, P. van Asbrock, Belgium
(66) Running Deer Teams, Sweden
(67) Running Deer, Individual, O. G. Swahn, Sweden
(68) Running Deer, Double Shot, W. Winnans, United States
(69) Clay Birds, Individual W. H. Ewing, Canada
(70) Clay Birds, Teams, Great Britain, No. 1, Team

XI. Swimming (Stadium)

(71) 100 metres, C. M. Daniels, United States
(72) 400 metres, H. Taylor, United Kingdom
(73) 1,500 metres, H. Taylor, United Kingdom
(74) High Diving, H. Johannsen, Sweden
(75) Fancy Diving, A. Zurner, Germany
(76) 200 metres, Team, Great Britain
(77) 200 metres Breast Stroke, F. Holman, United Kingdom
(78) 100 metres Back Stroke, A. Bieberstein, Germany
(79) Water Polo, Great Britain

XII. Tennis (Queen's Club, West Kensington)

(80) Winner, Jay Gould, United States

XIII. Wrestling (Stadium)

(81) Catch as Catch Can, Bantam, G. N. Mehnert, United States
(82) Catch as Catch Can, Feather, G. S. Dole, United States
(83) Catch as Catch Can, Middle, S. V. Bacon, United Kingdom
(84) Catch as Catch Can, Heavy, G. C. O'Kelly, United Kingdom
(85) Græco-Roman, Light, F. Porro, Italy
(86) Græco-Roman, Middle, F. W. Martenson, Sweden

XIII. Wrestling (Stadium)—continued

(87) Græco-Roman, Light Heavy, W. Weekman, Finland
(88) Græco-Roman, Heavy, R. Weisz, Hungary

XIV. Boxing (Northampton Institute, Clerkenwell)

(89) Bantam Weights, H. Thomas, United Kingdom
(90) Feather Weights, R. K. Gunn, United Kingdom
(91) Light Weights, F. Grace, United Kingdom
(92) Middle Weights, W. H. T. Douglas, United Kingdom
(93) Heavy Weights, A. L. Oldman, United Kingdom

XV. Football (Association) (Stadium)

(94) England

XVI. Hockey (Stadium)

(95) England

XVII. Lacrosse (Stadium)

(96) Canada

XVIII. Rowing (Henley)

(97) Eights, Leander Rowing Club, United Kingdom
(98) Fours, Magdalen College, Oxford, United Kingdom
(99) Pairs, Leander Rowing Club, United Kingdom
(100) Sculls, H. T. Blackstaffe, United Kingdom

XIX. Skating (Prince's Rink, Knightsbridge)

(101) Ladies' Competition, Mrs. Syers, United Kingdom
(102) Gentlemen's Competition, Salchow, Sweden
(103) Special Figures, Panin, Russia
(104) Pair Skating, Byer and Fräulein Hübler, Germany

XX. Yachting (Ryde and the Clyde)

(105) 6-Metre Boat, *Dormy*, T. D. C. Meekin United Kingdom
(106) 7-Metre Boat, *Heroine*, C. J. Rivett-Carnac, United Kingdom
(107) 8-Metre Boat, *Cobweb*, B. O. Cochrane, United Kingdom
(108) 12-Metre Boat, *Hera*, T. C. Glen Coats, United Kingdom

SPORT ANCIENT AND MODERN

ATHLETICS

Middlesex ranks first of all the counties of England in this branch of sport, containing, as it does, some of the oldest and most important athletic clubs in the country; many clubs in the county indeed are able to boast of an unbroken existence of nearly half a century.

Foremost among athletic clubs in Middlesex is the London Athletic Club. Founded in 1863 under the title of the Mincing Lane Athletic Club, it took its present name in the spring of 1866. It held its first athletic meeting at the Beaufort House grounds at Brompton on 9 April 1864, and a second on 21 May of the same year. It continued to meet there until 1869, having in 1867 had sports at the Old Deer Park, Richmond, and at Beaufort House, Walham Green. After it moved its head quarters to Lillie Bridge in 1869 meetings were held there until 1876. In 1877 it again moved, this time to its own grounds at Stamford Bridge, Fulham. These grounds of six and a half acres were closed after the last meeting on 24 September 1904, and a new and larger track was made, partly on the same site, with a banked track for cycling and seating accommodation for 10,000 people. The new area of seventeen acres was still known as Stamford Bridge, and the L.A.C. opened with a meeting on 10 May 1905. During the winter months the ground is used by the Chelsea Football Club.

The L.A.C. has been fortunate in securing the support of many prominent men in the management of its affairs, such names as those of Lord Alverstone and the Earl of Jersey (both famous athletes of a bygone day) appearing, among others as famous, on its list of officers. Its present president is Mr. Montague Shearman, K.C., a well-known runner at Oxford University, who afterwards won the amateur championship both at 100 and 440 yards. The L.A.C. now holds four afternoon and two evening meetings a year at which races open to all amateurs, approved by the committee, are included as well as races for challenge cups and other events open to members. In addition the club holds an extra meeting in the spring, chiefly confined to contests at various distances for the Public Schools Championships. The club also competes annually against Oxford and Cambridge Universities, on the lines of the inter-University sports, and these meetings act as an interesting and useful trial for the teams about to compete in the more important event at Queen's Club. The membership of the L.A.C. now totals about 400, a number far exceeded in the early years of the last quarter of the nineteenth century, when athletics were more popular than they are at the present time. The club, however, has done yeoman service in the past in the cause of athletics.

Another old and still prominent club holding its meetings at Stamford Bridge is the Civil Service Athletic Club, whose members are drawn from the various branches of his Majesty's Civil Service. This club held its first meeting in 1864 at Brompton and, like the L.A.C., moved to Lillie Bridge in 1869, and finally to Stamford Bridge, where it held its forty-fourth meeting in June 1907. The Civil Service Athletic Club includes several open events in its programme which always attract good entries from the best athletes of the day.

The United Hospitals Athletic Club, founded in 1867, also holds its meetings at Stamford Bridge. Its chief attraction is a competition for a challenge shield between members of the various London hospitals.

Many notable performances have been done both at Lillie Bridge and Stamford Bridge from time to time, and though all the old amateur records made at Lillie Bridge have now been beaten, the following records, accomplished at Stamford Bridge, still stand to-day :—

W. P. Phillips, 120 yds. in 11$\frac{4}{5}$ sec. . . . . on 25 Mar. 1882
C. A. Bradley, 120 yds. in 11$\frac{4}{5}$ sec. . . . . „ 28 Apr. 1894
A. R. Downer, 120 yds. in 11$\frac{4}{5}$ sec. . . . . „ 11 May 1895
J. W. Morton, 120 yds. in 11$\frac{4}{5}$ sec. . . . . „ 24 Sept. 1904
C. G. Wood, 150 yds. in 14$\frac{4}{5}$ sec. . . . . „ 21 July 1887
E. H. Pelling, 200 yds. in 19$\frac{4}{5}$ sec. . . . . „ 28 Sept. 1889
A. R. Downer, 200 yds. in 19$\frac{4}{5}$ sec. . . . . „ 14 May 1895
C. H. Jupp, 200 yds. in 19$\frac{4}{5}$ sec. „ 4 June 1904
C. G. Wood, 220 yds. in 21$\frac{4}{5}$ sec. . . . . „ 25 June 1887
E. H. Pelling, 250 yds. in 24$\frac{4}{5}$ sec. . . . . „ 22 Sept. 1888
C. G. Wood, 300 yds. in 31$\frac{2}{5}$ sec. . . . . „ 27 July 1887
H. C. L. Tindall, 440 yds. in 48$\frac{1}{2}$ sec. . . . . „ 29 June 1889
(At A.A.A. Championship Meeting.)
E. C. Bredin, 440 yds. in 48$\frac{1}{2}$ sec. . . . . on 22 June 1895

W. E. Lutyens, 1,000 yds. in 2 min. 14⅘ sec. . . . . on 5 July 1898
J. Binks, 1 mile in 4 min. 16⅘ sec.. . . . . „ 5 July 1902
(At A.A.A. Championships, Lieut. H. C. Hawtrey only being beaten by a yard in this race.)
A. Shrubb, 3 miles in 14 min. 17⅗ sec.. . . . . . . on 21 May 1900
F. Appleby, 15 miles in 1 hr. 20 min. 4⅗ sec. . . . . „ 21 July 1902
W. G. George ran 11 miles 932¼ yds. in 1 hr.. . . . „ 28 July 1884
G. Crossland ran 20 miles 440 yds. in 2 hrs . . . . „ 22 Sept. 1894

After W. G. George became a professional runner he ran a mile in a match with W. Cummings on 23 August 1886, at Lillie Bridge, in 4 min. 12¾ sec., which stands as a world's record to this day. As an amateur he had twice beaten the mile record, once at Stamford Bridge and again at Lillie Bridge.

The Universities of Oxford and Cambridge have held their sports in London since 1867; but, when the Lillie Bridge grounds were closed, they founded the Queen's Club at West Kensington in 1877. Here is a splendid cinder track of rather over three laps to the mile, and this ground has since been the *venue* of the University Sports, which are always looked upon as one of the chief athletic attractions of the year.

The following are the inter-University records at the present date:—

100 yds. by J. P. Tennant, J. G. Wilson, and G. H. Urmson, all of Oxford, 10 sec.
120 yds. (hurdles), K. Powell, Cambridge, 15⅗ sec.
440 yds. W. Fitzherbert, Cambridge, 49⅗ sec.
880 yds. K. Cornwallis, Oxford, 1 min. 54⅘ sec.
1 mile, C. C. Henderson-Hamilton, Oxford, 4 min. 17⅘ sec.
3 miles, F. S. Horan, Cambridge, 14 min. 44⅗ sec.
High jump, M. J. Brooks, Oxford, 6 ft. 2½ in.
Long jump, C. B. Fry, Oxford, 23 ft. 5 in.
Putting the weight (16 lb.), W. W. Coe, Oxford, 43 ft. 10 in.
Throwing the hammer (16 lb.), R. H. Lindsay-Watson, Oxford, 148 ft. 10 in.

An athletic meeting between Oxford and Yale Universities was held at Queen's Club on 16 July 1894, Oxford winning by five and a half events to three and a half. Oxford and Cambridge met the combined Universities of Yale and Harvard on the same ground on 22 July 1899, when the Englishmen won by five events to four. Yale and Harvard wiped out this defeat at Berkeley Oval, New York, on 25 September 1901, by six events to three, and repeated their victory at Queen's Club on 23 July 1904, again winning by six events to three. At the latter meeting W. A. Schick, of Harvard, won the 100 yds. race in 9⅘ sec., which is a record for an English track.

The Amateur Championships prior to 1879 were controlled by the Amateur Athletic Club, which was formed in 1866. It held its first championship meeting in London in that year and continued to do so until the management was taken over by the Amateur Athletic Association in 1880. The Amateur Athletic Club held its championships at Lillie Bridge immediately after the Oxford and Cambridge Sports, and they were chiefly patronized by the runners from those Universities. Owing to the growth of the L.A.C. and provincial clubs it was felt that the general body of athletes would be able to compete on more equal terms if the championships were held in the summer. With this end in view, the L.A.C. held an extra championship meeting in the summer of 1879 at Stamford Bridge. On 4 April 1880, a meeting of representatives of the chief athletic clubs in the country was held at Oxford, and the Amateur Athletic Association was then formed, with its head quarters in London. The A.A.A. is now the governing body for all amateur athletic clubs in England. All athletic clubs of any standing are affiliated to the Association and hold their meetings under its laws. It has branches in the North and Midlands, and controls the championships which are held alternately in London, the North and Midlands.

Middlesex also contains some important cross-country clubs. The Highgate Harriers, founded in 1879, held the National Championship in 1899, 1902, 1904 and 1905, and won the Southern Counties Championship in 1899, 1900, and from 1903 to 1907 without a break. The Finchley Harriers, also founded in 1879, won the National Championship in 1900, and were Southern Counties Champions in 1887, 1888, 1891, 1892, and from 1895 to 1897. The Hampstead Harriers, founded in 1890, the Polytechnic Harriers, whose head quarters are in Regent Street, and the St. Bride's Institute Athletic Club also run across country.

TOPOGRAPHY

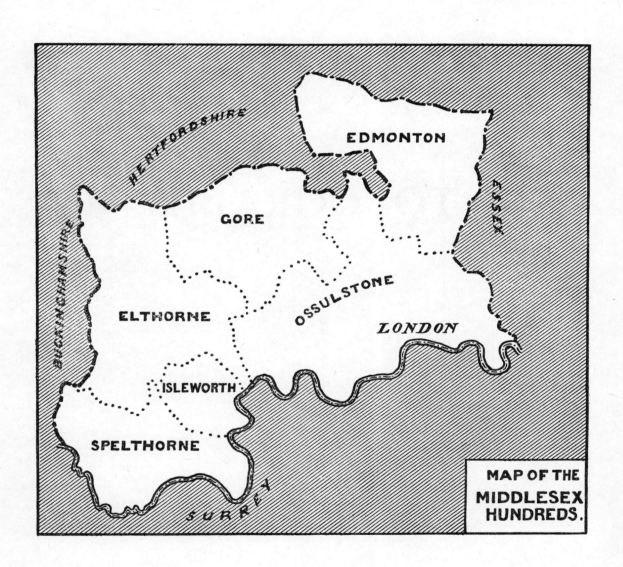

HERTFORDSHIRE

BUCKINGHAMSHIRE

ESSEX

EDMONTON

GORE

ELTHORNE

OSSULSTONE

LONDON

ISLEWORTH

SPELTHORNE

SURREY

MAP OF THE
MIDDLESEX
HUNDREDS.

THE HUNDRED OF SPELTHORNE

Spelthorne (Spelethorne, xi cent.) Hundred was already formed at the time of the Domesday Survey,[1] and contained, as it has since contained, the following parishes :—

ASHFORD

EAST BEDFONT with HATTON

FELTHAM

HAMPTON with HAMPTON WICK

HANWORTH

LALEHAM

LITTLETON

SHEPPERTON

STAINES

STANWELL

SUNBURY

TEDDINGTON

Littleton is the only place that is not mentioned in the Domesday Survey ; it was included, however, in Laleham.[2]

The hundred has always been held by the Crown, but the jurisdiction of the king's sheriff was largely curtailed until the Dissolution by the extensive franchise of the Abbot and Convent of Westminster. The principal manor held by Westminster was that of Staines, of which Ashford, Laleham, Halliford, Shepperton, Teddington, and Yeveney were appurtenant manors or members.[3] In the reign of Edward I, the Abbot of Westminster claimed the right to hold pleas of the Crown, view of frankpledge, the amendment of assize of bread and ale, and all pleas which the king's sheriff had in the county except appeals and outlawries, and to have market, fair, and toll, in Staines and its members.[4] The abbot based his claim on a charter of Henry III granting sac and soke, toll and theam, infangenthef and utfangenthef, and other privileges to the monastery, which charter had, he said, been inspected and confirmed by Edward I.[5]

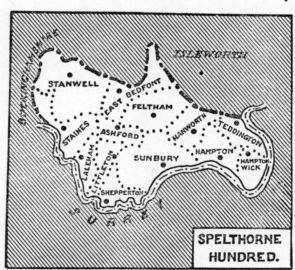

SPELTHORNE HUNDRED.

After the Dissolution, view of frankpledge was held in these parishes by the respective lords of the manors. It was held also in Teddington by the lord of the manor.[6] Hanworth lay within the liberty of the honour

[1] *Dom. Bk.* (Rec. Com.), i, 127–31.
[3] Cott. MS. Faust. A. iii ; Titus, A. viii.
[5] Ibid.
[2] See Littleton.
[4] *Plac. de Quo Warr.* (Rec. Com.), 479.
[6] Feet of F. Div. Co. Trin. 15 Chas. I.

of Wallingford, and was attached to the view of frankpledge held for that honour at Uxbridge.[7a] Stanwell and East Bedfont were included in the honour of Windsor. The Prior of Holy Trinity, Hounslow, had view of frankpledge in Littleton until the Dissolution.[8a] In 1540, Ashford, Feltham, Laleham, Hanworth, Teddington, and Sunbury, were annexed to the honour of Hampton Court.[9a]

ASHFORD

Ecclesforde, Exeforde (xi cent.) ; Echelesforde, Echeleforde (xiii–xiv cent.) ; Echelford, Assheford, Asheford (xvi–xviii cent.).

Ashford derives its name from the River Ash, which runs through the western corner of the parish, and from a ford over the river on the road which enters the parish from Staines and Laleham. A stone bridge was built over the ford in 1789 by the Hampton and Staines Turnpike Trust, and is still known as Ford Bridge.[1] The parish lies to the east of Staines, between the main road from London and the Staines and Kingston road, which form respectively the northern and southern boundaries. The country is low, lying only from 45 ft. to 50 ft. above Ordnance datum, and is nearly level throughout.[2]

The aspect of the whole parish is rapidly changing. Until a few years ago it was almost completely rural. Now, what was formerly the village street is being transformed by the erection of modern shops, and an entirely new town has arisen about the station to accommodate a population of the artisan class. To the east of the older part of the town is a group of private houses, standing in their own gardens. To the south, fields still alternate with woodland, stretching over what used to be Ashford Common. Before the inclosure of the parish in 1809 this was a favourite ground with George III for military displays.[3]

The hamlet of Ashford Common is composed of an inn, a smithy, and a few cottages, which cluster about the cross-roads from Staines, Kingston, Littleton, and Feltham. Here, again, building operations are in progress, and a few hundred yards to the west there are already several streets laid out on which workmen's houses are being built.

The parish church of St. Matthew stands by the side of the main street of the old village, and there is a mission room belonging to the Church of England at Ashford Common. A Congregational chapel was built in 1891, and there is also a Wesleyan Methodist mission hall in the parish. The West London District School, opened in 1872, lies near the western boundary towards Staines.

The land is the property of many small owners. There are 1,401½ acres in the parish, and of these 495¼ acres are arable, and 398¼ acres are grass.[4] The principal crops are oats, wheat, barley, turnips, and peas. The soil is gravelly, and the subsoil gravel.

The following place-names occur in mediaeval documents :—Chikethorn, Hedenerworth, Longehedes, Shorechecleosworth, Rapelties, Scharpeland, Littlemede in Jordansheigh, Hightacres or Eytacres, Haymondsham, Gretechene, Sturfurlong, Markynger, and Warecroft, which was named after William de Ware, who held a croft in Ashford until about 1308.[5]

ASHFORD belonged from early *MANOR* times to Westminster Abbey, and has always been held in chief. It is said to have been given to the monastery by Offa, King of Mercia,[6] but the gift is mentioned only in a confirmatory charter of King Edgar, which is itself of doubtful origin.[7] It is at any rate certain that it belonged to Westminster in the time of Edward the Confessor,[8] and it may possibly have been held by the abbey at an earlier date. In the reign of Edward it was one of four appurtenances of Staines,[9] the most important manor held by Westminster in Spelthorne Hundred. Ashford is not mentioned as a manor in the Domesday Survey, but four berewicks are ascribed to Staines,[10] and as both before and after the Conquest Ashford was linked with that manor, it is more than probable that it was included as one of the berewicks.

In 1225 part of the monastery's estates were allotted by Abbot Richard de Berking to the support of the convent.[11] At first Ashford remained with the abbot, but in 1227 the monks complained that their share was insufficient, and by a composition made in that year, the manor of Ashford was ceded to the convent, with all the lands that had been brought into cultivation and other appurtenances.[12] The only exception made was in the case of a wood, which the abbot retained for himself and his successors in order that it might supply timber for the construction and repair of the ploughs on the manor.[13]

[7a] *Cal. Pat.* 1340–3, pp. 47–8 ; P.R.O. Ct. R. portf. 191, no. 42.
[8a] Pat. 7 Jas. I, pt. x.
[9a] *L. and P. Hen. VIII,* xv, 498 (36).
[1] *Rep. on Public Bridges in Midd.* (1826), 261.
[2] *Ord. Surv.*

[8] *Beauties of Engl. and Wales,* x (4), 514.
[4] Inf. supplied by the Bd. of Agric. (1905).
[5] Doc. in custody of the D. and C. of Westm. Chest D. no. 26783–26791.
[6] Cott. MS. Faust. A. iii, fol. 20 ; Titus, A. viii, fol. 4.

[7] *V.C.H. Lond.* i, 434.
[8] Cott. MS. Faust. A. iii, fol. 120 ; Titus, A. viii.
[9] Ibid.
[10] *Dom. Bk.* (Rec. Com.), i, 128.
[11] *V.C.H. Lond.* i, 448.
[12] Ibid. and Cott. MS. Titus, A. viii, fol. 356. [13] Ibid.

Ashford remained with the convent of Westminster until the dissolution of that house in January 1539–40,[14] when it was ceded to the Crown.[15] It was annexed by Henry VIII to the honour of Hampton Court in 1540,[16] and was leased in 1542 for twenty-one years to Richard Ellis, a member of the royal household.[17] In 1602 it was granted to Guy Godolphin and John Smythe.[18] Godolphin is said to have sold his interest in the grant to Smythe in the following year.[19] It is probable that the latter conveyed Ashford Manor, as he did the rectory of Staines which he received in the same way, to Urias Babington,[20] who died seised of the manor in February 1605–6.[21] He left it to his younger son, William,[22] who still held it in 1630.[23] The latter is said to have conveyed it in that year to Henry Field, whose widow continued to hold it after his death.[24] She was married a second time, to Edward Forset, and died in 1689.[25] It is said that by a deed executed in her first widowhood, the manor passed to her brother, Abraham Nelson, and that his widow Susanna, a daughter of Sir Brocket Spencer,[26] held it after his death.[27] She died in 1712, when, according to the same deed, the manor went to Richard grandson of Abraham Nelson.[28] Richard Nelson certainly held it in 1719.[29] He is said to have died intestate, and to have been succeeded by his sisters and co-heirs, Frances and Mary, who also died intestate and unmarried.[30] The manor then passed to Sir John Austen, son of Thomas Austen and Arabella, daughter and heiress of Edward Forset by the widow of Henry Field.[31] In 1741 Sir John sold the reversion of the manor after his death and after that of Mary Wright, spinster (who was residuary legatee under his will),[32] to Peter Storer.[33] Sir John died in March 1741–2,[34] and Mary Wright in 1753, and Peter Storer, son of the original purchaser, then came into possession.[35] He died in 1760, having left the manor to his sister Martha, the wife of William Baker.[36] It was inherited by their son Peter William Baker,[37] who held it in 1777[38] and as late as 1800.[39]

WESTMINSTER ABBEY.
Gules St. Peter's keys or.

There is little further record of the manor. It was held by Solomon Abraham Hart from 1870 to 1882, but the estate is now broken up among many small owners, and all trace of the manor lost. A grange belonging to the abbey of Westminster is mentioned as early as 1278.[40] It was apparently rebuilt some ten years later,[41] about which time a considerable amount of building was in progress on the manor, including a house, a dairy, and piggeries.[42] A mill is mentioned in 1277 and the succeeding years, but seems to have been disused after 1309.[43] There was also a dovecot which, was built about 1369, and which was kept up until the end of the century.[44] An extent of the manor taken in 1312 shows that the capital messuage was then held by William le Palmer,[45] whose family held land for a considerable period in Ashford.

The estate was at first generally managed by a reeve,[46] who appears to have been elected in the manor court by the homage.[47] During the 14th century it was more often under a serjeant (*serviens*) appointed by the monastery.[48] The demesne lands were farmed from 1379 to 1387 by Ambrose de Feltham,[49] who had already acted as serjeant from 1372,[50] and who continued in that capacity until 1392.[51] After twenty years of his administration, the tenants sent a written complaint (in French) to Westminster.[52] They represented to the abbot that not only did his ' poor tenants ' suffer great wrongs and evil impositions at the hands of his bailiff, but that they were called ' thieves, dogs and other villainous and horrible names.' Further, they declared that Ambrose had falsified the accounts of his stewardship, and that he kept back the best animals for his own use, so that his sheep and lambs were finer and better (*plus nobles et bones*) than the lord's. It was probably in consequence of their complaint that his term of office came to an end, and that he appears no more among the bailiffs of Ashford. His place was taken by Richard atte Crouch, who acted as serjeant till 1402,[53] after which the demesne lands were again farmed, the tenant acting also as collector of rents.[54]

Until the middle of the 14th century the manor court was generally held three times a year, at intervals of about four months.[55] After that time it was more frequently held twice a year, one

[14] *Pope Nich. Tax.* (Rec. Com.), 13 ; *Plac. de Quo Warr.* (Rec. Com.), 479 ; *Feud. Aids,* iii, 372 ; Docs. in custody of the D. and C. of Westm. Chest D. ; Dugdale, *Mon.* i, 280.
[15] *Valor Eccl.* (Rec. Com.), i, 415, 422.
[16] *L. and P. Hen. VIII,* xv, 498, p. 36.
[17] Ibid. xvii, 704.
[18] Pat. 44 Eliz. pt. xxii, m. 6.
[19] Lysons, *Environs of Lond.* (1800), v, 244.
[20] Ibid.
[21] Chan. Inq. p.m. (Ser. 2), ccxcii, 186.
[22] Ibid.
[23] Feet of F. Midd. East. 6 Chas. I.
[24] Lysons, *Environs of Lond.* v, 1,

citing information supplied by the steward of the manor (1800).
[25] Ibid.
[26] G.E.C. *Complete Baronetage,* ii, 200.
[27] Lysons, op. cit. v, 1.
[28] Ibid.
[29] Recov. R. Mich. 6. Geo. I, rot. 241.
[30] Lysons, op. cit. v, 2.
[31] G.E.C. *Complete Baronetage,* v, 21.
[32] Ibid.
[33] Feet of F. Midd. Hil. 14 Geo. II.
[34] G.E.C. *Complete Baronetage,* v, 21.
[35] Lysons, op. cit. v, 2.
[36] Ibid. ; Feet of F. Midd. Hil. 33 Geo. II.
[37] Lysons, op. cit. v, 2.
[38] Recov. R. Mich. 18 Geo. III, rot. 368.

[39] Lysons, op. cit. v, 2.
[40] Doc. in custody of the D. and C. of Westm. Chest D. no. 26656.
[41] Ibid. no. 26667.
[42] Ibid. no. 26660–7.
[43] Ibid. no. 26655–97.
[44] Ibid. no. 26769–807.
[45] Ibid. no. 26703.
[46] Ibid. no. 26655–73.
[47] Ibid. no. 26734.
[48] Ibid. no. 26674 sqq.
[49] Ibid. no. 26786–801.
[50] Ibid. no. 26775, sqq.
[51] Ibid. no. 26801–8.
[52] Ibid. no. 26808.
[53] Ibid. no. 26812–32.
[54] Ibid. no. 26833–47.
[55] Ibid. no. 26655–748.

court, at which the view of frankpledge was taken, always falling within the octave of Trinity, while the second was held in the late autumn.[56] The values of the courts appear to have varied from about 4s. to 16s.

The only court roll extant for this period is dated 1368,[57] and is preserved by the Dean and Chapter of Westminster Abbey. A roll of courts held in 1542 and 1545 is at the Public Record Office.[58]

The right to hold court leet, court baron, and view of frankpledge, is mentioned in a grant of the manor in 1777.[59]

Free fishery in the Rivers Brent and Thames was also among the appurtenances of the manor at that date.[60]

The Manor Farm, which lies near the southern boundary of the parish, is now used as golf links by the Manor Farm Golf Club, the farm-house having been converted into a club house for the members.

Ford Farm, which is near the old ford on the road to Staines and Laleham, belonged in the reign of William III to Ann Batkins of Ashford, and was held of her by John Bett and William Ellary, husbandmen, on lease, touching which they brought an action against Ann Batkins in 1700.[61]

In 1086 the Count of Mortain held 1 hide in Ashford. It had been held formerly by Alvric, a vassal of the Abbot of Chertsey, and had lain within the jurisdiction of Staines.[62] It was now attached to the count's manor of Kempton, in which it probably became merged. A piece of land known as Ashford Marsh was part of Kempton Manor in the reign of Elizabeth.[63]

The parish church of *ST. MAT-CHURCH THEW*, built in 1858, is at least the third church built on the site, the previous one being built of brick in 1796, and replacing an older building of brick and stone, dedicated in honour of St. Michael, with a 12th-century south doorway; it consists of chancel 28 ft. by 19 ft. wide, north vestry and south chapel forming transepts, a nave 60 ft. by 20 ft. with aisles 11 ft. wide, and a small tower built over the porch on the south-west. It is built of stone with red-tiled roofs. The tower is in three stages, with a red-tiled pyramidal roof.

The chancel has a steep-pitched roof, and the east window is of three lights with 14th-century tracery; the south transept is also lighted by a three-light window in the south wall.

The nave has north and south arcades of five bays, and at the west end a large four-light tracery window. In the nave is a coffin-plate of the Hon. George Hay, Earl of Kinnoull (died 1758), and near the door a brass to Edward Wooden and his wife, 1525, with effigies of them and their eight children.

There are three bells, the treble by Bryan Eldridge, 1620, the second by William Eldridge, 1668, and the tenor by Thomas Mears, 1797.

The communion plate consists of a chalice 'the gift of Mr. Wm. Munden 1716,' the hall-marks being illegible; a standing paten, inscribed 'the gift of Wm. Munden in memory of the fire at the ford, Jan. 1716,' date letter 1715; a large chalice with date mark 1812; and a standing paten of the same year, given by R. Govett, vicar.

There are two books of registers previous to 1812, the first, evidently a copy of others made when Ashford was a chapelry of Staines, contains the baptisms, burials, and marriages of Staines from 1696 to 1710, 1706, and 1707 respectively; the baptisms and burials of Laleham from 1696 to 1704 and 1708; and the baptisms and burials of Ashford between 1699 and 1708, 1709; this book is bound in an old, almost illegible indenture. The other book contains printed marriages from 1754 to 1812 inclusive.

ADVOWSON Until comparatively recent times Ashford Church was a chapel dependent upon the church of Staines. It belonged until the Dissolution to Westminster Abbey.[64] It is first mentioned in 1293, when the rector of Staines and of the chapels of Ashford and Laleham was acquitted of the sum of 3½ marks which he owed for the tenth granted to Edward I for the relief of the Holy Land.[65] Ashford is enumerated among the chapels of Staines in the institution of that vicarage by William, Bishop of London, about 1426, and the vicar of the mother church was bound to appoint suitable curates to officiate at each of the chapels.[66]

After the suppression of the monasteries, the advowson of Ashford was separated from that of Staines, which remained with the Crown, and was granted in 1542 to the newly-founded cathedral church of Westminster.[67] The dean and chapter apparently presented Roger Gryffyn, who was vicar of Ashford in 1548.[68] On the foundation of the collegiate church of St. Peter, Elizabeth granted the advowson of Ashford to the dean and chapter.[69] It was then called a free chapel, but there is no mention of any presentation being made by St. Peter's.[70] Under the Commonwealth the benefice is described as a vicarage, and the 'minister' George Bonieman was 'brought in by consent and presentation of the parish,' being supported by the small tithes and glebeland.[71] There is apparently no further record of the church until 1760, when it appears as a chapel of Staines in the presentation to that vicarage by the Crown.[72] From that time it seems to have been served by a curate of Staines. During the early part of the 19th century the same priest officiated both at Laleham and at Ashford, and consequently service was held only on alternate Sundays at either church. The living is

---

[56] Doc. in custody of the D. and C. of Westm. Chest D. no. 26749–844.
[57] Ibid. no. 26847.
[58] P.R.O. Ct. R. portf. 188, no. 41.
[59] Recov. R. Mich. 18 Geo. III, rot. 368.
[60] Ibid.

[61] Exch.Dep.Mich.12Will.III,rot.36.
[62] *Dom. Bk.* (Rec. Com.), i, 128.
[63] *Midd. Co. Rec.* i, 40.
[64] Doc. in custody of the D. & C. of Westm. no. 16782, 16811.
[65] Ibid. no. 16776.
[66] Lond. Epis. Reg. Gilbert, fol. 177.

[67] *L. and P. Hen. VIII*, xvii, 395.
[68] Chant. Cert. 34, no. 138.
[69] Pat. 2 Eliz. pt. xi, m. 19.
[70] Newcourt, *Repert.* i, 735.
[71] P.R.O. Surv. of Church Livings, iii, m. 6.
[72] P.R.O. Inst. Bks.

described as a perpetual curacy from 1860 to 1865, in the gift of the Lord Chancellor,[73] since which date it has been a vicarage under the same patronage.

The rectory belonged with the church and manor to Westminster Abbey [74] until it was ceded to the Crown at the Dissolution, after which it was separated from the advowson,[75] and has since followed the descent of the manor (q.v.).

In 1610 the chapel was endowed with a house, and a 'backside' containing 28½ acres 2 yds. of glebe land.[76] In 1650 the parsonage or great tithes were valued at £60 per annum, and the vicarage with glebe and small tithes at £24.[77] In the survey of 1548 it was found that an acre of land had been given for the maintenance of a lamp in the church at Ashford.[78] The land was in Stanwell parish, and was then in tenure of John Beauchamp at a rent of 16s. yearly. He held also another acre of land worth 12s. per annum which had been given to the same church.[79]

CHARITIES It appears from the benefaction table that Mrs. Mary Reeve, by her will dated in 1679, devised land in the common field of Laleham and of Feltham, the rents to be applied in the distribution of bread to the poor of Ashford attending church in the proportion of 12d. per week, and the residue in bread to the poor of Laleham. Upon the inclosures in the respective parishes about 3½ acres in Laleham and 2 acres in Feltham were allotted in respect of the lands so demised, which are let at £14 a year. In 1906 bread was given to four recipients in Ashford and twenty-two in Laleham. There was also a sum of £36 13s. 7d. in hand, derived from sale of gravel.

The Poor Allotment or Coal Charity consists of 17 acres in Ashford, let at £8 10s. a year, and four cottages let on weekly rents producing about £22 a year, which were acquired under the Ashford Inclosure Act.[80] The trust is regulated by a scheme of the Charity Commissioners of 24 August 1877.

In 1723 Jerrard Tomlin, by will, devised an annuity of £1 3s. for the payment of 10s. 6d. to the parson for preaching a sermon on the anniversary of his death, 2s. 6d. for the clerk, and 10s. to be distributed in twopenny loaves to the poor attending to hear the said sermon. The charge was redeemed in 1902 by the transfer to the official trustees of £46 2½ per cent. annuities.

The Sunday School Fund.—In 1817, as appeared from the vestry book, a sum of £250 was subscribed by the principal inhabitants towards defraying the expenses of a Sunday school, which, with a legacy bequeathed by Zacharias Foxall for the same purpose, was invested in Government stock.

In 1866 a sum of £200, and subsequently a further sum of £100, were authorized by the Charity Commissioners to be expended in the building of a schoolhouse, thereby reducing the trust fund to £100 consols, which is held by the official trustees, and the dividends are remitted to the national school fund.

The charity of Anne Webb, locally known as the 'Dog' Charity.—The donor, by her will dated in 1801, and by the codicil thereto dated in 1807, proved in the P.C.C., bequeathed several charitable legacies to take effect after the death of her little dog Don, which event—as appears from the Chancery proceedings in the matter—happened on 27 October 1808 ! The trust fund for this parish consists of a sum of consols in the name of the Paymaster-General to the credit of the suit 'Attorney-General v. Smith, the Ashford Charity.' In 1906 the sum of £5 14s. 8d. was received in dividends, and distributed in accordance with the trusts between the three oldest men and the three oldest women in the parish. The vicar is entitled to deduct one guinea on filling up a vacancy.

EAST BEDFONT WITH HATTON

Bedefunde (xi cent.) ; Estbedefonte (xiii cent.) ; Bedefonte, Estebedefounte (xiv cent.) ; East-bedefounte (xvi cent.).

East Bedfont lies in the level country to the east of Staines. The parish stretches along the great main road from London to the south-west of England, narrowing about the village, to the east of which it spreads southward towards Ashford, while westward and northward a long tongue of land includes the hamlet of Hatton and reaches as far as Cranford on the Bath road. The land for the most part is laid out in fields and is but sparsely wooded. The village lies on the broad London to Staines road, the houses standing well back from the highway, leaving ample space for a green with

fine trees, which lies before the church. In front of the south porch are two very curiously cut yew trees, of the most fantastic shape ; the date 1704 forms part of their ornament. In coaching days East Bedfont stood midway in the second stage out of London, between Hounslow and Staines. The inns were described in 1826 as 'respectable and yielding good accommodation.'[1] The Black Dog Inn, about 1¼ miles along the London road, was then the receiving house for letters. A public hall, to seat 300 persons, was built in 1884 by the Bedfont Public Hall Co., Ltd. There is a Baptist chapel, which was erected in 1903. The Windsor line of the London and South Western Railway runs through the southern

---

[73] Clergy Lists, passim.
[74] Doc. in custody of D. and C. of Westm. no. 26751 sqq.
[75] L. and P. Hen. VIII, xvii, 704.
[76] Newcourt, Repert. i, 735.
[77] Ibid.
[78] Chant. Cert. 34, no. 138.
[79] Ibid.
[80] 49 Geo. III, cap. 17.
[1] Pigot, Lond. and Provincial Directory, 1826.

part of the parish. East Bedfont has no station, the nearest being that at Feltham, 1½ miles away. Besides the main highway from London to the south-west, roads from Hatton and Cranford, from Stanwell, and from Feltham converge on the village. 'The Duke of Northumberland's River' cuts in a straight line across the parish from west to east. It is a branch of the Colne, which leaves that river near Longford, and running in an artificial channel falls into the Thames near the Duke of Northumberland's house at Syon. It is said to have been made by the convent of Syon in the time of Henry V.[2] The more wandering course of the 'Queen's or Cardinal's River' enters the parish at almost the same point, and passes out

east of East Bedfont. It forms a junction for the many byways which radiate north and south towards the Bath and the Staines roads, and for this reason it is said to have been a favourite haunt of highwaymen in days gone by. It then stood on the borders of Hounslow Heath, and either road was easily accessible from the old inn, the 'Green Man' where the hiding-hole behind the chimney is still shown.

Two fairs, held respectively about 7 May at Bedford and 14 June at Hatton, were abolished by the Home Secretary on the representation of the Justices of the Peace in April 1881.[3a] It does not appear how long it had been the custom to hold the fairs.

BEDFONT CHURCH, FROM THE SOUTH

to the south towards Feltham. It supplies water for Hanworth and Bushey Parks and for Hampton Court,[3] and is said to have been made by Cardinal Wolsey's orders. The latter river is crossed by the London road at White Bridge, and the road to Hatton is carried over both rivers within a few score yards of one another by the Two Bridges. The River Crane forms the most easterly boundary of the parish, and near its junction with the Duke of Northumberland's River are the Bedfont Powder Mills, which are now disused. There is a gravel pit by the road to Ashford.

The hamlet of Hatton lies 2 miles to the north-

There is a Baptist chapel in Hatton, and a licensed mission room of the Church of England.

New Bedfont is a small hamlet consisting of an inn, a smithy, and a few cottages on the road between Hatton and East Bedfont.

The soil and subsoil are gravel; the crops consist mainly of garden produce. There are 1,926½ acres in the parish, of which five-sixths are under cultivation, the remainder being grass, with about 4 acres of woodland[4] and 18 acres water. The parish was inclosed under an Act of 1813.[5] A mill is mentioned in the taxation returns of 1291 as belonging to the abbey of Westminster.[6]

[2] Lysons, *Env. of Lond.* (1800),iii,82.
[3] Firth, *Midd.* 18; Lysons, *Supplement to Env. of London,* 71.

[3a] *Lond. Gaz.* 29 April 1881.
[4] Inf. supplied by the Bd. of Agric. (1905).

[5] Slater, *Engl. Peasantry and the Enclosure of Common Fields,* 287.
[6] *Pope Nich. Tax.*(Rec. Com.), 1?.

Most of the principal landowners of the parish are resident. Mrs. Reed lives at St. Mary's, and Mr. Henry Barnfield at Oakdene on the Ashford Road. Temple Hatton, once occupied by Lady Pollock, is now the St. Antony's Home for Boys. Mr. Alfred Barnfield lives at Pates Manor.

The following place-names occur : Goddard, Parrette, le Tabber.

MANORS *EAST BEDFONT* was assessed at 10 hides in the time of Edward the Confessor.[7] Eight and a half of these were held by Azor, and lay within the jurisdiction of his manor in Stanwell. The remaining $1\frac{1}{2}$ hides were divided equally between three sokemen, vassals respectively of Edward the Confessor, of Earl Lewin, and of Azor. The whole 10 hides were granted as a manor by William I to Walter Fitz Other, castellan of Windsor.[8] His descendants took the name of de Windsor, by virtue of their hereditary office as keeper of the castle.[9] East Bedfont owed the service of one knight's fee in the honour of Windsor in 1212,[10] and still continued to owe service to that honour in the 15th century.[11] It was probably included in the surrender to the Crown of the Windsor lands in Middlesex in 1542, and from that time it was held in chief.[12]

WINDSOR. *Gules crusily or a saltire argent.*

In 1086 the tenant of East Bedfont was one Richard.[13] It seems to have then given name to a family of under-tenants, for Walter de Bedfont held a knight's fee under Windsor in 1166,[13a] and Henry de Bedfont held one in Bedfont under him in 1198.[13b] The manor was held of the Windsors in the year 1212 by Nicholas de Aune,[14] the king's clerk and possibly also clerk to Richard Earl of Cornwall.[15] It is not clear how it came to John de Nevill who held it early in the reign of Edward II.[16] He was probably one of the Nevills of Essex, and was a distant connexion of the Windsors, through the marriage of his ancestor Hugh de Nevill with the heiress of Henry de Cornhill,[17] who himself had married

the descendant and heiress of Robert Lord of Little Easton, the second son of Walter Fitz Other.[18] John de Nevill conveyed his right in the manor of East Bedfont to the Trinitarian Priory at Hounslow.[19] It was confirmed to the master and brethren by Edward II in 1313,[20] and remained in their hands until the suppression of the monastery in 1530.[21]

In the reign of Elizabeth it was leased to Robert Sownes[22] but was granted in 1599 to Sir Michael Stanhope[23] of Sudbury, Suffolk, who in 1609 protested against the king's order for the erection of gunpowder mills and workmen's houses on the manor.[24] Sir Michael died in 1621, having settled the reversion of the manor six years previously on his second daughter Elizabeth, on the occasion of her marriage with George Lord Berkeley.[25] It was inherited by the latter's son George,[26] who conveyed it in 1656 to Algernon, Earl of Northumberland.[27] It has since descended with that title,[28] the representative of which was created Duke of Northumberland in 1766.[29]

PERCY, Duke of Northumberland. *Or a lion azure.*

At the time of the Domesday Survey the Count of Mortain held 2 hides in Bedfont, which lay in his manor of Feltham.[30] As there is no further mention of this land, it probably became merged in the parish of Feltham, which adjoins East Bedfont.

The so-called manor of *PATES* (Patys, Paytes, Patts, xvi cent.) was held of the manor of East Bedfont.[31] John Pate and Juliane his wife held land in Bedfont in 1403–4.[32] It was presumably the estate which was known later as the manor of Pates. The manor is said to have been held in 1498 by John Naylor and Clemence his wife,[33] whose daughter and heiress married Thomas West, leaving an only son Edmund West.[34] The latter left two daughters—Elizabeth who married John Bekenham, and Margaret, and these conveyed the manor in 1549 to Roland Page.[35] From them it passed in 1561 to Thomas Brend,[36] who conveyed it in 1575 to George Britteridge.[37] The latter died seised of the manor in January 1580–1,

[7] *Dom. Bk.* (Rec. Com.), i, 130.
[8] Ibid.
[9] G.E.C. *Complete Peerage*, viii, 185.
[10] *Red Bk. of Exch.* (Rolls Ser.), 542.
[11] *Feud. Aids*, iii, 380.
[12] *L. and P. Hen. VIII*, xvii, 285 (18).
[13] *Dom. Bk.* (Rec. Com.), i, 130.
[13a] *Red Bk. of Exch.* (Rolls Ser.), 315.
[13b] *Feet of Fines* (Pipe Roll Soc.), 9 Ric. I.
[14] *Red Bk. of Exch.* (Rolls Ser.), p. cclxxxii, 542 ; *Testa de Nevill* (Rec. Com.), 361.
[15] *Cal. Pat.* 1232–47, p. 456. He was alive in 1256, but apparently dead before 1265 ; *Excerpta e Rot. Fin.* ii, 233, 243.

[16] *Pat.* 6 Edw. II, pt. ii, m. 9.
[17] Morant, *Hist. of Essex*, i, 383.
[18] Collins, *Collections of the Family of Windsor*, 7.
[19] *Pat.* 6 Edw. II, pt, ii, m. 9.
[20] *Cal. Pat.* 1307–13, p. 578.
[21] *Feud. Aids*, iii, 372, 374, 380 ; *Inq. Non.* (Rec. Com.), 195 ; Dugdale, *Mon.* vi, 1563.
[22] *Pat.* 41 Eliz. pt. xvii, m. 16.
[23] Ibid. ; P.R.O. Rentals and Surv. portf. 3, no. 11.
[24] *Cal. S.P. Dom.* 1603–10, p. 537.
[25] Chan. Inq. p.m. (Ser. ii), ccccv, no. 161 ; W. & L. Inq. bdle. 63, no. 178.
[26] *Dict. Nat. Biog.* iv, 346.
[27] Recov. R. Hil. 1655, rot. 136 ; Feet of F. Midd. East. 1656.

[28] Feet of F. Div. Co. Hil. 3 & 4 Jas. II ; Recov. R. Hil. 3 & 4 Jas. II, rot. 166 ; Hil. 22 Geo. II, rot. 52 ; Hil. 57 Geo. II, rot. 363.
[29] Burke, *Peerage* (1907), 1234.
[30] *Dom. Bk.* (Rec. Com.), i, 129.
[31] Chan. Inq. p.m. (Ser. ii), cxcvi, no. 18.
[32] Feet of F. Lond. and Midd. 5 Hen. IV, no. 31.
[33] Lysons, *Environs of Lond.* (1800), v, 7, cites records of Christ's Hospital.
[34] Ibid.
[35] Feet of F. Midd. East. 3 Edw. VI.
[36] Ibid. Mich. 3 & 4 Eliz. Possibly these conveyances may have been only for a term of years.
[37] Ibid. Trin. 18 Eliz.

leaving it to his son and heir Edward, then ten years old.[38] Edward had seisin of his inheritance in 1594,[39] but Thomas Page, possibly a relation of Roland, seems to have had possession of the estate even during the minority of the heir, for in 1589 he conveyed two-thirds of the manor to John Draper.[40] The latter apparently left the same to his wife Barbara, and she with her second husband, Edward Pigeon, conveyed them in 1614 to Edward Hewlett.[41] The remaining third is said to have been sold in 1593 by Thomas Page to Philip Gerrard, who sold it in the following year to Henry Bell.[42] Henry and William Bell conveyed it in 1621 to Edward Hewlett,[43] who in 1623 gave the whole manor to Christ's Hospital.[44] The hospital still holds this property.[45]

CHRIST'S HOSPITAL. *Argent a cross gules with a sword gules erect in the quarter and a chief azure with a Tudor rose therein between two fleurs de lis or.*

The so-called manor of *FAWNES* was held of the manor of East Bedfont. It seems to have been conveyed to the Crown with the Windsor lands in Middlesex in 1542,[46] and from that date to have been held in chief.[47]

Richard Foun held land in East Bedfont by gift of Ralph de Bromland and Alice his wife, belonging to the latter, as early as the reign of Edward I,[48] and Alan Foun or Fawne held land there in the succeeding reign.[49] Robert Fawne, who was probably their descendant, and who is described as a citizen and skinner of London, held premises in the parish in 1428.[50] Ten years later a messuage and lands called Fawnes were pledged by William Edy, a draper, to John Derham of Windsor, for debt.[51] Fawnes is first mentioned as a manor in 1531, when it was in the possession of John Kempe.[52] The history of the manor is somewhat obscure. It was held by Anthony Walker as early as 1583 and at his death in 1590,[53] and was inherited by his son Thomas,[54] who still held it in 1603.[55] In 1618, however, it came into the hands of Felix Wilson,[56] in whose family it remained until 1654,[57] when it passed to Thomas Darling. Edward Darling held it in 1668,[58] after which date there is no trace of the manor until 1739, when Thomas Manning held it.[59] He seems to have been still in possession ten years later,[60] but by 1792 it was in the hands of Aubrey (Beau-

clerk), Baron Vere,[61] who succeeded to the dukedom of St. Albans [62] in 1787, and who held Fawnes in 1802.[63] It is now the property of Mr. William Sherborn.[63a] Fawnes stands on the south side of the village.

In 1086 Roger de Montgomery, Earl of Arundel, held 1½ hides in *HATTON*, which in the reign of King Edward the Confessor had been held by two sokemen, vassals of Albert of Lorraine.[64] This land belonged to the earl's manor of Colham, in which it probably became merged. A second entry in the Domesday Survey relates to a still smaller estate in Hatton, which was held by Walter Fitz Other, and which had been held formerly by two vassals of Azor.[65] It is probable that this land became merged in the Windsor Manor of East Bedfont, and was possibly granted to Hounslow Priory with the rest of that property. The priory certainly held land in Hatton in 1382,[66] and in 1599 it was granted, as land formerly belonging to Hounslow, to Sir Michael Stanhope,[67] and from that time has always been held with the manor of East Bedfont (q.v.).

Edward III seems to have built a house at Hatton, which was known as Hatton Grange. Richard II held this of the priory of Hounslow at a yearly rent of 50s.[68]

The church of *ST. MARY THE VIRGIN* consists of chancel 25 ft. 1 in. by 16 ft. 3 in., nave 54 ft. 3 in. by 16 ft. 3 in., north transept 26 ft. by 29 ft. 3 in., and west porch with a tower adjoining it on the west side. The earliest parts are the chancel arch, south doorway, and two small windows —one in the nave, the other in the chancel— which date from c. 1130, when the church consisted of a simple chancel and nave, both of the same width, but considerably shorter than at present. In order to give more light to the chancel two windows were inserted on the south side in the 13th century, but the church appears to have remained very small until the 15th century, when the chancel was lengthened 8 ft. 3 in. eastward, and probably the nave some distance westward; there is nothing to show how much the nave was increased, the western portion having been rebuilt in modern times, nor can any date be ascribed for the addition of a tower, as the present one is also a rebuilding.

The whole of the church except the north transept is built of pudding stone, of dark-brown colour, even to the quoins of the original chancel, but the doors and windows of both early and later

---

[38] Chan. Inq. p.m. (Ser. ii), cxcvi, no. 18.
[39] Fine R. 37 Eliz. pt. 1.
[40] Feet of F. Midd. Mich. 31 & 32 Eliz.; Recov. R. Mich. 31 Eliz. rot. 26.
[41] Feet of F. Midd. East. 12 Jas. I.
[42] Lysons, op. cit. v, 8.
[43] Feet of F. Midd. Trin. 19 Jas. I.
[44] Lysons, op. cit. v, 8.
[45] Inf. kindly supplied by Mr. W. Lempriere, sen. assist. clerk Christ's Hospital.
[46] *L. and P. Hen. VIII*, xvii, 285 (18).
[47] Chan. Inq. p.m. 33 Eliz. no. 230 (29).

[48] Feet of F. Lond. and Midd. 7 Edw. I, no. 66.
[49] Ibid. 10 Edw. III, no. 220; 18 Edw. III, no. 321.
[50] Ibid. 6 Hen. VI, no. 29.
[51] Early Chan. Proc. bdle. 10, no. 227.
[52] Feet of F. Midd. East. 22 Hen. VIII.
[53] Chan. Inq. p.m. 33 Eliz. no. 230 (29).
[54] Ibid.
[55] Feet of F. Midd. Trin. 1 Jas. I.
[56] Ibid. Hil. 15 Jas. I.
[57] Ibid. Mich. 16 Chas. I; Trin. 1654.

[58] Ibid. East. 20 Chas. II.
[59] Ibid. Div. Co. Hil. 12 Geo. II; Recov. R. Mich. 12 Geo. II, rot. 174.
[60] Feet of F. Midd. Mich. 22 Geo. II.
[61] Recov. R. Mich. 33 Geo III, rot. 302.
[62] G.E.C. *Complete Peerage*, vii, 6.
[63] Recov. R. East. 42 Geo. III, rot. 233.
[63a] Inf. from Mr. Sherborn.
[64] *Dom. Bk.* (Rec. Com.), i, 129.
[65] Ibid. i, 130.
[66] *Cal. Pat.* 1381–5, p. 131.
[67] Pat. 41 Eliz. pt. xvii, m. 16.
[68] *Cal. Pat.* 1381–5, p. 131.

312

work are in hard chalk. The tower is lined with brick, and the upper part is of timber with a projecting clock gable and surmounted by a four-sided shingled spire. The north transept is quite modern, built of yellow stock bricks with stone window-heads. Internally the whole of the church excepting the tower is plastered.

The chancel has a steep-pitched 15th-century roof, having tie-beams with king-posts moulded at the capitals and bases.

The east window is of the 15th century, with three trefoiled lights under a pointed segmental head and an external moulded label. In the north wall is a small deeply-splayed 12th-century light, and in the walling to the east of it can be seen the pudding-stone quoins of the contemporary north-east angle. In the south wall is a single trefoiled light under a square head, of the same date as that in the east wall, and to the west of it is a small square recess, its head made of the top of a small lancet window; it may have had a flue originally. To the west are a modern pointed doorway and two windows, one of one, the other of two lights, apparently 13th-century work, with double hollow chamfers on the outer face and internal rebates for a frame.

The chancel arch, c. 1130, has a semicircular head moulded with a single order of cheveron ornament and a chamfered label; at the springing is a chamfered string, below which the cheveron continues.

The west end of the nave has been rebuilt; on the north side are two modern two-light windows and an arcade of two bays resting on a round column with a capital and base in 14th-century style, and at the north-east angle of the nave are two pointed recesses, one in the east and one in the north wall, with a modern shaft in the angle. In the east recess is painted a Crucifixion, and in the other our Lord in judgement, and the dead rising, the date of the work being c. 1300. At the south-east of the nave is a 16th-century red-brick projection for a rood stair, lighted by a small four-centred window. To the west of it is a pointed segmental-headed window of the 16th century with three cinquefoiled lights and a moulded label, and to the west again a small original 12th-century window. The south door-way, c. 1130, is round-headed, of two orders with cheveron ornament. The west wall contains a modern pointed doorway in 13th-century style, and above it a circular window filled with plate tracery.

The modern transept is lighted by brick lancets with stone heads, and has a gallery at the north end; to the east is a small vestry.

There are no monuments of note, but in the chancel on the north wall is a brass with the figures of Matthew Page, 1631, and his mother Isabel, 1629. On the same wall is a 17th-century marble

scutcheon with a bend wavy and three lions rampant. In the south-west corner is a painted wooden panel to Thomas Weldish, who died in 1640, with his arms, Vert three running greyhounds argent, on a chief or a fox gules. In the graveyard to the east of the chancel is a slab to Matthew Page, 1678, with the arms, a fesse indented between three martlets; this used to be in the floor of the chancel, but has been replaced by a brass copy.

There are six bells, the treble and fourth by Richard Phelps, 1713, and the rest by Warner, 1870.

The plate consists of a small cup inscribed as the gift of I. F., with the date 1719, the hall-marks being illegible, a small standing paten from the same donor with the date-letter of 1719, a larger standing paten with no hall-marks, given by John and Serena Lee, 1756, with their arms, checky a lion rampant, and a cup of 1857.

The registers before 1812 are in four parts :— (i) burials 1678–1778 (with affidavits to 1725), baptisms 1695–1777, marriages 1695–1754; (ii) marriages printed 1754–1812; (iii) baptisms 1778–1813; (iv) burials 1779–1812.

ADVOWSON The advowson was granted to the priory of the Holy Trinity, Hounslow, with the manor, by John de Nevill before 1313,[69] and a vicarage was ordained and endowed by the Bishop of London in 1316, of which the master and brethren continued to be the patrons until the Dissolution.[70] After that time the advowson was in the hands of the Crown until it was granted to the Bishop of London, who first presented in 1568.[71] In 1591 and 1597 John Draper, who held a lease of the rectory,[72] was allowed to present to the vicarage by favour of the bishop.[73] The patronage belonged to the see of London until 1880, when it was transferred to the Crown by an exchange.[73a]

The church was rated at £5 6s. 8d. in 1291[74] and in 1428.[75] At the Dissolution the vicarage was valued at £12[76] and the tithes at £32. In 1650 it was worth £29 yearly.[77]

The rectory was held by Hounslow Priory until the suppression of the monasteries,[78] when it was ceded to the Crown. It came to the Bishop of London by exchange for other lands belonging to the see,[79] probably about the same time as the grant of the advowson. Bishop Aylmer gave it on lease in 1588 to John Draper of 'Luderworth' and his daughters Margaret and Cecilia, together with the tithes, the parsonage barn, and the Strawe-House, but saving the right of the vicar in the close known as the Old Vicar's Close.[80] It was to be held for the term of their lives at a rent of £8 13s. 4d. The rectory has always belonged to the patron of the living, but the tithes of sheaves and grain were granted to various persons at different times. They were conveyed in 1621

[69] Pat. 6 Edw. II ; *Abbrev. Rot. Orig.* (Rec. Com.), i, 211 ; *Cal. Pat.* 1313–17, pp. 162, 210.
[70] Newcourt, *Repert.* i, 574.
[71] Ibid.

[72] Lond. Epis. Reg. Grindal (Bancroft), fol. 329.
[73] Newcourt, *Repert.* i, 574.
[73a] *Lond. Gaz.* Sept. 14, 1880.
[74] *Pope Nich. Tax.* (Rec. Com.), 17.
[75] *Feud. Aids*, iii, 378.

[76] *Valor Eccl.* (Rec. Com.), i, 434.
[77] Lysons, op. cit. v, 9.
[78] *Valor Eccl.* (Rec. Com.), i, 434.
[79] Lond. Epis. Reg. Grindal (Bancroft), fol. 329.
[80] Ibid.

by Sir John Crompton to Edward Hewlett,[81] who then held the manor of Pates (q.v.), and in 1645 by James and William Hewlett to Francis Page.[82] Later in the same year a third of the tithes of grain was leased to Thomas Bartlett by William Norbonne for eighty years if the latter's wife Frances should live so long, the rent to be one peppercorn.[83] In 1691–2 the rectory and tithes were leased by John Clarke to Robert Goodyer.[84] Four-fifths of the rectory and tithes were conveyed to William Sherborn in 1789 by William Adams and others.[85] The rectorial tithes are now held by the Ecclesiastical Commissioners.

Hatton has always been ecclesiastically dependent on East Bedfont, though at the Dissolution Hatton Rectory was valued separately (at £4) among the possessions of Hounslow Priory.[86] It was held by the Crown after the priory was suppressed, and the tithes were leased under Elizabeth to Anthony Rowe, auditor of the Exchequer, and after his death to his three sons.[87] Probably the rectory

was granted with the advowson of East Bedfont to Bishop Aylmer. The tithes are mentioned with those of Bedfont in 1621.[88] They were held independently in 1726, when they were conveyed by John Page to Richard Burbridge,[89] and again in 1787, when apparently the co-heiresses of the Burbridge family conveyed them to George Webber.[90]

CHARITIES In 1631 Matthew Page, as mentioned in the Parliamentary Returns of 1786, bequeathed a legacy for the poor, which is now represented by £83 6s. 2d. consols, held by the official trustees. The dividends, amounting to £2 1s. 8d., are applied in the distribution of money in sums of 2s. or 2s. 6d.

The Fuel Allotment, acquired by an award made under the Inclosure Act of 53 George III, consists of 40 acres, let at £105 a year. In 1906–7 279 poor persons received 7½ cwt of coal each.

FELTHAM

Felteham (xi cent.); Feltenham, Felthenham (xvii cent.).

Feltham lies to the south of the main road from Hounslow to Staines, which runs just beyond and parallel with the northern boundary of the parish, The country is almost level, with a slight upward trend from south to north, but the highest point reached is only 73 ft. above ordnance datum.[1] The River Crane forms part of the eastern boundary, and ' the Queen's or Cardinal's River ' (v.s. East Bedfont) flows diagonally across the northern part of the parish, passing under the railway near the station, and a few hundred yards farther under the Feltham-Hounslow road, by a bridge which was built about 1800.[2] Of the 1,789½ acres in Feltham, about two-thirds are composed of arable land, and 371 acres are laid down in permanent grass.[3] There are only 20 acres of woodland,[4] and these lie mostly about the private houses in the north-east. The parish was inclosed in 1800 with Hanworth and Sunbury.[5] Until that date Hounslow Heath extended over the eastern part of the parish, and apparently the only roads which then existed were those from Ashford and from Hanworth. Even what is now the principal road, that which leads from the village to Hounslow, was not constructed till after this date.[6] The cross-road from Hatton, and the ways leading west from St. Dunstan's Church towards Bedfont and south through Feltham Hill, were also laid out at this time, the two latter following the courses of ancient tracks.[7]

The village is long and straggling, and extends for over a mile along the road to Hounslow. The older part lies towards the south, about the parish church of St. Dunstan. The houses stand close on to the narrow road, which curves sharply to the right, and then with a right-angled turn to the left proceeds past Feltham Farm to the central portion of the village. It is here known as the High Street, and widens out slightly before reaching the Red Lion Hotel, just beyond which a large pond lies to the right of the road. Northwards again are the more modern houses and shops, which are increasing year by year. Farther to the north-west is Southville, which at present consists of two streets of workmen's houses. The modern buildings lie within easy reach of the station, which is on the Windsor branch of the London and South Western Railway.

The spiritual needs of this growing population have been met by the erection of St. Catherine's Church, which was built in 1880 as a chapel of ease to the parish church, which stands at the upper end of the village. A north porch was added in 1890, and the tower and spire in 1898. There are two large Congregational chapels, one of which was founded in 1805 and rebuilt in 1865, while the second was built in 1905. A Wesleyan chapel was erected in 1870, and a Baptist chapel in the same year. A cemetery, extending over 1½ acres, was formed in 1880 at a cost of about £1,400. It has no mortuary chapels, and is now under the control of the Urban District Council.

[81] Feet of F. Midd. Trin. 19 Jas. I.
[82] Ibid. Hil. 20 Chas. I.
[83] Ibid. Mich. 21 Chas. I.
[84] Ibid. Hil. 3 Will. and Mary.
[85] Ibid. East. 29 Geo. III
[86] *Valor Eccl.* (Rec. Com.), i, 402.
[87] Pat. 27 Eliz. pt. xi, m. 19.

[88] Feet of F. Midd. Trin. 19 Jas. I.
[89] Ibid. Hil. 12 Geo. I.
[90] Ibid. Hil. 27 Geo. III.
[1] Ord. Surv.
[2] B.M. Egerton MS. 2356.
[3] Inf. supplied by Bd. of Agric. (1905).

[4] Ibid.
[5] Slater, *Engl. Peasantry and the Enclosure of the Common Fields*, 287 ; B.M. Egerton MS. 2356.
[6] B.M. Egerton MS. 2356.
[7] Ibid.

The convent of SS. Mary and Scholastica, belonging to an Anglican community of nuns living under the rule of St. Benedict, was founded in 1868 by Father Ignatius.[8] It was supported mainly by the sale of plain needlework and church embroidery worked by the sisters, and there was a small orphanage and day school attached to it. The establishment was broken up and removed in 1873.[9]

The hamlet of Feltham Hill lies on the southern borders of the parish, and is composed mainly of a few private houses standing in their own grounds. Mr. Alfred William Smith, one of the chief landowners in Feltham, lives at The Park in Feltham Hill. The old Manor House at Feltham is the residence of another landowner, Mr. Robert Smith.

William Wynne Ryland, the well-known engraver, who was the first to use the chalk or dotted line in his art, is buried in the churchyard. He was executed at Tyburn in 1793 for forging bonds of the East India Company.[10] Mrs. Frances Marie Kelly (Charles Lamb's 'Barbara S—'), actress and founder of the School of Acting in Dean Street, Soho, spent the last years of her life at Ross Cottage, and is buried at Feltham. She died in 1882.[11]

The parish is known chiefly for the Middlesex Industrial School for Boys, which occupies a large tract of ground in the south-west between the roads to Ashford and to East Bedfont. It was built in 1859 to hold about 1,000 boys, and consists of a large principal building, a chapel, infirmary, workshops, gas factory, residences for officers, and other detached buildings. About 70 acres of land are cultivated by the institution. There are ivory works near the village, and a cartridge factory stands on the banks of the River Crane. Saw mills have been erected near the station, and there is a large gravel pit lying near the railway line. A considerable portion of the parish is cultivated by nursery and market gardeners. The soil is gravel on a subsoil of gravel. The following place-names occur :—Swanne, Fullers and Loom Pit Closes, Mark Corner, the Greth.

FELTHAM is mentioned in a
MANORS charter of King Edgar as one of the members of Staines which had been given to Westminster Abbey by Offa King of Mercia.[12] This charter is, however, of doubtful origin,[13] and though Feltham may have belonged to Westminster at an early date, yet it is not mentioned among the manors belonging to Staines in the confirmatory charter of Edward the Confessor,[14] the authenticity of which is not questioned.

According to the Domesday Survey there were two manors in Feltham before the Conquest ; one consisting of 5 hides was held by a vassal of King Edward, the other, consisting of 7 hides, was held by a vassal of Earl Harold.[15] Both were given by the Conqueror to Robert Count of Mortain, and were held by him as one manor.[16] The Mortain lands were forfeited to Henry I after the rebellion of Count Robert's son, William, in 1104.[17] Feltham seems to have been granted shortly after to the Redvers family, who held it of the king in chief. The grant was probably made to Richard de Redvers, who received many gifts of land in return for his services to Henry I before the latter's accession,[18] and Richard's son, Baldwin de Redvers, held land in Feltham, while his daughter Hawise de Roumare, Countess of Lincoln, gave the church to St. Giles in the Fields.[19] The manor apparently descended in the direct male line, and came eventually to William de Vernon,[20] also known as de Ripariis, or Rivers, the second son of Baldwin de Redvers, who succeeded to the family estates and title of Earl of Devon after the death of his elder brother's sons, the youngest of whom died in 1184.[21] William de Vernon died in 1216,[22] and Feltham seems to have passed through the marriage of his daughter Joan[23] to Hubert de Burgh,[24] the justiciar of England. In 1228 the latter conveyed all his right in the manor to Henry III, together with his right in Kempton Manor in Sunbury parish, in exchange for the manors of Aylsham in Norfolk and Westhall in Suffolk.[25] From this time Feltham was closely associated with Kempton, and as part of that manor lay within the jurisdiction of its larger neighbour.[26] In 1245 Richard de Ponte, by virtue of his office as custodian of Kempton Manor, was granted an exemption from all customs and services due from 2 virgates and $1\frac{1}{2}$ acres of land in Feltham, with a reduction of rent from 11s. $5\frac{1}{2}d.$ to 5s.[27] In 1440 Robert Manfield, then keeper of the manor, and William Pope were granted 12s. a day from the profits of the towns of Feltham and Kempton by reason of their office of bearing the rod before the king and the Knights of the Garter at the Feast of St. George.[28] The king extended the protection in 1445 to all the men, tenants and residents in his manor of Feltham, with the assurance that their corn, hay, horse and carriages and other goods and chattels should not be seized for the king's use during a term of ten years.[29]

Feltham was annexed by Henry VIII to the manor of Hampton Court,[30] and it was held of that manor in 1594 and as late as 1631. In 1594 the 'perquisites and issues of the courts, all franchises, privileges, emoluments, and hereditaments' in Feltham were granted to Sir William

[8] Bertouch, *Life of Father Ignatius,* 393.   [9] Ibid. 539.
[10] *Dict. Nat. Biog.*
[11] Ibid. xxx, 349.
[12] Cott. MS. Faust. A. iii.
[13] *V.C.H. Lond.* i, 434.
[14] Cott. MS. Faust. A. iii ; Titus A. viii.
[15] *Dom. Bk.* (Rec. Com.), i, 128.
[16] Ibid.

[17] *Dict. Nat. Biog.* xxxix, 117.
[18] Orderic Vitalis, *Hist. Eccl.* iii, 51; iv, 95, 110.
[19] Harl. MS. 4015.
[20] *Cal. Close,* 1227–31, p. 149.
[21] *Dict. Nat. Biog.* xlvii, 385 ; G.E.C. *Complete Peerage,* iii, 101.
[22] Ibid.
[23] *Cal. Rot. Chart.* (Rec. Com.), i, 52.
[24] *Cal. Close,* 1227–31, p. 149.

[25] Ibid. pp. 133, 140 ; *Cal. Chart.* 1226–57, p. 82.
[26] P.R.O. Ct. R. portf. 191, no. 41, 42, 43.
[27] *Cal. Chart.* 1226–57, p. 287.
[28] *Cal. Pat.* 1436–41, p. 458.
[29] Pat. 24 Hen. VI, pt. i, m. 23.
[30] *L. and P. Hen. VIII,* xv, 498 (36); Pat. 36 Eliz. pt. xix, m. 22 ; Pat. 7 Chas. I, pt. vii, no. 2.

Killigrew with a lease of Kempton Manor and park for eighty years.[31] This grant was possibly made with a view to inclosures. Sir William's son, Sir Robert, obtained a grant in free socage of the same manor and park in 1631, presumably with the same rights over Feltham ; for the deed recites the grant to Sir William of the courts and profits of the courts, and other emoluments in Feltham, although in the ensuing confirmation to Sir Robert, Feltham is not mentioned by name.[32] His son and grandson, Sir William and Robert Killigrew, held manorial rights over Feltham together with the manor of Kempton in 1651, and conveyed them with the latter manor to Sir Brocket Spencer and William Muschamp.[33] It seems probable that the manorial rights over Feltham died out about the end of the 17th century. There is evidence that courts were held there by the lords of Kempton in 1676 and 1700.[34] The manorial rights probably died out very soon after.

The grant of jurisdiction in Feltham and Kempton to Sir William Killigrew in 1594 did not of course affect the king's possession of his lands in Feltham (vide supra). In 1631 Francis Lord Cottington received a grant through his trustees, Sir Henry Browne and John Cliffe, of these lands under the title of 'all lands, tenements, and hereditaments known as the manor of Feltham,' together with certain specified tenements.[35] A great fire broke out in 1634, which destroyed Lord Cottington's manor-house, together with thirteen dwelling-houses and sixteen barns, causing a loss of nearly £5,000.[36] Lord Cottington was on the king's side in the Civil War, and was amongst those excepted by Parliament from indemnity or composition.[37] His estates were confiscated, and were assigned in 1649 to John Bradshaw the regicide,[38] but they were recovered at the Restoration by his nephew and heir, Charles Cottington.[39] The latter sold Feltham in 1670 to Sir Thomas Chambers.[40] He died in 1692, and was succeeded by his son Thomas, who left two daughters.[41] By the marriage of the elder, Mary, Feltham came to Lord Vere Beauclerk.[42] It was inherited by their son, Aubrey (Beauclerk) Baron Vere, who succeeded his cousin in 1787 as Duke of St. Albans.[43] He still held the manor in 1802,[44] but it was sold probably after his death in 1803 to a

COTTINGTON. *Azure a fesse between three roses or.*

Mr. Fish, who himself died before 1816.[45] It came before 1874 to Thomas and Edward Barnet, and Peregrine Birch, by whom with others it is still held.

By an order stated in the court roll for 1676 no person was allowed 'to bring or recieve into the parish of Feltham or to entertain there any foreigner or stranger as an inhabitant' without the consent of the majority of the parish, and without giving security to the churchwardens or overseers of the poor for the care of any such 'foreigner.'[46] Any one transgressing in this manner was liable to a fine of 11d. to be paid to the lord of Kempton manor. The parish not being inclosed at that time there was a great expanse of common pasture for pigs, and consequently two 'hogg-drivers' were appointed for the year in the manor court.[47] One of their duties was to give warning to the owners of every 'un-ringed' hog or pig which they found in the commons or fields, and if after two days the warning was still disregarded, they were entitled to 4d. for each hog and 2d. for each pig over and above the amount of the fine paid by the owner to the lord of the manor.[48]

THE RYE (Reye, Ray, Raye, xvi and xvii cents.) was held of the lords of Feltham. William de Vernon gave land in Feltham to the convent of Cheshunt,[49] and the gift was confirmed by Hubert de Burgh as lord of the manor of Feltham before 1229.[50] Land was held of the convent by Agnes de la Rye, who was probably the daughter or the widow of Richard de la Rye.[51] Whether he took his name from the land or the land was named after him, it seems to have been known as the Rye from that time. At the instance of Dionysia, Prioress of Cheshunt, and as the result of a lawsuit which was perhaps collusive, Agnes conveyed her land in 1257 to John the Warrener of Kempton, to hold at a yearly rent of 7s. from the convent.[52] In 1311 Alice de Somery, who was then prioress, released all the convent's right in the land to John,[53] who seems to have added to it to a considerable extent ; this sub-tenancy is here lost sight of.[54] The Rye, having passed as part of the manor to the Crown in 1228,[55] was granted by Henry VIII to the Hospital of St. Giles in 1524, in return for other lands in Feltham which Henry VII had taken for the enlargement of Hanworth Park, and for which no recompense had been made.[56] The Rye then consisted of a barn and toft, a croft, a close, and 30 acres of land.[57] After the lands of St. Giles had been ceded to the Crown in 1537, the Rye was granted to John Welbeck in 1543, on a lease of twenty-one years.[58]

[31] Pat. 36 Eliz. pt. xix, m. 22.
[32] Pat. 7 Chas. I, pt. vii, no. 2.
[33] Feet of F. Midd. East. 1651 ; Recov. R. East. 1651, rot. 123.
[34] B.M. Egerton MS. 2351, fol. 3–4, 104.
[35] Pat. 7 Chas. I, pt. viii, no. 2.
[36] Lysons, *Environs of London* (1800), v, 45, quoting Strafford Papers, i, 227.
[37] Dict. Nat. Biog. xii, 393.
[38] Cal. of Com. for Compounding, 146.
[39] G.E.C. Complete Peerage, ii, 384 ;

Feet of F. Div. Co. Hil. 18 & 19 Chas. II.
[40] Close, 22 Chas. II, pt. ii, no. 1 ; Feet of F. Midd. Trin. 22 Chas. II.
[41] Lysons, *Environs of London*, v, 97 ; G.E.C. Complete Peerage, vii, 6.
[42] Lysons, *Environs of Lond.* v, 45 ; G.E.C. Complete Peerage, vii, 6.
[43] G.E.C. Complete Peerage, vii, 6.
[44] Recov. R. East. 43 Geo. III, rot. 233.
[45] *Beauties of Engl. and Wales*, x (4), 516.

[46] B.M. Egerton MS. 2351.
[47] Ibid.   [48] Ibid.
[49] Cal. Close, 1227–31, p. 149.
[50] Ibid.
[51] Feet of F. Lond. and Midd. 41 Hen. VIII, no. 362.   [52] Ibid.
[53] Ibid. 29 Edw. I, no. 294 ; 33 Edw. I, no. 311.
[54] Anct. D. (P.R.O.), C. 2433.
[55] *v.s.* manor.
[56] Pat. 16 Hen. VIII, pt. ii, m. 30.
[57] Ibid.
[58] Aug. Off. Misc. Bks. ccxv, fol. 51.

It was included in the grant of the manor to the trustees of Lord Cottington in 1631,[59] and was at that time, as it had been in 1543, divided into two parts—the Great Rye, containing a barn, two closes and 4 acres of pasture and woods ; and the Little Rye, which consisted of 3 acres.[60] Both were included in the manor in 1670.[61] Rye Close was still known in 1800.[62] It lay on the southern borders of the parish to the east of Feltham Hill.

An estate called *HAUBERGERS* in Feltham was apparently held in chief. John le Hauberger held a considerable estate in Feltham in the reign of Edward II. About 40 acres of land had belonged to Thomas atte Brugge, who held of the king, and these had been acquired by John le Hauberger from Thomas le Spenser in the preceding reign.[63] As the transaction had been carried out without gaining the consent of the king, the lands were taken into the king's hands. On payment of a fine, however, the offence was pardoned, and John le Hauberger was allowed to enter again into possession in 1326.[64] He died about 1335, and in common with his wife Margaret he held a certain amount of land in Feltham of the king at a yearly rent of 15s., payable to the manor of Kempton.[65] He held also a smaller estate of the Hospital of St. Giles,[66] and both were inherited by his son Edward le Hauberger, who was born and baptized at Feltham.[67] It was probably these lands which were known later as Haubergers or Lucyes. A farm of this name was bought from Nicholas Townly by Francis Lord Cottington in the 17th century,[68] and descended with the latter's manor to his nephew Charles Cottington.[69] The manor was sold to Sir Thomas Chambers in 1670, but Haubergers was specially excepted.[70] It was the cause of litigation shortly afterwards between Charles Cottington and Francis Philips, who held Kempton Manor,[71] and the farm was finally sold to the latter in 1674 for the sum of £150, and in consideration of the release of £29 13s. 4d. which Cottington owed him as costs and charges in the foregoing suit.[72] It was then known as Feltham Farm,[73] and seems to have descended with the manor of Kempton, for in 1800 it was supposed to form part of the property of Edmund Hill, who had bought Kempton in 1798.[74] The present Feltham Farm lies on the main road near the older part of the village.[75]

The *RECTORY MANOR*, which was also known as the manor of Feltham, was held of the king in chief. The Hospital of St. Giles in the Fields received a grant of land in Feltham at an early date from Earl Baldwin de Redvers.[76] The gift has been ascribed to the reigns of Richard I and John,[77] but no member of the family named Baldwin was living at that time,[78] and it was probably made by the Baldwin de Redvers who was son and heir of Richard de Redvers, and first Earl of Devon,[79] whose daughter gave the church of Feltham to the hospital.[80] In this case the grant must have taken place before 1155, the year in which Baldwin died.[81] It was confirmed to the hospital by Pope Alexander IV in the time of Henry III.[82]

In the reign of John the master and brethren of St. Giles granted land in Feltham to Robert Simple at a yearly rent of 14s.[83] When any of the brethren passed through Feltham he was bound by the terms of his lease to receive them in the house (*hospicium*), and to give them such food as he had. He was also to give to the hospital a tenth of the produce of the land, and a third of all his chattels at his death, in return for which the land was secured to him and his heirs, though he could neither pledge nor alienate it, and the hospital undertook to compel the villeins on the estate to work for him.[84]

It was perhaps the same house which was mentioned in 1307 as in the custody of Robert Simple. An inquiry was then made as to the advisability of stopping up a way in the village of Feltham which led to the village well through the middle court of the house belonging to St. Giles.[85] The village seems to have been just within the king's manor of Feltham,[86] but on condition that the hospital made a new and equally convenient approach to the well they were allowed to stop up the old way.[87] The alteration really benefited both parties, for not only did the hospital ensure the privacy of their house, but also the new way was considerably shorter and broader than the old.[88]

The Hospital of St. Giles held the rectory manor until 1537, when, in exchange for the manor of Burton Lazars, it was ceded to the king.[89] All the land which the hospital had held in Feltham was granted in 1544, after the dissolution of the house, to John Dudley, Viscount Lisle, the son of the Earl of Northumberland.[90] He sold it in May 1545 to John Welbeck,[91] who conveyed it during the same month to John Leigh of London, probably in mortgage,[92] as Welbeck had licence to alienate to Andrew Bury in the following December.[93] It is uncertain how the rectory came to Edward Bashe or Baeshe, who died seised of it in 1587.[94] He had settled it the preceding year on his son and heir Ralph, on the latter's marriage with Frances daughter of Edward Cary.[95] Ralph

59 Pat. 7 Chas. I, pt. viii, no. 2.
60 Ibid.
61 Close, 22 Chas. II, pt. ii, no. 1.
62 B.M. Egerton MS. 2356.
63 Inq. a.q.d. 19 Edw. II, no. 71.
64 *Cal. Pat.* 1324–7, p. 312.
65 Chan. Inq. p.m. 9 Edw. II (1st nos.), no. 10.
66 Ibid.
67 Ibid. 12 Edw. III (1st nos.), no. 56.
68 Close, 26 Chas. II, pt. ix, no. 9.
69 Ibid.
70 Ibid. 22 Chas. II, pt. ii, no. 1.

71 Ibid. 26 Chas. II, pt. ix, no. 9.
72 Ibid.   73 Ibid.
74 Lysons, *Environs of Lond.* v, 45.
75 *Ord. Surv.*
76 Harl. MS. 4015 ; Parton, *Account of Hosp. and Par. of St. Giles in the Fields*, 32, 61.
77 Parton, op. cit. 61.
78 *Dict. Nat. Biog.* xlvii, 385.
79 Ibid.
80 Harl. MS. 4015.
81 *Dict. Nat. Biog.* xlvii, 385.
82 Harl. MS. 4015.

83 Ibid.   84 Ibid.
85 Inq. a.q.d. 1 Edw. II, no. 35.
86 *Feud. Aids*, iii, 372.
87 *Cal. Pat.* 1307–13, p. 135.
88 Inq. a.q.d. 1 Edw. II, no. 35.
89 Parton, op. cit. 31.
90 Pat. 36 Hen. VIII, pt. ix, m. 29.
91 *L. and P. Hen. VIII*, xx (1), 846 (93).
92 Close, 37 Hen. VIII, pt. iv, no. 7.
93 Ibid. xx (2), 1068 (52).
94 Chan. Inq. p.m. 29 Eliz. no. 215 (269).   95 Ibid.

and Frances conveyed it in 1595 to Walter Gibbes and Elizabeth his wife.[96] By his will (dated 7 June 1612) Walter settled it on Elizabeth for twenty-one years.[97] She apparently died before May 1620, for Walter Gibbes, eldest son and heir of the elder Walter, came into his inheritance at that time.[98] He conveyed it in 1626 to William Penfather, from whom it passed to Francis Lord Cottington,[99] who had a grant of the reputed manor of Feltham in 1631 (q.v.). From that time the rectory and manor have passed through the same hands.

CHURCH The church of *ST. DUNSTAN* has a nave and chancel of equal width, built in 1808, with a west tower and wooden spire covered with shingles. North and south aisles, in a feeble Romanesque style, were added in 1853, and to the north of the chancel is a vestry. The whole is built of yellow and purple stock bricks, with round-headed windows, and has no architectural merit; but being set in a thickly-planted churchyard, with a path shaded by yews leading to its principal doorway in the west wall of the tower, can hardly be said to detract from the simple charms of its surroundings. It retains its high pews, and a western gallery, and has nothing worthy of note beyond a tablet to Sir Thomas Crewe of Steane, Northamptonshire, 1688.

There are three bells by Thomas Mears, 1803.

The plate consists of a flagon of 1801, 'the gift of Henry Capel to Feltham 1802,' two chalices of 1787, a paten of 1769, and a credence paten of 1777, all presented in 1802; there is also a large secular Georgian salver of 1769 presented in 1900.

The registers previous to 1634 were burnt in a fire in that year, and the earliest now existing are in two books in which those from 1634 onward are placed in irregular order; a third contains baptisms 1711 to 1806; a fourth marriages from 1754 to 1812 in printed forms, and a fifth burials 1754 and 1812.

ADVOWSON The church is first mentioned in a 12th-century grant, when it was given to the Hospital of St. Giles in the Fields by Hawis, the wife of William de Roumare, Earl of Lincoln,[100] the sister of Earl Baldwin de Redvers who gave other lands (v.s. rectory manor) in Feltham to the same hospital.[101] The gift of the church was confirmed by Henry II, and about 1221 by Eustace, Bishop of London, and again by Pope Alexander IV, and later by Edward I.[102] Before 1322 a vicarage was ordained and endowed, to which the warden and brethren continued to present until the Dissolution.[103]

In 1293, when the brethren of St. Giles were resisting the claim of the Bishop of London to exercise jurisdiction over the hospital and all its possessions, a special exception was made in the case of Feltham, and it was stated that as the church was quite outside London, yet in the diocese of London, the bishops had been wont to make visitation there, and apparently they continued to do so.[104]

In 1398 Richard II gave the Hospital of St. Giles, with the church of Feltham, to the abbey of St. Mary Graces by the Tower of London.[105] It is doubtful, however, if the grant took effect, and in either case, the custody of St. Giles was confirmed to the monastery of Burton Lazars by Henry V.[106]

When the master of Burton ceded the rectory manor of Feltham to the king in 1537 the church was excepted from the grant,[107] and probably did not come to the Crown until the suppression of the monastery in 1539.[108] From this time onwards the advowson was held with the rectory manor (q.v.).

On the confiscation of Lord Cottington's estates in 1649 the advowson was assigned with the manor to John Bradshaw.[109] On receiving the tithes of Feltham he issued an address in 1651 to the inhabitants of the parish, stating that his anxiety 'touching spyrituals' had led him to provide and endow a minister for them without putting them to any charge.[110] He left a bequest in his will for maintaining a good minister at Feltham,[111] but all his property was confiscated under the Act of Attainder of May 1660,[112] and the advowson was restored to Lord Cottington's nephew and heir, Charles Cottington.[113]

It continued with the manor (q.v.) for over a century,[114] and thus was held by the Duke of St. Albans in 1802,[115] but it seems to have been separated from the manor early in the 19th century. The Rev. Joseph Morris held it from about 1816 to 1840,[116] after which it was held by the Rev. P. P. Bradfield until about 1850. It then came to Charles E. Jemmet, after whose death it was held by his executors. It now belongs to Mr. E. J. Wythes of Copped Hall, Essex, whose father married Catharine Sarah, daughter of Mr. C. E. Jemmet.

CHARITIES The Poor's Stock, which, as appeared from the table of benefaction, formerly consisted of payments made to the overseers of £2 6s., £2, and 12s. annually, and carried to the poor rates, has ceased to be paid.

In 1798 Robert Lowe by his will bequeathed £200 stock, the dividends to be applied in bread. The legacy is now represented by £202 13s. 4d. consols, producing £5 1s. 4d. a year, which, together with certain fixed payments amounting to

96 Feet of F. Midd. Mich. 37 & 38 Eliz.
97 Chan. Inq. p.m. (Ser. 2), cccxxvii, no. 128.
98 Fine R. 18 Jas. I, pt. i, no. 57.
99 S.P. Dom. Chas. I, ccclxxvii, 177.
100 Harl. MS. 4015, fol. 5–9.
101 Dict. Nat. Biog. xlvii, 385; xlix, 314.
102 Harl. MS. 4015, fol. 5–9.
103 Newcourt, Repert. i, 602.
104 Cal. Pat. 1388–92, p. 458.
105 Ibid. p. 475.
106 Dugdale, Mon. vii, 635; Parton, Account of Hosp. and Par. of St. Giles in the Fields, 27.
107 Parton, op. cit. 31.
108 Dugdale, Mon. vii, 635.
109 Cal. of Com. for Compounding, 146.
110 Athenaeum (1878), 689.
111 Ibid.
112 Dict. Nat. Biog. vi, 179.
113 G.E.C. Complete Peerage, ii, 384; Feet of F. Div. Co. Hil. 18 & 19 Chas. II.
114 Ibid. Midd. Trin. 22 Chas. II; P.R.O. Inst. Bks.
115 Recov. R. East. 43 Geo. III, rot. 233.
116 Clerical Guide.

£1 5s. a year, granted in 1774, is duly applied by the vicar.

In 1804 almshouses for poor and aged inhabitants were erected on a piece of land formerly part of Feltham Common, in pursuance of a resolution of the vestry, and endowed with £202 0s. 6d. consols. They are further maintained out of the income of the Poor's Land. See below.

In 1844 Mrs. Mary Anne Paine (as recorded on a tablet in the church) gave £100 consols to be laid out by the vicar and churchwardens in bread to be distributed among twenty aged poor persons during January, February, and March.

In 1852 William Paine by a codicil to his will bequeathed £179 12s. 2d. consols, one moiety of the dividends to be annually applied for benefit of a clothing club, the other moiety annually in January in purchase of clothes to be distributed amongst ten aged poor persons regularly attending services of the Church of England at the discretion of the vicar and churchwardens. The dividends, amounting to £4 9s. 8d., are duly applied.

In 1867 John Ashford by will, proved at London 10 April in that year, bequeathed a legacy, represented by £618 9s. 4d. consols, the dividends to be applied at Christmas time in the purchase of fuel, clothes, meat, or bread for distribution among old men and women. The dividends, amounting to £15 9s., are distributed in meat and clothing under the title of the Ashford and Moore Charity.

In 1826 Thomas John Burgoyne by deed dated 9 December (enrolled) assigned to trustees a piece of ground in St. Pancras, with a messuage thereon for the residue of a term of twenty-one years, and subject as therein mentioned to accumulate the rents to form a fund, the income thereof to be applied towards the salary of the organist, repair of organ, and for the encouragement of psalmody, or of the church music. The trust fund consists of a sum of £404 0s. 2d. consols. The sum of stock has by an order of the Charity Commissioners been apportioned equally between this parish and the parish of Potton, Bedfordshire.

The several sums of stock are held by the official trustees.

The Poor's Land or Fuel Allotment, acquired by an award made under the Inclosure Act, 40 Geo. III, consists of 30 a. 3 r., known as the 'Gibbet Ground,' awarded to the lord of the manor of Colkennington *alias* Kempton, and the vicar, churchwardens, and overseers of Feltham for providing fuel for the poor. In 1890 2 acres were purchased for £324, and in 1902 land with greenhouse and buildings erected thereon and five greenhouses at Bedfont were purchased for £425, provided by sale of stock, with the official trustees, leaving in their name a sum of £478 18s. 5d. consols.

In 1905–6 the gross rental of the real estate amounted to £217, and the dividends to £11 19s. 4d.

The charity is administered under the provisions of a scheme of the Charity Commissioners of 18 July 1890, whereby the net income is applicable primarily in defraying the cost of supplying with coal deserving and necessitous poor residents in the parish, one-twelfth of the residue in defraying the expenses incidental to letting of lands in allotments, and one-twelfth of such residue in maintenance and repair of the almshouses above referred to, and for the benefit of the inmates.

HAMPTON

Hamptone (xi cent.) ; Hamtonet (xiii cent.).

Hampton is a large parish on the banks of the Thames, which forms its southern and western boundaries and divides it from the neighbouring county of Surrey. It is a low-lying district, nowhere rising over 50 ft. above the Ordnance datum, and was formerly open country, part of which now remains as Hounslow Heath. The soil is light and gravelly, and there is little indigenous timber.[1] There is still some pasture land, but most of it has been built over, except in the royal demesne of Hampton Court, which forms a considerable proportion of the parish.[2] The area, including the ecclesiastical district of Hampton Hill, is about 7,036 acres of land and 62 acres of water. The district called Hampton Wick[3] on the east, which was made a civil parish in 1831, contains 1,235 acres of land and 69 acres of water. An ancient British canoe made of the trunk of a tree was found in the Thames opposite the palace, and is now in the British Museum. A row of oak piles also found in the river has been considered Roman, but is probably the remains of an old weir of later date.

The main road to Kingston-on-Thames is a branch from the Portsmouth Road, which it leaves at Esher, passes through East Molesey, crosses the river at Hampton Court by an iron bridge erected in 1865,[4] and proceeds outside the wall of the 'Tilt Yard,' and between the Home Park and Bushey Park to Kingston, whence it continues to Richmond and London. Another road branches from the Kingston road opposite the 'Lion Gates,' to the north of the palace, and goes through the

---

[1] A few old oaks, now much decayed, in the Home Park, and some of the famous 'thorns' in Bushey Park are said to be indigenous.

[2] See pp. 386 et seq. for acreage of parks, &c. The manor and parish were originally coterminous.

[3] Hampton Wick includes the Home Park, part of the palace gardens and the eastern portion of Bushey Park. It is spoken of as 'The Wick' from an early period. See p. 325.

[4] See further account of ferry and bridge, p. 322.

A HISTORY OF MIDDLESEX

chestnut avenue of Bushey Park to Teddington, Twickenham, and Brentford.[5] It is well known that these roads and all the district surrounding Hounslow Heath were once infested with thieves and footpads. In 1667 Lord Bridgman's children were robbed going from Teddington to Tunbridge, and the Dowager Lady Portland between Twickenham and Hampton.[6] The Staines road, which leads north-west from Hampton Court Bridge to Hampton town, following the course of the river, passes several interesting houses; opposite them lie 'the Green' and Bushey Park. At the foot of the bridge is an old hotel, 'The Mitre,' probably the successor of 'The Toy,'[7] which originally stood on the opposite side of the road, near the 'Trophy Gates' of the palace. It was built in the time of Henry VIII, and is mentioned in 1653 in the Parliamentary Survey of Hampton Court as a 'Victualling house, worth by the yeare seaven pounds.'[8] This house was famous for the convivial meetings held there by the 'Toy Club,' of which William IV, then Duke of Clarence, was president. The club included many well-known names among its members.[9]

The first house on the road to Hampton is said to have been occupied by Sir Andrew Halliday, kt., the famous physician, and the second, known as 'Old Court House,' is that which Sir Christopher Wren rented of the Crown for £10 a year in 1708 and almost entirely rebuilt.[10] It was originally only of timber and plaster, but is now a solid brick house, and remains very much as it was when the great architect died there in his sleep after dinner on 25 February 1723, in the panelled room on the east side of the house.[11] There is a garden going down to the river, and the old tree under which Wren used to sit is still there, and so is the tool-house he built. After his death the house became the property of his son and grandson successively, and after passing through many hands[12] was eventually leased to Mr. James Fletcher, a well-known inhabitant of Hampton Court, who held it for many years and died in 1907.

The next house but one was occupied by Pro-

fessor Faraday the scientist, to whom it was given in 1858. He died there in 1867,[13] and the house was afterwards granted to Lady MacGregor, widow of Sir John Atholl Bannatyne MacGregor, bart., and daughter of Sir Thomas Hardy, Nelson's flag-captain at Trafalgar.[14] It is now the residence of the Princesses Dhuleep Singh. Several houses on this side of the Green are probably of about the period of Wren, if he was not actually concerned in building them, and they have charming slips of old-fashioned garden going down to the river. They are all Crown property; some are occupied by tenants and some held by 'grace and favour.' A little further up the road, beyond a large new private hotel, is the range of low Tudor buildings surrounding a square courtyard, which constituted the 'Royal Mews,' built by Wolsey and enlarged by Henry VIII.[15] These buildings, it is said, were at one time used as an inn, called 'The Chequers.'[16] They are now granted by the king to private individuals; one suite of apartments was occupied by the late Mr. Charles Maude, Assistant Paymaster-General,[17] others of smaller size being allotted to pensioners of Queen Victoria's household. The adjoining building to the west is Queen Elizabeth's stables, built in 1570.[18] Some of the remaining stables are made use of by the ladies of the palace. There are one or two more modern houses, and to the right, on the Green, just before the paling of Bushey Park commences, is a square building of the time of William III, now used as supplementary barracks.[19] From this point the road used to be a pretty one, lying between the river and Bushey Park. The electric tramway now spoils its picturesque appearance. Nearer to Hampton, on the river side, is a large, comparatively modern house called the Cedars, which it appears that David Garrick, the actor, bought and bequeathed to his nephew.[20] It is now the property of Mr. J. W. Clayton, one of the partners in the firm of Messrs. Day & Martin.[21] It has a pretty terraced garden on the bank of the river. The next house is a picturesque building called 'St. Albans.' It was originally built

[5] This was probably the route followed by the king's coach. The present route through Eaton Square (Five Fields), Sloane Square (East Field and Great Bloody Field), and so along King's Road, represents the sovereign's private way from St. James's Palace to Hampton Court and Windsor, in later times to Kew. In 1719 Sir Hans Sloane, as lord of the manor, petitioned the Treasury for right of way, but the Commissioners of Woods and Forests did not relinquish rights in the private road till 1829, when it became a public thoroughfare. *Midd. and Herts. N. and Q.* i, 195 (1896).
[6] *Hist. MSS. Com. Rep.* vii, App. 486; 'Sir H. Verney's Papers.'
[7] Pulled down about 1852. There were some buildings adjoining which remained and were occupied as apartments till 1867. Ernest Law, *Hist. Hampton Court Palace,* iii, 490.
[8] Parl. Surv. of Hampton Court, P.R.O. Midd. no. 32. Trade tokens of

the house are still extant. Larwood and Hotten, *Hist. of Signboards,* 505; cit. Law, *Hist. Hampton Court Palace,* iii, 190; Henry Ripley, *Hist. and Topog. of Hampton-on-Thames,* 83.
[9] Law, op. cit. iii, 330 et seq.; Houston, *Memories of World-known Men,* i, 35, 36, 41.
[10] Lysons, *Midd. Parishes,* 76; Rec. of Office of Woods and Forests; cit. Law, op. cit. iii, 228.
[11] Wren, *Parentalia,* 346; Elmes, *Life of Wren,* 523.
[12] Colonel Sir Henry Wheatley, K.C.B., father of Colonel Wheatley, late Bailiff of the Royal Parks (? Faraday House). Colonel Braddyll, probably the Colonel Braddyll, Coldstream Guards, who had rooms in the palace (*vide* Law, op. cit. iii, 457), and others are among the tenants of Wren's house; Ripley, op. cit. 11.
[13] *Dict. Nat. Biog.* It is now called 'Faraday House.'

[14] Law, op. cit. iii, 489. Lady MacGregor's son, Sir Evan MacGregor, G.C.B., was Permanent Secretary to the Admiralty from 1884 to 1907.
[15] Chapter House Accts.
[16] Ripley, op. cit. 9, &c.
[17] Son of the late Colonel Sir George Maude, K.C.B., Crown Equerry to Queen Victoria. (See below, p. 387.) Mr. Charles Maude died in April 1910: the rooms are now occupied by his widow.
[18] Nicholls, *Progresses of Queen Elizabeth,* i, 263, 274, &c.
[19] Less than a hundred years ago there used to be a gate across the road from the 'New Barracks,' with a watchman in a box near the river, to open it for passengers. It was called 'Bob's Gate,' and was intended to prevent cattle from straying off the Green.
[20] Ripley, *Hist. and Topog. of Hampton-on-Thames,* 12.
[21] Ibid.

for Nell Gwyn by Charles II. The local tradition is that it was occupied at a later period by George Fitzclarence, 1st Earl of Munster, son of William IV, who, with his wife, is buried in Hampton Church.[22] One of his children, a boy, was drowned by falling into the river from the lawn of St. Albans. Lytton Bulwer, afterwards Lord Lytton, lived there for a time,[23] and after him Sir William Wightman,[24] who married a niece of John Beard the singer,[25] an old resident of Hampton, who is also buried in the church. The present tenant is Mr. Robert Graham.

Beyond this house, but on the opposite side of the road, is 'Garrick's Villa,' formerly called 'Hampton House,' which David Garrick bought in 1754[26] from Mr. Lacy Primatt. The portico was built on to the original house by Garrick, from a design by Robert Adam.[27] In the garden is a small brick building with a dome and a porch, supported by four pillars from the Adelphi Theatre. This used to be called the 'Temple of Shakespeare,' and a life-sized statue of the poet by Roubiliac stood in it.[28] Part of the garden is divided from the house by the road, but can be reached by a passage underground. The river side of the garden, where the 'temple' stands, is well known to frequenters of the Molesey Regatta, which takes place opposite the lawn. Horace Walpole wrote of Garrick's entertainments at the house, and mentioned on one occasion that he met there at dinner the Duke of Grafton, Lord and Lady Rochford, Lady Holderness, 'Crooked' Mostyn, and the Spanish Ambassador.[29] In the *Rambler* of 1797 is an account of Garrick's charity and generosity to the poor people of Hampton. On 1 May he always opened his grounds to the children of the parish, and entertained them with 'cake, buns and wine.' Both he and his wife were fond of planting trees about their property; Mrs. Garrick lived there for many years after her husband's death, until she died at the age of ninety-nine in 1822. Mrs. Hannah More used to visit her there.[29a] All Garrick's collections, furniture, and pictures were sold after Mrs. Garrick's death.[30] In 1869 the house became the property of Mr. Grove, a retired tradesman, and his widow lived there till 1905, when the place was sold to the London United Electric Tramway Company, and was until recently occupied by Sir E. Clifton Robinson, the manager.

There are several houses in Hampton which claim to have been designed by Wren: among them Walton House, near the church, at present occupied by Colonel George Stevens. Beveree is also a good house of that period

standing in a charming garden, occupied by Captain Christie-Crawford, J.P. Castle House is one of the oldest houses in Hampton, the tenant is Colonel Graham, late 16th Lancers. The Elms is another of the Wren houses, now tenanted by Dr. Tristram, K.C., Chancellor of the Diocese of London. Opposite the Elms is one of the largest houses in the parish, Grove House, surrounded by a high wall and with fine trees in the garden, which extends to Bushey Park. It is now the property of Mr. Stretfield. The Manor House (so-called) stands back from the road in wooded grounds, on which small houses have lately begun to encroach. It was the property of the late Mr. James Kitchin, and is now untenanted.

The vicarage is a modern house, built within the last thirty years on the site of an older one; the present vicar is the Rev. Digby Ram, rural dean and Prebendary of St. Paul's. Hill House, near the station, was originally a private school, at which the late Lord Dufferin and Field-Marshal Earl Roberts were educated; but it has now been demolished, with other good houses in the district, to make room for the Grand Junction Waterworks, which monopolize a considerable acreage on the road from Hampton to Sunbury. There was a picturesque Tudor building used as an inn, called The Red Lion, almost opposite the church, but it was demolished in 1908.

The district of Hampton Hill contains no houses of any historical interest. Bushey House, Bushey Lodge, the Stud House, the Pavilion, the Banqueting House, and Wilderness House are all in the precincts of Hampton Court, and will be dealt with under 'Parks and Gardens.'[31] There is one other large house on the north side of the Green called Hampton Court House, overlooking Bushey Park, of which a wing is said to have been designed by Wren. It was at one time the property of the late J. E. Sampson, City editor of the *Times*,[32] and at a later period of Mr. James Campbell, who added a large room as a picture gallery. It was afterwards bought by Mr. A. de Wette, and is now for sale. The Ivy House, which is practically in the palace gardens, with a terrace overlooking the Broad Walk, is a picturesque building of uncertain date: part of it is probably old, like the house next to it, which belongs to the King's Arms Hotel. The Ivy House is the property of Colonel Walter Campbell, son of Mr. James Campbell, who formerly owned Hampton Court House. There are various houses, some of them fairly old, and others new and uninteresting, on the Kingston Road looking

[22] Ripley, *Hist. and Topog. of Hampton-on-Thames*, 12; Parish Register of Hampton.

[23] Ripley, loc. cit.

[24] Ibid.

[25] Born 1716, died 1791. He was one of the 'children of the Chapel Royal,' afterwards one of the singers in the Duke of Chandos' chapel at Cannon. He became manager of Covent Garden Theatre. His first wife was Henrietta, daughter of the first Earl

Waldegrave, and widow of Lord Edward Herbert. He was a well-known and popular singer.

[26] *Dict. Nat. Biog.*

[27] The house had a high wall round it until recently, when part of the garden was given up to make the road wider. The granite posts in front of the house come from the foundations of old London Bridge. Ripley, op. cit. 17.

[28] R. Snagg, *A Description of the Co.*

of Midd. (1775) 192–3. The statue is now in the entrance hall of the British Museum. Ripley, *Hist. and Topog. of Hampton-on-Thames*, 13, &c.; Horace Walpole, *Letters* (Ed. Toynbee), iii, 329.

[29] Ibid. iii, 331.

[29a] Ibid. xiii, 151; xiv, 29, 290.

[30] Ripley, op. cit. 16, 78; *Dict. Nat. Biog.*

[31] See pp. 385 et seq.

[32] Ripley, op. cit. 9.

into the Paddocks and Bushey Park. Most of them are Crown property. In 1707 Steele either rented or built himself a house called The Hovel at Hampton Wick,[33] to which there are numerous allusions in his letters to his wife, but the house has probably been pulled down, as it is not possible to identify it now.[33a]

Besides the River Thames there is a considerable amount of ornamental water in the parks and gardens of the palace, and the Longford or King's River (now known according to the Ordnance map as the 'Queen's or Cardinal's River') which was cut in the reign of Charles I[34] for bringing a better water supply to the palace.

The ferry from the Surrey side of the river to Hampton Court[35] used to be an important holding, farmed out on lease with the ferry opposite Hampton Church. The office of ferryman was looked upon as a lucrative appointment, though 10s. a quarter for ferrying over all the workmen and labourers to the palace does not seem a great sum ;[36] but the 'fines due (to the king) for leasing the manor of East Molesey, Surrey, the two ferries called Hampton Court ferry and Hampton ferry and the fishing in Cobham River,' amounted in the 17th century to £448.[37] It was not till 1750 that a petition was presented to the House of Commons for permission to build a bridge across the Thames at Hampton Court. A Bill was passed in April 1750,[38] and the bridge was built and opened for the use of the public in December 1753.[39] There are two prints, published in 1753 and 1754, which show the picturesque structure of the first bridge, composed of seven wooden arches, but it seems to have been extremely defective and unpractical, and in 1778 it was replaced by a more solid though equally picturesque erection which consisted of eleven arches,[40] also of wood, standing on piles and surmounted by a low parapet. It remained till 1865, when it was removed, and the present inartistic iron bridge was erected in its place.[41] The tolls levied were on an exorbitant scale, and brought the owners a yearly income of about £3,000. In 1876 the Metropolitan Board of Works purchased the bridge for £50,000, and on 8 July 1876 it was declared 'free for ever.'

Hampton Court Station (London and South

Western Railway) is on the Surrey side of the river near the bridge, in the parish of East Molesey. Hampton Station (Thames Valley line) is on the west side of the parish, beyond Hampton Church. There is also a station at Hampton Wick (London and South Western Railway branch line).

The Wesleyan chapel in Hampton was built in 1880, and will hold about 400 people. In Hampton Hill are Congregational and Primitive Methodist chapels.

HONOUR OF HAMPTON COURT.—In 1539 Hampton Court was created an 'Honour' by Act of Parliament.[42] It was among the 'statutory' as opposed to 'feudal' honours[43] created by Henry VIII.[44] The lands annexed to Hampton Court were partly confiscated monastic property, but some of them were obtained by purchase or attaint.

The following are the manors and lands annexed to the manor of Hampton Court by the Act creating the honour. In Surrey the manors of Walton on Thames, Walton Leghe, Oatlands (with lands in Weybridge, Walton, and Chertsey) ; the manors of Byfleet and Weybridge (with lands and tenements in Walton) ; East Molesey, West Molesey, Sandown, Weston, Imworth (or Imber Court), and Esher ;[45] lands at Heywood and the fee-farm of the borough of Kingston-on-Thames. In Middlesex the manors of Hanworth and Kempton, Feltham, and Teddington, with the parks of Hanworth and Kempton, and lands in Hampton, Kempton, Feltham, and Teddington.[46]

In the following year further manors were attached to the honour, i.e. Nonsuch, Ewell, East and West Cheam with lands in Coddington, Ewell, and Maldon ; the manors of Banstead, Walton on the Hill, Sutton, Epsom, Beddington and Coulsdon, Wimbledon with its members, Dunsford, Balham, Wandsworth, and Battersea, all in Surrey ; and in Middlesex, Haliford, Ashford, Laleham, Isleworth with its members, the site of the late monastery of Syon, and other lands in Hampton, Sunbury, Walton, Hanworth, Shepperton, Feltham, Kingston on Thames, Brentford, Hounslow, and Hanworth.[47] At later dates additional manors and lands were annexed, such as Norbury Manor in Croydon,[48] Rockingham Forest in Northamptonshire,[49] the manor of Billets in

[33] Aitken, *Life of Richard Steele*, i, 216, 343–4.

[33a] A custom, which has now entirely died out, was instituted in 1876 of holding a monster meeting of bicycles on the Green every year. They were the old high bicycles before the 'Safety' patent was invented. The Green used to be covered with shining wheels like the inside of a mammoth watch. The great joke of the occasion was the attempt of crowds of bicyclists to carry their machines past the toll-keeper on the bridge, and pay only the small fee of foot-passengers ; Ripley, op. cit. 138.

[34] *Hist. MSS. Com. Rep.* vii, App. 77 (House of Lords Calendar, 1653).

[35] The earliest lease seems to be one in 1545, to Thomas Sheparde of 'Mul-sey Surrey,' in which the 'mill called Stentemyll' is also mentioned ; *L. and P. Hen. VIII,* xix, 55.

[36] Harl. MSS. 1656, F. 232 (temp. Chas. II).

[37] *Cal. S.P. Dom.* 1667, pp. 88, 145, 462, 527.

[38] *Gent. Mag.* xx, 41, 186 ; Lysons, *Midd. Parishes,* 75.

[39] Law, *Hist. Hampton Court Palace,* iii, 286 et seq. The owner was a Mr. James Clarke, who held the lease till 1775.

[40] Brayley, *Hist. of Surr.* ii, 307.

[41] It was then the property of Mr. Thomas Newland Allen, and its building cost £11,176. The engineer was E. T. Murray, of Westminster Chambers.

[42] Stat. 31 Hen. VIII, cap. 5.

[43] Comyn, *Digest of Laws,* iv, 459

et seq. 'Honours' ; Madox, *Baronia Anglica* (ed. 1736), 8 ; Pollock and Maitland, *Hist. Engl. Law,* i, 260 ; Jacobs, *Law Dictionary,* 'Honour' (1829).

[44] Stat. 31 Hen. VIII, cap. 5 ; 37 Hen. VIII, cap. 18 ; 14–15 Hen. VIII, cap. 18 ; 23 Hen. VIII, cap. 30 ; 33 Hen. VIII, cap. 37, 38.

[45] Esher was the property of the see of Winchester, bought by Henry in 1538 ; *L. and P. Hen. VIII,* xiii (1), 778 ; (2), 444 ; Close, 30 Hen. VIII, pt. i, m. 27 d.

[46] *Stat. of Realm,* iii, 721 et seq. (31 Hen. VIII, cap. 5).

[47] *L. and P. Hen. VIII,* xv, 498 (36).

[48] Ibid. xix (i), 647.

[49] *Cal. S.P. Dom.* 1601–3, p. 131.

Laleham.[50] There is also mention of a mill called 'Stentemyll,' and a ferry over the Thames to Hampton Court from East Molesey.[51]

The original statute creating the honour provided also for the making of a new forest or chase for the king, to be called 'Hampton Court Chase,' 'for the nourishing, generation, and feeding of beasts of venery and fowls of warren,' in which the king was to have 'free chase and warren.'[52] It was also enacted that the same liberties, jurisdictions, privileges and laws, that belonged to the ancient forests of the kingdom, should also apply to this 'the newest forest in England.'[53] The limits of the chase were clearly defined in the Act, and were to extend from the River Thames on the south side of the manor of Hampton Court to Cobham and Weybridge, thus including all the Surrey lands originally annexed to the honour.[54] The chase was to be surrounded by a wooden fence, and there is an early grant of £600 to Sir Anthony Browne, for 'paling, ditching, and quick-setting of the King's chase of Hampton Court,'[55] besides payments for stocking the chase with deer,[56] and precautions to be taken for preserving them there.[57]

Sir Anthony Browne was the first 'Lieutenant and Keeper of the Chase,' an office held always with that of 'Chief Steward of the Honour and Manor of Hampton Court and Feodary of the Honour.'[58] With these offices were also generally held that of Housekeeper of the Palace and the rangerships of Bushey Park, the Middle Park, and the Hare-Warren Park. The rangership of the 'House' or 'Home' Park was usually separate. The last holder of that appointment was the Duke of Gloucester.[59] Sir Anthony Browne[60] died in 1548, and was succeeded by Sir Michael Stanhope, who was also Keeper of Windsor Forest and Lieutenant of Kingston on Hull. He was implicated in the affairs of the Protector Somerset, and was beheaded in 1552.[61] Successive holders of the office were William Parr, Marquis of North-

ampton;[62] Charles, the famous Lord Howard of Effingham, afterwards Earl of Nottingham;[63] James, second Marquis of Hamilton;[64] George Villiers, first Duke of Buckingham,[65] the favourite of both James I and Charles I; and Christopher Villiers, first Earl of Anglesey.[66] During the Commonwealth the office appears to have been in abeyance, but on Cromwell's death in 1658 George Monk, afterwards first Duke of Albemarle, the celebrated Parliamentarian general,[67] was appointed, and his appointment was confirmed by Charles II on his restoration. Monk held it till his death, and in April 1677 the stewardship of Hampton Court and rangership of Bushey Park were given to Barbara Palmer, Duchess of Cleveland,[68] who held them for her life in the name of her trustee, William Young.

In June 1709 Charles Montague first Earl of Halifax[69] was made keeper, and was afterwards succeeded by his nephew George Montague, also Earl of Halifax[70] by a later creation, and his son George Montague Dank second earl of the later creation.[71] On his death Anne, Lady North, afterwards Countess of Guildford,[72] was granted the offices, which she held for her life. In 1797 they were granted to H.R.H. William, Duke of Clarence,[73] and from the time of his accession to the throne in 1830 they have remained in abeyance.[74]

The chase seems to have been very unpopular from the beginning, and as early as September 1545, the 'men of Molsey and other towns in the chace of Hampton Court' were emboldened to lay a complaint before the Privy Council when it met at Oatlands, asking for redress on account of damage done by the deer, and other losses incurred by commons and pastures being inclosed.[75] Their petition was referred to Sir Nicholas Hare,[76] witnesses were allowed to appear before the Council, and were 'generally examined of their losses,' but no reparation seems to have been made at the time. In 1548, soon after the death of Henry VIII, a

---

[50] Pat. 4 Jas. I, pt. xxi, m. 35. Billets may have been included as 'Laleham' in 1540. L. and P. Hen. VIII, xv, 498 (36). This does not attempt to be a full list of the manors annexed to the honour at later periods.

[51] Ibid. xx (i), 1336 (55).

[52] Stat. of Realm, iii, 721; 31 Hen. VIII, cap. 5.

[53] Manwood, Forest Laws (ed. 1598), 11–12.

[54] It has been supposed that the honour and chase were identical, but the chase did not include any part of Middlesex. Stat. of Realm, iii, 721, &c. 31 Hen. VIII, cap. 5. See supra.

[55] L. and P. Hen. VIII, xiii (2), 457 (12). See also Chapter House Accounts, C. 6/3, fol. 226, &c.

[56] L. and P. Hen. VIII, xiii (2), 1280.

[57] Ibid. xx (i), 512.

[58] Ibid. xv, p. 539. Pat. 4 Chas. I, pt. i, no. 3. The patent of the Earl of Anglesey, in which his predecessors are mentioned; Lysons, Midd. Parishes, 57, &c.

[59] Ibid. Law, op. cit. i, 215, &c.

[60] Master of the Horse to Hen. VIII. He held among other appointments that of justice in eyre of all the king's forests north of Trent. He married, as his second wife, Lady Elizabeth Fitzgerald, 'The fair Geraldine,' see p. 339; Dict. Nat. Biog.

[61] Ibid. Sir Thos. Cawarden was also appointed, apparently by Edw. VI; Hist. MSS. Com. Rep. vii, App. 606a.

[62] He was born in 1513, died in 1571. The brother of Catherine Parr, last wife of Henry VIII; Dict. Nat. Biog.

[63] Born 1536, died 1624. Lord High Admiral of England.

[64] Born 1589, died 1625.

[65] Born 1592, died 1628. See p. 350, under Palace. Pat. 4 Chas. I, pt. i, no. 3.

[66] Born 1593, died 1630. Pat. 6 Chas. I, pt. xiii, mentions former holders of the office.

[67] Born 1608, died 1670. Pat. 12 Chas. II, pt. iii, no. 7.

[68] Born 1641, died 1709. Pat. 29 Chas. II, pt. iii, no. 7.

[69] Born 1661, died 1715. Chancellor of the Exchequer, &c. Dict. Nat. Biog.; Pat. 8 Anne, pt. i, no. 3.

[70] Died 1739. Created Earl of Halifax in 1715, on the death of his uncle; G.E.C. Peerage, iv, 136.

[71] Ibid. Born 1716, died 1771. In 1748 he held the chief justiceship in eyre of the Royal Forests and Parks south of Trent. Dict. Nat. Biog.

[72] Dict. Nat. Biog. Lysons, Midd. Parishes, 57.

[73] Ibid.

[74] Vide Declared Accounts Audit Office. P.R.O. Index, bdle. 247b, no. 288, &c.

[75] L. and P. Hen. VIII, xx (2), 278. Acts of P.C. 1542–7, p. 239. In April of that year a mandate had been issued that the red deer from the king's chase which had strayed into 'woods and bushes between Cobham and London' were not to be molested; ibid. 512.

[76] Master of the Rolls, &c. Dict. Nat. Biog.; Wriothesley, Chron. (Camd. Soc.), i, 101.

further petition was brought before the Lord Protector and Council, by 'many poor men' of the parishes of Walton, Weybridge, East and West Molesey, Cobham, Esher, Byfleet, Thames Ditton, Wisley, Chesham and Shepperton, complaining that 'their commons, meadowes and pastures be taken in, and that all the said parishes are overlayd with the deer now increasing largely upon them, very many Households of the same Parishes be lett fall down, the Families decayed, and the King's liege people much diminished, the country thereabout in manner made desolate, over and besides that his Majesty loseth yearly, diminished in his Yearly Revenues and Rents to a great Summe.'

The Lord Protector and Council examined twenty-four men of the parishes, and they were also interrogated by Sir Anthony Browne, Master of the Horse and Chief Keeper of the Chase, and it was decided that after Michaelmas that year the deer should be put into the Forest of Windsor, the pale round the chase taken away, and the land restored to the old tenants, to pay again their former rents.[77] A proviso was however entered 'that if it shall please his Majesty to use the same as a chase again,' the order was not to be taken as prejudicial to the sovereign's rights. These lands are therefore still technically a royal chase, and the paramount authority over all game within its limits is vested in the Crown.

In 1639 Charles I appears to have wished to make a new 'forest' by inclosing a tract of about 10 miles of country between Hampton Court and Richmond as a 'hunting ground for red as well as fallow deer.'[78] He even began building the wall to make this inclosure, but so much indignation was aroused among the people at the idea of their commons and pasture lands being taken from them that Archbishop Laud is said to have dissuaded the king; and a new 'Hampton Court Chase' was not made.[79]

MANOR In the time of Edward the Confessor **HAMPTON** was held by Earl Algar. It was granted by the Conqueror to Walter de St. Valery, who also received the neighbouring manor of Isleworth and considerable property in other parts of England.[80] In 1086 he held 35 hides in Hampton, 18 hides being in demesne, the rest farmed by tenants.

For considerably over a century Hampton remained in the hands of the St. Valerys. In 1130 Henry I remitted to Reginald de St. Valery, probably grandson of Walter,[81] the sums of £10 10s. of his *Danegelt*, and £11 16s. 2d. of the *auxilium comitatus* in Middlesex.[82] He appears to have held the office of *dapifer* to Henry II before his accession.[83] From 1158 to 1163 Reginald was still holding lands in Middlesex and other counties.[84] In 1173–6, a Bernard de St. Valery, presumably son of Reginald, is mentioned as holding what appear to be the same lands.[85] In 1201–2 Thomas, probably son of Bernard, held the property,[86] and seems to have been in possession till 1218–19, when Henry of St. Albans was permitted by Henry III to retain the manor of Hampton, which he held of the gift of Thomas de St. Valery, notwithstanding that all the lands of the said Thomas de St. Valery had been taken into the king's hands.[87] It has been suggested that Thomas joined the rebel barons in the reign of King John, and if he did not submit on the accession of Henry III, his lands may have been forfeited after the battle of Lincoln in 1217.[88] He died in 1219, leaving only a daughter, Annora, whose first husband, Robert de Dreux, possessed the other St. Valery manor of Isleworth in right of his wife.[89]

Henry of St. Albans, who thus became lord of the manor at some period before 1218–19, was well known as a merchant and citizen of London, and was one of the sheriffs in 1206.[90] He only held Hampton for a short time, as in 1237 he sold it to Terrice de Nussa, Prior of the Hospital of St. John of Jerusalem in England, for 1,000 marks,[91] he and his wife Sabine quitclaiming all rights in the manor to the prior and his successors. The prior seems to have made some claim to the property at an earlier date, as in the Close Rolls of 1230 a 'contention' is mentioned between H. de St. Albans and the prior concerning 'the house of Hampton;[92] and

THE KNIGHTS HOSPITALLERS. *Gules a cross argent.*

[77] Harl. MSS. 6195. 'Extracts from Council Bk. of Edw. VI,' fol. 2 d.–3 d. *Acts of P.C.* 1547–50, p. 190, &c.

[78] Clarendon, *Hist. of Rebellion*, i, 100 ; Law, op. cit. ii, 126.

[79] Ibid. Grove, *Hist. of Wolsey*, iv, 186 n.

[80] *Domesday Bk.* (Rec. Com.) ; *Pipe R.* 4, 8, 9, 19, 22, Hen. II (Pipe R. Soc.) ; *Rot. Canc.* 3 John (ed. Hardy), 105 ; ed. Round, *Cal. of Doc., France*, i, 385 ; Dugdale, *Baronage*, i, 454. Planché, in *The Conqueror and His Companions*, and Lipscomb, *Hist. of Bucks.* i, 367, give pedigrees of the St. Valery family, which trace its descent from Ric. II, Duke of Normandy, and 'Papia,' his second wife ; *vide Gen.* iv, 239. For the St. Valerys in Normandy at a later period see Round, *Cal. of Doc. France*, i, 6 et seq.

[81] It is generally thought that there was a Guy or a Bernard who was the son of Walter and father of Reginald ; *vide Gen.* iv, 239 ; Dugdale, *Baronage*, i, 454.

[82] Pipe R. 31 Hen. I, m. 29 d. (Midd.).

[83] Round, *Cal. of Doc. France*, i, 519 (1151).

[84] *Pipe R.* 4 Hen. II (Pipe R. Soc.), 114 ; 8 Hen. II, 8, 14, 19, 27, 36, 42, 44, 49, 67, 71 ; 9 Hen. II, 19, 49.

[85] Ibid. 19 Hen. II, 170 ; 22 Hen. II, 29. In 1189 a Reginald de St. Valery and Bernard his son are mentioned as confirming a grant of lands in Glouc. to the Abbey of Fontevrault ; Round, *Cal of Doc. France*, i, 286, 380, 385. This Bernard is said to have been killed at the siege of Acre in 1190. Planché, *The Conqueror and His Com-*

panions ; Lipscomb, *Hist. Bucks.* i, 367 ; *Gen.* iv, 239–41 ; Banks, *Dorm. and Ext. Baronage*, vi, 174 ; Dugdale, *Baronage*, i, 454 ; Law, *Hist. Hampton Court Palace*, i, 8.

[86] *Rot. Canc.* 3 John (ed. Hardy), 102, 105.

[87] *Rot. Lit. Claus.* (Rec. Com.), i, 385b.

[88] Law, op. cit. i, 8.

[89] *Vide* Planché, op. cit. ; Lipscomb, op. cit. ; Dugdale, op. cit. ; *Gen.* iv, 241.

[90] Harl. MSS. 4015, 80, 80b, 81 ; *Cal. Pat.* 1216–23 ; *Cal. Roy. Letters, Reign of Hen. III*, 254 (1225) ; R. R. Sharpe, *Cal. Le ter Bks. of Lond.* F, 27.

[91] Feet of F .Lond. and Midd. 21 Hen. III, no .148.

[92] *Cal. Close*, 1227–31, p. 451. What the 'contention' was is not explained.

there seems to have been a preceptory of the order at Hampton as early as 1180, when the sisters of the order were removed from their several commanderies to Mynchin Buckland in Somersetshire. 'Sister Joan' is mentioned in the Mynchin Buckland charter as the sister from 'Hampton in Middlesex.'[93]

In 1250 Henry III made a grant to the prior and brethren of free warren 'in their manor of Hampton,' which was confirmed by Edward I in 1280.[94]

Nevertheless, in 1292, Sabine of Durham claimed the property as the heiress of her grandfather Henry of St. Albans,[95] disputing the right of the then prior, Brother Peter of Hagham, to the manor, saying that her grandfather had been unjustly disseised of the property. The pleading of the prior is curious, as he denies that Henry ever was in seisin of the said manor, and the jury found that the prior and his predecessors continually held it 'for fifty years past and more.' The actual sale, which seems to have taken place when Henry quitclaimed his rights to the prior and his successors for 1,000 marks, is not mentioned, and eventually as a compromise Sabine agreed to accept 100 marks, and quitclaimed for herself and her heirs ' all her rights and claims in the said manor to God, St. John the Baptist, the prior and brethren of the hospital and their successors.'[96]

Henry of St. Albans had a son William, who is mentioned, with his wife Alice, in 1232, as holding a messuage at Newton in Middlesex, but he and his heirs never seem to have claimed Hampton.[97] The only other person who is mentioned as having held the manor 'for her life' before the Knights Hospitallers sold it to Wolsey, is Joan, the widow of Robert de Grey, kt. Tanner and Dugdale have both made the mistake of supposing that Joan de Grey was herself the donor of the manor of Hampton to the Knights Hospitallers.[98] What really happened seems to have been that Joan de Grey inherited the manor of Shobington in Buckinghamshire from her father Thomas de Valognes, it having been part of the dowry of her mother Joan de Valognes. This manor in 1298–9 Joan de Grey granted in mortmain to the Knights Hospitallers, but with their permission retained

her life interest in it, and at the same time had granted to her by them a life interest in the manors of Hampton in Middlesex and of Raynham in Essex, possibly in return for or in acknowledgement of the actual gift which she had made to them of Shobington.[99]

There is record of two further gifts of land in Hampton to the Knights Hospitallers. In 1303 Walter de Wyke and Maud his wife granted them a messuage, 100 acres of arable land, 1 acre of meadow, and 20s. rent.[100] Christine Haywood also gave them 60 acres of land with appurtenances in Hampton, and the 'Wike' (Hampton Wick.)[101]

In 1338 the report of Prior Philip de Thame to the Grand Master of the Order gives an account of the 'Camera' of Hampton as comprising a messuage with a garden, a dovecote, and 840 acres of land, chiefly pasture, yielding altogether £83 13s. 10d. annually.[102] The house was evidently small, as the total expenses, including the stipends and clothing of the brother in charge, ' a chaplain to serve the Chapel,' a corrodyman of the king, and other members of the household, were only £30 7s. 2d. per annum. A charge of 20s. a year is mentioned for maintaining a weir, which was used for fishing, and farmed at a rent of £6. There is also a yearly charge of 68s. 4d. arising out of a composition for tithe made with the vicar of Hampton,[103] and further expense seems to have been incurred by the entertainment of guests going to and coming from the Black Prince's house, either at Sheen, or more probably at Kempton (Kennington), about a mile from Hampton Court.[104] There are few further references to the house before it became the property of Cardinal Wolsey. Fox, Bishop of Winchester, in a letter to Wolsey, mentions that Henry VII had used it as a ' cell ' or subsidiary house to his neighbouring palace of Richmond.[105] The manor was leased in 1505 for ninety-nine years at £50 a year, to Giles, Lord Daubeny, Chamberlain to Henry VII,[106] who died in 1508, leaving in his will the remainder of the lease to his wife, who survived him,[107] but this agreement is not mentioned in the lease granted to Wolsey in 1514.

By an indenture dated 11 January 1514–15, Sir Thomas Docwra, Prior of the Hospital of St.

[93] Chart. R. 1 John, m. 17; Thos. Hugo, Hist. of Mynchin Buckland, 8, 9. It is said in the charter that the sisters were all removed to Mynchin Buckland in 1180, but there is a grant in the Chart. R. of 1227 to the prior and brethren of 'the right of having their dogs unlawed in their house in Hamtonet in the King's warren of Stanes —in which house the sisters of the said order dwell.' Cal. Chart. R. 1226–57, p. 30 (Mar. 1227).

[94] Chart. R. 8 Edw. I, no. 73; vide Cal. Close, 1279–88, p. 515, &c.

[95] Sabine was the daughter of John Vyel, sen., and Margery daughter of Henry St. Albans. Sabine married William of Durham, mercer and citizen of London. Both Vyel and Durham were well known, and had considerable property in London. John Vyel was sheriff 1218–20; R. R. Sharpe, Cal.

Letter Bks. of Lond., F. p. 277. William of Durham was sheriff in 1252 (ibid. p. 279), alderman in 1277; ibid. A, p. 15; Stowe MS. 942, no. 6406; Cal. of Midd. Wills. i, 66; Anct. D. (P.R.O.), C 2890, C 1910; Cott. MSS. Nero, E vi, fol. 26, 27.

[96] Assize R. Midd. 544b, d. (1292–3).

[97] Cal. Close, 1231–4, p. 133.

[98] Dugdale, Mon. vi, 802, 832; Tanner, Not. Mon. Midd. ii.

[99] Inq. a.q.d. 27 Edw I, F. 29, no. 16; Cal. Close, 1307–13, p. 491; Feet of F. Div. Co. 27 Edw. I, no. 45; 28 Edw. I, no. 51; De Banco R. Mich. 3 Edw. III, 279, m. 18 d. It seems impossible to trace that Joan had any hereditary claim on the manor, as has been suggested. Her mother Joan de Valognes may have been the daughter or granddaughter of Henry of St. Albans, but this is only conjecture.

[100] Cal. Pat. 1301–7, p. 157; Inq. a.q.d. file 43, no. 26 (31 Edw. I); Cal. Inq. p.m. (Rec. Com.), i, 185.

[101] Dugdale, Mon. vi, 832.

[102] Larking, The Knights Hospitallers in Engl. (Camd. Soc.), 127. 'Report of Prior Philip de Thame for A.D. 1338.'

[103] Larking, op. cit. 128.

[104] Ibid.; Lysons, Midd. Parishes, 271; Law, op. cit. i, 13.

[105] L. and P. Hen. VIII, iii, 414 (1519). Elizabeth of York went there in 1503 for a week, to pray for her safe delivery, just a month before her child was born and she herself died. Nicolas, Pivy Purse Expenses of Eliz. of York, 94, 95; Law, op. cit. i, 14.

[106] Cott. MSS. Claudius, E vi, fol. 46.

[107] Will, Somerset House, P.C.C. Bennet, 16; Dict. Nat. Biog. 'Giles, Lord Daubeny.'

A HISTORY OF MIDDLESEX

John of Jerusalem, and the brethren of the order granted a lease for ninety-nine years of the manor of Hampton Court with all appurtenances to Thomas Wolsey, Archbishop of York, and his assigns, at a rent of £50 a year, the lease to take effect from 24 June 1514.[108] The prior and brethren were to allow £4 13s. 4d. yearly to the archbishop for a priest to perform divine service in the chapel of the manor, and also four loads of wood and timber from St. John's Wood yearly for the repair and maintenance of the weir.

WOLSEY. Sable a cross engrailed argent with a lion passant gules between four leopards' heads azure thereon and a chief or with a rose gules between two Cornish choughs therein.

By the terms of the lease Wolsey was to build, rebuild or alter as he chose, and at the expiration of the term was to leave a thousand couple of 'conys' in the warren, 'or else for every couple that shall want 4d.'

The exact date, or the exact manner in which Wolsey, probably actuated by signs of the king's jealousy and displeasure, surrendered the manor and the splendid house he had built to Henry VIII is not known.[109] It became the king's property before the rest of the cardinal's lands were escheated to the Crown after his attainder in 1529.[110]

A letter from Jehan le Sauche, the Austrian Ambassador, to 'Madame' (Elizabeth of Austria), is now in the Vienna archives, and speaks of the gift having been made as early as June 1525.[111] Stowe and Cavendish both say that the king made an exchange of Richmond for Hampton Court with the cardinal.[112] Lord Herbert of Cherbury stated that Wolsey only finished the palace in 1525, and exchanged it with the king for Richmond in 1526.[113]

Wolsey himself, in writing to the king as early as 1521, dates his letter from 'Your house of Hampton Court,'[114] but as late as 1528, in writing to others, continued to speak of it as 'my manor of Hampton Court.'[115]

In 1527 Laurence Stubbs, Wolsey's paymaster

of the works, wrote to him, 'your buildings—at York Place, Hampton Court, Oxford, &c., go forward.'[116] In a letter from Fitzwilliam to Wolsey in 1528 he said, 'The King will be glad to be at your manor of Hampton Court on Saturday next—as I told him you could not conveniently remove by that day, he wished to be at your house on Saturday or Monday at furthest, where he will spend three or four days before his repair to Greenwich.'[117] In 1527, however, it was generally considered to be the king's property. Dodieu (the French Ambassador's secretary) wrote of it as 'a handsome house built by Wolsey, and presented by him to the king,'[118] but Wolsey certainly continued to live there, to receive private visits there,[119] and probably to bear all the expense of the upkeep, and continued building[120] until the time of his disgrace in 1529.[121]

The idea has usually been accepted that on the suppression of the order of St. John in England in 1539 the reversion of the lease of Hampton Court escheated to the Crown with the other property of the Order,[122] but this was not the case. In 1531 the king made an exchange with Sir William Weston, then prior, of 'the Manor of Hampton or Hampton Courte, Middlesex, for the advowson of the prebend of Blewbery in Salisbury Cathedral, lands at Stansgate, Essex and a messuage in Chancery Lane in the suburb of London.'[123]

Sir William Paulet, Christopher Hales, Attorney-General, Baldwin Malet, and Thomas Cromwell were appointed as trustees, to receive the manor 'to the King's use.'

From that date, 5 June 1531, Hampton Court became the property of the Crown or the State, and has so continued to the present day, with one short interval, during the Commonwealth,[124] when the fee of the manor and honour

THE KING OF ENGLAND. Azure three fleurs de lis or, for FRANCE, quartered with Gules three leopards or for ENGLAND.

was sold to Mr. John Phelps of London, gentleman, for £750.[125] Bushey Park and its appur-

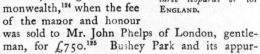

---

[108] Cott. MSS. Claudius, E. vi, fol. 137 (the original lease); Close, 6 Hen. VIII, pt. i, no. 38. The lease is printed in full in Law, Hist. Hampton Court Palace, i, App. B.

[109] The legend is that Henry with some anger asked the cardinal 'why he had built so magnificent a house for himself at Hampton Court?' Wolsey is supposed to have made the ready answer, 'To show how noble a palace a subject may offer to his sovereign,' but there is no historic warrant for the story, which is given in all the old guide books, &c. Vide Law, Hist. Hampton Court Palace, i, 99.

[110] In the inquisitions taken after Wolsey's attainder there is no mention of Hampton Court. Inq. p.m. (Ser. 2), lii, no. 35b, 102b; lx, no. 62; lxxvii, no. 26; Exch. Inq. p.m. (Ser. 2), file 1220, no. 12b.

[111] Cal. S.P. Spanish, iii (1), 209.

[112] Annals, 526 (ed. 1616); Harl. MSS. no. 428; Cavendish, Life of Wolsey (ed. Singer), i, 226.

[113] MS. Coll. by Mr. Shaw, an architect (1827); penes Mrs. Edwin Lascelles.

[114] L. and P. Hen. VIII, iii (1), 1192, 7 Mar. 1521.

[115] Ibid. iv (2), 275b. Letter to Jermingham, 16 Jan. 1528.

[116] Ibid. iv (2), 1369.

[117] Ibid. iv (2), 4766.

[118] Ibid. iv (2), 3105, (60). Cromwell says that the king purchased Hampton Court. This may refer to the later transaction with the Knights Hospitallers. Vide infra; ibid. x, 513.

[119] Ibid. iv, 4332, 4391. Letter from Warham, Archbp. of Canterbury.

[120] Chapter House Accts.; L. and P. Hen. VIII, iv (1), 1369.

[121] Ibid. iv (3), 5754.

[122] Porter, Knights of Malta, 340; Stat. 32 Hen. VIII, cap. 24.

[123] L. and P. Hen. VIII, v, 133, 285, 627, App. no. 12; Stat. 23 Hen. VIII, cap. 26.

[124] The questions in Parliament, the way in which the sale was carried out, &c., will be referred to more fully in the history of the palace, p. 354.

[125] It was repurchased for £750. The exact sum for which it was sold does not appear. Cal. S.P. Dom. 1654, pp. 180, 223. Warrant for purchase, p. 452; 10 Aug. 1654. Phelps was clerk to the House of Commons, he was included as one of the regicides on the accession of Charles II, and was obliged to leave the country; Dict. Nat. Biog.

tenances were sold to Edmund Blackwell for £6,638 7s., and the Middle Park to Colonel Norton for £3,701 19s. In February 1654 they were all re-acquired for the use of the State, on the return of the purchase money and the payment of £1,200 surplusage,[126] made necessary because some of the lands had already been sold again.[127] John Phelps appears on the Court Roll as lord of the manor from 14 May 1652 to 2 June 1654.[128] No further courts are recorded till 2 April 1657, when the Lord Protector's name appears.[129] After the death of Cromwell a bill was introduced into Parliament to settle the honour and manor of Hampton Court on General Monk, but this was not carried, and on the restoration of Charles II it became once more the property of the Crown.[130]

CROMWELL. *Sable a lion argent.*

HAMPTON COURT PALACE: HISTORY.[131] —There is no doubt that the preceptory of the Knights Hospitallers of St. John of Jerusalem stood on the site of the present palace at Hampton Court, but it seems to have been almost entirely destroyed by Wolsey when he began his new building.[132] At the end of Wolsey's lease is a curious list of the goods of the brethren, which were left in the house when he took possession of it.[133] They were of the most meagre description : even in the chapel the chalice alone was of silver. An item of twenty-two beds gives an idea of the number of people the house could contain. In the hall were some forms, two tables, and a cupboard. There were also some chests, and two bells in the 'toure,' one of which, the sole remaining relic of the order in the palace, still rings for service in the chapel, and has the following inscription on it :—

✠ STELLA ✠ MARIA ✠ MARIS ✠ SUCCVRRE ✠ PIISIMA ✠ NOBIS ✠

(Mary most gracious, Star of the Sea, come to our assistance)

The date of the bell is fixed by the letters 'T. H.' stamped on it, which are the initials of a famous bell-founder, Thomas Harrys, who lived about 1479.[134]

From the date of Wolsey's purchase to the reign of George III the history of Hampton Court Palace may almost be said to be the history of England. Besides its intimate connexion with the private lives of kings and statesmen, there were few questions of political importance that were not discussed by the Privy Council, which met frequently within its walls, and innumerable letters and documents which have made history are dated from it.[135]

Wolsey's political services in the successful campaigns against France and Scotland in 1513 had secured him a high place in the king's favour.[136] At this date or shortly afterwards he held the offices of chancellor and grand almoner,[137] and many minor dignities, and was besides bishop of three English sees and one French see.[138] From the revenues of these offices he amassed considerable wealth, and his ambition led to the design of building for himself a great palace.[139]

He was influenced in his choice of Hampton Court as the site for his great house, not only by the proximity of London and the convenience of the river as a 'swift and silent' highway, but by the exceptional healthiness of the neighbourhood. Afterwards, when the 'sweating sickness' and the plague raged in London, only 20 miles off, Hampton and Hampton Court remained singularly immune from infection.[140]

Henry VIII and Katherine of Arragon paid their first recorded visit to Hampton Court in March 1514, probably to see the property which Wolsey intended to acquire.

Giovanni Ratto, an emissary of the Marquis of Mantua, took the opportunity to present some very fine horses which his master had sent to the king—a present highly appreciated by Henry.[141] A little later in the same year (June 1514) Wolsey took possession of the property, and immediately began his extensive works on the site of the old manor-house.[142]

In May 1516 the building was so far advanced that he was able to entertain the king and queen at dinner,[143] but he did not stay there for any considerable period before 1517,[144] and it was

[126] *Cal. S.P. Dom.* 1653–4, pp. 300, 356, 385 ; Feet of F. Midd. Trin. 1654.

[127] *Cal. S.P. Dom.* 1653–4, pp. 300, 356, 363, 385, 397, 408, 409. These transactions are printed in full in Law, op. cit. ii, App. B.

[128] Land Rec. Ct. R. (Misc. Bks.), iii, bdle. 40, no. 3, 'Court Roll of Hampton Court.'

[129] Ibid. The Court Roll of the manor exists only from 1640 to 1792. *Cal. S.P. Dom.* 1654, p. 32.

[130] White Kennet, *Hist. Engl.* 67 ; *Hist. MS. Com. Rep.* vii, App. 463 ; *Journals of the House of Commons,* 15 and 16 Mar. 1660 ; S.P. Dom. Chas. II, x, 2. Manorial courts are still held annually, up to 1908 at the 'Red Lion,' Hampton on Thames. The number of copy-holders is now reduced to about two hundred. (In-

formation from Mr. F. G. Mellish, bailiff of the manor).

[131] The writer wishes to express her indebtedness to Mr. Ernest Law's *Hist. of Hampton Court Palace* for references to many of the works mentioned in this account.

[132] There is an idea that Wolsey retained the original hall, afterwards rebuilt by Henry VIII. Foundations of an older building have been discovered under the hall. See Architectural acct.

[133] Cotton MSS. Claudius, E. vi, fol. 137.

[134] Law, *Hist. Hampton Court Palace,* iii, 389, *vide* Stahlschmidt, *Surr. Bells.* Harrys was working at King's College, Cambridge, in 1479.

[135] *Vide L. and P. Hen. VIII* ; *Cal. S.P. Dom.* ; *Hist. MSS. Com. Rep.* &c.

[136] Creighton, *Life of Wolsey,* 29.

[137] At a later period he also held a Spanish see ; ibid.

[138] In 1515 he was made cardinal, and was appointed *Legate a latere* in 1518.

[139] For history of the architecture of the palace, see below p. 371 et. seq.

[140] *L. and P. Henry VIII,* ii (preface) ; iii, 1691 ; iv, 4436, 4542.

[141] *Cal. S.P. Venetian,* ii, 385 ; Haliwell, *Letters of the Kings of Engl.* i, 229.

[142] For Parks and Gardens, see p. 380 et. seq. ; *L. and P. Hen. VIII,* ii (1), 4662 ; Law, op. cit. i, 21.

[143] *L. and P. Hen. VIII,* ii (2), 1935.

[144] Ibid. ii (2), 3805 the first letter in the Calendar dated from Hampton Court. The first letter from Wolsey himself was written in Jan. 1518 ; ibid. 3886.

not till after the return from 'The Field of the Cloth of Gold' in 1520 that he seems to have considered the house practically complete and ready for the splendid entertainments which afterwards took place in it.[145]

It has been said that Wolsey was probably the greatest political genius that England has ever produced, and that 'he must be estimated rather by what he chose to do than by what he did.'[146] His designs were cast on a vast scale, and at a great crisis in European history he raised England to the leading position in international affairs which she has held practically ever since.[147] The field of action he deliberately chose was foreign policy, and all his schemes, and his magnificence, including the almost regal state in which he lived at Hampton Court and elsewhere must be understood as part, and not a small part, of his political design. The letters of the ambassadors from foreign courts, which have been preserved, show plainly the important share that the cardinal's splendour had in influencing their policy. It conveyed to their minds more rapidly than anything else could have done the power of the man—said to be the son of a butcher at Ipswich—who was not only making himself the master of England's fortunes, but who came very near to making himself master of the fortunes of Europe. Without this explanation, without some appreciation of the largeness of the plan into which the gorgeous entertainments of the cardinal's 'court' fit like the fine detail on some great building, without which it would be incomplete, a mere description of his magnificence shrinks into a meaningless list of somewhat barbaric festivities meant only to dazzle the populace. It is necessary to gain some insight into the vast interests he had at stake to appreciate at its full value the picture of the cardinal walking in his 'gallories, both large and long,'[148] meditating on affairs of State; giving unwilling audience to impatient petitioners during his moments of leisure in the garden,[149] or presiding over the princely fêtes he organized in honour of the king or his guests or the foreign ambassadors.

The political letters and documents of Wolsey's time, calendared in the *Letters and Papers of Henry VIII*, dated at Hampton Court or addressed there, are innumerable,[150] but the papers which most intimately touch Wolsey himself at Hampton Court Palace are his letters to his agents in Rome, concerning his candidature for the Papacy in 1523, on the death of Adrian III,[151] and those relating to the foundation of the cardinal's colleges at Oxford and Ipswich.[152] It is mentioned that the foundation charter of 'Cardinal's College' (afterwards Christ Church), Oxford, was granted in 'the south gallery at Hampton Court.'[153] The letters of Melancthon and Luther were among those discussed at Hampton Court, and there is some correspondence concerning them.[154] The majority of papers, however, dated from Hampton Court, until the matter of Henry's divorce has to be considered, are concerning foreign affairs.

Sebastian Giustinian, the Venetian ambassador, who constantly visited Wolsey at Hampton Court, writing to his Signory in 1519, gives the following description of the cardinal : 'He is but forty-six years old, very handsome,[155] learned, extremely eloquent, of vast ability, and indefatigable. He alone transacts the same business as that which occupies all the magistracies, offices and councils of Venice, both civil and criminal, and all state affairs likewise are managed by him, let their nature be what it may. He is pensive and has the reputation of being extremely just. He favours the people exceedingly, and especially the poor, hearing their suits and seeking to dispatch them instantly. He is in very great repute, seven times more so than if he were Pope. He is the person who rules both the king and the entire kingdom. He is in fact *ipse rex*, and no one in this realm dare attempt aught in opposition to his interests.'[156] His influence with Henry during the early part of the king's reign was almost unlimited, and Henry entertained a great affection for him personally, writing to him as 'mine awne good Cardinal,' expressing his gratitude for and appreciation of his Lord Chancellor's services, begging him to pay attention to his own health, and signing himself 'Your loving Master, Henry R.'[157] He seems also to have treated him with great confidence and unusual familiarity, walking with him in the gardens at Hampton Court arm in arm, and sometimes even with his arm thrown round the cardinal's shoulder.[158]

---

[145] *L. and P. Hen. VIII*, iv, *passim*.

[146] Creighton, *Life of Wolsey*, 2.

[147] Ibid.

[18] 'My Gallories were fayer, both large and long.
To walk in them when that it lyked me best.'
Cavendish, *Life of Wolsey* (ed. Singer), ii, 10.

[149] *L. and P. Hen. VIII*, ii (2), 3807. 'When he walks in the park he will suffer no suitor to come near, but commands them off as far as a man can shoot an arrow.' (Thos. Allen to the Earl of Shrewsbury.) Cavendish says he was accustomed to say Evensong with his chaplain as he walked in the garden. Cavendish, op. cit. i, 42, 233, 246. He also seems to have been in the habit of holding conversations with the ambassadors in the garden.

See Du Bellay's Letters. *L. and P. Hen. VIII*, iv (2), 4332, 4391, App. no. 158.

[150] The entries in the King's Bk. of Payments, for messengers carrying letters to the cardinal at Hampton Court are very numerous ; *L. and P. Hen. VIII*, iv (2), 3380.

[151] The references given are only typical, by no means exhaustive. *L. and P. Hen. VIII*, iii, 3389. Adrian died 14 Sept. 1523 ; ibid. 1892, &c.

[152] Ibid. iv (2), 4435 ; ibid. 3198, 4230, 4231, 4423, 4460, 4461, 5117 ; (3) p. 2552 ; 6748.

[153] Ibid. (2), 4461, 3 July 1528.

[154] Ibid. 2371-2, &c.

[155] Skelton, his implacable enemy, wrote of him (*Works* [ed. Dyce], ii, 315), as :—
'So full of malencoly,
With a flap afore his eye.'

Holbein, in the picture now at Christ Church, Oxford, painted him in profile, presumably because of a drooping eyelid. Much bitter and scurrilous literature was written concerning Wolsey not only by Skelton but by William Roy, a converted Franciscan friar (see *Rede me and be not wrothe* [Arber Reprints], 37 et seq.).

[156] Brewer, *Reign of Hen. VIII.* i, 60. Giustinian, *Despatches*, i, 137, 215. 'Though he might be called proud cardinal and proud prelate by those who were envious of his power, there is no trace throughout his correspondence of the ostentation of vulgar triumph or gratified vanity.' Brewer, *L. and P. Hen. VIII*, i, Pre. p, lxxxvii.

[157] Ellis, *Orig. Letters* (Ser. 3), i, 190.

[158] Law, *Hist. Hampton Court Palace*, i, 43.

Wolsey, who 'passed for an old man broken with the cares of state' before his fall, and died when he was only fifty-five, seems to have failed in health from an early date. In 1517 he suffered from the 'sweating sickness,' and was still ill at Hampton Court in December of that year. It was stated that his life had been in danger, and so great was the fear of infection that Giustinian said, 'None of those who were once so assiduous ever went near him.'[159] It was not, however, by any means only as a health resort that the cardinal used his great house; there is a contemporary description by Hall[160] of a characteristic masquerade given by Wolsey at Hampton Court, to entertain the king in 1519; he says: 'There were as many as thirty-six masquers disguised, all in one suite of fine green satin, all over covered with cloth of gold, undertied together with laces of gold, and making hoods on their heads: the ladies had tyers made of braids of damask gold, with long hairs of white gold. All these masquers danced at one time, and afters they had danced they put off their vizors, and then they were all known.' Their supper was 'of countless dishes of confections and other delicacies,' and afterwards, 'large bowls filled with ducats and dice were placed on the table for such as liked to gamble; shortly after which the supper tables being removed, dancing commenced,' and lasted, as it often did on such occasions, 'till long after midnight.'

Cavendish says that when the king repaired to the cardinal's house 'for his recreation, divers times in the year, there wanted no preparation or goodly furniture with viands of the finest sort that could be gotten for money or friendship,' and tells an amusing story of the king's coming 'suddenly thither in a masque with a dozen masquers all in garments like shepherds (sic) made of fine cloth of gold and fine satin . . . with vizors of good proportion and physiognomy.' He goes on to say that they startled the cardinal and his guests with 'the noise of guns—they sitting quiet at a solemn banquet'—and that Wolsey entertained them as strangers, and to the great joy of king and court mistook which was the king, and went up to one of the gentlemen of the court, hat in hand.[161] Only Shakespeare could do justice to these scenes of simple yet magnificent festivity, with the figure of the great cardinal moving through the gay courtiers that thronged his stately courts, unmindful of the jealousy already at work to undermine his power and his influence with the king.[161a] It was in 1522 that Anne Boleyn returned from France, and in 1524 Skelton's satire, *Why come ye not to Court?* was published, in which he drew

attention to the vast crowd of suitors who followed the cardinal rather than the king.[162]

It is impossible here to follow the course of Wolsey's diplomacy during the following years, though Hampton Court was the scene of many of his negotiations.[163] In 1515 he had received the cardinal's hat, and in 1517 was made papal legate. His moment of greatest success was perhaps in 1518, when universal peace was concluded among the European nations, but his path was beset with difficulties from the time of Maximilian's death in 1519, and in the course of the next few years his great design to maintain the peace of Europe and the position of England as mediator in the politics of the Continent was overthrown.[164] He continued to work for peace, and an important treaty was signed at Hampton Court in 1526 by Wolsey on behalf of Henry VIII, and by the French ambassador on behalf of Francis I, to the effect that neither king should unite with the emperor against the other, and that the King of England should endeavour to procure the liberation of the French king's sons, then held as hostages in Spain.[165] Wolsey had been working for some time to arrange a separate peace with France, and his letter to Henry from Hampton Court three days later expresses his satisfaction with the agreement.[166] In the following year the French commissioners, Gabriel de Grammont, Bishop of Tarbe, Francois Vicomte de Turenne, and Antoine le Viste, president of Paris and Bretagne, arrived in England to arrange a further alliance between the two kingdoms and a marriage between Francis I and Henry's daughter Mary, then only ten years old. Dodieu, the secretary to the French embassy, gives a detailed account of the negotiations.[167] The ambassadors seem to have stayed in 'the village at the end of the Park,' probably Hampton Wick. They were taken to the palace, where the king and queen were staying, and received by Wolsey, afterwards having an audience of the king 'in the hall.'[168] In the evening, after dining with Wolsey and other members of the council, they were admitted to the queen's 'chamber,' and talked with the king on indifferent matters, discussing Luther and his heresy, and the book that Henry had lately written; the king showing himself, as Dodieu says, 'very learned.'

The ambassadors and Wolsey afterwards discussed the subject of the treaty at length in the 'Cardinal's own room.'[169] They went back to London, and it was some time before a final conclusion was reached, and the treaty signed by Henry at Greenwich in April 1527.[170] It was ratified at Amiens in September, when Wolsey went

[159] Giustinian, *Despatches*, ii, 90; *L. and P. Hen. VIII*, ii, Pref. p. ccxxvi.
[160] Hall, *Chron.* 595 (ed. 1809).
[161] Cavendish, *Life of Wolsey* (ed. Singer), i, 49.
[161a] *Hen. VIII*, Act i, Sc. 4.
[162] Skelton, *Works* (ed. Dyce), ii, 276–320.
[163] See *L. and P. Hen. VIII*, 1518, &c.
[164] Creighton, *Life of Wolsey*, 51 et seq.

[165] *L. and P. Hen. VIII*, iv (2), 2382.
[166] Ibid. 2388.
[167] Ibid. 1406.
[168] Not the present 'Great Hall,' which was built by Henry VIII afterwards, and the room in which the queen interviewed the ambassadors no longer exists; but there seems to be little doubt that Wolsey kept a suite of rooms for Katherine on the second floor in the eastern side of the 'Clock'

Court, which was afterwards transformed and partly rebuilt by George II. The entrance to these rooms remains, with traces of the cardinal's coat-of-arms in the spandrels of the doorway; Law, *Hist. Hampton Court Palace*, i, 101–2.
[169] Architecture, see p. 371 et seq.
[170] *L. and P. Hen. VIII*, iv (2), p. 1413, Dodieu's narrative. For terms of the treaty see Rymer, *Foedera*, xiv, 195.

to meet Francis I. On account of the negotiations having been carried on there, it is known as the 'Treaty of Hampton Court.'[171]

Perhaps the most wonderful, as well as the last, of all Wolsey's regal entertainments at Hampton Court took place in the autumn of 1527, when a special embassy, consisting of the Grand Master and Marshal of France, Anne de Montmorency du Bellay, the Bishop of Bayonne, the president of Rouen, and M. d'Humières, followed by a retinue of a hundred 'of the most noblest and wealthiest gentlemen in all the Court of France,' and a guard of five or six hundred horse, came to England to ratify the agreement finally, and to invest the king with the order of St. Michael.[172] It is of their visit to Hampton Court that Cavendish gives a de-

and furnishing the same with beds of silk and other furniture apt for the same in every degree. . . . Then the carpenters, the joiners, the masons, the painters, and all other artificers necessary to glorify the house and feast were set to work. There were fourteen score beds provided and furnished with all manner of furniture to them belonging. . . .'[173]

On the day appointed 'the Frenchmen' assembled at Hampton Court and rode to Hanworth (2 or 3 miles away), where they hunted till the evening, and then returned to the palace, where 'everyone of them was conveyed to his chamber severally, having in them great fires and wine ready to refresh them. The first waiting chamber was hanged with fine arras, and so were all the rest, one better than another, furnished with tall

HAMPTON COURT PALACE : WOLSEY'S KITCHEN

lightful account. He begins by describing how the cardinal sent for 'the principal officers of his house, as his steward, comptroller, and the clerks of the kitchen—whom he commanded to prepare for this banquet at Hampton Court, and neither to spare for expenses or travail'—that the guests may make 'a glorious report in their country.' 'The cooks wrought both day and night in divers subleties and many crafty devices—the yeomen and grooms of the wardrobe were busied in hanging of the chambers with costly hangings,

yeomen. There was set tables round about the chambers banquet-wise, all covered with fine cloths of diaper. A cupboard of plate[174] parcel gilt . . . having also in the same chamber, to give the more light, four plates of silver, set with lights upon them, and a great fire in the chimney. The next chamber, being the chamber of presence, hanged with very rich arras, wherein was a gorgeous and precious cloth of estate hanged up, replenished with many goodly gentlemen ready to serve . . . the high table was set and removed beneath the

[171] Leonard, *Recueil des Traitez de Paix*, ii, 286 ; cit. Law, op. cit. i, 103 ; Rymer, *Foedera*, xiv, 195.

[172] *Memoires de Martin du Bellay*, ii, 30.

[173] Du Bellay also mentions 280 beds, as quoted in *Mag. Brit.* 1724 ; *vide* also 'accounts for expenses at Hampton Court when the French

ambassadors were there ;' *L. and P. Hen. VIII*, iv (3), 6748.

[174] *L. and P. Hen. VIII*, v (2), 3041.

cloth of estate. . . . There was a cupboard—in length the breadth of the chamber, six desks high, full of gilt plate, very sumptuous, and of the newest fashions ; and upon the nethermost desk garnished all with plate of clean gold, having two great candlesticks of silver and gilt, most curiously wrought, the workmanship whereof, with the silver, cost three hundred marks, and lights of wax as big as torches burning upon the same. The plates that hung on the walls to give light in the chamber were of silver and gilt, with lights burning in them, a great fire in the chimney, and all other things necessary for the furniture of so noble a feast. . . . My lord's officers caused the trumpets to blow to warn to supper . . . the service was brought up in such order and abundance, both costly and full of subtleties, with such a pleasant noise of divers instruments of music, that the Frenchmen, as it seemed, were rapt into Paradise. . . .

'Before the second course, my Lord Cardinal came in among them, booted and spurred, all suddenly, and bade them *proface* (welcome). My Lord commanded them to sit still—and straightways being not shifted of his riding apparel, sat down in the midst—laughing and being as merry as ever I saw him in all my life. . . . Then my Lord took a bowl of gold, which was esteemed at the value of 500 marks, filled with hypocras—putting off his cap, said, "I drink to the king, my Sovereign Lord and Master and to the king your master," and therewith drank a good draught. And when he had done he desired the Grand Master to pledge him cup and all, the which cup he gave him, and so caused all the other lords and gentlemen in other cups to pledge these two royal princes. . . . Then went my Lord to his privy chamber to shift him ; and returned again among them, using them so nobly, with so loving and familiar countenance and entertainment, that they could not commend him too much.'

Cavendish goes on to describe that every chamber had 'a bason and a ewer of silver, some gilt and some parcel gilt, and some two great pots of silver in like manner, and one pot at the least with wine and beer, a bowl or goblet, and a silver pot to drink beer in—a silver candlestick or two—and a staff torch ; a fine manchet, and a chetloaf of bread. . . . In the morning of the next day (not early) they rose and heard mass, and dined with my Lord and so departed towards Windsor, and there hunted, delighting much in the castle or college, and in the Order of the Garter.'[175]

On another occasion the king expressed his plea-

sure in hunting with Wolsey, 'and wished him to come again that they might have the pastime together two or three days.'[176]

Wolsey at first seems to have encouraged Henry's desire for a divorce in order to further his own foreign policy,[177] but 'the greatest political genius that England has ever seen' was no match for the ambition of Anne Boleyn, supported by the king's passion. From the moment that Anne became Wolsey's political rival his doom was sealed.[178] His enemies began to make themselves felt when his efforts to obtain the decree of divorce from the Pope failed,[179] and the royal favour was withdrawn from him. His gift of Hampton Court to the king was doubtless made at a moment when he first realized that his influence was declining. The satirists, Skelton and Roy, expressed public opinion when they dared to publish reflections on his name and fame.[180]

Meanwhile the cardinal continued to live at Hampton Court, to receive private visits there, and to transact business. The ambassadors continued to wait upon him, notably Du Bellay, the French ambassador, who stayed at the palace in June 1528, and mentions in his dispatches the various conversations he had with Wolsey, often while he was 'walking in his gardens.'[181] It was at Hampton Court, too, that he saw the Netherlands ambassadors, and there that eventually a truce for eight months was arranged with the Low Countries, and signed 15 June 1528. On 17 June it was solemnly confirmed in the chapel, Wolsey, the envoys of the Netherlands, Du Bellay, and the representatives of the emperor being present.[182] This truce, which must not be confused with the peace mentioned before, is also known as 'The Truce of Hampton Court.'

After this, the troubles which were gathering fast about Wolsey, and the prevalence of the 'sweating sickness,' seem to have prevented him from offering further hospitalities. During June, July, and August 1528 he was at the palace, attended only by a few followers, instead of by the train of noble and gallant gentlemen who had hitherto clustered round him.[183] On 3 July 1529, Du Bellay wrote that 'Wolsey is hidden at Hampton Court, because he knew nowhere else to go. He has fortified his gallery and his garden (? against the sickness). Only four or five are allowed to see him.'[184] The king seems to have stayed with him there again in September and December 1528,[185] and in March, April, and July 1529.[186] The last time that Wolsey himself was at Hampton Court was in July 1529. In November of that year a

[175] Cavendish, *Life of Wolsey* (ed. Singer), i, 134–5.
[176] *L. and P. Hen. VIII*, iv (2), 4766, Sept. 1528.
[177] Gairdner, in *Engl. Hist. Rev.* Oct. 1906.
[178] Creighton, op. cit. 160, 213.
[179] *Dict. Nat. Biog.* 'Wolsey,' 339 ; *Trans. Roy. Hist. Soc.* (Ser. 2), xiii, 75, 102. The various lords who had long been jealous of Wolsey's influence with the king were ready to take Anne

Boleyn's part against him ; Friedmann, *Anne Boleyn* ; Thos. Gairdner, 'New Lights on Divorce of Henry VIII,' *Engl. Hist. Rev.* July 1890, Oct. 1906.
[180] See p. 328, n. 155.
[181] *L. and P. Hen. VIII*, iv (2), 4332, 4391, App. no. 158 ; Le Grand, *Histoire du Divorce*, iii, 130–6 ; cit. Law, *Hist. Hampton Court Palace*, i, 113.
[182] Le Grand, *Histoire du Divorce*, iii, 129 ; *L. and P. Hen. VIII*, iv (2), 4566. The representatives of France and Spain

'touched hands in token of amity,' though one of the terms of the truce was that hostilities with Spain were not to be entirely suspended.
[183] An account of the 'sweating sickness' gathered from the *L. and P. Hen. VIII* is given in the preface to vol. ii, p. ccvii et seq.
[184] *L. and P. Hen. VIII*, iv (i), 1940.
[185] Ibid. (2), 4766, 5016.
[186] Ibid. (3), 5476, 5681, 5806.

bill of indictment was preferred against him in the King's Bench.[187] He was told that the king wished him to retire to Esher, where he had built a small house, of which a part still remains.[188] He only lived for about a year longer, and Hampton Court is not concerned in the final details of disgrace of him who :—

> Once trod the ways of glory,
> And sounded all the depths and shoals of
>   honour.[189]

Henry was already at the palace when he sent for Cavendish to speak with him about the cardinal's death. Cavendish's account shows plainly the profoundly self-seeking character of Henry. Wolsey's faithful servant was summoned to attend the king, who was engaged in archery in the park. As Cavendish stood against a tree, sadly musing, Henry suddenly came up to him and clapped him on the shoulder, saying, 'I will make an end of my game, and then I will talk with you.' He afterwards went into the garden, but kept Cavendish waiting for some time outside. Their interview was long, and the king said he would 'liever than twenty thousand pounds that the cardinal had lived.'[190] He nevertheless inquired anxiously about £1,500, apparently all that remained of his favourite's great fortune, which he had sent Sir William Kingston[191] to claim from Wolsey on his death-bed.[192]

It is possible to obtain a very clear idea of the wonderful collection of furniture, pictures, tapestries, and plate which Wolsey had at Hampton Court from an inventory of his belongings taken after his attainder,[193] from an Augmentation Office Roll now in the Record Office ; from Cavendish's

Life ; and from the Venetian ambassador's accounts of his plate.[194]

Venier, the Venetian ambassador in 1527, estimated what he saw at Hampton Court alone as worth 300,000 golden ducats, or £150,000. Giustinian valued the silver he saw in 1519 at the same amount, and says that the cardinal always had a sideboard of plate worth £25,000, in any house where he might be, and in his own room a cupboard with further plate to the amount of £30,000.[195]

The number of the cardinal's retainers, as estimated in contemporary records, varies, but consisted probably of about four hundred persons.[196] In Cavendish's different MSS. the numbers vary from one hundred and fifty to eight hundred. The first assessment of his household in a subsidy roll (No. 204) at the Record Office gives the number as 429 people ; another, dated 1525, makes the total not more than two hundred and fifty ;[197] but an assessment, taken apparently after his attainder in 1530, gives the number again as 429.[198] The expenses of his household were something over £30,000 a year in modern reckoning, but of course this 'included the entertainment of numerous gentlemen of good family, a very considerable retinue, and all the expenses of the Chancery.'[199]

Henry did not take possession of Hampton Court until Wolsey was actually banished. Up to that time the 'King's Manor' of Hampton Court was apparently a figure of speech, but one of his first acts was to erase the cardinal's badges and to mark the whole building with his own arms and monograms.[200] In the Chapter House Accounts for 1530–2 there are numerous items for fixing, carving, painting, and gilding the king's heraldic

[187] His last interview with the king seems to have been at Grafton Regis in Sept. 1529 ; *Dict. Nat. Biog.* 'Wolsey.'

[188] In the grounds of Esher Place, now the property of Sir Edgar Vincent; Cavendish, op. cit. ii, 247 ; *L. and P. Hen. VIII,* iii, 414. The *Gent. Mag.* for 1877 contains an interesting article on 'Cardinal Wolsey at Esher ' by —Walford.

[189] Shakespeare, *Hen. VIII,* Act iii, Sc. ii. Respect for tradition claims mention of the 'Cardinal Spider,' which is said to be peculiar to Wolsey's part of the palace, and to be connected in some strange fashion with his tragic fate. It is of a reddish brown colour, and often attains a very large size. Respect for truth claims mention that the species *Tegenaria Guyonii,* or *Domestica,* is to be found in other parts of the Thames Valley ; Blackwall, *Hist. of the Spiders of Great Britain and Ireland,* 160 et seq. ; cit. Law, *Hist. Hampton Court Palace,* i, 115. Tradition also has it that the cardinal haunts the scenes of his former greatness, and an amusing story is told of a housekeeper of the palace early in the last century, who, when asked if she had ever seen or heard of Wolsey's ghost, replied with nonchalance that she seldom went through the cloisters without ' brushing against his Eminence.' Another

story is told of a room near that which is now shown to the public as ' the Cardinal's Oratory.' A party of young people were playing at cards in this room, and the door continued to burst open constantly without any reason. One of the players, becoming tired of getting up to shut it, said, impatiently, ' If it is the Cardinal who keeps on opening that door, I wish he would sometimes shut it again.' The door immediately closed of itself, quite quietly. (Local traditions.)

[190] Cavendish, op. cit. i, 328 ; *L. and P. Hen. VIII,* iv, Introd. p. dcxx–i.

[191] Constable of the Tower.

[192] Cavendish, op. cit. i, 328–31 ; Creighton, *Life of Wolsey,* 206–7 ; *L. and P. Hen. VIII,* iv, Introd. p. dcxv.

[193] Harl. MSS. 599.

[194] Aug. Office Roll ; cit. *L. and P. Hen. VIII,* iv (3) ; *Cal. S.P. Venetian,* 1527–33, no. 205, &c. ; Giustinian, *Despatches,* ii, 314, &c. ; *L. and P. Hen. VIII,* ii, Introd. p. ccxlvii, &c. For detailed account see Law, *Hist. Hampton Court Palace,* i, 57–82 ; Law, *Guide to Hampton Court Palace,* 1907 ; Inventories of plate are printed in Gutch, *Collectanea Curiosa,* ii, 283, 334.

[195] *Cal. S.P. Venetian,* 1527–33 ; Giustinian, *Despatches,* ii, 314, &c. ; *L. and P. Hen. VIII,* iv (3), 6186,

6748, &c. ; Add. MS. B.M. 24359, fol. 42.

[196] *L. and P. Hen. VIII,* ii, Introd. p. ccxlvii, n.

[197] Ibid. Brewer suggests that Wolsey's household, as well as the house at Hampton Court, had been made over to Henry in 1525, but the return to the larger number at a later date is inexplicable on this assumption. There are entries in Wolsey's accounts for the entertainment of the French ambassadors at Hampton Court as late as 1527 ; *L. and P. Hen. VIII,* iv (3), pp. 3041–3.

[198] Ibid. (3), 6185.

[199] Brewer, op. cit. ii, Introd. p. ccxlvii, &c. Wolsey's personal attendants numbered 160 persons, including his high chamberlain, vice-chamberlain, 12 gentlemen ushers, daily waiters, 8 gentlemen ushers, and waiters of his privy chamber, 9 or 10 lords, 40 persons acting as gentlemen cup-bearers, carvers, servers, &c. ; 6 yeomen ushers, 8 grooms of the chamber, 46 yeomen of his chamber 'daily to attend upon his person,' 16 doctors and chaplains, 2 secretaries, and 4 counsellors learned in the law. As Lord Chancellor he had a separate retinue ; Law, op. cit. i, 86, 87.

[200] See Henry's arms in the First, or Base, Court, which still remain, also in the chapel, at the chapel door, &c.

devices, which are still to be seen in some parts of the palace.[201] It was not till the following year that he made the exchange of lands with the Prior of St. John of Jerusalem by which the manor of Hampton Court became legally Crown property.[202] The proceedings for the king's divorce had been going on for some time, and as early as 1528, while Wolsey was still at the palace, the French ambassador, Du Bellay, wrote that 'Melle de Boulan' had been given a 'very fine lodging near the king,'[203] and mentioned that 'greater court was paid to her than has been to the queen for a long time.'[204] Katherine, however, accompanied Henry in the beginning of February 1530, when he first went to Hampton Court after Wolsey's disgrace,[205] and they were said to treat each other

and Princess Mary the ground floor.[208] There are also many entries of a later date in the Chapter House Accounts for 'the lady Anne's lodgynges,'[209] but it is not possible to say exactly which rooms they were. The king's 'Privy Purse Expenses' give an idea of the numerous presents he made to her. They spent Christmas 1530 at Hampton Court, and the king gave her, besides other things, £100, and further sums 'to play with' at bowls and other games.[210] In September 1532 he had some of the Crown jewels sent from Greenwich to Hampton Court for her.[211] She was allowed her own suite of attendants,[212] and Henry treated her with the greatest consideration. He rode with her,[213] walked in the park or the gardens with her, and taught her to shoot at the target.[214] Katherine

HAMPTON COURT : TENNIS COURT FROM THE WEST SIDE

in public with the 'greatest possible attention.'[206] The king at this time inhabited the first floor in the Clock Court, the queen the rooms previously allotted to her by Wolsey on the floor above,[207]

meanwhile remained constantly with the king while he enjoyed his 'usual sports and royal exercises' at Hampton Court[215] until 14 July 1531, when he left her at Windsor and rode to Hampton Court.[216]

[201] Chap. Ho. Accts. C. $\frac{6}{10}$, fol. 1–261; C. $\frac{6}{13}$, passim. For Henry's other alterations and improvements see p. 372.

[202] See p. 326, descent of the manor; L. and P. Hen. VIII, iv (1), 627, App. no. 12.

[203] 'Anne Bouillayne's lodgynges at Hampton Court' are mentioned in the Chap. Ho. Accts. for 1528; C. $\frac{6}{10}$, fol. 110. It is generally said that this 'lodgynge' was at Greenwich; Cal. S.P. Spanish, iii, 863; L. and P. Hen. VIII, ii, 5177, 5211.

[204] L. and P. Hen. VIII, iv (2), 2177.

[205] Ibid. iv (3), 6227.

[206] Cal. S.P. Venetian, iv, no. 584, 637, 642.

[207] See p. 327.

[208] Cal. S.P. Venetian, iv, no. 584.

[209] Chap. Ho. Accts. C. $\frac{6}{13}$, fol. 121, 196, 597, 615, &c.

[210] Nicolas, Privy Purse Expenses of Hen. VIII, Introd.

[211] L. and P. Hen. VIII, v, 1335. They are described as '7 carkaynes of gold set with diamonds and other stones.

A George garnished with 16 small diamonds, and a rocky pearl in the dragon's belly. A gold chain, Spanish fashion, enamelled white, red and black.'

[212] Le Grand, Histoire du Divorce, iii, 137, 251.

[213] Cavendish, op. cit. i, 75, 80; L. and P. Hen. VIII, v, 308.

[214] Nicolas, Privy Purse Expenses of Hen. VIII, 91.

[215] Cal. S.P. Venetian, iv, 637, 642.

[216] Hall, Chron. fol. 781 (ed. 1548).

From that day he never saw her again. The accounts of Henry's sojourns at Hampton Court read like the shifting scenes of one long pageant of joy and revelry, yet in the background are the meetings of the Council, the dispatches daily submitted to the king, the discussions of foreign policy, and the masterly manipulation of one of the greatest revolutions England has ever seen, the detachment of the National Church from the Church of Rome.[217]

Hampton Court was, however, chiefly the scene of the king's pleasures. At the time of the Dissolution of the Monasteries he created the 'Honour and Chase of Hampton Court to improve his hunting.'[218] The king was also fond of fishing, and in his privy purse expenses are several entries for his rods to be brought to the palace, and for payments to the fishermen who attended him.[219]

A large 'Tilt Yard' was made on the north side of the palace, about 9 acres in area,[220] with five towers in which the spectators might sit,[221] and there numerous jousts and tournaments took place, in which Henry often distinguished himself 'in supernatural feats, changing his horses and making them fly rather than leap, to the delight and ecstasy of everybody.'[222] Giustinian gives an account of one of these tournaments held at Hampton Court, and says that when the king himself appeared a grand procession was formed, headed by the marshal of the jousts on horseback, dressed in cloth of gold, surrounded by thirty footmen in liveries of blue and yellow. Then followed the drummers and trumpeters, all dressed in white damask; next forty knights and lords in pairs, all in superb attire, and many in cloth of gold; then 'some twenty young knights, on very fine horses, all dressed in white, with doublets of silver and white velvet, and chains of unsual size, and their horses barded with silver chain-work, and a number of pendent bells.' Next came their pages, on horseback, their trappings, half of gold embroidery and half of purple velvet, embroidered with stars; and then the jousters, armed, with their squires and footmen. Last of all came his Majesty, armed *cap-à-pie*, with a surcoat of silver bawdakin, surrounded by some thirty gentlemen on foot, dressed in velvet and white satin, and in this order they went twice round the lists.'[223]

Another favourite pastime of the period was archery, in which Henry also excelled, and amused himself by teaching Anne Boleyn, and perhaps other ladies of the Court, to shoot. Lord Roch-

ford, Anne Boleyn's brother, won large sums from the king at this sport.[224] The butt stood in what was called 'The Great Orchard,' to the north of the palace.[225]

The tennis-court, or 'close tennis play,' at Hampton Court must also be mentioned, as it is the oldest court of the kind in England, and Henry was a skilful and graceful player.[226] There seems to have been also an 'open tenys play,' no doubt a forerunner of lawn tennis, and an open and two close bowling alleys. One of these alleys existed until about a hundred years ago, and was 270 ft. long, with windows on both sides. It stood apparently behind the tennis court, and there was another near the river.[227] Henry was an inveterate gambler, his losses at dice, backgammon, shovel-board, &c., in one year amounted to £30,000.[228] At the same time, his great versatility must be acknowledged, for, besides his encouragement of artists,[229] and numerous entries of payments to the king's minstrels for playing before him at Hampton Court,[230] he seems to have been a musician himself (some of the songs he composed are still extant)[231] and all witnesses speak of his skill in singing. He had also some taste for literature, and spoke several languages. The king's 'libarye' at Hampton Court is often mentioned in the Chapter House Accounts, and he filled it with books from York Place.[232]

BADGE OF QUEEN ANNE BOLEYN

[217] *L. and P. Hen. VIII*, iv–xxi.

[218] See under 'Honour.'

[219] Nicolas, *Privy Purse Expenses of Hen. VIII*, 65, 83.

[220] Now a nursery garden, rented from the Crown by J. Naylor.

[221] The old wall still remains, and one of the towers; *vide* Law, op. cit. i, 135 et seq.

[222] Giustinian, *Despatches*, ii, 102.

[223] Ibid. ii, 101.

[224] *L. and P. Hen. VIII*, v, 755; Nicolas, *Privy Purse Expenses of Hen. VIII*, 145, 'Item, the same day (8 July 1531) paied to my Lorde

de Rocheforde for shooting with the King's Grace at Hampton Corte, £58.'

[225] Chap. Ho. Accts. C. $\frac{6}{12}$, fol. 481, &c.

[226] See p. 290 for description of tennis court. Giustinian gives a flattering account of his appearance : 'It is the prettiest thing in the world to see him play, his fair skin glowing through a shirt of the finest texture ;' *Despatches*, i, 27. He also had other clothes made on purpose for playing, including 'tenys cotes' of blue or black velvet to put on when he rested ; Strutt, *Manners*

and Customs, iii, 87; cit. Law, op. cit. i, 139.

[227] Law, op. cit. i, 140.

[228] Nicolas, *Privy Purse Expenses of Hen. VIII*.

[229] See Chap. Ho. Accts.

[230] Nicolas, op. cit. ; *L. and P. Hen. VIII*, v, 307.

[231] MS. in possession of Mrs. Lamb, cit. *Arch.* xli, 371 (by W. Chappell, F.S.A.).

[232] Nicolas, op. cit. 89 ; 'Item, paied to Joly Jak for bringing the king's books from York Place to Hampton Courte—5s., Nov. 26, 1530.'

Hampton Court Palace : Arms of Henry VIII and Jane Seymour

Anne Boleyn was crowned in June 1533, and in July she came to Hampton Court, where a series of magnificent 'revellynges' took place in her honour. Besides joining in hunting, dancing, gambling, and other diversions,[233] she seems to have shared Henry's love of music, and to have amused herself and her ladies by doing needlework, of which specimens were to be seen at Hampton Court for many years after her death.[234] As well as his other additions to the palace Henry caused a new suite of rooms to be erected for Anne, instead of the 'Queen's Old Lodgynges'; but she never occupied the splendid apartments designed for her.[235]

There were great rejoicings at the birth of Elizabeth, but Henry very soon made manifest how all-important he considered the birth of a son. It becomes sufficiently apparent what the dominating motive was for the vast labour, time, trouble and expense lavished on obtaining his divorce. Anne was too slight a creature to retain any sort of influence over the king when she thus failed to satisfy his ambition. In January 1536, possibly at Hampton Court, it is said that she made her first discovery of Jane Seymour's attraction for Henry,[236] and her remonstrances only completed her estrangement from the king, who had apparently for some time previously contemplated the possibility of annulling his marriage with her.[237] Four months later, on 19 May 1536 she was executed on Tower Green, and the general sentiment of the country was one of joy at her death.[238]

A fortnight before her execution Henry left York Place for Hampton Court, and on 11 May Cromwell visited him there and settled with him the details of the coming trial; returning the same night.[239]

Jane Seymour was sent to Sir Nicholas Carewe's house, about seven miles from London, but was shortly removed to a house on the Thames nearer to the king.[240] The following week, when the death of Anne was announced to Henry, he immediately went by barge to the house where Jane Seymour was staying. A dispensation for the marriage was obtained from Cranmer on the very day of Anne's execution.[241] The next morning at six o'clock Jane secretly joined the king at Hampton Court, and there, in the presence of a few courtiers, they were formally betrothed,[242] not married as has sometimes been stated. Ten days later they were married in the 'Quene's Closet at York Place.'[243]

BADGE OF QUEEN JANE SEYMOUR

The new apartments not being finished, Jane Seymour does not seem to have resided at Hampton Court during the first year of her reign,[244] but in September 1537 she retired there to await the birth of the anxiously-expected heir to the throne.[245] The king accompanied her, and was present when on Friday 12 October, the vigil of St. Edward's Day, 1537, at two o'clock in the morning, the long-desired prince was born.[246] How much the evil of a disputed succession was dreaded is shown by the extreme joy of the whole nation.[247] A circular announcing the birth, signed by Jane Seymour, was sent to 'all the estates and cities of the realm. Given under our signet at My Lord's Manor of Hampton Court, 12 Oct. 1537.'[248] By tradition the room in which Edward VI was born is one on the first floor in the south-east corner of the Clock Court. This room was partially rebuilt and altered in the reign of

---

[233] Friedmann, *Life of Anne Boleyn,* i, 213.

[234] Wyatt, *Memoir of Anne Boleyn,* in Cavendish, *Life of Wolsey* (ed. Singer), ii, 442. There is a gateway still known as 'Anne Boleyn's Gateway,' p. 376.

[235] See architectural account, plan at All Souls' Library, &c.

[236] Wyatt, *Memoir of Anne Boleyn,* 443; *L. and P. Hen. VIII,* x, 103, 201, 245.

[237] It is not within the scope of this paper to enter into the question of Anne's guilt or innocence, even in such details as may be connected with Hampton Court; *vide L. and P. Hen. VIII,* x, 879, &c.; Friedmann, *Anne Boleyn,* vol. ii; Wyatt, *Memoir of Anne Boleyn,* &c. She is said to haunt a cer-

tain staircase in the palace, near the 'Quene's Lodgynges' which she never inhabited. The staircase itself is part of Wren's building, but joins the older part.

[238] *L. and P. Hen. VIII,* x, 377.

[239] Sir W. Paulet to Cromwell 11 May 1536, P.R.O. Cromwell Corresp. xxxiv; Chapuys to Chas. V, Vienna Archives P.C. 230, i, fol. 82; cit. Friedmann, *Anne Boleyn,* ii, 269.

[240] *Dict. Nat. Biog.* 'Jane Seymour.'

[241] *L. and P. Hen. VIII,* x, 915.

[242] Ibid. 926.

[243] Ibid. 1000, *vide* Pref. to vol. x, pp. xxxi, xxxii (Gairdner). Betrothal at that period was often considered quite as binding as marriage. Hence the frequency of divorces on the plea of pre-contract.

[244] The Chap. Ho. Accts. C. $\frac{6}{15}$, fol.

283, &c.; C. $\frac{6}{15}$, fol. 98, &c., show a considerable amount of work done in altering the arms and initials of one queen for the other.

[245] *L. and P. Hen. VIII,* xii, 41, 1164. Great precautions were taken about 'the death,' which at the time was 'extremely sore' in London; *L. and P. Hen. VIII,* xii, 839.

[246] Wriothesley, *Chron.* 11 (Camd. Soc.); *L. and P. Hen. VIII,* xii, 889; *Lit. Remains of Edw. VI,* i, pp. xxiii, clv.

[247] 'Incontinent after the birth Te Deum was sung in Paul's and other churches of the city, and great fires [were made] in every street, and goodly banqueting and triumphing cheer with shooting of guns all day and night'; Add. MSS. B.M. 6113, fol. 81.

[248] *L. and P. Hen. VIII,* xii, 889.

George II,[249] but the queen's rooms appear to have been among those destroyed to make way for Wren's new building. The bed in which Edward VI was born and Jane Seymour died was to be seen in the palace in Queen Elizabeth's time.[250]

The christening took place on the Monday following in the chapel at Hampton Court, and a long account is given in the 'Preparations ordained for the said christening at Hampton Court,'[251] in which the course of the procession, the decorations of the chapel, and the positions occupied by the Officers of the Household are minutely described.[252]

The procession[253] started from the 'Prince's Lodgynges,' situated to the north of the Chapel

HAMPTON COURT PALACE : CLOCK COURT FROM THE COLONNADE

Court, and passed through the 'Council Chamber,' where it was joined by the Officers of the Household, the children and ministers of the chapel, the king's council, and the other great lords, spiritual and temporal, the ambassadors and their suites, the chamberlains of the king and queen, and the Lord High Chamberlain of England, Cromwell, Lord Privy Seal, the Lord Chancellor, the Duke of Norfolk, and the Archbishop of Canterbury.

The 'chrysom richly garnished' was borne by the Lady Elizabeth, the king's daughter, being herself carried by Lords Beauchamp and Morley. The prince was carried by the Marchioness of Exeter, 'assisted by the Duke of Suffolk and the Lord Marquis her husband.' A rich canopy was borne over the prince by four gentlemen of the King's Privy Chamber.[254]

'The Lady Mary, the king's daughter, was appointed for the lady Godmother,' and a vast number of ladies of honour and gentlewomen followed her.

The procession, leaving the Council Chamber, passed through part of the room now known as 'the Haunted Gallery,' and so into the 'King's Great Watching Chamber' at the upper end of the Great Hall. They entered the hall through a door, now hidden by tapestry, and passed down the stairs under Anne Boleyn's Gateway into the Clock Court, and so through the cloisters to the chapel door.[255] All the way was lined with men-at-arms, attendants and servants holding torches. The ground of the courtyard was strewn with rushes, and barriers, covered with rich hangings, were erected to keep back the spectators, who were all inhabitants of the palace, as access to the court was forbidden to others on account of infection from the plague which prevailed at the time.[256] The decorations of the entrance and of the chapel itself were of 'rich cloth of gold or arras and tapestries,' the floor 'boarded and covered with carpets,' the 'high altar richly garnished with plate and stuff.' In the middle of the choir the font of 'solid silver gilt was set upon a mount or stage,' and over it 'a rich canopy.' The *Te Deum* was sung by the choir, and then the prince was baptized with the usual elaborate ceremonial. After the christening the torches were all lighted, and Garter King-at-Arms proclaimed the prince's name and style. The procession then re-formed, carrying with them the christening gifts, and proceeded to the queen's bedchamber, where the king and queen awaited their son, and he 'received the blessing of Almighty God, Our Lady and St. George, and his father and

[249] Now private apartments occupied by Mrs. Keate, widow of the late R. W. Keate, successively Governor of Trinidad, Natal, and Western Africa.

[250] Hentzner, *Journey into Engl.* (ed. 1757), 81–2.

[251] *L. and P. Hen. VIII*, xii, 911, from Add. MSS. B. M.6113, fol. 81 ; Nichols, *Lit. Remains of Edw. VI*, p. cclv.

[252] For description of the chapel see p. 388. Only the roof now remains as it was then.

[253] For a full account of the ceremony see Nichols, op. cit. ii, p. ccliv.

[254] See engraving in Law, op. cit. i, 187.

[255] This part of the palace (the cloisters, &c.) is totally different from what it was at that period.

[256] Nichols, *Lit. Remains of Edw. VI*, p. cclxii.

mother.' The trumpets meanwhile 'standing in the outer court with the gate, there blowing and the minstrels playing, which was a melodious thing to hear,'[257] but it is hardly surprising that the excitement proved too great for the health of the queen. She did not die, as has been sometimes stated, at the birth of her son, or two days after,[258] but on 24 October, nearly a fortnight later.[259]

The king may have been sincerely distressed by her death ; he 'retired to a solitary place to pass his sorrows,'[260] and wrote to Francis I of the 'bitterness of the death of her who brought me this happiness.'[261] Her body was embalmed, and her heart, &c., 'were honourably interred in the chapel.' On 26 October the corpse was laid on a hearse, surrounded with tapers, in her room, and all the ladies and gentlemen of the court 'doing on their mourning habit and white kerchers hanging over their heads and shoulders,' knelt about it during mass and *Dirige*. A watch was kept about it till the last day of the month, when it was removed to the chapel with much ceremony. 'The great chamber and galleries leading to the chapel and the chapel itself were hung with black cloth and garnished with rich images.' The hearse prepared in the chapel had eight banner-rolls with 'rachments and majestye.' 'The king's officers and servants stood in double rank with tapers lighted, and the procession formed, first the cross, with priests two and two, then gentlemen, esquires, pursuivants, and heralds, then the noblemen, then Garter, then the Earl of Rutland the Queen's Chamberlain, and the Duke of Norfolk, then the corpse, then the chief mourner (Lady Exeter representing the Princess Mary) assisted by two noblemen as earls, then eight noble ladies, mourners. The corpse was received in the chapel by the prelates and placed in the hearse, Lancaster Herald said with a loud voice "Of your charity pray for the soul, &c." Then *Dirige* was sung and all departed to the Queen's Chamber.'[262] Solemn masses were sung every day, and a constant watch kept—at night by the gentlemen, in the day by the ladies of the household—until Monday, 12 November, when the corpse was removed in a chariot drawn by six horses, with four banners borne by four barons. A long account of the procession is given in the *Letters and Papers*, and the route through Colbrooke and Eton to Windsor described, many people coming out to meet it with signs of mourning. On the following day the late queen

was solemnly buried in St. George's Chapel at twelve o'clock in the morning.[263]

Orders were sent to all the peers and noblemen 'to attend at Hampton Court and so to Windsor for the Queen's funeral, on 9 November.'[264] Jane Seymour's arms still remain, impaled with those of the king, at the entrance to the chapel.[265]

Henry seems for a time to have left the palace as a sort of nursery for his son.[266] The ambassadors were occasionally invited there to see the prince.[267] In November 1539 the king came to Hampton Court while waiting for the arrival of Anne of Cleves.[268] He never brought her there, but she stayed there by herself for some days before the decree of divorce was pronounced in July 1540.[269] She then retired to Richmond, and Henry arrived shortly afterwards to spend his honeymoon with Katherine Howard. They had been married privately at Oatlands on 28 July,[270] and on 8 August she appeared openly as queen, and sat next to the king in the royal closet in the chapel.[271] She afterwards dined in public at one of Henry's characteristic Hampton Court banquets, and the Princess Elizabeth appeared, apparently for the first time in public, with her.[272] Henry and Katherine then started on a royal progress, visiting the king's numerous palaces and other places, and returning to Hampton Court on 19 December.[273] They remained there in some seclusion for several months.[274] The Privy Council, with the king presiding, met almost daily during this period. A chapter of the Garter was held at Hampton Court, apparently for the first time, on 9 January 1541, when the Earl of Hertford was elected to a vacant stall in the order.[275] There is an amusing entry of six pasties of venison being solemnly presented to the king by Marillac, the French ambassador, who went to Hampton Court on purpose, and the king told him the next day that he had 'tasted the venison and found it marvellously good.'[276] Marillac also writes of a great excitement when two gentlemen of the court were unexpectedly 'led prisoners from Hampton Court to London, with their hands bound, and conducted by twenty-four archers to the Tower.'[277] Marillac was not certain of their identity, but they seem to have been Sir Thomas Wyatt and Sir John Wallop, the friends of Cromwell, who were accused of a 'traitorous correspondence' with Reginald Pole, but they both received the king's pardon shortly afterwards.[278]

[257] Law, op. cit. i, 190.
[258] Hall, *Chron.*; *L. and P. Hen. VIII*, xii, 970-1, 1060.
[259] Ibid.
[260] Ibid.
[261] Ibid. 970.
[262] Ibid. 1060, from a Heralds' College MS. i, 11, fol. 27.
[263] Ibid.
[264] *L. and P. Hen. VIII*, xii, 1612, &c.
[265] Henry had just completed the Great Hall and the alterations in the chapel. It is perhaps worthy of remark that Jane Seymour was the only one of his queens for whom Henry wore mourning, and according to his own directions he was buried by her

side at Windsor ; *Dict. Nat. Biog.* 'Henry VIII' and 'Jane Seymour.'
[266] For early life of Edw. VI passed at Hampton Court see p. 340.
[267] *L. and P. Hen. VIII*, xiii, 323, 388, 402 ; xiv, 126, &c.
[268] Ibid. xiv, 508, 607.
[269] Some of the proceedings about the divorce took place 'in a certain lofty and ornate chamber within the honour of Hampton Court'; ibid. xv, 925.
[270] *Rep. Pub. Rec.* iii, App. ii, 264.
[271] Stowe, *Ann.* fol. 581 (ed. 1631) ; Wriothesley, *Chron.* (Camd. Soc.), 122, On 15 Aug. she was prayed for in all the churches as queen ; *Dict. Nat. Biog.* 'Katherine Howard.'

[272] Her appearance at the christening of Edward VI was really the first, but she was then a child in arms.
[273] *Proc. of P.C.* vii, 93.
[274] Ibid. 93–150.
[275] *L. and P. Hen. VIII*, xvi, 218.
[276] Ibid. xvi, 449, Jan. 1541. In Mar. 1541 the king was laid up with an illness at Hampton Court, and seems to have conceived a great distrust of his advisers, caused no doubt by news of a fresh rising in the north. 'Shrovetide was spent without recreation'; ibid. xvi, 589.
[277] Ibid. xvi, 227, 466.
[278] *Dict. Nat. Biog.* 'Sir Thomas Wyatt'; 'Sir John Wallop.'

In January 1541 Anne of Cleves sent the king a New Year's present of two large horses with violet velvet trappings, and came herself to Hampton Court with her suite, accompanied only by the Duke of Norfolk's brother, who 'happened to meet her on the road.' She was graciously received by the king and queen, and after supper she and the queen danced together. The next day they all three dined together, and the king sent, through the queen, a present to the Lady Anne of a ring and two small dogs. She then returned to Richmond.[279]

The king and queen were again away, and returned to Hampton Court in October 1541.[280] The day after their arrival the king heard mass in the chapel, 'and gave most hearty thanks for the good life he led and trusted to lead with his wife; and also desired the Bishop of Lincoln, his ghostly father, to make like prayer and give like thanks with him on All Souls' Day.'[281] The Privy Council were 'given permission to go to their country houses for change of air.' On All Souls' Day (November 2) they were to meet again.[282]

It was on the occasion of this return that Henry found his son, the Prince of Wales, 'sick of a quartan fever, an unusual malady for a child of three or four years.' Henry summoned 'all the physicians of the country' to advise, and was told that the fever would put the child in danger. One of the physicians secretly told Marillac, the French Ambassador, that the 'Prince was so fat and unhealthy as to be unlikely to live long.'[283] It is possible that this incident throws a lurid light on Henry's subsequent treatment of Katherine, to whom he had been married for over a year without any signs of the issue he always desired so ardently.[284] No one has ever hidden a more crafty and subtle mind under a bluff and genial outward demeanour than Henry VIII. It is impossible to doubt the guilt of Katherine, but it is difficult to believe that Cranmer and the other members of the Council would have dared to bring the matter before the king if they had known that the news would be altogether unwelcome to him.[285] He received the first intimation of it, made to him by a paper put into his hand by Cranmer while he was hearing mass in the chapel at Hampton Court, with extreme horror, and showed himself overwhelmed with rage and distress.[286]

He professed to refuse to believe the account brought to him, and constrained himself, as Marillac says, 'to be as gay as ever with the ladies,' while a further investigation was going on; but on Sunday, 6 November, he left Hampton Court on pretext of hunting, dined 'at a little place in the fields,' and at night came secretly to London,[287] where the Council was called at midnight, and did not disperse till 4 or 5 a.m. on Monday.[288] The palace was closely guarded and Katherine was informed of the charges against her by the Archbishop of Canterbury and other members of the Council. Cranmer's letter to Henry gives an affecting account of a private interview he had with her afterwards, and of her state of terror and despair.[289] To the Council she denied all, but confessed to Cranmer, hoping thereby to obtain the royal pardon. In the midst of this harrowing conversation she heard the clock strike six, and gave way to an outburst of grief, saying it was 'for remembrance of the time; for about that hour Master Heneage was wont to bring her knowledge of the king.'[290]

The Council sent instructions to Cranmer to declare the whole miserable state of affairs to the queen's household, which he did, in the 'Great Watching Chamber.'[291] The household was then dismissed, and Katherine herself sent to Syon House, Isleworth, under an escort. She remained there a few weeks, hoping in vain for Henry's pardon, which Cranmer certainly endeavoured to obtain for her.[292] From Syon House she was taken to the Tower, and was executed on Tower Hill on 13 February 1542.[293]

The best-known ghost story of the palace is connected with Katherine Howard. The 'Haunted Gallery,' part of the Tudor building on the right-hand side of the way down the 'Queen's Great Staircase,' is so called because Katherine's ghost is said to run shrieking through the room. The legend is that she attempted to make her way into Henry's presence as he was hearing mass in the royal closet in the chapel. She ran down the gallery and reached the door, where the king's guard seized her and carried her back, while her husband remained in the chapel listening to her

---

[279] L. and P. Hen. VIII, xvi, 217. A malicious piece of gossip was circulated concerning this meeting of the king and Anne of Cleves; ibid. no. 1414. Later on 'two honest citizens were imprisoned for having said that the Lady Anne of Cleves was really the king's wife and that she had had a child'—a rumour widely believed; ibid. no. 1441. She visited the king again at Hampton Court in 1546; Acts of P.C. 1542–7, p. 239.

[280] They returned on 24 Oct. and the Privy Council met there on the same day. L. and P. Hen. VIII, xvi, 1281.

[281] Proc. P.C. (Ed. Nicolas), vii, 352.

[282] L. and P. Hen. VIII, xvi, 1292.

[283] Ibid. xvi, 1297. Letter from Marillac to Francis I, 29 Oct. 1541.

[284] Vide letter to Francis I, on rumours concerning Katherine; L. and P. Hen. VIII, xvi, 1332. See also what is said about her coronation, which apparently never took place; ibid. 712, 1183.

[285] Chapuys, the Spanish ambassador, certainly believed at the time that the whole matter had been arranged for the king's convenience, and suggested that for political reasons he wished to annul the divorce from Anne of Cleves. Chapuys wrote to Charles V of rumours of a reconciliation with Anne as early as January of that year; L. and P. Hen. VIII, 1328.

[286] Nicolas, Proc. P.C. vii, 354–5. 'Letters of the Council to the English Ambassadors abroad'; L. and P. Hen. VIII, xvi, 1334, &c. (12 Nov. 1541).

[287] Chapuys says by barge; ibid. xvi, 1328.

[288] Ibid. There are two accounts in the L. and P. Hen. VIII of this affair, one by Chapuys the Spanish ambassador, and one by Marillac the French ambassador. Marillac's account is considered the more correct. Vide Gairdner, L. and P. Hen. VIII, xvi, pref. p. xliii.

[289] Ibid. 1325, 1328, 1332.

[290] Ibid. 1325. The clock was no doubt the curious astronomical one which is still to be seen in the clock tower. It had been put up about the time of Katherine's marriage.

[291] Ibid. 1331–33; Wriothesley, Chron. i, 130, the 'Great Watching Chamber' is the room behind the great hall.

[292] On the plea that she had entered into a 'pre-contract' with Francis Dereham and that therefore her marriage with the king was void.

[293] Dict. Nat. Biog. 'Katherine Howard.'

screams unmoved. This strange scene her unquiet spirit is supposed to enact over and over again, and her screams are said to have been heard by several ladies who at different times inhabited the neighbouring apartments.[294] The great objection to the story seems to be that Katherine was not informed of the charges against her until after Henry had left the palace. Marillac mentions particularly that he maintained an unmoved demeanour and left Hampton Court 'secretly.' Even if Katherine suspected what was going on it was not likely, until the circumstances were made public, that the guards would have dared to use force to prevent the queen from entering the king's presence.

Nothing seems to have changed Henry's affection for the place. He returned there in December 1541 after Katherine had left, and he was there in the summer of 1542, entertaining at different times both the Imperial and French ambassadors,[295] when an offensive and defensive alliance was sworn between the king and the emperor on Trinity Sunday (May 1542).[296] Chapuys wrote to the Queen of Hungary in December following that some slight advantages gained against the Scots had rejoiced the king, who had 'continually shown himself sad' since he heard of the conduct of his last wife, and 'nothing has been said of banquet or of ladies, but now all is changed, and order already taken that the Princess (Mary) shall go to court at this feast, accompanied with a great number of ladies; they work day and night at Hampton Court to finish her lodging. It is possible that amidst these festivities the king might think of marrying, although there is yet no bruit of it.'[297]

Henry chose to return to Hampton Court with his last bride, Catherine Parr, widow of Lord Latimer.[298] Their marriage took place 'in an upper oratory called the Quyne's Pryvy Chapel' on 12 July 1543. The ceremony was performed by Stephen Gardiner, Bishop of Winchester, in the presence of about twenty witnesses, including the Princesses Mary and Elizabeth.[299] Christmas of that year was spent at Hampton Court, and on the Sunday before Christmas Eve the queen's brother, Lord Parr, was created Earl of Essex, and Sir William Parr, her uncle, Lord Parr of Horton.[300] The ceremony is described at much length—how 'the king went to his closet to hear high mass'—and the new peers 'went to the

pages' chamber, which was strawed with rushes, and after sacring of high mass, when the king was come into the chamber of presence under cloth of estate, the Earl of Essex was led into the chamber under cloth of estate, by the Marquis of Dorset and the Earl of Derby, Viscount Lisle bearing the sword, and Garter the Letters Patent, which were read by Mr. Wriothesley.' The usual ceremonies then took place, and the Baron (Lord Parr of Horton) was afterwards led in by Lords Russell and St. John, Clarencieux (in default of a baron) bearing the robe, and Garter the Letters Patent, which were read by Mr. Pagette. The new earl and baron afterwards dined in the Council Chamber,[301] and their styles were proclaimed.[302]

On Christmas Eve, after the court had attended grand vespers in the chapel, a chapter of the order of the Garter was held, and Sir John Wallop was made a member of the order.[303] There is also an account of Sir Thomas Wriothesley being created Baron Wriothesley at Hampton Court on 1 January 1544.[304]

The Earl of Surrey was among the knights who attended the chapter on this occasion, and it must have been about this time that he first fell in love with the 'fair Geraldine,' as he says in the famous sonnet giving the 'Description and Praise of his Love':

Hampton me taught to wish her first for mine.

In another poem he speaks of

The large green courts where we were wont to hove (hover)
With eyes cast up into the maiden's tower.

Surrey, whose picture, attributed to Holbein, is in the palace, was at this time about twenty-five years of age, and had been married at the age of eighteen to Lady Frances Vere. Lady Elizabeth Fitzgerald, who has been identified as the 'fair Geraldine,' belonged to the Princess Mary's household, and was then only about fourteen.[305]

The Christmas festivities were carried on into the following week, when the king received in state 'Ferdinand de Gonzaga, Viceroy of Sicily, Prince of Malfeta, Captain-General of the Chivalry and Army of the Emperor Charles,' who came in pursuance of the alliance sworn between the king and the emperor the year before,[306] to arrange

---

[294] Law, op. cit. i, 223–4. Mrs. Russell Davies, the well-known spiritualist, visited the Palace for the special purpose of 'interviewing' the ghosts of Katherine Howard and Jane Seymour. See her amusing account of these séances in Borderland, iv, 425, (1897).

[295] L. and P. Hen. VIII, xvii, 363, 371, 500; xviii, 44.

[296] Ibid.; Hall, Chron. 857; vide Law, op. cit. i, 288–9. It is impossible here to enter into the questions of policy which caused some jealousy between the ambassadors.

[297] L. and P. Hen. VIII, xvii, 1212.

[298] The plague was so bad at this time that a proclamation was issued at Hampton Court July 1543, forbidding

Londoners from entering the gates of any house 'wherein the king and queen lie,' and forbidding servants of the court to go to London and return to court again. L. and P. Hen. VIII, xviii, 886.

[299] L. and P. Hen. VIII, xviii, 873 (from the original notarial certificate at the Record Office).

[300] G.E.C. Complete Peerage, iii, 284; vi, 191; Hall, Chron. 859. Sir William Parr was chamberlain to his niece in 1543. He died in 1546. The peerage became extinct.

[301] The rooms mentioned were chiefly those built by Henry himself, and afterwards destroyed by Wren.

[302] L. and P. Hen. VIII, xviii, 516.

[303] See ante, p. 337; L. and P.

Hen. VIII, xviii, 517; Curtis, Reg. of Order of the Garter, i, 437–9 (ed. 1724).

[304] L. and P. Hen. VIII, xix (i), 1.

[305] Law, Hist. Hampton Court Palace, i, 232. Surrey's picture gives a fair idea of the magnificent dress of the courtiers of Henry VIII. It was probably painted by Holbein's imitator, Guillim Stretes. The picture is engraved in Fairholt, Costume; also in Law, op. cit. i, 233. Surrey was executed on a charge of high treason in 1547.

[306] L. and P. Hen. VIII, xviii, 603. May 1543. Treaty dated Feb. 1543 (though it is said to have been arranged the previous summer).

about the renewal of the war with France.[307] Henry eventually left Katherine Parr and his three children at Hampton Court, and went himself to take command of the English army in France.[308] The queen remained at the palace during his absence ; some of her letters are extant, informing him of the health of the prince and other children.[309] He rejoined her in October, and they continued at Hampton Court for some time. The picture, attributed to Holbein, of Henry VIII and his family sitting in the cloisters at Hampton Court, which is now in the State Apartments (No. 340), was probably painted at this period, about 1546.[310]

The last of Henry's great 'revellynges' took place in the summer of 1546, when the French ambassador, Claude d'Annebaut, Admiral of France, came to ratify the peace recently concluded between England and France. He went by river to Hampton Court from London, and was met by the young Prince Edward, attended by the Archbishop of York, the Earls of Hertford and Huntingdon, and 'a retinue of five hundred and forty in velvet coates ; the Prince's livery with sleeves of cloth of gold, and half the coats embroidered also with gold.' At the outer gate he was met by the Lord Chancellor and all the Council. The next day he had an audience of the king, 'and in great triumph went to the Chapel, where the king received his oath to perform the articles of the league as covenanted.'

After that followed six days of 'banquetings, huntings and triumphings, with noble masques and mummeries.'[311] This was the end of the gay scenes at Hampton Court which Henry had loved. A little later his health failed entirely ; he left the palace for the last time before the end of 1546, and died at Westminster on 28 January 1547.[312] Though Henry VIII himself left the palace on the death of Jane Seymour, and did not return there till the following year, the infant prince remained, and a regular household was appointed for him in March 1538.[313] It consisted of a chamberlain— Sir William Sydney—a vice-chamberlain, a chief steward, a comptroller, a lady mistress,[314] a cofferer, a dean, and several others, including the nurse and rockers.[315] An elaborate code of regulations was drawn up for the use of these officials.[316] The rooms allotted to the young prince were on the second floor on the north side of the Chapel Court, facing the gardens to the east.[317]

His nurse was Sibell Penn, daughter of William Hampden, and wife of David Penn. She was appointed in October 1538, having been recommended by her brother-in-law, Sir William Sydney, the prince's chamberlain.[318] She apparently continued to live at Hampton Court after Edward's death, and died there on 6 November 1562, of smallpox, at the time when Queen Elizabeth suffered from the same disease.[319] Mrs. Penn was buried in Hampton Church, and her monument is still to be seen there, a life-sized recumbent effigy, under a marble canopy. On the tomb are the date of her death, her coat of arms, and a quaintly-rhyming epitaph. Her ghost is the best authenticated of those that are said to haunt the palace.[320]

[307] Hall, *Chron.* fol. 857 ; Holinshed, *Chron.* iii, 19 (ed. 1809).

[308] *L. and P. Hen. VIII,* xix, Pref. p. x, &c. ; *Dict. Nat. Biog.* 'Henry VIII.'

[309] Commission of Regency to the queen and others was drawn up 11 July 1543 ; *L. and P. Hen. VIII,* xix, 864, 889.

[310] Law, op. cit. i, 238 ; *The Royal Gallery of Hampton Court,* 129-30.

[311] Holinshed, *Chron.* iii, 975 ; Fabyan, *Chron.* 708. *L. and P. Hen. VIII,* xxi (1), 693, et seq.

[312] *Dict. Nat. Biog.* 'Henry VIII.' It is said that he became so unwieldy that at last he could only be moved from one room to another in the palace 'by the aid of machinery' ; Lingard, *Hist. of Engl.* vi, chap. v.

[313] *L. and P. Hen. VIII,* xiii, 579.

[314] The earliest 'Lady Maistres' to Henry's three children seems to have been Margaret daughter of Humphrey Bourchier, Lord Berners, and wife of Sir Thomas Bryan, kt. ; *Lit. Remains of Edw. VI* (ed. Nichols), i, p. xxxii ; Stowe, *Surv. of Lond.* i, 1760 ; ii, 114, Strype's App. ; in which her will is given.

[315] The Chapter House Accounts include items for the 'Rocking Chamber' ; cit. Law, *Hist. Hampton Court Palace,* i, 201 ; *Lit. Remains of Edw. VI,* i, p. xxix.

[316] Ibid. p. xxvii, et seq.; *Treasury Papers* (Exch.), (Ser. 1), 750. A transcript is in the Cott. MSS. Vitellius, C. i, fol. 65.

[317] They are now private apartments occupied by Mrs. Thomson, widow of the late Archbishop of York.

[318] He wrote to Cromwell about his wife's sister : 'I doubt not but that she is every way an apt woman for the same, and there shall be no lack of goodwill in her' ; *L. and P. Hen. VIII,* xiii, 524. It is not certain that Sir William's letter refers to Mrs. Penn, though she must have been appointed about that time (1538) (ibid. 1257), but his wife appears to have been a daughter of Sir Hugh Pagenham, and from the coat of arms and inscription on her monument in Hampton Church it is clear that Mrs. Penn was born a Hampden ; Law, *Hist. Hampton Court Palace,* i, 196. Sir Clements Markham refers to her as the daughter of Sir Hugh Pagenham, and says that 'the second nurse was Mrs. Jackson— Mother Jak' ; *King Edw. VI ; An Appreciation* (1907), 4. A picture by Holbein, now at Windsor, of Edward VI and his 'wet nurse Mother Jak' is said to resemble the effigy of Mrs. Penn at Hampton, but it seems probable that she succeeded 'Mother Jak' ; *Dict. Nat. Biog.* Henry VIII rewarded her faithful service with some of his monastic spoils, making her a grant for her life of lands in Bucks. which originally belonged to the monasteries of Burcester and Godstow and Chacombe Priory. These lands were confirmed to her and her heirs by Edward VI ; *L. and P. Hen. VIII,* xiii, 1258 n. ; Orig. R. 7 Edw. VI, ii, rot. 49.

[319] Edward VI, and afterwards his sisters, Queen Mary and Queen Elizabeth, always continued to treat Mrs. Penn with great kindness and liberality ; *Lit. Remains of Edw. VI,* i, pp. xxxiii, ccxv ; *Cal. S.P. Foreign,* 1547-53, no. 1053.

[320] Her monument was moved when the old church was pulled down in 1829, and from that time it was said that her spirit returned to haunt the scenes of her former life. The sounds of someone using a spinning-wheel, and of a woman's voice murmuring as she spun, were said to be heard in one of the rooms in an apartment in the south-west wing of the palace. They are now private apartments occupied by Lord and Lady Wolseley. Inquiries were made, and a disused room was discovered in which was an ancient spinning-wheel. The oak floor was found to be worn away by the action of the treadle. At a later period she is supposed to have appeared at night to a sentry on guard, as well as to others. The usual description given of her ghost, as seen by strangers who knew nothing of the tradition, is said to correspond accurately with the figure on her tomb ; Law, *Hist. Hampton Court Palace,* i, 200. There seems to be absolutely no known reason why she should have haunted that wing of the palace. A further legend runs that she only appears when a child of royal descent is to be born in the palace, and her appearance foretells disaster. See p. 389.

The foreign ambassadors were occasionally invited to the palace to visit the prince, before Henry returned there himself.[321] Princess Mary, then living at Richmond, also came over sometimes to see her brother, by barge or on horseback.[322] Although Edward was sometimes at Hampton Court after his father's marriage to Katherine Howard,[323] and later when he and his sisters were there with Katherine Parr,[324] he and Princess Elizabeth were brought up together chiefly at 'Havering-atte-Bower,' Romford, Essex, and afterwards at Hunsdon in Hertfordshire. Very few of his letters which are still extant are dated from Hampton Court before his accession.[325]

His first return to the palace as king was in June 1547.[326] Edward was, of course, still entirely under tutelage. He himself gives an account of his walking with the Lord Admiral (Seymour of Sudeley) in 'the gallery' at Hampton Court; the Lord Admiral tried to urge the young king to assert himself 'that within three or four years he should be ruler of his own things,'[327] he also said that his uncle had told him he was 'too bashfull in myne owne matters.'[328] Meanwhile Somerset's splendour and arrogance increased. The people became discontented and the Council alarmed. In September 1549 the Lord Protector and his party[329] were with the king at Hampton Court, while the Council met secretly in London, hoping to arrange measures to bring Somerset to reason.[330] He heard of their meetings, and becoming suspicious of their intentions, caused all the armour to be brought down from the armoury in the palace, to arm his own men and the king's servants.[331] He also drew up a proclamation, which Edward signed, and it was issued in all directions on 5 October, commanding the king's 'loving subjects with all haste to repair to His Highness at His Majesty's manor of Hampton Court, in most defensible array, with harness and weapons to defend his most royal person and his entirely beloved uncle the Lord Protector, against whom certain have attempted a most dangerous conspiracy.'[332] Edward in his journal says simply, 'Peple came abundantly to the house,' and also mentions that the 'gates of the house were impared,' but it is said that the moat was filled, the gates fortified, and every preparation made for withstanding a siege.[333] The people came in numbers, probably chiefly from curiosity, for Somerset was not popular. They were gathered in the 'outer green court'—now called the 'barrack yard'—and the Lord Protector brought the king out to the first or Base Court, where their armed force was probably drawn up, and then took him to the gate where the people could see him.[334] After making him say 'I pray you be good to us and our uncle,' Somerset harangued the people himself, assuring them that he and the king would stand or fall together. Apparently he was not satisfied with their reception of his speech, as at nine or ten o'clock that night he hurried Edward off to Windsor 'with al the peple.'[335]

The council had assembled, meaning to 'repayre to Hampton Courte accompanyed with their ordynary number of servantes to have had friendly communicacion with the Lord Protector about the reformacion of the State,' but 'as they were booted and redy to have mounted upon their horses' they received the information that he had 'suddenly raysed a power of the communes to thintent if their Lordschippes had come to the Courte to have destroyed them.'[336] The council wisely 'determyned to stay at London,' met at Ely Place and sent forth letters requiring the nobles and gentlemen of the realm not to obey the Protector's commands.[337] Their action must have been successful,[338] for in five days' time Somerset was forced to submit without striking a blow, and was sent to the Tower. Edward, who did not like Windsor, was brought back to Hampton Court, or ''Ampton Court,' as he always wrote it.[339] After three months' imprisonment Somerset was pardoned. He was at Hampton Court with the king in July 1551, when the 'sweating sickness' had driven the royal household from London.[340] Maréchal St. André,[341] the envoy of

[321] L. and P. Hen. VIII, xiii, 323, 388, 402; xiv, 126, &c.

[322] Some of the times recorded were in Nov. 1537, and in Mar. Apr. and May 1538; Nicolas, Privy Purse Expenses of Princess Mary, 61, 64, 69.

[323] See p. 338.   [324] See p. 340.

[325] Lit. Remains of Edw. VI, i, 1–98; Clements Markham, op. cit. 4; Copies of seven original letters from Edw. VI (ed. Horace Walpole, 1772).

[326] There is a curious item for 32s. among the king's expenses, 'for grene bowes for the Kinges Maiesties pryvie chamber and galleries at Hampton Courte.' They may have served as blinds in the windows. Lit. Remains of Edw. VI, i, p. xcvi.

[327] Seymour of Sudeley had his own reasons for disliking his brother's supremacy; Burghley Papers (ed. Haynes), 87; Lit. Remains of Edw. VI, i, 58; Tytler, Engl. under Edw. VI and Mary, i, 111.

[328] Lit. Remains of Edw. VI, i, 59. 'Deposition of Edward.'

[329] Holinshed, Chron. iii, 1014. The party included Cranmer, Paget, Cecil, Petre, Sir Thomas Smith, and Sir John Thynne; Dict. Nat. Biog. 'Edward Seymour, Duke of Somerset.'

[330] Lit. Remains of Edw. VI, ii, 233, 'Journal'; Froude, Hist. Engl. v, 230; Acts of P.C. 1547–50, p. 330.

[331] Lit. Remains of Edw. VI, ii, 235, 'Journal.' Edward says there were '500 harnesses.'

[332] Ibid.; S.P. Dom. Edw. VI, ix, 1–9. Acts of P.C. 1547–50, p. 330 et seq. 'Council Register.'

[333] Burnet, Hist. of Reform. ii (2), 12; cit. Law, Hist. Hampton Court Palace, i, 850.

[334] Lit. Rem. of Edw. VI, ii, 235, 'Journal'; also i, p. cxxx. Wriothesley, Chron. ii, 25; Tytler, Engl. under Edw. VI and Mary, i, 249; S.P. Dom. Edw. VI, ix, 33. 'Letter of the Council to the King's Sisters.'

[335] Ibid.; Lit. Rem. of Edw. VI, ii, 235, 'Journal'; Wriothesley, Chron. ii, 85.

[336] Acts of P.C. 1547–50, p. 330, 'Council Register.'

[337] Ibid.

[338] Ibid. 337, 'Council Register.'

[339] Lit. Rem. of Edw. VI, i, p. cxxxi; ii, 241, 'Journal'; S.P. Dom. Edw. VI, ix, 42; Acts of P.C. 1547–50, p 344. Edward is reported to have said of Windsor, 'Methinks I am in prison, here be no galleries or gardens to walk in.' Lit. Rem. of Edw. VI, i, p. cxxxi. In May 1550 the French ambassador came to Hampton Court to a 'great banket and pastime on the water of Thames and Maskinge after'; the first mention of any entertainment on 'the water of Thames.' Wriothesley, Chron. ii, 40.

[340] Lit. Rem. of Edw. VI, ii, 330, 'Journal.'

[341] Jacques d'Albon, Marquis de Fronsac, Seigneur de St. André, a Knight of the Order of St. Michael, Maréchal of France in 1547; ibid. ii, 231, n. 2.

the King of France, who was staying at Richmond with a retinue of four hundred gentlemen, came to the palace on 14 July to present Edward with the order of St. Michael. He was received by the Duke of Somerset at nine o'clock in the morning at the 'wal end,' according to Edward's 'Journal,' probably at the end of the park.[342] The 'Journal' mentions that after his audience he went 'to his chamber on the quene's side, al hanged with cloth of arrase, and so was the hal and all my logeing.' After dinner St. André had some conversation with Edward, assuring him of the friendship of the King of France. The next day the king received the order of St. Michael with great ceremony. He was first arrayed in the robes and collar in his 'privy chamber,' and then proceeded in state to the chapel, with St. André on his right and de Gyé on his left, where Edward recorded in his journal that 'after the Communion celebrated eich of them kissed my cheke.' Various entertainments afterwards took place, such as coursing, hunting and shooting, in which the Maréchal and his staff joined.[343] They also heard the king play on the lute, and attended his 'arraying' as he called it, in his state bedchamber. At their last interview they dined with the king, 'after dinner saw the strenght of the English archers,' [344] and St. André received 'a dyamant from my finger worth by estimation 150 li.' [345] The Scotch ambassador was at Hampton Court on 19 July to receive the treaty 'for a better understanding with Scotland in the peace between France and England,' dated 10 June.[346] The Marquis of Northampton also came to the palace to be given final instructions concerning his embassy to France to present the Garter to Henri II, and to make proposals for the Princess Elizabeth of France on Edward's behalf, she being at the time five years old.[347]

On 18 July 1551 was issued from Hampton Court the famous proclamation of the council to the bishops and clergy, desiring them 'to exhort the people to a diligent attendance at Common Prayer, and so to avert the displeasure of Almighty God, He having visited the realm with the extreme plague of sudden death.' [348] At a council held on 9 August the Princess Mary's chaplains were inhibited from celebrating mass in her house or elsewhere, and five days later her comptroller and others were brought before the council for not informing the princess and causing this decree to be obeyed. She afterwards refused to obey,

and three of the gentlemen of her household were sent to the Tower.[349]

The Duke of Somerset was absent from the court on account of sweating sickness in his household when the new permanent ambassador from France arrived at Michaelmas, and was especially invited to be present in the chapel when the king and council received the Sacrament, 'wherein he seeth and understandeth the great difference betwixt our reverence in our religion and the slanders thereof usually spread by evil men.' [350] On the day following the council asked Somerset to return, and on 11 October he was present at the gorgeous ceremonies in the Great Hall, when, among other promotions in the peerage, the Earl of Warwick, his mortal enemy, was created Duke of Northumberland, and the Marquis of Dorset Duke of Suffolk.[351] Charges against Somerset had been made secretly by Sir Thomas Palmer on 7 October. On 13 October the king was informed of these accusations and left the palace. Somerset attended the council at Hampton Court on the following day, but a few hours after the meeting he was accused of treason and felony and removed to the Tower. Six weeks afterwards the late Lord Protector was found guilty of felony and condemned to death, but was not executed till 22 January 1551–2.[352]

During the autumn of 1551 the Queen Dowager of Scotland was entertained at Hampton Court on her way from France to Scotland. She had an escort from Portsmouth [353] of the gentlemen of Sussex and Surrey,[354] and arrived at the palace on 31 October.[355] She was received 2½ miles from the house by the Marquis of Northampton with 120 lords and gentlemen.[356] At the gate she was met by Lady Northampton and sixty other ladies, and the 'Journal' mentions that all the 'logeings' in the house and the 'hale' were 'very finely dressed.' A banquet with dancing and other diversions took place in the evening. On the next day 'the Dowager perused the house of Ampton Courte, and saw some coursing of dere.' [357] On 2 November she came by water from the king's palace and landed at 'Pawles Wharfe,' on her way through London. It is said that she afterwards expressed her appreciation of the young king's 'wisdom and solid judgment.' [358]

Hampton Court plays but a small part in the history of the remaining three years of Edward's reign. He was there apparently twice again :— namely in June and September 1552.[359]

[342] *Lit. Rem. of Edw. VI*, ii, 330, et seq. 'Journal'; Wriothesley, *Chron.* ii, 50.

[343] *Lit. Rem. of Edw. VI*, ii, 332–3, 'Journal.'

[344] Ibid. ii, 335, 'Journal,' July 26. [345] Ibid. [346] Ibid. 333–4.

[347] Ibid. ii, 333–4, 'Journal,' i, p. cliv.

[348] S.P. Dom. Edw. VI, xiii, 30. It is impossible to enter here into all the Reformation questions dealt with by the council at Hampton Court, *vide* S.P. Dom. Edw. VI; *Acts of P.C.* &c.

[349] *Acts of P.C.* 1550–2, pp. 333, 340, 347; *Lit. Rem. of Edw. VI*, ii, 337, 339–40, 'Journal.'

[850] S.P. Foreign, 1547–53, no. 451. 'Letter of the Council to Sir Wm. Pickering.'

[851] *Lit. Rem. of Edw. VI*. ii, 350–1, 'Journal'; S.P. Dom. Edw. VI, xiii, 56; Tytler, op. cit. ii, 29; Wriothesley, *Chron.* ii, 56.

[852] *Lit. Rem. of Edw. VI*, ii, 390, 'Journal'; Burnet, *Hist. of the Reformation*, ii (2), 67.

[853] 'She was driven by tempest to Portsmouthe & soe she sente worde she wolde take the benefite of the safeconduite, to goe by land & to see me.' *Lit. Rem. of Edw. VI*, ii, 356. 'Journal'; S.P. Foreign, 5 Nov. 1551.

[854] *Lit. Rem. of Edw. VI*, ii, 358, 'Journal.'

[855] Ibid. 359.

[856] *Acts of P.C.* 1550–2, p. 397. 'Letters to dyvers noblemen & ladies to attend uppon the Ld. Marques of Northampton and the Lady Marques his wyeff, for the receyving of the Quene Dowagier of Scotland at Hampton Courte.'

[857] *Lit. Rem. of Edw. VI*, ii, 360, 'Journal.'

[858] Strype, *Eccl. Mem.* ii, 284, cit. *Lit. Rem. of Edw. VI*, i, p. clv.

[859] S.P. Dom. Edw. VI, xv, 10.

There seems to be no record that Mary ever made Hampton Court her residence until she went there to spend the first part of her married life with Philip of Spain. On 23 August 1554, a few days after their state entry into London, they arrived at the palace, and, the court being in mourning at the time, lived in a very retired manner for some weeks.[360] It was perhaps the happiest period of Mary's ill-starred existence, but the people had become accustomed to the gorgeousness of the Tudor display, and her retirement did not make the marriage more popular.[361]

In April 1555 Mary returned to Hampton Court, to await the birth of her child,[362] all preparations were made, the nurseries were opened, and 'a cradle sumptuouslie and gorgeouslie trimmed' was ready.[363] Copies of the letters drawn up to announce the child's birth to all the foreign powers are still extant among the State Papers, ' from her Majesty's Manor of Hampton Court,' but with the date left blank.[364] There is an account in Holinshed's *Chronicle* of a scene on St. George's Day, 23 April 1555, when Philip, after attending high mass at the chapel in state, wearing his robes as Sovereign of the Order of the Garter, with the Lord Chancellor (Bishop Gardiner) in his mitre, the other knights of the order, and the lords of the council, also in their robes with crosses, ' and clarkes and prestes,' went in procession round the cloisters and courts of the palace, the thurifers swinging censers and the clergy in copes of gold and tissue. They marched through the old Inner Court—where the present Fountain Court now stands—and Mary, wishing to show her reverence for the ceremony, watched the procession from a window, so that she was seen ' by hundreds.' This was considered a serious breach of etiquette.[365] It was at this time that Elizabeth arrived at the palace, and the much-discussed reconciliation took place between the sisters. Thomas Wharton, in his *Life of Sir Thomas Pope*, gives a picturesque account of Elizabeth's reception at Hampton Court at Christmas 1554 ; he describes ' the Great Hall iit with a thousand lamps curiously disposed,' and Elizabeth's dress of ' white satin strung over with large pearls,' but there is no evidence for this.[365a] Philip and Mary were in London for Christmas 1554, and Elizabeth was still a prisoner at Woodstock.

She was summoned to Hampton Court, and arrived on 25 April, under the escort of Sir Henry Bedingfeld.[366] She found herself regarded as a prisoner, entered by a back gate, was taken to her apartments, and closely guarded.[367] The rooms she was given appear to have been in the water gallery, where there was a building isolated from the rest of the palace.[368] There she was visited by Philip, and afterwards by her great-uncle, Lord William Howard, but she was otherwise kept in solitude, until she had interviewed Gardiner, then Lord Chancellor, and the other lords of the council, who tried without success to make her acknowledge complicity in the Wyatt rebellion. After she had been at Hampton Court about three weeks she was summoned by the queen one night at 10 o'clock, and was conducted across the garden by Bedingfeld and one of the queen's ladies, while the gentlemen ushers and grooms carried torches before her.[369] She was taken to the queen's bed-chamber, where she found Mary alone, seated on a chair of state. Elizabeth, as usual, acquitted herself with great courage and prudence, maintaining stoutly her innocence. The queen ended the interview by saying ' Sabe Dios '—' God knows,' and then added, ' Whether innocent or guilty I forgive you.'[370] A week after Elizabeth was set at liberty, allowed to have a separate establishment, and treated with deference as heir to the throne,[371] although to the end of her life Mary refused to abandon her hope of a child. Her health had broken down completely, and the accounts of the ambassadors who visited her at Hampton Court give a terrible picture of her physical and mental condition.[372] Elizabeth remained at the palace, attended mass in the chapel, and otherwise affected a complete submission to her sister ; but when Mary left for Oatlands on 3 August, Elizabeth asked and received permission to retire from court.[373] A curious incident is recorded by Machyn, that when Mary left the palace on this occasion, as she went through the garden to enter her barge, she met a cripple, who was so much overcome by his joy on seeing her that he threw away his crutches and ran after her. Mary appears to have looked on this as a miracle, and gave him a reward from her privy purse.[374]

Mary and Philip were at Hampton Court again

[360] They left on 28 September, *Machyn's Diary* (Camd. Soc.), 69.

[361] There was some considerable ceremony on 2 September, when Sir Anthony Browne was created Viscount Montague. He was Master of the Horse, and Lieutenant of the Honour of Hampton Court ; *Cal. S.P. Dom.* 1547–80, p. 63.

[362] Courtenay was admitted to kiss hands before his departure as ambassador to the Netherlands, and the Duke of Alva paid a short visit to Philip ; Wiesener, *Youth of Queen Eliz.* ii, 154, 158, &c.

[363] Holinshed, *Chron.* (ed. 1808), iv, 69.

[364] S.P. Dom. Mary, v, 28, 32.

[365] *Machyn's Diary* (Camd. Soc.), 85.

[365a] It is also mentioned with further

detail in Mr. Shaw's MS. coll., but he does not give his authority.

[366] Wriothesley, *Chron.* ii, 128.

[367] Heywood, *England's Eliz.* 191; *vide* also Wiesener, *La Jeunesse d'Élisabeth* (ed. 1878), 310 ; Friedmann, *Dépêches de Michiel*, 36.

[368] A few years ago remains of the ancient water-gate, or rather of its foundations, were found under the towing-path, just beyond the present water-gallery, which dates from the time of William and Mary.

[369] Holinshed, *Chron.* ; Heywood, *England's Eliz.* ; Foxe, *Acts and Monuments*, viii, 621, cit. Law, *Hist. of Hampton Court Palace*, i, 274.

[370] Foxe and Heywood (*vide supra*) both declare that Philip was concealed behind the arras on this occasion and

heard all that passed. He was said to be fond of such tortuous methods of obtaining information ; *vide* Strickland, *Lives of the Queens of Engl.* iv, 108.

[371] Leti, *Vie d'Élisabeth*, 267.

[372] *Cal. S.P. Venetian*, 1553–4, p. 532; Holinshed, *Chron.* iii, 1160 ; *Cal. S.P. Foreign*, Introd. p. lxxiii ; *Ambassades de Noailles*, iv, 342, cit. Law, op. cit. i, 277. In Mary's will, dated seven months before her death, she made provision for settling the Crown on her issue ; Madden, *Privy Purse Expenses of Mary*, App.

[373] S.P. Dom. Mary, v, 48 ; *Machyn's Diary* (Camd. Soc.), 92.

[374] *Machyn's Diary* (Camd. Soc.), 92.

in August, but left on the 26th by barge for Westminster on their way to Greenwich.[375] Six days later Philip returned to the Netherlands, and did not rejoin his wife for two years. He and Mary paid their last visit to the palace during his second brief sojourn in England in June 1557, when they came down with several members of the council to hunt in the park, but it was only a flying visit, as the household was left at Whitehall.[376]

Though Hampton Court was not the scene of any great historic events during the reign of Elizabeth, it was the background for many festivities.[377] Elizabeth inherited to the full the Tudor love of splendid ceremonial and gorgeous pageantry. In June 1559 Winchester[378] wrote to Cecil[379] that he had made a survey of Hampton Court, and pointed out the alterations and improvements that he thought should be made for the queen. 'The grounds,' he said, 'will be laid out with as many pleasures as can be imagined.'[380] The queen arrived there for the first time after her accession on 10 August 1559, from Nonsuch.[381]

The question of Elizabeth's marriage was already the cause of anxiety to her advisers. The Earl of Arran, eldest son of the Duke of Châtelherault,[382] was the suitor at this time most favoured by Elizabeth and her Protestant advisers. Arran was a fugitive from France, hiding in Switzerland. He came over to England and concealed himself at Cecil's house in the Strand. In August he came to Hampton Court, crossed the river secretly, and was brought by Cecil into the 'Privy Gardens' where a sort of clandestine interview took place between him and the queen. The romantic touch no doubt appealed to Elizabeth, but Arran did not please her personally, and he returned to Scotland.[383] The meeting was kept profoundly secret, though de Quadra, the Spanish ambassador, discovered it.[384] The next turn of the political wheel brought him a message from the queen to say that she was disposed to consider favourably a marriage with the Archduke Charles, the son of the Emperor Ferdinand. De Quadra hastened to Hampton Court,[385] and a strange story was told him about a plot which had been discovered to murder the queen and Lord Robert Dudley, and put Mary Stuart on the throne.

It is necessary to mention here some of the scandals about Elizabeth and Leicester.

Many years after Elizabeth's death a man appeared in Madrid who declared that he was their son, and told a circumstantial story of his birth at Hampton Court in 1562. 'He was,' he said, 'the

reputed son of Robert Sotheron, once a servant of Mrs. Ashley, of Evesham.' By order of Mrs. Ashley, Sotheron went to Hampton Court, and was told that Mrs. Ashley wished him to provide a nurse for the child of a lady of the court, whose honour the queen wished to preserve. 'Being led into the gallery near the royal closet (? the "Haunted Gallery") he received the infant from Mrs. Ashley, with directions to call it Arthur; entrusted it to the wife of the miller at Moulsey,' and afterwards conveyed it to his own house. He treated the child as his own son, and only on his death-bed revealed to the boy his real parentage.[386] The old mill at East Molesey still exists. The story is discussed at length, with all the evidence, in Martin Hume's *Courtships of Queen Elizabeth*, and dismissed as improbable. 'Arthur Dudley' was most likely only a carefully coached spy. A curious story of the very familiar terms on which Dudley and the queen were is told by Randolph, writing to Sir William Throckmorton. The queen was sitting in the dedans of the tennis court at the palace, watching a game between the Duke of Norfolk and Leicester, when 'My lord Robert being verie hotte and swetinge tooke the Quene's napken oute of her hande and wyped his face, which the Duke seinge saide that he was to sawcie, and swore yt he wolde laye his racket upon his face. Here upon rose a great troble, and the Queen offendid sore with the Duke.' It can hardly be said that he was more courtly than Dudley. Nevertheless Elizabeth understood when to let her favourite know 'that there was only one mistress in England and no master.'[387]

The autumn of 1562 was a period of great political anxiety in England,[388] and in October Elizabeth lay ill at Hampton Court suffering from a dangerous attack of smallpox. On the night of the 15th she was thought to be dying, and the council came in haste to decide on measures to be taken in the event of her death. Froude's description of the scene, taken from the Simancas MS., is very graphic. On recovering from a state of unconsciousness that had lasted for hours, she found the council gathered round her bed, waiting to hear what she might say of the succession. Her first thoughts appear to have been of Dudley, who she begged might be made protector of the realm, and she asked that provision might be made for others of her relatives and attendants. This probably took place in the room on the south side of the palace, which still has Elizabeth's crown and cipher over the window. The worst part of

[375] Wriothesley, *Chron.* ii, 133.

[376] *Machyn's Diary* (Camden Soc.), 139.

[377] Law, *Hist. Hampton Court Palace*, i, 280.

[378] John Paulet, 1st Marquis of Winchester, Lord Treasurer.

[379] William Cecil, Chief Secretary of State, afterwards Lord Burghley.

[380] *Cal. S.P. Dom.* 1547–80, p. 131.

[381] *Machyn's Diary* (Camden Soc.), 206.

[382] James Hamilton (1530–1609),

eldest son of James, 2nd Earl of Arran, and Duke of Chatelherault. He was presumptive heir to the throne of Scotland.

[383] *Cal. S.P. Foreign*, 1558–9, no. 1274, 1293; Froude, op. cit. vii, 97, 140; *Sadleir Papers*, 417, cit. Law, op. cit. i, 282; Teulet, *Relations Politiques*, i, 343–47, 357–61, &c.

[384] *Cal. S.P. Foreign*, 1558–9, no. 1116.

[385] On 7 or 8 Sept. 1559.

[386] Ellis, *Orig. Letters* (Ser. 2), iii,

135; S.P. Spanish, Eliz. iv; S.P. Venetian, viii, 4 April 1587; Lingard, *Hist. Engl.* vi (n. E.E.); Law, *Hist. Hampton Court Palace*, i, 288.

[387] *Cal. S.P. Scotland*, x, no. 31a.

[388] Relations with Scotland were strained. The agitations of the Roman Catholic party had increased. The plots of Arthur Pole had been discovered. Troops had been dispatched to take part in the civil war in France. *Dict. Nat. Biog.*; Law, op. cit. i, 289.

her illness seemed, however, to be over, and the queen recovered rapidly. By 11 November she was sufficiently well to be moved to Somerset Place.[389]

Elizabeth still continued to welcome suitors for her hand. Hans Casimir, the eldest son of the Elector Palatine, asked Sir James Melville, the Scotch envoy, who was going from the Electoral Court to London, to carry his portrait to the queen, in April 1564. Elizabeth received Melville at Hampton Court, and he brought her the pictures of the 'Duke Casimir' and of his father and mother to see. The next morning she met him in the garden, and gave him back the portraits : 'She would have none of them,' Melville said, and wrote to the duke and his father 'dissuading them to meddle any more in that marriage.'[390]

In October Melville returned to Hampton Court on a special mission from Mary Queen of Scots,[391] and stayed at the palace for nine days, seeing Elizabeth constantly, and trying to appease her insatiable curiosity about Mary.

Like Wolsey, Elizabeth often made appointments with the ambassadors to meet her in the gardens, where she habitually walked every morning at eight o'clock, being careful, when she was likely to be observed, not to walk with undignified haste ; 'she, who was the very image of majesty and magnificence, went slowly and marched with leisure, and with a certain grandity rather than gravity.'[392]

Melville tells a story of his being taken by Lord Hunsdon to hear the queen play on the virginals. He was apparently led into 'a quiet gallery,' where he might hear without being seen, but after a time pushed aside the tapestry which hung over the door and entered the room where she sat. She stopped playing when she found that she was not alone, and expressed surprise at his entrance, but made him 'kneel on a cushion,' and at last drew from him the compliment the old courtier had hitherto skilfully evaded, as he was obliged to own that she played better than his own queen did.[393] He also conceded that Mary 'danced not so high or disposedly as she did.'[394] She was really fond of music, and always had a great number of musicians to play and sing while she dined or supped, as

well as on state occasions, at masquerades, balls and banquets.[395] She was also particular about the music in the chapel at Hampton Court, and used to send sometimes to tell her organist Tye that 'he played out of tune,' to which he returned, in uncourtier-like phrase, that 'her ears were out of tune.'[396]

In 1568 an important council was held at Hampton Court on 30 October, to decide on the further action of England with regard to the conference then being held in London concerning the chances of reconciliation between Mary Queen of Scots, who was a prisoner at Carlisle, and her rebel lords.[397] It was probably on this occasion that Elizabeth was made aware of the growing excitement among her Roman Catholic subjects, and the likelihood of a rising in the north on Mary's behalf.[398] The queen gave Mary's commissioners an audience at Hampton Court on 23 November, and assured them that the proceedings were to be in no way judicial.[399]

During the sitting of the conference Elizabeth remained at Hampton Court, where she received the new French ambassador, La Motte Fénelon, and also the Cardinal de Chatillon, brother of Coligny, who was the envoy of Condé and the Huguenots.[400]

On Friday 3 December Mary's commissioners again appeared at Hampton Court, and protested against the attitude of the Regent Murray and of the English commissioners.[401] An answer was not given at once, and they returned to the palace the next day, when they asked to see Leicester and Cecil, and suggested a compromise.[402] On 8 December the celebrated Casket letters were produced by Murray and laid before the English commissioners, and a great council of peers was summoned at Hampton Court to discuss the proceedings of the conference and to see these proofs.[403] The first meeting was on 13 December, the opinion of the peers was not unanimous, and for some time afterwards negotiations were carried on incessantly between Elizabeth and Mary's commissioners.[404]

Before Murray's departure[405] he had an interview with the Duke of Norfolk in the park, talking with him and encouraging him in his aspirations

---

[389] Froude, *Hist. Engl.* vii, 429. De Quadra wrote that 'when the Queen feared she might die she protested solemnly before God that although she loved Robert dearly nothing unseemly had ever passed between them.' *Cal. S.P. Spanish,* 1562, i, 190, *vide* Martin Hume, *Courtships of Queen Eliz.* 68.

[390] Melville, *Memoirs,* 79.

[391] He was sent to apologize to Elizabeth for an angry letter written to her by Mary, because Elizabeth had suggested a marriage between the Queen of Scots and Lord Robert Dudley. When Melville left the palace he was conveyed by Dudley in his barge from Hampton Court to London. He asked what the Queen of Scots thought of the proposal that she should marry him, but Melville answered 'very coldly,' and Lord Robert declared the

proposal an invention of his enemies ; Melville, *Memoirs,* 97, 101.

[392] Digges, *Compleat Ambassador,* 300 ; Melville, *Memoirs,* 97.

[393] Melville, *Memoirs,* 101.

[394] She asked him constantly whether she or Mary were the more lovely, the taller, the better dancer, &c.

[395] Nichols, *Progresses of Queen Eliz.* i, 487, 529.

[396] Ibid. i, 293. In Hawkins's *Hist. of Music,* v, 201, he says that 'in the hour of her departure she ordered her musicians into her chamber and died hearing them.'

[397] Goodall, *Examination of the Letters of Mary Queen of Scots,* ii, 179.

[398] Froude, *Hist. of Engl.* ix, 335, quoting a letter from Cecil to Sir H. Sydney. MSS. Ireland, P.R.O.

[399] Goodall, op. cit. ii, 189.

[400] *Dépêches de la Motte Fénelon,* i, 1–16.

[401] The Bishop of Ross was spokesman for the Scottish commissioners. Froude, *Hist. of Engl.* ix, 344 ; Goodall, *Journ. of P.C.* 223.

[402] These proceedings at Hampton Court were more or less private, and not meetings of the conference ; Law, *Hist. Hampton Court Palace,* i, 307, n. 3.

[403] The Earls of Westmorland, Northumberland, Derby, Shrewsbury, Worcester, Huntingdon, and Warwick, besides members of the Privy Council, Sir Nicholas Bacon, Clinton, Leicester, Cecil, &c.

[404] *Hist. MSS. Com. Rep.* iv, App. 209–10.

[405] Hosack, *Mary Queen of Scots and her Accusers,* i, 425.

for the hand of Mary. Norfolk, with good reason, did not trust the Regent. 'Earl Murray,' he said, as they parted at the postern gate, 'thou hast Norfolk's life in thy hands.'[406] In less than a year Murray had betrayed to Elizabeth all that Norfolk had said to him.

The queen continued to visit Hampton Court annually, and to spend some time there, but her visits were usually only occasions for rest or amusement. In the autumn of 1569, when Norfolk's rebellion in the north was at its height, she was at the palace,[407] and also in July 1571 and September 1572.[408] On the last occasion she again suffered from smallpox, and was so ill that 'my lord of Leicester did watch with her all night,' but the illness lasted a very short time, and she was soon able to go to Windsor.[409] At Christmas she returned to Hampton Court, and kept the season gaily with a long series of the revels in which she rejoiced as much as her father before her.[410] Masques and plays were presented before the court almost every evening in the Great Hall. The *Accounts of the Revels at Court*[411] contain many details of such performances, and show that the stage scenery of those days was not really so primitive as is generally thought. There are entries for 'painting seven cities, one village, and one country house,' and for bringing in trees to represent a wilderness.[412] The method of illumination by stretching wires across the open roof of the hall and hanging on them small oil lamps is also described in the accounts.[413] In 1576 and 1577[414] she again spent Christmas with great cheer at Hampton Court, and in 1576 six plays were presented before her by 'the Earl of Warwick's servants,' 'the Lord Howard's servants,' 'the Earl of Leicester's men.' The most interesting of these is 'The historie of Error showen at Hampton Court on New Year's Day at night, enacted by the children of Powles.'[415] It has been conjectured that this play was the foundation of Shakespeare's 'Comedy of Errors.' There is a little picture of Elizabeth at the palace in 1576, which shows a less pleasant side of her character, contained in a letter from Eleanor Bridges to the Earl of Rutland: 'The Queen hath used Mary Shelton very ill for her marriage. She hath telt liberall bothe with bloes and yevell wordes and hath not yet graunted her consent. . . . The Court is as full of malice and spite as when you left.'[416]

The queen's hospitality was practically boundless. The sum total of the charges for the upkeep of her household amounted to £80,000 in one year, but this very enormous sum for the period was exclusive of charges for Christmas and other feasts.[417] In January 1579 John Casimir, Count Palatine of Rhene and Duke of Bavaria, hunted in the park while he was staying with the queen.[418] She was also at the palace during 1580, and again in 1582.[419] In 1592 the Duke of Würtemberg came to shoot and hunt in the parks, and described his sport as 'glorious and royal.' He also described the palace as 'the most splendid and magnificent to be seen in England, or indeed in any other kingdom.'[420] In Shirley's *Deer and Deer Parks* are some interesting accounts of Elizabeth's own love of hunting and of turning every occasion into a scene of pageantry.[421] For Christmas 1592[422] and 1593[423] she was again at Hampton Court. In February 1593 a considerable robbery of plate and jewels took place, which is thus described by a gentleman of the court : 'Bryan Annesley, Francis Hervey, James Crofts, and John Parker, all four gentlemen pensioners, three days agone were robbed, and in their absences at six o'clock at night their chamber door, which is in one of the five towers of the Tilt Yard,[424] was broken open, and all their trunks likewise, out of all of which the thieves took and carried away of jewels and ready money, from these four, to the value of £400, and no news heard of them since.'[425] The chief perpetrator, John Randall, was afterwards discovered and hanged.[426]

At about the same time a plot was discovered to murder the queen, her Spanish Jew physician, Dr. Lopez, having been bribed by the Governor of the Netherlands to put poison in her medicine. The plot was discovered by Essex ; some of the investigations were carried on at Hampton Court, and at first Elizabeth, who was still at the palace, was very angry with Essex for bringing such an accusation against an apparently innocent man. Essex retaliated by shutting himself up in his own room for several days, until Lopez's guilt having become more evident, the queen sent repeated apologies and affectionate messages to her offended favourite. Lopez was afterwards found guilty and executed.[427]

In 1599 Elizabeth paid her last visit to Hampton Court,[428] as determined as ever to be young

---

[406] The interview did take place, and this remark may have been made. If true it would be interesting if the 'postern gate' could be identified. Hosack, op. cit. i, 480, &c.

[407] *Hist. MSS. Com. Rep.* iv, App. 210.

[408] Digges, *Compleat Ambassador,* 112–15.

[409] *Life of Sir Thomas Smith,* 'Letters from Sir T. Smith to Walsingham.' Elizabeth herself wrote that it was not smallpox, though there were symptoms resembling it ; *Progresses of Queen Eliz.* i, 322.

[410] Digges, *Compleat Ambassador,* 310; *Life of Sir Thomas Smith,* 239.

[411] Published by the Shakespeare Soc. (ed. P. Cunningham).

[412] For many interesting details see Law, op. cit. i, 318–20.   [413] Ibid.

[414] *Acts of P.C.* 1575–7, p. 121. Warrants for payments for 'bringing a game before Her Majesty,' and for presenting two plays before her in 1575–6. At the end of 1575 she entertained the ambassadors of France and of the Netherlands. The embassy from the Netherlands came to offer her the sovereignty of the Low Countries ; Nichols, *Progresses of Queen Eliz.* ii, 3.

[415] Cunningham, *Accounts of Revels at Court,* 101. The 'children of Powles' were the choir of St. Paul's Cathedral.

[416] *Hist. MSS. Com. Rep.* xii, App. iv, 107.

[417] Nichols, *Progresses of Queen Eliz.* ii, 47.

[418] Ibid. ii, 277.   [419] Ibid. ii, 392.

[420] Rye, *Engl. as seen by Foreigners,* cit. Law, op cit. i, 326.

[421] Shirley, *Deer and Deer Parks,* 40; Gascoyne, *Book of Hunting ;* Nichols, *Progresses of Queen Eliz.* i, *passim.*

[422] *Memoirs of Robert Carey, Earl of Monmouth,* 61 (ed. 1808), cit. Law, op. cit. i, 330.

[423] Nichols, *Progresses of Queen Eliz.* iii, 216–32.   [424] See p. 334.

[425] S.P. Dom. Eliz. ccl, 2 ; ccli, 50.

[426] Ibid.

[427] Birch, *Memoirs of Queen Eliz.* i, 150–5.

[428] S.P. Dom. Eliz. cclxxii, 94.

and frivolous. She was seen through a window dancing 'The Spanish Panic (? pavane) to a whistle and *tabourem* (pipe and tabor), none being with her but my Lady Warwick.'[429] The Scottish Ambassador also reported that when she left Hampton Court she wished to go on horseback as usual, though she was 'scarce able to sit upright,' and 'the day being passing foul, my Lord Hunsdon said "It was not meet for one of Her Majesty's years to ride in such a storm." She answered in great anger, "*My* years! Maids, to your horses quickly," and so rode all the way.' As she passed Kingston an old man fell on his knees praying God 'that she might live a hundred years, which pleased her so as it might come to pass.'[430] Three and a half years later Elizabeth died at Richmond Palace.

James I came to Hampton Court for the first time about four months after his accession.[430a] On 17 July 1603 he issued from there a general summons to all persons who had £40 a year in land or upwards to come and receive the 'honour of knighthood'; the payment of the necessary fees in return being understood, or a fine in default.[431] The first two of those who had this 'honour' thrust upon them were Mr. John Gamme of Radnorshire and Mr. William Cave of Oxfordshire, who were knighted by the king at Hampton Court on 20 July.[432] On 21 July the king created eleven peers, and the ceremony took place with much magnificence in the Great Hall at Hampton Court.[433]

A Roman Catholic plot to seize the king, and so to enforce some change in his policy towards the recusants, was betrayed by John Gerard, a Jesuit,[434] and the proclamation for the apprehension of the chief conspirators was issued from Hampton Court on 16 July.

James apparently determined to keep up Elizabeth's habit of spending Christmas at Hampton Court with suitable festivity. In December 1603 he and the queen returned to the palace, and a grand 'masque' called *The Vision of the Twelve Goddesses* was specially written for the occasion by Samuel Daniel.[435] Lady Arabella Stuart, in a letter dated 18 December 1603, says, 'The Queen intendeth to make a masque this Christmas, to which end my Lady Suffolk and my Lady Walsingham hath warrant to take of the late Queen's best apparel out of the Tower at their discretion.'[436] Sir Dudley Carleton also wrote of a 'Merry Christmas at Hampton Court,' and said that 'the Duke (of Lennox) is *rector chori* of one side (of the masques about to be produced) and the lady Bedford of the other.'[437] The exchequer accounts for the queen's royal household and wardrobe[438] give an idea of the preparations in the Great Hall and 'Great Watching Chamber' for this masque, and in a copy of the first edition, now at the British Museum, in the King's Library, the names of the twelve ladies who took part in it are inserted in a contemporary handwriting, thought to be that of Lord Worcester.[439] The representation took place in the Great Hall on Sunday, 8 January 1604, at nine or ten o'clock in the evening. All the ambassadors were entertained at court this Christmas, and were present at the masque. A letter from Sir Dudley Carleton, printed in Mr. Law's *History*, speaks of the banquet afterwards as being 'despatched with the customary confusion.'[440] Shakespeare belonged to 'the King's Company of Comedians,'[441] and it is extremely probable that he took part in some of the numerous plays presented before the king and queen in the Great Hall at different times.[442]

The first political difficulty with which James had to deal related to the necessity for a recognized form of religion. James was anxious to make a satisfactory compromise, and consented that a conference should be summoned at Hampton

---

[429] An unpublished report of Lord Semple of Beltreis to the King of Scots, in possession of Sir John Maxwell of Polloc; cit. Strickland, *Lives of the Queens of Engl.* iv, 710.

[430] Ibid. 709–10.

[430a] In 1602 Philip, Duke of Stettin Pomerania, travelling with his tutor through Europe, visited Hampton Court, which he described at length in his diary. The diary is still extant. *Trans. Royal Hist. Soc.* (new ser.), vi, 1, et seq.

[431] Rymer, *Foedera*, xvi, 530. The 'noble order of Baronets' was founded later, also as an expedient for raising money. They each had to pay a fee of £1,000.

[432] Nichols, *Progresses of Jas. I*, i, 204.

[433] S.P. Dom. Jas. I, ii, 72. During his reign he conferred 111 peerages, about seven times as many as Queen Elizabeth had created in a reign twice as long.

[434] *Dict. Nat. Biog.*; S.P. Dom. Jas I, ii, 54 (1603).

[435] For an account of the masque see Law, *A Royal Masque at Hampton Court* (1880), in which is a reprint of *The Vision of the Twelve Goddesses*.

[436] James was determined to make use of the late queen's wardrobe. Before he left Scotland he wrote asking that her dresses and jewels might be sent to his wife. Elizabeth is said to have left 500 gowns, all of the greatest magnificence; Law, *Hist. Hampton Court Palace*, ii, 7; Nichols, *Progresses of Jas. I*, iv, 1060.

[437] S.P. Dom. Jas. I, v, 20. The plague which raged in London at the time was one reason for being at Hampton Court. The deaths in London during the autumn had amounted to three or four thousand a week.

[438] Exch. Q.R. Household and Wardrobe Accts. bdle. 82, no. 1.

[439] Law, op. cit. ii, 9–22. Lady Suffolk, the queen, and Lady Rich were Juno, Pallas, and Venus. The Ladies Hertford, Bedford, and Derby represented Diana, Vesta, and Proserpine. The Ladies Hatton, Nottingham, and Walsingham were Macaria, Concordia, and Astraea. Lady Susan Vere, Lady Dorothy Hastings, and Lady Elizabeth Howard took the parts of Flora, Ceres, and Tethys. Inigo Jones is said to have designed the scenery.

[440] *Vide* Winwood, *Mem.* ii, 44.

Daniel, the author of the masque, was afterwards made 'Master of the Queen's Children of the Revells,' a post for which there appears to be evidence that Shakespeare himself applied.

[441] The warrant for enrolling the King's Company of Comedians is among the Chapter House Privy Seal Papers, no. 71, now in the Record Office Museum, dated 7 May 1603. Shakespeare's name is the third on the list. It was rather the queen than the king who rejoiced in and encouraged these revelries; Dudley Carleton remarked that 'he takes no extraordinary pleasure in them. The Queen and Prince (Henry) were more the players' friends.' S.P. Dom. Jas. I, vi, 21 (1604).

[442] Halliwell-Phillipps, *Life of Shakespeare*, 205; Collier, *New Facts about Shakespeare* (ed. 1835), 48; *Extracts from Revels Accts.* (Shakespeare Soc.). Mr. Law says that 'Unfortunately the career of the masque, though brilliant, was short-lived. With the decay of the drama in Charles I's reign, masques entirely died out, and were not revived when the taste for the theatre returned with Charles II'; Law, op. cit. ii, 29.

Court, when the bishops and other clergy of the Church of England and some of the great divines of the Puritan party were appointed to discuss the questions at issue. Those present for the Church were Whitgift, Archbishop of Canterbury, the Bishops of London, Durham, Winchester, Worcester, St. David's, Chichester, Carlisle, and Peterborough, the Deans of the Chapel Royal, St. Paul's, Chester, Salisbury, Gloucester, Worcester, and Windsor, the Archdeacon of Nottingham and Dr. Field · for the Puritans Dr. John Reynolds and

Dr. Thomas Sparks of Oxford ; Mr. Chaddeston and Mr. Knewstubs, of Cambridge.[443] It is not proposed here to do more than mention the fact that the Hampton Court conference took place in January 1603–4, and that a first meeting[444] was held on Saturday 14th in the king's privy chamber,[445] one of the large rooms built by Henry VIII on the east side of the Clock Court, which was altered in the reign of George II. The Puritans did not attend this meeting, but the conference met formally on the following Monday and Wednesday, and James's theological learning received the approbation and support of the bishops ; though the Puritan party can hardly have appreciated the forcible style of his language.[446] James was pleased with the opportunity to display his own erudition, and wrote to a friend in Scotland, 'I have peppered thaime soundlie.' One effect of the conference at the time was no doubt to emphasize the hostility which developed later into the Great Rebellion.

The most lasting consequence was that the decision to make a new translation of the Bible gave the nation the 'Authorized Version.'[447]

For eight or nine months in 1604 Henry Prince of Wales with his tutors and household remained at the palace, and there are accounts of his skill at tennis and his prowess in hunting while he was there.[448] From this time forth the king came to Hampton Court always in the autumn, the time when it is generally considered that the Thames Valley is at its worst ; but he was also there for

HAMPTON COURT PALACE :
THE HALL, LOOKING TOWARDS THE SCREENS

443 Neal, *Hist. Puritans*, ii, 10.

444 A private meeting between the king and the bishops was held the day before.

445 The chapel was first suggested as a meeting place.

446 In a letter from an eye-witness, Sir John Harrington, he says that 'the King talked much Latin and disputed with Dr. Reynolds, but he rather used upbraidings than arguments. The bishops seemed much pleased, and said His Majesty spoke by the spirit of inspiration. I wist not what they mean, but the spirit was rather foul-mouthed.' *Nugae Antiquae*, i, 181 ; 'Harrington's Breefe Notes.'

447 Barlow, *Sum and Substance of the Conference* (1603) (reprinted in the *Phoenix*) ; Whitgift, *App. of Rec. Bk.* iv, no. xlv ; Dodd, *Church Hist.* iv, 21 ; Fuller, *Church Hist.* x, 267 ; Gardiner, *Hist. Engl.* vols. i–v ; *Dict. Nat. Biog.* 'James I'; *Hist. MSS. Com. Rep.* iv, App. 418, 'Emmanuel Coll. Cambridge.'

448 Birch, *Mem. of Prince Henry*, 75, cit. Law, op. cit. ii, 47. There is a curious picture at Hampton Court of Henry Prince of Wales and the Earl of Essex. The prince (aged eleven years) is drawing his sword to cut the throat of a stag which Essex is holding. It is said that on one occasion when they were playing tennis together Essex threatened to strike the prince across the face with his racket for calling him the son of a traitor ; *Secret Hist. of Jas. I*, i, 266.

hunting in the spring, and often spent Christmas there.[449]

Up to the time of her marriage in 1610 the unfortunate Lady Arabella Stuart was constantly at Hampton Court with the king and queen.[450]

In September 1605, on Michaelmas Day, Dr. Bancroft, Archbishop of Canterbury, was sworn a Privy Councillor at Hampton Court, and the king remained there till October,[451] just before the famous meeting of Parliament after the discovery of the Gunpowder Plot. He was also there in December while the trial of the conspirators was going on.[452]

In August 1606 the queen's brother, Christian IV of Denmark, came to England and visited Hampton Court with the king and queen, they 'dyned and there hunted and killed deare, with great pleasures.'[453] The King of Denmark also saw a play 'presented by his Majesties' Players in the Great Hall.'[454] Sir John Harrington wrote an astonishing account of his convivial manners and habits.[455]

James always enjoyed associating the frivolities of the court with theological discussions, and in the autumn of 1606 he invited several of the leading ministers of the Presbyterian Church of Scotland to attend him at Hampton Court, and chose four eminent English divines to preach before them, 'for the reduction of . . . the Presbyterian Scots to a right understanding of the Church of England.'[456] Between the sermons the king received the Scottish ministers in private audience and argued with them at much length, no doubt to his own satisfaction; 'in effect they returned to Scotland of the same opinion, no good end having been served by their visit.'[457]

While they were still at the palace Francis Prince of Vaudemont, third son of Charles Duke of Lorraine, also arrived with a great retinue.[458] One of the gentlemen of the court wrote to the Earl of Shrewsbury that 'this night the Earl of Vaudemont will be here, with his crew, *plus clinquant que le soleil.*'[459] He stayed at Hampton Court for a fortnight, being 'very royally entertained and feasted, and rode a-hawking and hunting with the king to divers places, and then returned.'[460] Lord Shrewsbury's correspondent also described the 'dancing in the Queen's Presence Chambre,' when 'my lady Pembroke carried away the glory.'[461]

The following year saw a different scene when the queen went to Hampton Court alone, after the death of her infant daughter Mary, and 'the Court officers had leave to play, and are gone every one to his own home, only Lord Salisbury went to Hampton Court to comfort the Queen.'[462]

There are two contemporary accounts of Hampton Court in the reign of James I,[463] one written by Prince Otto, the son of the Landgrave Maurice of Hesse, who came there in 1611, and gives a long description of the palace, the tapestries, pictures, and other curiosities. Among the rooms he mentions one called 'Paradise—within which almost all the tapestry is stitched with pearls and mixed with precious stones.'[464] The Duke of Würtemberg had described this room in Elizabeth's reign, and mentioned a table-cover in it worth fifty thousand crowns, and the 'royal throne studded with . . . diamonds, rubies, sapphires, and the like.'[465] The German traveller Hentzner also spoke of it at that time, and said it 'glitters so with silver, gold, and jewels as to dazzle one's eyes.'[466] The other account is by Ernest, Duke of Saxe-Weimar, who was at the palace in 1613.[467] He was also astonished by the 'Paradise' room, and adds the detail that 'all the apartments and galleries were laid with rush matting.' He further described a 'great hunt' he had with the king, who was devoted to the sport. On 9 September 1609 the king issued from Hampton Court a stringent proclamation against 'Hunters, stealers and killers of Deare, within any of the king's Majesties Forests, Chases or Parks.'[468] Anne of Denmark shared this taste, and Ben Jonson called her 'the Huntress Queen.'[469]

[449] So unvarying were the king's habits that an observant courtier is said to have remarked, 'Were he asleep seven years and then awakened he could tell where the king every day had been and every dish he had at his table'; *Secret Hist. of Jas. I*, ii, 5.

[450] Lodge, *Illustrations of Engl. Hist.* iii, 236; *Progresses of Jas. I*, i, 457. In Feb. 1610, Arabella, after suffering much for no reason but her nearness in the line of succession to the throne, engaged herself to William Seymour, son of the Earl of Hertford. In March they were summoned before the Privy Council and promised not to marry without the king's consent, but in July were privately married. They were immediately separated by the king's orders, and after Arabella had made a desperate effort to escape to France disguised in a man's clothes on 4 June 1611, she was brought back to the Tower and remained there till her death in 1615. *Dict. Nat. Biog.*; Cooper, *Life and Letters of Lady A. Stuart*.

[451] Howe, *Chron.* (continuation of Stowe, *Chron.*); Nichols, *Progresses of Jas. I*, i, 577; *Cal. S.P. Dom.* 1603-10, p. 234.

[452] S.P. Dom. Jas. I, xvii, 7-32 (the 'examination' of those implicated in the plot). Nichols, *Progresses of Jas. I*, iii.

[453] *England's Farewell to the King of Denmark*, cit. Law, op. cit. ii, 50; Nichols, op. cit. ii, 81. There is a portrait of Christian IV in the palace, by Vansomer.

[454] Cunningham, *Extracts from Accts. of the Revels at Court* (Shakespeare Soc.), p. xxxviii.

[455] *Nugae Antiquae*, i, 348; *Dict. Nat. Biog.* 'James I.'

[456] Wood, *Athenae*, ii, col. 507 (ed. Bliss).

[457] Spotswood, *Hist. Ch. of Scotland*, 496-8; Wood, *Athenae*, ii (ed. Bliss); Gardiner, *Hist. of Engl.* The four preachers were Bishops Barlow of Lincoln and Andrews of Chichester, Dr. Buckeridge and Dr. King. A few copies of the sermon preached by Dr. Buckeridge are still extant, and one is in Mr. Law's collection at Hampton Court. Law, op. cit. ii, 53.

[458] Howe, *Chron.* (continuation of Stowe, *Chron.*), 887.

[459] Nichols, *Progresses of Jas. I*, ii, 96.

[460] Howe, *Chron.* 887.

[461] Law, op. cit. ii, 57; Lodge, *Illustrations*, iii.

[462] Ibid. iii, 324.

[463] They are given at length in Law, *Hist. Hampton Court Palace*, ii, 65 et seq.; W. B. Rye, *Engl. as seen by Foreigners*, 144; Nichols, *Progresses of Jas. I*, ii, 424.

[464] Law, op. cit. ii, 72.

[465] Ibid. i, 328-9; from Rye, op. cit. 19, &c.

[466] Hentzner, *Journey into Engl.* (ed. 1757), 82.

[467] Law, op. cit. ii, 72.

[468] S.P. Dom. Jas. I, xlviii, 23; see the account of James's love for hunting in Law, op. cit. ii, chap. v, vi, p. 73 et seq.

[469] Ibid. There is a picture of her at Hampton Court, no. 444 in the Picture Galleries, by Vansomer, in a fanciful green hunting dress, standing by her horse, with two little greyhounds jumping round her.

On 20 September 1613 James wrote the order at Hampton Court for the removal of the remains of his mother Mary, Queen of Scots, from Peterborough to Westminster Abbey.[470] The court was at the palace again in December 1614,[471] and in April 1615.[472] In June 1616 George Villiers, afterwards Duke of Buckingham, was appointed 'Keeper of the Honour of Hampton Court for life.'[473] In September 1617 was solemnized in the chapel the marriage of Buckingham's brother, Sir John Villiers, with Frances, daughter of Lord Chief Justice Coke. The wedding was followed by a great banquet and masque,[474] when the king and his courtiers ran about the palace and played extraordinary pranks. According to the strange custom of the period, early the next morning the bride and bridegroom were given a *réveille-matin*, the king himself jumping and rolling on their bed 'in shirt and nightgown.'[475]

In 1618 Anne of Denmark became seriously ill, and after a short stay at Oatlands moved to Hampton Court,[476] in the hope of regaining her health away from London. She was evidently consumptive, and by the end of February 1619 grew rapidly worse. On 1 March 'all the Lords and Ladies went to Hampton Court, but very few were admitted.'[477] The physicians,[478] the Prince (Charles) of Wales, and the Bishop of London were called to her hastily in the early morning of the following day, and at four o'clock she died.[479]

Her body was embalmed and taken by water in a royal barge to Somerset House. She was afterwards buried in Westminster Abbey.[480]

One of the curious economies of James I was the refusal to grant 'lodgings' in the precincts to any of the ambassadors, but in 1620 he allowed Gondomar, the Spanish ambassador, to take up his residence in one of the detached towers of the palace.[481] Inigo Jones was surveyor of the Royal

Works at the time,[482] and a letter which is said to be the only one of his that has been preserved is from Hampton Court, and is addressed to the Earl of Arundel and Surrey, concerning the 'lodgings intended for the ambassador.'[483]

In January 1620–1 the French ambassador was invited to the palace, and 'nobly entertained with hunting and hawking,' probably to prevent any jealousy concerning the Spaniard. Charles, Prince of Wales, returned to Hampton Court in September 1623, after his romantic journey to Spain, to make his own proposals of marriage to the Infanta, or rather perhaps to test the sincerity of the professions of the Spanish government.[484]

The negotiations were broken off very soon after Charles's return, and in September 1624, when the chargé d'affaires for Spain, in the absence of the ambassador, came to the palace, he was received with great coldness,[485] and did not even see the prince, who had had a severe fall while hunting in the park a week or two before, and remained in his own room.[486] There is no record that James I was at Hampton Court again before his death on 27 March 1625.

During the earlier part of the reign of Charles I[487] Hampton Court was chiefly the scene of his many difficulties with regard to Henrietta Maria's household,[488] and the record is one of succeeding misunderstandings, quarrels and reconciliations with her and with the diplomatic agents of France. The lady in waiting who had the greatest influence over the queen, and therefore inspired great distrust in Charles and his advisers, was Mme. de Saint Georges. Charles seized the opportunity, both in going to Hampton Court for the first time with his wife, and on leaving it for Windsor, to exclude Mme. de Saint Georges from the coach which carried himself and the queen. De Tillières, who was Henrietta Maria's chamber-

---

[470] Stanley, *Mem. of Westm. Abbey,* App.

[471] *Cal. S.P. Dom.* 1611–18, p. 263.

[472] Ibid. 282.

[473] Ibid. 374.

[474] Nichols, *Progresses of Jas. I,* iii, 440.

[475] Campbell, *Lives of the Chief Justices,* i, 303 ; *Progresses of Jas. I,* i, 471 ; iii, 255 et seq. The history of this marriage is a romantic one, too long to be given here.

[476] *Progresses of Jas. I,* iii, 441. She was not too ill to remember her old favourite, Sir Walter Raleigh, and wrote from Hampton Court to try to obtain a pardon for him, but without success. He was executed on Tower Hill on 29 Oct. 1618.

[477] 'Letter from Mr. Chamberlain,' *Progresses of Jas. I,* iii, 531.

[478] Sir Theodore Mayerne, who had attended Prince Henry in his last illness, was one of the physicians. There is a portrait of him in the palace. His MS. note-books are in the Brit. Mus.; Law, op. cit. ii, 83.

[479] There is an ancient tradition to the effect that she died exactly as the clock struck the hour, and that ever since it has always stopped when an old resident dies in the palace. Many corrobora-

tive coincidences have been noted, but no record has been kept of the dates when the clock stopped without any death having taken place.

[480] An account of her death, by one of her attendants, is printed in the *Miscellany of the Abbotsford Club,* i, 81, 84; see also letter from Mr. Chamberlain in *Progresses of Jas. I,* iii, 531; Law, op. cit. ii, 83, 87. James was at Newmarket when she died. The portrait of him at Hampton Court, by Vansomer, in black clothes, was probably painted while he was wearing mourning for the queen. There is another portrait of him in the palace, by the same painter, in robes of state.

[481] S.P. Dom. Jas. I, cxvi, 61, 20 Aug. 1620.

[482] He remained Surveyor in the time of Charles I ; *Cal. S.P. Dom.* 1637–8, p. 376.

[483] Collier, *Life of Inigo Jones,* 23, *vide* Law, op. cit. ii, 92, where the letter is printed in full ; S.P. Dom. Jas. I, cxvi, 65.

[484] *Dict. Nat. Biog.* 'James I' ; Hardwicke, *State Papers,* vol. i. James seems to have been alarmed by the suggestion that Charles should remain in Spain for a year, and to have signed the articles agreeing to the marriage,

chiefly in order that his son might return to England.

[485] *Cal. S.P. Dom.* 1623–5, p. 349.

[486] *Progresses of Jas. I,* ii, 1005. Charles and the Duke of Buckingham were the real rulers of the kingdom during all the latter part of James's reign.

[487] He first came to the palace after his accession in July 1625, two or three weeks after his marriage. The plague was raging in London at the time, and all through this reign constant precautions were necessary to prevent communication with London and the spread of the infection. Only one death from plague seems to have taken place at Hampton Court in 1636 ; *Hist. MSS. Com. Rep.* iv, App. 78 ; ibid. xi, App. 24 ; *Cal. S.P. Dom. Chas. I,* 1636–7, p. 57, &c. ; De Tillières, *Mémoires* (ed. Hippeau, 1862) ; S.P. Dom. Chas. I, iv, 13. On 7 July 1625 Charles received a deputation from both Houses of Parliament, who presented a 'Petition concerning Religion'; ibid. 20 ; Clarendon, *Parl. Hist.* iv, 377.

[488] It must be remembered that Henrietta Maria was only fifteen years old at the time.

lain, says that as he was conducting the queen down the steps of the Great Hall, when they were leaving the palace, he heard the king and the Duke of Buckingham speaking about it, and that Charles made Lord Hamilton take a seat inside the coach that Mme. de Saint Georges might be excluded.[489] The quarrels were no doubt rather between Buckingham and the lady-in-waiting than between Charles and his queen.[490] Jealousies that arose from the presence of the king's chaplain and the queen's Roman Catholic confessor also led to trouble. One day when the king and queen were dining together in the 'Presence Chamber' at Hampton Court, 'Mr. Hacket (chaplain to the lord-keeper) being there to say grace, the confessor would have prevented him, but that Hacket shoved him away; whereupon the confessor went to the queen's side, and was about to say grace again, but that the king, pulling the dishes unto him, and the carvers falling to the business, hindered. When dinner was done' they both started saying grace aloud together, 'with such confusion that the king in great passion instantly rose from the table, and taking the queen by the hand, retired into the bedchamber.'[491] Such a scene at the king's table seems hardly credible in these days.

As the virulence of the plague kept the court away from Whitehall, and a proclamation was issued to prohibit communication between Hampton Court and London,[492] the French ambassador, M. de Blainville, was very anxious to be lodged in the palace, and he tried in various ways to overcome the king's reluctance. Sir John Finett, the Master of the Ceremonies, told him that 'his Majesty would be loth to make a "President," that would hereafter . . . beget him so great a trouble as this was like to be.'[493] The rooms were at last granted to him, and 'Mr. Secretary' Conway writing to Buckingham from Hampton Court complains much of the expense and trouble caused thereby.[494]

In 1626 Paul Rosencrantz, the Danish ambassador, was received twice at Hampton Court,[495] and an ambassador from Bethlem Gabor, 'the Prince of Transylvania,' also had an audience.[496] On 6 October Laud was appointed Dean of the Chapel Royal, and took the oath in the vestry of the chapel

at Hampton Court before the Lord Chamberlain.[497] Eventually the difficulties concerning Henrietta Maria's household arrived at such a pass that Richelieu sent the Marquis de Bassompierre to try to arrange a compromise. On Sunday, 11 October, he arrived at Hampton Court in one of the king's coaches. A splendid repast had been prepared for him, but neither he nor his suite would touch it. To enter into the details of his mission is not possible here; de Bassompierre acted with tact and discretion, but ineffectually,[498] and on 31 July 1626, after a final scene with the queen, Charles insisted on her French attendants being turned out of Whitehall. On 8 August they re-embarked for France.[499]

Charles continued to visit Hampton Court at intervals, and the Duke of Buckingham was constantly with the king there up to the time of his own assassination in 1628.[500] The usual court ceremonies, and the usual plays performed by the king's players, took place from time to time, and it is interesting to find two of Shakespeare's plays among them—the *Moore of Venice*, on 8 December 1636, and *Hamlet* on 24 January 1637.[501]

In June 1636 Strafford came to Hampton Court to 'kiss hands' on his appointment as Lord Deputy of Ireland.[502] In 1639 Charles caused the canal called the 'King's' or 'Longford' River to be cut for the supply of water to the palace;[503] he also interested himself in the gardens and in the decoration of the interior. The catalogue of his pictures was compiled by Vanderdoort in the same year, and he also attempted once more to make a 'chase' and inclose it with a wall; but, as before, the inhabitants objected so strongly to the encroachment on their lands and commons[504] that the scheme had to be given up; and political difficulties were thickening rapidly round the king so that he had little further time to devote to private or domestic interests. He was at Hampton Court in December 1641, when Parliament presented to him 'the Grand Remonstrance.'[505] He refused to answer it immediately, and Parliament caused the text of the declaration to be published at once, much to the king's annoyance. Three days later he entertained seven of the city aldermen at the palace, and knighted three of them in the hope of reviving personal loyalty to himself in the

[489] De Tillières, *Mémoires* (ed. 1863), 92; *Memoirs of Henrietta Maria*, 1671, p. 13.

[490] Charles seems at first to have made Buckingham his intermediary with the queen, and Buckingham's arrogance and insolence served to increase the difficulty. Charles's private letters to 'Steenie,' many of them dated from Hampton Court, show how determined they both were to get rid of the 'Monsers,' without much regard for Henrietta Maria's feelings or wishes. *Vide* letters in Hardwicke, *State Papers*, iii, 2, 3, 12, &c.; Ellis, *Orig. Letters*, iii, 224, &c.

[491] Letter from Mr. Mead to Sir Martin Stuteville, Oct. 1625; Sloane MSS. no. 4177, cit. Law, *Hist. Hampton Court Palace*, ii, 101.

[492] Rymer, *Foedera*, xviii, 198.

[493] Eventually he was given rooms 'next the river in the garden,' which were the same as those occupied by Queen Elizabeth as a state prisoner in the reign of Queen Mary; see p. 343. De Tillières, op. cit. pp. 88–150; Finett, *Philoxenis*, 166.

[494] Hardwicke, *State Papers*, iii, 6. The charges for the ambassador's household amounted in a month or two to over £2,000; S.P. Dom. Chas. I, ix, 54.

[495] Finett, *Philoxenis*, 181–5.

[496] Ibid. 187.

[497] Laud, *Diary*, 84.

[498] Disraeli, *Chas. I*; Finett, *Philoxenis*, 187–9; *De Bassompierre's Embassy to Engl. in 1626*, p. 37 (ed. Croker).

[499] Ibid. *Dict. Nat. Biog.* 'Charles I'; *Hist. MSS. Com. Rep.* xi, App. i, 24.

[500] A picture of George Villiers, 1st Duke of Buckingham, with his family, attributed to Honthorst, is at Hampton Court; Law, op. cit. ii, 119.

[501] Cunningham, *Revels at Court*, p. xxiv; S.P. Dom. Chas. I, ccclii, 55; Collier, *Annals of the Stage*, ii, 12.

[502] S.P. Dom. Chas. I, cccxxxvi, no. 11.

[503] Ibid. cccc, 70; ccccxli, 144; Lysons, *Midd. Par.*; also 'Enrolled Accounts' in the Record Office.

[504] Law, op. cit. ii, 125–6; see also p. 324.

[505] Husband, *Coll. of Remonstrances*, 24; Heath, *Chron. Civil Wars*, 25; Clarendon, *Hist. Rebellion*, 200 et seq.; Evelyn, *Diary*, App. 'Correspondence of Sir Edw. Nicholas and King Charles I'; Kennet, *Hist. Engl.* iii, 112.

City ;[506] but the time to remove difficulties by such means was past.

In January 1642 Charles made his untoward attempt to arrest 'the Five Members' in the House of Commons, and, alarmed by the menaces of Parliament and people, the king and queen, with their family, fled from London to Hampton Court, where their arrival was so unexpected that they and their three eldest children had to share one room.[507] This ill-judged flight led to the final breach between king and Parliament. It meant practically the surrender of London, with all its arsenals and stores, to the Parliamentary party. Colonel Lumsden, who had commanded the royal escort, realized the danger, rode on to Kingston with his squadron, and took possession of the magazine of arms in the town. Lord Digby drove over from Hampton Court the next morning to thank him for what he had done, and to suggest further measures. For this Lord Digby was afterwards attainted of treason for 'levying war,' and Lumsden was arrested by the Parliamentary party and sent to the Tower.[508]

On 12 January 1642 the king moved to Windsor for 'greater security,'[509] and only returned to the palace for one night, at the end of February, when the queen was on her way abroad, until he was brought back, five years later, as a prisoner.[510]

After the battle of Naseby, in 1645, Hampton Court had become the property of the state, seals were affixed to the doors of the state apartments, and Sir Robert Hadow gave orders for the destruction of the religious emblems in the chapel. All the pictures, the stained glass in the windows, and the altar-rails, were pulled down and destroyed.[510a]

Charles returned, as a prisoner, on 24 August 1647, and remained for about two months, receiving honourable and dignified treatment.[511] He dined in public in the 'Presence Chamber' as he had done formerly, and any gentlemen who wished to show their loyalty might attend and kiss his hand. John Evelyn, the diarist, was among them.[512] The king's old servants and faithful followers were allowed to confer with him ; Mr. John Ashburnham and Sir John Berkeley, though voted delinquents by Parliament, were permitted to return and to be constantly with the king.[513] He also had his own chaplains, and his two younger children, who were then with the Duke of Northumberland at Syon House, were brought over to see their father, and sometimes to stay with him. He also played at tennis and hunted in the parks,[514]

but the Parliamentary Commissioners were living in the palace, and a guard of soldiers, under a Parliamentary officer, Colonel Whalley, was kept in attendance.[515] The head quarters of the army was at Putney, and Cromwell, with other superior officers, came over to see the king. It was noticed that Fairfax kissed his hand, but Cromwell and his son-in-law, Ireton, though they expressed themselves in a loyal manner, declined the ceremony.[516] Charles's prospects really looked brighter than they had done for some time previously ; Cromwell had long conferences with him of a friendly nature, and he received Mrs. Cromwell very graciously.[517] One of the most interesting of the historical scenes of which Hampton Court has been the background is that of Charles and Cromwell walking together, in friendly converse, through the galleries or in the gardens of the palace.[518] It is generally thought that Cromwell at the time sincerely wished to come to terms with the king,[519] but Charles's fatal love of intrigue, and of what he considered 'king-craft,' entirely destroyed any prospect of compromise, and the Parliamentary officers gradually ceased to come to Hampton Court.[520]

Charles understood the difference in his position, and was warned that he was in danger of assassination while he remained in the palace.[521] He eventually withdrew the promise that he had made to Colonel Whalley not to attempt to escape.[522] Ashburnham was dismissed, and the guards were doubled, but in other ways the king was allowed the same liberty as before, and his daughter Elizabeth came to stay with him in October.[523] She complained of the noise made by the two sentinels stationed in the gallery into which her bedchamber, as well as that of the king, opened, perhaps in the hope that they might be removed ; but Colonel Whalley only gave stricter orders to the soldiers to move quietly, unless the king 'would renew his engagement' not to escape, but this Charles refused to do.[524] Ashburnham and Berkeley were chiefly concerned in arranging for the king's escape, which took place on 11 November, 1647.[525] On the day before, Whalley had shown him the letter from Cromwell, which has always been quoted to prove that Cromwell did not wish to prevent the king's escape, but meant to use it against him.[526] From Colonel Whalley's official narrative of the event read in the House of Commons, it appears that after showing Charles the letter Whalley withdrew, leaving the king to carry

[506] *S.P. Dom. Chas. I*, cccclxxvi, 29 ; Civil War Tracts, B.M. ; cit. Law, op. cit. ii, 127.

[507] Clarendon, *Hist. Rebellion*, v, 142–52 ; Whitelocke, *Mem.* 54 ; Gardiner, *Hist. Engl.*

[508] Heath, *Chron. Civil War*, 27 ; Clarendon, *Hist. Rebellion.*

[509] Disraeli, *Chas. I*, ii, 333.

[510] *S.P. Dom. Chas. I.* cccclxxxix, 19.

[510a] See Architecture, pp. 376–7.

[511] Whitelocke, *Memoirs*, 267 ; Hutchinson, *Memoirs*, 305 (ed. 1846) ; Sir Thomas Herbert, *Memoirs of the two last years of the reign of Chas. I*, 47, 48 ; *Hist. MSS. Com. Rep.* vii, App.

594, a list of plate 'for the service of his Majesty at Hampton Court,' 23 Sept. 1647.

[512] Evelyn, *Diary*, 10 Oct. 1647.

[513] Clarendon, op. cit. v, 470 ; Heath, *Chron. Civil Wars*, 147.

[514] Whitelocke, op. cit. 267 ; Sir Thomas Herbert, *Memoirs*, 49.

[515] *Hist. MSS. Com. Rep.* ix, App. ii, 394.

[516] Godwin, *Hist. Commonw.* ii, 395 ; Clarendon, *Hist. Rebellion*, iii, 52, 67.

[517] Herbert, *Memoirs*, 49.

[518] Law, op. cit. ii, 136.

[519] The army began to murmur at the conciliatory attitude of the generals.

An impeachment was even threatened against Cromwell ; Disraeli, *Chas. I*, ii, 497 ; *Memoirs of Col. Hutchinson*, 305.

[520] Clarendon, *Parl. Hist.* iii, 778 ; Ashburnham, *Narrative*, ii, 98.

[521] *Lady Fanshawe's Memoirs*, 66.

[522] 'Whalley's Narrative to the Speaker,' *House of Commons' Journ.* ; Ashburnham, *Narrative*, ii, 100.

[523] Ellis, *Orig. Letters* (Ser. 2), iii, 328.

[524] Law, *Hist. Hampton Court Palace*, ii, 141–2.

[525] Ashburnham, *Narrative*, ii, 111 ; Berkeley, *Memoirs*, ii, clxiv.

[526] Carlyle, *Cromwell* (ed. 1904), i, 285 ; Rushworth, *Hist. Coll.* vii, 871.

on his correspondence as usual, as it was mail-day. He waited till six o'clock 'without mistrust,' and then, as there seemed no sign of the king's appearance for the evening meal, and his door remained locked, Whalley spoke to the king's gentleman-in-waiting, who tried to reassure him, but at seven o'clock he became, according to his own account, 'extreme restless in my thoughts, lookt oft in at the key-hole to see whether I could perceive his Majesty, prest Mr. Maule to knock very oft—he still plainly told me he durst not disobey his Majesty's commands'—which were that he had important letters to write, and was not to be disturbed on any account.[527]

Meanwhile, in the early darkness of the November evening, Charles had already left the palace, with Colonel Legge, passing through the room called 'Paradise'[528] by the private passage spoken of as 'the vault,' to the river-side,[529] where he was met by Ashburnham and Berkeley, with horses, and so made good his escape.[530] It has never been satisfactorily decided whether they crossed the river at Thames Ditton, and went thence through West Molesey to Oatlands,[531] or whether they rode to Hampton and over Walton Bridge to Oatlands.[532] In the first report to the House of Commons, the Speaker said that 'the king went last night, with nine horses, over Kingston Bridge.'[533] Colonel Whalley became desperate at about eight o'clock, called Mr. Smithsby, the 'keeper of the Privy Lodgings,' and with him went by the back way, 'through the Privy Gardens to the Privy Stairs, where he had sentinels stationed.[534] . . .

We came to the next chamber to his Majesty's bed-chamber, where we saw his Majesty's cloak lying on the midst of the floor, which much amazed me.' Whalley then sent for the Parliamentary Commissioners to go with them, and the king's servant, Mr. Maule, went into the bed-chamber and declared that the king was not there. On his table were found three letters, one addressed to Colonel Whalley, one to the Parliamentary Commissioners, and one to both Houses of Parliament.[535] He assured Whalley that it was not Cromwell's letter which had caused him to take this step, but confessed that he was 'loath to be made a close prisoner under pretence of securing my life.' The rest of the letter is chiefly concerning the 'household stuffe and moveables,' which the king still looked upon as his own. It does not appear that he realized at all the extreme significance of the step he had taken. Whalley immediately sent out soldiers to search the lodges in the park, and Colonel Ashburnham's house at Ditton, and informed the generals at head quarters, then at Putney, of the occurrence. Cromwell rode over to Hampton Court at once,[536] and wrote to the Speaker of the House of Commons from the palace at twelve o'clock the same night. His letter, and that of the king, were laid before the House the next day. This was the last departure of Charles I from the palace.[537]

Immediately after the execution of the king a Bill was introduced into Parliament to provide for the sale of all the property of 'the late Charles Stuart.' This Bill was passed on 4 July 1649,[538]

[527] *Journ. of the House of Commons*, v, 356, &c. ; Reprinted in Peck, *Desiderata Curiosa*, ix, 374.

[528] See *ante*, p. 349.

[529] Ludlow, *Memcirs*, 92 ; Law, op. cit. ii, 147–57.

[530] There is an interesting story given by Mr. Law (*Hist. Hampton Court Palace*, ii, 147–9), of a book which was dropped by Charles in the mud while he was escaping from the palace. The volume in question, with the stains of mud on its leaves, is now in the Brit. Mus., no. 100 of the Thomason Collection of Royalist and Parliamentary tracts, known as the 'King's Tracts.'

[531] *Commons' Journ.* v, 356, &c. ; Clarendon, *Parl. Hist.* iii, 788 ; Heath, *Chron. of the Civil Wars*, 148. Sir Thomas Herbert, the king's groom of the bedchamber, says that 'they passed through a private door into the Park, where no Centinel was, and at Thames Ditton crossed the river' ; Herbert, *Memoirs*, 53.

[532] The account in a contemporary newspaper quoted by Mr. Law leads to this conclusion. *Mercurius Anti-Pragmaticus*, Thursday 11 Nov. to Thursday 18 Nov. 1647.

[533] Clarendon, *Parl. Hist.* iii, 788. Clarendon says that the king's escape was not discovered till the following morning, but this is evidently an error. For a graphic account of the escape, and a detailed comparison of different contemporary documents concerning it, *vide* Law, op. cit. ii, chap. xii. From Oatlands Charles and his party made

their way to the Isle of Wight, and by the time that the Commons heard Colonel Whalley's account of his escape he had already surrendered to Colonel Hammond, the governor of the island, and was once more a prisoner in Carisbrooke Castle.

[534] It is considered probable that the room from which Charles escaped was one of those still existing in the south-west part of the palace, overlooking the 'pond garden.'

[535] Rushworth, *Hist. Coll.* vii, 871.

[536] Rushworth, op. cit. vii, 871 ; *Commons' Journ.* v, 356. Cromwell's letter certainly conveys the impression that he was not unprepared for the event.

[537] A Royalist rising took place at Kingston-on-Thames under the Earl of Holland, while the king was still at Carisbrooke, in July 1648. Holland was joined by the Duke of Buckingham and his brother Lord Francis Villiers, and a force of about six hundred horse. They advanced towards Reigate, but were compelled to retreat to Kingston. In their last skirmish Francis Villiers was killed ; Whitelocke, *Memoirs*, 317, 318, 320 ; *Journ. of House of Lords*, 367 ; *Journ. of House of Commons*, 35 ; Aubrey, *Hist. Surrey*, i, 46 ; Law, op. cit. ii, 158 et seq. Mr. G. A. Sala, in his historical novel *Captain Dangerous*, introduced an episode setting forth that Lord Francis and a 'Mr. Grenville' had been taken prisoners and brought to Hampton Court, where they were shot in one of the courtyards. The

discovery in 1871 of two skeletons under the cloisters in the Fountain Court led to an idea that they might have been the bodies of these young cavaliers, but Mr. Sala himself disavowed any historical warrant for his story ; *The Times*, 4 Nov. et seq. 1871 ; *N. and Q.* Nov. 1871. Lord Francis's body was buried, after the Restoration, in Westminster Abbey. A story is told of the lady who occupied the apartments near to which these skeletons were found having been much disturbed by what she thought were ghostly or supernatural noises. She addressed a formal complaint to the Lord Chamberlain, who politely referred her to the Board of Works. The Board, it is said, refused to interfere, on the ground that 'the jurisdiction of the First Commissioner did not extend to the Spirit World, and that there were no funds at the disposal of the Board for any such purpose.' When the skeletons were discovered in Nov. 1871, and were afterwards buried at Hampton, the lady in question thoroughly believed that the mystery was solved. 'Of course these are the two wretched men who have been worrying me all these years, and the Board never found it out !' Law, op. cit. ii, 161–8. Who the men were, or why they were buried in that place, has never been discovered. It would be interesting to know if any burial-place or vaults connected with the chapel could have extended so far.

[538] Scobell, *Coll. of Acts and Ordinances*, 1649, ii, 46 et seq.

and a very full and ample inventory was made of all the furniture, plate, jewels, pictures, tapestries, &c., in Hampton Court Palace. The inventory is still preserved in the British Museum,[539] under the title 'Goods viewed and appraised at Hampton Court, in the custody of William Smithsbie, Esq., Wardrobe Keeper, 5 Oct. 1649.' The sum at which each entry was valued, and the price for which it was sold, are entered, together with the name of the purchaser. A certain number of the tapestries,[540] pictures, &c., were fortunately eventually kept 'for the use of the Lord Protector.' The sale lasted for nearly three years.[541]

A rough survey of the manor was also made in view of its being sold for 'the benefit of the Commonwealth.'[542] The palace was valued at £7,777 13s. 5d.[543] The total value of the manor, including the parks and other inclosures, was computed to be £10,765 19s. 9d.

The Council of State, however, concluded that Hampton Court, Whitehall, Westminster, and a few other places were 'to be kept for the public use of the Commonwealth.'[544]

In October 1651 Cromwell installed himself in the palace, but in November 1652 a Bill for the sale of the late king's houses and lands hitherto exempted was brought before Parliament, and it was resolved that Hampton Court, 'together with the Parks, the Harewarren and Meadows—with appurtenances—be sold for ready money.'[545] Further debates took place on the subject,[546] and it was even offered to Cromwell in exchange for 'New Hall' in Essex,[547] but at that time he refused the proposal, and the parks were put up for auction on 15 November 1653, the fee of the honour and manor having been previously sold.[548] Cromwell was proclaimed Lord Protector in December 1653, and immediately proceeded on behalf of the State to buy back the palace and surrounding property.[549] On 30 August 1654 Mr. Phelps,[550] to whom the manor had been sold, re-conveyed it to Cromwell; in 1657 the Lord Protector's name is entered in the Court Rolls as lord of the manor.[551]

Cromwell was constantly at Hampton Court

after this, and one of the early records of his time is concerning a Royalist plot to assassinate him on his way to or from London to the palace, frustrated by his receiving a timely warning and returning by another road.[552] He transacted affairs of state at Hampton Court, and the members of the council came down to him on such occasions as they had done during the late king's reign.[553] Mrs. Cromwell, the 'Lady Protectress' as she was sometimes called, seems to have attempted, somewhat awkwardly, to hold a sort of court in the palace. In a scurrilous pamphlet entitled The Court and Kitchen of Joan Cromwell her household and habits are commented on in no kindly spirit. It is said, among other accusations, that she had little labyrinths and trap-doors made for her, 'by which she might at all times, unseen, come unawares upon her servants, and keep them vigilant in their places.'[554] Occasionally, however, public entertainments had to take place, and some of the old state was revived, such as the Protector's bodyguard of halberdiers attending in the banqueting room, and the old court ceremonials being observed in bringing up the dishes to the table. On 25 July 1656 the Swedish ambassador dined and hunted with Cromwell at Hampton Court[555] quite in the old manner, but this return to ceremony was by no means relished even by his friends and supporters.[556] A curious picture of his familiar ways with his officers and ordinary associates is given by both Whitelocke and Heath. Heath says, 'His custom was now to divert himself frequently at Hampton Court . . . here he used to hunt . . . his own diet was very spare, and not so curious, except in publique Treatments, which were constantly given every Monday in the week to all the officers of the Army not below a Captain, where he dined with them and shewed them a hundred Antick Tricks, as throwing of cushions and putting live coals in their pockets and boots . . . he had twenty other tricks in his head.'[557] He was fond of music, and instruments of one kind or another were always played during his banquets at the palace. He also had two good organs put up in the Great Hall, on which no doubt his secretary, Milton,

[539] Harl. MSS. no. 4898, fol. 238. If not the original list it is a contemporary copy, and consists of a very large volume of nearly 1,000 pages. The Hampton Court list fills about seventy-six pages.
[540] Law, op. cit. 278–90.
[541] Ibid. ii, 165–6.
[542] P.R.O. Midd. no. 32 dated 1649. Printed in Law, op. cit. App. 258 et seq. It was afterwards elaborated into a more detailed account, and completed in April 1653.
[543] For the acreage and valuation of the parks, see account of Parks and Gardens, pp. 380–8.
[544] Ludlow, Memoirs, 329; S.P. Dom. Commonw. i, 29; ii, 91, May and August 1649.
[545] Journ. of House of Commons, 1652.
[546] S.P. Dom. Chas. I, cxiv, 18; Scobell, Acts and Ordinances of Parl. ii, 227; Lysons, Midd. Parishes, 65; Journ. of House of Commons, 307.

[547] New Hall, an estate belonging to the Duke of Buckingham, had been sequestrated by the Parliament and bought by Cromwell in April 1651; Clarendon, Parl. Hist. xx, 223; Morant, Hist. Essex, ii, 15; Bruton, Diary, i, p. xi; Journ. of House of Commons.
[548] See descent of the manor, p. 326.
[549] Cal. S.P. Dom. Commonw. 1652–3, p. 405; 1653–4, pp. 299–300, 363, 385, 396, 408–9.
[550] Ibid. 'Warrants of the Protector and Council.'
[551] Ct. R. P.R.O.; S.P. Dom. Commonw. lxvii, 88.
[552] Cromwelliana, 144; Thurloe, State Papers, ii, 248. Cromwell generally wore a coat of mail under his other clothes, so much did he consider himself always in danger of such attempts; ibid. i, 708.
[553] Perfect Proceedings, no. 300, cit. Law, op. cit. ii, 175.
[554] Noble, Memoirs of the Cromwells,

i, 127–30 et seq. Even her moral character was assailed by those pitiless writers.
[555] Whitelocke, Mem. 649.
[556] Ibid. 656; Heath, Flagellum, 164.
[557] Heath, loc. cit. Cromwell seems to have had some appreciation of art, and kept Mantegna's great cartoons in the 'Long Gallery,' near his own rooms; it is to him that the preservation of any pictures and tapestries at this time is owing. There is no proof that he actually bought the great quantity of furniture and fittings which had originally belonged to the palace, and which was claimed by his family as private property at his death. He probably merely took possession of what he found there. The inventory of the goods thus claimed by the Cromwells is among S.P. Dom. Commonw. vol. ciii, 41. Printed in full in Law, Hist. Hampton Court Palace ii, App. C.

used to play.[558]   There is also record of sermons preached before him in the chapel, where the rich ornamentation of the Tudor roof of Henry VIII must have been strangely out of keeping with the severity of the Puritan preaching.[559]   Cromwell's third daughter Mary was married to Lord Falconbridge in the chapel on 17 November 1657. This public marriage was solemnized by one of Cromwell's chaplains, in accordance with the rite accepted by the Puritans, but they also seem to have been married privately on the same day by Dr. Hewitt, with the Church of England ceremonial, partly to please Mary Cromwell, who was still a member of the Church, and partly no doubt that there should be no question of the validity of the marriage in the event of a Restoration.[560] Cromwell always seems to have amused himself on such occasions with the 'anticks and tricks' mentioned by Heath.[561]

The accounts of conspiracies and plots against the 'Lord Protector's' life read like the records of a modern anarchist society.   In 1657 it was actually proposed that he should be blown up by a sort of 'infernal machine' at Hammersmith, on his way to Hampton Court.   The Duke of York, writing to Charles II, says calmly that the plan was 'better laid and resolved on than any he had known of the kind.'[562]   In the same year a Captain Thomas Gardiner was also 'taken in the gallery at Hampton Court with two loaded pistols and a dagger.'   Such discoveries naturally had some effect on Cromwell, and Heath says he was always 'shifting and changing his lodging, to which he passed through several locks; when he went between Whitehall and Hampton Court he passed by private and back ways, but never the same way backward and forward; he was always in a hurry, his guards behind and before riding at full gallop, and the coach always filled with armed persons, he himself being furnished with private weapons.'[563] He seems to have felt himself safer at Hampton Court than in London, and was constantly there with his children and grandchildren, to all of whom apartments in the palace were assigned.[564] Only one of his sons-in-law, Fleetwood, who lived near Hampton Court, was avowedly Republican, and refused to allow his wife to visit her father.[565] Cromwell's favourite daughter was Elizabeth Claypole, and she died at Hampton Court, after a short illness, on 6 August 1658,[566] to the inconsolable grief of her father.   Dr. Bates, Cromwell's physician, who attended her, testifies to her great distress and agony of mind, and declares that on her death-bed she implored her father to make atonement for his disloyalty by taking steps to ensure the restoration of the king.[567]   Her body was taken by water to London and buried among the kings and queens in Westminster Abbey.

A week after her death Cromwell himself was dangerously ill,[568] and though he recovered sufficiently to ride in the park on 17 August, George Fox, who came to the palace to present a petition on behalf of the Quakers, says that 'he looked like a dead man.'[569]   He shortly afterwards again visited Cromwell, but found that he had become too ill to see anyone.[570]   On 24 August he was confined to his room; the doctors evidently thought that he was dying,[571] and 'a public fast was ordered for his sake and kept at Hampton Court';[572] but two days later he was well enough to receive Whitelocke, who dined with him.[573]   However, the improvement did not continue, and he was removed to Whitehall,[574] where he died on 2 September 1658, the eve of his 'fortunate day,' the anniversary of the battles of Worcester and Dunbar.[575]

Richard Cromwell probably desired to keep Hampton Court as his private property; the Cromwell family certainly endeavoured to take possession of some of the contents, and an inventory [576] was immediately made by the Parliamentary Commissioners, who did not acknowledge Mrs. Cromwell's claim.[577]   Richard Cromwell was also ordered not to kill deer in the parks.[578]   A resolution was once more passed in the House of Commons for the sale of Hampton Court and other royal manors and parks,[579] but Ludlow seems to have considered the place 'very convenient for the retirement of those in public affairs, when they should be indisposed in the summer season,'[580] and he was successful in preventing the sale.   In February 1660 a Bill was introduced in the 'Long Parliament' to settle Hampton Court on Monk, the Parliamentary General,[581] but he looked on it as a bribe, and induced his friends to have the Bill rejected.   On 15 March 1660 a sum of £20,000 was voted to him, together with the custody and stewardship of Hampton Court Manor and Park for his life,[582] an

[558] Hawkins, *Hist. of Music*, iv 44; Noble, op. cit. i, 314; Thurloe, *State Papers*, 12 Apr. 1654; 'Inventory of Cromwell's Goods,' *Gent. Mag.* 1877, p. 753. One of the organs is said to have been brought from Magdalen College, Oxford. It was returned to the authorities there at the Restoration, and is now at Tewkesbury Abbey; S.P. Dom. Chas. II, xi, 57; Law, op. cit. ii, 183–4.

[559] There is a copy of one such sermon in the Ashmolean Museum, no. 826, 2544; *vide* Law, op. cit. ii, 184.

[560] Noble, *Memoirs of the Cromwells*, i, 143–4.

[561] Ibid. 155; *Cromwelliana*, 169.

[562] *Cromwelliana*, 160; Thurloe, *State Papers*, ii, 666.

[563] Heath, *Flagellum*, 193.

[564] Noble, op. cit. ii, 155; *Cromwelliana*, 174.

[565] Bates, *Elenchus Motuum Nuperorum in Anglia*, Pars Secunda (ed. 1676), 327.

[566] Thurloe, *State Papers*, vii.

[567] Bates, op. cit. 327; *Mercurius Politicus*, cit. Whitelocke, *Mem.* 674.

[568] Thurloe, *State Papers*, vii, 320, 340.

[569] G. Fox, *Journ.* 127 (ed. 3, 1765).

[570] Sewel, *Hist. of the Quakers*, i, 242.

[571] Bates, op. cit. (pt. 2), 275; Thurloe, *State Papers*, vii, 367, 376.

[572] Echard, *Hist.* 824.

[573] Whitelocke, *Mem.* 674.

[574] Thurloe, op. cit. vii, 355.

[575] Ibid. 373; Peck, *Cromwell*, 39.

[576] See p. 354; Harl. MSS. no. 4898, fol. 238; *Cal. S.P. Dom. Commonw.* 1658–9, p. 380.

[577] *Parl. Intelligencer*, 7, 14 May 1660; *Mercurius Politicus*, 10, 17 May 1660; cit. Law, op. cit. ii, 199, n. 1.

[578] *Cal. S.P. Dom. Commonw.* 1658–9, p. 367.

[579] *Journals of the House of Commons*, Oct. 1659.

[580] Ludlow, *Memoirs*, 286 (ed. 1771).

[581] White Kennet, *Hist. of Engl.* 67; *Public Intelligencer*, 25 Feb. 1660, no. 6; Philips, *Chas. II*, 714.

[582] *Hist. MSS. Com. Rep.* vii, App. i, 463; *Journ. of House of Commons*, 15–16 Mar. 1660; *Cal. Treas. Bks.* i, 461, 659.

office in which he was confirmed by Charles II almost immediately after his restoration.[583]

Charles II made a great many alterations in the palace,[584] and frequently went backwards and forwards between Hampton Court and Whitehall, riding down early in the morning to play tennis, and returning the same day.[585] From 1662 to 1667 many applications for offices about Hampton Court were made to the Crown. The 'Housekeeper of Hampton Court,' the 'Keeper of the Standing Wardrobe,' 'Keeper of the Still House,' 'Keeper of the Game about Hampton Court,' are a few of the coveted titles.[585] One claimant, Clement Kynnersley, Yeoman of the Wardrobe of Beds, seems to have been afraid that his services would not be sufficiently appreciated. He not only claimed £7,000 for 'arrears of salary,' but declared that 'he had, by his exertions, preserved £500,000 worth of His Majesty's goods together at Hampton Court from sale and embezzlement.'[587] Edward Progers, Groom of the Bedchamber to the king, received a great many of these appointments, chiefly of privileges granted in and about Hampton Court. He rebuilt the Upper Lodge in Bushey Park, spent £4,000 on it,[585] and had some difficulty in getting a warrant for the payment of the amount.[589] De Grammont declares plainly what the extremely equivocal services were for which he was thus rewarded by the 'Merry Monarch.'[590]

The marriage of the king and Catherine of Braganza took place at Portsmouth on 21 May 1662,[591] and they arrived at Hampton Court on the 29th.[592] Their progress, judging from the contemporary etchings by Dirk Stoop, must have been stately and dignified. They probably alighted at the foot of the Great Hall Stairs under Anne Boleyn's Gateway, and in the Great Hall itself were received by the Lord Chancellor Clarendon,[593] the Lord Treasurer, and the Councillors of State.

In the Presence Chamber they were met by the foreign ministers, the peers, and the lords and ladies of the court, who came to do homage to the new queen.[594] The Duchess of York also came by barge from London, and was received at the 'Privy Garden Gate' by the king himself.[595] Two days after, John Evelyn the diarist records that he was taken by the Duke of Ormonde to be presented to the queen, and saw her dining in public.[596]

Like Henrietta Maria before her, and in the same place, Catherine suffered on account of her retinue, who were quite unable to adapt themselves to their gay surroundings,[597] and were described by de Grammont as 'six frights . . . and a Duenna, another Monster.'[598]

At first, however, the king and queen amused themselves with entertainments out of doors, balls, plays and music indoors. Evelyn gives an account of their going on the river in a gondola, a present from the state of Venice, and on another occasion mentions 'the Queen's Portugal music, consisting of fifes, harps, and very ill voices.' He also describes the queen's bed, 'of embroidery of silver on crimson velvet, and cost £8,000—a present from the States of Holland . . . and the great looking-glass and toilet of beaten and massive gold given by the Queen-Mother. The Queen also brought over with her from Portugal such Indian cabinets as had never been seen here.'[599] Pepys was also much struck by the 'noble furniture.'[600] His diary and other records are full of gossip concerning occurrences at Hampton Court,[601] and he expressed the discontent of the people at the length of time during which 'the King and new Queen minded their pleasures at Hampton Court.'[602] As it happened in the palace it is necessary to mention the insult Charles was weak enough to offer the queen, by unexpectedly bringing the notorious Lady Castlemaine into her presence before the whole court.[603] The scene ended in the utmost confusion, for the queen fainted, and afterwards maintained her absolute refusal to receive Lady Castlemaine. Clarendon has described all that followed,[604] and to his own dishonour was persuaded by the king to use his influence with the queen, not only to receive Barbara Palmer, but to make her a Lady of the Bedchamber. For some time Catherine persisted in her refusal, and Clarendon says that 'Everyone was glad . . . they were still at Hampton Court and that there were so few witnesses of all that passed. The Queen sat melancholic in her chamber in tears, except when she drove them away by a more violent passion in choleric discourse ; and the king sought his diver-

[583] *Cal. S.P. Dom. Chas. II*, 1660–1, p. 174.
[584] The accounts for these alterations may be seen in Harl. MSS. no. 1618, 1656, 1657, and 1658, Dec. 1663, printed in Law, op. cit. App. D ; S.P. Dom. Chas. II. lxi ; *Cal. Treas. Bks.* i, 1660–7.
[585] *Hist. MSS. Com. Rep.* v, App. 168 (8) ; Marshall, *Annals of Tennis*, 89 ; Pepys, *Diary*, 4 Jan. 1664 ; see also account of Gardens, pp. 380 et seq.
[586] S.P. Dom. Chas. II, cxxxvii, 145 ; clxxxviii, 69, &c. [587] Ibid. xxii, 171.
[588] He was appointed Keeper of the Middle or North Park in reversion after the Duke of Albemarle ; *Hist. MSS. Com. Rep.* xv, App. ii, 304.
[589] S.P. Dom. Chas. II, lxxxvi, 78 ; cii, 27 ; cv, 125.
[590] De Grammont, *Memoirs*, 217 (ed. 1906), 231 n.

[591] *Cal. Treas. Bks.* i, 376.
[592] Heath, *Chron.* 509 ; Echard, *Hist. Engl.* iii, 8. There is a series of seven plates by Stoop, a Dutch engraver, illustrating Catherine of Braganza's progress from Lisbon to Hampton Court and London. A set of these etchings is in the Sheepshanks Collection at the Brit. Mus.
[593] From Lord Sandwich's journal it seems possible that Lord Clarendon was prevented from being present.
[594] *Journ. of Lord Sandwich* ; White Kennet, *Hist. Engl.* (ed. 1728), 699 ; *Memoirs of Lady Fanshawe*, 144 et seq.
[595] Strickland, *Life of Catherine of Braganza* (ed. 1851), v, 520–1. Miss Strickland had access to unpublished Portuguese documents.
[596] *Diary*, 31 May 1662.
[597] Clarendon, *Autobiography* (ed. 1760), ii, 80 ; Law, op. cit. ii, 212 et

seq.; Strickland, *Lives of the Queens of Engl.* (ed. 1851), v, 537–8.
[598] De Grammont, op. cit. 109.
[599] Evelyn, *Diary*, 9 June 1662. There are some Indian cabinets still in the state apartments, but whether they were Queen Catherine's is not known.
[600] *Diary*, 12 May 1662.
[601] Ibid. 22 June 1662, &c.; Estcourt & Payne, *Engl. Catholic Non-jurors of 1715*, p. 342.
[602] Note at end of diary for June.
[603] Barbara Villiers married Roger Palmer, who became Earl of Castlemaine. She was created Duchess of Cleveland by Chas. II.
[604] *Autobiography*, ii, 80–6; *Letters of Philip, second Lord Chesterfield*, 122 ; *Secret Hist. of Chas. II*, i, 447. See letter from Charles to Clarendon, dated at Hampton Court.

tisements in that company that said and did all things to please him.' Catherine's Portuguese attendants were sent away; she was told, not truly, that her dowry was in arrears; and the Portuguese ambassador was 'so grossly insulted that he left Hampton Court and retired to his own house in the city.' Lady Castlemaine had apartments assigned to her in the palace, and received greater homage than the queen herself. At last the pressure brought to bear on Catherine had its effect, and she yielded to the king's wishes; Clarendon being the first to blame her for the 'downfall' he himself had been instrumental in bringing to pass.[605]

On 28 July the king and queen went to meet Henrietta Maria at Greenwich, and on their return to Hampton Court supped together in public that their reconciliation might be understood.[606] Two days later the queen mother arrived at the palace, which she had not visited since the fatal flight from London in 1642.[607] She alighted at the foot of the stairs leading to the Great Hall, where she was received by the queen, and they sat together in the Presence Chamber, under the 'Cloth of State.' The king and the Duke of York had to act as interpreters, for Catherine could not speak French, nor Henrietta Spanish or Portuguese.[608] She shortly afterwards returned to Greenwich, but Charles and Catherine remained at Hampton Court till 23 August, when they made their state entry into London by river.[609] Pepys and Evelyn both describe the scene of the journey, the number of spectators, the barges and boats that covered the river, the splendid reception given to the king and queen.[610] It can hardly be hoped that all this magnificence was much comfort to Catherine; from that time forward a suite of apartments was always kept for Lady Castlemaine at the palace, and in 1666 was fitted up again for her.[611]

Several distinguished travellers who visited England at this time have left records of their impressions of Hampton Court, among them the Duc de Monconys and M. de la Molière, in 1663.[612]

In 1665 the king and queen were at the palace, in quarantine from the plague, the deaths in London amounting to 267 a week.[613] They remained at Hampton Court for a month, the king transacting business with the council at Syon House, probably that they might not come to the palace from London.[614] Pepys gives an entertaining account of his being at Hampton Court on 23 July, 'where I followed the king to chapel and there heard a good sermon.' He was distressed because no one invited him to dinner, but was eventually entertained by Mr. Marriott the housekeeper, in whose house he found 'good dinner and good company, amongst others Mr. Lilly the painter.'[615]

On 26 July the king and queen went by river to Greenwich, and thence proceeded to Salisbury and afterwards to Oxford, where Parliament had been summoned to meet on account of the plague in London. In January of the following year it was thought safe for the king to return to London; he stayed at Hampton Court for a week; Pepys and Evelyn record their visits to him there.[616] The queen also stayed there for a couple of days on her way back from Oxford in February.[617] In September 1666, at the time of the Great Fire of London, many of the king's valuables were sent by water to Hampton Court for safety.[618]

Towards the end of his reign Charles was not often at the palace, but he sometimes came down to play tennis, or for stag-hunting,[619] and he retired there with the Duke of York in August 1669, when they received news of the death of their mother, Queen Henrietta Maria.[620] There is also an account of a council held in the palace in June 1679, when Charles, to the dismay of the majority of those present, ordered the Chancellor to prepare a proclamation for the dissolution of the Parliament then sitting, and a writ for calling together a new one.[621] At another council in the palace on 23 May 1681 an order was issued by Charles forbidding 'the king's servants to frequent the company of the Duke of Monmouth,' whose conduct had become so overbearing as to excite the displeasure even of his father.[622]

Charles never stayed at Hampton Court for any length of time after 1666, though he continued to pay short visits and to hold councils there.[623] Concerning one of these visits a story is told by Walpole of the reckless extravagance of Verrio the painter, who had done much work in the palace, and had received large sums from Charles, which did not prevent him from constantly asking for more. On one occasion at Hampton Court, when he had but lately received an advance of £1,000, he found the king in such a circle that he could not approach him. He called out: 'Sire, I desire the favour

[605] Law, op. cit. ii, 230-9.
[606] Ibid. 'Unedited Portuguese Records,' trans. Adamson, cit. Strickland, op. cit. v, 536-7; Hist. Casa Real Portuguesa, cit. Law, op. cit. ii, 239.
[607] After the attempted arrest of the 'Five Members,' see p. 352.
[608] Strickland, op. cit. v, 537.
[609] Echard, Hist. iii, 84; Evelyn, Diary, 24 Aug. 1662; John Tatham, Aqua Triumphalis (1662).
[610] Evelyn, Diary, 24 Aug. 1662; Pepys, Diary, 24 Aug. 1662.
[611] Harl. MSS. no. 1658, fol. 138, Feb. 1666.
[612] De Monconys, Voyage d'Angleterre.

[613] Pepys, Diary, 29 June 1665; Clarendon, Autobiography, ii, 403.
[614] Evelyn, Diary, 7 July 1665; Pepys, Diary, 24 July 1665.
[615] Pepys, Diary, 24 July 1665. It was about this time that Lely, commissioned by the Duchess of York, painted all the beauties of the court. These portraits now hang all together in the 'King's Bedchamber' at Hampton Court. They were for some time at Windsor.
[616] Pepys, Diary, 28 Jan. 1665-6; Evelyn, Diary; S.P. Dom. Chas. II, cxlviii, 38.
[617] S.P. Dom. Chas. II, cxlviii, 38.
[618] Antiq. Repository, ii, 154.
[619] Magalotti, Travels of Cosmo III,

Duke of Tuscany (ed. 1821), 208; Hist. MSS. Com. Rep. xiii, App. vi, 263. ('Lord Anglesey's Diary.')
[620] Mem. of Henrietta Maria (ed. 1671), 89.
[621] Diary of Henry Sidney, 21; Hist. MSS. Com. Rep. vii, App. 473; Temple, Works, ii, 511-12. The House of Commons thus summarily dismissed had passed a Bill excluding the Duke of York from the succession, and was further proceeding to inquire into the 'bribery and corruption' which existed among members of Parliament.
[622] Reresby, Memoirs, 264.
[623] Hist. MSS. Com. Rep. vii, App. 352b, 363a, 405b, 410a; ibid. xii, App. viii, 160.

of speaking to your majesty.' 'Well, Verrio,' said the king, 'what is your request?' 'Money, sir, money; I am so short of cash that I am not able to pay my workmen; and your majesty and I have learnt by experience that pedlars and painters cannot give long credit.' The king smiled, and said he had but lately ordered him £1,000. 'Yes, sir,' replied he, 'but that was soon paid away, and I have no gold left.' 'At that rate,' said the king, 'you would spend more than I do, to maintain my family.' 'True,' answered Verrio, 'but does your majesty keep an open table as I do?' [624]

James II never appears to have lived at Hampton Court during his reign, though he held a council there on 29 May 1687, when 'the militia was put down, and the licensing of ale-houses was put in other hands than the justices of the peace.' [625] He was, however, often at Hounslow, where he encamped in 1687 with an army of 16,000 men, a force which apparently only met with derision. [626]

The reign of William and Mary opens a new era in the history of Hampton Court Palace, as under their auspices more than half the original Tudor building was pulled down. Wren's new palace was erected, and the whole place assumed very much the appearance it has now. [627] The quietness of the situation, the distance from London, and perhaps something congenial to William's Dutch taste in the formal lines of the avenues and the long canal, formed no doubt part of the attraction which the place evidently had for him. Mary has never been given credit for any feelings of sympathy for her father, and has often been censured for her apparent heartlessness, but perhaps one reason for her affection for Hampton Court was that James II had never lived there as king, and she could have had no memories of the place connected with him. From the beginning of their reign Mary and her husband paid frequent short visits to the palace, [628] and one of William's first acts was to offend the religious susceptibilities of a large proportion of his subjects by refusing to continue the ancient custom of 'touching for the king's evil,' a practice which he had the blunt common-sense to denounce as a 'silly superstition.' [629] At Easter as usual a crowd

of diseased folk arrived at the palace, but had to be content with the customary dole and no ceremony. [630]

William seems to have decided at once that the old palace was inconvenient and ill-arranged. Queen Mary wrote to a friend in Holland that it had been much neglected, [631] and almost immediately after their first visit Christopher Wren was appointed architect and the works began. [632] Wren's building will be dealt with in another place, [633] but while plans and elevations were being prepared, and the work of demolition had actually begun, the king and queen still passed a great deal of time in the palace. On 31 March 1689 they publicly received the sacrament in the chapel from the Archbishop of York, in preparation for their coronation at Westminster on 11 April. [634] They soon afterwards returned to Hampton Court, and the Princess Anne joined them there. [635] The routine of their life was sufficiently simple; Queen Mary superintended everything herself, inspecting the building and the gardens, making fringe, and playing 'Bassett.' [636] In May a declaration of war with France was issued from Hampton Court, and during that month the king and Prince George of Denmark went from the palace to inspect the fleet at Portsmouth. [637] The king hunted in the parks, and occupied himself during the first summer by visiting the camp formed on Hounslow Heath on 13 August. He rode over from Hampton Court to review the troops there on 17 August. [638]

An alarm was caused in July by intelligence of a supposed plot to attempt the king's life, to set fire to Whitehall and other places in London, and to seize the Tower. [639] Several companies of foot and horse were kept under arms all night round the palace, the guards were doubled, and stringent measures taken to prevent the entry of suspicious persons, but nothing further seems to have happened. The king, however, remained constantly at Hampton Court, and the life of the court was so quiet as to cause great dissatisfaction among the people. [640] Lord Halifax took upon himself to inform William that 'his inaccessibleness and living so at Hampton Court altogether, and at so active a time, ruined all business,' and remonstrated with him on the loss of time caused to the ministers, who took five hours to come and go. The king

---

[624] Horace Walpole, *Anecdotes of Painting* (ed. 1849), ii, 470.

[625] *Hist. MS. Com. Rep.* vii, App. 504.

[626] *Antiq. Repert.* i, 230.

[627] Certain alterations, notably in the clock court in the reign of George II, took place at a later date, but the main features are practically the same as they were left by Wren.

[628] Luttrell, *Relation of State Affairs*, i; *Diary of Henry, Earl of Clarendon* (ed. 1828), ii, 267; *Conduct of the Duchess of Marlborough* (ed. 1742), 115; Evelyn, *Diary*, Mar. 1689.

[629] Macaulay, *Hist. Engl.* chap. xiv, quoting *Athenian Mercury*, 16 Jan. 1691; *Paris Gazette*, 23 Apr. 1691.

[630] Queen Anne afterwards 'touched,' Samuel Johnson among others, for the

'King's Evil,' but the practice fell into disuse, and was not revived by the House of Hanover; *Cal. Treas. Papers,* 1702–7, p. 142; *Hist. MSS. Com. Rep.* 'Wentworth Papers,' 359, 375.

[631] *Lettres de Marie, Reine d'Angleterre* (ed. Countess M. van Bentinck), 116.

[632] Aud. Off. Declared Accts. (P.R.O.) bdle. 2482, R. 294; Wren, *Parentalia* (ed. 1750), 326; *Hist. MSS. Com. Rep.* xiv, App. ii, 431.

[633] See account of architecture, p. 377 et seq.

[634] Luttrell, op. cit. i, 520; Lamberty, *Mémoires de la Dernière Révolution en Angleterre*, ii, 235. The queen suppressed the fiddlers and other musicians who used to play in the chapel. William adhered to the Dutch custom of wearing his hat in church.

[635] She had her own suite of apartments, but William treated her with scant courtesy, refusing to pay her allowance and acting inconsiderately in other ways; Aud. Off. Accts. (P.R.O.) bdle. 2448, R. 122, Apr. 1688, Mar. 1689; Lamberty, op. cit. ii, 468; *vide* also *Conduct of the Duchess of Marlborough* (ed. 1742), 24–30, 33–5.

[636] Ibid. 115.

[637] Luttrell, op. cit. i, 533; *Lond. Gaz.* 17 May 1689, cit. Law, op. cit. iii, 9; Lamberty, op. cit. ii, 385.

[638] Luttrell, op. cit. i, 570–1.

[639] Ibid. 561; Lamberty, op. cit. ii, 512; *Hist. MSS. Com. Rep.* xii, App. vii, 252, 'Newsletter, 23 July 1689.'

[640] Burnet, *Hist. of His Own Times,* ii, 2.

answered, peevishly, 'Do you wish me dead?'[641] The 'Bill of Rights' was being debated at the time, and no doubt William's presence in London was highly desirable. The vexed question of the succession was for the moment set at rest by the birth at Hampton Court, on 24 July, of the Princess Anne's son, William Henry, afterwards known as Duke of Gloucester. He was baptized in the chapel on the evening of Saturday, 28 July, just a hundred and fifty years after the last christening there of an heir to the throne,[642] and from the first seems to have been a very weakly child.[643] The usual routine of the court was observed; William's adherents were knighted, and the ambassadors were received. On 29 August, George Walker, the hero of the defence of Londonderry, was given an audience by the king and queen, who made him a present of £5,000.[644]

troller,'[645] and the queen wrote constantly to the king during his absences in Ireland and Holland, complaining of the delays caused by 'want of money and Portland stone.'[645a] Pending the completion of the new state apartments Mary installed herself in the building known as the 'Water Gallery,' where Queen Elizabeth had been lodged as a State prisoner,[646] and it is recorded that Mary made of it 'the pleasantest little thing within doors that could possibly be made, with all the little neat curious things that suited her conveniences.'[647] The interior was decorated for her by Wren in the style that appears in his state apartments, with painted ceilings and panels, carved doorways and cornices,[648] oak dados, hangings of tapestry, and the characteristic corner fire-places with diminishing shelves in tiers above them. Mary first introduced the taste for 'blue and

HAMPTON COURT PALACE : WILLIAM THE THIRD'S BUILDINGS FROM THE SOUTH-EAST

The history of the palace during this reign is chiefly the history of the new building, which absorbed all attention when William and Mary were there. Quarrels occasionally arose between Wren, the 'surveyor,' and Talman, the 'comp-

white' oriental china into England; many of her quaint specimens are still to be seen in the palace. She had James Bogdane, a fashionable painter of animals, to decorate the 'Looking Glass Closett' for her;[649] she also had a 'Marble Closett,' finely

[641] Renesby, *Memoirs*, 5 May 1689 (?). William's reserved and somewhat morose temperament added to the general feeling of dissatisfaction; *Dict. Nat. Biog.*; Evelyn, *Diary*, 29 Jan. 1689.

[642] The Duke of Gloucester's untimely death was perhaps the origin of the superstition concerning Mrs. Penn. See p. 340.

[643] Jenkin Lewis, *Queen Anne's Son* (ed. 1881), 14.

[644] George Walker (1618–90), governor of Londonderry, defended that town against the Jacobites at the end of 1688. He was killed at the Battle of the Boyne in 1690; Macaulay, *Hist. of Engl.* chap. x; Luttrell, *Relation of Affairs of State*, i, 575; *Dict. Nat. Biog.* 'George Walker'; *Hist. MSS. Com. Rep.* xii, App. vii, 252.

[645] *Cal. Treas. Papers*, vi, no. 37; Aud. Off. Declared Accts. bdle. 2443, R. 124.

[645a] Dalrymple, *Memoirs*, pt. ii, App. 139; Aud. Off. Declared Accts. bdle. 2482, R. 295. The account from 1 Apr. 1689 to 31 Mar. 1691 reached the sum of £54,484.

[646] See below, p. 343.

[647] Defoe, *Tour through Gt. Britain* (ed. 1738), i, 245.

[648] Sometimes carved most exquisitely by Grinling Gibbons in limewood.

[649] Aud. Off. Declared Accts. bdle. 2482, R. 297.

painted, and a ' Bathing Closett ' fitted with a white marble bath.[650] She also had a dairy in which she took much pleasure.[651] There is something very modern in the picture of her life thus presented. Her chief employments were her constant consultations with Wren,[652] who seems to have found her taste excellent, about the building, superintending the garden, making her botanical collection,[653] and working with her needle. Burnet says 'she wrought with her own hands—sometimes with so constant a diligence, as if she had been to earn her bread by it.'[654] Specimens of her needlework remained in the palace up to a comparatively recent date.[655] The queen, inspired no doubt by Lely's paintings of the beauties of the court of Charles II, also started making a gallery of portraits of the ladies of her own court, painted by Sir Godfrey Kneller.[656] When the ' Water Gallery ' building was destroyed after Queen Mary's death, because it spoilt the view from the windows of the new palace, these pictures were placed in a room under the king's guard-chamber, known thenceforth as the ' Beauty Room,' and sometimes used by William as a private dining-room.[657] They are now in William the Third's ' Presence Chamber,' with other examples of Kneller's work.[658]

In 1690 William commanded the army in Ireland during the summer, and in 1691–4 he was absent for summer campaigns in the Netherlands.[659] During these numerous absences Mary was appointed regent, and affairs of State kept her chiefly in London, but she wrote constantly to report the progress of the new building at Hampton Court to the king.[660] The expenses of the war made it difficult to obtain sufficient funds from the Treasury to carry on the work, and Mary wrote on 12 July 1690 that the deficit had become 'so just a debt that it ought to be paid.'[661] Wren, in the *Parentalia*, says that the ' two royal apartments ' were not finished till 1694, shortly before Mary's death;[662] they were sufficiently advanced when the king and queen visited them on 30 December 1691 for their magnificence to be fully appreciated,[663] but Mary never occupied the apartments in which she had taken such keen

interest,[664] and William's final alterations and improvements were not finished till twelve years later. The king's pleasure in the place was much diminished by the loss of his wife, and for some years the work languished,[665] until, in January 1698, the palace of Whitehall was burnt down, and William once more turned his attention to the completion of Hampton Court.[666] He never attempted to rebuild Whitehall.[667]

In 1695 Sir Christopher Wren, who had become Grand Master of the Freemasons, initiated William into the mysteries of the order, and the king often presided over a lodge at Hampton Court during the completion of the building.[668] His apartments were finished and furnished in the style of stately if somewhat heavy splendour characteristic of the period towards the end of 1699; on 17 November he came down to stay for five days,[669] and a further estimate for furnishing and decorating the rooms not included before was laid before him.[670] It may be noted that the ' Queen's State Rooms ' were not decorated at all during this reign.

William returned to the palace directly after the House had risen for Christmas, ' to divert himself during the holydays,'[671] and refused an audience to the French Ambassador, the Comte de Tallard, on the plea that he ' could not be troubled with business at Hampton Court.'[672] His diversions did not include the long series of balls, banquets and masques which would have taken place in Tudor or Stuart days. He disliked display and ceremonial,[673] but enjoyed superintending the alterations and improvements in the building, and his only other amusement seems to have been hunting or coursing in the parks. On 5 January he returned to town.[674]

Early in 1700 William was at Hampton Court again, just after what he termed ' the most dismal session ' he had ever experienced.[675] He had given a reluctant consent to the Resumption Bill,[676] and immediately afterwards prorogued Parliament and retired to the palace for about six weeks of strict seclusion, though having lately been reconciled to the Princess Anne he entertained her occasionally at dinner.[677]

[650] No doubt one of the inconvenient contrivances honoured by the name of 'bath' which still exist in the state apartments; see 'Queen Mary's Closet,' &c.

[651] Defoe, *Tour through Gt. Britain* (ed. 1738), i, 245; Burnet, *The Royal Diary* (1705), 3.

[652] Wren, *Parentalia* (ed. 1750), 326.

[653] The catalogues of Mary's botanical collection are in B.M. Sloane MSS. no. 2928, 2370–1, 3343.

[654] Burnet, *The Royal Diary*, (1705), 3.

[655] Apelles, *Britannicus*, bk. i, p. 8.

[656] Kneller was knighted and received a medal and chain worth £300 for this service; Walpole, *Anecdotes of Painting*.

[657] This room is now known as the ' Oak Room,' and is used by the residents in the palace for entertainments.

[658] Law, *Royal Gallery of Hampton Ct.*, et seq. They were originally twelve

in number, but only eight now remain at Hampton Court. They were engraved in mezzotint by John Faber, jun.; Law, *Hist. Hampton Ct. Palace*, iii, 30, 32; Challoner Smith, *Brit. Mezzotint Portraits*, pt. i, 309; *Dict. Nat. Biog.* 'Godfrey Kneller.'

[659] *Dict. Nat. Biog.* 'William III.'

[660] Wren, loc. cit.; Dalrymple, *Memoirs of Gt. Brit. and Ireland*, pt. ii, App. 14.

[661] Ibid. App. 139; Aud. Off. Declared Accts. bdle. 2482, R. 295.

[662] Wren, loc. cit.

[663] Luttrell, *Relation of Affairs of State*, ii, 308, 324, 584; iii, 39, 115.

[664] She died of smallpox at Kensington Palace on 28 Dec. 1694.

[665] Switzer, *Ichnographia Rustica*, i, 75.

[666] Ralph, *Hist. Engl.* ii, 783. Wren's estimate for fitting up the rooms at Hampton Court is printed in the *Dep.*

Keeper's Rep. viii, App. ii, 200–1; Luttrell, op. cit. iv, 328.

[667] Grimblot, *Letters of Will. III*, i, 144; Macaulay, *Hist. Engl.* chap. xxiii.

[668] Larousse, *Grand Dictionnaire Universel du xixe Siècle*, viii, 765.

[669] *Lond. Gaz.*; Luttrell, op. cit. iv, 583; Grimblot, op. cit. ii, 379.

[670] *Cal. Treas. Papers*, 1697–1702, p. 349 (28 Nov. 1699).

[671] Luttrell, op. cit. iv, 596–7.

[672] Grimblot, *Letters of Will. III*, ii, 389.

[673] Luttrell, op. cit. iv, 599.

[674] *Lond. Gaz.*; *Hist. MSS. Com. Rep.* xii, App. ii, 393.

[675] Grimblot, op. cit. ii, 398; *Hist. MSS. Com. Rep.* xiv, App. ii, 618.

[676] Concerning forfeitures and grants of land in Ireland, reported on in Dec. 1699.

[677] Luttrell, op. cit. iv, 599.

On 23 April a meeting of the Privy Council was held to discuss the question of reducing the army, for which Parliament had voted very inadequate supplies,[678] and two days afterwards to consider alterations in the Commissions of the Peace,[679] one of the proceedings aimed at the ministry, and especially at Lord Chancellor Somers, who was accused of being partial in his appointments. He was present at this meeting as Chancellor for the last time.[680]

Many of the intrigues and interviews described by Burnet took place no doubt at Hampton Court.[681] The king remained at the palace, and Serjeant Sir Nathan Wright received the Great Seal at a meeting of the Privy Council at Hampton Court on 21 May 1700.[682]

William had already begun to carry into execution his plan to receive the foreign ambassadors only at Hampton Court, and in April 1700 he received the envoys of Spain and France,[683] who came to present a petition on behalf of the Roman Catholic priests in England, against whom an Act of great severity had been passed in the preceding session.[684] The Envoy Extraordinary of the Grand Duke of Tuscany was also received at Hampton Court in May.[685] A Chapter of the Order of the Garter was held in the palace soon after for ' electing the Earl of Pembroke and Montgomery, Lord President of the Council, and the Rt. Honble. Arnold Joost, Earl of Albemarle, Master of the Robes to His Majesty, Knights of the Garter in the room of the late Kings of Sweden and Denmark.'[686] William's attachment to Albemarle was the cause of much of his unpopularity, and that he should ' lavish away a Garter on his favourite ' was the text for many severe reflections.[687] In April 1700 the Duke of Shrewsbury decided to resign the office of Lord Chamberlain, on account of his health, in spite of the opposition of the king, who could ill afford to lose a friend near his person,[688] and on 24 June at Hampton Court the Earl of Jersey was appointed Lord Chamberlain in his place.[689]

It was noticed in June that the king was not in his usual health,[690] and he became very anxious to go to Holland in his customary manner, but was delayed by various affairs of state,[691] among them the question of the Scottish colony at Darien.[692] The king received the Scottish lords on Sunday 9 June, and the commissioners of the Lower House on 11 June. The physicians could not agree about him, and John Locke, the philosopher, who came to resign his commissionership at the Board of Trade,[693] was asked as a scientific expert to give an opinion on the king's state of health. He was sufficiently recovered to start for Holland on 7 July, after holding a Grand Council at the palace the day before, which was attended by the Lords Justices who were to administer the government in his absence.[694]

William went straight to Hampton Court when he returned in the autumn, but after holding one Privy Council there decided that they should meet at Kensington in future, for the greater convenience of the Lords.[695]

The Lord Mayor and Aldermen of London came to the palace to congratulate the king on his safe return, were entertained with ' a very splendid dinner,' and returned to the City with great satisfaction.[696] It was at about this period that William made up his mind, as he wrote from Hampton Court, to the ' absolute necessity of calling the House of Hanover to the succession, and of announcing the fact openly.'[697] On 1 November he received at Hampton Court the unexpected news of the death of the King of Spain,[698] an event which caused the utmost consternation in Europe, taking place as it did before the Second Partition Treaty had been completed.[699] Louis XIV, in violation of his most solemn pledges, accepted the late king's will in favour of the Duke of Anjou. William wrote to Heinsius from Hampton Court on 5 November,[700] expressing his extreme dissatisfaction, and his astonishment at the state of public opinion in England. ' It seems as if it were a punishment from Heaven,' he said, ' that people here are so little sensible to what passes without the island.'

In pursuance of a policy which it is impossible to follow here, the king dismissed the Whigs from office and sent for Lord Godolphin,[701] who had not been to court for four years. He attended the Cabinet Council held at Hampton Court on 1 December, and was appointed First Commissioner of the Treasury. Other Tory appointments followed, and on the 19th the king in Council at Hampton Court dissolved Parliament and ordered

[678] Luttrell, op. cit. iv, 636–7 ; Kennet, *Complete Hist. of Engl.* 1676–1700.

[679] Ralph, *Hist. Engl.* ii, 843.

[680] Burnet, *Hist. of His Own Times*, iv, 433, &c. ; Ralph, op. cit. ii, 908 ; Campbell, *Lives of the Lord Chancellors*, 148, &c.

[681] Burnet, op. cit. iv, 434, &c. ; Cole, *Memoirs*, 125.

[682] Campbell, *Lives of the Lord Chancellors*, iv, 241, 243 ; Luttrell, op. cit. iv, 646 ; *Lond. Gaz.* Hampton Court, 21 May 1700.

[683] There are three letters from William to Heinsius concerning his interviews at Hampton Court with de Tallard, the French ambassador, while the Second Treaty of Partition was being considered ; Grimblot, *Letters of Will. III*, ii, 407–12.

[684] Burnet, op. cit. iv, 409 ; Luttrell, op. cit. ' Diary.'

[685] *Lond. Gaz.* 7 May 1700.

[686] Luttrell, op. cit. iv, 645 ; *Lond. Gaz.*

[687] White Kennet, *Hist. Europe*, iii, 782 ; Oldmixon, op. cit. ii, 209.

[688] *Shrewsbury Correspondence*, 624.

[689] Luttrell, op. cit. iv, 645.

[690] Vernon, *Correspondence*, iii, 69.

[691] Kennet, *Complete Hist. of Engl.* (1702) 52 ; Grimblot, *Letters of Will. III*, ii, 416.

[692] Luttrell, op. cit. iv, 655 ; Vernon, *Correspondence*, iii, 77.

[693] Prior, *Hist. of His Own Times* (ed. Bancks), 179. Matthew Prior had been constantly at court, amusing himself and looking out for a post. He succeeded Locke at the Board of Trade.

[694] *Lond. Gaz.* 27 June 1700 ; Vernon, *Correspondence*, iii, 107. Vernon gives a detailed account of the king's illness. Kennet, *Hist. of Europe*, vol. for 1702, p. 52, also gives a minute description of the same, with the doctor's report on his illness.

[695] Luttrell, op. cit. iv, 707 ; *Lond. Gaz.* [696] *Lond. Gaz.*

[697] *Shrewsbury Correspondence*, iii, 143.

[698] Grimblot, *Letters of Will. III*, ii, 453.

[699] Hardwicke, *State Papers*, ii, 397.

[700] Grimblot, op. cit. ii, 477.

[701] Godolphin, with Shrewsbury, Marlborough, and Russell, had been accused of complicity in the Fenwick plot in 1696 ; *Dict. Nat. Biog.* ' James Vernon.'

writs for the election of a new one to be issued immediately.[702]

On 3 December the court had been ordered to go into mourning for the King of Spain,[703] and Count de Tallard, the French ambassador, who the year before had signed the Second Partition Treaty on behalf of France, arrived at the palace on the same day, bringing a letter from Louis XIV. An audience was arranged for him on the 11th, but without waiting for it he came to the palace the day before, and insisted on making his bow to the king. It is related that William only gazed out of the window and observed 'M. l'Ambassadeur, le temps est bien changé.'[704] De Tallard no doubt felt the truth of the remark when he came to have his final audience the next day, and William would scarcely notice him at all. The interview lasted hardly five minutes, and the court followed the king's example.[705] De Tallard delivered Louis' letter, but seems to have disagreed with the policy pursued by France. For a time he avoided Hampton Court, but eventually appeared there once a week, by way of putting the best face he could on the strained relationship between his own country and England. Meanwhile, the Emperor's ambassador, Count Wratislaw, was received with many tokens of friendship and respect, though William, hampered by internal politics and the state of public opinion at home,[706] was unable to adopt any measures for carrying out the provisions of the treaty so cavalierly ignored by Louis.[707]

William's constant state of political disappointment and anxiety affected his health, and Vernon, the Secretary of State, wrote that his various symptoms were chiefly to be ascribed to his 'great thoughtfulness in relation to the public.'[708] He remained at Hampton Court in seclusion, undergoing a course of treatment, which included such strange prescriptions as 'crabs' eyes and hogs' lice.'[709]

The state of excitement in the country after the meeting of the new Parliament in February 1701 can hardly be said to affect the history of Hampton Court, though the attack on the Whig ministers was one of the many subjects which engaged William's attention at the time.[710]

An address to the king on behalf of the Whig peers was brought to the palace on 16 April by the Duke of Devonshire and the Earl of Ramsay. It was presented to William with much formality,

but he did not vouchsafe any answer, a course of action which puzzled the promoters of the address considerably.[711] The king's real statesmanship was much impeded by purely party considerations, and Rochester's[712] dictatorial and assuming manner so much offended him that on one occasion after a consultation in the king's closet at Hampton Court he said to Lord Jersey, ' If I had ordered him to have been thrown out of the window, he must have gone ; I do not see how he could have prevented it.'[713]

William's health again kept him at the palace, and on 1 June 1701 he was there when he reluctantly appointed ' John, Earl of Marlbough,' commander-in-chief of his Majesty's forces in Holland,[714] and soon after made him Ambassador Extraordinary and Plenipotentiary to carry on negotiations at the Hague for treaties to be made with other powers against France.[715] On Monday 30 June the king himself left Hampton Court for Holland. He returned somewhat unexpectedly on 5 November, and arrived at the palace about eight o'clock, ' much tired with his journey, so that he went immediately to bed.'[716] James II had just died, and Louis XIV had instantaneously restored all William's popularity in England by acknowledging James's son as king of England. William was almost overwhelmed even on the day after his return by deputations from ' cities, counties, and universities,' assuring him of the loyalty of his subjects and their devotion to his crown and person.[717] He probably received them in the new ' Presence Chamber,' one of the most stately of Wren's rooms, which remains practically the same as it was then. The original canopy of crimson damask is still fixed to the wall, with its rich embroidery of silver and gold somewhat dimmed by time. One of the most beautiful of the great silver chandeliers is also in this room, embossed with the royal emblems.[718] Kneller's large picture of William III landing at Torbay in 1697, hung then, as it hangs now, opposite the canopy. ' We can imagine,' says the historian of Hampton Court Palace, ' the ceaseless throng passing up Verrio's resplendent staircase, making their way through the stately guard-chamber, and surveying with curiosity all the magnificence of the new palace, of which so much had been reported, and then approaching the feeble but high-spirited king, who stood to receive them, pale, haggard, and coughing.'[719]

[702] Cole, *Memoirs*, 249 ; Grimblot, op. cit. ii, 471.

[703] *Lond. Gaz.* ; Luttrell, op. cit. iv, 713.

[704] Boyce, *Hist. of Will. III*, 466.

[705] Cole, *Memoirs*, 271 ; Luttrell, op. cit. iv, 717.

[706] William was sensible that he had failed to conciliate either political party. He told Halifax that ' all the difference he knew between the two parties was, that the Tories would cut his throat in the morning and the Whigs in the afternoon' ; Ralph, *Hist. Engl.* ii, 908.

[707] Luttrell, op. cit. iv, 723.

[708] Cole, *Memoirs*, 279. Vernon was a staunch Whig, and viewed with great

apprehension the vexed question of the succession after the death of the Duke of Gloucester in 1700. He proposed that the king should marry again, and that the succession should be settled, in default of issue, in the Hanoverian line, assing over Anne entirely ; *Dict. Nat. Biog.*

[709] White Kennet, *Complete Hist. of Engl.* (1702), 52.

[710] Somers, Halifax, Oxford, Portland, and other Whigs were impeached ; Ralph, op. cit. ii, 944 ; *Dict. Nat. Biog.* 'William III.'

[711] Ralph, op. cit. ii, 944–5 ; Luttrell, op. cit. v, 40–1.

[712] Laurence Hyde, Earl of Rochester

(1641–1711), Lord Lieut. of Ireland ; *Dict. Nat. Biog.*

[713] Lord Dartmouth, *Notes*, cit. Law, op. cit. iii, 146–7.   [714] *Lond. Gaz.*

[715] *Hist. MSS. Com. Rep.* viii, App. i, 12 (26 June 1701).

[716] White Kennet, op. cit. vol. for 1702, p. 66 ; *Corresp. of Henry Hyde, Earl of Clarendon*, i, 419 ; *Lond. Gaz.*

[717] *Lond. Gaz.* ; Clarendon, *Corresp.* ii, 420.

[718] The rose, thistle, fleur de lis, harp, and the cypher W.R., all crowned, appear in the design, on both canopy and chandelier.

[719] Law, *Hist. of Hampton Court Palace*, iii, 154.

William wrote to Heinsius that he was 'quite exhausted by the labour of hearing harangues and returning answers.' [720] The first day, after all this fatigue, he afterwards walked for two hours in the garden at Hampton Court.[721] Macaulay writes of this time that 'the whole kingdom, meanwhile, was looking anxiously to Hampton Court. Most of the ministers were assembled there. The most eminent men of the party which was out of power had repaired thither, to pay their duty to their sovereign, and to congratulate him on his safe return. . . . Both Whigs and Tories waited with intense anxiety for the decision of one momentous and pressing question—Would there be a dissolution ?' [722]

William, as he owned to Heinsius, had some difficulty in making up his mind, but on 11 November 1701 he announced in council his intention to dissolve Parliament, and the proclamation to that effect, calling together a new one to meet on 30 December, was issued from Hampton Court at 11 o'clock p.m.[723]

The king continued at the palace, with Portland and Albemarle, who perceived, as he did himself, that his health was breaking down rapidly, though he carried on all the business of the state as usual, and even continued to hunt in the parks, but when he returned he had often to be carried upstairs to his own apartments.[724] When Parliament met he was obliged to return to London, and the night of Monday, 22 December 1701, was the last that he spent at the palace. He afterwards came down on Saturdays to hunt, and on 21 February (1701–2), though he had not been well that morning, he came as usual, and met with the accident which no doubt accelerated, if it did not cause, his death.[725] He was riding a favourite horse called Sorrel, who appears to have stumbled on a mole-hill, and the king was thrown on his right shoulder. His collar-bone was broken, but was immediately set by Ronjat, his serjeant surgeon, who happened to be at Hampton Court. In the evening, William, contrary to the doctor's advice, insisted on returning to Kensington, and it seems that the broken bone had to be set again.[726]

Even the date and time of the accident are recorded differently in contemporary accounts. The newspapers described it as having happened 'near Hampton Court,' but the exact locality has not been preserved even by tradition,[727] though twenty or thirty years ago a spot was still pointed out in the Home Park, near the cork-trees at the end of the Long Water,[728] as being the scene of the

machinations of the 'little gentleman in black velvet,' as the Jacobites called the mole which was said to be the cause of the horse's stumble.[729] No serious alarm concerning the king's fall seems to have been felt at the time, but unfavourable symptoms appeared later, and he died at Kensington Palace on Sunday, 8 March 1701–2.

Hampton Court was left to Queen Anne with accumulated arrears of debts against the Crown amounting to thousands of pounds.[730] Her association with the palace is accurately summed up in Pope's lines :—

Here thou, Great Anna ! whom three realms obey,

Dost sometimes Counsel take—and sometimes tea.

In the early part of her reign Anne used often to preside over meetings of the Privy Council in the Cartoon Gallery, otherwise known as 'The Great Council Chamber' or 'King's Gallery,' where the seven great cartoons of Raphael hung in the room built for their reception.[731] In 1702 councils were held there twice in July, three times in August ; in 1703, once in June, once in July, and once in August ; in 1704 on 1 June, and 'generally in the summers of succeeding years.' [732] After 1707 the queen does not seem to have been at Hampton Court till 1710, at a time when she had quarrelled with the Duchess of Marlborough, and wrote to Harley for help in her troubles and perplexities. She appears to have been afraid that the letter might fall into the hands of Godolphin or the Marlboroughs, so that she sent it by 'one of the under-labourers in Hampton Court Gardens,' and it was eventually delivered in a very grimy condition.[733]

On 4 May 1710 Queen Anne entertained 'some Indian kings' in the palace,[734] in June she came down twice a week 'for the air,' and on 26 September arrived with the whole court for a fortnight, the longest time she had spent there since her accession.[735] On 26 October a curious episode took place when the newly-appointed 'Lieutenancy' dined at the palace. Lord Halifax wrote to the Duke of Newcastle that 'the preparations were very great and magnificent, there were a hundred and fifty covers and a hundred and fifty dishes, but the day did not pass very cheerfully, for the Lord Mayor offered the names of five persons to be knighted . . . but the Queen remained fixt and would not knight any of them ; [736] . . this resolution in the Queen was so great a mortification

[720] Cit. Macaulay, Hist. Engl. (ed. 1861), v, 300.

[721] Luttrell, op. cit. v, 107–8.

[722] Macaulay, Hist. Engl. loc. cit.

[723] Luttrell, op. cit. v, 108; Lond.Gaz.

[724] Boyne, Hist. Will. III, iii ; White Kennet, op. cit. iii, 826 ; The Royal Diary (1705), 87; Luttrell, op. cit.v,110; Grimblot, Letters of Will. III,i,327,352.

[725] Luttrell, op. cit. v, 145, 147, 150 ; Vernon, Corresp. iii, 164 ; White Kennet, op. cit. vol. for 1702.

[726] Ibid. ; Ranke, Hist. of Engl. v, 297 ; Burnet, Hist. of His Own Times ; Dict. Nat. Biog.

[727] Law, op. cit. iii, 168.

[728] E. V. Boyle, Seven Gardens and a Palace, 286.

[729] Miss Strickland, in her life of Queen Anne, has drawn a vivid but quite unauthenticated picture of the occurrence ; vide Law, op. cit. iii, 168, n. 2. It is notable that there are no moles in the park now.

[730] The Treasury Papers are full of these claims ; Cal. Treas. Papers, 1702–7, pp. 38, 50, 143, 168, 169, 172, 216, 230, 343, 365, 438, 526. Verrio was among the creditors : he died at Hampton Court in 1707 ; Walpole,

Anecdotes of Painting (ed. 1849), ii, 471.

[731] Law, op. cit. iii, 171. They are now in the South Kensington Museum.

[732] Luttrell,op.cit.v,192,202,205,207, 303,333,430,470; vide also Lond. Gaz.

[733] Swift, Works (ed. 1824), iii, 182, 'Memoirs relating to the change of Ministry in 1710.'

[734] Luttrell, op. cit. vi, 599.

[735] Add. MSS. B.M. 100, 101, fol. 73 ; Luttrell, op. cit. vi, 633.

[736] It was apparently thought that one of them—Carse—had been concerned in some plot.

to these gentlemen that Sir W. Withers and some others went away before dinner. . . . The Duke of Somerset came to Court on Friday night, had a long audience and a very rough one on his part, and went away on Monday.'[737]

Swift came to Hampton Court once or twice while the queen was there, the first time on 2 October to dine with Lord Halifax at his 'lodgings,' in the highest story of the south side of the Fountain Court, overlooking the private gardens.[738] He went to the queen's drawing-room afterwards, where he met 'acquaintance enough.'[739] On another occasion he described his visit as follows : 'We made our bows, and stood, about twenty of us, round the room, while the Queen looked at us with her fan in her mouth, and once in a minute said about three words to some that were nearest to her. I dined at Her Majesty's Board of Green Cloth. It is much the best table in England, and costs the Queen £1,000 a month while she is at Windsor or Hampton Court, and is the only mark of magnificence or royal hospitality that I can see in the Royal household.'[740] The queen again held councils in the palace in October and November 1710.[741] In November she also held a chapter of the order of the Garter before she returned to London. After Christmas she came back to Hampton Court for some days.[742] She had drives, or 'chaise rides,' made for herself in the parks at this time, and Swift said that she hunted in a chaise with one horse, 'which she drives furiously, like Jehu.' He also said that on another occasion she hunted the stag till 4 o'clock in the afternoon, and drove in her chaise no less than 40 miles.[743]

A trivial incident which took place at Hampton Court about this time will always be remembered, as it led to the composition of Pope's famous poem 'The Rape of the Lock.'[744] The queen entertained the envoys of the King of France at the palace in the autumn of 1711, and also an ambassador from 'the Czar of Muscovy.'[745] Swift complained of the difficulties of going there himself, 'they have no lodgings for me—the town is small, chargeable and inconvenient.'[746] By 'the town' he meant the few houses which then existed near the palace.[747] That year Anne stayed at Hampton Court longer than usual: she received the Duke of Marlborough there on his return from abroad on 18 November,[748] and from there on 13 November she issued the proclamation by which she hoped to reform 'the indecencies and disorders of the stage.'[749] No further occurrence

of any importance took place at Hampton Court up to the time of Anne's death in 1714.

George I arrived at the palace about nine months after his accession, and finding it more to his taste than his other English palaces, lived there in great retirement, with Madame Schulenberg (afterwards Duchess of Kendal) and Mme. Kilmansegg (afterwards Countess of Darlington and Leinster). These ladies added considerably to George's unpopularity with his subjects. One reminiscence of them possibly remains at Hampton Court in the name of the 'Frog Walk,' under the west wall of the Tilt Yard, where it is said that they used to promenade, whence it was designated the 'Frau,' afterwards corrupted to 'Frog', Walk.[750]

In 1716 the Prince of Wales was appointed Regent during his father's absence in Hanover, and was allowed to live at Hampton Court in the suite of apartments still known as 'the Queen's State Rooms,' on the east side of the palace. The prince and princess endeavoured to hold a court which should contrast with the dull and stiff formality which was the king's idea of regal dignity. It was probably Caroline who encouraged the world of wit and learning as well as that of birth and beauty, to come to Hampton Court. The reminiscences of Walpole and Swift, the poems of Pope and Gay, which commemorate this epoch in the history of the palace are too well known for it to be necessary to quote them in this limited space. It will be enough to mention a few of the more famous frequenters of this young court, where gaiety and amusement reigned as it never seems to have done when George and Caroline came back as king and queen for the last of the regal courts destined to be held in the palace.

The most famous of the wits who thus made the court brilliant was Philip Dormer, fourth Earl of Chesterfield, who had been appointed Gentleman of the Bedchamber to the Prince of Wales, though he cannot be numbered among the beauties ; Lord Hervey called him 'a stunted giant.'[751] Carr, Lord Hervey, was also among the wits. He was said to be a cleverer man than his better-known brother John, who succeeded to the title, and was afterwards celebrated as the friend of Queen Caroline and of Sir Robert Walpole.[752] He began his career at court while the prince and princess were at the palace, and no doubt then began also his courtship of the princess's beautiful and vivacious maid of honour, Mary Lepell, whose praises were sung by all her contemporaries, including Pope and Gay, Pulteney and Chesterfield. Even Vol-

[737] *Hist. MSS. Com. Rep.* xiii, App. ii, 223. It is not said that Somerset had come to expostulate with the queen on her action, though it is implied.

[738] Now private apartments, occupied by the Dowager Lady Napier of Magdala, widow of the late Field Marshal Lord Napier of Magdala, G.C.B., &c.

[739] *Journ. to Stella,* 2 Oct. 1710.

[740] Ibid. 8 Aug. 1711.

[741] Luttrell, op. cit. vi, 640.

[742] Ibid. vi, 667.

[743] *Journ. to Stella,* 31 July, 7 Aug. 1711.

[744] Law, op. cit. iii, 193, where a full account is given of the incident, when Lord Petre cut off a lock of Miss Fermor's hair ; Elwin, *Pope's Works,* ii, 145.

[745] *Lond. Gaz.*

[746] *Journ. to Stella,* 8, 14, 25 Oct. 1711.

[747] Even in the present overcrowded days it can hardly be described as a 'town.'

[748] Swift, op. cit. 15, 22 Nov. 1711.

[749] *Lond. Gaz.* 13 Nov. 1711.

[750] Law, op. cit. iii, 205. It is pos-

sible that the *Frauen* who gave it this name were the ladies in attendance on the wife of the Stadtholder of Holland, who took refuge at Hampton Court in 1795.

[751] Born 1694, died 1773, the famous Lord Chesterfield, wit, politician, and letter-writer.

[752] Hervey, *Memoirs,* i, 266. He said that he entertained the queen at Hampton Court while 'other people were entertaining themselves with hearing dogs bark and seeing horses gallop.'

taire wrote verses in her honour. She married Lord Hervey in 1720.[753] Lord Chesterfield admired her good breeding, and said that 'she knew more than was necessary for any woman, but had the wit to conceal it.' A letter she wrote to Mrs. Howard (Lady Suffolk) twelve years later draws a pleasant picture of the gaiety and lightness of heart that existed at Hampton Court in those early days.[754]

Mary Bellenden was another charming maid of honour, of whom Horace Walpole wrote that 'she was never mentioned by her contemporaries but as the most perfect creature they had ever known.'[755] She married Colonel John Campbell,

one of the Grooms of the Bedchamber, long afterwards fourth Duke of Argyll. The 'giddy and unfortunate' Sophia Howe, who died in 1726, was another of the maids of honour who amused herself mightily at the palace.[756]

Lady Bristol, mother of the two Herveys, was also among the wits,[757] and Sir Robert's first wife, Lady Walpole, was one of the ladies of the court.[758] Among others were Mrs. Clayton, afterwards Viscountess Sundon, the Princess of Wales's intimate friend; Mrs. Selwyn, mother of the well-known George Augustus Selwyn,[759] and the notorious Mrs. Howard, afterwards Countess of Suffolk,[760] a woman of some ability and beauty,

HAMPTON COURT PALACE : FROG WALK

[753] John, Lord Hervey of Ickworth (1696–1743), second son of John first Earl of Bristol. He was distinguished in the world of politics, but only received office after the death of Queen Caroline, whose vice-chamberlain he was. Sir Robert Walpole for many years ruled the queen through him and the king through her. His extreme delicacy and effeminacy are often mentioned by his contemporaries. Sarah Duchess of Marlborough described him as having 'a painted face and not a tooth in his head.' Pope called him 'Lord Fanny.' Dict. Nat. Biog.; Hervey, Memoirs.

[754] Lady Suffolk's Letters (ed. 1824), i, 320 (31 Aug. 1728).

[755] Walpole, Reminiscences and Memoirs of Geo. II, 153; Gay, Poems, 'Welcome to Pope from Greece'; Lady Suffolk's Letters, i, 62. There is a story.

connected with Hampton Court, that she suffered from the unwelcome attentions of the Prince of Wales, who seems to have attempted to excite her avarice by constantly following her about counting her money, and refusing to accept her most pointed rebuffs, until one day at Hampton Court she sent his guineas rolling on the floor and ran out of the room, leaving him to pick them up. Lady Sundon's Memoirs, i, 97; Lady Suffolk's Letters, i, 62; Walpole, op. cit. 153.

[756] Hervey, Memoirs, p. xxx; Lady Suffolk's Letters, i, 41; Pope, Poems, 'Lines in answer to the question "What is Prudery?"' Lady Hervey described the six maids of honour as 'six volumes originally bound in calf.' Lady Suffolk's Letters, i, 10.

[757] Hervey, Memoirs, i, p. xxi.

[758] Catherine Shorter, daughter of a

timber merchant, son of the then Lord Mayor of London. She appears to have been an extravagant woman of fashion who 'wasted large sums'; Dict. Nat. Biog.

[759] George Augustus Selwyn (1719–91), wit and politician, son of Colonel John Selwyn; his mother was a daughter of General Farrington, 'a vivacious beauty' and woman of the bedchamber to Queen Caroline; Dict. Nat. Biog.

[760] Henrietta, daughter of Sir Henry Hobart, bart., married Charles Howard, afterwards sixth Earl of Suffolk. Pope, Gay, and Swift frequented their house. She built herself a villa at Marble Hill, Twickenham, towards which the Prince of Wales contributed £12,000. Her first husband died in 1733, and in 1735 she married George Berkeley son of the fifth Earl of Berkeley, who died in 1747; Dict. Nat. Biog.; Hervey, Memoirs; Lady Sundon's Memoirs.

who encouraged Pope and his literary friends, and gained an ascendancy over the Prince of Wales which she never entirely lost till she retired from court in 1734.[761] Her supper parties in the rooms she occupied in the palace became celebrated. Her apartments were known to her friends as the 'Swiss Cantons,' and herself as 'the Swiss,' possibly from some political allusion.[762]

Lord Scarbrough, 'amiable and melancholy,'[763] Charles Churchill, natural son of the Duke of Marlborough's brother General Churchill, who afterwards married a daughter of Sir Robert Walpole,[764] Lord Bolingbroke, Lord Bathurst, as well as Pope, Gay, Pulteney, Arbuthnot, and latterly Swift, may be mentioned as among those who added to the brilliancy of the court.[765] The social life at Hampton Court was a constant round of amusement. In the morning it was the custom to go on the river in barges, gaily decorated and hung with silk curtains,[766] rowed by oarsmen in royal liveries. The prince and princess afterwards dined in public with the whole court in the princess's apartments. In the afternoon she received her guests and read or wrote, and in the evening walked for several hours in the garden. They also visited the four pavilions that stood at each corner of the bowling green, where chocolate was served and 'ombre' or 'commerce' played. Sometimes the princess would invite a party to play cards in the 'Queen's Gallery,' or to sup with her in the Countess of Buckenburgh's chamber, though all the Germans who belonged to the court disliked the English and abused them roundly.[767]

It must not be supposed that business and politics had no place at court. Sir Robert Walpole, Lord Methuen, the Lord Chancellor Finch, Lord Townshend, and Count Bothmar, George the First's Hanoverian minister, were constantly in attendance. Lord Sunderland, who was a friend of the king, and Lord Townshend both seem to have distinguished themselves by a want of consideration for the princess. A story is told of her having a heated controversy with Lord Sunderland in the Queen's Gallery, during which she told him to 'walk next the windows, for in the humour we both are, one

of us must certainly jump out at the window, and I'm resolved it shan't be me.'[768]

In October 1716 the court left the palace, going by water in a barge, and did not return till August in the following year, in attendance on the king, whose presence did not add to their gaiety.[769] Pope wrote on 13 September 1717 that 'no lone house in Wales, with a mountain and a rookery, is more contemplative than this court; and as a proof of it, I need only tell you Miss Lepell walked with me three or four hours by moonlight,[770] and we met no creature of any quality but the king, who gave audience to the vice-chamberlain (Hervey) all alone, under the garden wall. I hear of no ball, assembly, basset-table or any place where two or three were gathered together, except Madam Kilmansegg's, to which I had the honour to be invited, and the grace to stay away.'[771] The general state of ill-feeling between the king and his son, and still more between the king and his daughter-in-law, of whom he generally spoke as 'cette diablesse la Princesse,' at this time developed into an open quarrel, which attained such dimensions, though the actual cause is unknown, that the prince and princess departed from the palace in October, leaving the king in possession, and shortly afterwards the king put a notice in the *Gazette* to the effect that the prince's friends would not be received at court.[772] In 1718, when the king returned to Hampton Court in the summer, the prince was holding an opposition court at Richmond. George I had commanded the 'King's Company of Actors' to perform plays before him in the Great Hall twice a week during the summer, but the theatre not being ready in time only seven plays were acted in September and October.[773] Among them, on 1 October, Shakespeare's *Henry VIII* was represented on the very spot where so much of the action had really taken place.[774]

Richard Steele, who wrote a prologue for these theatricals, when asked how the king liked the play, replied, 'So terribly well, my lord, that I was afraid I should have lost all my actors; for I was not sure the king would not keep them to fill the posts at court that he saw them so fit for in the play.'[775]

[761] Pope wrote in her honour the well-known lines 'On a certain Lady at Court.'

[762] *Lady Suffolk's Letters*, i, 64, 411.

[763] *Lady Sundon's Memoirs*, i, 95. He afterwards committed suicide.

[764] Ibid. He is here called the duke's brother, but General Charles Churchill died in 1714; *Dict. Nat. Biog.*

[765] Hervey, *Memoirs*, i, p. xxxiii.

[766] *Lady Cowper's Diary*, 121 et seq.; *Lady Suffolk's Letters*, i, 376.

[767] *Lady Cowper's Diary*, 125.

[768] *Lady Cowper's Diary*, 123; Defoe, *Tour through Great Britain*, i, 5.

[769] *Lady Suffolk's Letters*, i, 15; *Memoirs of Lady Sundon*, i, 330.

[770] The maids of honour were on terms of great familiarity with Pope. They probably considered him as he was described by Aaron Hill, 'The ladies' plaything and the muses' pride.' Hervey, *Memoirs*, p. xx.

[771] Elwin and Courthope, *Life of Pope*, ix, 272, 4. Lady Orkney is mentioned as doing the honours both at Hampton Court and St. James's, and in 1718 'they had two plays and one ball every week at Court.' *Hist. MSS. Com. Rep.* v, 568; xii, App. iii, 186; Letter from Sir John Stanley to Vice-Chamberlain Coke.

[772] *Lady Suffolk's Letters*, i, 18; *Hist. MSS. Com. Rep.* v, 536; 'Newsletters,' 14, 27 Nov. 1717.

[773] This company of actors, otherwise known as the Drury Lane Company, included Colley Cibber, Barton Booth, Mills, Wilkes, Mrs. Oldfield, Mrs. Porter, and Miss Younger. They seem to have found that the absence of laughter or applause 'higher than a whisper' had a melancholy effect upon their acting; Colley Cibber, *Apology for his Life*. He gives an interesting account of the arrangements and expenses.

[774] Lysons, *Midd. Parishes*, 67; Colley Cibber, *Apology for his Life* (ed. 1740), 447; *Lady Suffolk's Letters*, i, 29; Law, op. cit. iii, 223.

[775] Montgomery, *Life of Steele*, ii, 170. The stage was never used again till 1731, when a performance was given by order of George II, for the entertainment of the Duke of Lorraine, afterwards Emperor of Germany; Colley Cibber, *Apology for his Life*, 447, 456; *Daily Advertiser*, 18 Oct. 1731, cit. Law, op. cit. iii, 240. The stage remained till 1798, when James Wyatt, Surveyor-General of the Board of Works, obtained permission from George III to have it removed; Lysons, *Midd. Parishes*, 67. In 1733 Kent made a design of the hall as it was in the time of Henry VIII, with the idea of persuading George II to do away with the disfigurement.

One of the most shameful and sordid acts of the inglorious reign of George I took place in 1718, when the patent of Surveyor-General of the Board of Works given to Sir Christopher Wren by Charles II, which he had held with conspicuous success under five different monarchs, was withdrawn on 26 April, to please the Hanoverian favourites of the king, who persuaded him to give the appointment to William Benson, an ignorant and incompetent person, who had succeeded better than the great architect in obtaining and making use of court influence. The pretext for this action was stated to be a desire to effect economy in the public service, that old and most fallacious excuse for showing ingratitude and parsimony to the servants of the Crown.[776] Wren retired to his house on the Green [777] and thence wrote a letter to the Lords of the Treasury which is a perfect example of courtesy and forbearance towards his enemies on the part of an upright man unjustly accused.[778]

He had not long to wait for his vindication, for Benson's incapacity and dishonesty very soon became apparent, and he was ignominiously dismissed from his post, after holding it only for a year.[779]

George I made an ineffectual effort to put down an abuse which had apparently become conspicuous during his reign. People who had no prescriptive right to occupy 'lodgings' in the palace [780] established themselves there, on one pretext or another, with the aid, no doubt, of some 'friend at court,' and so acquired a position from which it was afterwards difficult to oust them.[781] This practice had begun even in the time of Henry VIII, and it continued to flourish more or less openly until George III, who never lived in the palace himself, made a strict rule, which was henceforward enforced, that no one was to occupy rooms without a written authorization from the Lord Chamberlain.[782]

From about 1719 onwards we have no record of any royal visit to Hampton Court until after the accession of George II. His court first went into residence there in July 1728,[783] and for the ensuing ten years or so of his reign they came regularly to the palace for some months during each summer,[784] but the court had entirely lost its early brilliancy. A letter from Mrs. Howard to Lady Hervey says that 'Hampton Court is very different from the place you knew . . . *Frizelation, flirtation* and *dangleation* are now no more, and . . . to tell you my opinion freely, the people you now converse with (her books) are much more alive than any of your old acquaintance.' [785] No doubt Mrs. Howard suffered more than the rest from the endeavour to 'amuse an unamusable king,' [786] besides having to bear with the small indignities the queen liked to inflict upon her as bedchamber woman. The room in the palace where she attended the queen's toilet is much as it was then, though little of the furniture remains.[787] Her Majesty's private chapel is next to this room, and prayers were read there by her chaplains while she was being dressed,[788] the door being left slightly open. Lord Hervey has among his *Memoirs* a curious little drama or dialogue, entitled 'The Death of Lord Hervey, or, A Morning at Court,' which gives an entertaining if not very edifying picture of life and study of conversation at the palace in those days.[789] The only amusement that the king permitted himself or others was stag-hunting and coursing, which went on even in the summer. 'We hunt with great noise and violence, and have every day a very tolerable chance to have a neck broke,' [790] wrote Mrs. Howard on 31 July 1730, from Hampton Court. Her fears were not ill-founded, as is proved by an account in a contemporary newspaper of accidents in the hunting field on 25 August 1731, to the Princess Amelia, as well as to one of the pages and a groom.[791] A passing excitement was the scandal caused by the behaviour of Princess Amelia and the Duke of Grafton, who used to hunt two or three times a week, and occasionally separated themselves from their attendants and went off together. The princess was really devoted to hunting, and in defiance of court etiquette used to visit her horses in the royal stables on the Green.[792]

The king and queen generally dined together in public in 'The Public Dining Room,' one of the finest of the state apartments. In the evening the court played cards,[793] or receptions were held,[794]

---

[776] *Cal. Treas. Papers,* 1714–19, p. 416. Memorial to the Treasury concerning the 'abominable cheats so long practised to His Majesty's prejudice,' drawn up by Benjamin Benson, the brother of William, and Colin Campbell, who was evidently a mere agent of William Benson.

[777] See p. 320. He originally used some rooms in the palace. A little octagonal room on the west side of the Fountain Court with a skylight, and one window, is pointed out as his writing-room; now private apartments occupied by Mrs. Maxwell, widow of the late Col. Robert Maxwell, R.E.

[778] *Cal. Treas. Papers,* 1714–19, p. 448.

[779] Elmes, *Life of Wren,* 512. Court influence saved Benson from prosecution, and secured for him another post with a salary of £1,200 per annum.

[780] In the reign of William and Mary discussions about the rooms allotted often took place; *Buccleugh MSS.* (Hist. MSS. Com.), ii, 645–8, &c.

[781] George I wrote to the Lord Chamberlain on 5 May 1719, to require him 'not to permit any person to have Lodgings in our palaces of Hampton Court, Windsor, and Kensington, who are not by their offices entitled thereto'; Law, op. cit. iii, 232–3.

[782] Ibid. 304. The Lord Chamberlain at first granted permission by letter, and from about 1765 by warrant.

[783] George I died on 11 June 1727.

[784] *Lady Suffolk's Letters,* i, 299, 312; Elwin and Courthope, *Life of Pope,* vii, 129.

[785] *Lady Suffolk's Letters,* i, 328.

[786] Hervey, *Memoirs,* ii, 16; *Lady Suffolk's Letters,* i, 291.

[787] The tall marble bath, which looks as if it had been put up endways by mistake, is still there.

[788] Queen Anne had the same custom, and once 'ordering the door to be shut while she shifted, the chaplain stopped. The queen sent to ask why he did not proceed. He replied he could not whistle the Word of God through the keyhole.' Hervey, *Memoirs,* ii, 336, note.

[789] Hervey, *Memoirs,* ii, 333 et seq. (ed. Croker, 1884).

[790] *Lady Suffolk's Letters,* i, 376.

[791] Cit. Law, op. cit. iii, 241.

[792] Walpole, *Reign of Geo. II,* i, 157. Walpole also says that 'the good people at Hampton Court are scandalized at Princess Emily's coming to chapel last Sunday in riding clothes, with a dog under her arm' (June 1752); *Letters* (ed. Toynbee), iii, 101.

[793] 'The King plays at commerce and backgammon, and the Queen at quadrille;' *Lady Sundon's Memoirs,* ii, 231.

[794] Ibid. i, 212.

probably in the Queen's Audience Chamber, where a canopy of the royal damask still remains.[795] Lord Hervey gives an account of the dulness of these evenings, when 'the king walked about and talked (to Lord Lifford) of armies, or to Lady Charlotte (his sister) of genealogies, whilst the queen knotted and yawned, till from yawning she came to nodding, and from nodding to snoring.'[796] A further picture of the company is to be found in Pope's ballad, 'The Challenge,' and in a letter from Lord Hervey to Mrs. Clayton, although he begins by saying 'I will not trouble you with any account of our occupations at Hampton Court. No mill-horse ever went in a more constant track, or a more unchanging circle.'[797] The record of this last court, held every year at the palace until the death of Queen Caroline, is one of court intrigues of a sordid nature, and of the king's disagreeable manners and various flirtations, especially after the departure from court of Lady Suffolk.[798] The queen and Lord Hervey had interminable conversations and discussed every conceivable subject,[799] though when the king was present he took pains that none of the affairs that interested the queen should be mentioned.[800]

The most important domestic matter for a long time seems to have been the continual state of irritation and ill-feeling between the king and queen and their eldest son, Frederick, Prince of Wales. It came to an open climax, when the prince, apparently solely in order to offend his parents, and at the great risk of his wife's life, contrived to remove her secretly from Hampton Court in the evening of Sunday, 31 July 1737, so that the birth of their eldest child might take place at St. James's on the same night, without the knowledge or presence of the queen. Their departure took place at half-past eight, after they had dined with the king and queen. The unfortunate princess was dragged down the stairs behind the Prince of Wales' apartments in the north-east corner of the palace, hurried, probably through the cloisters past the chapel door, to one of the side doors in Tennis Court Lane, and was there put into a coach, accompanied by the prince, Lady Archibald Hamilton and some of the princess's attendants. They were driven at full gallop to London, arriving at St. James's at ten o'clock. Their daughter was born only an hour later.[801] A courier was sent back to Hampton Court to announce the state of affairs, and arrived at half-past one in the morning. By four o'clock the queen was at St. James's and heard the prince's account of what he had done.[802] She interviewed everyone concerned, and returned to Hampton Court by eight o'clock in the evening.[803] The king refused to see his son,[804] and Lord Carnarvon[805] was sent to Hampton Court with a letter, in very bad French, from the prince to express his grief and repentance for having incurred the displeasure of his father. The king's reply was to send Lord Essex with a curt message to Carnarvon, who was kept waiting in one of the galleries, refusing any further answer to the prince. This scene must have been remarkable, and is given at length in Lord Hervey's *Memoirs*. It is said by him to have taken place in the queen's bedchamber or dressing-room, the letter having been brought to the king while he was at dinner in the Public Dining-room. The prince was ordered to retire to Kew, his usual military guard was taken away as a sign of the king's displeasure, and it was notified to everyone likely to attend the prince's court that their doing so would be disagreeable to the king.[806] The court left Hampton Court on 28 October 1737, and on 20 November the queen died, and the history of the palace as a royal residence practically came to an end.

George II never actually lived at Hampton Court again after the queen's death, though he sometimes came down for the day with Lady Yarmouth[807] and some of the court.

'They went in coaches and six in the middle of the day, with heavy horse-guards kicking up the dust before them—dined, walked an hour in the garden, returned in the same dusty parade ; and his majesty fancied himself the most lively and gallant prince in Europe.'[808] Occasionally he stayed for a night or two,[809] and it is to be supposed that he sometimes had his grandchildren to visit him there, as to this period belongs the famous story of his having on one occasion boxed the ears of the young prince, afterwards George III, and so disgusted him that he could never afterwards bring himself to live in the palace where he had suffered such an indignity.[810]

From the time of the death of George II no king of England has occupied the palace. It has ceased to be the scene of historical events, though among its inhabitants at all periods are found the

---

[795] A great many of the rooms appear to have been redecorated at this time. In the Public Dining-room, and the Queen's Presence and Guard Chambers the ornamentation is clearly not from any design by Sir Christopher Wren.

[796] Hervey, *Memoirs*, i, 297 et seq.

[797] *Lady Sundon's Memoirs*, ii, 231.

[798] Hervey, *Memoirs*, i, 350, 426.

[799] Ibid.

[800] She took great interest in religious matters, especially in the new school of thought, which was considered advanced and daring at the time. She had also some taste for art and literature, and interested herself in gardening and architecture. The Princess Royal complained to Lord Hervey of the king's 'unreasonable, simple, uncertain, disagreeable and often shocking behaviour to the Queen ;' Hervey, *Memoirs*, ii, 87.

[801] Ibid. iii, 166, &c.

[802] 'The Queen kissed the child and said, "Le bon Dieu vous bénisse pauvre petite créature, vous voilà arrivée dans un désagréable monde."' Hervey, *Memoirs*, iii, 171.

[803] Ibid. 179.   [804] Ibid. 193.

[805] One of the lords of the Prince's Bedchamber.

[806] Walpole, *Remin.* (ed. 1819-21), 60-1 ; Hervey, *Memoirs*, 238, 239. The queen went so far as to say that she hoped she should never see her son again. She actually did not see him on her death-bed, though she sent him a message of forgiveness ; ibid. 238 ; Walpole, *Letters*.

[807] Amalie Sophia, Frau von Wallmoden (1704-65), created Countess of Yarmouth in 1740 by Geo. II ; *Dict. Nat. Biog.*

[808] Walpole, *Remin.* 62.

[809] The bed, hung with crimson silk, which he generally used on these occasions, is still in the state apartments.

[810] This story is said to have been repeated to Heneage Jesse, by the person to whom the Duke of Sussex related it, while passing through the state apartments ; Jesse, *Life of George III*, i, 10.

names of some who have 'made history.' Even before the accession of George III the absence of the court had left the place much at the mercy of the housekeeper [811] and deputy-housekeeper, who made a show of it and exacted fees from the visitors who came to look at it. Horace Walpole, whose house at Strawberry Hill was only 3 miles off, constantly visited Hampton Court and made notes on its history, its pictures and curiosities.[812] On 3 August 1751, in a letter to Sir Horace Mann, he told one of the numerous stories about the famous and beautiful Misses Gunning, who, he said, 'make more noise than any of their predecessors since Helen. They went the other day to see Hampton Court; as they were going into the Beauty Room, another company arrived, the housekeeper said "This way, ladies; here are the Beauties." The Gunnings flew into a passion and asked her what she meant; that they came to see the palace, not to be shown as a sight themselves.' [813]

From 25 October 1760, the date of the accession of George III, the history of Hampton Court Palace assumes an entirely new aspect. Up to that time it had been the background of important public events, or connected with the private lives of the sovereigns of England; but thenceforward it became interesting only as the private individuals to whom apartments were allotted by grace and favour of the king or queen happened to be interesting.

The state apartments were gradually dismantled during the long reign of George III, furniture and pictures were sent to other palaces, and perhaps this gradual despoiling of the place, continued through so many years, is one of the chief reasons that it has remained in its present condition.[813a] It was not till the reign of Queen Victoria that by her special kindness and thought for her people the picture galleries and gardens were thrown open to the public.[813b] At first the private apartments were often held by irregular and more or less surreptitious devices,[814] by begging a grant from the Lord Chamberlain, or by bribing the housekeeper, until George III made the proviso that no one should occupy 'lodgings' unless the rooms were exactly specified in a written grant from the Lord Chamberlain.[815]

It may be said here that whatever reasons may have counted originally in conferring apartments on those favoured by the king, for a great many years they have been granted, in almost every instance, 'in recognition of distinguished services rendered to the Crown and country by the husbands or near relatives of the recipients. Recently the privilege has been almost entirely confined to widows or unmarried ladies.' [816] Some misapprehension of the terms on which these apartments are granted has often arisen, i.e. that there is some unwritten 'rule' limiting the 'grace and favour' of the sovereign to making grants of rooms only to ladies—which is erroneous,[817] as the king may give them to anyone he pleases. Another misapprehension, arising perhaps from William the Fourth's playful method of terming the palace 'the Quality Poorhouse,' is that the inhabitants are entirely without means.[818]

A guard of honour, supplied by the cavalry regiment stationed at Hounslow, is always on duty at the palace, and occupies the long low line of buildings on the north of the west entrance. Divine service is regularly performed in the chapel by one of the king's chaplains,[818a] who occupies a suite of apartments, and who is appointed and partly paid by the Crown.[819] A clerk of the works, who is also assistant surveyor, is appointed by the Crown; [819a] the fabric of the building and the gardens are under the jurisdiction of the Office of Works, though the interior is ruled by the Lord Chamberlain, who still signs all the warrants issued to holders of apartments.

Society in Hampton Court Palace has never been without its own peculiar charm and interest, as perhaps the following short list of a few of the more celebrated inhabitants may testify.

Commodore Hon. Robert Boyle Walsingham, youngest son of Henry, first Earl of Shannon, was granted rooms on the ground floor on the south side of the Clock Court. He took the name of Walsingham on succeeding to the property. He commanded a squadron sent to the West Indies to reinforce Rodney in 1780, and was lost in H.M.S. *Thunderer* in October that year. He married in 1759 Charlotte daughter of Sir Charles Hanbury

---

[811] The 'Lady Housekeepers,' who received a salary of £250, with fees which made the office worth nearly £800 a year, date from about 1758, and were Mrs. Elizabeth Mostyn, Mrs. Mary Keete, Lady Anne Cecil, Lady Elizabeth Seymour, and Lady Emily Montague, who died in 1838; Law, op. cit. iii, 444. An amusing account is given in *Frazer's Mag.* Aug. 1846, of the way in which someone who refused to pay the necessary fees for seeing the palace was kept locked up in one of the rooms for some time by the 'lady housemaid.'

[812] See *Anecdotes of Painting*, &c.

[813] Horace Walpole, *Letters* (ed. Toynbee), iii, 68. The 'Beauty Room' is the one on the ground floor, facing the south, under the King's Guard Chamber. The Kneller pictures originally hung there. It is now called the 'Oak Room' and is used for entertainments by inhabitants of the palace.

[813a] *Letters of Horace Walpole* (ed. Toynbee), v, 208–9; xii, 109.

[813b] Her Majesty seems to have been impressed by the Report of a Committee 'On the Arts and their connexion with manufactures,' in 1836, and to have then decided that it was advisable to allow the cartoons of Raphael and other pictures at Hampton Court to be shown to the public. 'Letter from W. Ewart.' *Frazer's Mag.* iv, 479.

[814] See p. 367; Law, op. cit. iii, 302.

[815] See p. 367, n. 781–2. An exhaustive list of the successive inhabitants, as far as they can be traced, is given by Mr. Law, op. cit. iii, App. G. A copy of Miss Antonia St. John's MS. list, compiled from old letters and warrants, has also been seen by the writer (lent by Mrs. Marcus Slade).

[816] Law, *Hist. Hampton Court Palace*, iii, 413–14.

[817] A warrant to Admiral Sir Samuel Brooke-Pechell, bart., 19 Nov. 1844, is said to have been marked 'as being a special exception to the rule that no apartments are now granted to married men or widowers.' Law, op. cit. iii, 452. In 1892 the late Queen Victoria granted apartments to Major-General Dennehy, extra groom in waiting to the queen.

[818] Conditions of the tenure of apartments may be found in Law, op. cit. iii, 353 et seq.

[818a] The present chaplain is the Rev. A. Ingram, M.A. He occupies 'The Treasurer's Lodgings' in the north wing of the west front.

[819] Law, op. cit. iii.

[819a] The present clerk of the works and assistant surveyor is Mr. Edwin Chart. He has a separate house in Tennis Court Lane.

Williams, K.B., who, after her husband's death, bought a property at Thames Ditton and built Boyle Farm, opposite the Home Park at the end of the gardens.[820] The rooms are now occupied by Miss Gordon, daughter of the late Lord Henry Gordon, who has a long connexion with the palace.

Elizabeth Countess of Berkeley had the rooms in the top story on the east side of the Fountain Court. She married first Augustus, fourth Earl of Berkeley, K.T., and secondly Robert Nugent, afterwards Earl of Clare. She is chiefly remarkable for Horace Walpole's remarks on her character: ' Be doubly on your guard against her. There is nothing so black of which she is not capable. Her gallantries are the whitest specks about her.' [821] The rooms were granted to her in 1782. They are now occupied by Mrs. Henderson, widow of Colonel Henderson, C.B., late Commandant of the Staff College, and author of *Stonewall Jackson and the American Civil War*, &c.

Admiral of the Fleet Sir George Francis Seymour, G.C.B., born 1787, died 1870 ; son of Lord Hugh Seymour, a distinguished naval officer, the personal friend of William IV, who gave him the Guelphic Order. He served for a short time in Nelson's flagship the *Victory* as a midshipman in 1803, was wounded in the face off St. Domingo in 1806, and afterwards saw service with Lord Cochrane and Lord Gambier. He was sergeant-at-arms to the House of Lords from 1818 to 1841, and naval A.D.C. to William IV. He and his wife Lady Seymour held rooms in the north wing of the south front of Hampton Court Palace from 1820 till Lady Seymour's death in 1878. Sir George Seymour was the father of the fifth and grandfather of the sixth Marquis of Hertford. Among his daughters were Lady Harlech, Countess Gleichen, and Princess Victor Hohenlohe Langenburg.[822] The rooms are now held by Lady Gifford, widow of the second Lord Gifford.

Lady Albinia Cumberland, daughter of George, Earl of Buckinghamshire, married Richard Cumberland, Esq., son of the celebrated dramatic writer. He died in 1794, and she was granted ' The Maids of Honour's Gallery,' which she held till her death in 1850.[822a] The rooms are now occupied by the Hon. Mrs. Saunderson, widow of the late Colonel Saunderson, M.P.

Colonel Sir Horace Seymour, K.C.H., was a younger brother of Sir George ; born 1791, died 1851. He was one of the heroes of Waterloo, and is said to have been an unusually handsome man. He had the ' Secretary at War's Lodging ' on the south side of the west front from 1827. His eldest son became Lord Alcester, and his second son, Colonel Charles Seymour, was killed at Inkerman. His daughter Adelaide married Earl Spencer. He also received the Guelphic Order from William IV.[823]

Lady Sarah Maitland, born 1792, died 1873. She was the second daughter of the fourth Duke of Richmond and Lennox ; married in 1815 General Sir Peregrine Maitland, G.C.B., who died 1854. Lady Sarah was present at the famous ball in Brussels, the night before the Battle of Waterloo. Her two sons were afterwards severely wounded in the Crimea. She had the ' Cofferer's Lodgings,' in the north wing of the west front, from about 1857.[824]

The Countess of Mornington ; Anne daughter of Arthur Hill, first Lord Dungannon, married in 1759 Garrett, first Earl of Mornington, and was the mother of the great Duke of Wellington and of the Marquis Wellesley, the illustrious Governor-General of India, who used to visit her at the palace. The little garden adjoining her rooms (the Prince of Wales' lodgings on the ground floor in the north-east angle of Wren's building), retained for many years the name of ' Lady Mornington's Garden,' and the catalpa tree she planted still survives as a stump covered with creepers. The Duke of Wellington gave the name of ' Purr Corner ' to a nook in the east front of the palace where his mother and her friends used to sit basking in the sun.[825] Another son, the Hon. and Rev. Gerald Valerian Wellesley,[826] was chaplain of the palace, and also held apartments, the rooms known as the Princesses' Lodgings on the first floor, at the east end of the north range. Her daughter, Lady Anne Wellesley, afterwards Fitzroy, afterwards Culling Smith, lived in ' the Queen's Half Storey ' in the east front.[827] Lady Mornington was granted rooms in 1795, and died in 1831. Her rooms are now occupied by Lady Augustus Hervey, widow of the late Lord Augustus Hervey and mother of the present Lord Bristol.

Mrs. Sheridan was another inhabitant, the wife of Thomas Sheridan, son of Richard Brinsley Sheridan, who died in 1817 ; she was the mother of Frank and Charles Sheridan, and her daughters were the three famous beauties, Mrs. Norton, the Duchess of Somerset, and Lady Dufferin, grandmother of the present Marquis of Dufferin and Ava. She had ground-floor rooms on the north side of the palace, off ' the serving place ' opposite Wolsey's kitchen, which were given her in 1820 ; she died in 1851.[828]

Major the Hon. William Beresford is interesting as the last holder of the ancient office of ' Master of the King's Tennis Courts,' to which he was appointed at the age of eighteen. He had the ' Lodgings of the Master of the Tennis Court,' from 1849. They are now occupied by Mr. Marlow, superintendent of the gardens. Major Beresford died in 1883.

Lady Georgiana Grey, daughter of Lord Grey, of Reform celebrity. She acted as secretary to her father, and is often mentioned in the diaries and letters of ministers and literary men of that era.[829]

[820] Law, op. cit. 460.
[821] *Letters*, vii, 149, 16 Nov. 1778.
[822] Law, op. cit. iii, 449 ; *Dict. Nat. Biog.*
[822a] Law, op. cit. iii, 467 ; E. V. Boyle, *Seven Gardens and a Palace*, 269–76.
[823] Law, op. cit. iii, 447.
[824] Ibid. 452.
[825] Ibid. 328, 470.
[826] Ibid. 48b.
[827] Ibid. 473.
[828] Ibid. 333, 479.
[829] Trevelyan, *Life and Letters of Macaulay*, i, 229. *Memoirs of an ex-minister (Lord Malmesbury)*, i, 36 ; Law, op. cit. iii, 413, 469.

She had the 'Duke of York's Apartments' in the south-east angle of Wren's building from about 1861, and died in 1900 in her hundredth year. The rooms are now occupied by Mrs. Creighton, widow of the late Bishop of London.

H.R.H. Princess Frederica of Hanover, daughter of His Majesty the late King of Hanover, second Duke of Cumberland, K.G., married Freiherr von Pawel Rammingen, K.C.B., K.H., &c., and was given the 'Lady Housekeeper's Lodgings' in the south-west wing of the west front in 1880, soon after her marriage. Her daughter was born in this apartment, 7 March 1881, but died three weeks afterwards. Princess Frederica gave up the apart-

tress' and her attendants to uncouth attempts at regal dignity, and such alterations and losses as it has experienced in its existence of nearly four hundred years have assuredly not been due to neglect.

When Wolsey began his great work in 1514, the site was already occupied by a building consisting of a hall with a parlour, kitchen, buttery, and stable, and a chapel which had a tower containing two bells. After the fashion of the *camerae* of the Hospitallers, the buildings differed in no essential way from those of an ordinary mediaeval manor-house, except, perhaps, in the relative importance of the chapel. It is not likely that they were of sufficient importance to influence the setting-out of

HAMPTON COURT PALACE : ENTRANCE COURT, LOOKING TOWARDS THE MOAT

ment in 1898, and it is now held by Lady Wolseley, wife of F.M. Viscount Wolseley, K.P., &c.

ARCHITECTURAL DESCRIPTION With such a history as it can boast, having been built and furnished in the most magnificent and sumptuous manner that the taste and ambition of its first owner could devise, and having passed from him into the hands of a king whose love of splendid buildings became proverbial, it is not to be wondered at that Hampton Court has always been a favourite and carefully-maintained possession of the Tudor, Stuart, and Hanoverian dynasties. Even in the days of the Commonwealth its atmosphere and traditions moved the 'Lady Protec-

Wolsey's buildings, or that their incorporation in the new work was ever contemplated ; at any rate, they have long ceased to exist, leaving no trace behind them.

From 1514 to 1529 the work of building went on under Wolsey's direction and at his expense, although during the last few years the palace had become the property of Henry VIII, and it is hard to say at what point the king took up the cardinal's design. The general setting-out of the plan shows none of the passion for symmetry which was to influence the English architects of Elizabeth's day, although the first or base court follows a regular scheme, having a great gateway tower in the middle of its west or outer side, and a second gate-tower—the clock-tower—corresponding to it on the east. On the east side of the second or clock court is a third gateway, and the centre line of the building passed through a fourth gateway on the east front of the palace. The approach to the palace being from the west, this front is more regular than the rest, being flanked on the north and south by projecting blocks of building, which are, however, additions to the original design, and not of equal size, bearing only a superficial resemblance to each other. The apportionment of the various parts of the building followed that of other great houses of the time, the outer court being devoted to lodgings for guests, long rows of chambers opening to corridors running along the inner side of each wing; while the second court contained the principal sets of rooms, with the great hall on the north side, adjoined on the east by the great chamber, and on the north and west by the kitchens and domestic offices. The chapel stands to the east of the great chamber, separated from it by a small court, and approached by galleries.

The whole of the buildings are of brick, generally of a deep red colour, but by no means uniform in tint, and the wall-surfaces are varied by the insertion of black bricks set in a lattice pattern, often very irregular, and sometimes without any definite design. The string-courses, plinths and copings, and the masonry of doorways and windows, are of stone, for the most part called Reigate stone in the original building accounts, but Caen stone and Barnet stone are also mentioned. The bricks appear to have been made on the spot in vast quantities, and many references to them occur. A long series of the building accounts has been preserved, the earliest dating from 1514, but unfortunately there are many gaps in them between that year and 1529. After this date they are fairly complete up to 1540.[1] On one point of great interest they do not, however, give much information, that is, who occupied the position of architect or designer of the work. Certain overseers are mentioned, as James Bettes, 'master of the works'; Master Lawrence Stubbes, paymaster in 1515–16; and Mr. Henry Williams, priest, 'surveyor of the works,' the last-named probably more nearly fulfilling the duties of a modern architect than the others; but in no case is it clear that the actual designing was done by any of these. In 1536–7 one Mr. Lubbyns is mentioned as being paid £3 6s. 8d. as a half-year's wages, side by side with an entry for 'paper Riall for plattes' for his use; from which it would appear that he certainly set out details of the work if he did not design them.

It is clear that from the first the work was pushed on with great energy. In 1514 there is mention of the chapel and gallery, and in 1515 of the great chamber, the king's dining chamber, the new lodging without the gate, &c.; and by 1516 the buildings were so far advanced that Wolsey could entertain the king at Hampton Court. Labourers were collected from distant parts of the

country, Northamptonshire and Oxfordshire being mentioned; and in the accounts for 1514 is a payment 'for the statutes of the last parliament bought, forasmuch as in them were comprised the statute of labourers and artificers,' much as anyone proposing to build at the present day might arm himself with a copy of the London Building Act.

The absence of the greater part of the building accounts during the years when Wolsey was in possession makes it impossible to determine the order in which the various parts of his palace were set up, but it is reasonable to suppose that the principal buildings, the hall, chapel, great chamber, &c., would be undertaken first. Henry added to and rebuilt a certain amount of the cardinal's work, but his additions were for the most part at the south-east, on the ground now occupied by Wren's buildings; and it seems probable that when Wolsey finally left Hampton Court in 1529 its area was little less than it is at the present day. The outer or base court as it now stands, a good part of the Clock Court, the range of kitchens and offices on the north, including the Lord Chamberlain's Court, the Master Carpenter's Court, the Fish Court, &c., together with parts of the chapel and perhaps some of the range to the north of the Chapel Court, all seem to be in the main of his time. His Great Hall, though no doubt a fine building, was evidently not fine enough for the king, who pulled it down in 1530 and finished the splendid hall which now exists about 1535. At the same time Henry seems to have remodelled, and partly rebuilt, the fine range of rooms to the east of the hall and the eastern range of the Clock Court, and in 1535–6 he refitted the chapel, adding the organ chamber on the south, but apparently not rebuilding the chapel nor making any important structural alteration. It is, indeed, called in one place of the accounts the King's New Chapel, but this does not necessarily imply a rebuilding; and in the entry relating to the enormous sum of £451 spent on the wooden vault and the royal 'holyday closettes,' the heading is for 'payntyng, gyltyng, and varnesshyng of the vought,' and the making of pendants and other details.

The tennis court—the 'close tennys play' of the accounts—and a 'close bowling alley,' at the north-east of the palace, were among the first additions made by the king in 1529, and he also lost no time in adding new kitchens and offices, being evidently no more content with the cardinal's kitchens than with his Great Hall.

Of Henry's immediate successors neither Edward VI nor Mary has left any mark on the palace, and Elizabeth is only commemorated by a little work on the south front, close to the southwest angle of Wren's building, where a bay window bears her initials and the date 1568, and by another panel on the east side of the entrance gateway of the first court. Inigo Jones was appointed surveyor of Hampton Court, among other places, in 1615; and though there is no record of anything done about this time to the

[1] In the P.R.O.; Chap. House Accts. New Misc. Bks. Exch. T.R. no. 235–46. They are folios of about five hundred pages each, beautifully written, and giving most minute details of the work.

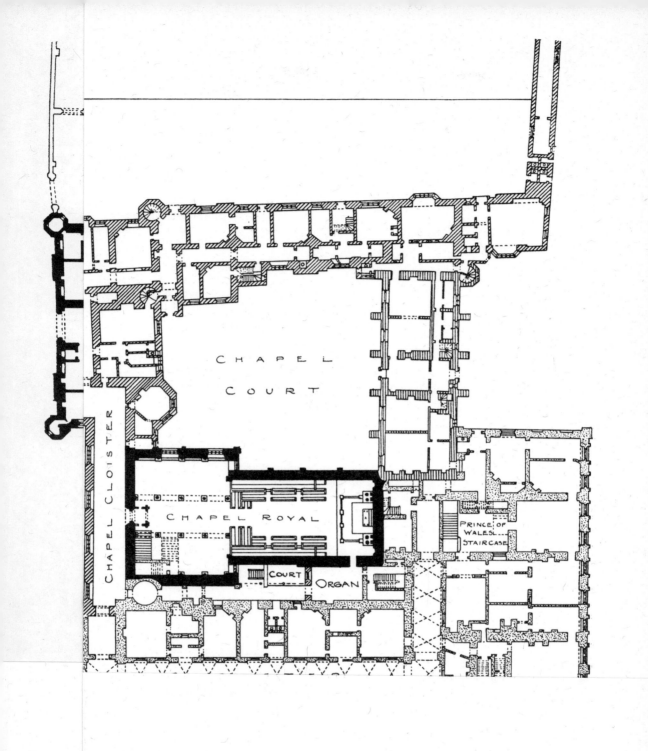

CHAPEL COURT

CHAPEL CLOISTER

CHAPEL ROYAL

COURT ORGAN

PRINCE OF WALES STAIRCASE

buildings, the block forming the east side of the Chapel Court shows detail belonging to the early years of the 17th century, and may preserve this evidence of Jones's supervision. Charles I, in the earlier years of his reign, was much occupied in furnishing and adorning the palace and gardens, but does not seem to have built anything of importance.

The extent of the buildings at the end of his reign is very clearly set forth in the survey taken by order of the Parliament in 1653, when it was proposed to sell the palace and its grounds in a number of separate lots, and to pull down all the buildings.

Beginning from the west, a green court inclosed, being the outer court, is first noted, from which a bridge led over the moat into the first court, also called a green court, that is, the present Base or outer Court. The ranges of buildings surrounding it are then noted, and a description of the Pond Garden, or Pond Yard, on the south follows. The Clock Court—then the Fountain Court—is next described, as 'paved with stone with a ffountayne standing in midst thereof,' with the buildings round it, the great hall being merely called a range of building like the rest. Then comes the Cloister Green Court, on the site of the present Fountain Court, with the Privy Garden and the Mount Garden to the south. The chapel, with its court and surrounding buildings, is summarized as 'severall other buildings, with the severall yards or courts lying betweene and amongst the sayd buildings.' The outlying buildings are then noticed, beginning at the north, though here again the tennis court &c. are not mentioned by name; then comes the Tilt-yard at the north-west, with its five buildings or towers, and then the projecting block at the south end of the west front, with a 'greate howse of easement,' now destroyed, standing over the moat. Finally the buildings on the south, towards the river, are surveyed, the Feather House and Hott House, with the Store Cellars, formerly the old Bowling Alley, between them, and the Stillhouse and Water Gallery to the east of them. On the south side of the Outer Green Court was the wood-yard, having to the west the Privy bakehouse, the Poultry Office, and the Scalding-house, and at the south-west angle of the same court a house called the 'Toye.'[2]

Hampton Court fortunately escaped the threatened destruction and became the residence of Cromwell and the scene of his sorry court, passing through the days of the Commonwealth with much loss of its furniture and treasures, both by the great sale which lasted from 1650 to 1653, and by the peculations of Cromwell's family after his death, but not suffering any material damage in its buildings.

Charles II made a good many internal altera-

HAMPTON COURT PALACE: CHAPEL COURT FROM SOUTH-WEST CORNER

tions, of which some evidence yet remains, and spent a great deal of money in refurnishing the depleted rooms. He paid special attention to the tennis court, which had evidently become somewhat old-fashioned, and the extent of his work at the palace may be estimated from the fact that in 1662 nearly £8,000 was paid over to Hugh May, master of the works, for charges and repairs.

In spite of all these changes, the buildings of Hampton Court remained to the outward view much as Henry VIII left them until the Revolution

[2] Pulled down in 1857. The bakehouse, poultry office, and scalding-house survived for a few years longer.

of 1688. William III was at once attracted by the quiet and secluded situation, but found the palace itself old-fashioned, and not at all to his taste, and soon decided to rebuild the old state apartments, whose historical associations stood for very little with him. Indeed, a far more extensive scheme of rebuilding, having for its object the making of a new approach to the palace from the north, on the line of the avenue in Bushey Park, was contemplated ; but, however fine the result might and doubtless would have been, it is impossible to regret its abandonment. As it is, the destruction of the Cloister Court, which must have been, after the hall and chapel, the finest part of the palace, is infinitely regrettable ; and though one would not willingly spare any part of the old buildings, it is to be wished that William could have decided to sacrifice almost any other court of the palace than this. The work was entrusted to Wren, who set out a new court, now known as the Fountain Court, on the old site, with great ranges of buildings on the south and east, 315 and 300 ft. long respectively, harmonizing to some extent with the older work in the use of red brick with stone dressings, and in themselves very charming examples of his work, but undeniably out of scale and character with the Tudor palace, to the picturesque irregularities of which their stiff classic lines cannot adapt themselves. In spite of various hindrances, quarrels with Talman the 'comptroller of the works,' and a good deal of injudicious meddling on the part of his royal client, Wren carried on the work, so that in 1691 it was in a fair way to completion. One source of delay had been the failure in the supply of Portland stone, owing to the presence in the Channel of a victorious French fleet. The fitting up and decoration of the new buildings was a lengthy and costly business, Grinling Gibbons and Caius Gabriel Cibber being employed among other less known sculptors, Laguerre among the painters, and to Jean Tijou and his assistant, Huntingdon Shaw, was given the work of making the well-known gates and screens of wrought-iron which inclosed the gardens on the south. The works were brought to a standstill for a time by the death of Queen Mary in 1694, but begun again after the burning of Whitehall in 1698, Verrio the painter being first employed, as it seems, in 1699, and the work of decoration was pushed on energetically. It seems that the scheme already referred to of building a great new entrance court on the north, and turning the great hall into a sort of vestibule, with flights of stone steps leading up to it on the north side, was now drawn up. It would have involved the destruction of the great watching chamber and all the eastern range of the Clock Court, as well as of the great kitchens and much of the work near them ; and though the palace would thereby have obtained a very stately façade and a dignified approach, the wholesale destruction of the Tudor work would have been an irreparable loss. There is ample evidence, too, that it would not have stopped here, and if William had lived he would probably have rebuilt the whole palace, and thereby destroyed a chapter of English history for which no master-

piece of Wren's creation could compensate us. The problematical 'little gentleman in black velvet' did good service to others than the Jacobites who drank his health. The year 1699 was marked by a further attempt by Talman to discredit Wren, which came to nothing, and when the king returned from Holland late in the year he was full of admiration for what had been done. Under Queen Anne the works continued, the most important item being perhaps the refitting of the chapel in 1710 ; but the unfortunate aversion of the queen to paying the debts incurred by her predecessor and herself made her reign a period of ceaseless 'dunning' by the various artists employed, such as Verrio and Tijou (who appears as John Tissue), and the builders and masons and sculpture-merchants. Under the Georges various works were carried on, and the fitting up of Wren's buildings may be considered to have been completed in the time of George I, which was otherwise and less pleasantly signalized, as already stated, by the disgraceful supersession of Wren in his old age in favour of the incapable Benson. George II has left his mark on the east range of the Clock Court, a good deal of work being done by Kent at the time, c. 1730. The scheme for altering the Great Hall was now again brought forward, but fortunately abandoned. After this time the interest in the buildings gradually declined, George III entirely abandoning Hampton Court, and leaving it neglected. In spite of this certain considerable repairs were carried out, such as the rebuilding of the Great Gatehouse in 1773, and the repair of the Great Hall in 1798. With the revival of interest in archaeology the buildings naturally received more attention, and at the present time everything is admirably and systematically cared for, about £5,000 a year being spent in repairs and maintenance. The beginning of the reign of Edward VII was marked by the making of a fine and complete plan of all the buildings, from which the plans which accompany this description are reproduced by special permission.

The approach to the palace is now, as always, from the west. The entrance to the precincts is through a gate with stone piers, the work of Kent, c. 1730, surmounted by lead figures of the lion and unicorn and trophies of arms. The roadway thence runs in a slanting direction to the main entrance, the gatehouse on the west side of the first court, passing on the left hand a long line of late 17th-century brick buildings of two stories, built for stabling and offices. In the past two years the appearance of the entrance front of the palace has been immensely improved by the clearing out of the wide moat between the wings at either end of the front, which had been filled in about 1690, and the uncovering and repair of the stone bridge crossing it. This bridge was built in 1536 by Henry VIII, replacing a bridge probably of wood, built by Wolsey, and from the full details remaining in the building accounts it has been possible to reproduce the lost portions, that is, the parapets, pinnacles, and shield-bearing beasts set thereon, with a high degree of certainty. The gateway to which it leads was largely rebuilt in

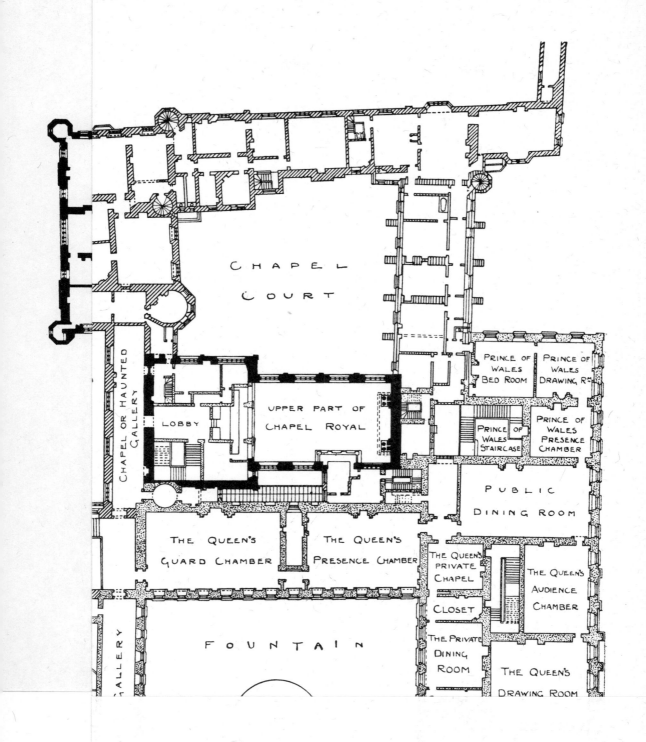

CHAPEL COURT

CHAPEL OR HAUNTED GALLERY

LOBBY

UPPER PART OF CHAPEL ROYAL

PRINCE OF WALES BED ROOM

PRINCE OF WALES DRAWING Rᵐ

PRINCE OF WALES STAIRCASE

PRINCE OF WALES PRESENCE CHAMBER

PUBLIC DINING ROOM

THE QUEEN'S GUARD CHAMBER

THE QUEEN'S PRESENCE CHAMBER

THE QUEEN'S PRIVATE CHAPEL CLOSET

THE PRIVATE DINING ROOM

THE QUEEN'S AUDIENCE CHAMBER

GALLERY

FOUNTAIN

THE QUEEN'S DRAWING ROOM

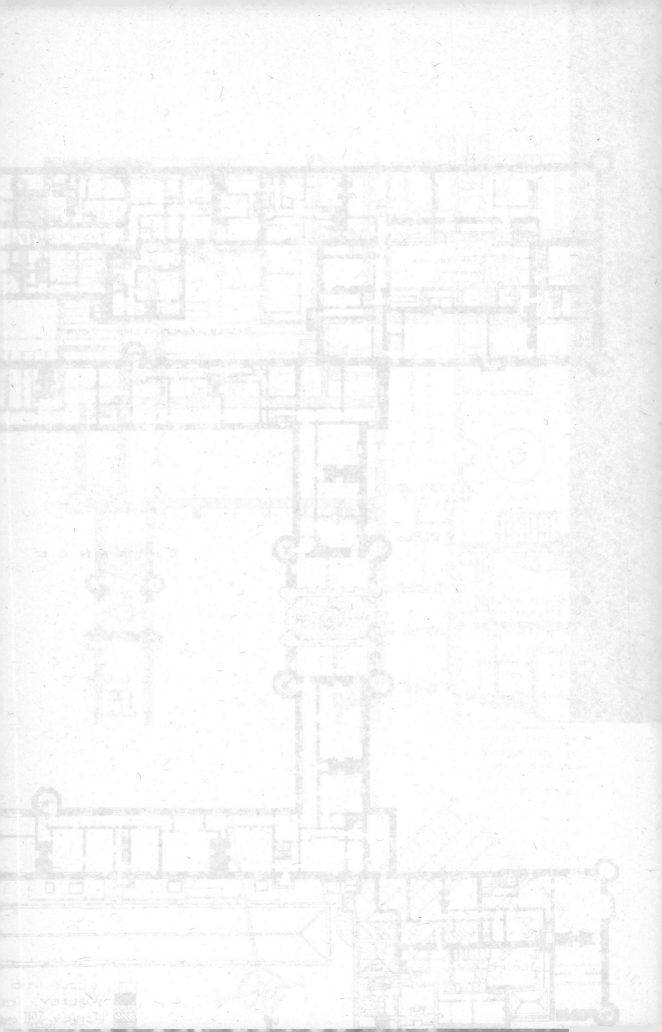

1773, losing greatly in dignity and interest thereby. The old gatehouse, of which several drawings exist, the most accurate being some measured drawings by Kent made about forty years before its rebuilding, was of five stories, and much taller than the present building. Instead of a single arch in the middle it had two arches, a large one for carriages and a small one for foot passengers, opening into the gate hall, and the large arch was in consequence not on the centre line of the gatehouse. This affected the oriel window over it, which, being set over the arch, was likewise not in the middle of the elevation. The openwork parapet above flanked by pinnacles has been reproduced in the present gateway, and the octagonal angle turrets stand on their old bases. About 1873 a stone vault was added to the gate hall, and the pinnacles of the parapet continued downwards as buttresses, precisely on the line of the parapets of the stone bridge, which, as now restored, butt against them.

As already noted, the wings at each end of the moat are additions to the original design, but are not of much later date, as the outer wall of the moat, built probably about 1537, is built against them. A staircase leads down into the south-west corner of the moat from the south wing, but there is now no evidence of any sluice for emptying the moat into the Thames, though something of the kind doubtless existed.

The buildings of the first court are of two stories with embattled parapets, the detail very simple, and the ornament confined to the pinnacles on the parapets and the chimney-stacks. The dark tint of the red brick walls is accentuated by the black pointing in the joints, an original feature, as may be proved by the entries in the building accounts for burnt hay for colouring the pointing of the walls. The windows are for the most part of three lights with uncusped four-centred heads. Their stonework has been very largely renewed, and none of the cut-brick chimney-shafts are old. The gateways are the chief architectural features, being of greater height than the rest of the buildings, and having angle turrets and panels of the royal arms over the archways. They are further distinguished by the large terra-cotta roundels with portraits of Roman Emperors, of which there were originally ten in the palace, made for Wolsey by Giovanni Maiano in 1521. These, with the fine panel of Wolsey's arms over the gateway in the Clock Court, are the only examples of terra-cotta now to be seen at Hampton Court; but that there must have been more of it originally is clear, both from documentary evidence and from the pieces of architectural detail now kept in the Great Kitchen,

having been dug up in the Round Kitchen Court not many years since. One very ornamental feature, now almost entirely lost, was the leaden cappings of the turrets; a good specimen still exists on the garden front of the Clock Court, with finial, crockets, and pinnacled buttresses. Such cappings are called 'types' in the building accounts.

Behind the north range of the first court lie three small irregular courts, the Chamberlain's, the Master Carpenter's, and the Fish Court. Though much repaired, and the least imposing part of the 16th-century palace—all being part of Wolsey's work—they are extremely picturesque, and at the east of them are the two kitchens, fine and lofty rooms with huge fireplaces, ovens, &c., and the remains of open-timbered roofs. The chimney stacks and stepped copings over the fireplaces towards Tennis Court Lane are particularly good specimens of Tudor brickwork, though the

HAMPTON COURT PALACE:
TERRA-COTTA PANEL OF WOLSEY'S ARMS

shafts of the chimneys are modern. To the east of the kitchens is the serving-place, a wide passage into which hatches open from the kitchen, and from which the dishes were taken to the north door of the hall, across the long corridor which connects the Round Kitchen Court with the three small courts at the west. The windows of the corridor are glazed, and have ventilating panes of pierced leadwork copied from old specimens.

The Clock Court, formerly called the Fountain Court, from a fountain set here by Wolsey and altered by Henry VIII, is in some ways the most interesting part of the palace, as giving some idea of the appearance of the destroyed buildings to the east of it, which contained the finest rooms other than the hall and chapel. On the west and south sides the work is Wolsey's, though the latter range is masked by Wren's colonnade; on the east Wolsey's work, much rebuilt by Henry, has been considerably altered and refaced in the time of George II, while the north side is taken up by Henry's Great Hall, which, except for much external repair and the loss of its lantern and minor fittings, remains in good preservation. Over the entrance gateway at the north-west is the dial of the clock from which the court takes its modern name, a fine piece of 16th-century work, lately repainted and repaired. The Great Hall stands over a range of cellars, and having its floor at a considerable height above the level of the court, is approached by a flight of stone steps from the gate-hall of the Clock Tower, leading to a fine door at the south end of the screens. A similar flight of steps on the north leads to the corresponding door, and served as the entry from the kitchens and butteries, &c., the disposition of the plan not allowing for these offices in the normal places at the lower end of the hall. There was, however, a pantry in this position, and the buttery was in the cellars under the west end of the hall. The hall measures 106 ft. by 40 ft., and is 45 ft. high to the plate and 92 ft. to the top of the gable. It is in seven bays, of which the eastern bay was occupied by the dais, the platform of which still remains, and is lighted by a splendid bay window on the south, rising to the full height of the wall, with a rich fan-vaulted stone ceiling and six tiers of lights with tracery above in the head of the window. The other bays of the hall have large four-light windows, and in the western bay are the screens with a gallery over them; in both gable ends of the hall are eight-light traceried windows, with smaller windows in the gable above. All these are filled with modern stained glass, nothing of the old glass now remaining. The screen is a very fine piece of woodwork, the treatment of its two openings, with large round pillars on either side having moulded capitals and bases, being unusual. The details of the work are Gothic, and the initials of Henry and Anne Boleyn sufficiently mark its date; it is to be noted that its carver was the same Richard Ridge of London who made the Italianate pendants in the roof above. The original front of the gallery over the screen was long since removed, but its place is now supplied by a modern front. The roof of the hall is well known as one of the richest and most splendid of English roofs; its construction and outlines are Gothic, but much of its ornament is Italian in style, though made by English craftsmen. It has hammer-beam trusses with arched braces springing from the hammer beams to strengthen the collars, while the spandrels above and below the collars, and below the hammer beams, are filled with tracery. The purlins are similarly strengthened by arched braces with pendants, and the whole surface of the roof is coved and panelled, and is everywhere enriched with carving, colour, and gilding. The most remarkable features are the sixteen great pendants, nearly 5 ft. long, below the hammer beams, carved by Richard Ridge in 1534-5, at a cost of 3s. 4d. each. The building accounts of this roof are well worth study as a glossary of mediaeval carpenter's terms. Externally the roof is leaded, and is of much flatter pitch in the upper

part than the lower; its appearance is much injured by the removal in the 18th century of the magnificent louvre or fumerel, a complete description of which can be obtained from the building accounts. Nothing equal to it is left to us.

To the east of the hall is the 'King's Great Watching Chamber,' which, with the vaulted cellar below it, was being built in 1534-5. It is lighted by a range of windows set high in the wall and a fine semicircular bay window on the south-east, and has a contemporary panelled ceiling with shields modelled in papier mâché at the intersections of the moulded ribs.

Jane Seymour's badge occurs twice on the ceiling, perhaps replacing that of Anne Boleyn.

At the north-west corner of the Watching Chamber is a smaller room known as the Horn Room; and in this, the Watching Chamber, and the hall are preserved the finest of the tapestries for which Wolsey's palace was famous. For a description of them see Mr. Law's *History of Hampton Court*.

On the east side of the Clock Court ran a series of five rooms opening from the Watching Chamber, the King's Presence Chamber and his private rooms, now so altered as to preserve little evidence of their former arrangement. For the disposition of the whole of Henry VIII's buildings round the Cloister Green Court, whose site is now occupied by the Fountain Court of William III, and the queen's lodgings on the east front of the palace, built for Anne Boleyn, but never occupied by her, the evidence of old drawings and an outline plan now at All Souls College, Oxford, and especially the many references to them in the building accounts, give very valuable materials which still await a thorough working-out. The great galleries of which mention is often made were evidently splendid examples of this peculiarly English feature, and of earlier date than any which have come down to our times; indeed, those which are recorded to have existed in Wolsey's palace, built about 1515-16, are the earliest of which any notice has survived in the kingdom.

To the east of the Watching Chamber is a small court known as the Round Kitchen Court, from a round building which, in its present condition, appears to date from the 18th century; drawings showing a scheme by Kent, c. 1730, for fitting it up as a latrine, are extant. On the north and east the court has a cloister, with a gallery over it, leading to the chapel, which is on the east side, and consists of a vestibule flanked by octagonal turrets, with the royal pew in a gallery above, and the chapel proper, an aisleless building of four bays with an organ chamber on the south-east. The walls are of Wolsey's date, but the organ chamber is an addition by Henry VIII; and the vaulted wooden roof is also of his time. The rest of the 16th-century fittings, except for a beautiful ceiling over the stairs to the royal pew, have been removed, after much damage in Cromwell's days, and the present fittings date from the time of Anne and later. The panelling of the vestibule and staircase, and the Corinthian altarpiece, are particularly good; but here, as in the

HAMPTON COURT PALACE : BRIDGE OVER THE MOAT

hall, the roof is the most notable feature, with its coffered vault and three rows of gilded pendants, round each of which are grouped four figures of angels playing pipes, singing from scrolls, or holding sceptres. The west door of the chapel, opening to the cloister, has on either side a large stone panel with the arms and initials of Henry VIII and Jane Seymour, supported by angels, though it seems that Anne Boleyn's arms were formerly here, and from the nature of the supporters Mr. Law suggests that the panels originally held the cardinal's arms. The entry of the carving of a crown for each of these panels in Henry VIII's time bears out this suggestion; but otherwise this work, though Italian in feeling, is notably inferior, and hardly what one would expect from Wolsey's workmen.

To the north of the chapel is the Chapel Court, bounded on the north by the range of buildings which were assigned to Prince Edward from 1537 onwards; they have suffered in recent years by fire, and contain nothing of their old fittings. Very little indeed remains in the palace of the magnificent decoration which was famous throughout Europe in the 16th century. In the west range of the Clock Court are some good linen-panelled rooms, and in the south range the rooms, traditionally Wolsey's private lodging, have some ceilings of the time; but the best idea of the splendour of Wolsey's ornament is to be gained from a room in the east range of the court, reached from the Mantegna Gallery on the first floor of the Fountain Court. This has a very rich geometrical ceiling, the panels of which have only recently been discovered to be of lead, with the 'gold and byse' colouring characteristic of its date, a narrow frieze with the cardinal's 'word' and badges, and below it some oil paintings on panel, of the Last Supper, the Scourging, the Bearing of the Cross, and the Resurrection, perhaps the work of Luca Penni or Toto del Nunziato. Below the paintings the walls were doubtless covered with hangings.

The south-east quarter of the palace is occupied by the Fountain Court, the work of Sir Christopher Wren. His buildings are in three stories, the ground floor towards the court being occupied by a cloister, and towards the gardens by ranges of rooms, now private apartments. Queen Mary seems to have used the walks of the cloister and part of the south range as a greenhouse and orangery, and Defoe mentions in his *Tour Through Great Britain* that 'the lower part of the house was all one as a greenhouse for some time.' The principal apartments are on the first or chamber floor, with a mezzanine or half-story over, the area of which is thrown into the largest rooms to increase their height. The third or attic floor has always been divided into suites of rooms, which still retain their official name of Galleries. The principal elevation is that facing east, 300 ft. long and 60 ft. high, divided into twenty-three bays, the seven middle bays forming a symmetrical composition, more elaborately treated than the rest and faced with Portland stone. The three in the middle have on the ground floor square-headed

gateways, opening to a vestibule leading to the cloisters of the Fountain Court, the piers between the gateways being of Portland stone with drafted joints, and serving as plinths for half-columns of the Corinthian order, which with their cornice frieze and architrave occupy the full height of the first floor, and carry a pediment whose apex reaches nearly to the top of the attic story. In each bay between the columns are tall stone-framed sash windows surmounted by cornices, and a band of carved ornament equal in depth to the capitals of the columns. The pediment incloses a group of sculpture by Caius Gabriel Cibber, 'The Triumph of Hercules over Envy,' carved between 1694 and 1696, for which the sculptor was paid £400. The two bays on each side of the middle three have square-headed windows on the ground story, and flat pilasters instead of half-round columns above. The cornice and band of carving beneath it is continued across them, and the attic stage above is divided by pilasters enriched with carving, carrying up the lines of the pilasters on the first floor. The attic windows are square, fitted with sashes like the others, the heavy sash-bars of which make a most attractive feature, and the whole is finished with a stone balustrade, divided into bays like the rest by panelled pilasters. On either side of the seven stone-faced bays are eight more simply treated, without pilasters and with red-brick walling. The ground-floor windows have low arched heads with prettily carved keystones, and the first-floor windows are like those in the middle bays, but over them runs a line of circular windows, lighting the half-story, and having carved keystones of very good style. Immediately above is a cornice ranging with that in the middle bays, but of much less depth and projection, and the treatment of the attic over has the same modifications of the design of the middle bays as that of the first floor.

The south elevation is of twenty-five bays, four at either end projecting 8 ft. in front of the rest, and has a stone-faced central composition of three bays with Corinthian columns on the first floor carrying a cornice inscribed 'Gulielmus et Maria RR.F.' The treatment is simpler than that of the east front, but, on the other hand, the seven bays on either side are not mere repetitions of each other, as on the east, but their middle bays have pediments over the first-floor windows surmounted by the royal arms of William and Mary supported by cupids, and the bays on either side have swags of fruit instead of the round half-story windows. The arms seem to be Gabriel Cibber's work, but much of the purely architectural decoration both here and on the east front was probably done by Grinling Gibbons, or under his supervision. Various payments to him between 1691 and 1696 show that a great deal of the ornament on Wren's building must be his work.

The least satisfactory part of the design is the sky line, now unbroken except by rows of singularly unattractive chimneys, but originally a little relief was given by four statues standing on the middle bays of the balustrades on each face; they were removed in the 18th century.

The elevations to the Fountain Court, although following the same lines as those of the fronts, are distinctly more attractive, partly no doubt from the contrast of light and shade which their four-square arrangement produces, but also because the horizontal lines of the cornices over the first-floor windows are here replaced by pediments, and the open arches of the cloisters beneath, with their well-carved keystones,[3] and lunettes filling the heads of the arches, are far more effective, backed as they are by the cloister walks, than the external range of windows of the ground story. The round half-story windows are here made the most ornamental

of view of planning, almost as much interest as those of the older buildings, both representing, it must be assumed, the best traditions of their time.

The State Apartments occupy the first and principal floor of the buildings on three sides of the Fountain Court, and their disposition shows little advance on those of the Tudor palace. The King's Great Staircase at the south-east corner of the Clock Court leads to the King's Guard Chamber in the projecting block at the west end of the south front, overlooking the privy garden, and from it a series of rooms runs eastward, opening one from another, the Presence Chamber, the second Presence Chamber, the Audience Chamber, the King's Drawing-room, and his State Bedroom. These occupy rather more than half of the width of the range, the other part towards the Fountain Court being taken up by the Great Gallery or Council Chamber, which can be entered from either end of the king's suite of rooms, at the south-east from the State Bedroom, and at the west, through an anteroom, from the second Presence Chamber. On the west side of the Fountain Court, and opening to the north side of the anteroom, is the gallery which leads to the Queen's Staircase and State Rooms. These are not so symmetrically arranged as the king's suite, the Guard Chamber and Presence Chamber, which occupy the north side of the court, opening through a lobby to the Public Dining-room at the east, from the south-east corner of which the rest of the Queen's Apartments are reached, consisting of three rooms, Audience Chamber, Drawing-

HAMPTON COURT PALACE:
FOUNTAIN COURT FROM THE NORTH-WEST CORNER

features of the elevations, being encircled by wreaths of foliage over which are hung lions' skins, arranged with a care for symmetry which is almost comic, especially in the treatment of the tail of the beast. The west elevation of the court is of two stories only, and consists of the cloister walk with a corridor above—the 'Communication Gallery' of the old accounts—masking the older buildings on the east of the Clock Court.[4]

The internal arrangements have, from the point

room, and Bedroom. These face eastward, and occupy the middle of the east front, having the Queen's Gallery to the south of them, while the west side of this range, facing towards the Fountain Court, is divided into a set of small rooms, the private apartments of the king and queen. The three small rooms and a staircase at the angle of the south-west wings are also private apartments, but open one from another, completing the passage round the outer side of the two fronts.

---

[3] The heads on nearly all these keystones were replaced about five years ago by careful copies of the original heads.

[4] One doorway in the Fountain Court has Wren's cipher above it; this is believed to be the only one in the place. See p. 367.

Hampton Court Palace: The Gateway

The north end of the east front, beyond the Public Dining-room, is occupied by a set of three rooms and a stair, known as the Prince of Wales's Apartments. Practically the whole of the State Apartments have now become picture-galleries, and the remains of their sumptuous decorations and furniture can claim at best only a divided attention. The grandiose wall and ceiling paintings of Verrio and Laguerre, however admired in their own day, have lost their vogue, and it is impossible to look at such decorations as those of the King's Staircase without a certain impatience at the riot of feeble allegory which they present. They are the work of Verrio. A banquet of the gods occupies the ceiling, and continues down the east wall, where it merges into a medley of Roman history, in which the twelve Caesars appear in the company of Æneas, Romulus, and the Wolf, presided over by the genius of Rome. On the north wall are Flora, Iris, Ceres, Pan, Apollo, and the Muses, in a crowd of cupids, nymphs, and river gods, and on the south wall Julian the Apostate is talking to Mercury. The Queen's Staircase is more simply, but not more attractively, treated in monochrome, with its ceiling painted to represent a dome, and scrollwork and 'property' figures on its walls, the work of Kent. Its wrought-iron handrails, however, like those of the King's Staircase, are another matter, and very beautiful work of their kind. The King's State Bedroom has a ceiling by Verrio, with Diana watching the sleeping Endymion, and a figure of Sleep, while in the King's Bedroom the ceiling shows Mars and Venus. It is in Queen Anne's Drawing-room, however, that the most important remains of Verrio's work are to be found, painted in 1704–5. On the ceiling the queen appears in the character of Justice, with scales and sword, attended by Neptune and Britannia ; on the west wall she is seated receiving the homage of the four quarters of the globe ; on the north wall her husband, Prince George, stands armed, and pointing to the British fleet ; and on the south wall Cupid is being drawn over the waves by sea-horses. The wall pictures having only been uncovered in 1899, after being hidden for more than 150 years behind canvas, are wonderfully fresh and brilliant, although a good deal of repair has been carried out. In the Queen's State Bedroom is a ceiling painted by Thornhill, with Aurora rising from the ocean in her chariot, and in the cornice are portraits of George I, Queen Caroline, George II, and Frederick Prince of Wales. The rooms are panelled either to the full height or on the lower parts only, the finest panelling being that of the Great Gallery in which Raphael's cartoons used to hang. This room was fitted up in 1699, and is no less than 117 ft. long by 28 ft. high, and 24 ft. wide, divided into six double bays by pairs of Corinthian pilasters carrying a rich cornice, above

which hang the tapestries which take the place of the original cartoons. All the details of the woodwork are admirable, and only equalled by their state of preservation, the oak being absolutely sound and perfect ; the carving is probably due to Gibbons and his assistants, and many other examples of equally beautiful work from his hand are to be seen throughout the State Rooms. A number of the chimney-pieces are, however, the work of Kent about 1730.

PICTURES The pictures in the State Apartments are chiefly remarkable as a collection made for all the kings of England since Henry VIII, by men of widely differing tastes, opportunities and knowledge. It is perhaps inevitable that a royal gallery should include more portraits than any other kind of picture—the 'king's painter' is almost invariably a portrait painter—and this adds to the interest of the series at Hampton Court. Contemporary portraits of historical personages have their own value apart from their artistic merits, and more than a third of these pictures are such portraits.

There are also a considerable number of old Italian pictures, chiefly by the less-known painters, whose works are rarely seen in England.[1] Among these may be mentioned two by Correggio, a 'Holy Family with St. James' (no. 430),[2] 'St. Catherine Reading' (no. 429), and 'A Shepherd with a Pipe,' said to be by Giorgione (no. 113), which Miss Logan considers 'the most precious picture at Hampton Court.'

Henry VIII began the collection, with some paintings on wood,[3] by Anthony Toto (Toto del Nunziato), but these no longer remain. Among the Tudor pictures are twenty which are said to have been painted by Holbein, but only three of them are recognized as genuine by the experts.[4] They are the portraits of 'Lady Vaux' (no. 270), and 'John Reskemeer (no. 265), of which the original drawings are at Windsor Castle ; and the portrait of 'Frobenius Erasmus,' printer (no. 280), but the authenticity of the last is doubtful. The other pictures, which are of Holbein's school, are none the less interesting, especially those representing historical subjects, such as 'The Meeting of Henry VIII and the Emperor Maximilian' (no. 445), the 'Battle of the Spurs' (no. 452), and the 'Field of the Cloth of Gold' (no. 455).[5] There is also the well-known group of Henry VIII and his family in the cloisters at Hampton Court, with Will Somers the Jester and 'Jane the Fool' in the background (no. 453) ; there are also several portraits of Henry, notably one said to be by Jost van Cleeg (no. 269), of Edward VI, Elizabeth and Mary, of Francis I (no. 264), and others of the period. The little copy of 'Henry VIII and Jane Seymour, Henry VII and Elizabeth of York' (no. 271) was painted by Rémee van Lemput in 1667, from the famous fresco by

---

[1] See Mary Logan, *The Italian Pictures at Hampton Court.*

[2] The numbers are given from Mr. Law's *New Authorized Historical Catalogue,* 1907, but the pictures are constantly moved and changed.

[3] The pictures painted on panel representing scenes in the 'Passion of Our Lord,' which hang in 'Cardinal Wolsey's Closet,' are possibly by Toto del Nunziato.

[4] Law, *The Royal Gallery of Hampton Court,* Introd. p. xx.

[5] These can all be identified from the inventory of Henry's possessions, made after his death and now in the British Museum.

Holbein at Whitehall, destroyed by the fire in 1698. There are several portraits of Queen Elizabeth, notably one in fancy dress, said to be by Zucchero (no. 309) ;[6] a startling allegorical picture of the queen with Minerva, Juno, and Venus by De Heere (no. 250), and two very characteristic portraits in all her glory of jewelled headdress, lace ruff, and wonderful strings of pearls ; one is said to be by Zucchero (no. 320), and one by Mark Gerrard (no. 619),[7] which represents her as an old woman, and is said to be her last portrait. There are also some comparatively inferior portraits of the statesmen of her reign, Walsingham, Leicester, Sir Nicholas Bacon, and Charles Howard, Earl of Nottingham. James I did not add much to the glory of the royal picture gallery ; there is a portrait of Mary Queen of Scots, a copy by Mytens, and one or two of James himself and of Queen Anne of Denmark ; two are by Vansomer (no. 515 and no. 521). There is also a fine portrait of the first Duke of Buckingham, by Janssen (no. 57). Charles I attempted to form a collection which could worthily be called 'royal.' The greater number of pictures at Hampton Court, including the best Italian examples, are from his 'gallery,' though many were scattered and lost during the Commonwealth. The equestrian portrait of Charles himself (no. 85) is probably from Vandyck's studio, and is a copy of the famous picture at Windsor. The only genuine work by Vandyck is a portrait of Mrs. Lemon (no. 317) ; and the only example of Rubens is a 'Diana and her Nymphs Reposing after the Chase,' in which the animals and background were painted by Snyders.

In 1628 Charles acquired the famous gallery of the Dukes of Mantua, including Mantegna's nine great cartoons, which form the most valuable part of the Hampton Court collection, and hang in the 'Communication Gallery' (or Mantegna Gallery) on the west side of the Fountain Court. They were painted (on twilled linen in tempera) by Mantegna for Ludovico Gonzago, Duke of Mantua, begun in 1486 and finished in 1492. They are said to have originally decorated a gallery in the duke's Palace of St. Sebastian, Mantua, and have been enthusiastically appreciated by many connoisseurs,[8] but are now much out of repair ; it is said that they were coarsely repainted by Laguerre in the reign of William III.

It must not be supposed that all the pictures collected by Charles I hung originally at Hampton Court, where the great rooms which now contain some of them had not been built ; they were divided, as the art treasures of the Crown are still divided, among the various dwellings of the sovereign. The king's pictures, sold after his death 'by order of the Parliament,' realized £38,000 ; the sale lasting about five years. From Hampton Court 382 pictures were disposed of for nearly £5,000 ;

among them Mantegna's 'Triumph' was valued at £1,000, but was saved by Cromwell, who also saved the great Raphael cartoons, for which Wren afterwards built a special gallery.[9] A certain number of the pictures were returned to Charles II by the States of Holland, from the collection of Van Reynot, who had purchased them at the sale.

The portraits of the Restoration period are well-known, and the collection of Lely's 'Beauties,' now in the 'King's State Bedchamber,' is famous. Kneller's portraits of Queen Mary's ladies were painted in emulation of the earlier set, and are more dignified, but far stiffer and less beautiful ; the large allegorical picture of William III landing at Margate in 1697 (no. 29) hangs in 'William the Third's Presence Chamber,' Pope's satirical lines perhaps describe it adequately :

'And great Nassau, to Kneller's hand decreed,
     To fix him graceful on the bounding steed.'

Queen Mary collected about twenty pictures by Baptiste, the well-known flower-painter of his time, and there are also a great many pictures of the German, Flemish, and Dutch schools. The collection of historical portraits by Benjamin West, chiefly of George II, George III and their families, formerly at the palace,[10] has been removed to Kensington Palace.

The paintings of Verrio and Laguerre on ceilings and staircases have already been described. Their 'meretricious magnificence' hardly suits the taste of the present day, but John Evelyn admired the work of Verrio enough to compare it with that of Raphael. The death-blow to his short-lived fame was given by Pope's couplet :

'On painted ceilings you devoutly stare,
     Where sprawl the saints of Verrio and Laguerre.'

Two paintings of the palace hang in the lobby of 'Cardinal Wolsey's Closet' ; one is a view of the old east front, showing the avenues and canal made by Charles II in 1665, by Danckers ; the other is a drawing of the south front in 1558, after Wynegaarde.

GARDENS The Knights Hospitallers had 'a garden and one dove-cote' belonging to their *camera* at Hampton.[1] Wolsey surrounded the parks, which then consisted of about 2,000 acres, with a red brick buttressed wall, part of which still remains ;[2] and the house and gardens with a moat The metrical version of Cavendish's *Life of Wolsey* gives a pleasant picture of the cardinal's garden :—

'My gardens sweet enclosed with walles strong
     Embanked with benches to sytt and take my rest.
The knots so enknotted, it cannot be expresst
     With arbors and alyes so pleasant and so dulce
To pestilent ayers with flavors to repulse.'[3]

[6] Mr. Law suggests that this is more probably a portrait of Arabella Stuart ; *Cat. of Pictures*, 65.
[7] Formerly no. 619, it has been removed, but apparently not re-numbered.

[8] See various authorities quoted in Law, op. cit. 275.
[9] They are now in the South Kensington Museum.
[10] They are included in Law, *Royal Gallery of Hampton Court*, 1898.

[1] Larking, *The Knights Hospitallers in Engl.* (Camden Soc.), 'Report of Prior Philip de Thame, 1338,' p. 127, &c.
[2] Law, *Hist. Hampton Ct. Palace*, i, 21.
[3] Cavendish, *Life of Wolsey* (ed. Singer), i, 32, &c.

The moat remained till the time of William III, and is mentioned as one of the defences when Edward VI and his uncle the Lord Protector caused the palace to be prepared for a siege.[4] Traces of the moat are still to be seen on the north side of the palace, and the passage leading to the Wilderness from Tennis Court Lane is known as 'The Moat Lane,' and the portion in front of the main entrance has now been cleared of the earth and rubbish which filled it, and has been restored to its former condition. There are numerous entries in the Chapter House Accounts which show that 'My Lordes garthinges at Hampton Courte' were laid out on a generous scale.[5] They were on the south side of the Base and Clock Courts, where a little inclosure, known as 'the Pond Garden,' no doubt retains some of the cardinal's style, though it was probably designed in something like its present form after Henry VIII had taken possession.[6]

Henry had also a 'Privy Garden' and a 'Mount Garden,'[7] which occupied the site of the present South or Private Gardens,[8] but no traces of them remain. There are accounts for roses (at 4d. the hundred), violets, primroses,'gilliver-slips,mynts, and other sweet flowers,' 'rosemary of 3 yeres old,' and Sweet Williams (at 3d. the bushel); but the chief decoration of a Tudor garden consisted of anything but flowers.[8a] In the walled parterres there were no doubt sheltered alleys and arbours ; among the items in Wolsey's accounts is one for 'twix to bind therber,'[9] but the embellishments were chiefly carved and painted heraldic 'beasts'[10] in stone or timber, on stone pedestals, and brass sundials, of which there

were an extraordinary number, though none now remain.[11] The flower beds were edged with wooden rails or trellis-work, painted white and green.[12] The plan adopted for the use of these edgings can be very well seen in the background of the picture, said to be by Holbein, of Henry VIII and his family, in the cloisters of Hampton Court.[13]

The Pond Garden is rectangular, surrounded by a low brick wall with stone coping, now surmounted by a hedge of trimmed lime trees, and laid out in three terraces following the shape of the garden and rising one above another, with retaining walls and copings, also of stone. On this stone can be seen the holes whereby the posts were fastened which sustained the thirty-eight fantastic beasts.[14]

HAMPTON COURT PALACE : THE POND GARDEN

[4] Nichols, Lit. Rem. of Edw. VI, 'Journ.' ii, 235 ; Cal. S.P. Dom. 1547–80, p. 23 ; Wriothesley, Chron. ii, 25 ; Acts of P.C. 1547–50, pp. 330, 337.

[5] Chap. Ho. Accts. C. bdle. 5, no. 9, fol. 689, &c.

[6] Law, op. cit. i, 206–7.

[7] See drawings by Antonius Wynegaarde (1558) in Bodl. Lib. reproduced in Law, op. cit. i, 201.

[8] They were kept private for the use of inhabitants of the palace for some time after the other gardens were opened to the public, but only a small portion is now retained.

[8a] Chap. Ho. Accts. bdle. 5. The flower garden properly so-called did not

become common till the reign of Queen Elizabeth ; Nichols, Engl. Pleasure Gardens ,105 et seq.

[9] Chap. Ho. Accts. C. bdle. 5, no. 9, fol. 762, &c.

[10] Ibid. One item is for 'makyng and entayllyng of 38 of the Kinges and Quenys Beestes in freeston . . . to stand about the ponddes in the pond yard at 26s. the pece. . . . Harry Corantt of Kyngston, carver,' seems to have been the chief sculptor, and also painted the devices on the shields or 'vanes' carried by these 'beestes.' Another item is for '17 beestes in tymber standing abowght the Mownte in the Kynges new garden' paid to

'Mych. of Hayles, Kerver'; Chap. Ho. Accts.

[11] No less than sixteen 'brasin dyalls' appear to have been required for the 'Kynges New Garden'; ibid.

[12] Ibid. There is an item for painting a great quantity of 'Rayle' and 'postes' in white and green for the 'Kynges New Garden.'

[13] No. 453 in the State Apartments.

[14] There were harts, lions, unicorns, greyhounds, hinds, dragons, bulls, antelopes, griffins, leopards, rams, tigers, and badgers ; Parl. Surv. 1653, the measurement of the Pond Garden is given as 120 ft. by 20 ft.

No doubt the beds were surrounded by the green and white railings, and the posts painted in those colours. In the centre is now one pond, with a jet of water flowing over a mound of moss in the middle of it. Originally there were apparently several ponds.[15] Opposite the entrance is an arbour of clipped yew.[16] There was an oblong building facing the river, called the 'Little Tower in the Glass-Case Garden,' which probably stood where the Banqueting House of William III now is.[17] The 'Mount' was also characteristic of the Tudor period. It was constructed in 1533, on a brick foundation, and planted with 'quycksetts' in the 'Tryangell.'[18] At the top was no doubt an arbour or pavilion. Judging from other 'Mount-gardens' of the period it was probably laid out in terraces.[19] It was certainly surrounded by a border of rosemary,[20] and embellished as usual with sundials and 'beestes' and painted railings. Henry had also kitchen gardens,[21] and two orchards, 'The Great Orchard' for which among others 600 cherry trees at 6d. a hundred were bought,[22] and the 'New Orchard,' where he built the banqueting houses and arbours, of which the roofs just appear in Wynegaarde's picture of the north of the palace.[23] These orchards occupied the space now known as 'The Wilderness,' and part of the nursery garden, which at present extends over all the 'Tilt Yard' as well.[24] They were separated by the moat, but with a drawbridge between them, decorated as usual with the 'Kinges Beastes.'[25] The 'Great Orchard' must always be memorable because it was there that Cavendish went to wait on Henry with the news of Wolsey's death, and found him shooting at a mark with Anne Boleyn.[26] One of the customs of Henry's gardeners[27] seems to have been that when Princess Mary came to the palace a basket of flowers or of strawberries was generally brought to her, a compliment she acknowledged by giving the sender a present of money.[28]

The next description of Hampton Court garden in the reign of Queen Elizabeth, refers to the 'sundry towers, or rather bowers, for places of recreation and solace, and for sundry other uses,' which were to be seen in the gardens, and also of the 'rosemary so nailed and planted to the walls as to cover them entirely.'[29] It was much the fashion at that time to trim and clip everything possible into wonderful and extraordinary shapes, 'that the like could not easily be found.'[30] Elizabeth was fond of walking in her gardens, 'to catch her a heate in the cold mornings,'[31] and she had them carefully kept up and improved,[32] though she did not actually alter or enlarge them. The Duke of Wurtemberg described the fountain she had erected in the garden as a 'splendid, high, and massy fountain, with a water-work by which you can, if you like, make the water play upon the ladies and others who are standing by and give them a thorough wetting.'[33]

Such flowers as 'lavender, spike, hissop, thyme, rosemary, and sage' are mentioned as among those in the queen's gardens at Hampton Court, Greenwich, and Richmond,[34] and another account describes the 'floures and varieties of curious and costly workmanship and also the rare and medicinal hearbes sought (? set) up in the land within these fortie yeares . . . ' at Nonesuche and Hampton Court.[35]

The great alteration in the gardens, which started them on an entirely new design, founded no doubt on the plan of Versailles, took place in the reign of Charles II. The park to the east of the palace is described by Evelyn in 1662 as 'formerly a naked piece of ground,[36] now planted with sweet rows of lime trees, and the canal for water near perfected.'[37] There is no record that the celebrated French gardener Le Nôtre ever visited England, but it is generally supposed that he designed the plan of St. James's Park and the alterations at Hampton Court.[38]

Le Nôtre's pupils, Beaumont and La Quintenye, assisted in the improvements at Hampton Court.[39] French gardeners were employed, and were under

---

[15] Chap. Ho. Accts. They are mentioned as 'the ponddes in the pond yerd.'
[16] Ibid. There is now a stone figure of Venus which stands in the arbour, and is quite out of keeping.
[17] Ibid. Add. Charters, B.M. 1262. Petition of Robert Trunkey to Queen Elizabeth for continuation of a pension because he built the 'Banquetinge House' and the 'Tower of Babylon' at Hampton Court for Henry VIII.
[18] Chap. Ho. Accts. The whole of this privy garden was more or less triangular in shape; see Kip's 'Birdseye View,' in the reign of Queen Anne; Law, op. cit. iii, 178.
[19] Nichols, Engl. Pleasure Gardens, 118. In the Parliamentary Survey for 1653 the size of the 'Privy Garden' and 'Mount Garden' is given as 3 acres and 1 rood. [20] Chap. Ho. Accts.
[21] L. and P. Hen. VIII, xvii, 1258. In Parl. Surv. the 'Kitchin Garden' is 3 acres.
[22] Ibid. The 'Old Orchard' 8 a. 2 r. The Tilt Yard 9 acres and 1 rood.
[23] Wynegaarde's drawing in Bodl. Lib. reproduced; Law, op. cit. i, 206.

[24] Ibid. 208. The nursery garden and the one remaining tower of the Tilt Yard were leased to Mr. Naylor.
[25] Ibid.
[26] See p. 332. The other orchard was sometimes called 'The King's Privy Orchard.'
[27] Thomas Chapman and Edmund Gryffyn were among the gardeners; L. and P. Hen. VIII, v, 1729, p. 760.
[28] Madden, Privy Purse Expenses of Princess Mary, 44, 45, 119, &c.
[29] Hentzner, Travels in Engl. (ed. 1757, 82.
[30] Rye, Engl. as seen by Foreigners, 18; 'Visit of Frederick, Duke of Wurtemberg.'
[31] Digges, Compleat Ambassador, 300.
[32] S.P. Dom. Eliz. xxxix, 64; Auditor's Acct. First Bk. of Privy Seals, 26 Eliz.
[33] Rye, Engl. as seen by Foreigners, 18.
[34] Cal. S.P. Dom. 1547-80, p. 171.
[35] Harrison, Descr. of Engl. (New Shakespeare Soc.), i, 332.
[36] This was the 'Course.' There does not appear to have been any garden on that side at an earlier date.

[37] Diary, 12 May 1662. A contemporary picture, by Danckers, shows the east front, with the newly-planted rows of lime trees, reproduced in Law, op. cit. ii, 217. See catalogue of pictures of James II in British Museum. The picture is now at Hampton Court.
[38] The gardens at Chatsworth, Bramham, and Holme Lacy have also been attributed to Le Nôtre. Nichols, Engl. Pleasure Gardens, 207, &c.; A. Amherst, Hist. of Gardening in Engl. 203. Switzer mentioned that Perrault, Le Nôtre's pupil, came to England, but not Le Nôtre.
[39] Beaumont was the designer of Levens in Westmorland, though his work there is hardly in the style of Le Nôtre. There is a portrait of him at Levens with the inscription on it :— 'M. Beaumont, gardener to James II and to Colonel James Grahme. He laid out the gardens at Hampton Court and at Levens.' Jean de la Quinteny, was a great French gardener and fruit grower. A. Amherst, Hist. of Engl. Gardening, 205.

the supervision of one Adrian May,[40] but John Rose, a protégé of the Earl of Essex, who studied at Versailles under Le Nôtre, was the most famous of the gardeners of Charles II ;[41] he planted some of the dwarf yew trees which were afterwards celebrated as among the finest in England, and it was probably under his auspices that the great sweeping semicircle of lime trees was planted before the east front, though Switzer declares that Charles himself made the design,[42] and it has been suggested that he meant it to be in the shape of a crown. It is now considerably altered, and the lime trees in front of the palace only form the segment of a circle, not a complete semicircle. Charles's design was technically described as a ' patte d'oie ' or goose-foot, from the three great double avenues which radiate from opposite the centre of the east front of the palace, and are linked together by the semicircular avenue.[43] The ' Long Water ' between the centre avenues extends nearly three-quarters of a mile (3,500 yds.) across the Home Park towards the river. It is 150 ft. wide, and is fed by the Longford River. It is so essentially part of the design of the garden that it is necessary to mention it here, though it is actually in the park,[44] but at that time it apparently almost reached the front of the palace,[45] and the ' rich and noble fountain,' mentioned by Evelyn,[46] with sirens, statues, &c., cast in copper by Fanelli, must have been in another part of the garden. It was afterwards removed by William III.[47] Possibly it was in the South Garden, as Evelyn at the same time described what is now known as ' Queen Mary's Bower,' and said that it was ' for the perplexed twining of the trees, very observable.'[48] He also spoke of ' a parterre, which they called Paradise, in which is a pretty banqueting-house set over a cave or cellar,' and suggested that ' all these gardens might be exceedingly improved, as being too narrow for such a palace,'[49] a criticism which might very well apply to that part of the grounds.

In 1669 the gardens were described by Cosmo III, Duke of Tuscany, as ' divided into very large, level and well-kept walks, which, separating the ground into different compartments, form artificial pastures of grass, being themselves formed by espalier trees, partly such as bear fruit, and partly ornamental ones, but all adding to the beauty of the appearance. This beauty is further augmented by fountains made of slate after the Italian style,[50] and distributed in different parts of the garden, whose *jets d'eaux* throw up the water in various playful and fanciful ways. There are also in the gardens some snug places of retirement in certain towers . . .'[51] The yew trees before mentioned were clipped into conical shapes and stood in geometrically-shaped beds.[52] Flowers are not mentioned among the ornaments of the garden of Charles II.

William and Mary devised the plan of a ' great fountain garden '[53] in the semicircular space inclosed by the lime trees. George London, a pupil of Rose, was appointed royal gardener, with a salary of £200 a year, and was also made ' page of the backstairs ' to Queen Mary,[54] but the chief alterations were apparently carried out after her death in 1699–1700. There is an item in the Treasury Papers for 1699 for ' 1,060 ft. superficiall of circular Derbyshire marble in the coaping of the Great Fountain ' ;[55] there are also innumerable items for levelling ' the great fountain garden,' for laying turf and gravel, for planting borders with ' fine shaped evergreens,' and for ' planting all borders with box.'[56] A strange item is for the removal of ' 403 large Lyme trees ye dimensions of their girt from 4 ft. 6 in. to 3 ft.,' which cost over £200. Defoe says that they had been planted over thirty years, and that they bore their transplantation very well.[57] This shifting of the trees was necessitated by the extension of the gardens towards the river on the south, when the old water-gate and the building that stood there were removed because they blocked the view from the palace windows. To balance this the garden was also extended to the north, and the trees, instead of surrounding completely the ' Great Semicircular Parterre,' turn off on each side in a straight line 50 yards from the front of the palace. Two low return walls were built parallel with the line of the palace for about 210 ft. on each side, to complete the inclosure of the gardens and face the straightened-out avenues. The ' Bird's-eye view of Hampton Court as finished by William III,' from Kip's *Nouveau Théâtre de la Grande Brétagne*,[58] shows that his design is practically unaltered now, though the growth of trees and superficial re-arrangements of grass and flower beds have given it a slightly different aspect. The small canal opposite the northern wall which divides the East Garden from the Wilderness had been made in the time of Charles II, to bring water from the Longford River to the Great Canal, and a corresponding small canal was constructed in 1669 on the south side. The stately ' broad walk ' in front of the eastern façade of the palace, which extends from the Flower Pot Gate on the Kingston Road to the water gallery by the river, is 2,264 ft. in length (nearly half a mile) and 39 ft. in width. The levelling and making of this, and turfing the grass walks on each side of it, cost £600.[59] The flower-beds which appear in the prints of this period are filled

[40] *Cal. S.P. Dom. Chas. II*, 1661–2, p. 175.
[41] Walpole, *Observations on Modern Gardening* ; Law, op. cit. ii, 205 ; Blomfield, *The Formal Garden in Engl.* 59.
[42] *Ichnographia Rustica*, i, 75.
[43] The space inclosed was 9½ acres ; Law, op. cit. iii, 20.
[44] Law, op. cit. ii, 218.
[45] See Dancker's picture ; ibid. 217.
[46] *Diary*, June, 1662.

[47] The ' Great Fountain Garden ' was laid out by William and Mary in the semicircular piece of ground inclosed by the lime trees.
[48] Evelyn called them hornbeam. They are really wych elm.
[49] Ibid. June 1662.
[50] It is said that there were twelve smaller fountains.
[51] Magalotti, *Travels of Cosmo III in Engl.* 208.

[52] Amherst, *Hist. of Gardening in Engl.* 205.
[53] Defoe, *Tour through Gt. Britain* (ed. 1738), i, 246.
[54] Switzer, *Ichnographia Rustica*, i, 79.
[55] *Cal. Treas. Bks.* lxvii, no. 2.
[56] Ibid.
[57] Defoe, loc. cit.
[58] Reproduced in Law, op. cit. iii, 109.
[59] *Cal. Treas. Bks.* lxvii, no 2.

with geometric designs; it is impossible to say of what they consisted beyond the box edgings of which William was so fond. Henry Wise and George London,[60] who together superintended the royal gardens during this reign, were answerable for these improvements, and for the alteration of the privy garden in 1700. The Mount was levelled, and the 'lines of hornbeam, cypress, and the flowering shrubs' removed to the Wilderness.[61] The raising of the new terrace from the water gallery to the bowling green was also continued, from a design sent to the king at Loo, the terrace being made almost entirely from the old bricks of the original 'water gallery.' The bowling green

been offensive to the sight. This Labrynth and Wilderness is not only well-designed and completely finished, but is perfectly well-kept, and the espaliers filled exactly, at bottom to the very ground, and are led up to proportioned heights on the top; so that nothing of the kind can be more beautiful.'[64] In one part the espaliers took a spiral form, which was known as 'Troy Town.' The Wilderness has been considerably altered even during the last few years, and the stiff walks and hedges admired by Defoe vanished long ago. The 'Labrynth' or maze alone remains as an amusing memorial of the ingenuity of a past age. The winding walks in the maze amount to nearly half

HAMPTON COURT PALACE: THE LOWER ORANGERY

had a little 'pavilion' at each corner, of which only one, much enlarged and altered, now remains.[62]

Another avenue of lime trees was planted in the park beyond. On the north side of the gardens the old orchard was converted into a 'Wilderness.'[63] Defoe says, 'it was very happily cast into a Wilderness, with a Labrynth, and Espaliers so high that they effectually take off all that part of the old building, which would have

a mile, though the space covered is barely a quarter of an acre.[65] Switzer complained that it had only four stops, though he had designed one which should have had twenty.[66]

The beautiful iron gates designed by Jean Tijou and executed by Huntingdon Shaw, which have now been replaced in their original position in the south gardens near the river, were finished in this reign. Huntingdon Shaw is buried in Hampton Church, and there described as 'an artist in his

---

[60] Dict. Nat. Biog. 'Henry Wise.'
[61] Cal. Treas. Bks. lxxi, nos. 33, 35.
[62] See Kip's 'Bird's Eye View,'

Law, op. cit. iii, 108. The pavilion is now one of the private apartments, occupied by Mr. Ernest Law.
[68] Cal. Treas. Bks. lxxxiv, no. 109.

[64] Defoe, op. cit i, 247. See plans in Law, op. cit. iii, 75, 77.
[65] Arch. vii, 124.
[66] Ichnographia Rustica, ii, 219-20.

way.' Tijou also designed the screen of St. Paul's Cathedral.[66a]

Queen Anne retained Wise in her service as royal gardener, and her chief action with regard to the gardens was to cause all the box edgings which he and London had planted to be removed in 1704. She seems also to have done away with some of William's elaborations, as Switzer says that she caused the gardens ' to be laid into that plain but noble manner they now appear in.' [67] The small canals seem also to have been made wider during her reign.[68] Ralph Thoresby, a topographer of Leeds, who visited the gardens in 1712, was chiefly impressed by the ' noble statues of brass and marble,' and the ' curious iron balustrades, painted and gilt in parts,' which separated the gardens from the parks. The ' Lion Gates ' and ' a figure hedge-work, of very large evergreen plants in the Wilderness, to face the iron gates,' were also erected in 1714, the last year of Queen Anne's reign,[69] and show that the plan for a great north entrance to the palace, as designed by Wren, had been given up. The stone piers of the gates bear Anne's cipher and crown, but the iron gates, which are by no means worthy of the piers,[70] contain the initials of George I.

Queen Caroline, the wife of George II, was the next sovereign to leave some mark of her taste and the taste of her period on the gardens, as well as on the palace, and her designer was Kent, who was no more accomplished as a gardener than as painter or architect, but his influence was not so disastrous out of doors as it was within. His wide lawns are really an improvement on the former ' parterres and fountains,' although Pope stigmatized them as ' a field.' [71]

George III entrusted the gardens to Lancelot Brown, the famous landscape gardener, better known as ' Capability ' Brown, who had been appointed royal gardener in 1750 by George II. Fortunately he did not attempt to adapt them to the very different style which had then become the fashion, although the king wished him to do so. He replaced some of the terrace steps in the Privy Gardens by slopes of gravel and grass, ' because we ought not to go up and down stairs in the open air,' but he does not appear to have done anything more drastic. The ' Great Vine,' which is one of the best-known sights of Hampton Court, was planted by Brown in 1769. It is a ' Black Hamburgh,' and was a slip from a vine at Valentines, in the parish of Ilford, near Wanstead in Essex, which had been planted in 1758, and also attained a great size.[72] Twenty years after the Hampton Court vine was planted it was said to have produced 2,200 bunches, which weighed on an average a pound each. The stem was already 13 in. in girth, and the main branch 114 ft. long.[73] At its best period (about 1840) the vine yielded on an average from 2,300 to 2,500 bunches every year, but it fell off very much for a time ; in 1874 the crop was only 1,750 bunches. Under better care it improved again,[74] but has not been allowed of late years to bear more than about 1,200 bunches, as many as 2,000 bunches being sacrificed sometimes to improve the quality of the rest. The stem now measures 3 ft. 9 in. in girth,

HAMPTON COURT PALACE : HUNTINGDON SHAW'S SCREENS

and the branches cover a space of 2,300 square feet. The vine house is 90 ft. long.[75] There are, of course, larger vines in Britain, all of the Black Hamburgh variety,[76] the largest being one at Kinnel House, Breadalbane, Scotland, which covers 4,375 ft. of wall space.

' Capability ' Brown lived for many years at Hampton Court. He was much esteemed by George III, who made a personal friend of him, and was also received familiarly by the Duke of Northumberland at Syon House, and Lord Chatham wrote of him that he was ' an honest man, of sentiments much above his birth.' [77] ' Wilder-

[66a] Rice, *Arch. Journ.* lii, 158, 172 (1895).

[67] *Ichnographia Rustica*, i, 83. See p. 387 for her alterations in the parks.

[68] *Cal. Treas. Bks.* cxxvi, no. 21, 12 Oct. 1710.

[69] Ibid. clxxix, no. 35.

[70] Defoe, op. cit. (ed. 1742), i, 240.

[71] Pope, *Works*, ' Epistle to the Earl of Burlington.' He does not actually refer to Hampton Court, but to the taste of the period.

[72] *Notes and Queries*, xii, 404.

[73] Lysons, *Midd. Parishes*, 72. The house was said to be 72 ft. long and

20 ft. wide the year before ; B.M. Add. MS. no. 6341, fol. 2b.

[74] Under the present gardener, Mr. Jack.   [75] Law, op. cit. iii, 297 et seq.

[76] Barron, *Vines and Vine Culture* (ed. 1883), 188.

[77] *Chatham Correspondence*, iv, 179, 430 (cit. Law).

ness House,' on the north side of the Wilderness, was occupied by Brown.[78]

The Banqueting House, now private apartments, stands on the south-west of the palace facing the river. The walls and ceilings are painted, probably by Verrio.

PARKS Wolsey inclosed with a wall about 2,000 acres as a park for his house.[79] Henry VIII had a large rabbit or hare warren in the park, where he also reared pheasants and partridges.[80] This domain was then as now divided into two parts by the Kingston road. These divisions are at present known simply as Bushey Park and the Home Park, Bushey lying to the north and the Home Park to the south-east of the palace. Henry had further inclosures made, taking in part of the heath near Hampton, and divided the north park into three

Bushey Park was sold to Edward Blackwell, and the Middle Park, 'called Jockey's Park,' to Colonel Richard Norton,[82] but they were repurchased with the palace for Cromwell in 1653–4.[83] In the inventory of Cromwell's goods made in 1659 it is mentioned that there were about 700 deer in the Home Park, in Bushey Park 1,700, and about thirty red deer.[84] In the paddocks and stables on both sides of the Kingston road the royal stud was kept for many years. It was started by William III, who was fond of racing, and continued by Queen Anne, who ran horses in her own name.[85] The stud was maintained by the first three Georges,[86] but George IV was the real founder of the afterwards famous Hampton Court Stud.[87] In 1812 he established a stud for riding horses of good strain, intending that they should all be grey; but in 1820, when he came to the

HAMPTON COURT PALACE : THE LION GATES

parts, i.e. the Hare Warren to the east, the Upper (or Bushey) Park to the extreme west, and the Middle Park in the centre. The Home Park contained only the 'Course' near the Kingston road and the Home Park itself, with the river on the south.[81] At the time of the Commonwealth some of the parks were sold apart from the house, and the 'fee of the honour and manor,' in which the Home Park and the Course were included.

Throne, they were all sent to Tattersall's. The Duke of York then kept a stud for breeding racehorses at the paddocks until 1827, Moses, the Derby winner of 1822, being the most famous horse.[88]

George IV then began breeding his own racehorses at Hampton Court, and spent considerable sums of money on his stud. He had thirty-three brood mares there, and some famous stallions. William IV endeavoured to improve and keep up

[78] It was so used till 1882, when it was given to Lady Adam, C.I., widow of the late Rt. Hon. William Adam, of Blair Adam, co. Kinross, M.P., Lord of the Treasury, First Commissioner of Works, and Governor of Madras. The rank and precedence of a baronet's wife were given to his widow, and her eldest son was created a baronet. She died in 1907, and the house was granted to her daughter Elizabeth, widow of Major the

Hon. Lionel Fortescue, 17th Lancers, who was killed in the Boer War. The present head gardener, Mr. Marlow, occupies the rooms originally inhabited by the keeper of the tennis court. See p. 370. [79] See p. 380.
[80] Chap. House Accts.
[81] See Hist. of Honour and Chase.
[82] Parl. Surv. 1653, P.R.O. Midd. no. 32.
[83] Cal. S.P. Dom. 1653–4, p. 356.

Other proceedings printed in Law, op. cit. ii, 272–6.
[84] For recent numbers see p. 247.
[85] Cal. Treas. Bks. lxxx, no. 100 ; lxxxv, no. 89.
[86] Ibid. cccii, no. 29 ; cclxix, no. 18.
[87] The Strangers' Guide to Hampton Court (1825) says that 'he spent many gay hours at the stud-house.'
[88] Law, op. cit. iii, 335.

the stock,[89] but he knew very little about horses, and a story is told that when Edwards his trainer asked what horses were to go to Goodwood, the king said 'Take the whole fleet; some of them will win, I suppose.' Three of his horses started for the Goodwood Cup on 11 August 1830, and came in first, second, and third in the race,[90] there being six other starters. On the death of William IV in 1837, the entire stud was sold for 15,692 guineas.[91]

General, then Colonel, Peel and Mr. Charles Greville were then allowed to keep a breeding stud in the paddocks. General Peel sold his stock in 1844, and Mr. Greville remained in possession, after 1851 conjointly with Queen Victoria. Her Majesty's first managers were Major Groves and Mr. Lewis. The royal stud was afterwards under the skilful and successful management of Colonel Sir George Maude, K.C.B., Crown Equerry, and became famous and lucrative. Large sums were realized from very early days by the sale of yearlings. In the reign of George IV and William IV they were generally sold at Tattersall's on the Monday in Epsom week for sums varying from £150 to £200 apiece.[92] The sale afterwards took place on Saturday in the week after Ascot in one of the Bushey Park paddocks, and the highest prices reached were in 1889 and 1890. In 1889 twenty-eight yearlings were sold for 11,745 guineas, an average of 420 guineas apiece. In 1890 twenty yearlings fetched over 14,000 guineas, an average of 700 guineas each. The famous La Flèche was sold to Lord Marcus Beresford for 5,500 guineas at this sale.

The racing stud was eventually sold in 1894, and there now only remains a small establishment for carriage horses and the famous cream-coloured ponies which draw the king's state coach. They are descended from horses brought over by George I from Hanover, and the breed has been carefully preserved. They are showy and powerful animals; and some of them have lived to a great age.[93]

The STUD HOUSE in the Home Park was originally the official residence of the Master of the Horse. It was at one time granted to Mrs. Keppel, the illegitimate daughter of Sir Edward Walpole, and widow of the Hon. and Rev. Frederick Keppel, fourth son of the second Earl of Albemarle, Dean of Windsor and Bishop of Exeter.[93a] Afterwards it was held by the Master of the Horse, or Master of the Buckhounds, of the period. From 1853 to 1865 it was granted to Lord Breadalbane, K.T., Lord Chamberlain, and in 1865 to Col. Sir George Ashley Maude, K.C.B., Crown Equerry. He died in May 1894, and the

house was given to Colonel Sir Alfred Mordaunt Egerton, K.C.V.O., C.B., Treasurer to the Household and Equerry to the Duke of Connaught, who relinquished it in 1907, and it is now held by Lady Sarah Wilson, daughter of the seventh Duke of Marlborough, and wife of Major G. C. Wilson, Royal Horse Guards. Besides this house there are only cottages and keepers' lodges in the Park.

Henry Wise laid out BUSHEY PARK in its present form, making the great central road through the park, which is a mile long and 60 ft. wide. Near the Hampton Court gate it forms a circle, round the great 'Diana' fountain, 400 ft. in diameter, and only 5 ft. in depth. The fountain itself was removed from the 'Privy Garden' in 1712–13, and was mentioned by Evelyn as being designed by Fanelli. In the inventory of Cromwell's goods made in 1659 the statue is said to be of Arethusa.[93b]

The great avenue of horse chestnuts, flanked by four rows of lime trees, borders this main road through the park, and there are two other avenues, each originally about three-quarters of a mile long, one leading towards the paddocks and the Kingston road and one to Hampton. The number of trees planted was 732 limes and 274 chestnuts. The whole cost only £4,300.[94] The idea of this magnificent avenue was of course that it should form part of the grand north approach to the palace designed, but never carried out, by Wren.[95] Fishponds and decoys were also made in the park, and Luttrell says that the deer were to be removed for the sake of the hare warren and pheasantry.[96]

The house now know as BUSHEY HOUSE, on the west side of the park, behind the chestnut avenue, near the Teddington Gate, was originally known as the 'Upper Lodge' and was rebuilt in the reign of Charles II by Edward Progers.[97] The existing house was built in the reign of George II by Lord Halifax. The Rangers of the park appear to have inhabited, or at all events had possession of, this house. William IV, then Duke of Clarence, was appointed Ranger in 1797, and lived almost entirely at Bushey House until his accession to the throne. He amused himself by looking after a farm he had made in the park and took a leading part in all the interests and amusements of the neighbourhood. Queen Adelaide was granted the house after his death in 1837, and lived there quietly till she herself died in 1849. One of the rare visits paid by the late Queen Victoria to Hampton Court was in 1844, when she and the Prince Consort, the King and Queen of the French, the King and Queen of the Belgians, the King of

[89] Colonel Wemyss was in charge of the stud.

[90] Day, The Horse and how to Rear Him, p. 48 (cit. Law).

[91] Christie Whyte, Hist. of the Brit. Turf, ii, 288.

[92] List of prices in June issue of New Sporting Mag. 1836 (cit. Law).

[93] Law, op. cit. iii, 339–40.

[93a] Horace Walpole, Letters, iii, 155. She was the sister of Lady Waldegrave, afterwards Duchess of Gloucester, the

mother of the three beautiful Ladies Waldegrave, whose famous portrait by Sir Joshua Reynolds is known to all the world. Lady Waldegrave occupied 'The Pavilions' at the time that her sister was at the Stud House. Law, op. cit. iii, 314–15.

[93b] Cal. Treas. Pap. clxxxii, 18 ; S.P. Dom. Commonw. cciii, 41, also Evelyn Diary, June 1662.

[94] Cal. Treas. Bks. lxvii, no. 14.

[95] See facsimile of plan from H.M.

Office of Works in Law, op. cit. iii, 79.

[96] A plantation opposite Bushey House ; Luttrell, Relation of Affairs of State.

[97] See p. 356. Vide Law, op. cit. ii, 206. for a picture of the house as it appeared at that time. S.P. Dom. Chas. II. The keeper of Bushey Park had rooms in the Palace, after the new building had been completed. Law, op. cit. iii, 463.

Holland and others were entertained by Queen Adelaide. Bushey House was afterwards lent by Queen Victoria to the late Duc de Nemours. It is now the National Physical Laboratory, and is occupied by the Director, Mr. R. T. Glazebrook, D.Sc., F.R.S.

There is another house in the park known as *CHARLES THE SECOND'S LODGE*, at present occupied by Lady Alfred Paget, widow of the late General Lord Alfred Paget, second son of the first Marquis of Anglesey, Equerry and Clerk Marshal of the Royal Household, who originally had the house granted to him. He died in 1888.

The one or two smaller houses in the park are keepers' lodges of a later date.

THE CHAPEL ROYAL. In Wolsey's lease of the manor of Hampton Court a stipulation was made for a yearly sum to be paid by the Knights Hospitallers for the maintenance of a priest to serve the chapel.[1] When the manor became royal property the chapel was served by the 'Chapel Royal,' or 'King's Chapel' establishment, which has no existence as a corporate body, resembling the dean and chapter of a cathedral, but has existed according to its present constitution for a considerable period before the Reformation.[2] The 'Establishment of the King's Chapel' in the time of Henry VIII consisted of a Master of the Chapel, thirty-two Gentlemen of the Chapel, and Children of the Chapel. The total expenses of the same being £424 13s. 4d. per annum. In the time of Edward VI the allowances and fees amounted to £476 15s. 5d.[3]

At the Coronation of James I the following officers are mentioned besides the Dean and Sub-Dean of the Chapel Royal :[4] the Ministers, the Master of the Children, Clerk of the Check, Doctor in Musicke, Gentlemen of the Chapel, Officers of the Vestry. At the coronation of Charles II the same are enumerated with the addition of grooms and yeomen and a Serjeant of the Vestry.

James II added a 'Confessor' and a 'common servant.' At the coronation of William and Mary two Organists and a 'Bellringer for the House-hold' are also mentioned.[5]

Strictly speaking, this establishment belongs to no fixed place, but is commanded to attend the sovereign wherever he may be. The services of the officers were required chiefly in London, formerly at Whitehall, and afterwards at what is now considered their head quarters, the Chapel Royal, St. James's,[6] but also at Greenwich, Hampton Court, and other royal residences.

In 1671 a petition was made to Charles II by a Doctor Thomas Waldon, physician, John Jones, apothecary to the household, and Captain Henry Cooke, master of the children of the Chapel Royal, ' that the Surveyor might provide lodgings for them when His Majesty removed to Hampton Court, as those they had were so decayed that they had to be pulled down.'[7] The Bishop of London is Dean of the 'Chapels Royal,'[8] and in 1699–70 asked for necessaries for the chapel from the Lord Chamberlain.[9]

At present the Chapel within St. James's Palace with the minor chapels within Hampton Court and Kensington Palaces constitute what are usually termed ' The Chapels Royal,' governed by the Dean, the Sub-Dean, and the Clerk of the King's Closet (the Bishop of Ripon), and there are various Chaplains, Preachers, Readers and other officers attached to them.[10] The Chapel Royal, Hampton Court, is served by a chaplain. The first chaplain appointed to Hampton Court as a separate office was the Rev. Gerald Valerian Wellesley, D.D., the brother of the first Duke of Wellington. He was appointed in 1806.

The plate is of silver gilt, and consists of a cup with paten and an almsdish 2 ft. in diameter, all of 1668 ; two flagons of 1687 with silver gilt linings of 1873 and 1874, all having the arms of William and Mary and the royal cipher ; a dish of 1736 with the arms of George II ; two cups of early 19th century unmarked ; a spoon of 1850, and a white metal almsdish.

CHURCHES The church of *ST. MARY THE VIRGIN* was opened for divine service in 1831, and succeeded a building which was entirely taken down in 1829. This had a mediaeval chancel of flint and stone, a nave with north and south aisles (the former built in 1726), a south porch, a west tower built in 1679, a building on the north side of the church which communicated with the north aisle, and which was used as the parish school, and a vestry at the north-west, built in 1726. There was a wooden turret on the north-east corner of the tower in which was hung a small bell, and in the bell-chamber were six bells which had been recast in the reign of Charles II ; there were galleries in the church on the north, south, and west sides, and in addition at the west end was a singing loft. There was a three-decker pulpit and a royal pew at the front of the north gallery.

The present church is a very unattractive product of the Gothic revival, rectangular in plan, 63 ft. long by 66 ft. wide, with north and south aisles ; at the east end is a modern sacristy, at the west end a tower, under which is the principal entrance, and to the north and south other entrances, with staircases leading to the galleries. There is a vestry at the east end of the south aisle, and the body of the church is under one low-pitched roof. It is built of brickwork.

---

[1] Cott. MSS. Claudius, E. vi, fol. 137. In the *L. and P. Hen. VIII* are many entries for sums paid to friars and others for preaching before the king at Hampton Court. A list of the chapel plate in 1530 is also given. Ibid. iv (3), 6184.

[2] *Old Cheque Bk. of the Chapel Royal*, 1561–1744 (Camden Soc. 1872).

There is a later cheque book preserved at St. James's.

[3] Introd. p. ix. citing Lansdowne MSS. no. 171.

[4] Ibid. pp. 64, 70, &c. The dean or sub-dean frequently held a 'chapter' in the vestry at Hampton Court.

[5] Ibid.

[6] Ibid.

[7] *Cal. S.P. Dom. Chas. II*, 1671, p. 264.   [8] *Clergy List*, 1908.

[9] *Buccleuch MSS.* (Hist. MSS. Com.), ii, 636.

[10] *Clergy List*, 1908. The Chapel Royal Savoy is the only one under the sole direction and control of the Crown and not within the jurisdiction of the Dean of the Chapels Royal.

HAMPTON CHURCH: MONUMENT TO SIBELL PENN

In the north entrance lobby is the effigy, under a canopy supported by Corinthian pillars, of Sibell Penn, daughter of William Hampden of Dunton, who was nurse to Edward VI, and died in 1562. On the base of the tomb are the arms of Penn, Argent a fesse sable with three roundels argent thereon, separately and impaling the Hampden coat. The tomb is simple but of excellent detail, with a fine strapwork soffit to the canopy, and an inscription of ten rhymed couplets on a panel at the back. The effigy is well wrought, but curiously stiff, in a long straight-sided gown with side pockets and a short cloak over the shoulders. It is the ghost of this lady, dressed exactly as she appears on her tomb, which is said to haunt a certain part of Hampton Court to this day. In the church are many mural tablets, the most interesting being an undated one to Edmund Pigeon, yeoman of the Jewel House to Henry VIII and Clerk of the Robes to Elizabeth ; another to his son, who succeeded him and died in 1619; to Thomas Smithesby of the Inner Temple, Keeper of the Privy Seal under the Protectorate, died 1655; a restored monument to Huntingdon Shaw, 1710, who worked under Jean Tijou on the well-known wrought-iron gates and screens at Hampton Court ; and one at the east end of the south aisle to Susanna Thomas, 1731, daughter and heiress of Sir Dalby Thomas, Governor of the African Company's settlements.

There are eight bells in the tower by Mears, 1831.

The plate consists of a communion cup of 1704, a cup and flagon of 1820, a cup of 1836 presented by Edward Johnson in 1845, two salvers of 1828, and a modern silver-gilt chalice and paten.

Of the registers, Book i contains baptisms 1554 to 1656, and burials 1554 to 1650 ; Book ii baptisms 1656 to 1725, marriages 1657 to 1703, and burials 1656 to 1677 ; Book iii baptisms 1726 to 1749, marriages 1726 to 1754, and burials 1726 to 1768; and Book iv baptisms 1656 to 1812. The fifth is the printed marriage register, 1754 to 1812, and the sixth contains burials 1768 to 1812.

The church of ST. JOHN, HAMPTON WICK, was built at the same time as the parish church of Hampton, and was intended as a chapel of ease to it ; upon its completion, however, the district was made a separate parish. It is a plain building of yellow brick with stone dressings consisting of a rectangular nave and chancel with side galleries, and is in the same spiritless Gothic style as Hampton Church. The register of baptisms dates from 1831 and of marriages from 1832.

The church of ST. JAMES, HAMPTON HILL, built in 1863 and enlarged in 1878, is of red brick in 13th-century style, and consists of

chancel, nave of five bays, aisles, organ chamber, south porch, and embattled tower at the south-western angle with pinnacles and spire, and containing four bells. The register dates from 1863.

ADVOWSON The church appears to have been originally appropriated to the Abbey of St. Valery or Valeric in Picardy, as part of the possessions of the Priory of Takeley in Essex. The temporalities were seized by Edward III during his wars with France,[1] and in the reign of Richard II the advowson of Hampton, with all the other property of the Abbey of St. Valery in Middlesex, was alienated in frankalmoign to the 'warden and Scholars of St. Mary's College of Winchester.'[2] In 1543 it came by exchange to Henry VIII.[3] The rectory and advowson were leased to Richard Bennett[4] in 1546, and in 1562 to Edmund Pigeon and Joan his wife,[5] afterwards, in 1574, to Robert Nicolls,[6] who held them till 1585, when they were leased to John Cely[7] for twenty-one years. In 1607 James I granted the rectory in fee to Michael Cole and John Rowden, with the advowson of the vicarage.[8] They conveyed it to Edmund Pigeon, said to have been the grandson of the Edmund Pigeon who held it in 1562.[9] His sisters and co-heirs Elizabeth Kyme[10] and Frances Dorman afterwards held the rectory in moieties.[11] The whole became eventually vested in the Dormans, and was again divided between their heirs Frances Clarke and Mary Dorman, who respectively sold their moieties to John Jones in 1675[12] and 1684.[13] In 1692 John Jones bequeathed the glebe and rectorial tithes to charitable uses for the benefit of the parish.[14] The advowson of the vicarage was reserved, and apparently reverted to the king, as in 1674 the 'impropriate rectory with tithes and advowson' was leased to James Nayler, but in 1679 the living[15] was once more in the gift of the Crown, and it has so remained to the present time.[16]

The new ecclesiastical district of Hampton Wick was formed in 1831, and that of Hampton Hill in 1864.[17]

CHARITIES The Hampton Parochial Charities were by a scheme of the Charity Commissioners dated 3 August 1894 consolidated, and comprise the following charities, namely :—

1. The Parish Lands, the earliest record extant being surrenders, 1659 and 1662, made at a court held for the honour and manor of Hampton Court; the trust estate consists of two houses known as 'The Feathers,' with a garden opposite, and 'River View,' and cottage and garden ; 'two allotments awarded under the Inclosure Act, 1811,

[1] Cal. Pat. 1343-5, pp. 8, 14, 143 ; 1348-50, pp. 303, 428.
[2] Ibid. 1388-92, pp. 413, 414, 417.
[3] L. and P. Hen. VIII, xii (2), 849 ; xviii (1), 981 (46) ; Pat. 35 Hen. VIII, pt. viii, m. 6.
[4] Pat. 37 Hen. VIII, m. 7 (6 Oct.).
[5] Pat. 4 Eliz. (26 June).
[6] Pat. 16 Eliz. pt. ii.
[7] Pat. 28 Eliz. pt. x, m. 9.
[8] Pat. 5 Jas. I, pt. xxvi.
[9] Lysons, Midd. Par. 83. Probably the Edmund Pigeon to whose memory there is a mural tablet in the church, see supra.
[10] Feet of F. Midd. Hil. 1658.
[11] Ibid. Trin. 26 Chas. II (1674).
[12] Ibid. Trin. 27 Chas. II.
[13] Ibid. Hil. 36 & 37 Chas. II.
[14] Deeds belonging to the parish.
[15] Inst. Bks. P.R.O. 1679.
[16] Ibid. 1679, 1716, 1752, 1762-3, 1798, 1803.
[17] Lond. Gaz. 1830-83. For the whole history of advowson vide Newcourt, Repert. Eccl. i, 62 ; Lysons, Midd. Par., 83, &c. Hampton Wick is a vicarage in the gift of the Lord Chancellor, and Hampton Hill is also a vicarage in the gift of the vicar of Hampton.

containing together 3 a. o r. 11 p., known as 'Cannon Field'; Hall's Platt, consisting of five cottages and gardens, known as Barrack Row, and a meadow containing 1 a. 3 r. 20 p., and the New Almshouses; the trusts of the original almshouses at the 'Four Hills' are mentioned in an admission on the Court Rolls, 1729, recited in an admission of 1823,[1] and a sum of £1,376 19s. 8d. consols, arising from sales of land from time to time;

2. Parochial Quit Rents, recently redeemed, represented by a sum of £369 2s. consols; and the charities of

3. Mary Harris, founded by will 1676, consisting of 3 acres, known as Holly Bush Close;

4. Mary Gavell, will, 1746, trust fund, £135 8s. consols;

5. John Turner, will, 1753, trust fund, £332 17s. 2d. consols;

6. Cyrus Maigre, codicil to will, 1777, trust fund, £74 2s. 2d. consols;

7. William Cole, will, 1807, trust fund, £630 consols;[2]

8. Mrs. Eva Maria Garrick, codicil to will, 1821, trust fund, £358 14s. 11d.;

9. School of Industry, otherwise the Girls' School, including the subsidiary charities, known as Roll's Gifts and Mrs. Wallace's Gift, comprised in a scheme of the Charity Commissioners of 25 August 1862. The trust funds consist of £1,009 2s. 11d. consols; and

10. Charity of John Jones for Poor, will, 1691, trust fund, £960.

The governing body constituted by the scheme consists of six *ex officio* trustees, being the vicars and churchwardens of the parish of Hampton, and of the ecclesiastical district of Hampton Hill, St. James; eight representative trustees and two co-optative trustees.

The scheme provides (*inter alia*) that out of the income of the charities 1 and 2 £50 shou'd be paid to the churchwardens of Hampton and £25 to the churchwardens of Hampton Hill, St. James, for the repair of the respective churches.

That one-third of the income of Mary Harris' Charity (no. 3) should be paid to the trustees of the Hampton Wick Parish Lands (see under Hampton Wick).

That the income of the charity no. 9, and so much of charity no. 3 as should not be required for apprenticing, should be applied in aid of any fund applicable in the parish of Hampton by a local authority for the purposes of technical instruction.

That the residue of the income of the remaining charities should be applied in providing stipends of not less than 5s. or more than 8s. a week for the almspeople and for the benefit of the poor of the parish of Hampton, exclusive of Hampton Wick, but inclusive of Hampton Hill, in such manner as the trustees should consider most conducive to the formation of provident habits.

In 1905 the income from the real estate amounted to £216 5s. and the dividends from the sums of stock, which are held by the Official Trustees, to £131 2s. 4d., making an aggregate income of £347 7s. 4d. The sum of £75 was paid to the churchwardens, £104 8s. 8d. as stipends of seven almspeople (including nursing), £10 for apprenticing, £12 to pensioners, and £25 6s. to the Local Technical Education Committee.

In 1873 Thomas Beer, by will proved 6 February, bequeathed to the vicar and churchwardens £450 2s. 9d. consols (with the Official Trustees), the dividends to be applied for the benefit of the poor of the parish of Hampton. The income, amounting to £11 4s. a year, is distributed in articles in kind.

In 1873 James Annett, by will proved 15 August, bequeathed to the vicar and churchwardens a legacy, now represented by £700 consols, with the Official Trustees, the dividends to be divided equally among eight respectable men, who should ring a peal on the bells of Hampton parish church on Sunday mornings from 10.15 to 10.45. The dividends, amounting to £17 10s., are duly applied.

The Hampton Endowed School. This school is regulated by a scheme made under the Endowed Schools Acts, 26 October 1896.

HAMPTON HILL, ST. JAMES

In 1881 the Rev. Fitzroy John Fitz Wygram, by will proved 26 October, bequeathed a legacy to the incumbent of St. James, to be applied by him according to his uncontrolled discretion in relieving the educational and bodily needs of the poor. The legacy is represented by £452 5s. 2d. consols, with the Official Trustees, producing £11 6s. a year, which in 1905–6 was applied in the payment of £6 6s. to a parochial fund for the poor, and £5 to the District Nurse Fund.

In 1892 William Blanchard, by will proved 22 March, bequeathed to the vicar and churchwardens a legacy, now represented by £411 Great Western Railway 4 per cent. debenture stock, with the Official Trustees, upon trust, to distribute the dividends among the poor. The annual income, amounting to £16 8s. 10d., is distributed in articles in kind.

HAMPTON WICK

The Endowed School.—The Board of Education by order, dated 1 August 1907, has established a scheme, including appointment of trustees, altering previous schemes made under the Endowed Schools Acts, whereby a special fund for elementary purposes was directed to be established, to be called 'The Elementary Education Fund,' which amounts to a sum of £2,290 3s. 7d. consols and £24 19s. India 3 per cent., with the Official Trustees.

In 1695 Thomas Burdett, by his will dated 29 February in that year, bequeathed to the poor of Hampton Wick the sum of £50, the

---

[1] The enfranchisement of the copyholds was completed in 1890.
[2] For other part of charities numbered 5, 6, 7, and 10, see under Hampton Wick.

profits thereof to be laid out in coals or wood and distributed yearly on St. Thomas's Day for ever. The legacy is now represented by £91 6s. 3d. Metropolitan Consolidated 3 per cent. stock with the Official Trustees, producing £2 14s. 8d. a year.

The Parish Lands and other subsidiary charities are regulated by schemes of the Charity Commissioners, dated respectively 1 May 1888, 6 August 1897, 10 January 1899, and 20 January 1903, and comprise the following charities, namely :—

1. The Parish Lands. The trust estate consists of sixteen houses, Park Side, Sandy Lane, let on long leases at annual rents amounting to £78 16s.; the Grove Inn, let at £70 a year, and £240 2½ per cent. annuities, and £169 9s. 10d. consols. The charities of :—

2. John Turner (part of), trust fund, £166 8s. 7d. consols ;

3. Cyrus Maigre (part of), £37 1s. 1d. consols ;
4. William Cole (part of), £315 consols ;
5. John Jones (part of), £480 consols ; and
6. Mary Harris, one-third of rent of Holly Bush Close, £6 13s. 4d.[3]

The several sums of stock are held by the Official Trustees.

The governing body constituted by the scheme of 1888 (as varied by scheme of 1899) consists of six representative trustees, nominated by the Local Board, the School Board, and by the governors of the Endowed School.

In 1906–7 the net receipts amounted to £160 3s.

Under the scheme of 1897 the income of the charities 2 to 5 is applicable in pensions on terms similar to those regulating the Hampton Parish Lands ; and out of the general income £50 was paid to the churchwardens, £55 for nursing, and £36 for educational purposes.

[3] For other part of charities numbered 2 to 6 see under ancient parish of Hampton.

HANWORTH

Haneworde (xi cent.), Hanewrthe (xiii cent.), Haneworth (xiv and xv cents.), Hamworth, Haneworth (xvi and xvii cents.).

Hanworth is a small parish lying to the east of Feltham. The northern boundary is formed by the River Crane, on which two large reservoirs have been built. The Queen's or Cardinal's River (vide East Bedfont) flows diagonally across the parish from the north-west. The land, which is apparently almost level, slopes gently from north to south, and lies between 70 ft. and 40 ft. above Ordnance datum. It is laid out almost entirely in

LYCH GATE, HANWORTH

nursery and market gardens, which give employment to a large proportion of the population. Of the 1,372½ acres in the parish, 543 acres are arable land, and 237¼ acres are grass.[1] The village is composed of detached houses mostly lying about the cross roads in the southern part of the parish. The church of St. George stands at a little distance from the village, near the ruins of Hanworth Castle. There is a Wesleyan chapel, which was built in 1867. The most distinctive feature of the parish is Hanworth Park, which occupies the north-east corner and extends over the boundary into Feltham parish. It contains many fine trees, which are the more remarkable as the rest of the parish is but sparsely wooded.

The parish was inclosed in 1800, together with Feltham and Sunbury.[2] The following place-names occur: Le Pille, Le Yawe, Ham-acre, Grewclose, Andymeres Land, Rice, Lott-meadow, Livershaw.

HANWORTH **MANOR** was held in the time of Edward the Confessor by Ulf, a 'huscarl' of the king.[3] It was granted by William I to Roger de Montgomery, Earl of Arundel, under whom it was held by one Robert.[4] Earl Roger's English estates were inherited by his second son Hugh de Montgomery, but after the latter's death in the Mowbray conspiracy of 1098 they passed to the eldest son Robert de Bellesme, who in turn rebelled against the king in 1102, with the result that all his lands were confiscated.[5] It is likely that the overlordship of Hanworth came in this way to the Crown. It was probably attached to the honour of Wallingford during the reign of Henry II,[6] and formed part of that honour apparently until 1539.[7] In 1540 it was annexed to the honour of Hampton Court.[8]

The family of Dayrell of Lillingstone Dayrell, Buckinghamshire, held the manor for several generations of the honour of Wallingford by the service of half a knight's fee.[9] It is uncertain when they were first connected with Hanworth. According to an ancient pedigree, Robert Dayrell, who lived during the latter part of the 12th century, is styled

DAYRELL. *Azure a lion or with a crown gules.*

'of Hanworth.'[10] Ralph Dayrell his son[11] held half a knight's fee of the honour of Wallingford, which probably represents Hanworth, from about 1166 to about 1210.[12] His son Henry Dayrell certainly held Hanworth about 1212,[13] and his grandson,[14] also named Henry, who held the manor in the reign of Edward I, certified that his ancestors had been lords of Hanworth time out of mind.[15] He died in possession of the manor in 1303, holding it jointly with his wife Alice.[16] The manor was settled for the term of her life on Alice,[17] who was still living in 1316.[18] Henry Dayrell left a son and heir named Henry,[19] who was sixteen years of age at the time of his father's death.[20] He was alive in 1307–8, when he made a feoffment of the manor.[21] In 1316 the king was holding in Hanworth,[22] probably on account of the minority of the younger Henry's heir, who seems to have been John Dayrell.[23] The latter certainly held the manor in 1335,[24] and was still in possession in 1353.[25] He was succeeded by his son Sir Roger Dayrell.[26] In 1377 Roger conveyed all his rights in Hanworth to Alan Ayete of Shalderton, and John Chamberlayn, clerk.[27–8]

Later in the same year Alan Ayete surrendered his claim to John Chamberlayn,[29] who then granted the manor to Thomas Godlak.[30] The latter enfeoffed Thomas Walyngton, Gilbert Manfield, and William Makenade,[31] and these again enfeoffed John de Macclesfield, the king's clerk.[32] The manor was occupied at the will of the lord by Sir Nicholas Brembre.[33] Sir Nicholas was Lord Mayor of London for part of 1377 and again in 1377–8. He was the strong supporter of Richard II among the London merchants, and was knighted for his services during the peasants' march on London in 1381. He was again mayor in 1383–4, representing the king's party; and was also a member of Parliament for London. He narrowly escaped impeachment in 1386; but in November 1387 he was accused of treason by the lords appellant, and was hanged at Tyburn in February of the next year.[34]

After his execution Hanworth was taken into the king's hand, but as it was found that Sir Nicholas had no real estate there, but was only a tenant at will, the right of John de Macclesfield was restored in 1391.[35] Idonea, the widow of Sir Nicholas Brembre, bought back a large proportion of her husband's personal property in July

[1] Inf. supplied by the Bd. of Agric. (1905).
[2] Slater, *The Engl. Peasantry and the Enclosure of the Common Fields,* 287.
[3] *Dom. Bk.* (Rec. Com.), i, 30.
[4] Ibid.
[5] Stubbs, *Const. Hist.* (1891), i, 334.
[6] *Red Bk. of Exch.* (Rolls Ser.), 310.
[7] Ibid. p. lxxxiii, 140, 145, 543, 595; Chan. Inq. p.m. 28 Edw. I, no. 44; P.R.O. Ct. R. bdle. 212, no. 2, 6–8, 18–19.
[8] *L. and P. Hen. VIII,* xv, 498 (36).
[9] *Red Bk. of Exch.* [Rolls Ser.], p. cclxxxiii, 145, 310, 543, 595.
[10] Lipscomb, *Hist. of Bucks.* iii, 31.
[11] Ibid.

[12] *Red Bk. of Exch.* (Rolls Ser.), 145, 310, 595.
[13] Ibid. 543.
[14] Lipscomb, *Hist. of Bucks.* iii, 31.
[15] *Plac. de Quo Warr.* (Rec. Com.), 477.
[16] Inq. a.q.d. 2 Edw. II, no. 98; Chan. Inq. p.m. 31 Edw. I, no. 26; Feet of F. Lond. and Midd. 22 Edw. I, no. 208; Lipscomb, *Hist. of Bucks.* iii, 31.
[17] *Feud. Aids,* iii, 372.   [18] Ibid.
[19] Ibid.
[20] Chan. Inq. p.m. 31 Edw. I, no. 26.
[21] Inq. a.q.d. 2 Edw. II, lxxiv, no. 8.
[22] *Feud. Aids,* iii, 372.
[23] Lipscomb, *Hist. of Bucks,* iii, 31.

[24] Chan. Inq. p.m. 9 Edw. III (1st nos.), no. 10.
[25] *Feud. Aids,* iii, 375.
[26] Lipscomb, op. cit. iii, 31.
[27–8] Feet of Lond. and Midd. 51 Edw. III, no. 540; Close, 51 Edw. III, m. 5.
[29] Close, 1 Ric. II, m. 24 d.
[30] Chan. Inq. p.m. 12 Ric. II, no. 78, 90.
[31] Ibid.
[32] Pat. 14 Ric. II, pt. ii, no. 31.
[33] Chan. Inq. p.m. 12 Ric. II, no. 78, 90; Feet of F. Div. Co. 8 Ric. II, no. 129.
[34] *Dict. Nat. Biog.* vi, 255–6.
[35] *Cal. Pat.* 1388–92, p. 379.

1388. Amongst the forfeited goods and chattels in the manor of Hanworth she was so prudent as to purchase a brass pot for 18*d.*, a leaden pot for 2*s.*, fourteen oxen, and other commodities to the value of £54 5*s.* 4*d.*[36]

John de Macclesfield may have lost his lands after the fall of Richard II, as in the early 15th century the manor was apparently occupied by a fresh owner.

The manor was held in 1428 by Henry Somer,[37] warden of the Mint under Henry VI.[38] He died about 1450,[39] and his right in Hanworth probably reverted to the Crown. Later in the same century the manor came into the possession of Sir John Crosby,[40] alderman of London, and founder of Crosby Hall.[41] After his death in 1475 the custody of the manor was granted during the minority of his son John to Thomas Rigby and William Bracebridge.[42] Sir John Crosby the younger died in 1500–1 in possession of the manor which had been settled previously on Thomas Winterbourne and other trustees for the use of John and his wife Anne, with remainder in default to Peter Christmas the next of kin. The latter being already dead in 1500–1,[43] John Crosby's heir was found to be the posthumous son of Peter Christmas, aged six months.[44] His trustees appear to have conveyed the manor during the same reign to Sir John Huse, and by an exchange of land in 1512 Hanworth came to the Crown.[45] In 1521 the lands of the manor, excluding the manor house, were let to Sir Richard Weston,[46] and in 1530 Stephen Gardiner[47] received the reversion of the same property, together with the site and all other appurtenances, to hold for life.[48] In 1532 these patents were surrendered, and the 'manor of Hanworth,' except the manor house, was granted to Anne Boleyn for 99 years; a month later the house was granted to her for life.[49] In 1536 Gregory Lovell was appointed to the office of keeper of the manor.[50] Hanworth was settled in 1544 on Katherine Parr, sixth and last queen of Henry VIII.[51] After her death it is said to have been granted, probably for life, to Anne Duchess of Somerset,[52] who was certainly living there with her second husband, Francis Newdigate, in August 1563, when her son the Earl of Hertford was removed to Hanworth from the Tower,[53] where he had been imprisoned on account of his marriage with Lady Katherine Seymour.[54] In 1594 the manor was leased to William Killigrew, groom of the privy chamber under Elizabeth, for about eighty years on surrender of a former grant for life.[55] He was succeeded by his son Robert, who conveyed the remainder of the lease to Francis Lord Cottington.[56] The manor was granted by the king in 1627 to Sir Roger Palmer and Alexander Stafford,[57] who acted as trustees for Francis Lord Cottington.[58] The latter was a prominent figure in the reigns of James I and Charles I. Having accompanied Sir Charles Cornwallis, the English Ambassador in Spain in 1609, and afterwards acted as English agent and consul,[59] Cottington was much in request on his return on account of his knowledge of Spanish affairs.[60] He was concerned in the question of the Spanish marriage,[61] and though disapproving of Prince Charles's journey to Spain, he was sent with him and took part in the negotiations at Madrid.[62] He acted as ambassador to Spain from 1629, and as a reward for negotiating the secret treaty of 1631[63] he was raised to the peerage as Baron Cottington of Hanworth,[64] receiving the honour 'at Greenwich in a very solemn manner.'[65] As the Civil War drew near he declared himself an active member of the war party, and after hostilities had broken out he joined the king at Oxford.[66] He was excepted by Parliament from indemnity and composition, and spent the remainder of his life abroad, dying in Spain in 1652.[67] His estates were assigned in 1649 to John Bradshaw the regicide,[68] but were recovered at the Restoration by his nephew and heir Charles Cottington, son of his elder brother Maurice.[69]

Charles Cottington did not keep Hanworth long, for he sold it in 1670 to Sir Thomas Chamber.[70] The latter died in 1692 and was succeeded by his son Thomas. Thomas Chamber left two daughters and co-heiresses, and Hanworth passed, through the marriage of the elder, to Lord Vere Beauclerk,[71] who was created Baron Vere of Hanworth in 1750.[72] The manor was inherited by his son Aubrey Lord Vere[73] in 1781, who succeeded his cousin as Duke of St. Albans six years later.[74] He still held the manor in 1802,[75] but conveyed it very shortly after to James Ramsey Cuthbert.[76] Frederick John Cuthbert was lord of the manor in 1816, but it passed before 1832 to Henry Perkins.

[36] Cal. Pat. 1385–9, p. 481.
[37] Feud. Aids, iii, 381.
[38] Cal. Pat. 1422–9, p. 72.
[39] Chan. Inq. p.m. 28 Hen. VI, no. 21.
[40] Cal. Pat. 1476–85, p. 7.
[41] Dict. Nat. Biog. xiii, 211.
[42] Cal. Pat. 1476–85, p. 7.
[43] Chan. Inq. p.m. (Ser. 2), xxi, no. 10.
[44] Ibid.
[45] L. and P. Hen. VIII, i, 3284.
[46] Ibid. v, 1139 (32).
[47] Dict. Nat. Biog. xx, 420.
[48] Ibid. 1207 (7).
[49] Pat. 24 Hen. VIII, pt. ii, m. 12–14.
[50] L. and P. Hen. VIII, xiii (1), 573.
[51] Ibid. xix (1), 644 ; P.R.O. Ct. R. portf. 191, no. 1.

[52] Lysons, Environs of Lond. (1800), v, 95.
[53] Engl. Hist. Rev. xiii, 305.
[54] Dict. Nat. Biog. li, 310–11.
[55] Cal. S.P. Dom. 1591–4, pp. 547, 559.
[56] S.P. Dom. Chas. I, ccclxxvii, 177.
[57] Pat. 3 Chas. I, pt. iii, no. 1.
[58] S.P. Dom. Chas. I, ccclxxvii, 177. The docquet conveys the manor to the trustees for 47 years; but the patent roll grant is made to them and their heirs.
[59] Gardiner, Hist. of Engl. ii, 134, 151.
[60] Dict. Nat. Biog. xii, 293.
[61] Narrative of Spanish Marriage Treaty (Camd. Soc.), 111.
[62] Dict. Nat. Biog. xii, 293.
[63] Gardiner, Hist. of Engl. vii, 176.

[64] G.E.C. Complete Peerage, ii, 384.
[65] Cal. S.P. Dom. 1631–3, p. 107.
[66] Dict. Nat. Biog. xii, 293.   [67] Ibid.
[68] Cal. of Com. for Compounding, i, 146.
[69] G.E.C. Complete Peerage, ii, 384 ; Feet of F. Midd. Hil. 18 & 19 Chas. II.
[70] Feet of F. Midd. Trin. 32 Chas. II ; Close, 22 Chas. II, pt. ii, no. 1.
[71] G.E.C. Complete Peerage, vii, 6 ; Feet of F. Midd. East. 3 Geo. III.
[72] G.E.C. Complete Peerage, viii, 26.
[73] Feet of F. Midd. Mich. 33 Geo. III. ; Recov. R. Mich. 33 Geo. III, rot. 302.
[74] G.E.C. Complete Peerage, vii, 6.
[75] Recov. R. East. 42 Geo. III, rot. 233.
[76] Beauties of Engl. and Wales x (4), 517.

After the death of his heir Algernon Perkins, before 1866, it was in the hands of his devisees, but was bought before 1887 by Messrs. Pain & Bretell, solicitors, of Chertsey, who are lords of the manor at the present day.

Henry Dayrell claimed the right to hold a view of frankpledge and amends of assize of bread and ale in the reign of Edward I.[77] The king's attorney said his claim dated from the grant by Henry III of the honour of Wallingford to Richard Earl of Cornwall and King of Almain. The jurors said that the Dayrells had, before that grant, held a meeting of all their tenants in Hanworth, and had taken the amendment of assize of bread and ale, and all that appertained to the view of frankpledge; and that after Henry III had given the honour of Wallingford to the Earl of Cornwall the latter's bailiff had attached all the men of Hanworth to the view held for that honour at Uxbridge. It appears that although the Dayrells obviously had no chartered right to hold the view, yet their right which accrued from custom was allowed.[78] Yet it seems as though a rent was paid in 1303 to the Earl of Cornwall for the view,[79] and in the 15th and 16th centuries the view seems always to have been held by the overlord.[80]

Fishing rights were among the appurtenances of the manor in 1303.[81] Lord Cottington had a grant of free warren in Hanworth Park in 1638[82] (v.s. park).

A water-mill belonging to the manor is mentioned in 1303.[83] In 1340 there was a mill known as Eldeford in Haneworth,[84] which apparently stood near the dyke called 'the Mersdich,' which ran between Hanworth and Kempton. Litigation took place concerning this dyke and the foot-bridge which crossed it and led to the mill. In the early part of January 1338–9 Roger, Bishop of Coventry and Lichfield, complained that though he was not liable to repair the dyke except in proportion to the use made of it by his yokes of oxen (pro averiis spannatis) and had done his part sufficiently therein, and though he ought not to repair the foot-bridge by the mill, yet he had been amerced by the sheriff to the amount of 38s. 8d. on the pretext that the dyke was not properly cleansed nor raised nor the foot-bridge repaired.[85] The sheriff was accused of having fined him on insufficient evidence, and was accordingly commanded to appear before the king, and to bring with him four good men from each of the four townships nearest the bridge. The sheriff appearing on the day appointed, said that the bridge was in a dangerous state by default of John Dayrell, lord of Hanworth, who was bound to repair it as his ancestors

had been used to do within the memory of man. The four men from the townships could not attend, as the order had come too late, and the case was adjourned to a later date. It was again respited to midsummer, when, the bishop, sheriff, and four men from each of the townships of Twickenham, Hampton, East Bedfont, and Feltham being present, it was found by the jury that the bridge was not for the common use, but only a little bridge by Eldeford mill for the easement of the miller and those of the neighbourhood who came to grind corn; and that the lord of Hanworth was not bound to repair it. The bishop recovered the amount of his amercement, while the sheriff was declared to be in mercy for taking presentment without his jurisdiction, it being found that one end of the bridge leading to Hanworth was within the liberty of the honour of Wallingford, and the other within the liberty of Queen Philippa's manor of Isleworth.[86]

HANWORTH PARK is not mentioned before the beginning of the 16th century, so that it may have been made either by the Crosbys or by the king. It was held as part of the manor of Hanworth, and became a royal seat in the reign of Henry VIII, 'where,' says Camden, 'he had the diversion at all times of the buck and hare.'[87] The park had been enlarged in the preceding reign by the addition of a considerable amount of land in the adjoining parish of Feltham.[88] Much care seems to have been expended both on the house and gardens under Henry VIII.[89] The office of keeper of the park was granted to Sir Richard Weston, who held it early in the reign,[90] and on the occasion of Princess Mary's residence at Hanworth in 1522 sent her a New Year's present of twelve pairs of shoes.[91] The park was granted with the manor-house to Stephen Gardiner in 1530,[92] and to Anne Boleyn in July 1532.[93] In 1544 it was settled for life on Katherine Parr,[94] who continued to live there after the king's death, with her second husband, Sir Thomas Seymour.[95] The Princess Elizabeth, whose education was entrusted to Katherine, came to live there at the age of fifteen. Seymour indulged in such familiarities with the princess as to lay himself open at his impeachment to the charge of having attempted to gain the affections of Elizabeth with a view to seating himself on the throne as Prince Consort, after he should have rid himself of Queen Katherine.[96]

After the queen's death in 1548 the custody of the park is said to have been entrusted to William, Earl of Pembroke.[97] It came in 1594 into the hands of William Killigrew,[98] who was a person of some importance under Elizabeth and

77 *Plac. de Quo Warr.* (Rec. Com.), 477.
78 Ibid.
79 Chan. Inq. p.m. 31 Edw. I, no. 26.
80 P.R.O. Ct. R. portf. 212, no. 2, 6, 7, 8, 18, 19.
81 Chan. Inq. p.m. 31 Edw. I, no. 26.
82 Pat. 13 Chas. I, pt. xxiv, no. 2.
83 Chan. Inq. p.m. 31 Edw. I, no. 26.
84 *Cal. Pat.* 1340–3, p. 47.

85 Ibid.
86 Ibid.
87 Camden, *Mag. Brit.* (ed. Gough), ii, 2, 13.
88 Pat. 16 Hen. VIII, pt. ii, m. 30.
89 *L. and P. Hen. VIII,* xiv (2), 236; iii, 2214; xvi, 380; xvii, 258; xviii, (2) 231.
90 Pat. 24 Hen. VIII, pt. ii, m. 12–14; 37 Hen. VIII, pt. iii, m. 16.

91 *L. and P. Hen. VIII,* iii, 2585.
92 Pat. 24 Hen. VIII, pt. ii, m. 12–14.
93 Pat. 24 Hen. VIII, pt. ii, m. 12.
94 *L. and P. Hen. VIII,* xix (1), 644.
95 *Dict. Nat. Biog.*
96 Heyne, *Burleigh Papers,* 99.
97 Lysons, *Environs of Lond.* v, 94.
98 *Cal. S.P. Dom.* 1591–4, pp. 547, 559.

James I. Besides being groom of the privy chamber, he was granted the right to farm the profits of the Queen's Bench and Common Pleas, in return for which he supported the court interest in Parliament, where he represented various Cornish boroughs in succession.[99] In 1600, during his keepership of the park, Elizabeth visited Hanworth, and remained some days, spent mostly in hunting in the park.[100] Sir William Killigrew died in 1622, and his son Sir Robert transferred the remainder of the lease of Hanworth Park to Lord Cottington.[101] Of the various members of the Killigrew family who were born or baptized at Hanworth three suffered to a severe extent for the royal cause. Sir Robert's elder son William was gentleman-usher to Charles I. He compounded for his estates in 1653 and was restored to his position at court under Charles II.[102] His brother, Henry Killigrew, D.D., a prebendary of Westminster, suffered many hardships during the Interregnum. He recovered his stall at the Restoration, and was made almoner to the Duke of York, and died as rector of Wheathampstead in Hertfordshire in 1693.[103] Both he and his brother attained some fame as dramatists, and his daughter Anne Killigrew was a poetess of some note at the time.[104] Sir Thomas Killigrew, the son of William, was also probably born at Hanworth. He acted as page to Charles I, and accompanied Charles II in exile.[105]

When Hanworth Park came into the possession of Lord Cottington he effected several improvements. In 1629 he wrote to Lord Strafford: 'There begins to grow a brick wall all about the gardens at Hanworth, which though it be a large extent yet it will be too little for the multitude of pheasants, partridges and wild-fowl that are to be bred in it.'[106] And further that 'dainty walks are made abroad inasmuch as the old porter with the long beard is like to have a good revenue by admitting strangers that will come to see these varieties. It will be good entertainment to see the amazement of the barbarous northern folk who have scarce arrived to see a well cut hedge, when the fame of these varieties shall draw them thither.'[107] His wife Anne, daughter of Sir William Meredith and widow of Sir Robert Brett, took an equal interest in the park. He speaks of her as 'the principal contriver of all this machine, who with her clothes tucked up and a staff in her hand, marches from place to place like an Amazon commanding an army.'[108] In 1635 Lord Cottington entertained the queen and all her court in great splendour at Hanworth.[109] He received a grant of free warren here in 1638 as well as licence to inclose 50 acres of land.[110] When hostilities broke out between the king and Parliament, his Royalist sympathies led to a search for arms in his house at Hanworth.[111] Cottington himself was away, and the house was in the charge of his servants. These petitioned Parliament for the apprehending of the delinquents, who had come with swords and guns and had attempted to pull down the palings of Hanworth Park and to ransack and pillage the house 'under colour of a pretended power to search for arms by virtue of a warrant surreptitiously gotten as the petitioners conceive and was directed to none there present.'[112] There was a second attack on the house a few months later (January 1642–3), when a company of soldiers forced an entry and took away all the weapons they could find. When pleading for the restoration of the arms or for licence to furnish themselves with others, Lord Cottington's servants urged the need of means of defence against vagabonds, thieves and robbers, because 'the house stands removed from any neighbours and destitute from others in time of danger.'[113] The house, which stood near the church, was destroyed by fire in 1797. The moat and a few traces of the buildings may still be seen. The present house stands further to the south-east. It was built by the Duke of St. Albans shortly after the destruction of the older mansion.[114] In the 19th century it was well-known to bibliophiles for the fine library of old books and manuscripts collected by Mr. Henry Perkins, which was sold by auction in 1873. The house is now the residence of Mr. Alfred Lafone, J.P., to whom and to Mr. James Scarlett and others Messrs. Pain & Bretell sold the park about 1873.

CHURCH The church of *ST. GEORGE* is a modern building of stone in 14th-century style, and consists of an apsidal chancel 24 ft. 9 in. by 18 ft. 5 in., a nave 60 ft. 3 in. by 23 ft. 3 in. with north and south porches, a north transept 13 ft. 10 in. long by 14 ft. 3 in. wide, and a north-east tower with a tall broach spire. The ground stage of the tower is used as a vestry. The churchyard is inclosed by an iron railing on a dwarf wall, and is entered from the south-east through a well-designed wooden lich-gate.

There is one bell, by Thomas Mears, 1814.

The plate consists of a silver cup and paten (1632) bearing the arms of Francis Lord Cottington, the donor; a silver paten (1781); chalice (1874) and flagon (1882). The registers begin in 1731.

ADVOWSON The church is first mentioned in 1293, when the advowson occurs in a grant of the manor.[115] The living is a rectory, the patronage of which descended with the manor (q.v.) until it was sold by Henry Perkins to the rector, the Rev. Oswald Joseph Cresswall, before 1866.[116] It was in the gift of Mr. John Bagot Scriven in 1874,[117] from whom it passed to the Rev. John Lyndhurst Winslow, who was rector of Hanworth from 1879.[118] The advowson is now held by his widow.

[99] *Dict. Nat. Biog.* xxvi, 116.
[100] Nichols, *Progresses of Q. Eliz.* passim.
[101] S.P. Dom. Chas. I, ccclxxvii, 177.
[102] *Dict. Nat. Biog.* xxxi, 116.
[103] Ibid. 168.
[104] Ibid.
[105] Ibid.
[106] Lysons, *Environs of London* (1800), v, 52, quoting Strafford Papers, i, 51.
[107] Ibid.
[108] Ibid.
[109] Ibid. i, 463.
[110] Pat. 13 Chas. I, pt. xxiv, no. 2.
[111] *Hist. MSS. Com. Rep.* v, App. 43.
[112] Ibid.
[113] Ibid.
[114] *Beauties of Engl. and Wales,* x (4), 517.
[115] Feet of F. Lond. and Midd. 22 Edw. I, no. 208.
[116] *P.O. Dir.* 1866, Essex . . . Midd. 596.
[117] *Clergy List,* 1874.
[118] Ibid. 1879.

Adam de Brome, the founder of Oriel College, Oxford, was rector of Hanworth in 1315.[119] Of his early life nothing is known. He was Chancellor of Durham in 1316, Archdeacon of Stowe in 1319, and was made vicar of St. Mary's, Oxford, in the same year. He obtained a licence to found a college at Oxford in 1324, and died in 1332.

Samuel Croxall, D.D., whose well-known *Aesop's Fables* were published in 1722, was the son of the Rev. Samuel Croxall, rector of Hanworth, and of Walton on Thames.[120]

In 1548 there was a 'guild church'[121] in Hanworth, to which belonged a church-house used for the 'assembelling of officers of the guild to drinck and thereat to gather money for the reparacion of the church.'[122] This house may perhaps be the same as a tenement in Hanworth which was in the occupation of the guardian of the church for the support of a 'gildar' or 'church iles,' granted in 1562 to Cecilia Pickerell, widow of John Pickerell, in part payment of a debt owed to her late husband by Edward, Duke of Somerset, in whose household John Pickerell occupied the posts of treasurer and confessor.[123]

CHARITIES In 1745 the Right Hon. Lord Vere Beauclerk gave an annuity of £6 for the poor chargeable upon certain copyhold property. The annuity is paid by Mr. Alfred Lafone, of Hanworth Park.

Poor's Land.—Under the Hanworth Inclosure Act (40 Geo. III), 3 a. 1 r. 11 p. were allotted to the churchwardens and overseers, now represented by the parish council, let at £14 a year.

Fuel Allotment.—Under the same Act an allotment, containing 17 a. 1 r. 9 p., was awarded for the poor in compensation for the right of procuring fuel. The land is let at £60 a year, which, together with the income of the preceding charities, was in 1906 distributed in coals to 200 persons.

In 1820 the Rev. James Burges, D.D., gave £1,500 consols to the rector of Hanworth in trust to promote the education of youth. The charity is regulated by scheme of the Charity Commissioners dated 12 April 1878.

By an order dated 15 October 1897, made under the Local Government Act, 1894, £500 consols, one-third part thereof, was apportioned as the Ecclesiastical Charity of Dr. Burges, and £1,000 consols, two-third parts thereof, as the Educational Charity of Dr. Burges. The trust funds are held by the official trustees. The dividends of £12 10s. and £25 are applied for purposes connected with the Sunday school and for educational purposes respectively.

LALEHAM

Leleham (xi cent.); Lalham, Lelham (xiii–xv cent.); Laneham (xvi cent.).

The parish of Laleham lies on the level ground between the road from Staines to Kingston and the River Thames. It is long and wedge-shaped, the point of the wedge lying towards the south, and the Thames forms almost the whole of the western boundary. There is no railway line in the parish, and the nearest stations are at Staines, 2½ miles to the north-west, and at Shepperton, 2½ miles to the east. The main road from Staines to Kingston runs just within the northern boundary, and roads from Staines, Ashford, and Shepperton converge on the village. The parish is sparsely wooded, and is laid out almost entirely in fields. The village lies near the Thames, about midway between the northern and southern extremities of the parish. It is a typical river village of the kind that is found on the lower reaches of the Thames. The pleasant street, very quiet except in the summer months, winds among private houses and shops, and after passing round the church, widens out into the road to Ashford, and the houses continue northwards. A new street of small villas has been built towards the river, and there are a few houses of the bungalow type facing the tow-path. The Thames is here comparatively wide, and a fine open stretch affords good mooring for the house-boats which lie along its banks in the summer. There is no bridge over the Thames in this parish, Chertsey Bridge lying just beyond the boundary, but a ferry (punt) plies from a point near the village to the opposite Surrey bank.

A triangular piece of ground of about 200 acres on the Surrey side of the river is known as Laleham Burway. It is part of an island formed by an offshoot of the main stream, and is divided from the Abbey Mead of Chertsey on the south by a stream called the Burway Ditch, and by another stream from the meadow of Mixnams on the north. This land is included in Chertsey parish, and belongs to the manor of Laleham. It is mentioned as the Island of Burgh in the original endowment of Chertsey Abbey between 666 and 675,[1] and is described as separated from Mixtenham by water, which formed part of the boundary of the abbey lands,[2] but it is not clear which of the two lay within the bounds of the abbey. Tradition says that the Burway originally belonged to Chertsey, and that in a time of great scarcity and famine the inhabitants of Laleham supplied the abbey with necessaries which those of Chertsey could not, or would not provide, in return for which the abbot granted them the use of this piece of ground.[3] Whatever the truth of this

---

[119] *Dict. Nat. Biog.* vi, 392.
[120] Ibid. xiii, 246.
[121] Possibly this means that part of the church was used by the gild; or that they had a chapel there.
[122] Chant. Cert. 34, no. 167.
[123] Pat. 4 Eliz. pt. iii, m. 40.

[1] Birch, *Cart. Sax.* i, 55–6.
[2] Cott. MS. Vit. A. xiii.
[3] Manning, *Hist. of Surr.* iii, 204.

story, it is certain that the abbey of Westminster when lord of the manor of Laleham held land on the Surrey side of the river, and that in the time of Edward I it held part of the meadow called Mixtenham also, for in a dispute with the abbey of Chertsey in 1278, Westminster agreed to release their right in this meadow in return for 4 acres of pasture contiguous with that which they already held[4] In 1370 they still held some pasture in Mixtenham.[5] Laleham Burway appears in a grant of the manor during the 18th century.[6] At the beginning of the 19th century it is described as paying no tithes or taxes to either Chertsey or Laleham parish.[7] It belonged to owners of estates within the manor of Laleham, and the pasture was divided into 300 parts called 'farrens,' the tenants of which were entitled some to the feed of a horse, others to the support of a cow and a half. A horse-farren would let for £1 17s. 6d. a year, and pasture for one cow for £1 5s., and when sold a farren was worth about £40.[8] This land was not inclosed under the Act of 1773 for inclosing the common fields of Laleham Manor in Chertsey,[9] and was specially exempted from the Act of 1808 for inclosing Laleham and Middlesex.[10] It was finally inclosed under an Act passed in 1813,[11] when the Earl of Lucan, lord of the manor of Laleham, acquired by allotment and purchase about 70 acres. Before its inclosure many cricket matches were played here ' by ennobled and other cricketers.'[12]

Laleham House, the seat of the Earl of Lucan, stands to the south of the village in well-wooded grounds of about 23 acres. It was built by Richard, the second earl, who bought the manor in 1803. Maria, Queen of Portugal, who spent her minority in England, lived here from 1829. George, the third earl (1800–88), served in Turkey and in the Crimea, and attained the rank of field-marshal. The charge of the heavy brigade at Balaclava was made under his direction, and he was himself wounded by a bullet in the leg. Lord Raglan blamed him for the advance of the cavalry on that occasion, and in consequence he returned to England and vindicated his conduct in the House of Lords (19 March 1855).[13] He was succeeded by the present earl in 1888.

Thomas Arnold lived at Laleham from 1819 to 1828. He settled here to take as private pupils a small number of young men preparing for the uni-

BINGHAM, Earl of Lucan. *Azure a bend between cotises and six crosses formy or.*

versities, and besides his own studies and those of his pupils he spent his time in assisting in the care of the parish.[14] After his appointment to the head-mastership of Rugby he still hoped to return to Laleham after he should have retired from public life.[15] His house, which stood at the end of the village, was pulled down in 1864.[16] His eldest and most distinguished son, Matthew Arnold, was born here in 1822.[17] After the family had removed to Rugby, he returned to Laleham as pupil of his maternal uncle, the Rev. John Buckland (1830–6).[18] He lies buried in the churchyard here, together with Thomas Arnold his eldest son.

Among the present residents are Mr. Adolphus Govett, J.P., of High Elms, whose family has long been connected with this parish, and Gen. Sir Frederick Maunsell, R.E., K.C.B., who lives at the Boreen.

The inhabitants of Laleham are chiefly dependent on agriculture, and the population returns of the last forty years show a decrease of over twenty per cent. The soil is light, and the subsoil gravel. The chief crops are wheat, barley, oats, turnips, and mangold-wurzel. There are 1,301 acres in the parish, of which 550½ acres are arable, and 465 acres are laid down in permanent grass. Woods and plantations cover 36 acres.[19]

The following names of pastures occur in mediaeval times : Le Cottes, Watcroftes, Hotlowe, Henland, Charston, Chikenes, Middelwellethorn, Tuccemede. Churchwynnesland was originally held by a John Cherchwynn early in the 14th century.[20]

MANORS

LALEHAM is mentioned as one of the four appurtenances of Staines in the charter of Edward the Confessor granting and confirming lands to Westminster Abbey.[21] At the time of the Domesday Survey, the abbey still held Staines and four unnamed berewicks,[22] and it is likely that Laleham was one of the latter, as the abbey held a large amount of land there in 1291,[23] and about the same time Laleham is described as one of those members of Staines which had belonged to Westminster from time immemorial.[24] The abbey continued to hold it until the Dissolution,[25] when the manor was ceded to the king, who caused it to be annexed to the newly-formed honour of Hampton Court.[26] Laleham remained in the hands of the king throughout the 16th century. The site of the manor had been leased by Westminster Abbey in 1538 to John Williams for seventy-six years, and in 1588 the site was leased on the same terms to Thomas Kay,[27] and in 1608 to Sir Thomas Lake.[28]

[4] Anct. D. B. 1853.
[5] Doc. in custody of the D. and C. of Westm. chest D. no. 27151.
[6] Recov. R. Mich. 10 Geo. II, rot. 423.
[7] Manning, op. cit. iii, 204.
[8] Ibid.
[9] V.C.H. Surr.
[10] Ibid.
[11] Brayley, *Hist. of Surr.* ii, 172.
[12] Ibid.

[13] *Dict. Nat. Biog.* Suppl. i, 196.
[14] Ibid. i, 113.
[15] Stanley, *Life of Thomas Arnold,* 35.
[16] Firth, *Midd.* 116.
[17] *Dict. Nat. Biog.* Suppl. i, 70.
[18] Ibid.
[19] Inf. supplied by the Bd. of Agric. (1905).
[20] Doc. in custody of D. and C. of Westm. chest D, no. 27113.
[21] Cott. MS. Faust. A. iii.

[22] *Dom. Bk.* (Rec. Com.), i, 128.
[23] *Pope Nich. Tax.* (Rec. Com.), 13.
[24] *Plac. de Quo. Warr.* (Rec. Com.), 479.
[25] *Feud. Aids,* ii, 372 ; Doc. in custody of D. and C. of Westm. chest D. no. 27105–71 ; Dugdale, *Mon.* i, 326 ; *Valor Eccl.* (Rec. Com.), i, 410.
[26] *L. and P. Hen. VIII,* xv, 498 (36)
[27] Pat. 31 Eliz. pt. x, m. 20.
[28] Pat. 4 Jas. I, pt. ix, m. 17.

In 1612 James I granted the manor to Henry Spiller,[29] who was knighted in 1608.[30] He leased the site of the manor to a widow, Jane Thompson, and to Thomas Stapley, and litigation took place in 1630 touching the arrears of twelve years of rent and waste and spoil on the part of the defendants, Jane Thompson and others,[31] when it was alleged that the latter had neglected to give entertainment to the steward and surveyor of the manor and their servants, and had not provided 'fitt and competent meat drink and lodging for them.' Amongst other charges they were accused of not holding the manor courts, and of taking a new toll of 2d. for every team of large horses passing through the land of the Old Farm adjoining the river.[32]

SPILLER. *Sable a cross voided between four pierced molets or.*

In 1640 proceedings for recusancy were instituted against Sir Henry's wife, Lady Anne Spiller, and she was pronounced guilty on 5 May of that year.[33] Sir Henry took the king's side in the Civil War, and after being taken prisoner and confined in the Tower,[34] he proposed to compound for his estates for the sum of £8,611.[35] He died, however, in the early part of 1650, leaving half the fine unpaid, and James Herbert, who had married Jane Spiller, the granddaughter and heir-at-law of Sir Henry, and Sir Thomas Reynell of Weybridge, who had married Sir Henry's daughter Katherine, between them paid the remainder of the composition, and were admitted to the lands on 12 March 1652. Laleham was apparently assigned to Reynell, and was inherited by his son, also named Thomas.[36] It passed to the latter's daughter and heiress Elizabeth,[37] who, as her second husband, married Sir Richard Reynell, son of Sir Richard Reynell of East Ogwell, Devon.[38] The manor was held jointly by Richard and Elizabeth, and by Richard after his wife's death.[39] On his own death

REYNELL. *Argent masoned and a chief indented sable.*

in 1723 it was inherited by his son Sir Thomas Reynell.[40] The latter's son died unmarried in 1735,[41] and in the following year Sir Thomas conveyed the reversion to Sir Robert Lowther of Whitehaven,[42] sometime governor of Barbados.[43] Sir Thomas Reynell seems to have continued to hold the manor at any rate until 1741,[44] but by 1768 it was in the hands of Sir James Lowther,[45] who was the second son of Sir Robert, and was created Earl of Lonsdale in 1784. The year after his death in 1802[46] it was bought by the Earl of Lucan, in whose family it remains at the present day.[46a]

The grange belonging to the abbey of Westminster was apparently built about 1278.[47] It contained a room for the use of the monks.[48] A house was built about 1290, with stables for cattle and sheep, piggeries, and a garden.[49] The abbey already possessed one garden,[50] and apparently a good deal of fruit was grown in Laleham, for fruit to the amount of 23s. was sold to Roger the fruiterer of Wraysbury in 1385–6.[51] A smithy was built before 1300, but ceases to be mentioned after 1354.[52] There was a dovecote on the estate in the 13th century,[53] and as many as 189 doves were sometimes sold in the year.[54] The dovecote fell into disrepair in 1302,[55] and was still neglected in 1306,[56] after which there is no further mention of it.

There was a windmill and a grain-mill in the 14th century,[57] and pastures on Windmill Hill and Grundmullhull are occasionally mentioned.[58] The abbey had a water-mill on the Thames,[59] which was considerably repaired in 1276,[60] and which appears to have been moved to a fresh place in 1302.[61] A mill is mentioned in a grant of the site of the manor in 1608,[62] and a water-mill belonged to the manor when it was held by Sir Henry Spiller.[63]

A weir called 'Depewere' lay between Staines and Laleham, and was given to the Abbot of Westminster in the 13th century by Gilbert son of John de Monte, together with the fishery, and also with three cart-loads of timber and two of brushwood from the Abbot of Chertsey's wood, for its upkeep.[64] Weirs are mentioned in a grant of the site of the manor in 1600,[65] and there is now a weir just beyond the parish boundary in Staines, and a second weir at the southern boundary opposite Chertsey.

A sailing boat was made for the bailiff of Laleham in 1290, at a cost of £7 4s.[66]

29 Pat. 10 Jas. I, pt. vii, no. 13.
30 G.E.C. *Baronetage.*
31 Exch. Dep. Mich. 6 Chas. I, no. 38.
32 Ibid.
33 Midd. Co. Rec. iii, 154.
34 *Midd. and Herts. N. and Q.* iii, 45.
35 *Cal. of Com. for Compounding*, 1145.
36 Feet of F. Midd. Trin. 19 Chas. II ; G.E.C. *Baronetage*, iv, 212.
37 P.R.O. Ct. R. portf. 191, no. 46.
38 G.E.C. op. cit. iv, 212.
39 P.R.O. Ct. R. portf. 191, no. 46.
40 Feet of F. Div. Co. Mich. 2 Geo. II ; G.E.C. op. cit.
41 G.E.C. op. cit.

42 Recov. R. Mich. 10 Geo. II, rot. 423.
43 Collins, *Peerage*, Suppl. (ed. 5), 349.
44 B.M. fol. 21559, no. 58.
45 Ibid. no. 162.
46 Burke, *Peerage* (1906), 1032.
46a Ibid ; Firth, *Middlesex*, 165.
47 Doc. in custody of D. and C. of Westm. Abbey, chest D. nos. 27105–6.
48 Ibid. no. 27108.
49 Ibid. no. 27109.
50 Ibid. no. 27105–6.
51 Ibid. no. 27115.
52 Ibid. no. 27116–39.
53 Ibid. no. 27105.

54 Ibid. no. 27108.
55 Ibid. no. 27113.
56 Ibid. no. 27115.
57 Ibid. no. 27133, &c.
58 Ibid. no. 27119, 27121, 27128, &c.
59 *Hund. R.* (Rec. Com.), i, 431.
60 Doc. in custody of D. and C. of Westm. Abbey, chest D. no. 27105.
61 Ibid. no. 27113.
62 Pat. 4 Jas. I, pt. ix, m. 17.
63 Exch. Dep. Mich. 6 Chas. I.
64 Abst. of Chartul. of Westm. Abbey in possession of Saml. Bentley, no. 51.
65 Pat. 4 Jas. I, pt. ix, m. 17.
66 Doc. in custody of the D. and C. of Westm. Abbey, chest D. no. 27110.

From about 1294 to 1304 the manor courts seem to have been held almost monthly, and generally on a date towards the end of the month.[67] After 1331 they were held three times a year, the court held with view of frankpledge falling always near the Feast of the Conversion of St. Paul.[68] The reeve (*prepositus*), who was responsible to Westminster for the manor, appears to have been elected by the homage,[69] and to have been usually a native tenant of the manor. Though the manor was generally managed by a reeve, the abbey occasionally appointed a serjeant,[70] or a collector of rents.[71] There are four court rolls extant of the reign of Henry VI,[72] and twelve are preserved at the Public Record Office which date from 1690 to 1721.[73]

LA HYDE or *BILLETS.* In 1086 Robert Blund (Blunt) held 8 hides as a manor.[74] This land is ascribed to Laleham only, but it probably extended into the neighbouring parish of Littleton also, as the Blunts certainly held land there.[75] Littleton is not mentioned by name in the Domesday Survey, but as Westminster Abbey held the more important estate in Laleham, there would hardly be room in so small a parish for another manor estimated at as much as 8 hides. In the time of Edward the Confessor Robert Blunt's manor had been held by Achi, the king's servant, and it had then lain within the jurisdiction of Staines.[76] It was held of Robert Blunt by one Estrild, a nun.[77] Laleham is not mentioned again among the lands of the Blunt family, whose chief property lay in Suffolk, and who were barons of Ixworth in that county.[78] The last of this branch of the family, William Blunt, was killed at the battle of Evesham, and his estates were divided between his sisters, Agnes the wife of Sir William Criketot of Ovisdone, and Rose wife of Robert de Valoigne.[79]

In the reign of Edward III Robert de Eglesfeld held the manor of La Hyde in Laleham.[80] He held it by gift from his father, John de Eglesfeld, who was one of the heirs of John de Crokedayk.[81]

EGLESFELD. *Argent three eagles gules.*

The Eglesfelds and the Crokedayks were Cumberland families,[82] and it is possible that the latter represents a branch of the Criketots, and that the manor of La Hyde was part of the 8 hides held by Robert Blunt in 1086. There is, however, no actual proof of the connexion, nor is Laleham mentioned among the lands inherited by John de Eglesfeld from John de Crokedayk.[83] Robert de Eglesfeld son of John was chaplain to Queen Philippa, the consort of Edward III, and the founder of Queen's College, Oxford.[84] His manor of La Hyde apparently gave its name to a pasture known as the Hyde Acre. An extent taken in 1327 shows that it lay in Laleham, Littleton, and Staines, and that it had a house and garden, stables, a grange, and that there were in demesne $36\frac{1}{2}$ acres of arable, and 9 acres of pasture ;[85] the whole being worth £6 14s. $10\frac{1}{2}d$.[86] In 1328, Robert de Eglesfeld granted the manor to Edward III in exchange for Renwick or Ravenswyk, a hamlet in Cumberland.[87] The king added La Hyde to the manor of Kempton, in Sunbury parish, and gave it into the custody of John de L'Isle, the constable of Windsor Castle.[88] The capital messuage and garden and demesne lands were then held by Roger Belet, the pantler (*panetarius*) of the queen's household,[89] an office which seems to have been hereditary in the Belet family since the reign of John.[90] In 1337 these lands were granted to Roger to hold in fee by the services due,[91] though the estate still remained in the manorial jurisdiction of Kempton.[92] In 1366 Belet conveyed these and the reversion of all his lands in Staines, Littleton, and Laleham to the abbey of Westminster.[93] From this time it seems to have been merged in the abbey's manor of Laleham, and to have been distinguished under the name of Beletes tenement.[94] At the Dissolution it was probably represented by the 'manor' of *BILLETS*, which was valued separately from that of Laleham at the sum of £6 13s. 4d.[95] It was surrendered with the rest of the abbey's lands to the Crown, and was annexed to the honour of Hampton Court.[96]

The site of the manor was leased in 1538 to Thomas Cawarden, and later to Roger Rogers. In 1585 it was leased to John Keye (being described as 'Billets in Laleham'[97]), and in 1606 to Henry Spiller,[98] to whom it was finally granted, with the manor of Laleham, in 1612.[99] The history of the two manors from that time was identical, and they were generally described as the manor of 'Laleham and Billets,' otherwise 'Laleham Billets.' The name of Billets is not to be found now in the parish, but land known as the Billet

[67] Doc. in custody of the D. and C. of Westm. Abbey, chest D. no. 27111–14.

[68] Ibid. no. 27127, &c.

[69] Ibid. no. 27120.

[70] Ibid. no. 27119, 27133.

[71] Ibid. no. 27161–8.

[72] Ibid. no. 27169, 27170.

[73] P.R.O. Ct. R. portf. 191, no. 46.

[74] *Dom. Bk.* (Rec. Com.), i, 131.

[75] v.s. Littleton.

[76] *Dom. Bk.* (Rec. Com.), i, 131.

[77] Ibid.

[78] Croke, *Hist. of the Croke Family*, i, 100.

[79] Chan. Inq. p.m. 48 Hen. III, no. 25.

[80] Ibid. 1 Edw. III (1st. nos.), no. 1.

[81] Ibid.

[82] Ibid. 18 Edw. III (1st. nos.), no. 53.

[83] Ibid. 10 Edw. III, no. 24.

[84] *Dict. Nat. Biog.* xvii, 165.

[85] Chan. Inq. p.m. 1 Edw. III (1st. nos.), no. 1.

[86] Chart. R. 2 Edw. III, m. 24, no. 79.

[87] Close, 2 Edw. III, m. 34 d.

[88] *Abbrev. Rot. Orig.* (Rec. Com.), ii, 17.

[89] Mins. Accts. (P.R.O.), bdle. 916, no. 27.

[90] Cart. Antiq. II, 15.

[91] *Cal. Pat.* 1334–8, p. 410.

[92] P.R.O. Ct. R. portf. 191, no. 41.

[93] Abst. of Chart. of Westm. Abbey, no. 88, 89, 125, 134, 135 ; Chan. Inq. p.m. 40 Edw. III (2nd nos.), no. 20.

[94] Close, 3 Edw. IV, m. 11, 12.

[95] *Valor Eccl.* (Rec. Com.), i, 410.

[96] Pat. 4 Jas. I, pt. xxi.

[97] Pat. 27 Eliz. pt. v, m. 30 ; 27 Eliz. pt. xi, m. 33.

[98] Pat. 4 Jas. I, pt. xx, xxi.

[99] Pat. 10 Jas. I, pt. vii, m. 18.

estate lies on the borders of the neighbouring parish of Staines, and perhaps represents that part of the manor which originally lay in that parish.

At the time of the Domesday Survey, the Count of Mortain held two hides in Laleham.[100] This land had been in the time of Edward the Confessor in the possession of the abbey of Westminster, under whom it was held by the bailiff of Staines, who could not sell it out of the soke of Staines without permission from the abbey.[101] The Count of Mortain gave it to the abbey of Fécamp, and the abbot still held lands and rent in Laleham in 1134, which he exchanged for other lands in France with Nigel son of William, nephew (*nepos*) of Robert, Earl of Gloucester.[102] There is no further trace of this land, but it is probable that it came again into the hands of Westminster Abbey, and that it was then merged in the manor of Laleham.

The church of *ALL SAINTS*, a
CHURCH little ivy-grown brick-faced building, though containing some 12th-century work in the nave, has been so altered and rebuilt that little really old work is left; at the present time it consists of a brick-faced chancel 21 ft. 6 in. by 15 ft. 4 in., a north chapel belonging to the Earls of Lucan, 21 ft. by 13 ft. 9 in., faced with 17th-century brickwork, a nave 34 ft. by 15 ft. 4 in. of the 12th century, which had north and south aisles, of which the latter has been pulled down and the former rebuilt in modern times, and at the west end of the north aisle an 18th-century brick tower, covered with ivy, having a west doorway and round-headed windows.

There is no east window to the chancel, the space being occupied by a large picture of our Lord walking on the water with St. Peter; this is lit by a skylight above. On the north side the wall has been cut away towards the Lucan chapel, which is lit on the north and east by square-headed cut brick windows of three four-centred lights. On the south side of the chancel is a modern Gothic doorway.

The chancel arch is slightly pointed, of one chamfered order, with a chamfered abacus, all so covered with colour wash that it is impossible to be sure of its age. The nave has arcades of three bays of late 12th-century date, with edge-chamfered pointed arches on massive round columns with scalloped capitals; all the arches have chamfered labels, except the east arch of the north arcade. The label of the middle arch of this arcade has billet ornament on its label, re-used material from an arch of different radius. In the blocking of the south arcade are two modern two-light windows in 15th-century style, and in the western bay a doorway which looks like 14th-century work, leading into a red brick porch. At the west end of the nave is a gallery

containing an organ, which hides a modern three-light window.

The north aisle has three modern two-light north windows like those on the south of the nave; at the west end is a gallery, and the east end opens to the Lucan chapel by a plain chamfered pointed arch.

In the chancel is a monument to George Perrott, baron of the Exchequer, who died 1780, and his wife Mary, 1784, and there are others of the 19th century. The font, at the west end of the north aisle, is modern, in 12th-century style.

There are three bells by William Eldridge, 1663, and a set of eight tubular bells.

The plate consists of modern chalice, paten and flagon, and a standing paten, the gift of Samuel Freeman, 1767.

The registers date from 1538. Book (i) contains baptisms 1538 to 1690, burials 1538 to 1682, and marriages 1539 to 1643; (ii) baptisms 1690 to 1692, marriages 1682 to 1683, 1643 to 1690; (iii) printed marriages 1754 to 1789 and 1801 to 1812; (iv) burials 1804 to 1812, baptisms 1804 to 1812; (v) marriages and baptisms 1789 to 1801, and burials 1789 to 1802, having threepenny stamps.

Laleham was from the earliest
ADVOWSON times a chapelry of Staines,[103] with which it was probably appropriated, but until the 15th century it was served by a separate vicar appointed by the Abbot and Convent of Westminster, patrons of the mother church.[104] By an order made by William, Bishop of London, however (probably between 1426 and 1431), the vicar of Staines was in future to appoint curates to the chapels of that church, but it was provided that if there were any vicar who had been canonically appointed to any of the chapels, he should remain there during his lifetime.[105] Apparently the order came into force at Laleham during the latter half of the 15th century, for the last institution to the vicarage took place in December 1439, and in 1492 Laleham is mentioned as a chapel in the institution to the vicarage of Staines.[106] At the Dissolution the patronage of the latter fell to the Crown. In 1542 the advowson of Laleham was separated from that of Staines, and was granted to the dean and chapter of the Cathedral Church of Westminster,[107] but there is no mention of an institution to the vicarage, and in 1550 Laleham appears again as a chapel of Staines in the presentation of that living which was then the gift of the Crown.[108] In 1560 the queen granted the vicarage and free chapel of Laleham to the newly-founded Collegiate Church of Westminster,[109] but again there is no record of any institution.[110] In 1612 the advowson was given with the manor to Sir Henry Spiller,[111] from whom it descended to Sir Thomas Reynell,[112] who presented immediately after the Restoration and again in 1662 and 1663.[113]

100 *Dom. Bk.* (Rec. Com.), i, 129.
101 Ibid.
102 Round, *Cal. of Doc. France*, 42.
108 *Pope Nich. Tax.* (Rec. Com.), 17; Doc. in custody of the D. and C. of Westm. press 5, shelf 2, no. 16782, 16811; *Feud. Aids*, ii, 378.

104 Newcourt, *Repert.* i, 683; *Cal. Pat.* 1313-17, p. 459; 1381-5, p. 395.
105 Lond. Epis. Reg. Gilbert, fol. 177.
106 Newcourt, *Repert.* i, 683.
107 *L. and P. Hen. VIII*, xvii, p. 395.

108 Newcourt, op. cit.
109 Pat. 2 Eliz. pt. xi, m. 19.
110 Newcourt, op. cit.
111 Pat. 10 Jas. I, pt. vii, no. 18.
112 See manor.
118 Inst. Bks. (P.R.O.).

LALEHAM CHURCH : NAVE AND SOUTH AISLE

It descended with the manor (q.v.), and thus came by purchase to Sir Robert Lowther in 1736.[114] In 1773 and 1778, however, Laleham is again mentioned as a chapel of Staines,[115] and during the early part of the 19th century it continued to be served by a curate of the mother church. At that time services were held on alternate Sundays with Ashford, although it is mentioned in 1826 that 'the inhabitants have the benefit of other preachers, who officiate occasionally.' The living was a perpetual curacy in the gift of the Earl of Lucan from 1858 to 1865,[116] after which it is called a vicarage. The advowson still remains with the Earl of Lucan.

In the 14th century 10 marks from the church of Oakham were paid yearly to the Abbot of Westminster's household.[117] These were given up by Abbot Littlington to the convent, and 10 marks from the church at Laleham were granted instead, for the supply of plate.

The rectory, which was held by Westminster Abbey till the Dissolution, was granted in 1602 to Guy Godolphin and John Smythe.[118] Godolphin sold his interest to Smythe, who conveyed the rectory to Urias Babington.[119] The latter died seised of it in 1606, having demised it to his younger son William.[120] Under the Commonwealth it was held by George and Robert Holmes, who in 1650 and 1657 conveyed their respective shares to William Powell or Hinson.[121] Before 1682 it came into the hands of Robert Gibbon,[122] in whose family it continued until Mrs. Elizabeth Joddrell, daughter of Phillipps Gibbon, sold it to Mrs. Mary Jeffreson, who in 1733 alienated to Samuel Freeman.[123] The latter's daughter Martha married Captain John Coggan,[124] who held the rectory in 1782, and as late as 1800.[125] In 1836 Mr. Conosmaker, Mr. Hartwell,

and Mr. John Irving are mentioned as the impropriators,[126] but after this nothing can be learnt about the rectory.

CHARITIES
Charity of Ann Reeve for bread : see under Ashford.

In 1819 Mrs. Mary Hodgson, by will dated 4 September, bequeathed a sum of stock, now represented by £95 consols with the official trustees, the income to be given to the poor of the parish by the vicar and his successors to whom and in what manner he should think necessary.

The Poor's Land consists of 17 a. 2 r. acquired under the Inclosure Act, let at £22 10s. a year, the administration of which was regulated by a scheme of the Charity Commissioners of 4 August 1865.

In 1896 Dr. John Hearn Pinckney, by a declaration of trust dated 10 February, settled a sum of £120 London, Chatham and Dover Railway 4½ per cent. stock for the benefit of the National School.

By a scheme of the Board of Education, the Poor's Land and Dr. Pinckney's Charity were consolidated with the National School under the title of the 'Laleham School Foundation,' whereby the trustees were authorized to raise a loan of £300 by mortgage of the trust property, and to sell the railway stock for the purpose of the enlargement of the school buildings, at a cost of £500. A sum of £150 19s. 6d. was realized by the sale of the railway stock. The loan is subject to replacement within thirty years, and within the same period a sum of £174 consols has to be funded with the official trustees in lieu of the railway stock.

In 1906–7 the income of the charities (other than Ann Reeve's Charity) was used as a contribution to the School Enlargement Fund.

LITTLETON

Lutleton, Litlinton (xiii cent.) ; Lutlyngton, Littelyngton, Littelton (xiv cent.) ; Lytelyngton, (xvi cent.).

The parish of Littleton lies to the west of Laleham. The northern portion is roughly triangular in shape, the base about 2 miles long, lying along the road from Staines to Kingston, the sides narrowing gradually towards the village at the apex. The southern part is a mere slip of land about 1½ miles long and nowhere more than half a mile wide, which runs from the village to the River Thames. The curious shape of the parish may perhaps be accounted for by the fact that it probably formed part of Laleham until the end of the 11th century,[1] when this wedge-shaped piece was separated from the western part of the

latter, the dividing line being drawn at the River Ash. The ground falls gradually towards the Thames, and the higher and more northerly parts are well wooded, while two stretches of common, known respectively as Astlam and Littleton Common, fall within the northern boundary. The village is one of the least spoilt in the county. It is built almost entirely of red brick, and presents a cheerful and peaceful aspect as it clusters about the church. There has never been either publichouse or shop in the parish, and the only trade represented is that of the blacksmith. No railway line runs through the parish, the nearest station being at Shepperton, 1½ miles. A road from Feltham passes through the village from north to south, and joins the Laleham-Shepperton road,

[114] Recov. R. Mich. 10 Geo. II, rot. 423.
[115] Inst. Bks. (P.R.O.).
[116] *Clergy Lists, passim.*
[117] *Hist. MSS. Com. Rep.* iv, App. i, 171.
[118] Pat. 44 Eliz. pt. xii., m. 6.

[119] Lysons, *Environs of Lond.* (1800), v, 1.
[120] Chan. Inq. p.m. (Ser. 2), ccxcii, 186 ; Exch. Dep. Mich. 7 Jas. I, no. 25.
[121] Feet of F. Trin. 1650 ; East. 1657.

[122] Feet of Div. Co. East. 34 Chas. II.
[123] Lysons, *Environs of Lond.* v, 200.
[124] Ibid.
[125] Feet of F. East. 22 Geo. III.
[126] *Clerical Guide,* 1836.
[1] See descent of manor.

which runs across the narrow part of the parish, and from the latter a road leads southwards to Chertsey Bridge.

There was formerly a wooden bridge here connecting the counties of Middlesex and Surrey, of which either county maintained half.[2] About 1770 the Middlesex part was much out of repair, and the magistrates of Middlesex prevailed on those of Surrey to join in building a stone bridge. When the contractor had finished the number of arches he had undertaken, they did not reach to the Surrey shore, and it cost that county a large sum to make good the deficiency.[3]

Much land in the parish belongs to Captain Thomas Wood of Gwernyfed Park, Three Cocks, Brecknockshire. Littleton House, which was originally the family seat of the Woods, was burnt down in 1874. It was a large brick mansion, surrounded by a park and grounds of 600 acres, and is said to have been built during the reign of William III, by the workmen who were then employed at Hampton Court.[4] This seems all the more likely considering that the Thomas Wood of that time was ranger at Hampton Court.[5] Littleton House contained Hogarth's famous picture 'Actors Dressing,' which was destroyed when the house was burnt.[6] A portion of the house has been rebuilt, and is now the residence of Mr. Richard Burbridge. It stands behind the church to the south of the village, and the waters of the River Ash form a natural boundary to the grounds.

Another considerable house, 'the Manor House,' is the residence of Mr. Theodore Bouwens.

Littleton was inclosed in 1848 under the General Inclosures Act.[7] There are 1,138 acres in the parish, of which 325 acres are arable, 524 acres are permanent grass, and 270 acres are woodland, and 19 acres are water.[8] The population is principally dependent on agriculture. The soil is sandy loam, and the subsoil gravel. The chief crops are wheat, barley, clover, mangold-wurzel, peas, and beans.

A weir is mentioned in 1235, when it was conveyed by William le Sire to Robert de Beauchamp.[9]

LITTLETON is not mentioned **MANORS** by name in the Domesday Survey.

In the reign of Edward the Confessor it was probably included in the estate of Achi, a servant of the king.[10] The 'soke' then belonged to Staines. Achi's manor, assessed at 8 hides, passed to Robert Blund, to whom it belonged in 1086, when it was said to be in Laleham.[11] But it has been seen that the estate was probably too large to have been included as a whole within the present bounds of that parish,[12] and as the two parishes are contiguous, and as the descendants of Robert Blunt held Littleton in the time of Henry II,[13] it may be concluded that in the 11th century the latter formed part of the 8 hides ascribed to Laleham.

Littleton is first mentioned by name about 1166, when it was held as one knight's fee in the barony of William Blunt, Baron of Ixworth, by whom it had been inherited from his father Gilbert, who held it in the reign of Henry I.[14] It still formed part of the barony in the latter half of the 13th century,[15] but on the division of the Blunt lands after the death of William Blunt at the battle of Evesham (1265),[16] the mesne overlordship of the fee does not appear to have passed to either of his heirs. It appears to have been by 1316 in the hands of the Abbey and Convent of Westminster,[17] who had temporalities there as early as 1291,[18] and it is probable that the abbey may have received a grant of it towards the end of the 13th century. It was apparently held of them in 1528.

In 1166 Littleton was held of the Blunts by Robert de Littleton.[19] It apparently descended to Osbert de Littleton, who conveyed it in 1204 to Robert de Leveland,[20] the son of Nathaniel de Leveland and Desirea, his wife, of Leveland in Kent.[21] His family held the offices of custodian of the royal palace of Westminster and of the Fleet Prison,[22] which offices descended at this time with the manor of Leveland.[23] The Leveland inheritance came in the reign of Henry III to an heiress, Margaret de Leveland, who married first Giles de Badlesmere,[24] and secondly Fulk de Peyforer,[25] but having no issue by either marriage, her heir was found to be Ralph de Grendon.[26] On his death, which occurred about 1280, he was succeeded by his brother Stephen, who was also known as de Leveland,[27] and who left an only daughter and heiress Joan.[28] She married John Shenche or Sench, by whom she had a son of the same name,[29] who died in 1349 and was succeeded by Margaret his daughter.[30] Margaret died in 1361, and her heir was found to be Roger, son of Roger Sapurton,[31] who held the manor of Littleton,[32] and also the offices of custodian of Westminster Palace and the Fleet Prison.[33] After the death of Roger the manor

[2] Manning, *Hist. of Surr.* iii, 205.
[3] Ibid.
[4] Keane, *Beauties of Midd.* 178.
[5] Burke, *Landed Gentry* (1906), 1842.
[6] Firth, *Midd.* 167.
[7] Slater, *Engl. Peasantry and the Enclosure of Common Fields*, 185.
[8] Inf. supplied by the Bd. of Agric. (1905).
[9] Feet of F. Lond. and Midd. 19 Hen. III, no. 116.
[10] *Dom. Bk.* (Rec. Com.), i, 131.
[11] Ibid.; see descent of manor of Billets in Laleham.
[12] See descent of manor of Billets in Laleham.

[13] *Red. Bk. of Exch.* (Rolls Ser.), i, 409; *Lib. Niger* (ed. Hearne), i, 297.
[14] Ibid.
[15] *Testa de Nevill* (Rec. Com.), 360, 361, 362.
[16] G.E.C. *Complete Peerage*, i.
[17] *Feud. Aids*, iii, 372.
[18] *Pope Nich. Tax.* (Rec. Com.), 16.
[19] *Red Bk. of Exch.* (Rolls Ser.), i, 409; *Lib. Niger*, i, 297.
[20] Feet of F. Lond. and Midd. 5 John, no. 27.
[21] Round, *Cal. of Doc. France*, i, 488.
[22] Madox, *Hist. of Exch.* i, 514; *Rot. Cancellarii* (Rec. Com.), 99, 103;

Rot. de Oblat. et Fin. (Rec. Com.), i, 492.
[23] Hasted, *Hist. of Kent*, ii, 770.
[24] Pat. 40 Hen. III; MS. quoted by Madox, op. cit.
[25] Chan. Inq. p.m. 5 Edw. I, no. 17.
[26] Hasted, *Hist. of Kent*, ii, 771.
[27] Chan. Inq. p.m. 8 Edw. I, no. 16.
[28] Hasted, op. cit. ii, 771.
[29] Chan. Inq. p.m. 6 Edw. III, no. 65.
[30] Ibid. 23 Edw. III, pt. ii, no. 127.
[31] Ibid. 36 Edw. III, pt. ii, no. 33.
[32] Plac. in Canc. file 29, no. 1.
[33] Chan. Inq. p.m. 12 Hen. VI, no. 19.

was held by his daughter Elizabeth,[34] whose husband, William Venour, was keeper of the Fleet in 1440.[35] It came probably after the death of Elizabeth to Ellen, the daughter and heir of John Sapurton, brother of Roger, who married Robert Markham, with whom she conveyed it in 1528 to Anthony Windesore, representative of the family of Windsor of Stanwell.[36] Edward Lord Windsor sold it in 1563 to Francis Vaughan,[37] and it appears to have . come before 1573 to John Bartram, who transferred his right in it in that year to Thomas Newdigate.[38] The latter possibly acted for the Somerset family, as Francis Newdigate married Anne, Duchess of Somerset, the widow of the Protector,[39] and Henry Newdigate conveyed the manor in 1600 to her son, Edward, Earl of Hertford.[40] It was inherited after the latter's death by his grandson and heir William,[41] who succeeded to the earldom in 1621.[42] He conveyed it in 1627 to Daniel and Thomas Moore,[43] of whom Thomas conveyed it to Nathaniel Goodlad in 1648.[44] The history of the manor for the next hundred years is somewhat obscure. It is said to have come early in the 18th century to the family of Lambell,[45] the last of whom, Gilbert Lambell, certainly held it in 1749.[46] He died in 1783,[47] having sold the manor to Thomas Wood, whose family had held the manor of Astlam (q.v.) in this parish since 1660. His direct descendant, Captain Thomas Wood, holds the manor of Littleton at the present day.[48] Several members of the family have gained distinction in military service, of whom perhaps the most famous is General Sir

WOOD of Littleton. *Sable a bull passant argent.*

David Wood (1812–94), the son of Colonel Thomas Wood of Littleton.[49] He served in the Boer campaign of 1842–3, and commanded the Royal Artillery at Balaclava, Inkerman, and before Sebastopol, and the Horse Artillery in the Indian Mutiny.[50] The eighteen tattered colours of the Grenadier Guards, which now hang in the church, were placed there by the father of the present representative of the family, who was colonel of that regiment.

The Leveland family appears to have let the manor to tenants. Robert de Winton held it as a tenant of Robert de Leveland in 1209, paying a yearly rent of 1 lb. of pepper.[51] Edward de Winton owed the service of three-quarters of a knight's fee in Littleton during part of the 13th century.[52] It is uncertain how long the de Wintons held the manor, but it was probably until about 1335, when an Edmund de Winton presented to the rectory,[53] the advowson having been first granted to Robert de Winton in 1209.[54] Possibly the manor passed very shortly to William de Perkelee, who held the advowson about that time,[55] and tenants of the same name, who were presumably his descendants, held the manor in the reign of Henry VI, rendering the same yearly rent of 1 lb. of pepper by which the de Wintons had held.[56] Guy de Perkelee, citizen and fishmonger of London, appears to have held the manor in 1424.[57] A few years later Simon de Perkelee and his brother Guy, who were possibly his sons, held the manor together.[58] Simon, who was a citizen and scrivener of London, died in 1439, leaving a son William, then nineteen years of age.[59] Litigation took place in 1444, Guy and his sister Matilda, the wife of John Talent, having apparently taken possession of the manor, and their nephew William attempted to recover it from William de Bokeland, to whom they had conveyed it.[60] It is possible that William de Perkelee died before the conclusion of the suit, for in the following year the manor was divided, two-thirds being held by Guy and his wife, and one-third by Agnes, who was William's wife, with remainder to Guy. The latter, in that year,[61] conveyed his share and the remainder of the third part to William de Bokeland, who appears to have held the whole manor in 1458.[62] After this time the under-tenure seems to have lapsed.

The so-called manor of *ASTLAM* (Ashlam, Aschlam, Astelam, Astleham, xvii and xviii cents.) appears to have been held in chief. The name first occurs in 1600, when Katharine Ryse, widow, conveyed the manor to Francis Townley.[63] Nicholas Townley, who was probably the heir of Francis, and Joan his wife held it in 1650–1,[64] and in 1660 sold it to Thomas Wood, the son and heir apparent of Edward Wood, alderman of London,[65] who was the first of his family to settle at Littleton.[66] The manor remained with his descen-

[34] Plac. in Canc. file 29, no. 1.
[35] Cal. Pat. 1436–41, p. 422.
[36] Feet of F. Midd. Mich. 20 Hen. VIII.
[37] Recov. R. Trin. 5 Eliz. rot. 608 ; Com. Pleas D. Enr. Trin. 5 Eliz. m. 13.
[38] Ibid. Mich. 15 & 16 Eliz. This document is too much decayed to be inspected.
[39] G.E.C. Complete Peerage, vii, 174.
[40] Feet of F. Midd. Hil. 16 Eliz. ; Mich. 42 & 43 Eliz. ; Div. Co. Trin. 44 Eliz. ; Midd. East. 4 Jas. I.
[41] Ibid. Hil. 10 Jas. I ; Hil. 2 Chas. I.
[42] G.E.C. Complete Peerage, iv, 225.
[43] Feet of F. Midd. Hil. 2 Chas. I.

[44] Ibid. Mich. 24 Chas. I.
[45] Lysons, Environs of Lond. (1800), v, 202.
[46] Recov. R. Hil. 23 Geo. II, rot. 383.
[47] Lysons, op. cit. v, 202.
[48] Burke, Landed Gentry (1906), 1842.
[49] Dict. Nat. Biog. xii, 354.
[50] Ibid.
[51] Pipe R. 2 John, m. 6 d.
[52] Testa de Nevill (Rec. Com.), 360–2. It was then said to be held of the Blunts, but this was probably a mistake.
[53] Lysons, op. cit. v, 204.
[54] Pipe R. 11 John, m. 6 d.
[55] Newcourt, Repert. i, 688.

[56] Plac. in Canc. file 29, no. 1.
[57] Close, 2 Hen. VI, m. 14 d.
[58] Plac. in Canc. file 29, no. 1.
[59] Ibid.
[60] Co. Plac. Midd. no. 41 ; Feet of F. Lond. and Midd. 21 Hen. VI, no. 105.
[61] Feet of F. Lond and Midd. 23 Hen. VI, no. 120.
[62] Feet of F. Lond. and Midd. 36 Hen. VI, no. 185.
[63] Feet of F. Midd. Mich. 42–3 Eliz.
[64] Ibid. Hil. 1650–1; Recov. R. East. 1651, rot. 21 ; Feet of F. Midd. Mich. 1655.
[65] Close, 13 Chas. II, pt. xv, no. 23.
[66] Burke, Landed Gentry.

dants,[67] and was inherited by Thomas Wood, who bought the manor of Littleton (q.v.) towards the close of the 18th century. It is last mentioned in 1801,[68] after which time it was probably merged in the manor of Littleton. The name is still preserved in Astlam Common, which lies in the north-west of the parish.

According to an extent taken in 1660, there was a 'mansion house built with brick,' where the lord of the manor dwelt.[69] Belonging to it were outhouses, barns, stables, mill-houses, orchards, gardens, and 'back sides.'[70] A dove-house was built between 1600 and 1650, and dove-houses are mentioned in 1660.[71]

The Beauchamps of Hacche in Somerset held land in the parish for several generations. It does not appear of whom the land was held in early times, the only mention of an overlord occurring in 1360, when the Abbot of Westminster is named.[72] Robert de Beauchamp acquired land there in 1235 from Richard son of Bartholomew,[73] and in the same year a weir from William le Sire.[74] In 1341 John de Beauchamp, Baron of Hacche, the descendant of

BEAUCHAMP of Hacche. *Vair.*

Robert, received lands in Littleton from Henry de Roydone and Joan his wife, which were, however, held by Henry and Joan for the term of their lives for the yearly rendering of one rose.[75] In the same year Alice widow of William Raghener conveyed premises in Littleton to John de Beauchamp which she also held for life on rendering one rose yearly at the feast of St. John the Baptist.[76] The Ragheners, or Raheners, had held land in Littleton since 1283, when John Rahener acquired 8 acres from John Argent and his wife Margaret.[77] William Raghener held land there in 1310,[78] and William de la Lee conveyed certain premises there to him in 1321.[79] John de Beauchamp's lands were inherited by his son, also named John,[80] who died seised of tenements at Littleton in 1360.[81] His heirs were found to be his sister Cicely and his nephew John Meriet, the son of his second sister Eleanor by her first husband.[82] The Littleton lands apparently fell to the share of John Meriet.[83] In 1373 he released all his right to the 'manor' of Littleton to William Beauchamp and others, who were presumably acting as his trustees.[84] This is the only instance in which the estate was called

a manor. John Meriet died in 1391, leaving an only daughter and heiress Elizabeth, who married Urias Seymour.[85] The Meriet lands came in this way to the Seymours, as did the lands of the Beauchamps by the marriage of Cicely Beauchamp with Sir Roger Seymour,[86] and were inherited eventually by Edward Seymour, Earl of Hertford and Duke of Somerset, who acted as Protector in the reign of Edward VI, and who was created Baron of Hacche in 1536.[87] His son held the manor of Littleton (q.v.), and it is probable that the lands originally held by the Beauchamps became merged in that estate.

SEYMOUR. *Gules a pair of wings or.*

It is just possible that in 1340 Sir John de Moleyns held lands here, which were sometimes called a manor. In that year he obtained a confirmation of the manors of 'La Lee - - - Littleton,' and others.[88] He forfeited his lands in that year, and they were not restored until 1345.[89] No mention is made of this 'manor' in the records of the restitution. Possibly the lands had been granted to some tenant, not improbably to Augustine Waleys. On 26 March 1346 Augustine Waleys and Maud his wife conveyed the 'manor of Littleton' to John Gogh,[90] who conveyed it at midsummer of the same year to Edward de Bohun and Philippa his wife, with remainder in case of default of heirs to Guy de Brian.[91] It seems very likely that this estate was not really a manor. It probably came to Guy de Brian in due course, although there is no mention of a 'manor' belonging to him. Sir Guy already held lands in Littleton, part of which (one messuage and 1 acre of land) he had acquired in 1346[92] by conveyance from Sir John de Moleyns, who held it as early as 1340.[93] He received a grant of free warren in his demesne lands at Littleton in 1350.[94] The estate passed in 1390 to his eldest surviving child, Philippa, wife first of John Devereux, and then of Sir Henry de Scrope.[95] She died holding a 'toft and lands in Littleton' in 1407, when her property passed to her sister Elizabeth, wife of Robert Lovell.[96] About 1473–4 Robert Lovell was engaged in a lawsuit with one Katharine Palmer concerning these lands.[97] But they were never known as a manor, and are not traceable beyond this date.

[67] Feet of F. Midd. Trin. 16 Geo. III.
[68] Recov. R. Mich. 42 Geo. IV, rot. 124.
[69] Close, 13 Chas. II, pt. xv, no. 23.
[70] Feet of F. Midd. Mich. 42–3 Eliz. ; cf. Hil. 1650–1.
[71] Close, 13 Chas. II, pt. xv, no. 23.
[72] Chan. Inq. p.m. 35 Edw. III, pt. i, no. 36.
[73] Feet of F. Lond. and Midd. 19 Hen. III, no. 115.
[74] Ibid. no. 116.
[75] Ibid. 15 Edw. III, no. 143. .
[76] Ibid. no. 150.
[77] Ibid. 10 Edw. I, no. 120.

[78] Ibid. 3 Edw. II, no. 50.
[79] Ibid. 14 Edw. II, no. 272.
[80] Croke, *Gen. Hist. of the Croke Family*, ii, 205.
[81] Chan. Inq. p.m. 35 Edw. III, pt. i, no. 36.
[82] Ibid. ; Croke, op. cit. ii, 205.
[83] Fin. R. 36 Edw. III, m. 27, no. 83.
[84] Close, 8 Ric. II, m. 28 d.
[85] Chan. Inq. p.m. 15 Ric. II (1st nos.), no. 48.
[86] Croke, op. cit. ii, 205.
[87] G.E.C. *Complete Peerage*, vii, 174.
[88] Chart. R. 4 Edw. III, no. 30.
[89] *Cal. Pat.* 1343–5, p. 543.

[90] Feet of F. Lond. and Midd. 20 Edw. III, no. 221.
[91] Ibid. no. 214.
[92] Ibid. 20 Edw. III, no. 207.
[93] Ibid. 14 Edw. III, no. 135.
[94] Chart. R. 24 Edw. III, no. 145, m. 1, no. 3. Dugdale (*Bar.* ii, 145) says that Sir J. Moleyns held the manor of Littleton in Wilts. This is not substantiated by his reference to Chart R. 14 Edw. III, no. 30, where no county is mentioned.
[95] G.E.C. *Complete Peerage*, ii, 445.
[96] Chan. Inq. p.m. 8 Hen. IV. m. 54.
[97] Early Chan. Proc. bdle. 4, no. 112.

LITTLETON CHURCH: NAVE LOOKING EAST

CHEST IN LITTLETON CHURCH

The church of *ST. MARY CHURCH MAGDALENE* consists of chancel 39 ft. 2 in. by 17 ft. 6 in., nave 33 ft. 4 in. by 19 ft. 4 in., north aisle 6 ft. wide, south aisle 6 ft. 9 in. wide, west tower, and some buildings on the north of the chancel, which were burial-places for the Wood family, built in 1705, but are now transformed into vestries.

The chancel seems to date from the 13th century, and the plan of the nave is perhaps of the 12th, a south aisle having been added in the 13th century, and a north aisle in the 14th; the clearstory is of red brick, and probably of the 16th century; and the west tower except for its top stage, and the south porch are perhaps of the same date. The walls, except those of the clearstory and north aisle, are rough-cast, and the roofs are red tiled, with plastered coves.

The chancel has a modern east triplet of lancets, two original lancets on the north, to the east of which is a modern doorway into the vestries; and in the south wall three modern lancets, a window of two trefoiled lights at the south-east, and a south door between the first and second lancets from the east. The proportions suggest that it has been lengthened eastward since its first setting out.

The chancel arch is old work in two pointed chamfered orders, and at the springing is a modern moulded string; to the south of it, in the angle of the nave, is a lancet window inserted to give light to the pulpit, which looks like old work re-used.

The nave has a north arcade of two bays, with arches of two chamfered orders with a label, and an octagonal central column of 14th-century detail; the responds have a moulded string on the inner order only. The south arcade has two pointed chamfered orders with a large circular column, and semi-octagonal responds with plain capitals, probably cut down, and bases which show remains of 13th-century detail. The clearstory has two square-headed two-light windows on either side over the arches, of cut red brick with moulded labels.

The walling of the north aisle is rough rubble of stone and flint; in the west wall is an old lancet window, and to the south of it can be seen the angle of the earlier aisleless nave. In the north wall is a pointed 14th-century doorway with an external hood; it is now blocked, and contains a small window. To the east is a window of two trefoiled lights with a segmental head, the jambs being probably 14th-century work, while the tracery is modern.

The south aisle has an old lancet window at the west end, and a modern doorway and two-light window on the south. The porch has a four-centred outer order and moulded 16th-century beams in the ceiling.

The tower is in four stages; the top stage, which seems an 18th-century addition, has no roof, but a quatrefoiled opening in each wall. The third stage has two-light belfry windows in

red brick, and in the ground stage is a four-centred west door with a three-light window over it.

There are some simple 15th-century pews in the nave, and in the vestry is an old iron-bound chest of the reign of Henry VIII, ornamented with leather and nail work. The pulpit is good 18th-century work, and at the west end of the nave is a large organ. The font is octagonal on a round stem, and is ancient but extremely plain. Its pierced and domed wooden cover seems to include a little old woodwork.

In the north wall of the chancel is a brass inscription taken up from the floor, 'Here lyeth Lady Blanche Vaughan, sometyme wyfe of Syr Hugh Vaughan, knight, who lyeth buryed at Westmynst' whych Lady Blanche decessyd the VIII[th] day of deceber, An° Dni m[l] v[c]liii whose soules Ihu pdon.' Below is a shield with three castles and a fleur de lis, and on each side of the shield a double rose, having on their centres the words 'Ihu mercy.' There are several later monuments to the family of Wood.

In the church are eight pairs of colours of the Grenadier Guards, and two red ensigns belonging to the same.

There are three bells by W. Eldridge, 1666.

The plate consists of a chalice of 1632, engraved with three fleurs de lis in a border bezanty, quartering a fesse checky in a border engrailed, the whole impaling a quarterly shield: 1st, a bend bearing three stags' heads embossed on an escutcheon between six crosslets fitchy; 2nd, three leopards passant, a label of three points; 3rd, checky; 4th, a lion rampant; a flagon with date mark 1734, given by Mrs. Elizabeth Wood in that year; a small cover paten of 1632, engraved with a goat's or bull's head breathing fire; a standing paten of 1680; a chalice of the 1696 cycle; and an embossed salver marked

N
I.E.
1677.

The earlier registers are: (1) christenings 1579 to 1652, marriages 1564 to 1652, burials 1562 to 1651; (2) woollen burials 1678 to 1715, marriages 1678 to 1705, burials without affidavits 1698 to 1705; (3) printed marriages, 1754 to 1810; (4) baptisms 1664 to 1811, burials 1664 to 1812, and marriages 1664 to 1751.

ADVOWSON The church of St. Mary Magdalene is first mentioned in 1209.[98]

The living is a rectory, the gift of which appears to have been held in early times by the sub-tenant of the manor. It was conveyed by Robert de Leveland in 1209 to Robert de Winton,[99] and appears to have remained with the de Wintons for over a century, Edmund de Winton presenting in 1335.[100] It then probably passed to William de Perkelee, who presented on four occasions between 1321 and 1336.[101] Four years later, however, it was conveyed by Master John de Redeswelle, parson

[98] Pipe R. 11 John, m. 6 d.
[99] Ibid.
[100] Lysons, op. cit. v, 204, cites Stat. Major Eccl. St. Paul.
[101] Newcourt, *Repert.* i, 688.

of 'Goderushton,' to Sir John de Moleyns.[102] On Sir John's imprisonment in that same year [103] it was taken into the king's hand, Edward III presenting in 1343.[104]

In September 1345 Edward III gave the order to restore the advowson of the church of Littleton to Sir John.[105] At Easter 1346 the latter conveyed it to Sir Guy de Brian.[106] At midsummer in the same year a settlement of the advowson was made by John Gogh (apparently a trustee) on Edward de Bohun and Philippa his wife, with remainder in default of heirs to Guy de Brian.[107] This may perhaps be explained in connexion with Moleyns' recent forfeiture. The person represented by Gogh may possibly have had a grant of the advowson between 1340 and 1345, so that the rights of both parties may have been compromised in this act.

In 1355, however, the advowson of Littleton was settled by Edward de Bohun on his wife : [108] Edward died childless in 1362,[109] so that the last-mentioned settlement would be rendered ineffective by the former remainder in favour of Guy de Brian. The latter evidently came into possession, for he gave it in 1372 to the priory of Hounslow, for the remembrance of his own and his wife's anniversary.[110] It remained with Hounslow Priory until it was granted by Prior Thomas Hide to Edmund Windsor.[111] Andrew Lord Windsor presented in 1537,[112] the next presentation being made by his son's executor,[113] Roger Roper, in 1554.[114] The advowson was sold by his grandson, Edward Lord Windsor, in 1563, with the manor,[115] and came with the latter to Edward Seymour, Earl of Hertford, who first presented in 1572.[116] In 1610 the advowson was granted by the king to William Hughes,[117] who was probably a fishing grantee. Later in the same year he and his father Reginald Hughes conveyed their right to Francis Townley,[118] but the Earl of Hertford presented in 1616 and 1617.[119] Litigation ensued, and Francis Townley recovered the right of presentation from the earl,[120] and the rector, who had been inducted in 1617, was admitted a second time (in 1619) on Townley's presentation.[121] The Seymours, however, seem to have retained some right in it, for in 1637 Frances Countess of Hertford held the patronage for the term of her life,[122] after which it appears to have passed to the Townleys. Nicholas Townley held it in 1650,[123] and conveyed it in 1660 to Thomas Wood.[123a] It has remained with his descendants to the present day [124] and is now held with the manor by Captain Thomas Wood. In 1341 the parish was rated at £9 6s. 8d., but because the

land was sandy, and the inhabitants were unable to sow it on account of their poverty, only £6 could be raised.[125] The rectory was valued at £14 at the Dissolution,[126] and the same in 1548.[127] In an extent of 1610, a mill, house, dovecote, orchard, garden and fishing are mentioned as belonging to the rectory.[128]

A chantry was founded in 1324 by Thomas de Littleton, then rector of Harrow, and formerly rector of Spaxton.[129] By an agreement with the Abbot and Convent of Chertsey, the latter bound themselves to pay 5 marks yearly to a chaplain to celebrate divine service daily at the altar of St. Mary in the church of Littleton, in honour of the saint, and for the souls of the founder, of his parents, and of Simon de Micham. The chaplain was to be appointed by Thomas de Littleton, and after his death by Sir Geoffrey de Perkelee, the rector of Littleton, and his successors.[130] In 1548 the chantry was served by a French priest, Sir Philip Lyniard, who had a house, an orchard, and a little croft or close.[131] After the dissolution of the chantries in 1548 the land seems to have been held by the Crown until 1610, when it was included in a grant of the advowson of the rectory to William Hughes.[132] It has probably descended since with the rectory.

The Bread Charities.—In 1724 *CHARITIES* Mrs. Elizabeth Wood, by will, bequeathed to the minister and churchwardens £100 to be put out at interest, and the yearly income thereof to be laid out in bread to be distributed every Sunday among poor attending the church.

In 1737 Robert Wood, LL.D., by will, bequeathed £100 South Sea Annuity stock, the income thereof to be distributed in bread every Sunday by the minister and churchwardens.

These legacies are represented by a sum of £217 4s. 9d. consols, with the official trustees. In 1906 the dividends, amounting to £5 8s. 4d., were applied in the distribution of bread every Sunday to five families.

The school, formerly carried on in a room on the estate of the Wood family, was erected in 1872 in memory of the late Lieut.-General Wood. It is endowed with a sum of £382 13s. 7d. consols with the official trustees, producing £9 11s. 4d. a year, which arose from the accumulations of a legacy of £30 bequeathed by will of the Rev. Thomas Harwood, D.D., rector, dated in 1731, and from subscriptions in 1787 of £50 each by Thomas Wood, Thomas Wood, junr., Edward Elton, and the Rev. Henry Allen, D.D., rector.

---

[102] Feet of F. Lond. and Midd. 14 Edw. III, no. 135.
[103] *Dict. Nat. Biog.* xxxvii, 127.
[104] *Cal. Pat.* 1343–5, p. 158.
[105] Ibid. p. 543.
[106] Feet of F. Lond. and Midd. 20 Edw. III, no. 207.
[107] Ibid. no. 214.
[108] Ibid. 29 Edw. III, no. 334.
[109] Chan. Inq. p.m. 36 Edw. III, pt. i, no. 24.
[110] Ibid. 46 Edw. III.
[111] Pat. 7 Jas. I, pt. x, no. 9 ; the grant is said to have been made in 1536, but

Dugdale gives the dissolution of the monastery in 1530 (*Mon.* vii, 303).
[112] Newcourt, *Repert.* i, 688.
[113] Collins, *Coll. of the Family of Windsor,* 57.
[114] Newcourt, *Repert.* i, 688.
[115] Recov. R. Trin. 5 Eliz. rot. 608.
[116] Newcourt, *Repert.* i, 688.
[117] Pat. 7 Jas. I, pt. xv, no. 9.
[118] Common Pleas D. Enr. Mich. 8 Jas. I.
[119] Newcourt, op. cit. i, 688.
[120] Ibid. quoting Lond. Epis. Reg. Bancroft, 232.

[121] Newcourt, op. cit. i, 688.
[122] Ibid.
[123] Feet of F. Midd. Hil. 1650–1 ; Recov. R. East. 1651, rot. 21.
[123a] Close, 13 Chas. II, pt. xv.
[124] Inst. Bks. (P.R.O.)
[125] *Inq. Non.* (Rec. Com.), 199.
[126] *Valor Eccl.* (Rec. Com.) i, 433.
[127] Chantry R. 34, no. 184.
[128] Pat. 7 Jas. I. pt. x.
[129] *Cal. Pat.* 1334–8, p. 246.
[130] Ibid.
[131] Chantry R. 34, no. 184.
[132] Pat. 7 Jas. I, pt. xv, no. 9.

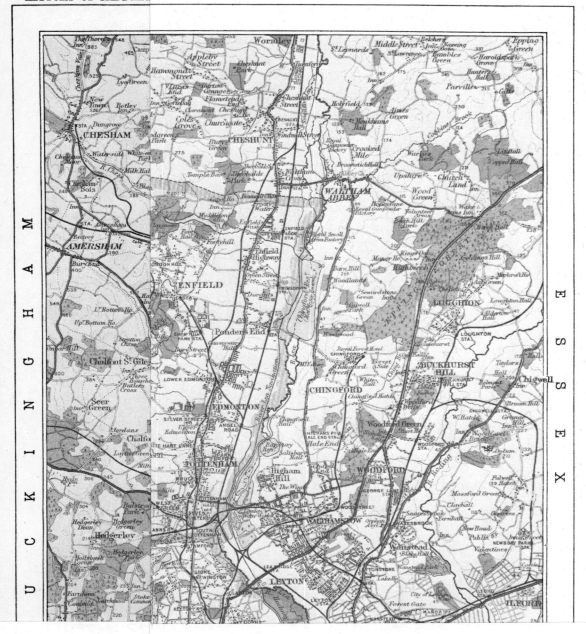